A Measured Pace

Toward a
Philosophical Understanding
of the Arts of Dance

Though the theoretical importance of dance has always been recognized, dance has been relatively neglected in the philosophy of art. In this sequel to *Off the Ground*, in which Professor Sparshott focused on the concept of dance in general, he considers the recognized classification of dance as art, its values, and its relationship to the other arts.

Sparshott begins with an explanation of the philosophical importance of the major classifications of dance and their basis. He examines dance as a mimetic and expressive medium, and reviews the major dimensions of dance form. He then explores the relationship of dance to three related fields: music, language, and theatre. Sparshott also discusses the major philosophical problems of dance as an art: the specific values of dance; the relation between the way the audience perceives dance and the dancer's self-perception; the ways in which dancing and dances are learned; the division of artistic creation between choreographers and performers; and the ways in which dances are identified and retain their identity through time. A concluding chapter on how dances are recorded considers how the media may change the nature of dance. *A Measured Pace* is a wide-ranging and substantial contribution to a philosophical understanding of dance.

FRANCIS SPARSHOTT is University Professor Emeritus, University of Toronto. He is author of numerous books of poetry and philosophy, including *Taking Life Seriously: A Study of the Argument of the Nicomachean Ethics*.

A Measured Pace

Toward a
Philosophical Understanding
of the Arts of Dance

Francis Sparshott

UNIVERSITY OF TORONTO PRESS
Toronto Buffalo London

© University of Toronto Press Incorporated 1995
Toronto Buffalo London
Printed in Canada

ISBN 0-8020-0510-1 (cloth)
ISBN 0-8020-6946-0 (paper)

Printed on acid-free paper

Toronto Studies in Philosophy
Editors: James R. Brown and Calvin Normore

Canadian Cataloguing in Publication Data

Sparshott, Francis, 1926–
   A measured pace : towards a philosophical
   understanding of the arts of dance

   (Toronto studies in philosophy)
   Sequel to: Off the ground.
   Includes bibliographical references and index.
   ISBN 0-8020-0510-1 (bound) ISBN 0-8020-6946-0 (pbk.)

   1. Dancing – Philosophy. I. Title.

   GV1588.S73 1995   792.8'01   C94-932461-2

University of Toronto Press acknowledges the financial assistance to its
publishing program of the Canada Council and the Ontario Arts
Council.

This book has been published with the help of a grant from the
Canadian Federation for the Humanities, using funds provided by the
Social Sciences and Humanities Research Council of Canada.

This book is dedicated to all my former students,
in gratitude for all they taught me.

Contents

Preface

This is the second of two books on a somewhat neglected topic: the philosophy of the art of dance. Their purpose is not to present a general theory of dance, or to recommend a specific philosophical approach to it, but to indicate the general character of the topic – and, incidentally, to explain why it has been neglected. They present materials, arranged in reasonably good order, which people presenting a general theory or philosophy of dance should know about, even if they choose not to discuss them. And I say enough about these materials to give a general idea of what, in my judgment, there is to think about.

The first of the two books (Sparshott 1988) had less to say about dance as an art than about dance generally: the concept of dance, whether one can say what dance is, and what words like 'dance' mean. The present book takes it for granted that dance is a well-established art form, and deals with the problems that arise from that. The discussions here do not depend directly on those in the previous book, though they are continuous with them. Unavoidably, there is some overlapping.

The present volume is related not only to its predecessor but to the whole of my previous work in aesthetics. It is one of a series of works produced in the course of a career that required me to teach that subject, a task that called for an account of how the subject held together. I could find no such account. My first problem (Sparshott 1963), necessary for a responsible teacher, was to show how the chaotic diversity of problems actually discussed in aesthetics related to each other. After that, I essayed a rationale for the then-popular equation of aesthetics with the theory of critical discourse – the key being that a work of art as such is an object-for-criticism, a 'performance' in a novel sense I introduced there (Sparshott 1967). This was something of a parergon; the next major task was to resolve the fundamental but insufficiently observed distinction between aesthetics (as the philosophy of criticism) and the philosophy of art as such. Disentangling the structure of the concept of art required me to show how a traditional discourse about the fine arts generated other sorts of discourse that were incompatible with it, though they could neither eliminate it nor be eliminated by it (Sparshott 1982c).

The background of the present book, then, is an extensive review of the general problematics of the philosophy of art, rather than any specific concern originating in the dance world. My concern with the philosophy of dance arose from my being rebuked for saying so little about dance in my general works. Reflecting on the justice of this rebuke soon led me to the realization that dance as a fine art is anomalous and that my major task would be to deal with this anomaly.

The attempt to deal with the anomalous nature of dance led me to the discovery that, in addition to the concept of art, a new tool was needed to deal with such phenomena: the concept of a *practice*, in a sense more general than those familiar in social and political philosophy, and a whole way of articulating the discussion of practices. In this way, unexpectedly, my foray into the philosophy of dance proved not to be a diversion or enclave within my explorations in aesthetics, but an essential continuation of them, diging deeper into their ground.

How could a philosopher with no special knowledge of dance contribute anything worthwhile to dance theory? People concerned with the performing end of the arts have asked me whether my work in dance aesthetics would take me all over the world, 'or would I be doing it all out of books?' – and this in a city where groups of dance performers come from around the globe. No analogous question is ever asked in connection with any other art; what is it about dance that provokes the enquiry? Is it the conviction that dance is inseparable from its cultural context? But, if it is, it would be futile to travel, for seeing the dance would give no insight into that context – one can, in fact, argue that a dance belonging to an alien culture cannot really be seen at all (Williams 1991, 8–12). The underlying feeling may rather be that there is no essential reality in dance, nothing but isolated phenomena and isolated texts describing them. Such feelings may be respected; but they are not to be relied on. My real subject, in any case, is the connections between ideas, aspects of the structure of the world of conscious culture. And then I am tempted to say that, as a railway worker can very well know how to join a truckload of rutabagas to a truckload of tape recorders without having a degree in either agronomics or electronics, so a philosopher can compose a discourse on the connections between (say) dance and music without being either a dancer or a musician. That analogy is not a good one, however, and would not help me if it were; so I will say only that every individual has a perspective from which something useful may be seen. I have explained elsewhere (Sparshott 1993) my understanding of how a multitude of disparate approaches can be intelligibly interrelated in a general mass of theorizing about dance.

In the world of dance theory, the time when the first draft of these reflections was produced (in 1980) is a remote past, almost a different era. A lot of good thinking has been done, and much fine work has been written. A lot of it applies established theories of art to the specifics of dance, often with illuminating results. There are still, to my knowledge, no general handbooks on dance aesthetics that combine broad scope with strenuous thought; but the sense of urgency I felt when I began my reflections would no longer be appropriate. The ambience of dance history and theory changes rapidly, like other newly cultivated academic fields, as each generation teaches the next and publication builds on publication.

The division of the text into sections and subsections is intended to show how the argument is articulated. Cross-references using section numbers refer only to the passage bearing the number in question, not to any of its subsections; for instance, '§9.2' refers only to §9.2 itself, and does not include §9.21, §9.211, and so on. References to a section *including* its subsections use the abbreviations 'f' and 'ff'; for instance, '§9.2ff' refers to §9.2 with all its subsections, from §9.21 to §9.22 inclusive. '§9' by itself refers to the portion of chapter 9 preceding §9.1.

I have many debts to acknowledge. First and foremost, I must thank Selma Jeanne Cohen, without whose initial promptings and continued encouragement I would neither have ventured into this territory nor remained in it so long. In addition to all the dancers and choreographers whose work has challenged, delighted, stimulated, frustrated, and instructed me for half a century, and the fellow-members of the Society of Dance History Scholars who have patiently set me right on so many things, I owe very special debts of gratitude to Selma Odom, Gregory Scott, and C. Anderson Silber for years of generous support and criticism. I am hugely indebted to the students and colleagues who contributed to my seminars at the University of Toronto and York University, in which my ideas were tested and improved; it grieves me that the poverty of my records and the weakness of my memory prevent me from recording all their names. I am indebted also to the University of Toronto Press for enabling me to bring my work so massively before the public, and to the Press's readers and editorial staff for helping me to improve its form and substance.

Preparation of this book was made possible by a Connaught Senior Fellowship in the Humanities for the academic year 1984–5.

A Measured Pace

Toward a
Philosophical Understanding
of the Arts of Dance

CHAPTER ONE

Introduction

This book is a contribution to the philosophy of dance. But what is the philosophy of dance? Many answers are possible; here is mine. Philosophy, unlike science and history, enquires into meanings and the meaningful. Scientists, within a given theoretical framework, seek to establish what is the case; historians, within the framework of a general view of human affairs, seek to establish what really happened and why. Philosophers mostly accept what historians and scientists say, and what 'everybody knows,' and try to make sense of it – or to explain why it makes no sense. The specific things that philosophers do contribute to, or follow from, this basic enquiry. Philosophers, committed to the 'pursuit of wisdom' that their name implies, try to avoid the two main sources of folly: failing to see what is there to be seen, and constructing arbitrary systems or pretentious theories. They try to deepen their understanding of things as they are. So the philosophy of dance consists bascially of attempts to make sense of dance – to explain how dancing is something it makes sense to do, or why it does not. It seems that people everywhere dance – is that really true, is there some one sort of activity all these people are engaged in, and, if so, what are they up to?

Much of the philosophy of dance concentrates on dance as an art, as putatively one of the 'fine arts' (like painting and poetry). The identification of the fine arts as one of the main areas in which human intelligence is exercised goes back to the eighteenth century, at about the same time as science and history were similarly identified as characteristic ways in which intellectual activity was organized and carried on. People began seriously to ask what important contribution, if any, the arts made to the life of the mind; and, if dance is one of the arts, how dance shared or could share in that contribution. As part of that enquiry, one goes on to ask how particular dances and ways of dancing are bearers of meaning. Or one could start at the other end, asking how particular dances are meaningful, and going on to generalize about what sort of meaning the art of dance exists to convey. Perhaps there is no such meaning? Perhaps dances are enjoyed, but there is nothing for anyone to understand or appreciate? It may be so; but then, either dance is not among the arts, or the arts themselves do not have the significance we attribute to them. These are among the possibilities that the philosophy of dance has to discuss.

To the extent that dance is not among the fine arts – and certainly not everyone who dances is thought of as an artist – the philosophy of dance has a different focus. We look now at what part dance plays in the lives of humans as makers and sharers of culture – not what has led people to dance, which is history, nor what psychic forces impel them to do so, which is science, but why dance is something it makes sense to do. Of course, there may be no answer to that, in which case the philosophy of dance is exhausted in discovering that there is no more to be said.

The philosophy of dance is not something most professional philosophers concern themselves with, especially in North America. There may be good reasons for that, but the mere fact that our subject is little studied does not mean either that it is unworthy of attention or that great things remain to be done in it. The only way to find out is to try and see.

As explained in the preface, the predecessor of this book dealt mainly with the concept of dance as such, and the problem of defining dance. The upshot of that initial investigation was equivocal. Dance could, of course, be made to fit the context of art, because that is where it nowadays plainly belongs. But difficulties remain. Dancing, both as concept and as practice, has an existence outside the context of art, and it was not clear that what gives dance its central importance is anything of an artistic sort – at least, as art is generally understood in the philosophy of art nowadays. It was not even quite clear that the focus of the idea of dancing is any sort of human practice at all, rather than a class of movements, or a sort of energy that is generically spiritual rather than human. It might even be suggested that the starting point of all thinking about dance should be the notion that the world in its entirety is most fittingly thought of as a dance, or as the product or domain of a dancing god. In Milton's *Paradise Lost* (v 618–27), the archangel Raphael tells Adam:

> That day, as other solem dayes, they spent
> In song and dance about the sacred Hill,
> Mystical dance, which yonder starrie Spheare
> Of Planets and of fixt in all her Wheeles
> Resembles nearest, mazes intricate,
> Eccentric, intervolv'd, yet regular
> Then most, when most irregular they seem:
> And in thir motions harmonie Divine
> So smooths her charming tones, that Gods own ear
> Listens delighted.

Such talk may strike us as merely quaint, but it has been widespread and pervasive (see Miller 1986). We have to recognize it as a dominant metaphor that colours thought about dancing in a way that has few obvious parallels in the other arts.

When I turned to a consideration of the human practice of dancing, I found that dance seems to be different from the other arts – though in fact the fine arts differ among themselves so widely and deeply that this was no startling discovery. The more I looked and thought, the more it seemed to me that dancing, when done for its own sake and not merely as a job or an exercise, tends to draw its significance from the fact that in it the dancer's self is transformed: to say that a dancer's body is either the medium or the instrument of dance, though not actually false, is misleading.[1] One does not *use* oneself, and if one truly used one's body one would do so not as a wholly embodied being but as a spiritual or cerebral entity to whom the body was extraneous. I return to this theme again and again.

The self-transformation in dance, I suggested, is partly analogous to the entry into an alternative way of being that is often felt to be central in the experience of music. But the contrast is as striking as the analogy. If music is a separate domain of experience, it is because the structures of musical works are superimposed on structures that are themselves purely musical. Music, like language, is artificial through and through; but, unlike language, it does not derive its musical meaningfulness from any relation or supposed relation to anything beyond itself – Derrida's conceit, that the extralinguistic reference in linguistic behaviour is a promise never fulfilled, does not alter the fact that without that reference language loses its point. Music is a self-contained mode of consciousness in which one seems to become nothing but music, but it is mostly as consciousness that one seems transformed. In dancing, one makes one's whole bodily self into that of a dancer, most centrally by performing movements that are nothing but dance, neither utilitarian nor (as in dramatic art) social. Music and dance are often said to be in principle inseparable, and there are practices in which they are so in fact, and part of what makes them so may well be that both involve entry into an alternative mode of being; but, if they are united, it is as inside and outside of the transformation. Some of these issues will be dealt with in chapter 12.

The structure of the book in which the foregoing thoughts were elaborated and supported was by no means linear and did not provide premises from which those thoughts could properly be derived as conclusions. But, to the extent that they could be supported, they did suggest that dance is pervasive and intrinsic to our human way of being in a way that other arts are not. And the metaphor whereby the whole world is a dance is one that includes the whole social order and all modes of personal interaction within its scope. But although dance is in this familiar way ubiquitous, in another way it is elusive – at least in modern industrial societies. Signs of actual dance practice are not conspicuous everywhere, as traces of the other fine arts are. As one walks through the city, indoors or outdoors, one is everywhere confronted with the worn-down forms of distinctively artistic activity. There is architecture all over the place, of course. But also there is music everywhere, a background privately or publicly generated; there are sculptural and graphic forms, and literary language. One is surrounded, not indeed by artistic masterpieces, but by signs and symbols used in ways that could not be what they are without the direct influence of self-consciously artistic practice. But there is no sign of dance anywhere, other than in actual dances which have to be located and sought out. Some young people will be wearing dance shoes, and there will be pictures of dancers here and there; but these are references to dance activity, rather than actual dance procedures. The only exception I can think of is the mannequins in the windows of clothing stores, which are almost always in dance poses. What else are the mannequins doing, if they are not dancing? So the upshot of the book may be that dance is everywhere and nowhere. Admittedly, that is not a very useful thing to say.

The present book is concerned not with the *quod* but with the *quale*, as people used to say – not with what dance *is*, but with what dance *is like*. It takes it for granted that dancing is a practice, a sort of thing that people do; that it has an aesthetic focus; and that it is centred on body movements that are in the first instance dance movements – however the status of 'dance movement' may be conferred. The centre of attention is the accepted art or arts of dance, the sort of thing people go to see in theatres and which professional dancers make a living by performing. It is the meaning of what goes on in that kind of performance art that will be my main concern.

As a philosopher, I discuss problems of principle – of what must be the case, or what cannot be the case, within my chosen domain. I am not trying to annex the terrain of critics and historians, or of expert practitioners. My procedures will, however, be philosophically impure. If philosophy has to do with meanings *rather than* facts, the meanings can only be the meainings *of* facts of some sort or other. In the philosophy of practice, one's starting point can only be the practice itself, what is actually done; and much of this is sure to be contingent, historically conditioned, even accidental. We cannot always know what there is about a practice that enables it to sustain itself. We cannot be sure of the grounds of its viability, or even of the description under which it is viable. There is, accordingly, good reason for philosophers to follow the model of Marxism, making their discussion a critique of the specific praxis of a historical place and time in the light of a well-supported view of social and practical dynamics in general. Two things stop me doing that. One is that no such general view is adequately sustained: exponents of such methods are too often reduced to merely wilful assertion. The other is that such historical hermeneutics always in fact exploit a more general, trans-historical understanding of the variables in terms of which actual changes are assessed; and it is on this more general level of intelligible relationships that I wish to operate.

In discussing 'what dance is like' within this restricted framework, I begin with the question: What kinds of dance are there? Debates about the right way, the best way, the *only* way to dance presuppose agreement about what the relevant ways of dancing are, among which choice is possible. We should expect some differentiations to impose themselves, given only the barest notion of what dance is; others to be contingent, but intelligible in the light of a systematic grasp of what dance is; others to be firmly anchored in the actual history of practice and tradition. Yet others may seem arbitrary, without foundation in theory or in practice; these I will try to ignore. But in practical matters one cannot invoke any definitions or canons to determine what is essential, what is significant, and what is trivial; one has to rely on the attentive and critical judgment of oneself and one's readers.

Among the ways of classifying dances, some are extrinsic, having to do with how dances are related to other contexts and aspects of life; others are intrinsic, different ways of dancing. Among the latter, a principal contrast is that between the formal, conceived in terms of the ways the dancers' bodies move, and the mimetic, conceived in terms of what a dance shows or represents. We will have to consider how the balance is held between these two aspects. Then we will have to consider, first, the modes of mimesis, and, second, the modes of body movement. Each of these classes of modes considers dances holistically, as units of behaviour; so the next task is to think about different modes of dance organization, the ways dances are put together from parts that are themselves formally or mimetically shaped and articulated.

Thinking about how dances are organized leads us in two directions. Obviously we cannot go in both directions at once. I choose to start with the relation between dance organization and other manifestations of symbolic order, notably music and language, each of which offers both significant likenesses to and differences from the order of dance, and each of which may be fused with dance in a common practice. Also, since dance as an art presented for a public is (commonly if not invariably) a theatre art, we must consider dance in relation to theatre.

The consideration of dance order leads, no less directly than it does to the relationship with these other orders, to the underlying principles of dance order itself: that is, to the question of dance values, and whether any or all of those values are distinctive of dance. That leads to the question how these values function in practice, which takes two special forms. First, what is the relation between dancer and spectator – between someone for whom the dance exists as something felt and done, and someone for whom it is something seen? And second, in view of this apparent split between what a dancer feels and what a spectator sees, how does one learn to dance, to be a dancer? And consideration of this apparent discrepancy in viewpoints leads to a consideration of choreography – the practice of making dances for some people to dance and others to watch, neither group being necessarily the same as the person designing the dance. This topic, though late in our order of treatment, is of capital importance, since it is the activity of the choreographer rather than that of the dancers that is at the centre of dancing as nowadays considered to be among the fine arts. So now at last we are in a position to ask, what is it that the choreographer creates? What are the identity conditions of dances? – a perennially debated topic, in practical application as well as in theory, in all performance arts. And that leads us, finally, to the question of how whatever is created is recorded and preserved, and how different ways of doing that may alter our ideas about what it is that is preserved.

That concludes my survey of topics for a philosophy of dance. As will be seen, they are related to each other; but each has its own integrity, and they are commonly discussed in isolation. I would expect readers to treat the chapters as independent, though I hope some will read the book as a whole.

By way of epilogue, I say something about the emblem of the Three Graces, because it would never do to leave them out.

PART ONE

Kinds of Dance

CHAPTER TWO

The Problem of Classification

What kinds of dance are there? All kinds of dances. The question makes no sense. One can hardly imagine a situation in which one would want to ask it, unless one were a librarian setting up a cataloguing system (see §2.2). Any characterization of a dance gives rise to a rudimentary classification. If I call a dance 'difficult,' for instance, I immediately establish a classification of dances into difficult and not-difficult (perhaps further differentiated into easy and moderate). If I say that a dance was danced after dinner, I implicitly classify dances into those danced before, during, and after dinner. And so on endlessly. There are innumerable ways of classifying things, no way of classifying those ways that promises enlightenment.

Things are not really as bad as that. If you want to know what plants are, for instance, you could hardly do better than look at a flora, a descriptive taxonomy of plants: it would show you what kinds of plants botanists recognized, how they were differentiated, how they were related. And, in so far as only one taxonomy prevailed in science, it would suggest that really there is only one currently viable way of talking about plants as plants.

Cultural phenomena and practices, it is true, do not yield straightforward taxonomies. A determinate taxonomy has to derive its definiteness and its stability from a single dominant point of view, which must itself be validated by some overriding practical purpose. But I have no such purpose here. I am only reflecting on ways classifications can be rooted and ramified.

That does not mean, however, that taxonomical discussions are futile.

Consider, for instance, Robert North's *Troy Game* (1974), as performed recently by the Canadian National Ballet. The programme says it was first performed by the London Contemporary Dance Theatre, and I observe that it is now being performed by a ballet company. It is, I see, for eight male dancers, plainly parodic and based on what the programme calls 'muscle-flexing and macho athleticism.' Since this is what I notice and read, I take it that these are all relevant features of the dance; and they tell me a lot. If this dance is for eight people, dances are either for definite numbers of people (and it matters how many), or they are not; if for males, dances are for males or (potentially at least) for females, for mixed genders, or unisex. Since the dance is parodic, presumably dances are either 'straight,' not referring to other practices, or, like this dance, referring to other practices; and then it matters whether the practice referred to is itself a dance practice or not, and whether the reference is mocking, or reverential, or what. I note from the programme that dances are relevantly classified by the date of composition and by the kind of dance company (ballet, contemporary) that introduces and performs them. Besides, though every characterization grounds a classification, the fact that the dance is presented under a certain description gives reason to think that some classifications are already in place, built into the organizing set-up of the practice, and hence take a certain priority. A characterization becomes a classification, denoting a *kind* of something, when the division it refers to falls within the determinate scope of an actual or possible practice and is conceived as belonging to a way in which the practice is articulated. The reason we do not look for a definitive taxonomy of a cultural practice is that we do not think the scope of such a practice is ever determinate and concede that different legitimate interests may call for different articulations of the same practice.

The ways we regularly talk about and describe dances show what dance is: if we say that a dance is *x* rather than *y*, we are implying that dance is the sort of thing about which it matters whether it is *x* or *y*. But now, suppose something you read or overhear puts you in mind of *Troy Game*, and you suddenly realize that the dance had a feature you didn't notice at the time, a feature you perhaps don't even have a word for. Your sudden realization that it is true and significant that the dance was 'like that' at once puts you in possession of a general classification of dances into those that are 'like that' and those that are 'not like that' – perhaps in recognizably various ways. This being a general classification, it not only is now in place but potentially was always in place: you have discovered a permanent feature of dances, that they are such that they significantly have or lack this newly recognized character. Of course, in most cases the significance is ephemeral, in the sense that it is not taken up into general discourse, and we ourselves soon forget it; but, if it is found usable and used, we have discovered a new fact about dance.

That the characterization and classification of dances become richer in this way is an important truth about cultural practices, one deeply explored by Arthur Danto (1981). What is most significant is not the mass of interrelated distinctions that we have actually at our disposal, but the underlying truths that we, as human beings, have an indefinite capacity for recognizing features, constructing distinctions, and incorporating them in our conceptual apparatus and that whenever such a distinction is made it becomes quite definite, with a fixed place in the discourse that surrounds and partly constitutes the practice of dance.

Even a miscellaneous and wayward listing of ways of differentiating dances would deepen and broaden understanding of what dance is about, and this understanding would be enhanced as we learned the ways in which the differentiations lent themselves to systematic classification or resisted such classification. But even though dance does not, like the vegetable kingdom, have a single (genetically derived) principle of organization, it does not consist simply of a mass of observable behaviours. In the first place, dances everywhere belong to systems of practice that are built into their culture. In the second place, the dances that will most concern us here are those done under the concept of art or as part of theatrical entertainment, and those two concepts can be expected to impose preemptive classificatory structures.

At this point we may invoke Plato, who thought more deeply about how to get an intellectual grasp on areas of human practice than anyone before or after him. His subtle dialogue *The Sophist* purports to place the practitioners of the elusive profession of 'sophist' in a general taxonomy of human pursuits. But it turns out that there is more than one way of doing this, depending on whether one considers it as a way of making a living or as a way of fulfilling social needs, and the various perspectives determine quite different configurations of activities and different saliences of relevant features. Any cultural practice must fit into alternative mappings of human enterprise, and there can be no one determinately correct mapping, since all the members of a society are real individuals with real interests and associations which they are not about to abandon. Some of the resulting configurations will be relatively constant in given social and cultural orders, but there is no reason to suppose that at any given time the most permanent ones and the most practically important ones will coincide. What is truly remarkable, though, is that although the alternative taxonomies Plato offers are constructed with satiric intent, and the society in which they are embedded has long vanished, we can still understand both of them and see a certain validity in them. Even the disjointed and messy articulations that follow here, though they amount to no system, cannot but reveal something of permanent applicability about what dance is and is like.

2.1 How Showbiz Did It

Classifications made for practical purposes join and separate things in ways other than those that science prescribes. A classification made to suit the needs of a particular practitioner will obviously be idiosyncratic. It will multiply distinctions in areas of preoccupation and leave huge gaps where interest was not taken; and the principle of classification is likely to be simple salience, so that the classes picked out will reflect different and disparate concerns and aspects. Such a scheme is determined by the accidents of the compiler's life and may make little sense beyond that. But similarly rough-and-ready systems of arrangement may arise within fairly stable bodies of practice (like the way merchandise is arranged on supermarket shelves), and something may be learned from them. Let us look at one such.

Bernard Sobel (1951, 50) tells us that vaudeville booking agents used to list dancing acts 'under the heading of Dutch, Irish, Plantation, Rough, Blackface, Neat, White-face, Grotesque, and Acrobatic.' The assumption is that within the class of show dancing suitable for vaudeville presentation there was an exhaustive set of genres, not expected to overlap. But the designations of the genres are not all of a piece. Whatever they stood for in practice, two of them take the form of ethnic designations, one ('Plantation') refers to a social setting, 'Blackface' and 'White-face' refer to mode of presentation, 'Rough' and 'Neat' designate gross style characteristics, and 'Grotesque' and 'Acrobatic' allude to types of movement picked out in ways that are not quite parallel. It is not clear from the context whether these labels determined a limited range of dance types, the only ones acceptable for the vaudeville stage, or offered a rough set of categories to one of which any dance would be assigned, for reasons of convenience, by agents and bookers. Nor is it clear whether every dance had to belong in one of these categories, for in the next paragraph Sobel writes: 'Everyone strove for novelty. The "pedestal" dancers, for instance, presented their number on a real pedestal in order to display their ability to defy gravity' – and we are left to wonder whether pedestal dancers are a subset of acrobatic dancers, or a new category that Sobel forgot to mention before; and, in any case, how the emphasis on novelty worked in relation to the limited range of accepted kinds of dance. But perhaps, as we put all these together, we begin to get some idea of what vaudeville dancing was all about. And, if we do, vaudeville dancing will turn out to be one kind of dancing, which, in conjunction with other such kinds, and with other kinds of dancing differentiated on other principles, will amount to an idea of what dancing is all about.

A sorting procedure similar to Sobel's appeared in the 1992 directory of my local dance association, Dance Ontario (it was changed in the following year). The compilers offered schools the following choice of classifications: Modern and Post-Modern, Ballet, Jazz, Cultural Specialty and Folk (specify), Tap, Other (specify), Ballroom and Social. We note that the list is in what could be a descending order of cultural prestige among display dances, with merely social dance forms in a sort of addendum after 'Other.' In the directory itself, we find individuals identifying their specialties as Acrobatics, Baton, Biblical Dance, Creative Dance, Creative Movement for Children, Dancercize, Kids' Dance, Musical Theatre, Stretch and Strength, T'ai Chi, Theatre Arts, and Therapy. The intent of these listings is strictly practical within a common professional understanding, and to interpret them as any sort of classification of dances as such we would need to know a lot about what is included in the scope of the sometimes-enigmatic labels, as well as about who seeks listing in such a directory; and we would have to remind ourselves that what is being classified is dance instruction rather than dance practice. But the two listings together offer a sort of vivid gestalt of professional dance instruction within a certain community, a world with whose organization and integrity philosophers of dance have seldom come to terms. The reality of dance largely depends on the clarity and continuity of such traditions of instruction, together with the institutions and handbooks that sustain them.

2.2 How Libraries Do It

Not all current schemes are as hand-to-mouth as the ones Sobel describes and Dance Ontario once used. Although it is no longer fashionable to design Maps of Knowledge, on which various fields of human endeavour could be located in relation to all other such fields, such maps do effectively exist, and intellectuals use them every day. In the academic world, the division of disciplines and subdisciplines and their distribution among departments, faculties, colleges, schools, and such represent a rigid articulation: it makes a difference whether a department of dance is part of a school of physical education or of a faculty of fine arts, or constitutes a separate faculty with its own dean. More pervasive and subtle is the influence exercised by library classification systems. What books are placed next to what other books? Consider the two most widely used systems, the Library of Congress and the Dewey Decimal System. The Library of Congress, originally an ad hoc system intended to order a specific collection and not to exemplify and impose a theory, firmly places dancing as a distinct category among physical recreations, and a long way from art.[1] Dewey, in contrast, worked his system out at his desk. He placed the fine arts and all forms of recreation in the 700s. The sequence is architecture – craftsmanship – visual arts – music – cinema – theater – games – sports. Dance is not a separate item but is divided between theatre and amusement, so that a dance encyclopedia may be divided from a work on ballet history by Hoyle on card games. Looking at the books on the shelves, it is hard to see what the system is, but in theory it goes like this. The 790s are devoted to 'Recreations and Performing Arts.' After 791, 'public performances,' we have 792, 'theater': 792.1 is tragedy and serious drama, 792.2 comedy and melodrama, 792.3 pantomime, 792.7 vaudeville, and 792.8 ballet. Then we come to 793, 'Indoor Games and Amusements,' including 'parties and entertainments' (793.2) and 'dancing' (793.3), including 793.32 'theatrical dancing.' These labels surely reflect very strong, and nowadays very unusual, opinions about what dancing is and how different sorts of dancing are related to each other. And where is ethnic dancing? One can see that folk dancing, if done for fun in a church basement, would fit the scheme, but dancing done outdoors, neither as amusement nor as a theatrical show, has no home. I imagine it would have to go into the 900s, under geography and travel. But it is to be noted that, unlike the vaudeville booking agent's pigeonholes, a librarian's classification has to be exhaustive: every book received has to be catalogued, and to be catalogued it must be given a number, and the number must be assigned in accordance with the operative classificatory system.

What the Dewey system represents is a bygone day, when 'ballet' meant a sort of show in which dances formed a large part but did not constitute the whole; when dancing was always light relief, recreation at a party or a divertissement in a theatrical show; and when the dancing done by Indians and Africans was part of their folkways or of their religion – exotic, having no real connection with anything *we* might do or watch. And it is this viewpoint that is built into every public library system I can remember using, in Britain or in Canada.

The methods of these general cataloguing systems would not be suitable to a library devoted specifically to dance. Such a library could not exist unless dance in some sense were a publicly recognized institution, apt to attract many books, and its focus would be on that institution. Accordingly, the library would be organized essentially by institutionalized traditions, bodies of lore handed down by teaching and enshrinable in publications. These would be traditions of dancing, of choreography, of teaching, and of presentation, with their appurtenances – costumes and sets, music and lighting, criticism – and supports (patrons and publics). Non-art and non-institutional dance would be peripheral to this central organization. All would be represented by exemplary types and prominent individuals. And there would be a penumbra of the ancillary: ideologies, theories, philosophies, programmes, autobiographies; diet, medicine, law. ... But in any case the articulation of the collection would have to follow that of the institutions that made the library necessary and possible.[2]

2.3 Dances as Individuals

The most important classification of dancing, and the most characteristic of dance as opposed to other practices, is by the names of specific dances, each peculiar to a specific culture or range of cultures. There is, for instance, a dance called 'the waltz.' It is exemplified in innumerable waltzes danced on different occasions. I dance the waltz with Matilda on Saturday 13 May 1948, at Lindsay Town Centre. The dance she and I (and no one else, at no other place and time) dance together is, in an obvious sense, one dance. But there is a no less obvious sense in which what we and all the other couples are there and then dancing is one dance – the seventh waltz of the evening. And all those seven collective waltzes, together with all the other waltzes danced on all the other evenings all over Europe and America and everywhere else, are the same dance: The Waltz. Dances have proper names, and one can capture most of dance practice by simply giving the names of all the dances there are, just as one can specify humanity by naming all the people. In fact, some people insist that no one can properly be said to be dancing unless one can specify what dance it is that they are dancing.

Things are more complex than that paragraph makes them seem. What I danced with Matilda was one specific variant of the 'the waltz' – perhaps 'The Viennese Waltz' as long current in ballrooms everywhere. But there are and have been many other variants on the waltz (lots of them invented by dancing instructors, hoping to sell the instruction sheets if not the lessons), all recognizably the waltz, but each having its own internal history. What we do at Lindsay Town Centre may not be *quite* the same as what they do at Albemarle Legion Hall, and will certainly not be exactly what our waltzing grandparents would have done where they came from. We may think of 'the waltz' as a scattered particular, the sum of all the dances designated as waltzes in relation to a recognizable development of music and movement; we can also think of it as a generic kind of dance that its own history articulates. There is also a third way of thinking of it, which I am told has become fashionable in biological circles. In the light of genetics and evolutionary theory, people say, what used to be called an animal or plant 'species' should be thought of as a sort of individual, constantly changing and having its own roughly identifiable origin and end, within which individual 'members of the species' are sub-individuals. This pattern of thought applies in a rather similar way – not quite the same, because patterns of learning and cultural influence follow different paths from those characteristic of gene pools – to culturally originated and transmitted practices such as the dance. A scattered particular, a historically articulated genus, a super-individual – the facts about the waltz support all three ways of describing it.

Because a dance like the waltz, on this understanding, consists of what a lot of different people choose to do in the light of a more or less clearly articulated schema, its formal and historical identity is bound to be shadowy at the edges. From this point of view, I will be reconsidering the matter when I come to discuss the problems of dance identity (§§19.4, 19.42). But we do think of it as one specific dance, distinguished from all other dances. That is how we most often think of dance and of most dances: the Charleston, the *kordax*, the Mexican Hat Dance, the Navajo Night Way Dance, sharply distinct cultural entities to be classified in the first instance only as dances *of* the culture in question. They are repeatable cultural forms. They can be classified, of course, in many ways: the waltz is in the first instance a ballroom dance as opposed to a theatre dance or an ethnic dance; Newcastle is a 'Playford' dance, which is a kind of country dance as opposed to a folk dance; and so forth.[3] Still, what I am dancing on a particular occasion is likely to be a named dance that I and others have danced and will dance many times. And, for the practice of dancing that dance to sustain itself, it is not necessary that it should be recognized as belonging to any particular classification, not even that it be thought of as 'dance.'

There is a noticable likeness and difference between the situation just described and the situation in music. In music, what I play or sing will probably be a song or a piece that others have performed and will perform; it is less likely that I will improvise. But the musical repertoire is larger than the available dance repertoire, and not distributed in the same way: I am likely to know more hundreds of songs than I know dozens of dances. It is not individual songs that are cultural monuments, so much as styles and composers. There is, of course, a limited international repertoire of musical masterpieces, as there is a limited international repertoire of world drama and a stable of balletic warhorses; but, in those cases, the limit is imposed by the status of classic, and exists against a more diffuse mass of occasional practice. What seems peculiar to dance as a phenomenon is that the cultural significance is everywhere borne by identifiable dances that function as recognizable constants within the cultural flow.

2.4 Dimensions of Meaning

Most people are more familiar with specific dances than they are with dance in general. To such people, the task of classifying dances must be less than compelling. Still, that is my present assignment. How should I set about it?

I have listed elsewhere some 'dimensions' of dance meaning – fundamental ways in which differences among dances may be found meaningful (Sparshott 1988, chap. 4). Any such list would underwrite a classification of dances and ways of dancing. Emphasis on one such dimension, or a profile of emphasized dimensions, would establish a significant kind of dance, even if it did not correspond to any emphasis recognized by practitioners or public. (Such an enquiry would work both ways, of course: acknowledged significances of actual dances or recognized kinds of dance would be strong candidates for our list of possible dimensions of meaning.) Then, within the scope of such a dimension, we would identify the range of actual meanings and significant contrasts.

Relevant materials from that earlier list will find their own place in what follows, but one thing needs to be said at once. One of the dimensions of variability was whether the meaningfulness in a dance was found in experience or in reflection. Similarly, an emphasis that generates a classification or a characterization may be either discovered in a dance or imputed to it. For instance, given the possibility of social or economic stratification (or lack of same) in societies, the dancers of any given dance must either share a definite stratum (or set of strata) or not. It is always open to a theorist to assert that this social/economic-stratification aspect of the dance in question is the most significant thing about it, whether the dancers or their public are aware of it or not. Such a determination may be entirely doctrinaire, or it may claim evidential support, direct or indirect. Now, new social, economic, or psychological theories may spring up at any moment, on excellent grounds or on shaky grounds or on no grounds at all. It follows that the task of cataloguing and classifying the ways of classifying and characterizing dances can never be completed, unless we choose to begin by stipulating some specific account of what dance is. There is nothing wrong with such stipulation, but it would obviously be out of place here.

2.5 Quality and Context

Roughly speaking, a dance consists of certain movements performed on a given occasion. It follows that there are two principal ways of classifying dances: by the movements, and by the occasions or contexts. The distinction is not perfectly clear-cut: the *movements* that make up a giraffe dance, for instance, may be determined principally by the requirement that they be recognizably giraffe movements; but, if that is so, there is an implicit *context* of a world in which giraffes exist and have a certain salience.[4] Accordingly, some people actually do say that mimetic dance is never pure dance, on the ground that the constituent movements are determined by the aspects of reality that the dancers have in mind rather than intrinsically by their movement qualities. This is an untidy issue, to which we must return in due course; but, meanwhile, it seems as legitimate as it is easy to distinguish roughly between what people actually do and the context of thought and fact in which they do it.

2.51 Global Concepts

The difference between quality and context is as marked as a difference could be. But many important kinds of dances are differentiated in both ways. The very reason for dancing on some particular occasion may also be a reason for dancing in one particular way rather than another; on another occasion, the reason for dancing may itself be a reason for dancing in some entirely different way. If that is so, it may never occur to the dancers to apply the same word ('dancing') to both activities, since they belong to quite different kinds of praxis. Many societies, in fact, have no single word that naturally applies to everything that we call dance (see Sparshott 1988, §8.4611). In such a society, what they call different activities we will identify as different sorts of dance. Conversely, their scholars will find that we conceptually confuse radically different sorts of activities by calling them all dances. This state of affairs will yield a lexicographical method of classification to set alongside our bibliothecal one (§2.2), and we will look at another aspect of it under the heading 'Self-defined and Other-defined' (§3.1).

One such global distinction among ways of dancing, one that is built into the cultural heritage of our civilization, is that between Hellenic *choreia* and *orchesis*.[5] Though specific to bygone thought and practice, it seems perennially significant. *Orchesis* was jumping, vertical, athletic, with a tendency to spontaneity and excitement. *Choreia* was horizontal, ordered, calm. *Orchesis* made a display of individual prowess and energy; *choreia* was an expression of social seemliness and cooperation.[6] *Choreia* tended to be cyclic; *orchesis* was more likely to be linear than not. In *choreia* the dancers moved from place to place within a designated location; *orchesis* might take place anywhere, because the significant movement was that of an individual's limbs in relation to the body. If *orchesis* had a meaning, it would be mimetic and gestural, tending to pantomime. The meaning of *choreia* would tend rather to be symbolic, figuring forth in its totality a hierarchic order (civic or celestial or both). In this, *choreia* displays a significance, while *orchesis* communicates a message.

The pair of terms we are distinguishing refer to different practices, but both practices are historically embedded in a way of life long abandoned. The fact that, despite this, we find the distinction clear and unproblematic should give us pause. It owes something to the depth of our own embeddedness in the classical thought-world and something to the influence of Hellenic literature on the patrons of dance in the formative decades of the modern age; but surely we do have here two different practices fulfilling different sorts of cultural needs, relating roughly to competition and cooperation respectively.

It is remarkable that although the two practices are so different, both in occasion and in meaning, the difference between the two Greek words is not maintained throughout the history of the very resilient language they both belong to. One might suggest that the words refer not to different kinds of practice but to different aspects of what is likely to be a single complex practice. *Orchesis*, on this showing, refers to the physical activity of dancing, and *choreia* to the social act of participating in a dance, and most dancers most of the time are doing both of these things. But that is not wholly convincing. It does seem rather that there were two basic sorts of practice in which a number of abstractly intelligible polarities were fused. What one does when one feels like dancing, and what one does when one recognizes that now is the occasion for entering into the dance, are likely to be very different things, and some such difference will remain *whatever* reasons and occasions may prevail in a given culture for doing either of those things.

The complex distinction between this pair of obsolete concepts has no current interest, but it exemplifies what may be a common phenomenon. Two or more named dances or ways of dancing may be systematically related in a culture in a number of ways, some of which tend to unite them and some to contrast them, and the relations among these may vary as unstably as alliances and hostilities among nations. Anyone concerned with the history or theory of dance has to come to terms with such unpredictable dynamics. It is no solution to throw up one's hands and confine oneself to mere description and chronicle, because in ignoring the dynamics one loses sight of what sustains the practice in existence.

CHAPTER THREE

Classification by Context

The primary context of a dance, as danced, is its historical and social setting; as choreographed, the historical and social setting of its creation. When we ask what sort of dance *Swan Lake* is, what first comes to mind is that it is a ballet; when we seek to classify it by its context, what we first note is that it is a product of the imperial Russian theatre of the late nineteenth century. If we want to know more about it, we learn more of its history. But, if we pursue this enquiry long enough, we find that we are no longer classifying the ballet but tracing the narrative of its singular history. Even our initial classification was rather misleading. What a historical account does is place a performance or a creation at a specific location in a continuous development, and what we took for classification was simply an approximate placement. To classify a work historically is to assign it to a 'period,' which commits us to the reality and distinguishability of historical periods – a commitment we might not want to make.

The conceptually suspect nature of historical classification need not make us abashed. We were right first time. *Swan Lake* is just what we said, a characteristic product of Russian imperial ballet-making at its best. Those ballets obviously had a lot in common – common properties, not just a common historical origin; but the handiest and most economical way of identifying those features is by that origin. That is partly because the easiest explanation of how those features came together and varied in relation to each other is the narrative of how it actually happened. The narrative serves as explanation, partly because it saves us from inventing reasons where none are to be found, but partly also because both the dance-makers and their public were intelligently responding to a real situation they shared. What they came up with, to the extent that it ceased to be a string of experiments and established itself as a solution, had a stable reality.

Such groupings of dynamically interrelated features, recognized and historically established, are what some philosophers of science have called 'natural kinds': we speak of a natural kind, as opposed to an artificial classification or an imposed unity, when we find a group of entities sharing a number of distinguishing features that cannot be causally attributed to a single agency. Grouping cultural phenomena by historical origin is both illuminating and classificatory to the extent that something like a natural kind seems to have emerged and stabilized itself in what would otherwise be the continuous flux of cultural process.

If a historical classification really works as a classification, it effectively picks out a group of distinguishing features. For that to be possible, the features in question must be in principle identifiable independently of their origin. Classifications by historical context thus necessarily cut across classifications by inherent distinguishable features. This works both ways. Classifying dances by distinctive features will be cut across and effectively cancelled by cultural associations. It may be true of two nations that each has war dances, and each has ecstatic dances; and these, fighting and ecstasy being what they have to be, may have a lot in common. But what war means, and what ecstasy means, to the one culture, may be quite remote from what they mean to the other.

The point made in the last paragraph is made in its strongest form by the anthropologist Clifford Geertz (1976). What art is, he says, varies according to the kind of being-in-the-world that it promotes and exemplifies, and this is something that varies radically from culture to culture. But this, he concedes, does not prevent it being a fact that, in some clear sense, all cultures and societies have art – does not prevent it because, I would say, every society obviously has some way or ways of being-in-the-world. I would add, though, that the concept of art itself is specific to our civilization, and hence to a certain way (or range of ways) of being-in-the-world, so that what can truly be said to be *done as art* covers a narrower range than what is done by one group and then said by another group to be art.[1] And this brings us to the first sort of classification by context that I will consider here.

3.1 Self-defined and Other-defined

Of all context-based classifications of dance, perhaps the most basic is that which rests on the way the dancers define themselves. Some dances are recognized by those who dance them as dances, or by some generic term of comparable scope and significance to our English word 'dance'; but much of the world's dancing is done by people in whose vocabulary no such term exists.

Since different languages, belonging to different civilizations of comparable reflectiveness and sophistication, have different conceptual groupings to cover what we call dance, and all of these (including our own) have considerable complexity, it would be foolish to set up a simple dichotomy between people who know that what they do is dancing and those who do not know that. If the concepts used by us as observers and by a group we were observing were sufficiently close, we could distinguish between, first, dances recognized as such by *us* (our scientific reference-group) but not by the dancers and *their* reference-group; second, dances recognized by the dancers and their culture but not by us; and, third, dances recognized by them as well as by us.[2] And we should bear in mind that the 'reference-group' for a group of dancers need not be uniquely determined, since they might be a subculture functioning within the ambit of some set of scientists or pundits whose authority was more or less contested or ignored.

It is indeed possible to make distinctions in such terms, but to avoid ethnocentricity (if indeed we wish to avoid it; for to avoid ethnocentricity may be to pretend to be someone other than one is, or no one at all) we would have to admit the possibility of something more complicated. We might consider drawing up a worldwide list of dance-like categories used by different cultural and linguistic groups and observing what set of criteria would be fulfilled by the dances of any given culture. But we might also differentiate dances and dance practices by the degree of self-consciousness they embodied. Some dances, and some sorts of dance, are deliberately engaged in under the concept of dance, as ways of dancing and ways of being dancers, as though inviting everyone else to 'see how *we* dance,' the whole point being that other ways of dancing are pointedly rejected. In other cases, the dancers do what they do more or less unselfconsciously, influenced only incidentally, if at all, by the knowledge that what they are doing is 'dancing' or that dancing is a preferred or a more-or-less acceptable designation of what they are doing.[3]

3.2 Forms of Life

If dances are strongly individuated and recognized by their cultural contexts, so that the most usual dance phenomenon is a named dance connected with a specific institutional or practical setting, one salient way of classifying dances will be by the 'life-forms' with which they are associated. What I mean by a 'life-form' (the term is borrowed from Ludwig Wittgenstein) is something more easily grasped and illustrated than explained.[4] Religion is an example of a life-form, involving a distinctive set of practices, ways of dressing, facial expressions and bodily comportments, ways of talking, publications and associated literary styles and typefaces, together making up a distinct part of people's lives, a part to which they and those who observe them unhesitatingly refer what pertains to it. Sport is another example: there are games to play and watch, but there are also haircuts, drinking habits, special sections of newspapers, types of clothing (not necessarily functional), and so on, which sports buffs go in for. Other examples of life-forms are sex and mating, art, theatre, education, politics, war – and, no doubt, dance, in so far as there is a dance world. These are not in any sense mutually exclusive, having the status of tendencies rather than domains: most people participate in all or many of them, and one may not always be sure at any given moment where (say) the sex ends and the religion begins. But they do afford highly recognizable and conventionally distinct contexts for action and speech, and we orientate ourselves by them. And there are dances belonging to all of them, even if dance does also constitute a life-form all on its own. Theatre dance, for instance, is a category recognized as sharply distinct from all others, even though many theatre dances also belong no less clearly to the life-form of art. There are war dances, mating dances, educational dances; and, though in any given society every such group of dances is likely to share distinctive characteristics of its own, the actual basis of the classification is not those characteristics but the life-form to which the dance is assigned.

Because they are conglomerative tendencies rather than niches, life-forms do not ground a systematic or exhaustive classification of dances, only a way in which dances may be assigned to classes. There is no reason to expect that every dance will find a box to fit, or will fit into only one box. Much dance in Europe and America belongs to physical culture, the world of the fitness buff; but physical culture is not separate from education, nor education from art, and dance departments that belong to the physical education centres of universities may lead ambiguous existences.

The concept of a life-form belongs to a grey area of conceptual sociology. But at least we can say that, wherever a dance can be unambiguously assigned to a life-form, that assignment will be one of the most important ways of classifying and characterizing the dance – characterizing as well as classifying, because it cannot but become tinged with the form to which it belongs.

The assignment of a dance to a life-form may, however, be a significant judgmental act with complex practical implications. Consider, for instance, the Sardana, the national dance of Catalonia. If we assign it to politics, we are conceptually politicizing a lot of Catalan recreation; if we assign it to 'folkways' or some such, we are downgrading Catalan nationalism. Similarly, to assign disco dancing to mating behaviour, though legitimate, is tendentious, introducing an emphasis of a kind that has in the past often been used to justify measures of social control.

3.3 Amateur and Professional

Dances for amateurs differ from dances for professionals. Among types of music, this distinction is fundamental and venerable: Aristotle's *Politics* (VIII vi) already points out that the part played in education by a sort of music that everyone can be expected to perform is very unlike that played by virtuoso performance and composition. In societies where all educated people can sing and accompany themselves on lute or piano, and can perhaps make up songs and accompaniments for themselves, acquisition of those skills will be a normal part of everyone's schooling. The sort of training undergone by operatic singers and violin virtuosi is different in itself, plays a different part in their lives, and finds it fruition in professional practice rather than in private recreation.

As with music, so with dance. In many societies, everyone acquires the steps of the best-known dances; people learn how to hold themselves and how to move with whatever the approved qualities are. But that has little to do with what ballet dancers and comparable professionals go through. John Locke, like other educationists in an age of 'polite society,' contrasted the elegance that a gentleman must acquire from his dancing lessons with the virtuosity that he must avoid (Sparshott 1988, 64). His contemporaries stigmatized the agility of the professional dancer as monkey-like; they felt it to be subhuman, because it did not pertain to any behavioural context in which civilized people might find themselves (cf. §15.22111 below).

Aristotle's distinction between types of music really had three aspects. First, it distinguished two levels of accomplishment – that which requires constant practice and that which does not. Second, it distinguished the kind of music that one makes a profession of, pertaining to the lifestyle of the professional musician, from that which is an embellishment of lives that find their centre elsewhere. And third, it distinguished between two separate instruments and repertoires: gentlemen play the lyre, professionals play the flute. The three distinctions do not necessarily go together. In our society, one might say, ballet dancing and ballroom dancing hardly overlapped in any way; movements and musics were different. The former was for professionals, the latter for amateurs. The former called for extreme skill, the latter did not. None the less, Vernon and Irene Castle danced ballroom dancing professionally and with professional virtuosity, and many children take ballet lessons without any thought that they might pursue the discipline into adolescence, much less do it for a living. Most skills can, after a fashion, be practised either amateurishly or intensively, in ways that fit into ordinary life or demand a lifetime's dedication. In some skills, however, extra dedication offers diminishing returns. It may have been a pity to lavish such care as the Castles used on such thin material.[5] In other skills, amateurishness is almost pointless. Ballet repays extreme efforts, but the efforts of casual participants might yield a better return if devoted to less complex and exorbitant routines. I at least find that there are few spectacles more disheartening than a third-rate ballet company, who have trained so hard for so many years to do such difficult things so badly.[6]

In its starkest, Aristotelian form, the contrast between amateur and professional dances divides those that belong to occasional, social or recreational dancers from those that are the perquisite of those who give their lives to dancing. And we have seen that this is a compound of various distinctions that need not go together. But not all who dance professionally, and whose dances belong to their profession, are professional dancers in that sense. In many parts of the world, including our own, there is a general profession of stage performer or 'theatrical,' who can act, sing, dance, juggle, tell jokes, do acrobatics and perhaps other 'turns' on demand, well enough to please an audience and collaborate with fellow professionals (see §14.12 below). The dances of such a person will be worked up as dance numbers and will recognizably belong to the professional stage and nowhere else (cf. §18.61).

I have spoken as if the distinction between amateur and professional were always between what belongs to a full-time career choice and what is practised as recreation or hobby. But things are not so simple. For one thing, the concepts of 'career' and 'hobby' apply to specific phenomena of our own society, which is not the only one within which amateurs and professionals are differentiated. But there are other complications closer to home. The Morris dance, before its revival by folk-dance buffs, was a professional dance in the sense that it was done by teams of skilled practitioners who did it for money – in the spring, for instance, to pick up some cash before the time of the hiring fair – but by no means as a steady living. To fulfil that role, obviously, the dance had to demand skill and training and practice together, but not the sort of constant daily study that the ballet dancer or the piano virtuoso needs.[7] Many genres of dance and music are practised at this level, with skill and devotion and in compliance with professional standards of artisanship, but not on a full-time basis, because there is no living to be made that way.[8] The crucial consideration is that the professional dance has standards of attainment and compliance that are not flexible by personal preference or taste or indulgence.

In the foregoing cases, the profession to which the dance pertains has been either dance itself or some wider genre of practice within which dance was a specialism. In such cases, the dancers' professionalism almost coincides with their technical prowess – almost, but not quite, because the professionals' attitude in their experthood makes a lot of the difference. But there are other cases that might be considered. A person's profession may, for instance, be that of priest, and that calling might include among its requirements performance of the sacred dances. Such priests are professionals because they dance ex officio, not because they professionally develop and exploit dancing skills. At the other extreme, among those whose professionalism does lie in their skill, we may single out as a special group those whose work requires the development of a special deformation or habit of the body itself. No doubt this is a matter of degree: all skills involve a transformation of the instrument. But in some the transformation is radical and conspicuous; it may even incapacitate one for other activities, and so lock one into one's profession. In any case, there are some dances one could not even attempt without laboriously making oneself into a special kind of body, and such dances are, in a quite distinctive way, not for amateurs.

The difference between amateur and professional involves a sort of gradient of self-consciousness that is relevant in various contexts, such as when considering the 'authenticity' of folk dances. I have already mentioned one sort of self-consciousness, in which the dancers are aware that what they are doing is to be conceptualized as 'dance' (§3.1). The sort of self-consciousness to which I now turn is that in which dancers are aware of how other people will see and think of the way they are dancing. At one extreme, one simply dances, without regard for whether or not anyone is looking on. Next, one may dance in the same way (and would be dancing anyway), but consciously showing others what one does. Next, one dances in the same way, showing what one does, and would not otherwise be doing it. Next, one *demonstrates* what one does, taking care perhaps that what one is doing is clearly visible and as close as possible to what one 'usually' does. Next, one dances in a way adapted for others to see, not merely to instruct others but to please them. Then, finally, one dances what one thinks the others want, conforming to their ideas of what one's dance is or what they take dance in general to be. But it is seldom easy, these days, to tell where on this scale what one is seeing (or doing) actually belongs; as a tourist in Oahu, I have found it a fascinating but baffling exercise to figure out just what the various presenters of 'traditional' hula dances thought they were showing, and what was actually being shown.

The gradient of self-consciousness has as its converse a gradient of artistic professionalism. At one extreme, one dances as a professional, accepting artistic and technical standards as one's own. But there are also gifted amateurs who are serious about their art but choose to exempt themselves from the severest challenges and obligations, amateur groups who enjoy themselves in the practice of the art without attempting to reach professional standards, and others again who simply play at the art. And these two gradations become fused when the 'onlookers' in the former gradient are thought of as the public for an art, with the standards of the art made vocal in its critics (see chapter 16).

As in music, the distinction between amateurs and professionals in dance is at odds with that between artists and virtuosi. The latter contrasts those who are appropriately judged by the primary standards of their art (expressiveness, or whatever it may be) with those who stand or fall by the secondary standards of technical accomplishment.[9] It may be found in the following remark by Théophile Gautier, who characteristically confuses it with a contrast between art and nature: 'The Spanish dancers, granted that they lack the finish, the precise correctness, the elevation of the French dancers, seem to me greatly their superiors in their grace and charm; since they work little, and did not subject themselves to those terrible loosening-up exercises which make a dance class resemble a torture chamber, they avoid that thinness (as of a horse in training) which confers on our ballets something excessively macabre and anatomical; they keep the contours and curves of their sex; they have the air of women who are dancing – not of dancers, which is something quite different.'[10]

Gautier seems to think that compliance with secondary standards precludes success by primary standards. This is a common but deplorable prejudice. But if we were to insist that, for instance, dance is essentially a matter of self-transformation, and dance artistry always a matter of how such transformations are achieved and shown, it would seem to follow that virtuosity could be expected to be at odds with artistry.

3.31 Style

The combination of the contrast between amateur and professional with that between artist and virtuoso leads us to consider the place of personal style in dancing.[11] An art such as dance progresses in depth and complexity by the successive discovery of ways in which the materials of the art can be made to bear meaning and systematically exploited and varied to that end. To master an art is to master every aspect of everything in the domain of the art that can be thematized – that is, singled out as something about which the artist can (and therefore must) do something in each work, even if the decision is to play it down or disregard it. Such artists have taught themselves to take systematically into account, and to handle in their work, many things; it is characteristic of learners, of bodgers, and especially of amateurs not even to realize that there is so much that one has to come to terms with, even if they have occasional brilliant successes. We ascribe such successes to 'beginner's luck,' not so much because they unexpectedly succeed in what they attempt as because their failure to attempt all sorts of relevant things turns out not to have spoiled their work.

What we mean by the individual 'style' of a professional artist is the acquired habit of handling each thematizable aspect of the art in a characteristic way and of relating those aspects to each other in an integral way that is equally personal and characteristic. Richard Wollheim (1979) argues that we do not take art seriously unless it is a manifestation of style in this sense. Style, then, is what differentiates professionals from amateurs among creators of dances, whether they be creative dancers or choreographers. Such a style need not be distinctive – one's personal way of working may not be markedly different from the way others do things; but it is necessary that one have developed a hierarchy of choices, in terms of which one works, and in which one is not at a loss.

The reason why Isadora Duncan overwhelmed artistic Europe and inspired young dancers, but was despised by many of the artists and advocates of the Russian ballet, may have been that she remained amateurish and never developed a style in the sense we are now considering: critics well versed as professionals in the art of dance were blind to what she could do, not just because they were hidebound and prejudiced, but because they could observe her failure to reach a level of accomplishment she did not even know to be possible.[12]

The foregoing paragraph is tendentious, as the implied critique of Duncan suggests. The idea of style it advances is a *beaux arts* ideal, that of a systematic education in an art in which progress is possible without loss. Its opponents might say that a style in that sense is not necessary; what one needs is only genius that knows no law. But people who say that will also be opposed to the idea of professionalism. And, since professional artists are for the most part intensely proud of their professionalism, the issue arouses strong and mixed feelings, as one can see by the remark quoted from Gautier in the previous section.

Without accepting the notion of unfettered genius, one might protest that the idea of style sketched here rests on a false model of an art as constituted by a determinate exfoliation of variables. An artist like Duncan has a style of her own, with its own set of variables and systems of choice. The critics of whom I spoke were as blind to the parameters of her dance as she was to the basics of ballet.[13] But the principle is unaffected. Wherever an art is professionally practised there must be a system of skills and related options that professionals master and amateurs do not.

3.4 Regular and Irregular

Some dances are tied to a particular occasion; others are not. Comparable distinctions hold in other arts as well. In painting, altarpieces and icons constitute separate classes of works, even apart from the fact that their use and place normally go with an appropriate iconography. In music, there is a difference between Christmas carols and harvest hymns, and in general between seasonal and ceremonial works that pertain more or less strictly to specific occasions and pieces that may be appropriately performed whenever their content is musically acceptable. Some such distinctions are observed more strictly than others – rood screens may be taken down and moved to museums, and Haydn masses are favoured concert pieces, whereas Christmas carols are seldom heard in midsummer; but in no case are they given pride of place in theoretical treatments of those arts. The corresponding distinctions among dances seem to be more important.

One of the big differences between arts is the extent to which the context of performance is divorced from the context of reception. A painting done for a church, once completed, becomes a decorative object that can in principle be moved; it can certainly be reproduced, and is most familiar as thus replicated. And it is as recordings that the world's music is most ubiquitous, so that we eavesdrop in our living-rooms on what a choir did – and now does timelessly – in its church on a festival. But dances, other than theatre dances, are characteristically social entities and tied to their occasions. Dances are not readily transportable or available in reproduction: an ethnic dance toured around the world is accepted as something wrenched from its context, a cut flower.

However firm and deep their social roots, dances do have distinct forms and accordingly are in one way or another repeatable. Kinds of dance differ according to the type and degree of uniqueness of the occasion they are tied to and the strength and strictness of the tie. Some are appropriate to very specific ceremonies and occasions, being performed, say, only at a specific annual celebration. Such a dance need not even be rehearsed – children and novices, who will probably in any case have seen the dance done, will tag along, encouraged and prodded into place by their elders. Other dances are proper to certain sorts of occasion: funeral dances, coming-of-age dances, and the like, to be done whenever and only when such an occasion arises. Others again are proper to seasons, and to other situations determined by time and circumstances rather than by a structured occurrence to which they are integral. And, finally, there are dances that are danced whenever one wishes to dance them or wishes to have them danced, for pleasure or profit, in response to the general wish for a dance or to the specific wish for this particular dance as the very dance it is.

This type of classification could, obviously, be elaborated, in ways the suitability of which would depend on rules observed by the dancers' society or divined by the analyst. In any case, it could work out in three ways. A dance could be linked to a particular season or occasion or festival simply because it was in fact danced only then. Nothing about village Morris dances made them suitable, or felt by anyone to be suitable, to the traditional occasions of their dancing: they simply were the dances that were traditionally danced then. Alternatively, a dance could be felt to be appropriate to its proper season (like Sir Roger de

Coverley at a Dickensian Christmas), without there being any way in which that appropriateness was articulated. And, finally, a dance might be suited to its occasion by dynamic or mimetic features, as a dance performed before battle might involve violent movements, threatening gestures, and even a waving of spears. In this last case, clearly, the contextual difference would be coupled with formal differences among the kinds of movement performed.

3.5 Audiences

Some dances exist for the dancers, some for an audience: dances for doing, and dances for showing. Chapter 16 deals generally with the relations between dancers and spectators. But many dances exist for a collective comprising both – one in which, for instance, the distinction between dancers and spectators is that between those of us who are now dancing and those of us who are not now dancing, but in which the dance falls short of full realization unless there is a sufficient audience at hand. And perhaps we should add a fourth category: dances that are acknowledged to be demanded by the nature of the world, and in which the world is, as it were, watching. Something like that could be the way the Hopi think of their dances.

I have noted above (§3.3) the gradation of self-consciousness from dancers concerned only with their own dancing to dancers putting on a show to please an audience. It is a commonplace of our civilization that the place of many dances is equivocal and contested. A dance developed by a dancer, out of the need to find personal expression or artistic fulfilment in dance, may find its outlet in public performance, and then become transformed into a show, so that in a way the dancer loses control over it.[14] A dance that fulfils a ballerina's technical or artistic ambition, developed to meet the exacting standards of connoisseurs, may be performed in the context of the Jockey Club's taste for the appearance of scantily dressed young women – and the precise form in which the artistic requirements are developed and fulfilled may have been modified by that constraint.[15] At dance performances, as at musical performances, there is likely to be a tension between art-lovers, virtuosity-lovers, and sensation-lovers – and, of course, in our eclectic age, among art-lovers of different stamps.[16] The essential difference is perhaps that between the appreciative and the unappreciative – between those who respond primarily to what they correctly take the artist to be appropriately achieving, and those who respond to something else – to the artist's vigour, or skill, or beauty, or human expressiveness. But today's public concerts depend on a self-renewing type of audience of varying taste, experience, and degree of commitment, to which any work of performance art must in fact look for its only possible realization (see the beginning of chapter 16). Such a work must be susceptible of appreciation from many viewpoints and at many levels.

The whole set of relationships among artists and audiences in a civilization in which the practices of dancing for fulfilment and dancing for display are both recognized to exist is bound to be different from that which prevails in communities in which audiences are not institutionalized, but dances are, and in which the satisfaction dancers take in their prowess is reinforced by the appreciation of fellow-dancers but not dependent on any possible source of applause.

3.6 Dancers

Just as different dances may be proper to different occasions, so different dances may be appropriated to different sorts of person. Some dances are for the old, some for the young, some for males only, some for females only.[17] These specifications may be merely matters of custom, so that if a man dances a woman's dance he acts oddly but not necessarily offensively; or there may be ritual stipulations, so that a man dancing a woman's dance is out of line and gives offence. In some cases the insistence on a particular kind of dancer – a virgin, or someone who has killed in battle, or the hereditary chief – may relate to definite social or ritual functions of the dance in question. But there are other dances that may be danced by anyone capable of making the movements (as in standard ballroom dances, and in any general-purpose social dance), and others in which preference for a particular age or sex prevails but is not felt to have any compelling force at all. Often the situation is equivocal or obscure. In Euripides' *Bacchae*, the aged seer Tiresias says that the god must be served by all, young or old, male or female; but the action of the play shows that in fact the dance in question was for adult women only, and the culmination of the dance in a ritual 'tearing' (*sparagmos*) relates to that fact.

I have picked out the differentiation of dancers by age and sex as being the most obvious sort, but it is certainly not the only possible one. Scottish reels are dances for Scots to dance: other people also dance them, but, as it were, in quotation marks, assuming honorary Scothood. There can be dances of particular ranks or statuses or callings: anyone can dance a sailors' hornpipe, but at one time only sailors did, and it is clear that it might have been prohibited for anyone else to do so. And dances for particular ranks, trades, professions, and other socially differentiated groups merge into dances reserved for particular individuals and officials – dances that may be danced, for instance, only by the high priest and the king;[18] and these in turn, because the dance of an individual is likely to pertain to what the individual does when officiating in some specific personal or official capacity, will merge into those dances that belong to particular seasons and times, a division that belongs to a different category (§3.4 above).

3.7 The Context of Art

When we focus on dance as art, or as artistic, many ways of classifying dance impose themselves: ways of distinguishing between what is art and what is not art; different ways in which a dance may count as art (by figuring in a ballet company's repertoire, for instance, or by being 'seen as dance' by some 1960s pundit); or such distinctions as that between being an art form, being artistic, and being considered from the aesthetic point of view. Any workable definition of art will generate a battery of such distinctions. Viktor Shklovsky, for instance, equates art with the defamiliarization (*ostranenie*, making strange) of objects.[19] If one accepted that definition, one could run through the familiar resources of the arts and consider how many ways of 'making strange' they include – distortion of form, novelty or oddness of content, unfamiliarity of the code used, superposition of code on code, freshness of juxtaposition or context, and so on – and then see how many of those sorts of device had been used, or might be used, in dance. Alternatively, one could look at dance, and see how much of its interest depended on some form of defamiliarization, and how widely that form was used (or could be used) in other dances. Other general views of art would generate similar possibilities. They would be worth pursuing, but I won't. I return to the general question of the values and standards of art in §15.212.

3.71 High Art

A nation's official culture identifies itself, in part, by its poets, architects, painters, and sculptors. It glories in them: they are advertised, subsidized, promoted, and so forth, in a quite distinctive way, to claim a place in the company of culturally gifted peoples, showing that one is civilized enough to prize such gifts. Supreme exponents of such arts may be identified as 'national treasures.' The arts in which prowess may achieve such recognition we may set aside from all others, not by the general and rather ambivalent term 'fine arts,' but as 'high arts.' The implication is that these arts enhance life in a way that warrants large expenditure of public energy and public funds. In our own civilization, ballet has fairly regularly been allowed such a place, and has been joined, especially in America, by 'Modern and Post-Modern' dance, an amorphous tradition marked out precisely by the aspiration to replace ballet as high art.[20] A branch of dance has clearly attained the status of high art if it gets a special subvention from the public purse, rather than lining up for an arts-council handout with the rest of the penurious art-world; a less equivocal sign of that status is that it can call on composers, painters, and poets from the other high arts to supply its scenarios, scenery, costumes, and music.

Virtually all 'high art' dance is theatre dance, partly because something like a theatre is needed as a display case for the gem. But by no means all theatre dance belongs to high art; the stage is hospitable to all sorts of entertainment or display dancing. Use of the term 'high art' is ideological, conceding the right to claim the deepest significance and the highest seriousness the term 'art' can be used to invoke. At least four kinds of value may be involved. First, there is the fine-arts value of technical accomplishment and finesse – a high art must be of exceptional difficulty or require exceptional gifts. Second is aesthetic value of an exceptional sort, the presumption that the accomplishment and finesse are devoted to something that repays a highly developed appreciative skill and personal involvement. Third is prestige value; the high arts are socially acceptable in some way that calls forth and celebrates distinction for their practitioners – if they are slaves, they are very expensive slaves. And, fourth, there is heritage value, the high arts permanently pertaining to whatever maintains and defines the cultural community. These four kinds of value are not always equally present, but it is their confluence that gives the notion of a high art such substance as it has.[21]

3.72 The Dance and Dancing

There is a general distinction to be made between, on the one hand, *the dance*, conceived in a given social context as a specific art, a specialized set of skills that have to be learned and developed, conjoined (in most cases) to an institution to which one stands in some definite form of membership relation, and, on the other hand, *dancing*, a form of activity that anyone can engage in. This distinction does not coincide with that between high art and the rest, or with that between professional and amateur: not every art is a high art, and an amateur may learn and practise an art. What distinguishes the dance from dancing is the need for focused learning. Dancing, in the present sense, is something that need not be learned at all, otherwise than in the way one learns the basic skills of language and operations that are diffused throughout one's culture and are the common possession of the people.[22]

In any art or practice that is recognized in a culture, if there is no taboo or exclusive role assignment to stand in the way, anyone may at some time feel called upon (or *be* called upon) to practice it in a rudimentary way. Anyone, in our society, may be called on to write a verse, or make a drawing, or dance, or get a sound from an instrument, or sing, or whittle, or darn a sock, or put up a shed. And one can make some sort of stab at it. Everyone has some sense of the appropriate form of care. One may neither possess the necessary skill nor know how to acquire it; but everyone has a rudimentary sense of *what it would be like* to develop it. A person who cannot play the flute will probably be unable to get any other sound from it than the sound of heavy breathing – flute-playing is not a common possession of the culture. Flautists are specialists. But music *is* a common possession: everyone knows enough to ask meaningfully, 'How do you play this thing?', has some sense of what a musical instrument is and what it is to play one. In the cases of dancing and versifying or singing, the specialist skills are refinements of and developments from the unspecialized skills and styles of body movement, voice production, and language use. In such cases, everyone can do something that will serve as a simulation of, and hence as an approximation to, a rudimentary degree of the skill of the art. In this sense, everyone can actually dance, sing, and versify, and may from time to time do so if nothing prevents.

Dancing, like the uses of other art media, may be art-related in three ways: by issuing from one of the recognized motivations or points of view of art; by constituting an actual practice of art as an institutional reality; and by having some other appropriate relation (simulation or resemblance, for example) to the practices of the art. Our present polarity separates dancing, conceived as an outgrowth from the abilities and concerns that anyone in a culture may be expected to have, from the

dance as an art that has to be learned. On a given occasion, what someone does is likely to partake of both: the practitioners of the art will be
humanly sustained by whatever it is that makes other people dance,
and people who share in the practice of dancing will behave in ways
that reflect their knowledge of an attitude to the dance, as dancers
dance it.

3.73 Spontaneous and Enforced

The distinction between dancing and the dance relates to a difference
between what individuals do as from their own resources and what
they do by way of conforming to a pre-existing structure of practice.
The difference can be made out to be illusory, because in each case the
people are doing what they have learned to do; but it does answer to
a real contrast in the way things are felt about and done. It shades into
yet another contrast, that between the spontaneous and the enforced.
There is a difference between children's skipping games, which are
perhaps rudimentary dances, and dances like Sir Roger de Coverley,
which (in my day) the same children would do at Christmas parties at
the instigation of presumably benevolent adults.[23] It is the difference
between activities organized from the top down and those organized
from the bottom up. Some pedagogical writings on dance distinguish
'educational dance' as one genre of dance among others: the idea is, or
should be, not only that physical education stands alongside therapy,
art, and ritual as one characteristic context in which dancing occurs, but
also that the presumed context of a uniformity authoritatively imposed
without regard to any spontaneity of the dancers (beyond their initial
submission to the curriculum) generates a recognizable set of ways of
dancing. What is imposed must be imposable – a drill.[24]

   Ideally, educational dance would be dance that contributed to education and thus liberated the students by putting them in control of their
own bodies and enhancing their sense of personal autonomy.[25] But, ever
since this ideal has been in place, critics have observed that it is the
school that defines the autonomy and prescribes its conditions – the
children are 'forced to be free.'

3.74 Learnable and Unlearnable

What is imposed must be imposable. Some dances can be easily and
completely learned; others cannot. In some sorts of communal dances,

such as an American square dance, anyone who has learned the steps can do them as well as anyone could. So long as one does not make a mistake or lose one's place, one's participation in the dance, as expressive or symbolic, is complete and perfect. The only relevant requirement is to get the moves right. Other kinds of dance must not only be done right, but done well. The difference is roughly that between dances conceived digitally and those conceived analogically. In the former, there are only a few simple choices to be made. Once one has memorized these, and what counts as exercising them, there is nothing more to learn; no other differentiations or variations count. This is very different from learning to perform movements gracefully, or exquisitely, or beautifully – a kind of learning in which there is no simple alternative of right or wrong and in which, consequently, the notion of *completeness* in learning has no application.[26]

Given that in a 'learnable' dance there is no place for refinements, two situations are possible. It is conceivable that such a dance should take place in a context in which no participant or judge has any concept of any other way of dancing; but it is more likely that those involved should also know of dances in which other dance values are relevant. In the latter case, it will be possible for someone to perform the 'learnable' dance in a way that is recognized by the dancer and by others as complying with some of those other values, converting the dance (so far as this individual dancer is concerned) into a display of elegance, or daintiness, or agility, or whatever. When that happens, two views may be taken of the matter. The aberrant dancer may be judged to be dancing the learnable dance badly, because it is inappropriate to make such a dance the occasion for displays of that kind. But, if one says that, it appears that we did not describe the learnable dance completely. It does, after all, make specific aesthetic demands, over and above those of compliance with the right choices: demands of propriety, unobtrusiveness, cooperativeness, modesty, and so forth. These are clearly aesthetic standards, though they are not specifically dance values, since they demand social tact rather than dancerly skill. The alternative view of the matter is that individual dancers may, if they please, make the learnable dance an occasion for the enjoyment or display of prowess, but that is irrelevant to the dance as such. Such a dancer is doing two sorts of dance in one, a communal dance and an uncovenanted solo. And this may very often happen, in a round dance that is done in public where there is someone watching whom the dancer wishes to impress. Such displays of 'strutting one's stuff' are likely to be regarded with indulgence or sympathetic amusement by the unbesotted, and may be felt neither to mar nor to enhance the dance, but to fall under the heading of 'by-play.'

3.75 Kinds of Art as Kinds of Dance

To the extent that dance is an art or a set of arts, any classification of works of art, of performances, of artists, of art forms, of functions of art, or more generally of kinds of art may engender a corresponding classification within the field of dance, unless it is such that all dance necessarily occupies the same place within it. I have elaborated many such distinctions elsewhere (Sparshott 1982c, chap. 7 and appendix B; Sparshott 1963, chap. 6). One might run through such classifications, in case some of them turned out to have specific relevance to dance. I will not do it here.

3.751 The Institutional Theory

Dance is a form of life (§3.2) – one of those domains, real but vaguely delimited, around which human affairs cluster. A dance could be equated with a performance or activity that pertained to that domain in a way that could be recognized, though we would not expect to be able to specify it in words.

Within the context of art, itself a form of life, we can go further. In that form of life there are objects – works of art – that are regarded and treated in a complex and distinctive way: subjected to interpretation and criticism, and so on. The form of life constitutes, or is centered on, the 'artworld' or 'Republic of Art,' which is institutionalized in that it has a coherent structure involving organs of education, presentation, preservation, discussion, and so on. An influential view of art has held that works of art cannot be defined otherwise than as artefacts (or, in extreme versions, *anything at all*) that are put forward as candidates for this sort of treatment.[27]

People deeply concerned with an art, exceptionally sensitive to it, and (as one might expect) practically involved with it as practitioner or promoter or critic, may be able to 'see as art' things that are not usually so seen, and may then claim for them the status of work of art. This is true especially in the art of dance, where there is no prescriptive medium other than the stillness and movement of human bodies – that is, everything anyone does. There is no limit on what one can meaningfully claim to be a work of dance art.

Institutional theories typically require us to concede that everything suitably brought within the ambit of the dance world is a work of dance art. But not all such claims are on the same footing (cf. chapter 13 note 10, below). Some may be frivolous; some are based on an artist's deep knowledge and sensitivity. Claims will not be taken seriously, of course, unless they rest on a real and shareable possibility of seeing and doing and understanding something in meaningful relation to what one has learned to appreciate as dance. But, more important, understanding of what it is to be dance, and what it is to see something as dance, could not be built up from random examples of action that are dance only because they are declared to be within the ambit of the dance world. There has to be a coherent body of skill and sensitivity with enough character of its own for meaningful extrapolation to be possible.

Given enough coherence in one's experience of dance for extrapolation to be a possible act of the understanding, the status of dance can be claimed for new candidates on quite different bases. One can simply regard the candidate as within the range of one's established acceptances. Or one can claim that one's understanding of dance should be so stretched as to include the candidate, so that in time it will form part of the normal base of the understanding of dance art. Or one can be simply carried away by the institutional theory itself, by the realization that *even this* can be seen as dance!' Unfortunately, neither devotees nor critics of vanguard movements in the arts usually pay any attention to the differences among these three. A generalization about the art of dance may then be met with a 'counterexample' which in fact derived its original point from its abnormality.

A philosophical approach to the arts of dance is reduced to nonsense both by including vanguardist ploys within the scope of dance and by excluding them. One needs to consider, in each case, on what grounds it was claimed to be dance, and on what grounds and in what sense it is now claimed to be dance or not to be so. Institutional theories of art are invaluable as articulating the structured way in which art is a form of life but risk distracting our attention from the different ways in which performances and artefacts enter into the structures.

3.76 Privileged and Unprivileged

Granted that a special status attaches to whatever counts as 'high art,' one often meets claims that one and only one kind of artistic dance is worthy of respect as truly dance, purely dance, fully dance, or authentically dance. The specific values embodied in those four adverbs are the following. First, some practices and art forms that pass for dance are, not really dance at all (under some preferred definition), but something else – mime, gymnastics, clowning, performance art, or something; however excellent by their own lights, these do not embody the specific values of dance. Second, some true dances are impure, combining (and contaminating or compromising) the values of dance with extraneous values: showmanship, spectacle, narrative, music, or whatever it may be. Pure dances, however rare and however unpopular, have a special place in the hearts and minds of true lovers of dance. Third (the converse of the second, in effect), some dances puristically confine themselves to what dance alone can achieve. But such dances do not attain the full richness of dance as we know and love it, in which an engrossing and affecting story, brilliantly danced, is embellished with sumptuous costumes, dramatic lighting, and spectacular athleticism. It is by the range and splendour of such opulent shows that the full potentialities of dance are revealed, and it is against them that more niggardly dance forms are to be judged. Fourth, a dance or dance form, however pure and austere (or rich and full) in its realization, may be inauthentic, working out some intellectual ideal or aiming at some visible effect conceived independently of dance as such. An authentic dance is the honest working-out of a pure dance idea.[28] Only such a dance really earns the reverence due to art.

Words like 'art' have both laudatory force and descriptive sense (cf. Sparshott 1982c, 213–15). The four adverbs whose implications I just looked at exemplified a common tendency to restrict both the force and the sense of such a term to a subset of the practices to which critics and public usually apply it. Such restriction raises three questions. Given that various practices are generally accepted as art and as dance, we ask, first, why anyone should think that only one form of dance can be artistically respectable; second, on what grounds one should decide what the privileged form should be; and, third, why anyone should want to assign positions of cultural privilege at all. I deal with the first two questions together.

Some of the reasons for privileging one dance form over others rely on beliefs about the shape and significance of history. Not all art forms, it is argued, form part of a significant practice, of which a rational history could be written. But humanity is nothing but human history; what matters to our common self-understanding is what enters into a rational unfolding of possibilities. Such a rational unfolding must take the form of a dialectic. If the dialectic of art is integral to the dialectic of history at large, there can at any one time be only one form of any true art that answers to the real development of humankind. What that form is, the philosophical student of history can at worst guess and at best divine. These are all very strong contentions, and as stated they seem to be beyond belief; but modest versions of them can be persuasive. Some stories are better than others, and some dance forms fit more easily into such stories than others. What doesn't fit is relegated by philosophical critics to the cosmic equivalent of 'Off Broadway.'

If we prefer not to invoke history in that way, we can invert the argument and look forward. Not all art forms contribute to the development of the possibilities of their art. Dance that widens the horizons of dance has a privileged position at the cutting edge of the art.[29] This view of the matter, however, does not impel us to extend privilege to only one dance form at any one time, for possibilities may simultaneously be opened up in several directions.

If we do not wish to trust either the overall shape of history or the opening up of the unforeseen, we can confine our attention to the situation confronted by any practitioner of an art at any given time. The present state of the art will pose certain questions, issue certain challenges; whatever answers those questions and responds to those challenges is clearly serious in a way that less engaged and responsive practices are not. Of course, any specific judgment in this area risks being in error, taking a fad for the true centre of artistic activity or misconstruing the inner import of what is correctly divined to be central. But, in any area in which it makes sense to ask what is really going on, readiness to take such risks is the measure of seriousness.

Historical reasons for assigning privilege to some dance forms and withholding it from the rest always assume that one can distinguish between the inner significance of what is going on and mere surface phenomena. If such a distinction is in place, privilege can be earned. Of course, it is not obvious that the distinction can always be made; but, if it cannot, it is hard to see how the practice of any art could be serious.

One may assign privilege to some dance forms and withhold it from others without appealing to the shape of time. For instance, one can argue that artistic significance, in dance or anywhere else, requires fine discrimination of specific differences within the scope of the art. Such discrimination can be learned only by long experience of, and close application to, a restricted subject matter. That calls for the development of limited forms and styles, both for practitioners and for audiences. Art forms that have in fact developed in such a way as to impose precise and stringent demands on artists and observers may, accordingly, be assigned a privileged place. The privilege depends entirely on the epistemic and appreciative structures they subtend, not at all on any connection with the state of the world, and not on any direction in which the art itself may be changing.

Again, it is argued that not all genres and styles can be equally well developed within the medium and formal resources of a given art. In dance, what lends itself to artistic exploitation may be thought to depend on what the human body is capable of; not all dance forms operate effectively within those constraints, and those that do may earn a privileged place.

Somewhat similarly, it may be argued that not all genres and styles of dance develop and make available the resources of meaning and emotional effect that are specific to the dance medium. Here, the scope of the art is conceived not as a set of constraints on what can be fruitfully attempted but as a set of possibilities to be exploited and limits to be overcome. A special esteem belongs to those dance forms that do one or the other, whatever position they may hold in the artistic or generally cultural hierarchies in which they flourish. As before, judgments that a given dance or dance form has succeeded in this way, or has failed by ignoring and violating real limitations, may well be parochial or biased; but such errors in judgment do not invalidate the grounds on which the judgments purport to be based.

Actual claims to a privileged status may be confused, as appears from a well-known article by Marshall Cohen (1983). He examines the rival claims advanced on behalf of two supposed tendencies in artistic dance – modernism and syncretism. The latter claim is based on comprehensiveness and advocates dance that appeals to the totality of perception and involves the enlistment of all the arts in the service of the dance experience; the former is based on clarity and purity, aiming at the quintessence of dance through the emphasis on the nature of the medium of dance (the moving body) and its inherent potential. These are, respectively, the 'richness' and 'purity' I mentioned above, and the fundamental values involved are, on the one hand, the social dimension of dance and its integration into the whole fabric of life, and, on the other hand, the capacity of an art as such to refine and develop a particular range of sensibility.

So far, all is clear. But this contrast is now confusingly combined with that between 'primitivism,' the supposed original condition of humanity before specialization and alienation set in, and 'modernism,' the supposed revolution in art practice that took place in the late nineteenth and early twentieth centuries – a confusion against which Cohen partly protests and to which he partly succumbs. He further conflates two issues: the dubious validity of arguments that seek to win one set of values an exclusive privilege over others, and the abuse of descriptions to attach the preferred values to a particular claimant. Cohen argues, and shows by many examples, that actual dances do not conform to these supposed norms. The arguments about privilege belong to the rhetoric that surrounds dance practice (what choreographers and their public-relations people say) and do not affect the mainsprings of that practice itself (what choreographers and dancers do). Such theories, says Cohen, stand in the way of 'an adequate account of the central manifestation and achievements of dance as we know it'; we need 'a more accurate description of its formal nature and its historical qualities' (Marshall Cohen 1983, 176–7).

Yes, but dance as who knows it? What Cohen knows is the New York scene, and what is central in the Big Apple may not be so in the great globe itself. How are we to describe manifestations and achievements, without knowing what kind of success choreographers are ready to stand or fall by? Cohen could argue that the very fact that one sees something evidently worth seeing and describing is assurance enough that one has achieved the appropriate point of view. Well, one has seen *something*; but there is room for a bit more dialectic here, as we will see later (§§12.3, 15.22, 17.5).

I have been looking at ways in which dances may derive privilege from their specific historical and cultural contexts. Since any dance phenomenon is what it is only because of its situation, there is no need for us to take any higher ground or breathe more rarefied air. Such stances are, however, possible. I name three.

First, human beings uniquely represent the corporeal presence of reflective sentience in and to the world – there could be other such beings, but we know of none. If only one form of dance can manifest this uniqueness, that form of dance will be important as no other dance can be. If all or many forms of dance share in the manifestation, they will share the privileged position to the extent that they do share it (Fraleigh 1987).

Second, human beings as such are capable of inherently expressive ways of moving their bodies. A form of dance that exploited these possibilities would be important as no other form of dance could be. No other art than dance exploits them so purely and directly, and there is nothing else that dance can do and no other art does.[30]

Third, a persistent philosophical tradition envisages the universe as a single self-knowing system (see Sparshott 1988, §9.1). If that ideal standpoint could really be taken, it would determine a place for ideal forms of every art and science. It is thinkable that dance as an art could occupy such a place. If it did, then that place might afford a privileged position for those dance forms that were appropriate to the place. Since this set of possibilities exercises a compelling attraction over some imaginations – those who are so attracted insist that it is impossible seriously to think the alternatives through – there is a persistent vogue for theories that draw postdated cheques on its eventual credit. The argument is that there is no real doubt about what sort of standpoint it would have to be, if only we could find the way through to it.

In general, people who would claim a privileged position of esteem for some dance practices over others might well argue that the alternative is not that all forms of dance are equally good, but that all are alike trivial, incapable of being related to serious human concerns. But one could retort that the most serious human concern of all is a respect for freedom, autonomy, and the uninhibited play of intelligence, to which any principle of privilege must be inimical.[31]

One of our three initial questions remains. Why would anyone want to establish a position of unique cultural privilege for any mode of dance, however serious? An argument for the importance, even the unique importance, of any sort of dance is not in itself an argument in favour of allowing it any privilege. 'The poorest he that is in England hath a life to live as the greatest he';[32] choreographers of high-school musicals arrange their numbers unabashed and unthreatened by the thought of Ashton or Graham. Does not the claim to privilege smack of elitism? But the answer to that is no, of course it doesn't, if by elitism you mean the ranking of preferences according to the social position of those whose preferences they are; and if you mean anything other than that, you should tell us what you do mean, and what you think is wrong with it.

Claims of privilege are in place wherever there is competition that cannot be suitably settled by the market. In dance, there can be competition for esteem and competition for material resources. Esteem, affection, and individual bounty can perhaps be left to the marketplace, but dominant institutions have to proceed on other principles. Foundation and government funding must go to some projects rather than others and cannot afford to seem capricious; critical space in the dominant organs of opinion is scarce and must be rationed on some principles or other. Arguments in favour of one dance form over all others amount to little more than claims to substantial reviews and sustaining grants; and the best such claims, because the most defensible in public, are those that appeal to worthiness as established by agreed and defensible principles. But no doubt the real battle for prestige is waged in the individual consciousness of dance people and in the collective consciousness of the dance world. The men must always be reassuring themselves that they have really killed the Father and are now patriarch of the horde, and no doubt the women reassure themselves that Earth Mother loved them best.

The intellectual and political battles of prestige and privilege are inevitable, not only because scarcity prevails in the world, but also because our hearts and minds are small. We have to have some way of restricting our concern, some way of establishing preferences among our preferences, and some basis for reviewing those second-order preferences themselves. But the public debates, like the famous old one between ballet and modern dance, or the one between formalism and eclecticism, or the one that Cohen speaks of between modernism and primitivism, have an air of absurdity about them. Is anyone going to argue ballet-lovers out of appreciating ballet? Is there any sense in which Martha Graham offers an *alternative* to Busby Berkeley, and vice versa? One doesn't quite see how.

3.761 Imperial Elites

I distinguished above between the vicious elitism that allows aesthetic privilege to art forms on the basis of the social position of their publics and the presumably benign system, whether it be called 'elitism' or not, that accords that privilege to those who succeed magnificently in doing what the rest of us are trying to do. But that distinction ignores the facts of sociocultural empires. What we call civilizations are not simply enlarged tribes but include within their scope all sorts of cultural enclaves that maintain their own ways of life, including their own arts. A civilization superimposes on these living unities a common administrative system that embodies a common understanding of how things are done, supported by a common education system (such as that epitomized in the worlds' universities today), incorporating an officially approved body of artistic practice. People nowadays often write of such common systems as if they were simply the local culture of one group whose political strength has enabled it to enforce privilege and prestige for its own tastes.[33] No doubt that is, often if not always, how the systems originate, but it is not how they function. The sort of dancing epitomized by the Kirov, the sort of music exemplified by the Vienna Philharmonic, simply is not the peculiar property of any ethnic group; it is part of a worldwide cultural system, like that of science. The point is not that it is necessarily better than what we do back home in the village or the suburb, but that it belongs to the coordinating system that makes the civilization a communicable unity.[34]

In relation to the educational and cultural system that defines the operative life of the civilization as a whole, other art forms may be defined as folk arts, which people practise in ways that are sustained by common local tradition without regard to any educational superstructure, or as ethnic arts, which are practised with the conscious aim of sustaining the common life and identity of a group that recognizes or claims common kinship. Within the arts built into the common 'official' educational system, one distinguishes between the metropolitan and the provincial, according to their proximity to the originating centres where power is concentrated and to which talent gravitates. These are not idle terms of praise and abuse; they reflect the ways in which cultural life in complex imperial systems is organized.[35]

3.77 The Sanskrit Alternative

Mandakranta Bose (1991) reviews the anatomy of the arts of dance recoverable from Sanskrit treatises, covering a millennium and a half and a subcontinent. As one would expect, the record is baffling, full of ambiguities and reversals. In that, it is no different from the history of theory in the West; but the lack of social and historical background would make it impenetrable, even if its categories were closer to our own. I will mention a few items from Bose's account, warning the reader not to rely on my interpretations.

The fundamental text in Sanskrit dance theory is the *Natyashastra*, from about the second century CE, which anatomizes the dance form *natya*, music dance drama based on traditional texts (Banerjee [1983] calls it 'ballet,' assigning both *natya* and the Western forms to the same remote origins in central Asia). Later texts accept the *Natyashastra* as authoritative and purport to be commentaries on it, even when they are being original.[36] The treatise also recognizes and anatomizes a purely aesthetic dance of beautiful movement, *nrtta*, but it does not acknowledge this as a separate art form – presumably there was no such practice of public performance, though making such movements and combining them in dances would obviously have to be part of a performer's training.

Later, *nrtta* was recognized as a separate practice, but was then (tenth century CE, p. 109) accompanied by a new term, *nrtya*, expressive dance as opposed to purely aesthetic dance. What was distinctive of *nrtya* seems to have been narrative content; *nrtta* would presumably not be inexpressive, but pervaded with *rasa* (cf. §15.21211, below). A later theorist (Samgadeva, Bose 57) recognizes the situation by introducing a generic term for dance, *nartana*, of which *nrtta*, *nrtya*, and *natya* are three categories; but this usage did not become general. In addition, Samgadeva maintains from the *Natyashastra* a distinction between two basic ways of dancing: *tandava*, athletic and masculine dance associated with Siva, and *lasya*, graceful and feminine dance associated with Parvati.

The distinction between *tandava* and *lasya* is variable and multiform, like the Western distinction between grace and vigour (§15.2211–15.22112). But it has been suggested (Bose 1991, 120) that it should not be seen primarily as one between two modes of sensibility: since Siva is maker and destroyer of worlds, the *tandava* should be beyond sensibility, a dance of sheer celebration, whereas *lasya* would be the dance of sensibility in general. But Bose observes (163) that in fact *lasya* 'appeared in the *Natyashastra* as a delicate movement used in dramatic presentations, and later became identified as a dance presentation, delicate, graceful and at times erotic as well, which has survived as a major feature of dancing till the present time.'

In addition to the foregoing, a distinction is made between *marga* and *desi* (cf. note 35 above). The distinction is basically that between classical dancing associated with the 'imperial' Sanskrit culture, and vernacular dancing. The former is included in the scope of the *Natyashastra;* the latter is not (194). But this does not work out, because later writers want to discuss *desi*, even though they subscribe to the *Natyashastra's* authority; accordingly, we find *desi* sometimes identified not as a plurality of regional dances and dance steps but as an alternative tradition within the scope of the *Natyashastra* itself (220ff). The result is a conceptual free-for-all that defeats an outsider's comprehension. According to Bose (258–9), the fact that *desi* dances were not mentioned in the earlier literary sources 'suggests that they could not have been of any great importance in the early period.' But, one asks, not important to whom?

The foregoing are the most persistent categories of dance, as they appear in Bose's review of the available sources. One other prevalent distinction is worth mentioning: that between dances that are rule-bound (*bandha*) and those that are not (*anibandha*). One might think that the latter would include free dancing, to accommodate any Indian Isadora Duncans, but this is not the case. The forms of unrule-bound dancing are themselves enumerated; as Bose observes (258), the difference must be between dances that are rigidly defined throughout and those that allow some latitude within a determinate framework.

In addition to the major classifications we have glanced at, the Sanskrit treatises are full of detailed descriptions of specific dances and dance practices, with terms that keep changing in usage and coverage. In this, they resemble the dance manuals compiled by Western dancing masters from the fifteenth to the eighteenth centuries, which show the same combination of basic principles with localized practical instruction. But the way the Sanskrit treatises do this belongs to a thought world very different from anything in the West. Reverence for authority and tradition is combined with a passion for abstract classification, enumeration, and definition; and both of these are accompanied by an extreme concreteness, so that each exposition is inseparable from a very specific praxis. This seems to be because scholarly and tradition-minded intellectuals are formulating practice and passing it on, one on one, to individuals who live and work closely with them. The combination of erudition with 'hands-on' training is as far as anything could be from the ruling patterns of the Western instructional system. And yet the conceptual apparatus that Bose outlines, however elusive in its detail and aroma, strikes a Western reader as immediately comprehensible, congenial both in its discriminations and in its emphases. We don't do things that way, but we can see that one might.

3.8 Motivations and Meanings

As dances are associated with different forms of life (§3.2), they may be associated with different typical motivations. How one dances may be expected to be governed by why one dances, and the kinds of satisfactions and meanings that can reasonably be attributed to a dance depend on the kind of dancing that is going on, so a classification based on motivations is almost as much intrinsic as it is contextual. But not quite.

There is a kind of motivation, which concerns me here, that is extrinsic and culturally controlled and need have no functional relation to what is actually danced.[37]

What I mean by the word 'motivation' here is, roughly, the meaning and purpose that the dancers ascribe to a dance, what they or their interpreters will give as the best answer to the questions 'Why is this dance being danced?' and 'What is the function or purpose of this dance?' All discourse about purposes and meanings is elusive and slippery, not because (as some philosophers say) it belongs to an outmoded folk psychology that misdescribes phenomena, but because it is not straightforwardly descriptive at all: it belongs to the strategic levels of practical discourse, declaring how one wishes one's behaviour to be taken. If I tell you why I am doing something, I am not offering a scientific hypothesis about my mental state, I am guiding you in how to react to my behaviour. In the present context, an extra layer of ambiguity is added by the difference between 'the dance' as a publicly institutionalized set of arts and 'dancing' as a mode of personal action. A dance that is an act of public penitence will have that meaning, even though it is danced by dancers none of whom are the least bit sorry for anything; but they *may* be sorry, and, if they are, their penitence may be expressed in the dance as fitting symbol, or as apt outcome, or as both. This sort of ambiguity in the arts is usually covered by the word 'expression' and more or less adequately explored in the many treatises on that topic;[38] it is also covered in recent discussions of textuality in literature, according to which what people mean by what they write must be distinguished from what is meant by what is written (and also, perhaps, from what they intend what they write to mean), and what different groups of readers read into what is written.

The following distinctions overlap Hegel's differentiation of three modes of art (and hence, by implication, of artistic dance): the symbolic, in which the assigned meaning is not sufficient to determine the form of what is done, so that generalized forms answer to vague significance; the classical, in which a fully developed idea is adequately expressed, and one does not distinguish between what a dance is and what it means; and the romantic, in which the assigned meaning fully determines the form of the dance but is not exhausted by it, so that the triumph of the art is to display its own infinite inadequacy (Sparshott 1988, §§1.331ff). My own treatment is confined to some widely recognized classifications, derived from types of meaning commonly supposed to be expressible in dance.

I begin by singling out dances of trance and ecstasy: dances that separate the dancer from the community and unite him, or her, with some individuating personal or superpersonal principle – alone to the alone.[39] The principle may be equated with God, or Society, or the Ancestors, or one's true Self, or whatever may be the local equivalent of the Transcendental Ego: it is not the metaphysics but the dynamics of the dance meaning that concern us here. There is a stereotype (of which I do not know the source) according to which trance-inducing dances are characteristically vigorous and continuous and accompanied by insistent and repetitive drumming or other music calculated to preclude relaxation – dances of ecstasy are perhaps dances of hyperventilation. Their movements are such as to induce causally, or to symbolize, abandonment or possession. (The dances complying with this stereotype may be contrasted with those alluded to in the following two paragraphs as typifying, respectively, *orchesis* and *choreia*.)

At the opposite extreme from dances of ecstasy are dances, characteristically sober and intricately patterned, that symbolize hierarchy. Sometimes the specific relations incorporated in the dancers' movements are held to symbolize cosmological or civic relations of ordered dependence; sometimes it is the mere fact of solemn intricacy that carries that meaning in a more generalized form. In either case, since neither social order nor cosmic order is in itself a matter of movements in space, the meaning, though it may be assigned to the dance in virtue of the dance movements it comprises, is one that is indeed assigned to it, rather than discovered or directly embodied in it.

As danced order may symbolize hierarchy, collaboration in dance has often been held to symbolize civic concord, or even to embody it. Any dance in which many people dance together in a ring, or in any other formation in which there is no precedence, may be assigned this meaning of solidarity. Some theorists (e.g. Elyot 1531) assigned it a priori to all such dances; they must have supposed either that the symbolism was inherent in the movements themselves, without regard to any observer or interpreter, or that anyone who danced them must feel that meaning in them, whether it was consciously articulated or not. But one may prefer to limit oneself to the meanings that are explicitly assigned to dances by their dancers (or some other preferred group), as well as being congruent with what the actual character of the dance movement is taken by the most relevant authority to be.

Historically, the dances that most notoriously symbolized political and cosmic hierarchy were the French court ballets. Mark Franko's

(1993) study of the burlesque ballets that became a feature of that genre, and in which he sees a covert revolt of the aristocracy against monarchic centralism, suggests the following reflections. Establishing a politically hierarchic meaning for dance automatically opens up a language in which alternatives to hierarchy can be affirmed, and in which hierarchy itself can be subverted by parody or by anarchy. This can be done in the organization and presentation of the dance performance, in the choreographic design, or, most important, by the bodies of the dancers themselves, either by sending up the choreography they are executing or simply by presenting the body itself as recalcitrant and individualistic. Such layering of meanings and motivations is pervasive in all performing arts (see chapters 14 and 18 below), as it must be wherever cooperative ventures are elaborately structured; we will return to it in various contexts.

Sometimes as a specialization of civic concord or of hierarchy, but perhaps more often and more truly as the case from which civic concord was generalized, many dances rather obviously and directly celebrate sexual selection. (Such celebration is not to be confused with practices whereby certain dances are customarily done at weddings or betrothals – or at divorces, for that matter, though divorce dances are not a common genre – or in which dances are performed as actual means to sexual congress, whether regular or irregular.) Paired dances almost inevitably have this meaning: they cannot always be held to lead to sexual union (despite some puritan diatribes), unless either all partnerings are for keeps or promiscuity prevails, and the pairing of bodies in movement invites no meaning more obviously than the sexual. As to the prevalence in our civilization of paired dancers, that may be thought of as an idiosyncrasy of a culture in which sexuality is overly emphasized. But it is a natural, not a cultural, fact that a person can only be face to face with one person, only look one person in the eyes; the pairing that is necessary to sexual union is also necessary to the deepest sharing of thought and feeling.

I have been treating paired dances as a special case of celebrations of concord or hierarchy. But it is a very special case indeed; the sense in which individuals are only an abstraction from the society within which their lives are lived is very different from the sense in which an individual is only half of a pair.

Whether the meaning of a dance be the solitude of the individual to be lost in the One, or the placing in a hierarchy, or the solidarity with a community, or bonding in a pair, it can be argued that a deep meaning of all dance is liminality – that the specialness of dance makes it apt to signify and celebrate a removal of the dancers from all social contexts, the better to return to the same context or move to another (see Sparshott 1988, §8.1). It may look as if this alleged common meaning militates against such distinctions as I making here. But it does not. The effective liminality of a dance does not preclude its having a social relation as its meaning – it only means that the relationship is symbolized and not realized, is held in suspense and made an object of reflection.

The meanings thus far considered in this section have to do with the ways in which dancers relate to other people, or to societies or other organizations and entities to which they are integral. Different from these are the magical meanings of dances, typically conjuring or apotropaic, relating the dancers to entities that are fundamentally other than themselves. A rain dance, wherever or however danced, either compels the rain to come or expresses the sense that rain is coming or prays that rain may come – these meanings are probably seldom distinct from each other. The meaning of such a dance is in any case to generate some power magnetically attractive to an invoked power. (To say that this is the meaning of the dance is not to say that the dance is actually expected, by everyone or by anyone, to have the effect in question.) Perhaps hardly to be distinguished from such conjuring dances are apotropaic dances to expel (or to express a sense of the imminent departure of, or to pray against) such evils as famines or floods or droughts or diseases. To avert one power is to invite its counterpart: to invite rain is to avert drought.

Such conjuring and apotropaic dances are typically communal activities. There are also conjuring and apotropaic dances that may be danced in private, as by a necromancer or a shaman; and these in their turn may be danced ex officio, as part of a social role of magic dancer, or as a means to private power. In either case the way they have meaning, and the meaning they can have, is radically different from what is available to the social dance, even if it is the same power that is called on to come or to go. A power invoked in private is essentially a secret force; a power invoked by the people (or for the people in the people's presence) is a part of their world, even if not a part in which they partake.

The residues of a lifetime's reading and listening have left me with the impression that, among conjuring dances, theorists assign a special place to hunting dances, in which (they think) the hunters typically dance out the actual movements of the animal to be hunted. The aim, they say, is not so much to attract the beasts or subject them to the power of the tribal arrows, or to put the tribe in a hunting mood, as to establish the proper rapport between hunter and hunted. Self-respecting hunting peoples know that what really happens in a hunt is not that an unwilling (or unwitting) victim is tracked down, but that a beast generously offers itself to its hungry cousins. The dance is the opening phase of a social transaction. Whether or not this is true of actual hunting communities, it is a persistent and powerful myth, elevating need to a level of ceremony of which the meaning may be enshrined in the literal ceremony of a dance (cf. Lonsdale 1981, chap. 4).

The magical meanings of dance I have been talking about have mostly concerned contingent events – or at least, what an agnostic would consider such. It is from this point of view that magic used to be called 'primitive science,' as though it purported to establish causal relations between kinds of doings and kinds of happenings. But there are also, as we have seen, cosmogonic dances, which re-enact the establishing of the world and, in so doing, sustain it in existence. We dance lest the world fail – what form of failure would follow from what manner of neglect is something we would rather not find out. The meaning of such dances is the contingency of the universe: they embody the sense that the world is not to be taken for granted but is maintained by a will or a power that the willed power of dance can enhance, or support, or celebrate. Hegel argued that such dances are really divorced from their meanings, because the actual things the dancers do can never be seen and felt to bear their supposed meanings but are connected to them by arbitrary and factitious conventions; but that argument belongs to his theoretical critique of the fine arts as embodying ideas in sensible form, not to a study of the affective dynamics of dancing. If the performers of such dances take a Hegelian view of what they are doing, and judge their dance by how it actually embodies the thought it should express, Hegel may be right in saying that they can be doing what they are doing only for the love of sheer dancing, for the sake of the movement quality and not for the sake of the world. But the practices I have described do not belong to the fine arts as Hegel conceived them, so his critique is beside the point. A meaningfulness that is simply accepted as factual, as part of the tradition, might still be the point of everything that is done and effectively suffuse the whole and every part with symbolic force.

Cosmogonic dances bring us round full circle to cosmological dances: nothing really separates celebration of a hierarchy on which we depend from celebration of an order within which we exist. It remains to consider dances that express how we relate to such orders – dances of attitude. Apotropaic and conjuring dances are dances about good and evil, the acceptable and rejectable. Ancient traditions, still meaningful to us, build the fundamental and necessary opposition between what threatens and what supports us into a multiplex scheme of affirmations and rejections. So there are dances of triumph and despair, of joy and grief, of welcome and repudiation. Interwoven with these are the polarities of vital dynamics: tension and relaxation, aggression and consolidation, changing and preserving, together with all the subtler oppositions that go with sexual differentiation, the yin and the yang. A classification that rests on such complementary polarities has a certain stability; a species whose life is built on eating and suffering must surely weave these polarities into its way of life and into its dancing. But that is not to say that it generates an adequate, or even a universally applicable, taxonomy of dance meanings. Such systematic taxonomies may be plausible, but as I suggested at the beginning of chapter 2, cannot be secured against competition or rebuttal, or even against a refusal to be convinced.

Jean Baudrillard (1972, 251) has argued that our environment today is not (as in the eighteenth century) the natural order nor (as in the high Victorian age) the socio-political order of culture but a universe of communications, the world of signs. In a way, this is little more than a facile example of the French fad for treating everything in terms of Saussure's theory of language. The point is that everything is what it is only by differentiation from other things, and that such differentiation is only possible within a sign system. Hence, things exist only as sign systems: actions, things, and persons do not exist. It is a good point, but points are good only within a matrix of truth in which other points, equally good, can be made; and it is notorious that if you engage proponents of such views to lecture for you they will expect to be really booked into actual hotels, with beds as comfortable as those the Victorians knew. Baudrillard has an interesting and entertaining angle on things, but an angle is all it is.

Anyway, if we differentiate dances by their meanings, and if Baudrillard is right, dances will exist only as signs within the sign system of meaningful dances, which are constituted by the interpretations that differentiate them from other possible dances and, indirectly, from other realms of articulated significance. A dance is made up of those of its movements that are identified as bearers of the relevant meanings. But Baudrillard is right only up to a point. The movements that are codified are movements made and learned by social beings, whose movings and learnings are already culturally meaningful in terms of an indefinite system of other codifications; it is because those other codifications are embedded in a cultural matrix whose meaningfulness they do not exhaust that the socio-cultural environment (which Baudrillard says is obsolete) is one with which we still have to reckon. And the socio-cultural matrix is itself superimposed on a physical reality that it does not supplant. Corporeality is not exhausted by the cultural develop-ments it sustains. Baudrillard's three environments are not mutually reducible, and neither nature nor culture is sublated in the supposed universe of communication. Dance is a practice marked by the thor-oughness with which it involves the dancer, and by the consequent completeness of the self-transformations that it involves and that under-lie the significance it may have. Because dancers dance with their own real bodies, and with other real people, it is in principle impossible that a dance should be reduced to the system of its specifically dance meanings.

CHAPTER FOUR

Mimesis

4.1 Quality: Intrinsic Classifications

Dances may be classified extrinsically, by the contexts they are referred to, or intrinsically, by the kinds of movement that make them up and the ways those movements are put together. This contrast between the contextual and the inherent is straightforward, but not so sharp as it sounds. Contexts are imputed rather than observed – they are not merely what happens to be in the neighbourhood, but what there is in the surroundings that we find it meaningful to relate things to. Now, movements of humans, and often of animals, are as readily classified by the actions they pertain to as in any other way: the movements one makes when screwing in a light bulb, for example, go together, forming an integrated unity; they are most easily identified and recognized as the movements one makes in the course of doing that thing. But actions themselves are identified by the contexts of practice to which they are referred. Saying that someone is screwing in a light bulb relates the action to the institutionalized practice of using electric power for illumination. In a world without electricity, there could be no such action. So perhaps to describe the movements anyone (for instance, a dancer) makes is always to say what the person is doing, and consequently to refer the movement to a context of meaning, so that our original dichotomy becomes compromised. That is a good point, but there is something factitious about it. We must not let it bamboozle us into forgetting the difference between what one knows one is actually doing, together with the movements one is making, and the significance of one's doing it, or between what one can see someone else doing, together with the way they move in doing it, and what they are doing it for.[1]

All dancers are doing the same thing – namely, dancing. Their movements all belong to the same action class – namely, dance movements. If they belong to actions other than dancing, they do so by simulation, or by quotation, or by reenactment, or by referring to them in some way. All such movements we may term 'mimetic.'[2] A dance is mimetic in this sense if the questions 'What are they doing?' and 'What are they being?' have answers substantially different from 'They are dancers dancing.' A first classification of dance movements, accordingly, and hence of the dances that comprise them, is by whether the movements of a dance are all mimetic, or some mimetic and some not, or none of them mimetic. With the mimetic we shall contrast the 'formal,' the set of movements that can be fully characterized by saying what bit of body goes where. Such a movement can often be described or specified in terms that refer to actions – 'Raise your arm as though you were putting a full jar of water on a high shelf' – but if the purpose of the description is merely to say how the arm moves, and not to include the described action in the meaning of the dance, it will count as completely formal.

In some ways, we might do better to classify dances in accordance with their emphasis on three dimensions derived from C.S. Peirce's categories of 'firstness,' 'secondness' and 'thirdness.'[3] First come the abstract qualities, the repeatable (and hence recognizable) features of what is observable as matter moving in space. These include directly affective properties (like the 'menace' of 'threatening' weather) not imputed to any consciousness or agency. Second comes activity – what is imputed to the agency of a sentient and purposive being. And third come mediation, representation, translation, and the like, whereby a movement is not merely locomotion and intentional movement but something that has a definite meaning in a system of interpretations. This division corresponds roughly, but not exactly, to the three dimensions of 'form,' 'expression,' and 'representation' commonly used in treatises on aesthetics.[4]

4.11 Dimensions of Art

Any work of art can be made out to have four 'dimensions.' First, there is the sheer presence of the work as it confronts one. Second, there is the internal structure of the work, its form, its perceptible properties in their mutual relations. Third, there is the semantic aspect of the work, what it portrays or represents, the scene it shows or the story it tells, the world it reveals or suggests. And, fourth, there is what the work expresses, the feeling it conveys.

Most writers who ascribe dimensions to works of art, however, mention only three. Since four are possible, it is not surprising that two alternative triads are proposed. The simpler and more familiar one is that suggested by Peirce's categories: form, representation, expression. 'Presence' here is elided into 'form': the triad essentially distinguishes between what is phenomenologically located in the work itself; what is related forward, as it were, to a reality beyond the work and referred to by it; and what is referred back to a sentient agency behind the work, from which it issues.

The alternative triad, proposed by Dufrenne (1953), is more subtle. First comes the sheer presence of the work. Second come the formal and representational features of the work together, because they relate it to a world beyond itself. The structures of the work, like the reality it depicts, could be extended beyond its confines. Other works could recognizably depict, or belong to, the same world. And third is the expressive dimension, which similarly evokes a creative sensibility from which other works might issue, different but bearing the stamp of what is phenomenologically the same personality.

All three ways of ascribing dimensions to works of art seem to me illuminating and rewarding. They supplement each other, rather than cancelling each other out, affording alternative ways of ordering one's experience. The way in which they overlap corresponds to the perceptual and semiotic richness that we look for, and often find, in art. They are discussed at greater length below (§15.2121). I introduce them briefly here because the simpler triad – representation, expression, form (the standard textbook version) – is the basis for the organization of the ensuing chapters.

4.12 Formal and Mimetic

The word 'mimetic' does not mean 'having the nature of mime.' Dance is one practice; mime is a different practice (Sparshott 1988, §7.72). Each is defined in part by its difference from the other, in any context in which both concepts are current. But much dance is mimetic, though some is not. The verbal confusion gives rise to a confusion of thought whereby it is taken for granted that mimetic dance is somehow not pure dance, or even that it is not real dance at all.[5] Real dance, on this view,

is dance to the description of which no reference to any kind of enactment or representation, no allusion to any agent or action other than the
movements the dancers make with their bodies, is directly relevant
(otherwise, that is, than as a way of saying how a movement is to be
made or how it is to appear). But this is simply a muddle: the terms in
which any contrast between the practices of dance and mime is drawn
have to do with the determinants of the presentations as organized
wholes and say nothing about whether dance should be representational
or abstract (it is a nice point whether there can be such a thing as
abstract mime, though I have seen things that might have been
examples of it).[6] If there are reasons for thinking that abstract or non-
representational dance is better, or more authentic, or more true to the
medium, than mimetic dance, we need to be told what they are (cf.
§3.76).[7] And then we will have to see if those reasons are better than the
reasons for holding the opposite view.

Frederick Ashton remarks: 'All ballets that are not based on the
classical ballet and do not create new dancing patterns and steps within
its idioms, are, as it were, only tributaries of the main stream. ... If the
ballet is to survive, it must survive through its dancing qualities, just as
drama must survive through the richness of the spoken word. In a
Shakespearean play it is the richness of the language and the poetry
that are paramount; the story is unimportant'.[8] But if that were true of
Shakespeare, there would not be so many plays, films, and ballets on
the themes of *King Lear* and *Romeo and Juliet*; Ashton may be right in his
emphasis on choreographic originality, but in the best ballets (including,
surely, Ashton's own) that originality is exercised on a strong narrative
or quasi-narrative armature.

One would expect a debate on the relative merits of mimetic and non-
mimetic dance, or the relative importance of mimetic and formal aspects
of dance, to duplicate the familiar debates about abstract and representational painting: that representational elements are literary rather than
pictorial (cf. note 7 to this chapter), that representation must be at odds
with formal quality (or need not be, or may enhance it), that representation cuts down on formal possibilities (or multiplies them), and so on.
In practice, the result in the pictorial field has been a tie: advocates of
representation have not shown to the world's satisfaction that abstract
art is meaningless or trivial, and advocates of abstraction have not
discredited representation as a source of pictorial meaning. Today's
artists practise either or both without thinking twice about it. Why
should the same position not obtain in the field of dance?

There is, in fact, a reason. In the graphic arts, the non-artistic use of the media in question (utilitarian, educational, and recreational) is mostly representational. One learns to draw things and people, and what one does in learning is what one will do when one has learned. Abstract art, other than pattern-making in the sense of the production of regular ways of variegating surfaces, is a recent and revolutionary development. The position in dance is quite different: social dance, recreational dance, and educational dance have often been abstract, if not predominantly so. In our society, representational dance has always existed, but never as the prevailing norm: when most people learn to dance, the substance of what they learn is to make dance movements and put them together – 'dancing,' not 'the dance' (§3.72). And, whereas in the graphic arts the domain of abstract art has been mostly in the more rarefied strata of the fine arts, in dance it was long thought that fine-art status depended on mimetic significance. Putting these two together, we get the stance developed in the eighteenth century and long maintained, in which what Gallini (1762) called 'sheer unmeaning dancing' (see Sparshott 1988, 19 note) was simultaneously identified as quintessentially dance and as an inferior mode of dance.

Like the notion that mimetic dance must be inferior to abstract dance, the idea that abstract dance must be meaningless and cannot be a vehicle of art stems from a simple confusion – in this case, from the unexamined belief that mental culture is identical with verbal culture. Isaac D'Israeli (1859) sneered at the pretensions of calligraphers to be artists; but all he did was quote their claims and follow them with repeated exclamation marks. As if punctuation were argumentation!!! His idea seems to be that to make an art of calligraphy is to divert attention from the substance of what is written to its form. But what is wrong with that? The content of what is written may be pernicious, or trivial, or dull. And we know that in Chinese and Islamic civilizations the art of calligraphy has been given an important place.

The confusion D'Israeli represents corresponds to my own transition, in what I have just written, from 'substance' to 'content' as the antithesis of 'form.' In a formal art, the form itself is the substance; and why should there not be a formal art? We need a convincing argument. One reason might be (as Hegel thought) that nothing is ultimately meaningful except the conscious articulation of the political and economic order, what can be translated into precept and edict. But that too stands in need of defence: the 'public realm' within which our lives are said to take resonance and shape could be merely a mythical disguise for police power and bureaucratic form-filling. As humans, we respond to human gesture, movement, and expression directly, without reducing them to what can be caught in words. Just as, in language itself, metaphor goes beyond literal meaning and reveals possibilities of reality that are no more reducible to what can be literally described than dreams are, and yet belongs to the substance of waking life as dreams do not, so the development of meaningful movement into the disciplines of dance enhances directly the possibilities of our lives in ways that are actual but not reducible to prose. A new form of dance, like a new form of music, its itself a new reality; we live in its light, and cannot know whether or how it affects our lives.

To see for the first time Balanchine's *Agon*, or the Sankai Juku troupe's presentation of *Kinkan Shonen*, is to be made free of an enlarged world of human possibilities. The revelation is not to be reduced to the discovery (exciting as that may be) that it is possible to dance in this unprecedented way, and has almost nothing to do with the fact that Amagatsu's choreography is said in the programme for *Kinkan Shonen* to represent 'A young boy's dream of the origins of life and death,' with an explicit narrative structure – what we experience is an enlargement of the world. What the old critics disparaged as 'sheer unmeaning dancing' was a mere display of agility with no such resonance. But to say that the abstract masterpieces of choreography can have such resonance only by being mimetic is empty dogmatism.

The question whether mimetic dance is really dance or not arises from a misunderstanding; the question whether mimetic or abstract dance is inherently superior or richer or more artistic we may brush aside. But can the distinction itself be maintained? A poem, a musical piece, a picture, is such only by being related to existing works of the same category, and is recognized and appraised by its likenesses to and differences from such works. It refers to its own tradition: if the artist does not consciously work with that reference in mind, the critics will. In Cartesian terms, its internal structure, its formal properties, may be what make the work clear, but the way it relates to other works is what makes it distinct.

Another way in which many dances may turn out to be mimetic was mentioned in §3.8. If people dance to avert rain, a principal meaning of their dance is that it refers to *there being rain*, the state of affairs it seeks to avert. We can distinguish both the state of affairs referred to and what the dance purports or proposes to do about it: avert, induce, represent, mock, celebrate, and so on. But the supposed mimesis in this case is contextual; if there is something about the movements that makes them especially fit for their purpose, the dance will be mimetic in a different way.

If we set aside references to tradition and to states of affairs that make a dance meaningful, what about abstract dances danced for their own sake? Such dances appear to lack referential meaning. But, if they are really dances, and not merely stretches of movement that somehow turn out to be dance-like in character, it is presumably possible to dance them right or to dance them wrong. If that is so, the dances may be thought to refer to the kind of movement they exemplify – otherwise there could not be a dance, there would be nothing that was identifiable and hence in principle repeatable.[9]

Among those who have adopted the view sketched in the preceding paragraph is Nelson Goodman (1968, 64–5): 'Some elements of the dance are primarily denotative. ... But other movements, especially in the modern dance, primarily exemplify rather than denote. What they exemplify, however, are not standard or familiar activities, but rather rhythms and dynamic shapes. ... To regard these movements as illustrating verbal descriptions would of course be absurd; seldom can the just wording be found. Rather, the label a movement exemplifies may be itself.' That is, the question 'What is that movement?' can be given a precise answer neither by a verbal description nor by saying what the movement stands for but by repeating the movement – another movement that is exactly like the first in all relevant respects. It is precisely because the dancer/respondent knows just what the relevant respects are that one can specify what the movement is. Nicholas Wolterstorff (1980, 346 note 59) finds Goodman's position 'mystifying': 'Why is it,' he asks, 'that Goodman thinks movements of modern dance typically refer to anything at all, let alone to themselves?' But Goodman did not say that they did. He said that some of them did. And the ones that do are, of course, those that are done precisely *as* the movements they are, that are singled out by dancers and presented to audiences as tokens of types. In relation to those movements, Wolterstorff's question has a simple answer. Not all features of movements or of movement-sequences have attention drawn to them, and thus function as meaningful. If they do, however, they invoke a system of meaning-bestowers, of labellers. But in the present case there is no label beyond the act of selection itself. Some leading practitioners of modern dance have said just this: that one develops a way of dancing by proceeding from naïve (and spontaneous and unrepeatable) expression to dance proper by training and perfecting the body as an instrument and by developing a style as a system of movements (with its own distinctive principles) that can be performed on that instrument (see Wigman 1975, 51ff).[10] The result will not coincide with what the audience sees, because the dances constructed in accordance with the developed system will be what Wolterstorff himself calls 'normative kinds.'

The fact that Wolterstorff's rhetorical question is readily answered does not mean that the protest it implies is not justified. I can see what someone means, and not disagree with that person, without holding that it was the right thing to say. In this case, one might argue that exemplification, as Goodman conceives it, is a very weak mode of reference. The dancer or choreographer is not just *giving an example* of a kind of movement, to satisfy the curiosity of the audience as to what the movement-type exemplified might be: the fact of exemplification as such is of no interest to performer or audience. On those somewhat exceptional occasions when exemplification is stressed, as when the dancer strikes a pose (adopts an attitude, performs an arabesque), the pose will most likely – as in these examples – have a name.

Just as we may doubt the mimetic or referential quality imparted to movements by the fact of their repeatability, we may question the legitimacy of saying that every work refers to the tradition in which it stands and from which it derives its meaning. There is rather a gradation. At one extreme, a work may actually be *about* the tradition or a part of it; the whole point of the work may be how it bears on its ancestry. Less extremely, a work may be consciously related to a tradition towards which it adopts a stance, without that stance being the central topic or motivation of the work. At the other extreme, a work and an artist may simply take their place within a tradition from which they derive their meaning, without making that place a topic or referring to it at all.

If one were to say that every dance is mimetic because it must refer to the tradition that gives it a distinct meaning, why not go further and say that every work is mimetic because it refers to *itself* – is reflexive, is meant to be what it is, so that the 'what it is' is postulated as an ideal object to which the work refers? The reason for not saying that is that it destroys the point of the concept of mimesis, which is that the form of a work depends for its intelligibility on something other than itself, to which it refers. One easily sees what is meant by speaking of an 'otherness' that separates the actuality of a dance from its ideal reality, but the effect is a quite factitious obscuring of an obvious difference. In short, the distinction between mimetic and non-mimetic dances is no more undermined by the multiplicity of ways in which all dances have a referential aspect than it is by the obvious and uninteresting fact that even the most fully mimetic dances consist of movements of which some exhaustive formal description could be given.

We may accordingly stay with the obvious fact that dances can be classified by the extent to which the focus of interest is on the form or on the reference of the dance and by the ways in which the two interact – whether, for instance, the formal properties are stylizations of representations, or the mimetic properties modifications of formal patternings.

I said we might 'brush aside' the question whether mimetic or non-mimetic dancing was inherently superior to the other. It is, however, tempting to assign inherent superiority to those dances in which the distinction between the mimetic and the formal aspects is hardest to make: in which the mimetic aspects are so thoroughly danced that there is nothing in them in which the mimetic quality takes on an appearance that is at variance with or even independent of characteristics that appear to respond to purely formal exigencies, and in which everything that has formal value is at the same time fully expressive.[11]

What does 'expressive' mean in this context? Not necessarily something that expresses a content that can be put into words (Tormey 1971), but something that is meaningful in a way referrable to human (or, in extreme cases, animal) subjectivity, to the courses of lives. Dance is expressive to the extent that it is a human person dancing (Peirce's 'secondness'), not a set of articulated limbs being set in motion. In this sense, dancing is expressive *as* mimetic. Inner feeling can be expressed, subjectivity can be shown, only through motion that amounts to action. But expressiveness is not achieved through *what* is done, so much as through the manner and style in which things are done. Let us suppose that a dance consists of a series of dance steps, describable most appropriately in the technical language of some developed dance system. It is not absurd to suppose that such a dance can be danced with complete technical precision and finesse by two dancers but that one should make of it a mere exercise and the other a movingly expressive dance – even if what it expresses is nothing other than the passionate perfection of the dance itself. It is not absurd, but of course it may never be true: the supposition that it could be true might be sentimental self-deception. If, however, it really is true sometimes, then the way I have set the whole discussion up guarantees that what makes the difference must be an expressiveness that is mimetic in character. To resist the temptation of putting things this way, I would need a different way of making the distinction I recognize.

Bournonville sometimes compares a ballet, as he conceives it in the light of Noverre's theories, to a string of beads on a narrative thread. But he also compares it to an opera, with mimed recitatives and danced arias. In this mood he writes (1865, 133); 'The art of *Mime* encompasses all the feelings of the soul. The Dance, on the other hand, is essentially an expression of joy, a desire to follow the rhythms of the music.' On the face of it, this is a confusion: how can joy be equated with the desire to follow the rhythms of the music?

What is it that Bournonville wants to bring to our notice? Presumably, that at the transition to aria or to formal dance two things happen in one. First, a stretch of singing or dancing that is articulated by a narrative interplay of actions, speeches, and feelings gives place to a unified stretch that is based on musical or dance structures per se; and, second, the feeling dimension of music or dance is not interrupted or abrogated in this transition, but takes on a different form: that of a unified expression of a single mood, or of a unified complex of moods that has itself a simple pattern. It is as if the narrative has reached a situation of which some aspect sings itself, or dances itself, timelessly rather than in the time sequence of the narrative, celebrating the mood or constellation of moods that has been established. Why 'joy'? Because the transition marks a moment at which a certain intensity has been reached (or has become suitable), and such intensities can only be paroxysms of acceptance or rejection. Moments are either positive or negative. But why 'joy' alone, rather than 'joy or grief'? Perhaps only because Bournonville is in the entertainment business; but more likely because the fact of dancing or singing is in itself a manifestation of positive feeling, an overplus of energy, so that what expresses desolation can do so only as a modification of ecstasy. In any case, the transition from the straightforwardly mimetic to the abstract represents not a loss of human feeling but a purification and enhancement of feeling that answers to a concentration and purification of movement.[12]

If the ideas I have been putting forward are correct, the concept of 'classical ballet' that figures in off-the-cuff writing nowadays carries with it a danger of confusion. The idea it conveys is that of a style of dance that aims at technical perfection and aesthetic beauty in the use of the fully developed repertoire of ballet movements and positions, without any admixture of anecdote or narrative or mimetic gesture – in fact, a wholly non-mimetic dance. (Compare the enthusiastic remarks of Vadim Gaevsky, quoted below in chapter 6 note 25.) But must such a dance be wholly inexpressive, unrelated to the humanity of the dancers? Must a choreographer tell the dancers how their bodies are to move, rather than how they are to move their bodies – let alone what they are to do? This would imply that 'sheer unmeaning dancing' – the achievement of technical perfection in the performance of exercises – was a sufficient ideal. It is sometimes suggested that in the heyday of St Petersburg this is what ballet connoisseurs valued and got (cf. note 7 to this chapter). Few critics, however, would refuse to make the distinction I suggested above, between dancers who appeared to be mere technicians in this sense and dancers who offered something more – a style, or a general expressiveness such as warmth or coldness. Only those capable of the latter are numbered among the supreme practitioners of the art of dance: a supreme technical mastery is put to the service of a rare artistry.[13]

But what is this distinction between technique and expression? Is stylistic expressiveness itself a perfection of technique – perhaps a development of 'right-hemisphere' as opposed to 'left-hemisphere' virtuosity? Or is one to say that the great artist puts technique at the service of a higher value, a pathos, a manifestation of life? It is the latter possibility that has been suggested here. On this view, the ideal of classical ballet would be that this realm of expressive value should not replace the use of a technical repertoire, but that it should be achieved only through the refinement of its proper use. There are to be no short-cuts. What is touching or terrifying in such a dance is not a way in which purity of line is compromised in the interest of melodrama, but something that is achieved, to all appearances, in the perfecting of the technique itself – in a way analogous to that in which individuality, in Hegel's philosophy or in Zen Buddhism, is recovered through the negation of personality and subjectivity.

4.21 Modes of Mimesis

4.211 How Mimesis Can Belong to Dance

Mime, or mimesis, may belong to dance in any of at least six ways. First, the performer may perform an action in an ordinary way – a way not modified by its forming part of a dance – but do it as a dance, by putting it in a context that makes it a dance, and in the light of a dance value. This holds no matter how such values and contexts are distinguished; it is only necessary that there be *some* way of distinguishing them.

Second, the performer may do something in an ordinary way, or in some other non-dancelike way, but do it as part of a dance that as a whole does have some determinate dance character. (Again, this holds *whatever* that character may be taken to be.)

Third, the performer may mime by doing something within a dance-ish dance, not in an ordinary way or in a generally dance-ish way, but in a special way that is traditionally assigned a referential meaning in that dance. This is a very common phenomenon within Western traditions of theatre dance, which have special forms of mugging and so on that are not strictly dancing but are indigenous to dance traditions and are found virtually nowhere else.

Fourth, the performer may do something in the course of a dance in a way that is neither ordinary nor undancelike nor special in the way just indicated, but is stylistically subordinated to the particular dance that is being danced. The performer does not break off the dance and do something else but continues the dance in a way that incorporates the something else as a distinguishable entity within the dance of which it forms a part.

Fifth, the performer may mime an action but do it in a generically dancerly way, transforming each of its components into a dance movement exercising the dancer's special skills.[14]

Sixth, and most subtly, the performer may do something that is a recognizable dance equivalent of a non-dance action, a modulation within an overall movement of which the major determinants are formally conceived.

4.212 Dimensions of Variation

Mimetic dances differ fundamentally along a variety of dimensions. Here as elsewhere, what differentiates dances may also differentiate parts and aspects of single dances.

4.2121 Mimesis as Communication

One difference lies in the way the mimesis functions as communication. Mimesis lies in the imparting of a resemblance or reference by a creator or performer and its recognition by a public. Normal or successful mimesis takes place when the dance-makers intend a reference of some sort and the appropriate audience recognizes just the intended reference in just the intended way. But there are many ways in which this can go wrong. One way is when mimesis is intended, but the mimesis, or even the intention itself, is not recognized by the proper public – or, in the extreme case, by anyone. And there are a variety of cases in which the intention is recognized but the target of the mimesis is not (very common in dance, and in mime as such – 'What on earth is she supposed to be doing?'), or in which the target is recognized but the purport of the mimesis is missed – ridicule is discerned where none was meant, or was intended but goes unnoticed (as often happens when satire is directed against something or someone the audience finds so ridiculous in the first place that they cannot tell whether it is being lampooned or done 'straight'). One may distinguish here, too, between cases where the failure is that of inept dance-makers, cases where it is unqualified audiences that are to blame, and cases where both are at fault. At the other extreme from cases where an intended mimesis misses its mark are cases where an unintended mimesis is successfully imputed by some relevantly authoritative group or public, whose grasp of history or psychology, or whose control of the media of exegesis, enables them to bestow meanings. There are also cases where philistines declare that a dance reminds them of this or that ludicrous behaviour; such belittlement is a facile and familiar mode of disparagement and has no particular significance except when a misreading is so widely shared as to indicate an important ignorance of social codes on the part of the dance-makers. In the last two sorts of case one ought not to speak of 'recognition,' since the use of that word implies that what is recognized has some prior authoritative status that is being acknowledged, rather than that a meaning is being conferred by creative interpretation; but in fact the authors of such creative misreadings often do seem to be claiming an authority that overrules the artist's conscious thoughts.

There is another way in which communication and interpretation are complicated. Consider Kurt Jooss's *The Green Table* (1932). The piece can hardly be seen otherwise than as a denunciation of war and international diplomacy. In its original context, reference to the First World War and its aftermath must have been definite and clear, but neither that nor any other specific allusion is built into the structure of the piece. In later presentations it can be taken in quite general terms; but in particular situations it could take on a new reference, and its performance might well be forbidden by a militant government on those grounds. But also, a performance of the dance might have a political effect, which could be quite unintended, resulting from an unanticipated relevance of some aspect of it to local circumstances. People might seize on the occasion of a performance of the dance to stage a protest; or again, a promoter might mount a performance of it by way of making a protest. Notoriously, in the days of absolute monarchies, censorships kept a close eye on all representations of kings in ballets and operas, suspecting covert subversive intentions in the artists and dangerous susceptibility to subversive imagery in the audiences.

4.21211 Recognizability

Representations may also be differentiated by their degree of recognizability.[15] At one extreme lie resemblances that are noticeable and recognizable without prior warning that mimesis is going on: one simply sees, without doubt or prompting, that the dancer is dancing a cassowary.[16] Then there are cases where one sees, without prompting, that something is being represented, but is not sure what it is – not an uncommon sort of case, actually, analogous to situations in which one hears someone talking and recognizes that language is being used but does not know what it is that is being said (or, sometimes, even what language it is being said in). Next, there are cases where a resemblance is visible provided that one knows beforehand that mimesis is taking place, but not otherwise – given that something is being represented, one can see what it is. And finally there are cases where a resemblance is recognizable only if one knows not only that something is being represented but what it is that the dance purports to represent. Within this last possibility there are two sorts of case: those in which, when one sees the likeness, one can also see how the resemblance is carried, can decipher the articulation of the mimetic means; and those in which one just sees the likeness without being able to tell what brings it about.[17]

4.2122 Objects of Representation: Entities and Events

Another fundamental difference among mimetic dances lies in what is represented, which may be either an event or an entity and, in either case, may be an individual or a kind. If an entity is represented it may be shown simply (one dances a horse) or in a situation or action (one dances a horse being tamed, or a horse bucking). Of course, an entity shown 'simply' will always be shown, implicitly, as situated in some way, if only as 'isolated' or 'in the void'; but that implicit situation is not what is being danced. At the other extreme, the entity may be shown as taking part in a definitely structured event.

The beings one dances differ significantly as being more or less homogeneous with the dancer, from a sailor dancing a sailor's hornpipe (or, even more extremely, an individual dancing 'me being angry' or even 'me dancing'[18]) to a civic choir dancing the planetary orbits. I will have more to say in chapter 16 about the ways in which some beings may be excluded from danceability, but one of these ways may be simple unimaginability. A learner might, I suppose, be given the task of dancing an egg-carton; but there is a limit at which one stops representing and starts faking or fantasizing. Is there really a way in which one can dance an egg-carton for oneself or for anyone else? One can dance a dance in which there are egg-cartonish features, which one can point out to one's instructor or any other interested party, and which may even be recognizable when pointed out, without there being any sense in which 'dancing an egg-carton' would be a reasonable account of what one was doing, as opposed to 'doing the best one can when told to dance an egg-carton.' In Balanchine's memorable phrase – known as 'Balanchine's Law' – 'There are no sisters-in-law in ballet': there is a clear sense in which what is not made clear in the dancing cannot be part of the dance.[19]

Someone who dances a horse does so by adopting poses and/or making moves that are in some sense specifically and determinately horsy. The significance of these may be that they are precisely the moves and poses they are, or merely that the dancer is 'being a horse,' just like that; or, as we said, a situation or action or fully formed narrative in which the horse (a specific horse; or some horse or other) is involved. One may dance 'a horse being tamed.' But, if that is possible, it is presumably equally possible for the point of the dancer's enactment to be the situation, the *being tamed*, without its being relevant whether what was being tamed was a horse or some other sort of wild thing; and even, in principle, that someone should dance a narrative structure as such, without its being relevant, or even evident, what sort of entities were involved in the narrative (cf. §11.1). In some of Martha Graham's dances, for instance, it may seem clear what sort of feelings are being expressed – rejection, aspiration, defiance, and what not – and there may be what appears to be a quite clear narrative line on which these feelings are being strung out, without its being in the least clear what sorts of people, or for that matter what sorts of entities, are involved in the narrative. We may take the dancing personae to be participants in an allegory of the unconscious mind, or dummies for memories of the choreographer's childhood self, or anything we please; but such assignments of meaning, whether on the part of a critic or spectator or of the dancers or choreographer, are interpretative acts, unreliably related to the data. What is danced is what is danced, and the movements may be orchestrated into actions, and the actions grouped into narratives, with little room for ambiguity.

How is one to dance an entity or an event? At this point we may fall back on any general treatment of representation in art, which will discourse on the limits of objectivity in likeness, on conventions of 'looking like,' and so on; particularly important is the extent to which the recognition of what is represented (and hence the creators' and performers' ability to do something recognizable) rests on the general skills of recognition learned in a society (the ability to 'use one's eyes' in the socially expected ways), or on possession of the society's actual stereotypes of recognizability for particular kinds of entity, or on knowing the general artistic conventions and stereotypes for mimesis used in the society, or on possessing the specific canons of representation in the art form involved.[20] Anything that we find in such a general treatment will be immediately applicable to mimetic dance (and therefore needs no discussion here), on one condition: that the means be such as to be realizable through specifically dance techniques, the dance steps and dance movement styles that are admitted by the dance art that is being practised. Nothing useful can be said in general terms about what this condition may involve: one simply has to learn in each case what restrictions are imposed and what restrictions follow automatically from the limitations of admissible technique.

In any case, dancing an entity and dancing an event may be interrelated in various ways. At one extreme a dancer may dispose of a technique for dancing entities, events, and emotions in general, in the same way that a painter can use paints to paint any sort of thing, person, scene, or event. Such a dancer may then decide, for instance, to dance a princess feeding a carrot to a horse; and to do this will be a single complex task, either to develop the appropriate impersonations and movements and build a dance from them, or to take a dance sequence and to modify it in the direction of that portrayal and depiction. The task will be complete to the extent that the dancer never moves outside the domains of dance, of princesshood, and of carrotic hippotrophy. The task may, of course, fall under Balanchine's ukase: carrot rather than celery, princess rather than duchess, may not be danceable directly and without using props, just as a painter may have to rely on a caption to explain aspects of what is painted that are not visually accessible; and there are likely to be complex rules, in both cases, that govern what is an admissible device and what no longer counts as a proper resource of the art. But the limits are pragmatic: it is a matter of the painter's or dancer's and choreographer's ingenuity, and the corresponding acumen of their appropriate publics.

At the other extreme, the representation of narrative and of person may fall apart, as they are said to do in some Asian dance-dramas. In such cases, the dancers' repertoire may contain a number of stereotyped figures, probably with appropriate masks, each of which always dances in the same way: being an old man, being the heroine, being the king, with little or no variation introduced by the action of the drama. A dancer may go through a whole performance without knowing which drama is being danced, and without the audience ever being aware of the fact. The narrative is danced independently of the presentations of the individual characters, merely by their collocations and confrontations. There is some analogy between this technique and the method of shooting film scenes out of sequence and without the actors knowing the script; but the analogy is partial, because the film actors are told what their motivation is, and the director, who tells them, does know the script if there is one.[21] There is also a partial analogy with the method invoked in Russian theories and experiments with film montage, in which, it was alleged, a brief shot of an actor's expressionless face would appear to take on whatever expression was required by the shots it was intercut with. But, again, the analogy is only partial, because in the film the standards of expectation were those set by naturalistic drama. In the dance dramas, the standards are those of dance, in which the audience are never to forget that what they are watching is a dance performance, and appropriate manifestations of power and pathos are not to be mediated by illusion.

4.2123 Modes of Representation

Modes of mimesis may vary along another axis – the relation between the subject of the mimesis and its object: impersonation, representation, mimicry, presentation, transformation, transfiguration, and so on. 'Representation' is the most general term: to represent something is to stand in for it, recognizably to take its place in some context of presentation. More specifically, a dancer may impersonate an entity, pretending to be it, assuming its identity; and this is not the same as becoming that entity for the duration of the dance ('transformation') or as being possessed by it ('transfiguration'). None of these is the same as giving an imitation of an entity, assuming its appearance, or as portraying it, using one's body to present its likeness.

Impersonation, representation, and portrayal may be done either with a straight face, or by way of making some sort of comment, most often satiric. I have already referred (§4.2121) to the subtle difference between giving a straightforward representation of a ludicrous person and a parodic representation of a normal person, a difference that may depend on stylistic cues or on a covert agreement between performer and audience as to the status of the target in relation to their shared assumptions about social normality. Possibilities here are too various, and depend on discriminations too fine, for a general map of the terrain to be possible; it makes more sense to note the variability and leave elaboration to descriptions of what goes on in particular cases and genres.

The sort of variability sketched here is not peculiar to dance. It is a common feature of all modes of performance art that have mimetic capabilities. The distinction between what is performed and the way it is performed immediately opens up a gap that invites exploitation. A pianist working from a score must play the music in some specific way, which must incorporate a way of understanding the music: there is no distance at all between this and thinking about the music and commenting on it in one's performance, and from this to making some aspects of one's own performance comment on other aspects of it. Similarly, actors have to choose among doing a play straight, hamming it up, sending it up, camping around with it, and so on. Dance, however, is in a special position, because although in the formal aspects of dance one can distinguish between performances that distance themselves in such ways and performances that do not, the mimetic aspects of dance are never direct and straightforward, simply because the dancers are dancing: the mimesis either supervenes on the dance or is modified into dance.

4.21231 Ways of Personalizing

Mimesis in ballet and similar dance forms is modified (or consists of modifications) in another way, which partly corresponds to the Indian theory and practice of *rasa*. In Indian drama, each dance has a flavour, corresponding to one of the main kinds of human passion: each movement, utterance, colour, and so on is chosen in a way that suits this (see §5.1 and §15.21211). Character dancing in ballet is suffused in a comparable way, in every detail, with the idea of the character being danced. Someone dancing Giselle or Quixote does everything in a way that is Gisellish or Quixotish, subtly suffused with the notion of what it is to be that character, in a way that is not reducible to anything simpler or more general.

Sanskrit poetics, I am told, recognizes this notion, which is also implicit in what Aristotle says of Achilles (*Poetics* xv 11): a character like Hamlet or Achilles is a sort of individualized type, and anyone acting (or writing!) the part must enure that Hamlet does and says everything in a Hamletish way. (Neo-classical dramatic theory coarsened this into the notion that kings must always be kinglike, peasants must always be peasantish, and so on.)[22]

4.2124 Mediation by Language

At least as fundamental as any of the distinctions I have made among mimetic modes is that between meanings that are directly mediated by language and those that are not. I count as directly mediated those gestures of which a definite verbal equivalent can be given, as in the *mudras* of Indian dance systems, in which one can read what the hands are doing almost in the way one can read a written text. Such gestures have to be learned, as one learns a foreign vocabulary, and are to be contrasted with gestures that function iconically, to be interpreted in the light of our experience of how people in our society show feelings and intentions. In the gambling scene in de Valois's ballet *The Rake's Progress*, for instance, the gamesters who are kept waiting by the Rake are instructed by the choreographer to shift on their chairs in the way that one would shift impatiently in such a situation. The audience are to recognize their impatience. The impatience is mediated by language, but indirectly, because the understanding of choreographer, dancers, and audience relies on their all recognizing a condition that they would classify as 'impatience,' even if that word had not been used in instruction.[23] And there is a less delimited but equally definite way in which a great deal of iconic mimesis is mediated by language: cases in which we specify what is shown by saying such things as 'It looks like ... ' or 'It is as if ... ,' followed by some simile or metaphor.

Beyond the range of meaning that we draw into the domain of verbal control by such figurative devices as saying 'It is as if ... ,' there is a further depth, in which we find meanings that cannot be articulated in words at all – but, of course, we cannot say what those meanings are; we have no way of identifying them otherwise than by dancing them for each other. Between this possible extreme and the *Rake's Progress* type of case, however, there may be a range of cases in which there is no actual verbal mediation, but a measure of verbal articulation is possible – meanings that are more readily shown that said but which do not elude speech altogether. The flourishing of mimetic dance depends on the importance of this intermediate realm, for it is here that mimetic dance fulfils a communicative need that is real and distinctive, and the distinctiveness of which can be stated and discussed.

Doris Humphrey (1962, 116) has pointed to the peculiarities of the use of social gestures in dance. 'Nothing says bow except bow' – the use of such a gesture can be described and explained, but it is so familiar and fundamental that it is itself a basic element in our vocabulary for social interchange, rather than something dependent on language. But, as she points out, just because such gestures are unique and basic, they can serve as the basis of variations: their standard meanings can be varied or negated by the manner in which they are performed. Something of the same sort happens in mime, of course, but not in quite the same way: a handshake in mime may be a strange or revealing handshake but remains a way of shaking hands; the same gesture in dance may allude to the social practice it embodies without actually exemplifying it.[24]

Something of the same sort is true of the Indian *mudras*. Unlike the basic social gestures just considered, they are the equivalents of verbal concepts rather than independent media of intercourse: one can say what they mean, and the gesture means no more than the words. But they have their own syntax and inflection: they are made in the course of more comprehensive movements that control their actual significance, are made with the hands in this or that significant position, and may have ambiguities that result from their formal use rather than from anything proper to their verbal equivalents (La Meri 1964). Someone using these gestures in a dance is not doing anything like conveying a message in American Sign Language but is performing a dance that is in part a dance of meanings of this special sort. There is a partial analogy with Wagner's device of the leitmotif, in which a particular musical phrase can mean 'the broken sword,' neither more nor less, on each occasion of its use, but is almost never used simply to *say* 'broken sword': it is built into the musical structure, modified by every musical means, combined with other musical devices of the same and different sorts, so that it not only becomes allusive in ways that defy linguistic reduction but functions from the beginning as a musical rather than a linguistic entity.

4.2125 Ideologies of Exemplification

In dismissing the thesis that every dance movement is mimetic in the extended sense that it refers to just the kind of movement that it is, and the associated thesis that a dance movement must take its meaning from other dance movements in the same and other traditions, to which it accordingly may be held to refer, I allowed that a specific dance may have such reference in a much more emphatic way: the fact that its formal movements are of a certain sort may be given ideological significance, by the choreographer or by others. Exemplification may then be a large part of its meaning; and, if it is not a mimetic aspect of the dance in a usual sense, it is certainly not a formal aspect.

The history of dancing in Western civilization has been shot through with ideological contrasts, some of which have exercised choreographers and dancers, and others of which (like the one singled out by Marshall Cohen, §3.76 above) have been the concern of critics and publicists more or less removed from practice. The predominant meaning assigned to a theatre dance by this or that group may be that it occupies a specific position in such a conflict. Avant-garde art, notoriously, and almost by definition (since the vanguard is defined by a presumption about the reality of progress and its direction), presents its works as illustrations of its manifestos; works of a different stamp may be presented or interpreted as rebuttals. Such dances are taken as essentially referring to the positions they are taken to exemplify.

The contrasts in question tend to overlap, and to combine in confusing ways. Among those that have recurred constantly is the contrast between upper body and lower body (arms and legs), the cultural and the physical, the expressive and the athletic. Is this a single contrast or a set of related oppositions? Who is to say? In any case, dance as athletic is danced by the human body in its nakedness, dance as cultural involves the social self, clothed and in its right mind. American modern dance owes its origin and allegiance to physical culture, to democratic and pragmatic nineteenth-century ideas about personal development; its proponents decried ballet as effete and aristocratic. Since ballet never had a smaller public than 'modern' dance, made as great demands on athletic prowess, and was cultivated no less strenuously as a means to physical culture, the difference was ideological; but it was no less real for that. The predominant meaning of a dance might be that it was affiliated with some particular stance in this complex of positions.

Just as the significance of a dance might be that it was the property of this or that party to an ideological dispute, so a dance might indeed refer to its own tradition – not to the cultural heritage it pertained to (as persons of Irish ancestry may go in for Irish dancing for the sake of its and their Irishness), but to the way of dancing itself. Authenticity becomes a dominant value, and the dance becomes a demonstration of a way of dancing, referring to the tradition it exemplifies as surely as a square of carpeting among a salesperson's samples refers to the roll of carpeting from which it was taken and, through it, to other like rolls.[25]

4.2126 Utterance and Affirmation

In one way, mimesis is like utterance. If I utter a sentence, I may wish to affirm what the sentence says, or I may be simply quoting. Suppose I do a cassowary dance: the purport of my doing so may be to impersonate a cassowary, so that I am pretending to be a cassowary or in some other way identifying myself with such a bird. But I may not be: I may simply be showing you a cassowary, or showing what a cassowary is like – or, at one more remove, showing you what a cassowary dance is like, or how one would dance a cassowary. I may, even, be simply doing that familiar dance, the cassowary dance. Just as, in the linguistic case, I use my own voice to utter a linguistic unit that I do not wish to affirm, so in the dance I may be using my own body to portray entities or persons with which I do not want to identify myself in any way. In any art that thus uses communicative means, a question arises on each occasion as to what use is being made of it by the artist: to produce an artefact, or to make a personal communication. A second and a third question then arise, as to how we ourselves shall take the artist's product, and as to what the cultural and professional proprieties are that should govern our common understanding, whether we choose to comply with them or not.

In dance, as in other performance arts, an extra layer of complexity is added. As we saw when we were considering *The Green Table*

(§4.2121), what the choreographer wishes merely to articulate the dancer may wish to affirm, and what the choreographer views as a manifesto the dancer may treat merely as an exercise to be performed. Or again, in a system of danced gestures, there may be a gesture that means something like 'hatred' and one that means something like 'I hate you.' If a dancer uses a gesture of the latter sort, the question arises as to who is said to be hating whom, and with what sincerity, and whether it is as part of a pretence or as part of a narrative. But with a gesture that conveys the bare concept of hatred such questions do not yet arise. There is, in any case, a distinction in principle between movements that *show* what the dancer is, or is supposed to be feeling or doing, and those that merely *inform* or convey propositional content.

The distinctions outlined in the last two paragraphs are singularly important in dance, because many theorists have held that dance is naturally expressive and a natural means of expression: dancing is something people naturally do to express their feelings, and it is natural to read every dance as expressing some feeling or other. The position seems to be rendered untenable by the consideration that, even if people may break into dancelike movements to give an outlet to their feelings, the actual arts and practices of dance are exercises of skills that are socially learned, and deployed on occasions that are socially structured. And, in choreographed dances, even if an intuitive choreographer may devise a movement on the basis of what she or he feels at the moment, the movement, once devised, becomes a stable part of the dance, and is retained and repeated without further consideration of how anyone may be feeling. It may be replied, however, that the practice of dancing exists always as a development and exploitation of naturally expressive movements, in which feeling takes perceptible form, and that all responses to dance are corresponding developments of a similarly spontaneous response to recognized expressiveness. This may be more a speculative thesis about the origins of dancing than an explanation of what dance is; but it does suggest that it is time to say something about expression.

CHAPTER FIVE

Expression

When I say something, my utterance has physical reality as a stream of sound, a wave formation in air. It has linguistic form as a string of phonemes, structured according to a linguistic code without regard to the meaning of what I say. And then there is my meaning, what I am talking about and what I am saying about it. But no matter what I am saying, my tone and gesture, and aspects of my choice of words, show, without saying, how I feel and what I am thinking. In a way, this is part of my meaning; in a way, it is not, for it is not what I mean *by what I say*.

A dance has three recognizably distinct aspects. There are its formal aspects, the movements of the dancers' bodies in space, considered in the light of their relation to other movements in the same dance or in other dances, similarly considered, as though a dance were a dynamic pattern of moving limbs. There are its mimetic aspects, what is portrayed or enacted, considered in the light of how the dance relates to the world outside the dance. And there are its expressive aspects, the felt quality of the life that is perceived in the dance and which the dance thus seems to embody. But are expression and mimesis really distinct? One reason for considering them together is that the 'quality of life' would have to be that of some person or persons (the dancers, the choreographer, some real or fictive collectivity) who actually lived that life in a real or fictional world to which the dance referred. If someone dances *The Dying Swan*, the dance refers to or expresses swanhood and the mood of resignation in a single dance act: it is absurd to say that the dancer 'represents' a swan and 'expresses' its resignation as two different acts. In so far as a dance is mimetic, the dancer enacts some entity (even if that entity is 'the dancer'), and this entity must be danced as active in some way and as in some psychological condition or other. But to this it may be replied that to mime a swan is one thing and to express resignation another; that we never have any difficulty making the distinction; and that one can express resignation in dance without the question 'whose resignation is being expressed?' needing to arise. We need not settle the dispute here, or even decide whether there is any real issue. In any case, every dance can be seen as expressing some individual state of sentience or other, and issuing from some social way of life or other. This may not be so (although it is often alleged to be so) in other arts, but it must be so in dance, because, if no other (assumed or fictive) subjectivity underlies the dance, that represented by the dancer must. The dance must be danced as the dance of someone, and to dance a dance *of no one* is itself a powerfully expressive act.[1] This expressive aspect of dance may be emphasized in some dances, which we may then single out as *expressive*; we have seen that such dances may be accorded artistically privileged status (§3.76). They could be classified according to what they express – by the feeling made manifest, by the way of life made visible, and so on – and by the entity, if any, to which the feeling is relevantly assigned: dancer as person, dancer as performer, entity or character represented, dance creator, humankind, or whatever.[2]

5.1 *Individual Expression*

All dance expresses feeling, in the broad sense sketched above – namely, that it must be danced *as* by a sentient being whose sentience must have some recognizable (though not necessarily nameable) character. The idea that 'all dance expresses feeling' seems, however, often to stem from the following simple and naïve idea. A person in a state of exuberant euphoria may give vent to it by bouncing and prancing. Such a person may be said to be 'dancing for joy.' The idea arises that this is the origin of all dance, and that the fact of dancing is first a sign of such exuberance, and then a way of indicating joy or, hence, the presence of grounds for joy. Dance now has a function as well as a cause, the function of *expressing* joy, as Bournonville suggests. But in mimetic dancing joy is no longer the unique object of expression. Sophisticated dance is accordingly assigned the function of expression feeling in general.

Expression of feeling has often been said to be the unique function of all art. The position is reasonable enough. An original artist can only be fulfilling an original idea – that is, an idea that originates in the artist's creative consciousness. Before the work is done, this idea can only have the status of a hunch or feeling, a set of unstable requirements to which the work is to conform. The work is judged complete when it seems satisfactory to the artist, when the 'feeling' is fully 'expressed.' This way of looking at things perhaps no longer passes muster as a general theory of the nature of artistic practice. But it does lend itself to the way of thinking about dance I have just mentioned. In the other arts, we have to stop and wonder why an urge to express feeling in artistic creation should issue in the specialized activity of painting or glass-blowing. But our bodies we have always with us, and the direct route from feeling to action is so plain that we have no difficulty in envisaging elaborations in which both the expressed feeling and the expressive act are refined into media and resources.[3] Dance is the art of which it is most naturally and obviously true that feeling is expressed in it, and it seems relevant to ask of a dance what feeling it expresses, even when we are not at all tempted to suppose that the feeling expressed is one that was felt as a part of the personal history of anyone involved in generating the dance, or will be felt by any member of the dance's public.

If the expressiveness of dance lies in the quality of conscious vitality (not referred to by it, but) manifest in it, it is not always appropriate to ask dancers what their dance expresses, or what they intend to express by it.[4] They will be able to respond reliably only if they are operating in terms of something like the *rasa* system, of which I will give a fuller description shortly. Otherwise, their ability to respond at all will depend on their degree of self-consciousness, and their ability to answer truthfully will depend on an unusual capacity for reflection. Dancers and choreographers are authorities on what their dance is about, or refers to; but they are experts on what it expresses only because they are more closely and responsibly acquainted with it than anyone else, not because it is a secret to which they alone have access. If what the dance expresses is not what is intended or referred to by it, but an aspect of what is manifest in it, that is something that can be observed only in and after the fact.[5]

The great dance critic John Martin (1939) based a whole theory of dance and dance appreciation on the idea that dance must be expressive if it was not to be trivial (formal) or inauthentic (mimetic). In each major field of art, he said, we distinguish between 'fine' and merely 'decorative' arts, the former being presumptively vehicles of deep meaning.[6] Tap dance and comparable forms of theatre dancing 'can be excellently, even exquisitely, conceived and executed' but remain at the same level as mystery stories in the domain of literature (20). The predominantly decorative character of nineteenth-century theatre dance has, however, had this effect: 'We have lost all awareness of the fact that movement can be and is a means of communication, of the objectification of inner feeling – in short, of art expression' (22). But 'Though all dance is essentially one in so far as it is the externalization of inner, emotional force of some kind in terms of bodily movements, there are different motives for such an externalization and as many different objects for it to accomplish' (26–7). Meanwhile, 'The spectator must also employ movement in order to respond to the dancer's intention and understand what he is trying to convey' (31). Primitive man, when frustrated, 'creates an imaginary environment in which he can realize these needs, at least temporarily,' and responds to this as if it were actual – 'that is, he reacts first in terms of movement, or in other words, he dances' (32). In fact, all perception is a matter of motor reaction, or it would be no more than 'sensation' (46), so that 'We have no experience of art until it has been transmuted into assimilable stuff, and this assimilable stuff is the stuff of life experience, which in its basic terms is movement' (34).

After identifying the 'inner man' as 'those elements of the organism which serve to maintain life and keep it functioning at a harmonious level,' and asserting that all 'higher' mental activity exists for this inner person (37), Martin goes on to tell us that 'the efforts of the outer man to carry out his orders from within constitutes the sum total of what we are aware of as the business of living' (42), and that 'the only function of sense impressions is to prepare the body for appropriate movement with relation to the objects reported upon. It follows, then, that we are made aware of any object only in terms of the appropriate movement we are prepared to make with relation to it' (42–3). Then, after expounding the old 'empathy' theory of aesthetic response as 'inner mimicry,' Martin concludes, not surprisingly, that 'The response to the dance ... is potentially the simplest of all art responses' (52). A dancer cannot 'make any movement which has not been either submitted to the inner man for his approval, or dictated by him in the first place. In other words, dance movements must inevitably have motor connotations' (52). Thus, we participate inwardly in the dances we see 'with all our musculature. Naturally these motor responses are rejected by our movement-sense receptors, and awaken appropriate emotional associations akin to those which have animated the dancer in the first place' (53).

All this theory-spinning makes the reader a bit dizzy. Martin never says what reasons he has for thinking that any of his assertions are true. Are they all on the same level, part of a single account? If so, is it a phenomenological description of what dance essentially is in the worlds of dancers and dance-goers, or is it a neurological description of the inner workings of movement-perception? If the former, who is this tyrannical 'inner man'? If the latter, what part are the neural mechanisms supposed to play in the work of artists and the appreciations of critics? It is not enough to say, as he says, that they may be put to many uses, for he describes them as necessary operations that would not admit of any sort of modification or conscious control.

The alleged mechanisms of emotional transfer by way of muscular movement are puzzling. The feeling aroused in the spectator cannot be the counterpart of the dancer's personal feeling, since the dancers dance the same way at every performance no matter how they may be feeling, and what they dance is what the choreographer (who may never have danced the whole thing through in person) invented for them; and the theory seems to preclude appreciation of a *pas de deux*, since the audience cannot inwardly simulate the muscular contractions of both dancers simultaneously.

Who, we may wonder, is the 'primitive man' who cannot tell the real world from his imagination? Why should we be interested in the delusions of such a klutz? And are we to think that all dancers are equally bemused? Is this primitive man a sort of externalized version of the alleged 'inner man'? But who is the inner man, anyway? He sounds like a reification of the Freudian 'primary process'; but, if he is, he should not be introduced apart from the theoretical package to which he belongs.

Martin was a fine critic, a person of great knowledge and discriminating intelligence. Why did he commit himself to this embarrassing farrago? He must have felt the need for some underpinning for discriminations and evaluations that seemed urgently necessary. No doubt his task as critic was to justify and explain the appropriate response to the American modern dance of the day, which relied on the authenticity and depth of the subjectivity communicated by an artist who was both dancer and choreographer. Martin's theoretical task was, accordingly, to effect a dynamic transition between gut response and artistic appreciation, between spontaneously expressive movement and the creation of artistic dances. If one tries, as I did, to articulate these relationships without making unwarranted theoretical commitments, one is in danger of ending by saying nothing. It is Martin's misfortune that the theories he invoked were already out of fashion and had never been well grounded; they represented 'degenerate research programmes,' lines of enquiry in which no progress is being made or prepared, so that we are not tempted to accept their promise to explain tomorrow what they have not explained today. Today's sophisticates may feel that they have a better kind of theory, one with a future, and one which Martin's essentially mechanistic account precludes. Martin has no place for 'cognitive science,' no place for codification and information processing: all of that stuff is relegated to a mere adjunct of the inarticulately emotive 'inner man.' And the split Martin implies between thought and feeling, an emotional real life overlaid by a cognitive veneer, is no longer allowed a central role in our models of self-knowledge.

Among theories of dance expression, the crude psychologism of Martin is at the farthest extreme from the classical theory of sentiments (*rasa*) in the Indian dance drama, first and most authoritatively articulated in the *Natyashastra* (cf. §3.77).[7] This is at least as much a practical poetic as it is a psychological theory, and one cannot say whether it is descriptive or prescriptive: it is presented as a divinely inspired account of effective practice, so that, as in all recipe books, recommendation and description coincide. It is best thought of as a theory of aesthetic propriety, based on congruences experienced in everyday life, worked out in professional practice, and embodied in cultural stereotypes.

'The dance is occasioned by no specific need; it has come into use simply because it creates beauty' (Ghosh 1967, IV 267). But beauty in art always has a definite affective tone – an expressive side, related to a dominant emotional mood or 'sentiment.' Just as Martin maintained in distinguishing fine arts from decorative arts, there can be no poetic meaning without a sentiment, which gives the work its characteristic flavour and, like literal flavours, results from the combination of appropriately flavoured ingredients (VI 31). In this classical version of the theory, the unity of a work depends on its being dominated by a single sentiment, and there are just eight of these: the erotic, the comic, the pathetic, the furious, the heroic, the terrible, the odious, and the marvellous (VI 15) – later theorists of a pietistic tendency added the serene.[8] Each of these sentiments is associated with a no less definite set of manifestations: in drama, a set of stories and event-patterns; in language, a vocabulary; in poetic, a set of images; in scene, a set of plants, beasts, and other objects; in music, a determinate set of rhythms and scales; and, of course, in dance, the appropriate ways of moving. The totality amounts to a comprehensive set of conventions for a work of musical dance-theatre but is applicable in the same way to literary works and to dances in a more restricted context.

What concerns us here is that the theory of *rasa* is presented as a theory of appropriate composition. It has nothing to do with how the performer feels or should feel, nor does it rely on simulation of feeling in order to evoke a sympathetic response. The audience is not supposed to be stimulated into a surrogate passion, but to be moved to a delight with a certain savour. Everything in the work is experienced as suffused with a specific sentiment, the sentiment that Western theory would say it expresses, because the appropriate character is methodically imparted to it.

The *Natyashastra* never distinguishes between cognitive factors and emotional dynamics, nor does it speculate on how the recommended procedures work, and how the lists of sentiments, durable psychological states, and so forth are arrived at. I, for one, do not feel the lack; but that is because I take it as an account of what has succeeded in a specific practice, not as a global theory of dance meaning and dance effect. From this point of view, it seems strictly complementary to the sort of thing that Martin does, which speculatively assigns a causal mechanism to the dynamics of emotional involvement in dance but makes no suggestion as to how the supposed mechanism should be related to the developed art of dancing. The *Natyashastra* describes the expressive aspects of dance meaning and lists the appropriate tools but does not raise questions about what goes on and why – unless the metaphor of 'flavour' itself has explanatory value.

The difference between the savourless and the savourful is that between the beauty we confront as mere spectators and admirers and that which involves us, concerns us, relates directly to the currents of our lives. The difference seems obvious – the difference between a seashell and a tragedy. But it can be made to seem difficult, as the controversial status of the ninth sentiment, the serene, may remind us. Passionless beauty concerns the courses of our lives as ideal, as object of a deeper concern. What strikes us as mere decoration or pattern, in Martin's terms, is trivial by contrast; but so too the everyday concerns of living, which do not arrest or deflect or accelerate the courses of our lives, are trivial.[9] So we are thrust back to the simplest terms of the contrast, between that which engages our personal concern in its beauty and that in which our approval is uninterested, external. It is just this aspect of the distinction that Martin wants to capture and explain by ascribing force to a psychological and physiological bond; but the postulated mechanism only arouses confusion and disbelief and stands as mere metaphor for Martin's wish.

In so far as the sort of life concern I have been speaking of is a recognizable reality, we can acknowledge it without further ado as an 'expressive' dimension in dance. No psychological or other speculation is called for. The presence or absence of expression as thus identified, and the extent to which it is emphasized, will be an important and irreducible, though intractable, basis for classifying dances; and a further classification will be afforded by a way (such as that of distinguishing eight or nine master sentiments) of classifying what is expressed, the ways in which vital concern may be engaged.[10]

5.11 Expressing Nothing

If expression is one of the dimensions of dance, one can always ask of any dance what kind of sentient agency is expressed in it. But if expressive dances are one kind of dance among others, the question may be inappropriate, or may receive the simple answer 'none.' And even if expression is a dimension, so that the question must have some answer, it does not follow that a given dance must be 'expressive of' something that could be identified.

There is a gradation, from expressing a named feeling ('the delight of tiptoeing through the tulips,' say), which belongs to Peirce's category of 'thirdness,' through expressing a feeling quality that has no name, to expressing some general quality of sentience (Peirce's 'secondness'). But some post-modern choreographers claim to abjure feeling altogether. According to Noël Carroll (1981, 96), they wish to create works that are 'non-expressive or even anti-expressive,' 'dances that are not representational or expressive, that is, neither referring to nor suggesting events or emotions, fictions or feelings. These dances are meant to show nothing above and beyond the specific movements employed in making the given dance.' However, as Carroll says (99), nothing prevents such dances being 'expressive' in some broad sense; historically, what Yvonne Rainer abjures in *Trio A* (see Rainer 1974, chap. 4), Carroll's prime example, is the sort of dance typified by Martha Graham (Carroll 1981, 101).

Rainer could, of course, be repudiating interest in the quality of sentience in the movements of her dances, expression in the broadest possible sense, in the interest of concentration on the movement as movement. But movement in what sense? Movements made by humans moving their bodies? Or physical movements of their bodies as merely solid objects in space? From Carroll's descriptions it would seem to be the former, since the movements are said to be learnable but difficult to perform, and audiences are said to find them hard to follow. That would not be possible unless the dancers were construed to be human beings making movements, but movements that conformed to no expectations and made no sense. As Paul Ziff said when commenting on Carroll's paper (Fancher and Myers 1981, 107), in expressing *nothing* the dance is expressing something. It is a very special quality of sentience, just as dancing *as no one* is (as I said at the beginning of this chapter) a powerfully expressive act.

Rainer cannot have it both ways: she cannot both make her dance a polemic against expression and also make it consist of movements performed simply as the movements they are. It is not surprising that she soon gave up dance-making altogether.[11]

5.2 Social Expression

I have been treating expression (and expressiveness) as an aspect of individual subjectivity, which is what it has to be so long as we focus our attention on one dancer observed in the act of dancing. The sentiments of *rasa* theory are likewise conceived in terms of individual emotional states, even though they are not manifested solely in individuals per se, but appear no less in their surroundings and interrelations. But a dancer dances as representative of humanity, and of any number of social and economic groupings, which are no less perceptibly manifested to the suitably instructed eye. These social modifications of subjectivity are aspects of expression to the extent that they are not referred to, or thematized, but simply shown in the quality of the dance. I have already mentioned, among contextual classifications of dance, their pertaining to such 'life forms' as sport and religion; and these affiliations may be thought of as expressed, in the sense I am using. The term 'expression' is more obviously suitable, however, to typical movement styles that give perceptible form to a whole way of life and thereby to the prevailing tone of a subjectivity as available to the observer. The fundamental importance of such styles was a tenet of educational dance theory in the early years of this century: 'Folk and national dances beneficially recapitulate man's neuromuscular history because they imitate human occupations such as sowing, hunting, and building. The dancer, according to this theory, experiences movements of his more primitive ancestors and the feelings that accompanied them.'[12] As the basis for what should be the most important and fundamental classification of dance styles, this notion was elaborated by Alan Lomax (1968) in a book devoted chiefly to a taxonomy of folk song – song, he says, 'can be defined as "danced speech"' (222).

Lomax starts with an 'initial hypothesis,' which might better be termed an assertion: 'Dance itself is an adumbration of or derived communication about life, focused on those favored dynamic patterns which most successfully and frequently animated the everyday activity of most of the people in a culture. ... The dance is composed of those gestures, postures, movements, and movement qualities most characteristic and most essential to the activity of everyday, and thus crucial to cultural continuity' (223–4). The taxonomic study of such basic movement forms and dance types, correlated with a typology of cultures, Lomax calls 'choreometrics': it 'does not describe a series of postures or steps, but the dynamic qualities that animate the activities of a culture' (224). 'We find many examples of the carryover of posture from work stance into dancing stance, of work-team shape into choreographic shape' (224–5). Thus Eskimo drum-dance movements, with their wide stance and diagonal strokes on the drum, echo the stance of a harpooner (226). 'A child joins his culture by learning how to move in the style of his culture' (228), with its ways of sitting, standing, walking, and so on; dance learning comes later, and is superimposed on this. Such constancies, of course, appear most clearly in rural communities, not in urban cultures subject to fads (230). And the function of this basic stylistic level 'seems to be primarily one of identification. The dance or song style proclaims what culture, age, and sex group those present belong to' (235). And he follows with some generalizations about specific congruities: there are seven basic kinds of transitions in movement, and the prevailing transition type is related to the level of productive complexity (240) – for instance, the 'complex, spiral approach to space,' common in the East, is characteristic of rice-planting (242), and the complexity of culture correlates with the number of body parts used in dance, of which 'an increase occurs with plant agriculture and a very sharp rise with irrigation' (243).[13]

Lomax's presentation combines two different theses. First, there is the contention that dance styles incorporate, and are variations on, the ways of movement learned within a society as part of its way of life. This is part of what I am calling the expressiveness of dance, something that appears in the dance as the way of living that is manifested in it. But there is a second thesis – that these aspects of style are the topic of the dance itself, serving consciously or unconsciously the function of cultural reinforcement.[14] Insofar as that is really the case, the way of life is not expressed in the dance but is referred to by it. If this entails that honest dancers would give something of this sort as an explanation of why they dance as they do, I do not believe it. If it is put forward as an observer's account of what causes them to dance in this way, assigning an unconscious ground for the satisfaction the dancers find in dancing just the way they do, I am not qualified to judge; but, if we suppose that the practice of dancing itself requires no explanation of this sort, the explanation of specific dance forms seems gratuitous, since whatever movements the dancers have learned must in any case be the raw material they have to work with when they come to develop dances. And some critics object that when people stop working and start dancing, the movements they have to make at work are just the movements they will want to avoid.

Lomax presents his work as the foundation of a new science of folk art. It has not achieved that status – Drid Williams (1991, 131–49) pulverizes it – but has the same sort of scattered and selective following that other theoretical constructions do. Kapilar Vatsyayan (1976, 263–4) uses a less abstract version in sketching a typology of Indian folk dance: hunters use stalking and short movements, fishermen and agriculturists use sweeps of the arm that are characteristic of net-casting and seed-sowing, respectively, while paddy growers do a lot of bending and retreating – and peoples who live by the sea make curved movements 'which recreate the waves and tides of the ocean,' whereas stilt dances tend to be found among marsh-dwellers. Social expressiveness is an aspect of dancing that is widely recognized; it lends itself more to plausible conjecture than to investigation, but it is not alone in that.

5.3 Being in the World

I have contended that dance as a practice and an art involves transformation of the dancer and that many meanings of dance belong to this way of looking at it. If that is right, the deepest (if not the most prominent and interesting) meanings of dance may be expected to relate to the deepest kinds of self-transformation involved. Our ways of being ourselves will presumably be our ways of existing in the world – primarily, our life-world, the objectivity that correlates with our subjectivity or the encompassing reality of which we are a sustained and contributing part; and, since dance rather obviously involves the corporeality of our being, it will be our ways of corporeally being in the world that dance most deeply signifies. This line of thought has been most deeply explored by phenomenologists such as Sartre and Merleau-Ponty and is suspect to philosophers of other persuasions, but I do not see how it can be denied that to be a living thing is necessarily to be related in some way or ways as a being to an ambience; when we are thinking about our lives, we cannot leave that way or those ways completely blank. It is entirely frivolous to ignore a philosophy because one finds its style of presentation distasteful, and the phenomenologists work out a legitimate point of view from which the most fundamental way of classifying dances is by the basic modes of engagement with the world that they embody or signify.

This way of classifying dances comes under our head of 'expression' alongside individual and social ways of expression, because what is taken to be signified in the dance is an aspect of the dancer's way of living a life – an aspect that is not peculiar to the individual or to a particular kind of social organization but is related to the human condition itself. That dances can be significantly classified in just this way has been brilliantly shown by Susan Leigh Foster (1986, chap. 1). But the underlying aspect of dance to which it refers is none other than the manifestation of 'virtual powers' that Susanne K. Langer (1953, chaps. 11–12) identified as that which dance existed to symbolize.

At what level are the distinctions that ground this classification to be manifested? Are they focused on, consciously, as objects of interest? Or are they hypothesized to explain what takes conscious form as interest or delight in what the dancer is manifestly doing? Can and do choreographers and dancers take alternative ways of being-in-the-world as the *subject* of their dances? And, if they do, do the dances exemplify them, or serve as metaphors for them? In either case, what assures choreographers and dancers that these exemplifications and metaphors will be understood as the object of their concern? Granted that many dance-makers do think of their creations as meaningful in this sort of way, can the meanings be made obtrusively visible, with the metaphors evidently carrying reference to such meanings, or do the audience have to read the dance-maker's manifesto in a programme note? And suppose we do have to read the manifesto, will the alleged meaning be one that we have to take on faith or one that we can see when it is pointed out to us but would effectively have appreciated the dance just as well without (as some people feel that the Masonic symbolism of Mozart's *Magic Flute* can be recognized once it is pointed out, but really adds nothing to the artistic or human value of the piece) – or will it be such that to see the dance properly one has to look for and recognize and respond to its ontological dimension?[15]

What of those dance-goers who find ontological reflection repugnant? Such resistance may be a sign of a shallow and unreflective nature, but it may not; it may rather reflect intellectual integrity, or a principled refusal not to compromise one's imagination by invoking a sense of reality. Do some dances belong to an esoteric art open only to the phenomenologically sensitized or the ontologically instructed? (And, we may nastily add, not too well instructed; artists of a philosophical bent often offend philosophers because their understanding of philosophical issues is so shallow.) And, if the dance has a surface meaning for the gallery and a deep meaning for the cognoscenti, will the latter be connoisseurs of dance, or of ontology, or of the art of dancing ontologically?

Even if dances are in principle to be classified by the ways of being-in-the-world which (or the meanings of which) they embody, it is not necessary that such meanings should be articulated. Dance-makers create, and dance-goers respond to, aspects of dances that they find deeply meaningful in ways that they need not, and perhaps cannot, describe. It is for the theorist to explain that these felt differences correspond to different ways of being human – differences that philosophers can expound, if only provisionally and only in terms of a set of philosophical categories that are themselves open to question.[16] If the human condition be conceived in certain terms the applicability, urgency, and poignancy of which seem beyond question, then certain alternatives and no others are open to us; and it may be that certain differentiations among dances, already recognized and found important, can be assigned with certainty among these alternatives. Philosophies of human nature, or of the human condition, seem to me to have this kind of provisional compellingness, and some people find some of them unprovisionally compelling (cf. Sparshott 1989). A classification of dances articulated on such principles could be important.

It may be, however, that the best way to put the matter would be as follows. It is obvious, on sensitive reflection, that humans, reflective and sentient beings living in a world, relate to that world in at least three principally significant ways: cognitively, as theorizers; affectively, as feeling perceivers; and conatively, as beings actively engaged with a world that serves as equipment for their active lives. It is to be expected that these three aspects will be involved in everything we do and at every moment of our lives, but in different ways. That will also apply to the ways we dance and the ways we are aware of dances. It is always a good and pertinent question about any dance how it engages these three kinds of concern, whether it engages all equally, or whether it is directed principally to one or two of them. But, just because this triplicity applies to every human life and every moment in such a life, it will not always be a particularly interesting question to ask about a given dance. That will be true even if the arts of dance are eminently the arts of which human being-in-the-world is prima facie the basis. The same considerations will apply whatever particular analysis of being-in-the-world we may adopt.

5.31 Corporeality

Different ways of dancing should express different ways of being in the world, if anything does. But we can be *in* the world, occupy places and move in a real world, only by being embodied parts of it. And most dances are most obviously placings and movements of dancers' bodies. It should then be possible to classify dances according to the styles of corporeality they expressively embody.

The fact that dance practice centres on movements of the body gives rise directly to many kinds of distinctions among dances. There are distinctions in body orientation, in body habit, in relation between dance rhythm and body rhythm, in degree and kind of emphasis placed on the body (as opposed to dances in which the body loses its identity). There are different understandings of 'the body,' as the clothed social entity or the wearer within the clothes;[17] there is a contrast between the 'turned out,' unfolded, and presented body in ballet and the infolded body, energized from the centre, implicit in Martha Graham's practice and in the systems on which she and her mentors drew.

Distinctions and classifications of these sorts are related to each other in subtle and intriguing ways. For instance, the contrast between body-emphasizing and body-losing dances intersects oddly with that between rhythms derived from the body and those imposed on the body (§9.211). One might suppose that a dance based on the body's impetus would be a body-affirming dance. But is that true? A dance that captures the body's rhythms might rather be one in which the body's movement goes beyond itself, is transcended in the dance; whereas a dance in which the movements are imposed on the body might rather emphasize the body as that of which the inertial forces were visible as external compulsions imperfectly overcome.

Many of these body-based distinctions have to do with formal properties of the body and its kinetics and will be discussed in their place (see chapter 7). The ones that concern us here are those that express different ways of being embodied and different attitudes to embodiment. Some dances celebrate embodiment;[18] some present it as a fate and a burden; some purport to transcend it, converting the dancer into a system of pure energy; some seem to deny it, making the body, as it were, an inert instrument of a manipulative instrument; some even seem to ignore it.[19] Many dances make the fates and fortunes of the body's ageing and mortality a theme of their action. Almost alone among American choreographers known to me, Bill T. Jones has, very movingly, presented the varying weights and shapes of bodily frames not as spectacle but dignified as the realities of lives. Several Japanese dance-makers have used their old age to express the weathered depth of a venerability like that of a rock buried in a garden. And, of course, since our way of being embodied in the world is pervasively and profoundly sexual in a way that has become obsessive in recent decades, this sexuality has formed a theme in the midst of the more general theme of 'gender' as social and political.[20]

5.311 The Dimensions of the Body

The phenomenology of human corporeality is most often associated with the work of Maurice Merleau-Ponty (1962, part I); but the less-known suggestions of Jean-Paul Sartre in this area offer a more immediately promising basis for a possible classification of dances, as well as what purports to be an analysis of what is present in all dances.[21]

According to Sartre, the body has three dimensions, corresponding to the three 'persons' of Indo-European grammars. There is *my* body, the first dimension, the body as I *live* it; there is the second dimension, corresponding to the way in which I am aware of the body of someone I am directly relating to (*your* body); and there is a third dimension, impersonal corporeality, the body as a part of an interpersonal world (*her* body, anyone's body). All of these dimensions are essential to my awareness of myself as a corporeal being.

The second dimension is that aspect of our awareness of ourselves that is derived from our awareness of other people as alive. We do not perceive them as masses of tissue within which a consciousness lurks, but as wholly vital: the moving form of the body is not distinguished from the consciousness and character of the embodied person. It is indeed possible for us to be aware of the other, and derivatively of ourselves, as *flesh*, a body not infused with life but dragged around by a living agency; but this is a morbid dissociation of the person, a mode of awareness and self-awareness at home in the desperations of sex and self-loathing.

'Nothing can be less in the flesh than a dancer, even when she is nude,' Sartre writes.[22] This is because dance is par excellence the kind of activity in which the body is transfused with visible vitality. Clearly, Sartre thinks of dance, as such, as celebrating the body's second dimension. And the second dimension is the body of the Other: it is by imagining ourselves as the Other's Other that we are aware of our own corporeal presence in this mode.[23] It seems to follow that the value of dance would be a value *for the spectators*, who, in awareness of the perfected freedom made visible in the dancer's movements or sheer presence, become aware of, and sustained in, the consciousness of their own corporeal puissance.

Before I can be a body for others, I must be a body for myself. The first dimension of the body is my immediate experience of my own corporeality; but my embodiment is not an object of my consciousness, it is the embodiment I live, the way I experience the world as one incarnate in it, situated at a particular place from which I have a unique perspective on it. I am embodied in the world by extending instrumentally into it. My location in the world is a matter of where my eyes and ears and hands (and tools) reach. This is the original meaning of my body, and it is by living this out unselfconsciously that I become a body for the Other's consciousness and thereby make available to the Other the awareness of being *objectively* embodied. The first dimension of the body does not in any way involve the boundary of the skin or the physiological mechanisms.

Can there be a dance of the first bodily dimension, as there is of the second? Not in so far as dance is display, since the first dimension is what is unselfconsciously lived. The first dimension is, indeed, involved in all corporeal activity, including all dance, because it is what makes the other dimensions possible; but that is apparent only to reflection. My awareness of the body-for-others is awareness of a life unconsciously (first-dimensionally) lived, but this dimension is not immediately present to me. Could there be a dance of the first bodily dimension, one in which the dancing presence has to be taken as a sign of unselfconscious incarnation? Only if there is a mode of my own first-dimensional embodiment that is dancelike in some other sense than that it is itself the realization of such a dance as made Sartre deny that the dancer was 'in the flesh.' Is there such a mode?

To the extent that my action in the world is guided by a proprioceptive awareness of which the object is not the innervated musculature, or whatever, but the sureness of my placement and effectiveness as I act in and on the world, my realization of this could be thought of as a dance of the first dimension, realized for others not as a gracefulness or agility, or other mastery of bodily movement, but as the manifestation of this sureness. It would be a dance of pure thereness and pure instrumentality. It would not be a dance within the scope of dance practice or dance appreciation as such; but it is the sort of phenomenon (or noumenon) in which an affinity to dance quality is customarily acknowledged, when need arises.

In addition to the ability to live a danceable world, there is a common sort of myth that relates to what could be a dance of the first dimension. Such myths tell of a dance in which a creator brings a world into being by mere proximity: the world comes into being around or before the god in recognition of the compelling presence and by the power of the dancing – but not in any literal sense as the *effect* of the dance. Orpheus plays his lute: he does not cause the trees to dance, nor do the trees dance to a music they hear, but the trees dance on account of the music.

According to a rather different mode of imagining, the world dances before or around the figure of a creative god; in this mode, the god dances, and the world exists. Such a dance needs no spectators, for it is one in which the worldliness or embeddedness of living is given imaginative force. We meet it again in my Afterword.

I may be making too much of this. One need not resort to myths of divine or heroic efficacy, or to overall modes of self-engagement, to find possible scope for dances of the first dimension. There could not be an *art* of such dance, for arts depend on conscious skills exerted on a medium, and in this case the medium must be the body as it could be for others before it is one's body for oneself. But is it not enough to say that whenever I dance simply to celebrate my presence in the world, my dance is of the first dimension, and the more properly so the more my actual way of dancing relates to this animating impulse? Many dances in which I dance as music makes me – in which I am moved to dance by an impulse from music, and what I dance is the meaning I find in the music – may really be of this sort. What I do is take from the music a new sense both of my presence and of the quality of my presence, which I express in the way I actualize my sense of stance and motion. In music, we are transposed into an alternative reality, because the music that fills our consciousness is made of nothing but musical items musically arranged; in dance, we ourselves are transformed. Such a transformation, immediately reflecting such a transposition, would surely amount to a radically new way of being in the world.

Perhaps, then, there are or could be dances of the first bodily dimension, as well as of the second. But what of the third? (Once more, we must remember that our corporeality is always fully three-dimensional; what is in question here is only which dimension of corporeality is essentially exploited in an act of dancing.)

The third dimension is that in which the body is lived as everyman's body, the body that can be weighed and measured and subjected to medical and gymnastic regimen, and for which the medical profession and other institutions can share our responsibility.[24] This is the least personal, the least vital, of the aspects under which I live my embodiment, but as a third dimension (the verbal felicity is more than a pun) it confers a solidity, a factuality; it closes the circle by providing a reifying context in which the more immediate first and second dimensions are eventually grounded. The third dimension is that whereby I have *a* body, as others do, and can fill a place prepared for me. So the solitary dancers of the first dimension and the dance artists of the second dimension, of which the former dance by themselves and not to others and the latter dance for others but not for themselves, contrive to be real dancers because they are all anchored in, and take their rise from, the practice of social dancing, whereby one shares the dance and the experience of others' dancing with others who share the dance one is dancing or who, breathless, wait or imagine their turn to take a place in the dance. Dances of the third dimension, then, are social dances, dances that one may do as well as someone else – and, in general, all dances in which one can tell the dancer from the dance.

CHAPTER SIX

Formal Principles of Movement

Dance movements may be mimetic, or expressive, or abstractly formal. They can be characterized and classified by which they (saliently) are; and, within each of the three, by the ways in which they are these, and by the operative distinctions within those ways. But every mimetic or expressive movement must itself admit of some abstractly formal description, though that description will not reveal what is mimetic or expressive about it, and it must accordingly be classifiable according to its formal properties, even when those are not salient.

If the art of dance is based on, and essentially consists of, the movements of the human body, an analysis of the ways the body moves must ground a relevant classification of dances (and hence a delineation of the nature of dance). But it may not directly determine such a classification. First, some differences may not be effectively danceable. Second, some theoretically danceable differences may not be recognized in any actual dance tradition, so that their relevance is at least doubtful. Third, the differences actually found significant in dance practice and criticism may be determined by a complex of traditional considerations, not readily reducible to any general classification of body movements. All the same, the general principles of differentiation of human movement must be relevant at some point, if only to show how they differ from the differences practically recognized.

Usually, when we look at people moving, we see them directly in expressive and mimetic terms. We see what they are doing and why, in its meaningful social and practical setting, and we see something of how they are feeling and what their intentions are. Accordingly, one would expect the formal possibilities for dance to be relatively limited. There would be, first and foremost, the development of refined skills in performing specific ranges of precise body movements (as it were, vocabularies and syntaxes of non-referring body languages) and correspondingly refined skills among connoisseurs, such as are cultivated among the practitioners and devotees of ballet, together with skill in controlling and perceiving body movement generally. Second, there would be a formal pattern-making using human bodies as elements. And third, there would be theatrical spectacle, to which the moving bodies made a contribution of the same order as that made by costume, lighting, and scenery.

In differentiating formally among dance movements, one would expect a polarity between differences in basic movement types derived from the possibilities of movement as such and differences based on what matters to dancers. The latter would be manifest in the ranges and orders of movement actually relied on by the major traditions of dance-making. These could, in principle, be anything at all, since human agency and culture are free, so that we would have an enumeration rather than a classification; but no doubt there are physical and psychological constraints on historical development and stylistic compatibility, which would make some sort of intelligible account possible.[1] At the opposite extreme, equally sure to be relevant but less likely to be of practical significance, are the most abstract shapes and movement types, conceived in Euclidean terms: lines or rings, two or three dimensions, curvilinear or rectilinear, and so on. But how should we fill the middle ground? Most obviously, with what is special to the human body. Toward the Euclidean pole, there will be matters dependent on the articulation and musculature of the human frame operating within a gravitational system; toward the traditional pole, the movements that depend on the ways dancers relate to each other and their audiences. What else?

The most relevant intrinsic differences in any field should be those that follow directly from the way the field is defined. I refuse to define dance, but an anthropologist gives the following working definition of a dance practice: 'Human behavior composed, from the dancer's perspective, of (1) purposeful, (2) intentionally rhythmical, and (3) culturally patterned sequences of (4a) nonverbal body movements (4b) other than ordinary motor activities, (4c) the motion having inherent and aesthetic value.'[2] Is there anything here we have left out? Purpose and cultural patterning we took care of under 'expression.' Values will be dealt with as a separate topic (chapter 15); questions about value might be expected to depend on questions of classification, rather than the other way around, and in any case I will not pre-empt that discussion here. What is missing from our treatment and present in Hanna's definition, though, is the concept of rhythm. Surely dances are differentiated by their rhythms as much by anything else – the tango, the polka the minuet. But rhythm, too, must have a chapter to itself (chapter 9), because fundamental conceptual problems are involved.

6.1 *Basic Movement Types*

Consider a sphere in space. It can move in any direction, and spin on any axis. It can change direction or axis in any way and at any rate, smoothly or jerkily. Its movement and/or spin may be at any velocity, and may accelerate or decelerate at any rate. It may stop and start at any times. These are the bases of locomotion. Any body of any shape can be reduced to a system of such spheres, which can move together or severally in these ways, in relation to each other or to a chosen frame of reference. This, I think, exhausts the possibilities of spatial movement, unless one counts it a movement in space when a sphere expands, or contracts, or changes its shape. But actual movements are not readily reduced to these terms. What we call 'simplicity' in a movement is not determined by ease of such analysis, but by the familiarity of the dynamics that give rise to it. I give three examples.

First, terrestrial movements involve width. Up and down are determined by gravitation; all movements at right angles to these are horizontal. Horizontal and vertical movements are significantly different, in type as well as in significance: horizontal movements in any direction cope with inertia in the same way, but vertical movements are helped or hindered by gravity.

Second, particular patterns of directional change, and of acceleration or deceleration, may be fastened on as significant; quality may be associated with such patterns in different styles of dance. Speed takes on significance, in relation to our normal expectation for the kind of movement in question, or in relation to other norms derived from our own body experience and perceptual capacities.

Third, movements may be assessed as departing from, or returning to, some position taken as normal (the 'centre'), or some other fixed position.

But what should I say next? It is not clear what the criteria for a satisfactory treatment of the topic of this section should be, partly because it is not obvious what movement types resist reduction to simpler terms, and partly because it is not clear where the line should be drawn between biological dynamics on the one hand and human volitions on the other. So I break off here.

6.11 Dimension of Movement

One basic classification of movements is by the dimensions involved in trajectories: one-, two-, or three-dimensional. All dance movements, unless we count those projected onto screens in shadow-plays, are three-dimensional, since the body is itself a solid object and its joints are not all in the same plane; but there may be differences in emphasis. There are no one-dimensional dances, that I know of: if there were, they would be limited to rhythmically complex backing and forthing (or up-and-downing). But there can be two-dimensional dances, in which the emphasized movement is in a plane. What advances on one or recedes from one is quite different from what moves at a right angle to one's line of vision, or is thought of as so moving: it is only the latter that can be observed with precision and without involvement.

Among dances two-dimensionally conceived, the basic distinction is that between vertical and horizontal. In fact, if one thinks of it, it seems only an accident that movements in these planes should belong to the same practice. Vertical movements, leaps and skips, seem proper to displays of individual force; horizontal movements, stepping out figures on a floor, are more social and cerebral. Again, horizontal movements tend to be those of the body as a whole unit, with the legs functioning only as transporters: vertical movements, movements visible from those in the dancer's plane, include movements of arms and head. In the history of our civilization, in the court ballets of the seventeenth century, dances were often designed planimetrically: they were danced in the body of a hall (which might be surrounded by a raised gallery) and conceived in terms of movements from one part of the floor to the other – movements of which the dancers would be aware (and could learn from following a plan) and which could be seen from galleries. In the later type of theatre, with a raised stage and a proscenium arch, the spectators in the body of the hall could not see such figures clearly but could follow precisely changes in the vertical profile of the dance.

In a dance conceived two-dimensionally in the horizontal plane, and envisaged from a position directly above or below, all directions are alike so far as the movement is concerned (though some position may be singled out as sacred, or as where the mayor sits, or as facing wind or sun or rain, or in some other socially or metaphysically or physically determined way).[3] In the vertical plane (seen or imagined, once more, at right angles), this democracy of position does not obtain, because verticality is initially conceived in terms of up or down or sideways: up is where the head belongs, but, more fundamentally, it is the direction away from the pull of the earth. Every movement in this plane is determined in its basic character by the way we struggle or connive with gravitation.

But what about two-dimensional movement in the same plane as oneself as spectator? Vertical movements, seen from above, must lose most of their force, since leaps merely peter out; seen from below, as through a glass stage – well, it might be a novel experience, but I don't know that anyone has thought it worth trying; the gravitational force is a constant, and the interest (voyeurism aside) would be limited to speculating on the strength of the transparent floor. The case of horizontal movements seen horizontally is very different. The inherent democracy of directions, to which I referred, leaves the relation to the spectator in the determining position. (Who is this 'spectator'? In a theatre dance, all spectators are notionally 'front and centre'; in other dances, it will depend on circumstances whether there is a privileged spectator – where the mayor sits – or whether each spectator may privilege himself or herself as focus.) A movement directly toward the spectator is an advance, threatening or offering; a movement away is a weak movement, withdrawing or enticing. Such movements necessarily have a strong mimetic component. Movement toward and movement away, even of inanimate objects, differ in important ways, as things move into or out of the range of this or that mode of observation or interaction: but with animals and people, which interact with us in more complex ways as agents or patients or partners, it matters which way they are facing. An animal that turns tail and flees is different from one that backs away; and a dancer's retreat has a very different quality, simply as perceived movement, depending on whether the back is turned or not. Movements observed or conceived as side-to-side, across the visual field, tend to be neutral in this regard; there are differences between right-to-left and left-to-right (away from or towards our more effective side), but they are hard to pin down. Finally, one might suppose that diagonal movements forward or backward would occupy an intermediate position, but this seems not to be the case. Such movements are not directed at or away from oneself, and this is a difference of kind, not of degree. The effect is rather an increase or decrease in tension, and the diagonal movement is displayed to view in a way that a movement directly toward one or away from one is not.

6.12 Energization and Orientation

Just as basic as the distinction between dimensions is that between movement regarded as centred on the body and movement as related to a containing space – or, as we have just seen, in relation to a fixed viewpoint. (Strictly, the latter alternative is a special case of a broader option, that in which the dance is considered from a viewpoint independent of the dancer's position, but this is an unnecessary complication – if one walks up and down during a performance, or is carried past it on a bus or something, one compensates for one's movement in the usual way by supposing what one would see if one stopped and looked; a dance to which one made a vital contribution by dodging about would involve one as participant, not as spectator.)

Laban's 'choreutics' (1974) analyses movements of the body as paths between the points of regular and semi-regular solids accessible to the limbs within a sphere concentric with the body (see further §8.2222). It makes no difference to such an analysis whether the centre of the sphere (and, accordingly, the dancer's body as a whole) is stationary or moving (in space, or in relation to any point in the environment). In one way, this is the dancer's normal viewpoint, since each person is the centre of that person's world, though in practice one is aware of oneself as getting from place to place within a world that differentially attracts and repels. An alternative analysis treats the dancer as a moving system with a definite location and orientation in a finite space, a stage or a dance floor. This is the spectators' normal viewpoint, though they may use (actual or notional) opera glasses to isolate the dancer as centre of a system.[4] These alternative views may be taken of any dance, or indeed of any moving thing – 'Copernican' and 'Ptolemaic' are really correlative terms for complementary analyses. But a dance may have been conceived, and may be more rewarding viewed, from one standpoint rather than the other.

It can be argued that one of these viewpoints is inherently more suitable to dance than the other or that dances of one sort are more authentically dances than the rest. Dance movement typically differs from dramatic movement, it is said, because, whereas actors take part in the

mimesis of a socially structured action, within an established stage
setting, a dancer's movement generates its own field of tension in such
a way that the dancer's body is the centre of its own space. A solo dancer
fills the stage (as light fills a room), and an ensemble dancer is part of a
field of force that collectively fills it, but in which each dancer is a centre
of force that repels the others even as it unites with them. The stage set
becomes a moving box pressing in on or receding from the dancer.

Like most theses about what is authentically dance, the contention
just advanced (to which I return in §14.1 and §14.2) attracts its proponents more than it convinces sceptics. Perhaps it comes to little more
than this, that solos in dance are more usual than soliloquies in drama.

Movements in the spectator's plane are observed as advancing, or
receding, or passing across, or bypassing diagonally (in ways that, oddly,
we have no special names for), and this stems partly from the fact that
the dancers are people (potentially involving) and animals (potentially
aggressive or victims) and partly from the mere fact that they are large,
heavy objects in motion. If we think of dance movement as centred on
the dancer's own body, a corresponding variation in character becomes
evident. Movements are centrifugal or centripetal, central or peripheral;
their trajectory can be traced through the body parts. These variations too
have a threefold meaning: in terms of human gesture, in terms of animal
vitality, and simply as functions of a dynamic system. Dances can be
thought of as systems of gestures in which these three aspects are
indissolubly fused; much modern dance belongs to this way of thinking.

Up and down, forward and back, left and right, have their own
meanings that cannot be got rid of. So do sudden and slow, prepared
and unprepared, tensed and relaxed, strong and weak, hurried and
leisurely. These terms, and many like them, refer to energy levels and
energy distributions. Nothing is more characteristic of a dance than the
way it is energized; in learning an exotic dance style, what one has
principally to master is how and where the energies go.[5] And, once
more, the differentiation is threefold: only a human being can be languid, but a languid movement is comparable to movements that an
animal might make, and to movements that might take place in an
inanimate mass.

6.121 In Place and through Space

The distinction between body-oriented and frame-of-reference–oriented
movement can be considered objectively, rather than in terms of domi-

nant viewpoint. It then becomes a difference between movement in place
and movement through space. To make this distinction, one must first
select a unit, with either a fixed boundary or a fixed centre, within which
internal rearrangements are possible.[6] Dances vary according to how
changes of place are distributed: dancers may move ceaselessly from
place to place, may remain in one place, may move between positions in
each of which they remain for a while, and may do so regularly or
irregularly. Which of these happens, and the way it happens, makes a
big difference to the character of the dance as experienced.

The relations between movements in place and through space are
greatly complicated when there is more than one dancer, because the
relevant unit may not remain the same. Internal changes of position
among dancers who function as parts of a whole (the corps, let us say)
differ subtly from those between dancers of whom each is an individual
unit conceived as moving separately through space. Leaving subtleties
aside, a group as a whole may continue to occupy the same space on
stage while its members move through space, interchanging positions
or circling, and a dancer may retain relative position within a group
that moves as a whole.[7]

6.1211 Spin

Between movements in place and movements through space, one kind
of movement holds a unique position: the spin. A person can, by wearing a special shoe on a ball bearing, spin while remaining entirely
motionless as far as limbs and muscles are concerned (whatever the
middle ear may make of it). Such a person is not really dancing, otherwise than by the context of movement or of presentation. But less
perfect spins form part of the regular repertoire of ballet and other
developed dance forms and take a central place in some trance-inducing
dances elsewhere.[8]

For one who spins, the world turns. Spins have been singled out
from all other movements by speculative philosophers, and more lately
(and on quite different grounds) by physicists: the difference between
left-hand and right-hand spins seems to be one of the few absolutes in
nature, and it is a difference that (as the reference to handedness indicates) is embodied in humans in a singular way. Clockwise and anti-
clockwise, deasil and widdershins, differ fundamentally and irreducibly.

The general theme of asymmetry is taken up later (§6.13). It also
matters whether a spin is vertical or horizontal (or oblique) in relation

to a gravitational system – as every child knows who has played with a top. Dancers can spin only vertically; they cannot generate enough angular momentum to offset the gravitational pull, as a gyroscope does. Could a dancer spin horizontally or obliquely, if both ends were supported on pivots? I suppose so, but who cares? A somersault is not a spin; enough horizontal rotations to constitute a spin can be generated by rolling on the ground, but rolling is not spinning, it is a means of locomotion.[9]

6.1212 Cyclic and Linear

We do not usually refer to a movement as a spin unless the spinning unit has an axis on which it turns, a motionless point that stabilizes the peripheral movement. A ring dance, in which the dancers move in a circle, does not count as a literal spin, whether or not there is an object (a maypole, a dance-leader) at the centre to form a focus around which they dance. One might dismiss this as a mere matter of usage: the group *is* spinning, whether we say it is or not. But that would be a mistake. Only a quite rigid body can spin, so that it can generate a true (conserved) angular momentum; a circling group has a quite different dynamic. If its members remain separate, each dancer is moving on her or his own curved track; if they hold hands, the tug on the hands is experienced as constraining what the movement would otherwise be. A whirl or a swirl neither looks like nor feels like a spin.

Whether the dancers in a circle dance are spinning or not, their movement has something in common with a spin: it returns to the point from which it began. More precisely and more significantly, the last portion of the movement is identical with the first portion of another movement of exactly the same kind. The movement is a homogenous cyclic movement, as is all movement in a circle; but not all cyclic movements are homogeneous. To say that a movement is cyclic is to say only that the completion of the movement is the initiation of another movement of the same general sort.

A movement that is cyclic is linear. History is linear, in that the fact that an event has taken place forms part of the past of all later events in the same history. Vital phenomena, in contrast, can usually be conceived as cyclic, since in the short run they form sequences the repetition of which maintains species and organism in existence. But then, in this light, history is cyclic again if we construe it as the birth, growth, maturity, decline, and death of civilizations, as Spengler and Toynbee did.

The sweeping generalizations in the preceding paragraph were meant to suggest that the distinction between cyclic and linear process and movement enters everywhere into our thinking about the world and ourselves. Consequently, the difference between linear and cyclic dances is bound to be very important. But it is also bound to be extremely complex. The development of species through natural selection, for instance, involves a sort of open-ended chain of cycles; a rondo in music is a cyclic recurrence of chains, in that the episodes between occurrences of the recurring section are defined only by their place in the sequence and by the initial and terminal modulations that integrate them in the cycle. Such complexities are easily realizable in dance forms. Cyclic and linear elements may be combined, sequentially and hierarchically, without limit and without confusion, for there is no formal property that is more familiar; and, wherever and however the distinction is manifested, it is always an important aspect of what is going on.

6.1213 Space and Place

When I distinguished between dances 'in place' and dances through space, I treated place as location in space. That is not always the right way to think of it. When we do, we differentiate between locations identified in relation to ourselves and those related to a point of origin supposed fixed in some coordinate system. But to say what *place* I am at is, normally, to say where I am in relation to some significant system of locations: to say I am at Aunt Bettina's is not at all like giving my latitude and longitude. Colloquially, what is 'out of place' is inappropriate to some aspect of the cultural or practical situation. In general, the concept of place has as much to do with mimesis and expression, including being-in-the-world, as it has with spatiotemporal location, so that much in the ensuing discussion would have been in place in the previous chapter.

Where a dance takes place is always a dance place, made a significant somewhere by the act of holding a dance there. But a dance place may be significant for other reasons, too: it may be a dance hall, or a studio, or the stage of a prestigious theatre, or a palace or a temple conferring social and religious dignity on what is done there.

A dance may move from one place to another, and the transition may be significant: sacred to secular, crowd to desert. Such a movement may form an episode (take place!) within a dance, or it may occupy the whole of it, as a processional. Processional dances exist as danced *from* one place *to* another, *through* some of the places between and *past* or *around* others (see §14.3 below).

A dance may differentially occupy places within a place. Such movements through space are meaningful dynamically as approaches, retreats, and passings-by and spatially as related to centre and periphery of the dance area; but they also represent different ways in which the dancers situate themselves. It is one thing for dancers not to change their factual position in a space; it is another thing for them to dance *in place,* purposely staying where they are. It is one thing for a body of dancers to start somewhere and end up somewhere else – if they have lots of room, they may do so without noticing. It is quite another thing for them to dance out of, and away from, one place, and toward, and into, a different place.

All the human ways of being in the world, as we saw, can be danced, by exemplification and by metaphor. Among the most powerful metaphors is that of place. We have (or lack) a home in the world, a home in which we dwell or from which we are exiled; and the world itself is our dwelling, we live in the world as inhabitants. We have, most of the time, firm ground under our feet, and the world sustains us in its inertness. We share a sky over our heads, or shelter from it indoors, and we are exposed to the world as to the impartial light of heaven. So dances may be centripetally home-centred or centrifugal, terripetal or terrifugal, open to the gods or closed against them. Whole traditions may be taken as celebrating different ways of placing oneself in the world. A friend who took lessons in baroque ballet told me that the first thing he had to master in that style was to dance onto and along the ground. In romantic ballet, one danced *away from* the earth. And in the African dance styles that have been carried all over the world and affected the way the world dances, one dances not only down onto the surface of the earth but as it were into the earth, drawing strength from it.

The language of the preceding paragraph was meant to be reminiscent of Heidegger. I alluded in chapter 5, note 15 to Sartre's (1943, part IV chap. 2 §1) adaptation of those themes, in which he interprets certain sports in terms that could apply to dance as well. According to Sartre's phenomenology, self-conscious beings such as humans cannot have a stable reality, for consciousness as such has no inertia; but they cannot function without one. The various styles of dealing with this impossible situation are policies for acting in the world, which imply control over the world and, hence, possession of it. Sartre's 'existential psychoanalysis' purports to show how different sports involve different ways of relating to the earth (via that piece of the earth where the game is played) and hence symbolically realize ways of mastering the reality that sustains us. In skiing, for instance, one glides over a smoothed-out terrain, marking it but not detained by it; in water-skiing, one does something rather similar, but the marks one makes soon vanish, though they make waves. And so on. In the same sort of way, every kind of dance manifests a specific mode of mastery over the dancing place of which it takes possession and thus realizes symbolically a basic strategy for combining absolute freedom with inert objectivization.

Illuminating and useful as Heidegger and Sartre may be, a more directly helpful treatment of space and place is Frye's differentiation of four 'cosmic levels' of space and time – more directly helpful because derived from literary structures, hence from the imaginative world proper to art.[10] The four levels are the divine (heaven), the unfallen world of paradise, the fallen world of experience, and the demonic (hell). These levels yield four spatialities. First is the 'here' of full and immediate presence, the circle whose centre is always here (because everywhere) and whose circumference is nowhere; second is the world of places, in which everyone and everything is either in its proper place or out of place; third is spatiality as the order in which all observables and observers, including ourselves, are mutually situated; and fourth is space as the empty gulf between self and other, the space of alienation. These are all aspects of myth, in Frye's understanding, and all are given in the experience of dance; we have no need of the cosmological instantiations.[11]

6.12131 Dance Space

Travel through space may be from one place to another. But it need not be. To be in a place is to be somewhere: places have character. Spaces are distances, and constructs from distances; as such, they are placeless. It is not incidental that we travel from place to place and pass through places, because *travelling* is changing places, and the places we pass through are places where we might stay, which attract or repel our staying. But not all movement is travelling. Movement as such is from point to point and passes through points that are, indifferently, points. To say that we are located in space is to say that we can or could move, or are prevented from moving, in every conceivable direction. As constructs of movement, dances are in space.

Because dancers have real bodies in a physical world, and are people interacting in a social world, the spaces in which they dance are multiple and heterogeneous – irrespective of the fact that they are also dancing in specific and significantly different places.

In the first instance, space is 'Euclidean' space, in which angles and distances are interpreted as in a characterless and self-contained system. There are no places in Euclidean space, only positions defined in terms of distance and direction from each other. If we choose one point to start measuring from, the choice is arbitrary; the point chosen cannot be assigned a location otherwise than by its relation to points that are identified by distances and directions from itself.

Space is distance – and direction; distance is distance in a direction. For an audience, distance in a dance is defined by sight and hearing: what looks or sounds near to or far from oneself or from something else seen or heard, and how far. For a dancer, as for any agent, distances are defined by how long and with what effort they are to be traversed and by the implications of the traverse. A long way up is a lot of climbing, a long way down is a long way to fall – and, it may be, a long labour to clamber back up.

A space is, as it were, a practical chunk of space. It is defined by limits and obstacles to movement or (for spectators) to vision. Spaces are confined or open – in a significant word, *roomy*. A dance space is the room one has to dance in, with leg room and elbow room and head room, and the room one has to be seen dancing in.

Euclidean space is what we measure in. There are other geometrical spaces, but they are of no everyday significance. More important, there are other kinds of distance than the ones geometries define, hence other spaces; but we know how to translate them into Euclidean space, and we do not know how to translate them into each other, or how to translate Euclidean space into any of them. Euclidean space is accordingly thought of as real space, or just as space. We get the dimensions in metres of studio or stage, and that shows us what room we have to move about in, what we have to fill. On that basis, we can work out for ourselves the other sorts of spatial relationship we have to take account of.

Given that a dance is what a dance is experienced to be, does a dance take place in Euclidean space? What are the alternatives? In practical terms, there are hodological spaces, where distances are defined by how long it takes by the routes that are (have to be) traversed. The freeway may be longer than the back road in kilometres, but a shorter because a faster drive; for walkers, hill paths are deceptive short cuts; distances as the crow flies are not distances as the trail meanders. Then there are social and personal spaces, spaces of reaching toward and avoidance. Face to face is not back to back; where people are in relation to each other is not to be measured by tapes. Crossing and passing are elastic.

E.T. Hall (1966) says that the space of interpersonal relationships has four regions: the intimate, the personal, the social, the public. There is a region of closeness that we allow only to lovers; a wider region that belongs to person-to-person exchanges; a region within which those present belong to the same group; and the widest region, compresence within which has no significance. The differences between these regions are qualitative; their implications for relationships are decisive. They are largely a function of distances in Euclidean space, but not entirely; the rules change on a crowded bus. And the distances vary from society to society: what is only personal in one culture may connote intimacy in another, a fact that makes for discomfort and awkwardness in cross-cultural exchanges. Intra-dance relations play on variations among the first three of Hall's regions: such variations are an important aspect of dance dynamics, and hence of dance space.[12] But these relations belong to virtual space, not to real space, as that distinction will be made below: the implications of proximities are exploited, but not experienced or exemplified by the dancers. The dancers throughout remain, or purport to remain, as professional colleagues united in the dance where the relevant regions of closeness are those generated by the requirements of physical and mental cooperation.

Because a dancer is a person, and related to other dancers and to the audience as a person as well as a dancer, the real and virtual distances in interhuman space are exploited in shifting and indeterminate ways. In an African dance in which it is important that the dancers are both dancers and members of the community in which and for which they dance, the social region may be exploited in the dance in one way and exemplified, in the real relation between the dancers and the bystanders, in another way. In a belly dance, if a dancer dances to individual male spectators, she generates for the nonce a virtual personal space at the same time as she implies a virtual intimate space, while the real space remains the public space in which the relationships are devoid of individual significance.

Complexities of the sort I have just sketched are real and important, but the descriptions seem factitious. One is driven to say that all this talk of interhuman spaces (and of all spaces other than real, measurable,

Euclidean spaces) must be metaphorical, because the only constraint on what one says is that it seems somehow to fit, and one can give no reason why something else might not fit better, or equally well in a different way. And that surely is the hallmark of metaphor – that no metaphor can claim privilege over another metaphor. But that way of putting the matter cannot be quite right. The facts of interhuman space are real facts, though complex and variable; and, since they are facts about relative closeness and distance, what they are facts about is something spatial.

There are interhuman space facts, then, and hodological space facts, and these facts belong to spatial systems. But there is also a dynamic space, or system of space facts, of human orientation, in which up is not merely the opposite of down, and in which up–down is really different from side-to-side; in which left is not right, and toward is not symmetrical with away-from. Dance-makers actively exploit such spaces, rely on them, generate the appearance of spatial constructions in their terms, and rely on their being palpably generated. But to *explain* to each other what it is that they do, we and they rely on our knowledge of Euclidean space and refer everything to its terms. It is only in the realm of explanation that Euclidean space has priority; for most people most of the time, it has no experiential reality.[13]

If a dance is a work of art, and works of art are such only under an interpretation, then the space of a dance is a virtual space, not a real space.[14] That is, it is a space that exists for the relevant experience, but the experience is one that has to be learned and can only properly be enjoyed in relation to works designed to be perceived and understood in the appropriate way. To take the most obvious case, in a landscape painting one sees the hills as *beyond* the trees, the rider as *astride* the horse, and so on; the relations hold between items in the painting as a painting, not between sense-data or between the patches of pigment of which the painting is made. A non-representational painting has to be seen as modelled in three dimensions, or in two dimensions (abjuring the third), and the relations thus modelled are not the same as those between portions of pigment. Similarly, to hear music is to hear tones and intervals in tonal relations, relations that exist only in constructed systems of musical meanings. Something similar must hold for a work of architecture, which is more than a pile of stones, even if we do not have a habitual language to discuss it in.

To see a dance is to see dancers in dance relations. These dance relations must similarly be virtual relations; this will be true even if we cannot see or specify any difference between these relations and those between the physical bodies. Just to see things as dance imposes another layer on what one sees, a distancing and unifying, like quotation marks round a quotation. So the dance is taken out of real space, in the sense that nothing matters except what is relevantly seen as part of the dance, and what is meaningfully relevant to that. Even if the virtual space coincides with real space, the identity is contingent. (It is contingent even if the two *invariably* coincide, though it is a funny sort of contingency, and just what we are to make of it will depend on the ramifications of our modal logic and epistemology.)

Could the extent to which dance space is real rather than virtual space be divined or illuminated by the differences between the presentation of a dance on video and its presentation live? Video changes scale and perspective, but it is the same dance one sees; so perhaps the virtual spatiality is what survives the move to the small screen. But this seems to be a mistake. I have remarked elsewhere (Sparshott 1984) how quickly and fully one adjusts in sportscasts to playbacks and slow-motion takes; one simply seems to be getting a second and better look at an event, as one would if one moved to get a different view of a perduring object. The miseries and glories of video change nothing, because the virtual space of the dance is mediated by real space, just as the third dimension in a painting is mediated by the actual brushstrokes on the flat canvas. I return to this matter in chapter 20.

If a dance is (experienced as) in virtual space, not in real space, does that mean that the measurable, 'Euclidean' space of our common measurement practices loses its privileged position? If so, does the exploitation of social, hodological, and dynamic (and perhaps other) spaces in dance directly affect the unified space of dance in a unique way? Not really. Euclidean space refers to perceptible phenomena only as mediated by techniques of measurement; in practical situations, the possibility of such measurement is always in abeyance, in the same sort of way as it is in dance.

All real-space relations have virtual-space counterparts, I suppose. The difference is one of ontology and of phenomenology. When one enters the dance, or leaves the dance, nothing need be different except that one is sometimes in the dance and sometimes not. (Usually, many things are different, and one joins the dance for their sake; but it need not be so.) And, even if we say that a dance is in virtual space, it is of course true that a dance is fully real only when it is being danced, and that whenever a dance is danced it is danced in real space. Above all, it is danced in *physical* space, with solid bodies on real boards under really shining lights and so on. That's where we start, all right. But it doesn't get us far, so we should not insist on it at the expense of a proper development of such genuine complexities as have occupied us in this section.

6.122 *Pose and Transition*

A movement that stays in place starts in one posture and ends in another, or starts in one orientation and ends either in another or in a return to the same. A movement through space starts in a posture at a place and ends in a posture at a place – different, or the same resumed. Sometimes interest lies in the trajectory or dynamic properties of the movement, with the positions at beginning and end being no more than unobtrusively suitable terminal points. Sometimes the movement is no more than a similarly decorous way of getting from one emphasized posture to another. In a complex theatrical dance, such as a ballet, interest shifts constantly: sometimes it lies in a movement in progress, sometimes in a pose being held, sometimes (in a lift, especially) in the shifting dynamics within a self-transforming pose.

Though theatre dances have the sort of complexity mentioned – a complexity that we seldom recognize as such, because that is simply the way one dances – there is a difference in principle between two possible kinds of dance, corresponding to different sorts of movement. One sort of movement consists of changes or happenings, with definite beginnings and ends.[15] Answering to it there would be a dance of transitions, definable as a series of poses or scenes or tableaux or vignettes. The other sort of movement is continuous activity, in which the interest is always on what is going on, never on what is being brought about. In a dance based on movement of this sort, interest would centre on the way the dancers moved, the quality of the changes themselves.

There is a point of view from which posture and movement are indistinguishable. At each moment, the body is in some position or other, and the position is what it is. The sequence *a-a-a-a* is no less a sequence than *a-b-c-d*. Stillness and movement can be interchanged by altering the frame of reference. But this point of view is one that only physicists take. Practically, our inertial bodies have an unchanging frame of reference – the earth's gravitational field. Poses must be *held*, movements must be *made*.

The iterated sequence *a-a-a-a* has a special significance. Living things are homeostatic. Because their mechanisms are set up as negative feed-back systems, their internal changes have to be construed as departures from and returns to a 'normal' condition of equilibrium, even if that equilibrium is never reached. So with theatre dance. The dancer's return to a securely held and maintained posture after an elaborate set of manoeuvres is a decisive moment in dance; some modern dance tech-niques can even be described as a constantly manipulated loss and recovery of balance (cf. §15.2121).

John Dewey's aesthetics (1934) was based on the achievement of an 'aesthetic moment' of order and balance from disorder, through organ-ized effort. His work retains authority because of the range of vital experience it brings to bear on the activities of art. But its application to artistic procedures themselves is never simple. The case of dance seems problematic: if it is an art of movement, the moment of rest can hardly be the moment at which aesthetic satisfaction is achieved. But that is not what Dewey meant: aesthetic success lies precisely in the fact that the movement itself, at every moment, constitutes a solution to the artistic problem. The conclusion in a return to fifth position, or whatever, is not what the movement was to achieve, but something else: it solves the problem of how to hold a pose – a pose from which other movements can begin. It is as it were a demonstration, or a celebration, of the quality of control that has been manifested all along. It invites the audience to applaud the quality of the dancing they have just witnessed – exactly as, at the end of an old-fashioned operatic aria, a sustained note from the singer, accompanied by an emphasized cadence and a repeated chord from the band, celebrates the eternal order of the har-monic structure through which singer and players have tunefully cavorted.[16]

6.13 The Asymmetrical Body

The difference between two directions of spin (§6.1211), manifested in the absolute difference between left-hand and right-hand spirals, takes on a special meaning in dance because, whereas the two kinds of spiral are entirely symmetrical, the human body and its organization are not.

A human body is not just *any* kind of material object. It has limbs, it is an organism of organs. Simply as a moving thing, the body is asym-metrical in three ways. Front and back are asymmetrical in one way: moving forward and moving backward are different in motor terms, as well as psychologically. The front is where the toes and knees are, which affects balance and locomotion; the front is where the eyes are, which affects steering. Top and bottom are asymmetrical in a second, quite different way: the parts of the body that are normally oriented toward the centre of gravity of the local inertial system have quite different movement properties from those oriented in the opposite direction and those oriented laterally.[17] Here, again, the physical differentiation is quite different from, though inseparably related to, the biological and psychological differentiations. And third, right and left depart from symmetry only by each being the mirror image of the other. From the point of view of movement as such, symmetry is perfect: for every left-hand or deasil movement there is a precisely corresponding right-hand or widdershins movement.[18]

Physiologically and psychologically, however, bilateral symmetry is not preserved. The internal organs are not perfectly symmetrical; the functions of the brain hemispheres differ and relate differentially to the sides of the body; and, more directly revealed in experience, handedness is a fact of life.

It is a curious fact that the asymmetry of dexter and sinister has little significance in the dances I know about; the possible contrast between an arabesque or an attitude and its mirror image is not marked.[19] Symmetrical groupings can be truly symmetrical. If this is really the case, it may be because, outside dance, it is practically and socially significant movements that require differentiation of right from left. There are all sorts of movements, not requiring a differential deployment of skills by the paired limbs (as when we hold an object in one hand and work on it with the other), in which neither agent nor observer notices which limb moves in which way.[20]

6.131 Symmetry and Asymmetry

Our bodies confront us with the fact that forms may be symmetrical or asymmetrical, that symmetrical items are sometimes interchangeable and sometimes not, and that symmetry may be departed from and recovered. Once introduced, this becomes an important formal resource, setting tidiness and dullness against untidiness and incident. And whenever we carry parcels in each hand we discover that balance and symmetry are strongly but subtly related. People who arrange items (such as a dance chorus) on a stage sometimes trade symmetry in for a sort of metaphorical balance, in which left and right of the stage are balanced, as it were, on a central fulcrum, by maintaining equality between the weight and distance of dance-person on either side. We may never notice that no physical lever exists and that, in reality, no balancing is going on.

6.2 Recapitulation

This chapter has covered what I wanted to cover in a reasonably order-ly fashion, but its order lacks cogency. Ideally, we should take several different runs at the same material until we feel at home there, like taking a number of walking tours through the complexly articulated streets of a city until one knows one's way around. Except that there (almost certainly) is no city, only streets created and connected by our perambulations.

Differentiating kinds of movement has its dangers. To avoid an inde-terminate and amorphous mess, one introduces system and, in doing so, implies a claim to have covered all possibilities. But by identifying these as 'possibilities' one suggests that they constitute a pre-existing, ordered set, among which choices had to be made.[21] I want to avoid that sugges-tion. But then, what can the task of this chapter be?

For there to be a movement, two things are necessary: a physical actuality, and a description (uttered or understood) by which the rel-evant actuality is isolated, identified, and characterized. But this is quite indeterminate. Anyone can do anything, and anyone can *say* anything. Despite Orwell and Wittgenstein, natural languages, with such resources as negation and metaphor, are designed to ensure that the unsayable can be said; otherwise they would be useless to a spe-cies chiefly characterized by its tendency to introduce and deal with novelty.

My task here, then, can only be to indicate some leading factors that generate preferred identifications and descriptions and say how and why they are 'leading', leaving it to others to propose supplements and alternatives. We can be sure there will be supplements and alternatives, as well as a lot of residual indeterminacy.

What is a dancer? Setting aside the phenomenological considerations about corporeality and being-in-the-world (§§5.3ff), we can say in quite mundane terms that a dancer is, normally, all of the following: (1) a material object, subject to the general laws of physics; (2) an animal body, metabolizing in an environment; (3) a human body, with the specific articulations of a vertical, bipedal mammal; (4) a human animal, its human body directed by a big brain; (5) a dancer, to be felt and seen as engaging in dance, whether that be determined by action pattern, by technique, by performance context, or by institutional context (at the minimum, being known to be a dancer); and (6) a human being, a social animal in its society, its movements describable in terms of human 'doings' even if the (mimetic and expressive) significance of those doings is not in point. I say a few words about each of these.[22]

(1) Material objects do not move but are moved or are in motion; their behaviour is thus not immediately relevant to dance. But dancers move their bodies *as* material objects, whether they think of them as such or not: their bodies are subject to the general laws of dynamics and mechanics. The movements a dancer makes are modulations of movements generated by physical forces, and the (willed) modulations themselves are exemplifications of forces studied in physics textbooks.[23]

(2) Animal bodies are integrated, organic systems, controlled by a central nervous system, acting and reacting, pursuing and avoiding, growing and decaying, and their effective functioning as such is associated with such qualities as agility, grace, vim, and stealth.

(3) The human body has its own characteristic size and proportions, articulations and rigidities, musculature and skeleton. The weight and structure of its limbs impose ranges of flexibility, natural rhythms of swing, limits of speed, norms not to be transgressed without special physical or mental effort. All these are in relation to an intricate perceptual system, with hierarchies of salient stimuli related to the sense organs and motor systems; the whole makes up a system for moving and staying in a variously enticing and threatening environment. The resulting movement, intimately related to a system of typical motivations, is inevitably expressive and mimetic in an indeterminate fashion, because it is the movement of a body all of whose possibilities are initially ways of responding to a meaningful environment. But, just because this is so, a movement that is straightforwardly expressive and/or mimetic is never exclusively so: a movement of head or eye in observation or apprehension will have definite formal properties in physical terms, as well as in terms of the overall vitality of the living animal.

(4) Since a human body is that of an animal with a big brain, with capacity for language and mathematics and elaborate information-handling capacities of which we do not fully understand the nature or the limits, any human movement is immediately seen as integrated into systems of memory and planning, hierarchical and parallel. A human movement can never be seen as a reflex or immediate response to an

identifiable stimulus. We know that a human being may always be up to something. A human movement is always seen with an aura of indefinite possibilities, with more going on than will ever meet the eye.

(5) Dancers, as such, move in terms prescribed by the dance or the style of dancing.[24] In the normal case, their movements are shaped-to-be-seen or shaped-to-be-made; in any case, they are 'virtual' movements in the sense that they are to be seen as to-be-seen-as-danced. But this very fact, whatever the original choreographic intention may have been, will tend to affect the real movements made, in various ways: in stylization or the avoidance of stylization, or in an apparently unaffec-ted elegance, and so on. Whenever possible and appropriate, what the dancers do will be construed as specifically dance movements or dance poses.[25] A dancer walking will be seen as doing a movement called 'walking,' if that is a possibility in that style. It is not an accident of history that ballet dancers everywhere use a special (mostly French) vocabulary for so many even of the simplest things they do; the parallel language is a constant reminder that everything is being not only done but danced.

(6) Animals mostly ignore other animals, unless the are related to them as prey or predator. Social animals, however, including humans, take cognizance of members of their own species. Human cooperations, conflicts, conversations, and gestures take place against a background of general cognizance; human interaction takes place in a sort of space in which people pass or encounter, meet or part, acknowledge or ignore each other. In addition to the specific miming that may take place in a dance, there is a level of meaning on which the dancers are all mutually related to each other as human, without anything in particular being expressed or conveyed. Face-to-face, dos-à-dos, à-la-main left or right are specific, danceable relations that can obtain only among people but have no definite meaning. No line can be meaningfully drawn between this sort of spatiality and the domain of expression. The complexities introduced into movement by the facts of humanity are uncharted and perhaps inexhaustible. I merely mention two.

(a) As athletes and acrobats, dancers perform feats of exertion and contortion, testing or displaying the limits of bodily prowess for them-selves or for humanity. These are neither expressive movements nor purely formal but relate to the real or supposed potentialities of the human as mobile agent.

(b) The system of positions in space whereby movement in general is charted becomes, in the human case, a system of places from which one is displaced and to which one returns, and so on. Such a space is elastic, with volitional vectors; some of these vectors are defined in relation to the stage, or other circumscribed dance space, and others are generated by the danced action. As humans watching humans, audiences cannot help construing what they see in terms of such fields.

However the dancers are seen, a dance is normally danced in a space. It is danced on a surface, which has a relevant character as a field for movement. It will be flat or tilted, rough or smooth, single- or multi-levelled, in various ways. The danceable surface will have or lack determinate boundaries. Its limit may be abysses or walls, or simply prohibitions (taboo areas), or conventions of abstention from dancing. The surface, if limited, will have a shape and proportions; even if unlimited, it may have contours of relative undanceability. Access to the dancing space may be limited for the dancers (by doors, wings, ramps, conventions of entry) or for the audience (physically by proscenium arch, thrust stage, amphitheatre; or conventionally, by understandings of what it is proper to see, and so forth).

With or without limited access, dance may be orientated. Dancers may dance toward, or away from, an audience or each other. People are built to move in the direction their eyes point but are able to move backwards; dancers may face in one direction and move in another.[26] Accordingly, dances may be focused on objects, dance *at* a victim or *for* a consumer.[27] A circle dance may be danced around an object or a person thereby defined as victim or as power centre; a linear dance, or one that is, as it were, polarized, may be danced at or for an audience or a revered object.

The movements and orientations mentioned in the last paragraph are those of a solo dancer or of a group dancing as a whole. But, if there are many dancers, movement may be *within* the dance as well as *of* the dance. Anatomical movements are themselves internally directional; the trajectory of a movement, for the dancer or for the audience, may pass through or among the limbs, or it may be centripetal or centrifugal; when there are many dancers, the line of a movement may pass from body to body harmonically or contrapuntally. One important kind of complex movement, accordingly, will be that in which what is part of a single dancer's body movement is also part of a movement pattern distributed among the group. What is special about such movements is that they belong to different energy systems; a hand moves as part of what the dancer is doing with her own body, but also as part of a pattern that the choreographer devised, and that the dancer has had to learn and memorize. In the latter respect, the reasons for making the movement as and when it is made have no kinaesthetic reality in her experience.

To conclude our enumeration or check list, we must recall the distinction between discrete movements and continuous activities. The prevailing use of blackouts instead of curtains to mark the beginning and ending of theatre dances has facilitated the conceptualization of performed dances as ongoing activities, of which the audience has seen a sample, in the same way that tunes in popular music genres in the 1960s might fade out with the performers still playing and singing (cf. §14.31 below). And if we think of a dance not as something to be begun and ended, but as a stretch of continuously interesting activity, we may also think of a dance (as Paul Valéry did; Sparshott 1988, 357–9) as an outflowing of pure energy, rather than as anything actual dancers actually do.

CHAPTER SEVEN

Anatomy

Mention of spinning as a basic type of movement led to the topic of handedness, and hence to the bilateral asymmetry of the body as a formal element in dances. This opens up a new topic: the use of different body parts as a prime resource in dance, the basis of a formal classification among dances.

The difference between the parts of the body as instruments of dance is not only formal. The limbs and other parts of the body do indeed have distinctive formal (and material) characteristics. Legs are heavier than arms, attached to the trunk differently, muscled and boned differently, function differently in relation to the body's support, move differently. Bellies, heads, hands and fingers, eyes and lips are similarly different. In so far as a dance is composed of abstract body movement, no part is substitutable for any other part. But, of course, the bodily parts function as parts of a distinctively human body, so that their movements have unmistakable human significance. Legs can, arms cannot, kick and stride; heads can nod, bellies cannot. We are aware of different parts in different ways, simply as moving parts, without regard to any mimetic or expressive significance they may also have.

Body movements are inescapably ambiguous in the foregoing way. They are also susceptible of another ambiguity, touched in on the last chapter. A movement in a formal or abstract dance may be transmitted from hand to hand of a number of dancers, whose hands or arms thus become as it were independent entities, relevantly seen without attending to the whole dancer whose limbs they are. Alternatively, a movement may be a function of the dancer's whole body, perhaps transmitted from leg through trunk to arm and hand. Such movement may still be seen abstractly, but in a different way, as the abstract movement of a person moving beautifully.

In addition, the movements of the body parts may take on quasi-mimetic significance: that is, they can have the nature of what one might do with that part of one's body, but without admitting any specific mimetic interpretation. Beyond that, we get into another whole range of meanings, the moving body as variously manifesting the corporeality of the living person. I treated these meanings as expressive, rather than formal: we engage the world in different ways through different parts of the body, we are different in them, they engage different worlds. None the less, parts of the body remain simple body parts. Because dances are based on movements of the bodies of living people, we are continually concerned with their different aspects: material, physiological, corporeal, animal, personal. ... It is the simultaneous inseparability and irreducibility of all these aspects that makes discussions of dance endlessly contestable.

Dances can be differentiated by the parts of the body that are involved. Such involvement could be of two kinds: that only certain parts of the body are moved, or that only the movements of those parts count as part of the dance. In the latter case, separation may be effected by conventions about where one looks, but it can also be brought about by such devices as masks, shields, fans, or spotlights. And masking works in two ways: it may assist spectators to direct attention in the appropriate way, or it may entice them to speculate about what is hidden (cf. §§14.32f).

As well as variations in involvement, there are variations in emphasis: the conventions of a dance may require us to concentrate on only some of the dancers' movements, or to regard them in different ways. In an Irish jig, in some traditions, the feet move nimbly while the torso remains immobile, and prowess requires combining the two. But they matter in different ways. Skill is not a matter of keeping still while the feet move but lies in how you move your feet – the immobility of the torso is a testimony to one's prowess rather than a component in it. Other variations in quality of attention are possible: it is at least thinkable that there should be a dance in which there should be one set of a dancer's movements that was a sexually alluring or aggressively intimidating spectacle, and another set that was aesthetically significant as dance.[1]

7.1 Feet and Hands

The first contrast is that between dances that emphasize the upper part of the body and those that emphasize the lower part. The contrast is a commonplace; it recurs throughout the history of Western dance writing as an ongoing polemic between dances that emphasize technical dexterity and athleticism and those that emphasize human meaning and expression.

It is with the head and the hands that humans habitually communicate meanings. We are centaurs, human only from the waist up; legs are merely mammalian. The other side of the polemic says that our legs are human legs, and only in dancing is their humanity completed: sentimental fools and rank amateurs can wave their arms about in a vaguely expressive manner and call it dancing, but only a true dancer can impart dexterity to the pedal extremities.[2]

The contrast between legs and arms has just been presented in such a way as to suggest the contrast between professional and amateur; but that is misleading. Most of the dances popular in the West have been defined essentially in terms of where the feet go, as sequences of steps; movements of arms and torso have been trivial, or matters of complete indifference. In the crudest terms, this has to be so: if your feet take you to the wrong place, you are either in the way or out of the dance altogether; misplaced arms are much less of a nuisance. In much ballroom dancing the postures of trunk and arms were relatively invariant, as though confined to expressing the social closeness of the dancers, and the dance as such was determined by where you put your feet. Hornpipes, jigs, tap-dances, and other such pastimes are essentially dances for legs and feet, the bodily posture being excluded from detailed notice as dance.[3]

The contrast between upper-extremity and lower-extremity dances has three aspects. In one aspect, it seems to be a version of a contrast between dances of expression and dances of agility, the ways in which the different limbs are involved being a natural consequence of the values and meanings sought. In a second aspect, it derives a meaning from the ways the different ends of our bodies function. The top end is dominated by the head, the control tower, and the clever hands; the bottom end is correspondingly crowned with the sexual organs. In the third aspect, the contrast between arms and legs in dance is a matter of mechanics. Hands are more flexible than feet, legs are thicker than arms; legs are supporting, arms are supported; fingers are cleverer than toes. The trunk tends to be relatively inert, functioning as the fulcrum on which head and limbs pivot.[4] The head is too heavy, and its contents too vulnerable, to do much wobbling, and head dances are not common. Arms and legs are what there is left, so there would inevitably be these two contrasted sorts of dance even if no symbolism were involved. The body contrast and the significance can be separated, even in civilizations in which it is habitual: one can gesture with the legs, walk on the hands, cultivate a *port de bras* in which arm movements are developed for purely formal properties. But a biped's a biped, for a' that.

7.2 Whole and Part

The contrasts between upper and lower, legs and arms, feet and hands are basic in dance but may be thought to mask a yet more basic opposition: that between dances involving the trained and expressive body as a unified instrument, and those in which the parts of the body are conceived as separate components separately movable. There are dances in which we concentrate (as dancers and designers or as spectators) on head and arms and treat the legs primarily as support, dances in which we watch the twinkling toes and let the arms dangle, dances in which the trunk is only a mass on which the limbs pivot. In such dances one might question whether dance has realized its full flowering as the art of the human body in motion. Surely the human body is an organic whole, and the body as human is the human person as corporeal. A truly artistic dance is one that is meaningful *through and through*; must this not mean one to which every part of the body contributes? On this understanding, if attention is directed to a specific part or function of the dancing body, the direction is itself a functional part of the dance: if a part of the body is excluded from choreographic concern, that exclusion itself has choreographic meaning. And a dance confined to a part of the body, rather than engaging the dancer's self as a dancing whole, could hardly effect the self-transformation that I have alleged to be important in dance; it would surely be a dance strictly for spectators. Can we not then say that dances that truly involve only a part of the body are amusements, trivial because the dancer as a whole is involved in them not as agent but as manipulator?

7.21 Focal Dances

The foregoing arguments should be resisted. The organic integration of the human body does not really impose a holistic character on serious dance. It is never a requirement of an art that all its resources be exploited in every work. It is certainly never a requirement on a specific *fine art*, as the fine arts have been developed and recognized as among the cultural resources of our civilization, that it develop everything revealed as capable of development by a priori reflection on what its medium ought to be. A fine art has as its nucleus a definite set of practices, themes, paradigms, and devices, historically developed, the extensive knowledge of which is the only basis for knowledge of the art. A fine art of dance need be no different. Theoretical concern for the unity of the body, and a locally developed preference for holistic choreography, do not preclude the legitimacy of dance arts and practices that confine themselves to limited movements of specific parts of the body.

Just as arts need not exploit the whole of their potential resources, and need not on any occasion deploy the whole of their repertoire, persons are not diminished in their humanity if on any given occasion, or in any particular practice, only a part of their bodies is engaged. Richness and fullness of life are not measured by completeness of bodily engagement. To put the whole of oneself into what one is doing is a matter of intensity of experience, rather than of exhaustiveness of muscular exercise.

We need, then, some special argument to show that a developed art of dance must be a dance of the whole body. Can such an argument be provided? Easily. The art of dance, like other activities, is necessarily symbolic, exemplary where not mimetic. Only a dance in which the body moves as a whole, in which every part of the body is constantly relevant even if not actively employed, can express humanity in its completeness; any dance that does not connote human completion connotes human diminution. A jig in which rigid head and torso counterpoise the energetic legs, a tap dance in which the cool relaxation of arms and the upper body ironically negate the eloquence of the footwork, project a single mode of human presence; a dance in which it really made no difference what the arms did could only amount to a set of tricks, not an imaginative life.

The foregoing argument is specious, however persuasive. It simply asserts that dance has to be seen in one way, and then states plausibly enough the implications of that viewpoint. But why should a dance be seen that way? To say that only a dance of the whole body could visibly represent a transformation of the whole person is tendentious. Dance practices are what they are, and the nerve of any such practice, even if such a nerve can be identified, is subject to change as the weight of life and the distribution of interests change; an argument based on a supposed value of self-transformation is cogent only to the extent that it is found to be persuasive. Nor is it true that our most intense moments are those in which attention and bodily movement are most widely diffused. We know that our whole self, our whole life, may be concentrated on a single action, a single point; why should this knowledge desert us when we are at the dance?

A dance must be meaningful through and through. But through and through *what*? The argument took it for granted that the appreciating eye is entitled to scan the entire body of the dancer for significance. But that assumption was unwarranted. All arts are governed by conventions for directing the attention – in the rich furnishing of the throne room in *The Sleeping Beauty*, we do not notice that there is no carpet on the floor. Nothing prevents there being dances in which only certain parts of the body are relevant, or only certain parts are emphasized.

Involvement of part or whole is really a matter of degree, in which we may differentiate five significantly different possibilities. At one extreme, it does not matter what the dancer does with any part of the body not involved in the dance, just as a singer may sing in any posture without affecting the song as a piece of music. There could be dances of eyes, or of fingers, that a dancer could perform equally well in any posture. At the other extreme, there are dances in which emphasis on any one part of the body is a mere episode within a holistic dance. The former of these extremes is more likely to be fully exemplified than the latter: a dance that literally involved *every* controllable part of the body would have to be performed naked, and potentially incorporate waggling of the ears and tightening of the scrotum. So let us interpret this extreme case more pragmatically, as holistic dances in which no part of the potentially dancing body is at all singled out for emphasis or suppression.

Close to the former of our extreme cases would be a dance in which only a part of the body was involved, but the uninvolved parts were in effect required to be undistracting and unobtrusive – it does not matter what the dancer does, so long as nothing indiscreet is done. Close to the holistic extreme are dances, of which belly dancing may be an example, in which the dancer dances as a whole, but a particular part of the body functions as focus for the interest of dancer and spectator alike. It might serve as such a focus in three ways: as bearer of the principal meaning of the dance; as formal focus, around which other movements were structured; or simply as displaying an exceptional or unusual skill – for it is at least possible that a 'belly' dance should appear as such, not because abdominal gyrations are its structural or symbolic centre but rather because most dances do not include them at all, so that they serve as a distinctive feature and become a cynosure for those more accustomed to dances in which they play no part.

The middle position between the extremes would be taken up by dances in which the demands on some part of the body are of a different order from those made on the rest: the dancer does indeed dance with the whole body, but in such a way that all movements other than those of the part to be emphasized are a mere background for that. There could be a dance in which the whole point of the dance, and a correspondingly special skill, focused on the fingers, though the dance made specific but unobtrusive demands on the body as a whole. The relation in such a case would be in a way analogous to that between a principal dancer and a member of the corps: every eye is supposed to be on the soloist, but each member of the corps is required at the same time to be dancing with extreme though inconspicuous skill.

I referred above to 'waggling the ears' as a kind of movement necessarily included in dances involving 'the whole body.' The reference has an incorrigibly facetious air: those who can perform that movement do so as a stunt, and we do not take seriously the suggestion that it might form a dance or part of one. Why not? Presumably because we start with a notion of the dancing body as an integrated totality of movable parts. The notion is hierarchical – though in a very complex way, as you will see if you try to work it out. Movements of the eyes play a small part in dances to be seen from a distance; movements of the big toe do not figure in traditions where shoes are worn, and are marginal even in barefoot dances among shoe-wearing societies such as our own, but may be an integral part of dances in countries where people are habitually unshod, though even there the toe movements are not usually the most prominent. But movements of the ears or scalp form no part of any tradition I am aware of; they do not enter into the articulation of the dancing body as such.[5]

The point prepared by the preceding paragraph is this. The notions of 'part' and 'whole,' of the body and its parts, with which we have been working, are not conceived in terms of the anatomical body and its musculature, but with reference to an unformulated background notion of the body and its mobilities as available for dance. Dances are conceived as holistic or as partial with reference to this set of potentialities. The result is that any talk about whole or part is deeply ambiguous. It may refer to use of the whole or part of the available range; or it may refer to a proposed revolution in which that range itself is expanded. A finger-dance might be a dance that involved only the fingers (under one of the modes of exclusion already considered); or it might (however unlikely) be the harbinger of a dance practice in which only the fingers were dancing parts. In fact, the old ideological battles about 'legs and arms' are less suitably thought of as concerned with ways of dancing than as about the scope and organization of the dancing body.

Another ambiguity has pervaded this chapter. I have sometimes written as if focusing attention on one part of a dancing body were a spectator's free choice of what to look at. And every spectator certainly has that freedom. But what is more important is that the dancer's energies may be concentrated on that part, or originate from it, and that a spectator's attention is directed or misdirected accordingly (Sawyer 1985, 209–10). And from this point of view the trunk, despite its relative immobility to the eye, takes on especial importance. The torso is likely to function as the source of movement as of stillness; it is always ready to dominate the dance.

One last complication awaits us. I said that a revolutionary movement that advocates dancing with 'the whole body' is promoting a revision in the way the dancing body is (thought of as) organized. The purport of such a revolution is very different in a community already prepared in principle for perspective shifts from what it is where the very idea is unprecedented. If 'modern' dance is thought of as involving such a revolution, it is worth noting that it arose in a world in which the art of painting was already undergoing a comparable revolution: ever since Hegel, the idea of *art in general* had held the potential of becoming a powerful solvent of all media and techniques in all the arts. When Graham told Fokine, on a famous occasion, that he knew nothing about movement, part of what was involved was just this: that Fokine's reforms had been modifications, however drastic, within the possibilities prepared by the education of a dancer's body, while Graham thought of the dancing body as in principle open to reinvention.[6]

CHAPTER EIGHT

Units and Systems

Are dances made up of movements? Not if a dance is an action, something people do. All proper parts of actions are themselves actions. If I am changing a car tire, that action can be broken down into smaller actions: jacking up the car, unscrewing the bolts, taking the wheel off, and so on. But the movements of the muscles in my fingers as I unscrew the bolts are not things I do, and are not parts of the action as such. Similarly, as I perform a dance, the parts of my action will all be things I do in dancing: my turns, lifts, and so forth, and not the ways my limbs move as I perform these actions.

In a sense, a dance that is an achieved work of art can have no proper parts at all: it is a seamlessly expressive whole.[1]

On the above ways of thinking, if you do not see my dance as an indivisible unity, you do not see it as a work of art at all; if you do not see the way my dance arises out of the separate things I do in dancing it, you do not see what I am doing, and therefore do not see my dance. Well, you may not see my dance, but there is something you do see, and what you see is the way my body moves. And there is nothing in my dancing but the way my body moves; the movements of the body are the medium of the dance. Analyses of dance movement are, in a sense, not about dance; but they are about what we see happening in dance. A dance, whatever else it is, is an articulated sequence of movement.[2]

Are all dances articulated in the same way? Perhaps not. One might think, to take a parallel case, that all literary texts are organized in a hierarchy: syllable, word, phrase, clause, sentence, paragraph, chapter.

But scriptural texts go by chapter and verse, and poetic texts go by line, stanza, canto, and so on.[3] Is anything comparable true of dance?

Perhaps in any organized way of dancing there must be a minimal level, a least recognizable unit of movement; then a least recognizable *meaningful* unit; then a least recognizable *danceable* unit; then a least recognizable danceable *figure*; then a least recognizable *dance* – or something like that. I don't know what these terms would mean, but it seems not impossible that a suitably informed person could work out some such scheme to fit all or a large class of dances; one could then classify dances by the different ways in which they fitted this scheme, or (if they did not fit at all) by which of a number of alternative schemes they *did* fit.

In any such scheme, we could not really start with irreducible units and combine them in ever more complex compounds. The units would normally be complementary to wholes of which they were proper parts, or systems in which they were proper elements. And surely such complementarities must be relevant to the dance practice in question; the units should be components of the action as performed, what would properly be said to be done from the point of view of the dance-maker's intention or a proper critical analysis. On the other hand, we cannot make that intention or analysis a fixed starting point: the fact that dancers use themselves (and themselves are used by choreographers) in dancing injects an element of human indeterminacy into the situation.

Janet Adshead (1988, 1) takes what seems to be the opposite view. The actual movements of a dance, she says, are a matter of observation. The system to which the movements belong can be divined: there will be one, and only one, way in which the movements fit together. Interpretations, however, must be devised, and can never be more than plausible, because they relate to the meaning of what is observed and divined, and rely on imputing intentions and adducing relevant practical contexts, which are always contestable. In a way, Adshead's position is persuasive: what the eye could see, an impersonal camera would show. But how the movement would break down into movement units the camera would not show, and the uninformed eye cannot be expected to see.

The articulation of a dance system of units in combination might be 'emic' or 'etic,' to use a piece of anthropologists' jargon – that is, it might be an articulation followed within the practice itself, or it might be one set up by outside observers.[4] And the articulation might follow the thinking of specific interest groups: of choreographers, or of dancers, or of informed spectators (connoisseurs), or of dance theorists, or of anthropologists. One would expect these to overlap, or even to coincide; but they might not. One must be prepared for surprises.

Whoever establishes the articulation, it can be made from the top down, or from the bottom up. In the former case, the whole dance is initially conceived as a unity, and the system of divisions imposed on it after the fact for one reason or another – perhaps to make it easier to teach, or to memorize, or to describe, or just to see if some hidden structure was present. Articulation from the top down need not arrive at a set of determinate units: since decisions must be made at each stage, it is likely that the further down one got the less reliable the articulation would be, and one might well be uncertain at what point (if at any) one had reached indivisible elements. Alternatively, the structure may be built from the bottom up, the dance practice consisting essentially of a repertoire of preferred or possible units ('steps,' for instance) and preferred ways of combining them – in which case the concept of a dance as a whole need not be present at all, just as possession of a vocabulary and a syntax enables one to talk on endlessly without one's discourse ever reaching a conclusion.

In practice there is also a third possibility: that the familiar practical units should be movement sequences, danceables, the analyst's task being to discover both how these could be broken down into elements and what the laws or norms of their combinability are. Also, unless one confines oneself to public performances of dance works, the possibility of improvisational dance opens up a further possibility. In musical improvisation, what I do takes on musical coherence in many ways. One way is that, at any given time and in any particular passage of my playing, what I play implies a thematic and harmonic background and a compositionally coherent continuation, so that it is to the listeners as though they were hearing the midst of an unfamiliar musical composition. But there is no composition, and as I go on playing the implicit background and continuation may change. Something similar could be true of improvisational dance: at every moment the dancer dances coherently in terms of an implicit set of options with an implied future and past; but, as the dance continues, the dancer's living dancerly intelligence continues active, the implicit options change – just as the project of one's life changes as one matures and ages, and the units in which one conceives past and prospect assume different magnitudes.

One would expect to find that a dance or a dance practice would admit of several alternative modes of analysis: it is possible that all dances and practices admit of all possible modes of analysis, including any yet unimagined, since we have no a priori rules for deciding inadmissibility. In the light of this variability, the important differences among dances should depend on what modes of analysis came most naturally. But what are the criteria of 'coming naturally'? Some modes might be normal within the dancing culture or tradition, or in influential subgroups of that; a different set of modes might be normal in the observing culture or tradition. But no doubt such remarks represent an arid scepticism. In real life, in artistic dance, only one articulation corresponds to the dance-makers' artistic use of the tradition within which they are working, and spectators simply do not see what the dancers are doing unless they see it in the light of this understanding. In social dance, similarly, the very existence of the dance is a function of the shared understanding among the participants of how they are to dance together, and a spectator who is ignorant of the terms of this understanding cannot see what is being done.[5]

Theoretically, then, though any dance can be broken down in endlessly many different ways, a dance, as learned and danced as a matter of practice, will almost certainly have its own proper articulation.

If one does decide to analyse dances in ways known not to be those internal to the practice, or without regard to whether they are so or not, one may do so in three ways: by articulations proper to some other dance practice; by articulations devised by dance theorists to be applicable to all dance practices; or by articulations conceived on some principle alien to dance. None of these, presumably, will classify dances otherwise than by their degree and manner of their resistance to the analysis imposed.

8.1 Units of Movements

Units are correlative with systems, elements with wholes. So it makes little sense to speak of 'units' by themselves. But it makes some. In our turbulent, polyglot, multicultural societies, much practice in the arts is inevitably eclectic, whatever the cultural mandarins may decree, and we can envisage a dance in which, whatever the imaginative unity of the whole, individual components were recognizably heterogeneous.[6] What distinctions are to be recognized here?

To begin with, natural movements may be distinguished from steps – movement-units that are conceived from the beginning as elements in dances. By 'natural' movements here I mean no more than movements that derive their identity from some context of activity other than the context of dance itself: they include work movements, sport movements, devotional movements, as well as those that belong to the general stream of life. This distinction between steps and natural movements is conceptual: there is a sense in which anyone might spontaneously take up the 'first position' without knowing it, and a sense in which this is not possible.[7] Blasis invented the 'attitude' by bestowing status on, and defining a repeatable identity for, a pose already famous from Greek sculpture; one could not be certain, from looking, whether someone was adopting that dance pose or demonstrating the posture of that sculpture.

Aside from this conceptual distinction, some movements are natural in the quite different sense that they come easily to the untrained body, and others are unnatural in being special or forced – movements one would never or rarely make unless one were dancing. Among the latter, a special place is occupied by movements that are unnatural in the stronger sense that most people cannot make them at all without special training; in dance forms like ballet, most or all movements may be of the latter sort. Leaving that last factor out of consideration, a movement such as a sideways skip might occur outside of dance, if one had occasion to skip sideways; but an entrechat would be most unlikely to do so, and an arabesque virtually never would.

Another distinction is that between movements that are gestural, in the sense that they are of a sort that is characteristically made in order to convey a meaning, and movements that are characteristically formal, to be specified in the first instance by what goes where. I say 'characteristically' here because it is possible to make gesture-like movements without gesturing (not waving, but drowning); a dance built from actual gestures, or exploiting gestural meanings, comes under our earlier heading of mimetic dance.

Among gestural movements we may distinguish between those that are also steps and those that are not. We may also distinguish movements that are gestural through an expressive quality – they look as though they meant something – from those that are gestural because they look as though they were elements in a language (a specific language, a known sign-system of which the character is approximated; or just some sign system or other, much as when an acute listener detects that an African talking-drum is doing something language-like, without actually knowing any Bantu language, and without guessing that an actual message is being conveyed). I say more about gesture in §13.2 below.

The most vital of the distinctions made here is no doubt that between dances made up from steps and those not so composed. In a sense, anyone can dance at any time, by beginning to move rhythmically and with aesthetic attention. In another sense, a person is not really dancing unless what is done imitates the movements conceived to be proper to some practice recognized as dance within that person's society. And people are not dancing properly unless they have mastered the vocabulary of dance, or developed such a vocabulary, and remade the body into an instrument capable of putting that vocabulary to effective and exclusive use. There is, as often, an analogy with music: anyone can make music of a sort by banging away and chanting, but music proper is made up of musical sounds (or musical intervals) constituted by their mutual relationships within a gamut. In a society that has developed such a music, nothing else really counts.

8.2 Movement Systems

Since dance is a practice, and dancing is something people do, dance movement cannot really be abstracted from the web of discourse and explanation in which it is embedded. However, in any dance that consists of steps, as here conceived, those steps must form part of a definite system, each step being defined in part by how it relates to other steps. In fact, in so far as a dance is not mimetic but assigned to a formal classification, and if it is to be recognized as a dance intrinsically (rather than contextually), it must either have some diffuse formal quality of dancelikeness or consist of movements recognizable as dance movements; if the latter is the case, there must be a determinate set of such movements, and these, being determinate, must be determinable. It may be possible to describe such a movement without referring to any other movement in the same dance system; but it must also be possible to say or show exactly how it differs from any other movement within the same dance practice.[8]

Any system of which that is true is called a 'notational' system; the logic of such systems has been definitively explained by Nelson Goodman (1968, chap. 4).

Dance, as Goodman points out (211–18), is not notational. For one thing, the stated condition is not fulfilled; art dances have to be recognized contextually, both because the idea of art requires openness to change and because art nowadays has to be seen as art and *nothing but art* (McFee 1992, chap. 4). If some one system of dance notation became canonical, dance would still not be a notational art unless the notated score became the sole authority for what did and what did not constitute a performance of the dance in question, which would mean substituting the score's analysis for the system of steps through which dances are learned, remembered, and taught. Within a dance tradition, a sequence is typically described by a series of names of positions and steps plus spatial and dancer-to-dancer orientations, together with descriptions or reminders ('then three of *those*') of such movements and positions as are not named in the system. Dance traditions vary greatly in their tolerance of novel, unnamed, and unrepeated elements. The fact that all or almost all ways of dancing that consist of discrete elements dispose of a repertoire of standard movement elements ('steps') related to each other in standard ways does not mean that such dances can be completely analysed into those steps. They may, or they may not. I return to this issue in §20.222.

8.21 Dance Traditions

Dance traditions do tend to develop systems of steps, of learned movements of varying degrees of subtlety and complexity. Some of these are in the first instance systems of gestures; others are more straightforwardly repertoires of special positions and movements, as in ballroom dancing and disco dancing. A prime example of a traditional system is that of ballet, developed over the centuries to become the dominant system in Western civilization. One author says that there are 'more than 1400' ballet steps (Deakin 1956, 65); I do not know how the enumeration was carried out, but it is evident that a set of movements of such a scope must be systematically differentiated from each other and must form a system, because they could hardly be memorized as independent vocabulary items.[9]

In principle, a movement scheme such as that of ballet is defined formally; but an element, or a complex pose or a sequence, may have a semantic meaning, which would confer on it the status of indissoluble unity so long as that meaning was retained. The status of such assigned meanings, operating within a formal system on which they are superimposed, is very different from the status of gestural meanings in systems where the semantic meanings come first and the formal differentiations follow the requirements of mimesis.

It is pointless to generalize much about traditional systems. Being traditional, they must be studied in their historical context and developing individuality. The actual workings and changes of dance traditions are most of what the student of dance systems has to learn and understand. The brevity of my discussions here does not reflect the insignificance of the topic, but its concrete magnitude.

8.22 Theoretical Analyses

Dance traditions develop movement systems in the form of repertoires of steps and positions, together with rules for combining them. But various theorists have worked out systems of body movement which, though applicable to dance, go beyond actual practice. Such systems abound and are based on the most various principles: muscular economy, the articulation of the limbs, the body as a dynamic organism, the differentiation of gestures, the range of physical possibility, the varieties of expression, the significances of orientation, the manifestions of spiritual power – who can say? But all have one thing in common. If their scope includes the whole range of possible movement, they cannot shed specific light on the range of choices and significances employed in any particular way of dancing (cf. Adshead 1988, 24). What explains everything in general explains nothing in particular: it is a reef on which many ambitious philosophies have foundered.

How, in general, *do* movements affect us? How do we find them meaningful? People have tried to construe human movement as a sort of code, within which observed differences would correspond to differences in significance (cf. §13.5). One such attempt is typified by René Descartes's theory of the emotions, according to which complex emotional effects should be analysable as combinations of a few basic feelings. In the middle of the eighteenth century, systematic attempts were made to construe the effect and meaning of musical compositions in these terms, so that the composer could discover the relevant rules and make them the basis of a musical rhetoric. Much the same thing was suggested for dance by John Weaver at the beginning of the same century.[10]

8.221 Weaver

Weaver's work in fact confronts us with a double system. His *Essay* of 1712 envisages an art of 'stage-dancing,' to be reconstructed according to the descriptions of ancient writers, essentially mimetic in character: '*Dancing* was (at least) of old, a form of Mute Rhetoric; while the *Dancer* by his Gestures, Motions, and Actions, without Speaking, made himself perfectly understood by the Spectators, in whom he rais'd the Passions of Anger, Pity, Love, Hate, and the like; which was as much as the Poets or Orators could pretend to effect by all the Force of their Tropes, and Figures' (Weaver 1712, 16). Among the required gestures, some are 'the *natural Effect* of *practical Causes*, as when Men are struck with Joy, they leap. ... [W]hen Grief assaulted them, they cast down their Heads; Anger and Admiration lifted up their Hands'; and so on (90–1). But, for the most part, a body of knowledge of the appropriate movements must be built up and studied.

> The Feet, and Steps, which seem to claim the greatest Share towards the Perfection of this Art, will not, as I shall show, appear so material a Qualification towards the Masterly Performance of it, as the *Address* of the Body, and just and regular *Movements* of the Arms; neither is it so difficult to obtain an Excellency in the former, as in the latter; for whereas the Feet require only Agility, and constant Practice, to arrive at the utmost Perfection; the Motions of the Body and Arms require a Judgment, and Knowledge in several Arts, to qualify them for a just Performance; for it is by the *Motion* of the Body and Arms, that he must express the *Design* and form the Imitation; For this Address, and Motion of the Body, is not, as some are willing to believe, an Air, or Manner, natural to some; but it is a Perfection acquired with Judgment, and altogether Artificial; and to arrive at this Perfection requires a long Experience gain'd from the Instruction and Observations of good Masters; ... (161–2)

In the preface to the scenario for his ballet *The Loves of Mars and Venus*, in which he sought to put his principles into effect, Weaver adds: 'Nature assign'd each Motion of the Mind its proper Gesticulation and Countenance as well as Tone; whereby it is significantly and decently express'd'; but he recognizes 'the Necessity of having both Dances and Spectators instructed by Degrees, with the Rules and Expressions of Gesticulation' (Weaver 1717, xii–xiii). He contributes to this end by listing in his scenario the gestures he has used for Admiration, Astonishment, Jealousy, Upbraiding, Anger, Threats, Power, Impatience, Coquetry, Neglect, Contempt, Distaste, and Detestation, as well as for Triumphing, Entreaty, Grief, Resignation, Forgiveness, Shame, and Reconciliation (21–3 and 28).

Four years later, however, in a series of lectures delivered to his fellow dancing-masters (1721), the emphasis changes. His concern is now not with theatre practice but with the 'common' dancing his colleagues teach their pupils. In dancing in general, the aim is to achieve beauty in Motion, Figure, and Measure (Weaver 1712, 86–8); the project of the lectures is to re-establish the traditional basics of dance instruction, and much of the substance of what he says is a digest or transcription of the most authoritative descriptions of the human bones and muscles, with the rudiments of Euclidean geometry and mechanics to explain what is actually involved in standing, walking, and jumping.[11] He trusts that rules based on such data will guarantee elegance and grace when followed by bodies that comply with established canons of proportion[12] and that the requirements of elegance will coincide with those of health (Weaver 1721, 89). He does add, however, that 'there is a certain Carriage of the Body and Limbs, in the Performance of almost all Steps in *Dancing*, which gives a peculiar Grace and Air to the Motion; which is not only very difficult to attain; but much more so, to lay down Rules for them' (Weaver 1721, 141).

Common dancing, unlike stage dancing, has no communicative function beyond that of displaying the dancer's elegance. The relative emphasis on agility and expression is accordingly reversed, and Weaver can say what he denied before, that 'the Carriage and *Movement* of the Arms depends more on the Fancy of the Performer, than on any certain rules. ...'[13] The lectures do say something of the expressive side of stage dancing. Now, however, the source of this lore is not said (as before) to be dance tradition, no doubt because the postulated tradition would be that of an ideal choreography and not that of the practical dancing masters who are now principally addressed. Rather, one is to study the art of rhetoric and the visual arts. It is not clear how the actual study of rhetoric will help, beyond providing an analogy for the elegant and moving use of gesture, and perhaps affording a list of the 'Passions and Affections' to be expressed;[14] for a usable repertoire of suitable movements and postures, the instructor is advised to study '*Paintings* and *Prints*' (Weaver 1721, 146).

Despite the support of the *Spectator*, to which he contributed, Weaver was never able to establish a theatre in which his ideas could have been consolidated; but his very advocacy of an art of dancing that should be based on the principles of mathematics, physics, physiology, and psychology established by the best contemporary science was ahead of the general tendency of its time.

8.222 The Nineteenth Century

Weaver's world is that of a polite society whose ideals are avowedly those of a privileged minority. Very different in inspiration are the systems worked out in the late nineteenth and early twentieth centuries. These take their origin in the rise of industrialism and the concomitant rise of science as a total enterprise. The social and economic background has two important aspects. First, there is the rise of mass societies and conscript armies, which bring to notice the proletariat, human beings seen by the educated classes as undeveloped members of what is really an alien species. Weak, sickly, and ignorant, they are to be trained and educated and must first be studied: traditional learning presupposes a shared culture with shared values, within which transmission and cultivation are to take place. Without that common background, one must consider afresh how the weak and sickly bodies of the new industrial population are to be developed, to be made fit for war or work. Physical training is to be carried out in the name of 'fitness.' But what does that involve? Freedom from disease and inanition, certainly. But beyond that the idea becomes civic and aesthetic: the ideal is that of a body fit for, and expressive of, the activity of a free citizen – a free citizen, because in the new societies each individual must be capable of taking any of a number of places in a functionally fluid social and economic order. We have, then, a motive for developing descriptions of free human movement, conceived in terms of the human body articulated at the will of a free human mind. When these ideas penetrated the world of dance, they tended to choose as their foil the idea of ballet as a servile and special way of moving, one that traps its exponents within its hierarchical system.

The sort of system of which I have sketched the motivation is ideologically democratic, though practically bourgeois: it outlines the life and education its proponents think proper for everyone and in practice are determined to secure for themselves. But the same epoch is that of the factory system and mass production, which require motions no less constraining and specialized than those of ballet, but determined by function rather than tradition. How can people work with machines? We must find out how the body can perform any task most efficiently; and that requires that we develop a general way of describing any movement, in relation to the capacities of bodies and the demands of tasks.

The foregoing two aspects of the rise of industrial mass societies are accompanied by a third, more technical factor. The same period was also the great age of transportation, its phases marked by the successive introduction of new ways of moving goods and people: stagecoach, canal, railway, bicycle, automobile, airplane, with their transformations.

Among these, the development of powered flight represented a unique challenge. How do birds and insects fly? How do wings keep them up, propel them forward, and allow them to manoeuvre at the same time? In the last half of the nineteenth century, this problem stimulated a widespread and intense interest in the mechanics of all animal and human movement.[15] These researches have now become the domain of 'kinesiology' as a branch of value-free physiological science – a general study of animal movement which is empirical, heteronomous, unsystematic, and unrelated to any practical interest; but their earlier stages generated an urgent excitement.

The names now remembered from this age of system-building in movement studies are Jaques-Dalcroze, Delsarte, Laban, and the now-rediscovered Souriau. They developed rational systems of movement analysis on the basis of defensible but mutually unrelated principles and with quite different aesthetic and semiotic implications. I am not conducting a historical enquiry here, but I will say enough about each to show that general systems of movement analysis not only can be but have been worked out and have influenced the theory and practice of dance.

8.2221 Delsarte

In the rethinking of the principles of meaningful movement, immense influence was wielded by the eccentric autodidact François Delsarte. He had no special interest in dance as such but approaches Weaver's problem of the systematization of gesture in art from the angle of a professional theatre innocent alike of the exact sciences and the fine arts and unconnected with aristocracy. He began from the perennial problem of teaching opera singers to act, went on to the techniques of theatrical expression in general, and ended by working out a complete system of gestural movement on the basis of the capacities of body parts and the inevitable meanings of socially interactive movement. The system was validated, he thought, by his decades of observation of people in all walks of life, but to our contemporaries it looks like an instruction manual for melodrama. The position of the torso, he urged, showed the basic attitude; the gross movements of the limbs represent the passions; the extremities answer to the intellect. On this basis, articulated by dynamic principles of direction and reaction, Delsarte works out a 'natural' language of movement in which each position of every independently movable part of the body is assigned a specific meaning. Presumably, though Delsarte seems not to have been quite clear on this, the resulting system of meanings is carried and guaranteed by the inescapable facts of human physiology and psychology and social interaction, and is readable by anyone capable of thinking away any conventional significances that may have preempted its functions.

The comprehensive system of posture that Delsarte provides is available for a dance practice that would be dramatic in abstraction from any specific mimetic content. As such, divorced from its pedagogic origins, it has had immense influence in America, in two directions.[16] It was developed into a system of gymnastic exercises by his younger colleague Steele MacKaye, under the name of 'harmonic gymnastics,' designed 'to give symmetrical physical development, and to take out the angles and discords, to reduce the body to a natural, passive state, and from that point to train it to move in harmony with natural laws.'[17] And on its original territory – dramatic education – it took part in the movement whereby elocution, which played a great part in American education from the 1820s, was expanded into a general training in 'expression' as women's education became important in the late nineteenth century. On this basis, Genevieve Stebbins developed an elaborate analysis of gesture and expression that became enormously popular and influential.[18]

The Delsartian system was taken up and touted as the basis of his own practice by Ted Shawn, who (in alliance with Ruth St. Denis) occupied a strategic position in the development of modern dance in America, and whose exposition of the system (1968) is the most accessible – Delsarte himself died in 1871 without arranging his work for publication (Stebbins 1902, 75). What mostly survives of it, I suppose, is the idea of a comprehensive, systematic, and fully defended method of meaningful movement analysis independent of any particular tradition or convention, together with one specific idea: 'The recognition of the torso as the source and main instrument of true emotional expression – and equally important, the use of successions, beginning in the torso and spreading outwards and downwards throughout the entire body' (Shawn 1968, 61). But a deeper significance lies in the fact that, as Ruyter points out (1979, xiii), the modern American dance was self-consciously intellectualized from its very beginning.

8.2222 Laban

To lend authority to his system, Delsarte invoked a supposed 'Law of

Correspondence': 'To each spiritual function responds a function of the body, to each grand function of the body corresponds a spiritual act.'[19] At the opposite extreme from this is the way of thinking about movement developed by Rudolf Laban half a century later. Laban imagines the body's centre as centre of a 'kinesphere,' that sphere any part of which a person can reach without changing stance, poised on one foot. Movements are conceived abstractly as paths around the circumference of the sphere, and centrifugally or centripetally along vertical, front-to-back, and lateral axes or along diagonals. Given these orientations, movements differ depending on whether they go all the way or half way. And, in addition to this, 'Movements can be executed with different degrees of inner participation and with greater or lesser intensity' (Laban 1974, 27).

Whereas Delsarte interpreted movements as the ways a spiritual force expressed itself in the articulation of the body, Laban reduces everything to the inherent dynamism and direction of the movement itself – it is not even necessary to specify what part of the body performs the movement (112); nor need a specific feeling content be ascribed to a movement, for the dynamics of its trajectory within the sphere carry their own meaning (100). Rather than looking to psychology or spirituality to give the system resonance, we look outward to the world: 'Our body is the mirror through which we become aware of ever-circling motions in the universe with their polygonal rhythms' (26). Above all, because the basis of the system is itself in terms of dynamic space and trajectories, the significances initially chosen for the leading forces and dimensions do not preclude indefinitely extended elaborations which need not be tied to the emotional life – which, endlessly complex and subtle as it is, is conceived from the beginning in terms that we have no reason to expect will correlate with the differentiations of movement as such. The result is that, though Laban, like Delsarte, was an originator rather than a systematizer, the latter's work persists only as a legacy within certain dance techniques, whereas Laban's has been carried on by others, especially through the development of the notation he originated.[20]

It is possible, though, that Laban could ignore emotional expression only because other analysts had already dealt with it. The abstractness of his movement analysis revealed its weakness when, in exile later in life, he turned to the problems of industry. For this purpose he had to introduce a new and independent way of dealing with how the body moves at work, gripping, hauling, and so on – an 'effort shape analysis' with which the dance world has been little concerned (Laban and Lawrence 1974).

8.2223 Souriau

The other two theorists I named are not interested in movement analysis as such. Souriau is concerned with the conditions in which motions are judged pleasant, and hence beautiful, by those who perform and perceive them. Pleasantness is always a matter of relaxation; unpleasantness and ugliness come from tension. At the lowest level, pleasure comes simply from awareness of muscular exertion; a higher level of pleasure comes from expressiveness and grace, the appearance that a movement has been undertaken in the easiest and most efficient manner. But the highest excellence of beauty comes (the inspiration is Kantian) from the recognition that a task has been analysed and the conditions (perhaps not evident) in which it can be most efficiently accomplished have been fulfilled. The height of aesthetic excellence is achieved, for Souriau, not in dance but in gymnastics. It follows from what he says that a true art of dance would break with the past and reconstruct itself on the basis of scientific culture. His view of dance aesthetics is functional and hence, in principle, alien to the idea of a vocabulary and syntax of unit steps – alien, but not opposed, for it can be seen that his ideas are continuous with those of Laban, as Laban's are with Delsarte's.

8.2224 Jaques-Dalcroze

Emile Jaques-Dalcroze's starting point was the teaching of music: he observed that his students played mechanically (as, he thought, ballet dancers danced) by forcing their fingers to make one memorized, mechanical movement after another. Like Delsarte, and many others, he believed that expressive movement should be a spontaneous manifestation of inner life; and, also like many others, he thought of music as properly a phenomenon of that inner life. Music education should therefore concentrate on training people to make their bodies the responsive instruments of their wills, so that they could follow flexibly and gracefully the most subtle variations in inner rhythm.[21]

Dalcroze wrote little but founded an influential movement and school called 'eurhythmics' – a misleadingly pompous translation of his own straightforward phrase *méthode rythmique*. In his own mind, this was primarily a use of physical training to inculcate musical sensibility; in the world of pedagogy it became, inevitably, a use of music to assist physical education.

Dalcroze comes into our story because his whole practice implies a condemnation of most existing dance, a condemnation that he explicitly endorsed: 'Dance must be completely reformed, and in this domain, as in so many others, it seems quite useless to try to reform what already exists. We must destroy from top to bottom the fallen art and form a new one on principles of beauty, purity, sincerity and harmony' (Jaques-Dalcroze 1917, 28). Who could quarrel with that? On the other hand, who could learn from it? Petipa did not set out to be a proponent of ugliness, impurity, insincerity, and discord. But we are being unfair. Dalcroze had just written that 'the real perception of movement is not visual, it is muscular' (25); if that is true, any dance system based on steps, and any movement analysis based on objective orientations in Euclidean space, must miss the values he invokes. To these ways of going wrong he adds another: the practice of borrowing postures from the visual arts. This paid homage to the supreme authority then generally accorded to Greek art and Greek civilization, but did it in the wrong way. A dance that paid true honour to Greek civilization would do so not by putting on Greek garments and pretending to be a frieze but by making music the basis of artistic expression and of all early education: 'There is no tradition of bodily movements, and, as we have seen, modern dancers borrow from the fine arts a cult of attitude which substitutes intellectual experiences for spontaneous feeling and puts dance in the second rank in the domain of art. There is only one way of giving back to the body the complete scale of its means of expression, and that is to submit it to an intensive culture in music, to give it complete control of all its powers of dynamic and agogic expression, to give it the power to feel all shades of tone-music and express them muscularly.'[22] It sounds like Isadora Duncan, in one of her phases. But it is not clear what Duncan thought she was up to, since the supposed priority of music seems to have been an afterthought to justify a style she had already developed. 'Did we not see the fine artistic efforts of Isadora Duncan, the fervent advocate of natural gesture, checked during the last few years of her life because of a lack of perseverance in acquiring new technical methods?' (Jaques-Dalcroze 1930, 35–6). He, by contrast, held the appropriate theory of music, the only theory that could justify his position: 'From its birth, music has registered the rhythms of the human body of which it is the complete and idealized sound image. It has been the basis of human emotion all down the ages'; the musical compositions of an age reveal 'the entire mental state of the period at which it was composed' (7).

There is deep confusion here. What is the relation between the desiderated spontaneity of expression and the 'new technical methods' that might have saved Duncan from banality? He says of the 'classical Italian ballet' specifically that its movements are jerky and disconnected and 'executed with an incredibly small range of tempi' (76–8). He concludes:

> If choreography is to be revivified, it needs to acquire new motor habits, brought into being both by instinct and by consciousness. Its technique need not be changed, but it should be supplemented by a knowledge of bodily nuances in relation to those of time. ... The art of dancing, if it still insists on union with music, should achieve the transmutation of sound into bodily movement and of movement into sound. It is not enough that moving plastic should be superimposed on music. It should spring forth from music as a spontaneous growth, adapt music's extended form and style to its own, and interpret all its shades of emotion. Such transposition is possible only through actual education, which is needed by even the most gifted and talented artists. (86-7)

What, then, are we to make of a disciple's report that at a demonstration at Hellerau in 1911 two of Dalcroze's pupils undertook (by coincidence) to realize the same Prelude of Chopin, 'But hardly a movement of the two interpretations was the same'? One girl lay on the ground almost the whole time, 'expressing in gentle movements of head, hands and feet, her idea of the music'; the second girl stood upright until the end, when 'she was bowed to the ground, in an attitude expressive of the utmost grief. In such widely different ways did the same piece of music speak to the individualities of these two girls'.[23]

The apparent discrepancy is reconciled when we realize that the demonstrating students are not dancers, probably not advanced students of music, either. All they are equipping themselves to do is to give flexible expression to the nuances of what a piece of music *happens to say to them*. To be good choreographers, they would have to be profound musicians, as Balanchine and Tudor were; to be dancers, they would have to equip themselves with such technical resources as ballet dancers acquire. The required revolution of the art of dance-making was that a dance should not be linked together out of sequences of routines, but should completely subdue the acquired ways of moving to a cultivated sense of rhythm. And that, after all, is the same reform that Fokine had in mind at the same period, and the same attitude to technique that it is nowadays conventional for adepts in all the arts to express.

What Dalcroze leaves us with is, in the end, a sense of what function steps fulfil in dance-making and what sort of system a dance movement system would be. The dominant concept here is that of rhythm, the topic of the next chapter.

8.223 Educational Dance

The home of part/whole analyses, such as have occupied us in this chapter, is neither practice nor appreciation but pedagogy. Delsarte, Dalcroze, and Laban were all primarily teachers and were influential by being absorbed into one or other branch of the education industry. Dance education is the topic of several books and deserves a chapter of its own here, including a discussion of whether the phrase 'educational dance' picks out one or more special kinds of dancing or refers only to the use of extant forms of dance for educational purposes. But I will be perfunctory.

If by 'education' we mean the totality of what is formally taught to the citizenry at large and supplemented by spontaneous continuations of that – what the Greeks called *paideia* – it is clear that education has several distinct functions into which dance and dance-related activities may enter. First, there is the initiation of individuals into ever higher levels of cultural and individual development. Second, there is the taming of infants in nursery schools and kindergartens, a social analogue of toilet training. Third, there is the acquisition of supposedly good habits, like reading poetry and saying one's prayers, which are inflicted on children but never practised by adults, who are old enough to realize that virtue and refinement are for other people. Fourth, there are the skills and competences required by adult vocations, in which the educational system's remit is to train the young differentially according to what level of expertness their mentors deem will suit their likely fate in the economic order. And, fifth, there will no doubt be pure teachables, things done in school because it is expected that schools will do them, and which persist, like legionnaire's disease in a modern hospital, because no one has yet traced the source of infection.

One position is taken up by Graham McFee (1994), who recognizes only the first of my five functions as legitimate and argues that schools should teach children to understand masterpieces of artistic dance. Since the context he assumes is that of a national school system with a common examination system, the analysis of dance education into testable teach-ables in relation to a unified understanding is a central preoccupation.

McFee's argument (chap. 10) is directed principally against those who effectively take the second view of education. He quotes from a government publication this thesis: 'Every child can dance. The sharpness of his sense and the intensity of his reactions frequently demand immediate expression' (DES 1972, 44, cited from McFee 1994, 162), and from an educational theorist that 'Dance is simply the art form of movement. It comes about when movement of any kind is so aestheticized that the prime intention becomes the presentation of aesthetic form' (Hirst 1989, 41, cited from McFee 1994, 105). If one puts those together, it is obvious that dance education is limited to stopping the kids from racketing around and teaching them to play nicely, after which they will dance as well as anybody could – a task they should have mastered by the time they start learning to read.

A version of this child-centred view of educational dance, compatible with our third category of educational enterprise, is developed by Laban (1963; cf. Redfern 1982) along the same lines as Dalcroze: the task of dance education is to liberate children from cramped and disunified movements: 'Dance training from its earliest stages is principally concerned with teaching the child to live, move, and express himself in the media which govern his life, the most important of which is the child's own flow of movement. This develops slowly, and in most cases never at all' (Laban 1963, 23). Such education can clearly continue throughout one's school years, and after, for Laban associates it with the European 'free dance' that he and his colleagues (like Mary Wigman) had helped to develop, and was himself instrumental in organizing mass dance festivals (balefully linked with the Nazi ethos); it sounds holistic, but Laban's practical suggestions extend to a curriculum based on a child's 'recognition of basic elements of movement' and so on (ibid).

Laban's work in Britain supervened on a practice of educational dance based on 'Greek' ideals, which the politics of historiography have left obscure to the laity. But on the other side of the Atlantic, Gertrude Colby and others kept seeking the principles of educational dance in the aftermath of Delsartism (Ruyter 1979, 50–1). 'One may readily ask,' Ruyter says, 'why the sources of dance have had to be discovered so often in the twentieth century, especially when no one worried about them before that,' and suggests that it may be due to the continuing influence of Duncan's distrust of formal rigidity. But John Dewey, the most important figure in the theory of progressive education, rejected principles altogether in the name of pragmatic adjustment; so one suspects that the search for 'principles' was an attempt to forge links between the theories about natural expression endorsed by psychology and a curriculum with enough concrete content to be sold to a local school board or a university department of physical education.

Debates about the proper scope of dance education are bedeviled by a widespread failure to recognize that, if a single system is going to take over all forms of organized upbringing, it must necessarily have radically different functions in relation to different social purposes and clienteles, and these can be only very loosely bundled.[24] Education as thus conceived is a merely adventitious congeries, and debates about the true nature of dance education are likely to be campaigns to secure money and teaching time that might otherwise be squandered on one's colleagues elsewhere in the system.

CHAPTER NINE

Rhythm

After discussing dances as kinds of movement in space, the next obvious topic is kinds of movement in time. The general word for that is
'rhythm,' an old Greek word: Plato (*Laws* 665A) defined it as 'the ordering of movement,' and the word he uses for 'ordering' is the ordinary
word for marshalling an army on parade.

Stereotypically, rhythmicality is one of the two excellences of dance:
poses should be graceful, movements should be rhythmical. The anthropologist Judith Hanna, as we saw above (p. 103), made intentional
rhythmicality one of the defining characteristics of dance. But what does
that mean, exactly? Since everyone agrees that the 'rhythm' of a dance
is one of the most important things about it, we would expect the
possibility of radical differences among dances to go with a corresponding indeterminacy in the concept of rhythm. And so it does.

9.1 The Conceptual Question

9.11 Ambiguity

Oddly enough, debates about rhythm include differences in interpretation of the Greek term. Presumably the disputants think that taking the
tradition hostage will help their argument. Some authors emphasize the
fact that Greek art criticism applied the term to statues as well as to
dances and say the term really meant well-proportioned division in
general, being applied to any sort of articulation of an ordered whole.
Others look to the etymological affinities of the Greek term with the

word *rhein*, 'flow,' and say that rhythm really means flowing (Sawyer 1985, 124) – which an examination of dictionary citations shows that it never does. But this difference in interpretation, after all, comes down to a matter of emphasis. If there is no articulation of a movement into parts, there is nothing to flow, only undifferentiated continuation – not even the *a-a-a-a* I spoke of in §6.122, but only endless *a*. If, on the other end, the parts are not inwardly linked in a meaningful succession, flowing one into the other, there is no movement, only isolated events. It is a difference among styles of dance and among foci of attention in criticism and appreciation.

9.12 Necessity

When Hanna made it a defining condition of dance that it be intentionally rhythmic, she cannot have meant that all dance-makers must use the concept of 'rhythm': many cultures may not have the concept of 'rhythm' at their disposition at all. All that could be meant would be that dance-makers everywhere intend their work to have a character that our own culture would identify as 'rhythmicality.' But what could this be? Not, surely, a recognizable quality of 'dancelikeness'; we have seen that, though there may be such a quality, it would not be something that all dances would have to have. The avant-garde being what it is, the specification of what the required property of 'rhythmicality' or 'dancelikeness' was would only serve as a challenge to choreographers to devise something that was undeniably a dance but lacked the property in question.[1] Undancelikeness in a dance context is a dance quality; so too must arhythmicality be, as we will see later.[2] So what *are* we to say?

A dance is inevitably ordered in time as well as in space. The word 'rhythm' picks out the order that it has, whatever that may be: the way the movement fits together sequentially as a divided whole. Significant kinds of rhythm will be significant kinds of sequence: orderly, disorderly; repetitious, varied; quick, slow;[3] jerky, smooth; insistent, understated. To say that rhythm is essential to dance is not to say that there is any specific quality or set of qualities that a dance must have; it is rather to say that it is always relevant to ask of any dance how its movement is ordered as a temporal sequence (or skein of sequences). To say that dance must be *intentionally* rhythmic should be to say only that, if one is not attending to this aspect of what one does, one is not engaging in the practice of dance, whether or not some critic or spectator judges that one is in some sense 'dancing.' Articulation and flow are to be thematized by dance-makers, focused on by critics and spectators in whatever they 'see as dance.'

The types of temporal order will be important types of dance; the kinds of such order that are recognized as significant by a dance culture, especially those that are named and of which the names are current and familiar, can be expected to correspond to a classification of dances that is highlighted in that culture. One can see that there can be innumerable ways of articulating movements for dance purposes, as for any other purposes; and one can see that there could be indefinitely many ways of classifying those methods of articulation themselves. The question of *how* the time of a dance is divided must have been thematic from the beginning: one cannot generalize a priori about dance rhythms, because the variability of the ways of varying movement is one of the principal resources that may be developed in an art of dance. Many writers do in fact make stipulations about how such variation in movement is to be organized and carried out, but though such stipulations may well describe the approved practice of some way of dancing (perhaps the only way that is accepted at some time) it is impossible that they should have any general validity.

9.121 Rhythmicality

All the same, there is such a quality as rhythmicality, which passes for a normal excellence in normal dance. What in general passes as rhythmical in a dance culture may be identified with what is accepted as practically 'danceable.' In our culture, this is clearly akin to what passes as practically singable and playable (so far as time goes) in music. But we meet precisely the same ambiguity and uncertainty in music as we did in dance. What is acceptable as music varies within the world of music; here too the avant-garde is ever on the watch for generalizations which may be confuted by constructing counterexamples. The hierarchical and artistic politics of the musical world, and the rules of avant-garde thought, leave it for detailed historical criticism to determine how closely the resulting ambiguities and uncertainties correspond to those in the dance world.

'Danceability' is an incomplete expression: it means 'danceable by' some group whose identity and relevance is taken for granted. So the word is really useful only where there is unanimity or accepted authority – or where a propagandist hopes to get away with pretending that there is. 'Rhythmical,' accordingly, is a value term, indicating both a recognizable quality that a movement has and the valuation that is placed on that quality; we look at it from that point of view in §15.2121. But there is a lot to be said about what danceability and rhythmicality come to in practice; I return to the question in §9.31 and §9.5.

9.2 The Basics

One tends to think of the equation of rhythm with a danceable rhythmicality as the old-fashioned, traditional view of rhythm. This naïve view has now been displaced, we think, by more sophisticated views. First came the modernist age of medium-conscious exploitations of artistic resources, free from traditional inhibitions; then came the post-modern era, in which we have learned that the concept of 'resources of the medium' is itself a structure of traditional inhibitions. But this version of history is misleading. So far as we can reconstruct it, the earliest account of rhythm in the Western philosophical tradition is as general in its principles as our opening remarks were. It is the work of Aristoxenus of Tarentum, a colleague of Aristotle and (one guesses) an alumnus of the Pythagorean school of his native city, and begins by elucidating the recognizable divisions of time.

9.21 Aristoxenus on Rhythm

The Greeks, in the dawn of philosophy, were not inhibited in the generality of their claims by cloying conventions and traditions, and their way of life was sufficiently unlike our own that they did not always share our views as to what was obvious. So we still find it useful to read them if we want to get our bearings in a field. The first book of Aristoxenus's treatise *The Elements of Rhythm*, or so it appears from the scraps that survive, is one such case.[4] It is the most general account of rhythm that we have and is based on the powerful analysis of the concepts of time and motion in Aristotle's *Physics*. Here is a sketch of what he says.

A rhythm, according to Aristoxenus, is (to use Plato's phrase) an ordering in time, and he works in terms of Aristotle's definition of time as the measure of change or motion. Consequently, a movement or immobility is not rhythmical at all if its continuity is uninterrupted and unvaried: there can be no rhythm unless there is a distinguishable 'before' and 'after.'

Not every ordering (*taxis*) in time in rhythmic: a movement is arhythmic if the ways its parts are put together are completely unknowable in every way. I take it that what Aristoxenus means by unknowability is something like randomness: an unknowable and completely arhythmic movement is one with no discoverable principles, so that it can be specified only by enumerating the positions occupied and how long it takes to move from each to the next.

A movement is 'enrhythmic' if its divisions have some discernible pattern that is strictly adhered to; a movement is 'rhythmoeidic' ('rhythm-ish') if its divisions have a discernible pattern but the pattern is not strictly adhered to – that is, there is a pattern from which the movement is discernibly deviating. For these terms to be applicable, a movement has to be divided into parts. Time, as here understood, cannot divide itself; for there to be a rhythm, time has to be divided by something that is itself initially 'rhythmed' – that is, divided into *recognizable* parts (*gnorimois meresin*): rhythm is a matter of making time and times *perceptible*. What is 'rhythmed' (*rhythmizomena*) can be divided into enrhythmic or arhythmic arrangements alike.

Aristoxenus distinguishes three rhythmed entities: speech, melody, bodily movement. Each divides time according to its own characteristic articulation. Speech does it by letters, syllables, words, and so on; melody does it by tones, intervals, and phrases; bodily movement does it by significant gestures (*semeia*), figures (*schemata*) – 'and any other such part of movement as there may be.' And these three are fundamentally different, though I do not find him saying so. The division of speech by syllables and such has to do with the basis of its intelligible structure and is not directly related to the time an utterance takes; the note divisions in a score show how a tune is structured and articulated in real time but correspond to a self-contained system of measures (cf. §12.42). The parts of bodily movements, by contrast, approximate real divisions in actual processes.

What Aristoxenus says here has the effect of ascribing indeterminacy to dance rhythm as such, unless we insist that dances must be divided into a set repertoire of gestures and steps, in the way that music and speech must be divided into their proper elements. Aristoxenus probably would accept that insistence; art dance nowadays would probably not. The point of his caveat here is that his remarks apply not to dance movement as such but to any bodily movement, which is inherently articulated just because we have limbs with joints.

Aristoxenus thinks (as we ourselves sometimes do) that an articulated system must be built up from minimal parts and (as we do not) that these parts must be not merely the smallest recognized units but actually incapable of being subdivided.[5] A 'primary time,' then, is indivisible – such that we cannot get two distinct sounds, or two distinct syllables, or two distinct gestures, into it. A time is 'divisible' if it will hold more than one of *any* of these sorts of units, 'mixed' if it is divisible by some but not by others. I think we would go at it the other way – at least, I would. If a movement is clearly articulated, there must be units in terms of which the theoretically minimal elements can be identified, but what these elements will be depends on the principle of articulation used and has nothing directly to do with physical or perceptual minima. It may be a truth of physics or of psychology that there is a least time in which a sound can be identified or a gesture recognized, but it is unlikely that these minima can be precisely and unequivocally identified – for instance, it must take longer to identify a low note than a high note – and certain that this will never be directly relevant to the analysis of rhythm. Rather, we say that rhythms relevant to dance may be based on units of any sort: in work dances, the units may be discrete phases of a task; in others, the movement phases ('steps') recognized in the style; in others again, the elements in the melody to which the dancers move.[6]

Aristoxenus assumes that rhythm is articulation in terms of discrete units, divided by rests, without which the items (syllables, tones, figures) could not be identified, and he says that in any sequence the units must be homogeneous – all syllables, or all figures, or all tones: a rhythm cannot switch from one kind of unit to the other, because they are in principle incommensurable (*Elements of Rhythm* I frag. 3). And I suppose, though I do not find this stated, that the rests by which they are separated are conceptually measured in the same way. In fact, they are 'rests' in rather different senses. A notional silence between syllables, a timed rest in music, and an interruption in a physical movement differ from each other in ways determined by the three kinds of temporality involved, as described above. The alternation of movement and rest is a dogma for Aristoxenus: if a movement unit seems to be followed directly by another unit, there must be an imperceptibly brief rest that serves as actual boundary, without which they could not be distinct units. I do not know why he thinks that; one of the most obvious ways to set up a rhythm is by repeatedly beating a drum to impose divisions on a continuous chant or drone (see §9.422).

As I read Aristoxenus, I wonder about two things. First, what is the relation between these articulations and what we nowadays tend to think of as preeminently rhythm – the rhythmical or swinging quality of insistent dynamism? In Aristoxenus's usage, it does not seem that rhythm could be a matter of degree, in the sense that one dance might be 'more rhythmical' than another. Being more rhythmical would not be having a more emphatically marked rhythm, which he could handle easily, or complying more closely with an implicit pattern, which he deals with, but having a more compelling or captivating rhythm, a quality rather than a quantity of movement. If we were using Aristoxenus's terminology, we should call such movements 'eurhythmic' rather than 'enrhythmic,' although in fact, unless the copyists of his manuscripts were at fault, he seems to use the terms interchangeably.

The second thing I wonder about is what Aristoxenus would say about movements in which the 'rhythm' is a matter of continuous modulation rather than articulation, analog rather than digital. That is of little interest to him, because he is really concerned with languages, in which phonemes are truly discrete parts, and their realization in music; but to someone whose interest is in dance the treatment seems inadequate – especially since the modern concepts of acceleration and deceleration, measuring rates of change in a rate of change, have made us think about movements in a quite new way. But Aristoxenus need only say that the word 'rhythm' itself, in his day, meant 'articulation' as a matter of linguistic usage. If we want to talk about something else, we can find another word and not spoil a word that already has a clear meaning of its own.

9.211 Kinds of Time

For Aristotle, time is the measure of change, and by change he meant physical change (because it was change in the natural world he was talking about). But Aristoxenus observed that the change that is temporally ordered in rhythm need not be physical: it could be the phonemic patterning of language, or the determinate system of musical time that is only loosely related to the actual duration of performances, as well as the physically patterned movements of bodies in space. But this should remind us that modern philosophy, more attentive to the phenomenology of experience, recognizes a variety of times and temporalities. There is the Cartesian ordering of unextended instants, measurably later and earlier than each other; there is the temporality that places us in an ever-changing but ever-present 'now' between anticipated or unforeseen future and remembered or forgotten past; there is the duration of lived time, the time that goes by like a flash or drags on interminably; there is the temporal *dasein*, the human situatedness between birth and death. And there is the time that the clock keeps, a pervasive aspect of modern life that should puzzle us more than it does (see §9.4221). And I do not know how many others there may be, recognized or discoverable in our own lives, or embedded in other cultures and alien to our own. Any of these may generate its own rhythm or may complicate or contaminate rhythms generated elsewhere. And, this being so, a dance may have several distinct rhythms. Arlene Croce observes (1987, 185): 'All dances have an inner time and an outer time. The outer time is the tempo of the steps, usually set by the music; the inner time is the rate at which meanings accumulate.'

9.2111 Frye

Discussing dance space, I mentioned Northrop Frye's cosmological distinction of four kinds of spatiality: a heavenly space of immediate presence, a paradisal space of proper places (and displacements), a mundane space of correlated positions, and a demonic space of insuperable alienation. Frye also distinguishes four corresponding temporalities. First, there is the 'now' of immediate experience (as in the supposed *nunc stans* of heavenly experience), in which we do not relate what is present to anything past or future. Next comes a paradisal temporality of 'exuberance or inner energy,' in which 'now' is experienced as the fulfilment of past and the promise of future moments, intrinsically dynamic. Then there is the mundane temporality of scientific discourse, as described first by Aristotle, a system of measurements whereby events can be correlated as simultaneous with, earlier than, or later than other events by specifiable amounts. The fourth, demonic temporality is the supposed system of mutually exclusive 'instants,' none of which has any duration. Demonic temporality annihilates change and movement, which it replaces by a vanished past, an unreal future, and a non-existent present. Of these four temporalities, the first three are applicable to dance, but the first allows no place (so to speak) for rhythm. The 'paradisal' time allows for a rhythmic dynamism that the energies of dance can both possess and symbolize; the everyday, Aristotelian time envisages the intricate patterning of change which, again, dance can both have and symbolize. But the demonic temporality, like demonic spatiality, cannot really be exemplified, though the incessant talk about the 'evanescence' of dance shows that it is among our relevant anxieties.

Evidently, there is a lot that Aristoxenus has not thought of, and we will have to deal with later. Meanwhile, the things he has thought of provide us with food for thought. But first I will just mention a distinction introduced by Paul Weiss (1961), between 'individual' and 'common' rhythms. The latter follow some principle of articulation that they share with other movements, as a dance may follow a metronome that observes clock time; but the former are articulated entirely by their own internal divisions. This is clearly a possibility opened by Aristoxenus's general view of time – that no sort of unit of change is incapable of grounding temporal order. If that is true, the units of a specific temporal pattern might well be *sui generis*.[7] However, having mentioned this possibility, I have nothing to say about it; it seems to be one of those useless possibilities, common in philosophy, that one bears in mind just to keep one honest – like the possibility that the world, complete with all the memories of all its inhabitants, came into existence five minutes ago, or the possibility that you, reader, might really be nothing but a brain, tended by a team of mad scientists, in a vat on a planet of Alpha Centauri.

9.212 Rhythm and Metre

What Aristoxenus analyses is not quite what we mean by rhythm. What is central to his concern is the musical setting of literary texts – a prosody that conventionally assigns determinate lengths to syllables – not the articulation of readily danceable movement. Our own prosody distinguishes between non-metrical and metrical rhythms. A metrical rhythm is one in which the articulation consists of a series of segments of one or more interchangeable units, such that the rhythm is that of a regular or semi-regular pulsing. The metrical segments ('feet') are themselves grouped in short sequences of fixed length ('lines'). This way of distinguishing metrical and non-metrical rhythms is not, however, in universal use. (I have a lot more to say about metres in §12.41, in the chapter on dance and music.)

The metre of a poem is sometimes simply identified with its rhythm, perhaps because people equate poetry with versification and versification with metricality, so that metre is the only rhythm proper to a poem as a poem. But sometimes a poem's metre is contrasted with its rhythm. When this is done, a distinction is made between the way a poem's syllables are formally patterned (or, more often, the formal pattern to which its 'rhythmoeidic' syllabic arrangement is properly held to approximate), which is its metre, and the way its sound is articulated in a proper reading, which is its rhythm.

The contrast between the rhythmic and the metrical is tricky. It is often said that the introduction of a mensural notation in music makes polyphony possible: it allows large numbers of musicians to keep time with each other as they cooperate in complex works. But the price of this is the introduction of bar lines and measured performance, hence an impoverishment of rhythm. The same consideration may be thought to extend to dance, which is often controlled (though not directly) by the rhythmic organization of music to which it is danced, with its metrical regimentation. But this point of view is hard to square not only with what we saw in Aristoxenus but, more important, with the whole long history of Greek and classical Latin metrics. For those metrics, rhythm is par excellence the organization of verse and song by syllabic units, feet, and stanzaic forms, all metrically determinate, and contrasted with the free flow of prose. Rhythm in that classical sense was not opposed to metre, but was the use of metre.

In distinguishing rhythm from metre, I several times used the words 'proper' and 'properly.' But the words were used equivocally. As applied to metre, the propriety is based on knowledge: one is supposed to know what an iambic pentameter is. In the case of rhythm, what is appealed to is artistic competence, a supposed skill in how to read poems. The latter requires judgment and taste, though it depends on knowledge of the speech cadences of the language the poem is in, of the current conventions of poetic reading, and of course of metrics as well. The former requires no taste, only information. It is the way Scottish children are, or were, required to read their metrical psalms: di-*dum*, di-*dum*, di-*dum*.

If one accepts the distinction between metrical (systematically iterative) rhythms and others, one may divide the former into those that involve metres and those that do not. A metre stipulates a named combination of named feet, with set rules for variation; but a poem may be metrical without being in a metre, by being composed throughout of correctly formed feet without using any such prescribed combination.

Augustine's *On Music*, a treatise immensely influential for an immensely long time, resembles Aristoxenus's work on rhythm in being largely a discourse on metre. The reason is that music, as a science, is a branch of mathematics, and, as a practice, was mostly a matter of setting poetic words in song, so that verbal metrics become a principal part of scientific music. But that way of thinking has vanished without trace, and for a long time now, otherwise than in hymn tunes, Western music is not conceived metrically. The apparatus of metrical analysis is not usually applied to it and is not a standard part of the composer's bag of tricks. Even less is the concept of metre used in talking about dance, though such terms as 'waltz time' and 'jig time' are in fact nothing other than names of metres. Why is this? Well, poetry can be metrical because the tongue is a little member. Stresses can be assigned to syllables, syllables can be given standard lengths, without physical strain: the metre can then have a recognizable reality of its own. Exactly the same is true in music: metricality is not impossible or difficult in music, it is merely uninteresting. But to dance metrically one would have either to coerce limbs of different properties into the same quantitative pattern, or to repeat the limb movements that made the pattern realizable. The former would most often be grotesque – there could be effective dances of such a pattern, but the notion verges on the bizarre – and the latter would be confined to formally minimal dances, such as the waltz is. None the less, aspects of metrically could be significant aspects of dance rhythms. It is only the place of metre as a key formative concept that seems to be ruled out.

The distinction between metrical and non-metrical rhythms includes that between the merely repetitive and the grouped. The minimal way of articulating time is by simple division into segments, as by the steady beat of a drum. But the drill-sergeant's endlessly repeated 'Left, right, left, right ... ' groups the impulses into pairs (just because feet are paired and drilled, soldiers are to march 'in step,' not only stamping in time but stamping with the same foot at the same time); most who follow that trade build the divisions into longer phrases ('Left; left; left, right, left!'). Of these marching orders, the former, I think, strikes one as bare repetition, in that the dyadic relation lacks all structural interest; the latter strikes one rather as a repeatable structure.[8]

This raises the general topic of repetition and repeatability, to which I will return (§9.4).

9.22 Density

I said that metre, a rhythm of precisely measured equivalences, is possible because the tongue is a little member, its agility unaffected by inertia. Musical instruments, too, may be designed to minimize resistances to agility. But the body is the body, the reality of its weights and sizes imposes constraints. But that was not quite the right way to put it. Rather, as Aristoxenus's treatment suggests, metre is proper to poetic discourse as such, measuring spoken and written words equally. Words in themselves are neither spoken nor written; they are medium-neutral and in consequence can have no inertia at all.

The actual rhythms of actual events, even in music, involve an actual medium. This means that physicality is always a factor, even in music, but it goes beyond that. A musical composition is not a string of tones but includes a tune with melodic tensions and releases and a harmony that is thick or thin, consonant or dissonant, and offers more or less resistance accordingly. Instruments have not only physical resistances (one cannot play a trill on a gong, and arpeggios on tubas are acts of heroism), but timbres that may retard the effect of movement if not its actuality. The dynamic rhythm of a piece of music is determined not by metronome speeds but by the audible qualities of every aspect of the composition.[9] The same is true of dance, but less obviously, because the physical resistances and facilitations of the body pre-empt our attention. The movement of a stagefull of heavily clad men may have a ponderousness that is not that of the temporal divisions and the physical resistances but is a quality of the rhythm of the movement in which they all share. Aristoxenus covered only half of his subject.

9.3 The Sources of Rhythm

The general account of rhythm that Aristoxenus gives, equating rhythm with the ordering of movement in time, provides that any exhaustively completable division of any sort of temporal sequence of units of any kind is equally rhythmical. I contrasted this notion with that of a specific quality of rhythmicality, which we have yet to discuss. Even without that, though, Aristoxenus's account is deceptive. If rhythm is going to be an invariable aspect of the practices of dance, rhythms must be detectable, so that they can be used and recognized, and they must be interesting, so that people will want to use them and respond to their use by others. They must be relatable to human life. That in itself is not a restriction, of course, because 'life' includes everything, including what is intrinsic to dance. But it suggests that we should look at the identifiable kinds and sources of rhythmic movement and the basic ways in which they relate to human activities.

The rhythm of a piece is the way it is meaningfully divided and articulated in time. But what ways are meaningful? The ways that are intended and recognized, or *might* be so intended and recognized, by dancers, choreographers, connoisseurs, critics, audiences, anthropologists, and any other groups or persons who are interested in ascribing meanings to, or discovering meanings in, dances. When Hanna's definition says that a dance must be intentionally rhythmical, we can take that as insisting that its dancers or choreographers must have some intentions about the way the movement is articulated; it does not follow that the intended rhythm coincides with the rhythm or rhythms that other qualified observers correctly find in it. We may, if we wish, stipulate that if a dance is successful the intended rhythm is definitively the rhythm that it has (or that the indeterminacy of its rhythm is definitively its intended indeterminacy); but we need not so stipulate.

However we define rhythm, I suppose it must be based on and be an expression of the human sense of order, our ways of arranging information and experience. One thing that is characteristic of humans is the generality of our intelligence, our capacity to deal with inputs of all sorts; this includes our 'sense of time,' our ability to invent and work with temporal sequences of all sorts. These will include regularities and irregularities discerned in the world and may be based on the patterns of movement and change that are easy or congenial or interesting for our bodies, on what our measuring intellects can pick out and respond to, and on the developments and changes of our emotional lives, as well as on the patterns of movement that are familiar from being imposed by the ways we interact with the working world. The criterion of what from the point of view of dance is ordered or orderly, or strikingly disorderly, and hence within the general domain of rhythm, must be pragmatic: what can in fact be so produced by dancers that it may come to be recognized, and being recognized accepted, as having some worthwhile significance.

One tends to think of rhythms as clock-generated, in the sense that the basic articulation is derived from the operation of a standard case of the maximal correlation system I will be describing later, of which the paradigms are mechanisms. It is as if (like the drill sergeant) we began with an iterated beat and introduced variations into it. But rhythms may be generated in other ways, and some of these are available for dance – more directly available than the metronome. A rhythm may, for instance, be task-generated, the units defined by the completion of basic operations and the subgroups by the fulfilment of partial tasks (Sparshott 1988, §7.1). It may be mind-generated, the units identified by an arbitrary and abstract analysis, so that discovering and following the rhythm is a purely intellectual matter. Or it might be generated in other ways, such as by changes in the emotive tone of successive episodes in a narrative. A dance rhythm may be derived from music, and very often is; but that raises the question of what musical rhythms are, and why we are interested in them, and the topic is better postponed to our chapter on dance and music.

9.31 The Human Sources of Rhythm

The most important divisions among rhythms would follow the basic ways in which humans relate to their movements and those of others. If we follow the old division of volition, cognition, and emotion, we can ask: Is this rhythm imposed by the will, by the intellect, or by the emotions? An insistent, pulsing beat may represent an iteration of self-assertion; a complex temporal pattern may interweave systems of division based on different intelligible principles; a changing, flowing movement may follow the ebb and flow of various feeling. In classical Indian dance, the *tandava* dance of Siva and the *lasya* dance of Parvati might be thought to embody conative and emotive rhythms, respectively – embody them, that is, not as the immediate cause of the movement but as the source of the character willingly imparted to it.[10]

Whichever of these categories a rhythm is assigned to, we can ask whether it is being assigned to something innately inherent in the human make-up; or culturally ingrained; or acquired by individual habituation. And we can ask whether the assignation itself is generically human, or a cultural convention, or an individual association.

9.311 The Human Engine

Most obviously, rhythms for dance can be directly generated and/or dominated by the tempi of human life, especially by the human body itself. Doris Humphrey remarks that human beings provide themselves with four separate sources of rhythmic organization. First is the breath, by the action of breathing itself and by the use of the singing and speaking apparatus, which provides us with the notion and practice of *phrasing* – a practice which, once learned, can be transferred to any part of the body. Second, there are the functional workings of the body, not themselves under voluntary control: the heartbeat, peristalsis, and the other fundamental controls of vital process. Third come the pendulum rhythms of the limbs, especially the legs. What we identify in dance as 'normal' as opposed to fast and slow time is derived from the motion of the legs in normal walking speed, not from the heartbeat and not from the breath. And, in addition to these three, there is the more elusive but inescapable rhythm of emotional variation, which is experienced not as belonging to the body but as the shape of living itself.[11] It is worth reflecting at leisure on the fundamental differences among these four types of rhythmic change as they enter into our experiences and into our activities, and on the fact that they enter into a single continuity of life. The richness, centrality, inexhaustibility, variety, and unity of dance are all there.

If rhythm in dance is derived in large part from the rhythms of life – the temporal patternings of change that are evident in our action and experience as embodied agents in social orders – and if dance is an art in which rhythm is emphasized, the rhythm of a dance may be expected to relate significantly to these rhythms from which it is derived. It might do this in several ways. It might simply isolate them for attention, as the patterns they are, with or without allusion to their vital sources. It might accentuate them. It might diminish them, or tame them. It might modify them. Or it might contradict them. In any of these cases, the effect might be simply a piquancy in the dance, or it might powerfully interact with that in us which grounds the life rhythm to which it relates.

From the specific point of view of dance, the art of body movement, the most important distinction among rhythms should in any case be that between rhythms that stem from the body and those that are imposed on it. It is true that the key terms 'stem from,' 'imposed on' and 'body' can be interpreted in different ways, so that the resulting classification is neither automatic nor unambiguous; but that does not matter, because whatever reading is most natural in a given context will automatically yield the most relevant version. Whatever counts as origination, whatever is felt as imposition, whatever is identified as the body, effect the distinction between two classes of rhythms: those that are experienced as native to the dancing body and those that are alien. Leaving subtleties aside, there is a sort of robust sense in saying that the physical construction of the body obviously makes some rhythms, those that consort with the dynamics of limbs and musculature and the energy replacement systems, congenial to it, whereas others, derived from movements generated by other physical systems, will be less congenial. One may hazard a guess, too, that the rhythms of orally transmitted music, being generated by humans for humans, will tend to be well adapted to these inherent impulses of the body. But we cannot be certain that this will be so, and the processes of musical invention and transmission in general are such as to blur distinctions in this area.

9.312 Rhythm and Life

Speaking more generally, there is one special sort of temporal order to which the word 'rhythm' is especially applied, a sort of movement that is recognizably congenial to the free movements of the body. It is this sense of 'rhythm' that forms the centre of Susanne K. Langer's philosophy of biology. The main source of functional continuity in the development of early life forms, she argues, must have been the establishment of rhythms in this sense: 'Rhythmic concatenation is what really holds an organism together from moment to moment ... ; a sequence wherein the subsiding phase, or cadence, of one act (or similar element) is the take-up for its successor' (Langer 1967, 323–4). The essential characteristic of rhythm is this energetic interflow of movements, not (as we shall find Dalcroze urging) periodic repetition; for not all repetitions are periodic, and not all rhythmic sequences are repetitious – especially not in dancing. Rather, 'The essence of rhythm is the alternation of tension building up to a crisis, and ebbing away in a graduated course of relaxation whereby a new build-up of tension is prepared and driven to the next crisis, which necessitates the next cadence.' Such rhythmic movement, Langer says, is the basis of all living form in life and art.

A position like Langer's seems to fit what we may still think of as *standard* dances, before the avant-garde took hold. Some such sense of what rhythm in general (especially dance rhythm) is lies behind the traditional identification of 'grace' as the supreme value of dance (see §15.22111).

The kind of rhythm that Langer describes is organic rhythm, and in a single organism such rhythms are interrelated (see §9.3121). The primary exemplification of organic rhythm in dance would be the rhythm derived from movements generated within the dancer's body (since all human bodies are variations on the same anatomical and physiological theme, these would not be 'individual' rhythms in Weiss's sense). But it is organic rhythm in general, the master pattern of life itself, that lies at the heart of the matter.

Body is traditionally contrasted with mind, and organic rhythms are almost automatically contrasted with rhythms intellectually conceived, in the manner of Aristoxenus. But this contrast is akin to that between 'feeling' and 'thinking,' a contrast that is hard to harmonize with the tripartition of conation, cognition, and passion or appetition, which I introduced above. Rhythms imposed by the mind on the body surely belong to conation, the active and forethoughtful planning of the will as opposed to the passive following of appetite and impulse. The blind will-to-power which Schopenhauer contrasted with formalization (or however one translates *Vorstellung*) is, from the point of view of human agency, mere passion as opposed to conation. This goes to show that these rough-and-ready classifications from traditional speculation fit only where they touch.

I have just contrasted rhythms derived from the body with rhythms imposed by the mind on the body; previously, I contrasted rhythms derived from the body with rhythms derived from other (presumably inorganic) physical systems. All this sounds as if it makes sense, but it could be deceptive. A rhythm my mind imposes on my body is, I suppose, simply something I don't feel like doing, and will be no less uncongenial if it is in itself a kind of movement my body often makes. Again, a movement 'imposed by the mind' may be one typical of some inorganic system (when, for instance, I try to act like a machine), or one with no natural dynamic instantiation (for instance, one derived from arbitrary interpretation of an algorithm). The resulting rhythms will differ widely among themselves in the kind of discipline I must impose on myself in order to carry them out at all, as well as in the kind of thinking and training I must do to make out of them something that I and my public will find acceptable as dance.

9.3121 The Dance of Death

Langer's thought about rhythm, I said, involves equating it with the organic articulation of movement. A small cyclic movement is captured by, and modifies, a larger movement so as to become integral to it, not as a mechanical subsystem, but in an elastic and responsive fashion. Movements generated from different sorts of internal determination become reconciled and adapted to one another in a single system in a way that is seen as characteristic of vitality, and a system of this sort is what we call an 'organism.'[12]

Authors who write of the 'Dance of Life' are likely to be thinking of cosmic processes in just this way: the cosmos is like a living organism to the extent that the orbiting of the planets, the succession of the seasons, and so forth form a single system of mutually responsive changes (Ellis 1923; cf. Sparshott 1988, §2.3). What makes an organism an organism, on this understanding, is just the prevalence of such mutual adaptation and assimilation.

If that is the dance of life, what about the dance of death? The traditional iconography is just what the foregoing would lead us to expect. 'Death,' represented as a skeleton – the part of a living figure that is purely mechanical in its articulation – compels the movements of its victims by playing a compulsive and metronomically repetitive tune on a fiddle, or drags them along with a chain. The movement imparted to the dying or dead bodies is imposed from outside and is not responsive to the internal impulses of their organic selves. Their motion is at best metrical rather than rhythmical (§9.212). It is called a dance for three reasons: the movement is ordered, it is a movement of bodies, and it is caused and coordinated by a *choragus*, a 'leader of the dance.'

9.4 Repetition, Pattern, and Flow

Dynamic rhythmicality is not simply a matter of the ordering of time but relates such ordering to our vital experience of life with exulting and recalcitrant bodies in an encouraging and resisting world. What can we say in general terms about such ordering, the pattern of dance itself?

9.41 Dance-generated Movements

Rhythms can be not simply person-generated in the ways we have just been considering, but dance-generated in a way specified by Maxine Sheets (1966, 97 and 104). She thinks of any dance, phenomenologically, as characterized by its 'dynamic flow,' 'the way forces are checked, released, gathered together, dispersed, their potency, their quickness,' and so on and identifies rhythm as the accentual pattern resulting from the dynamic interplay of forces. How does this differ from what Humphrey proposed? That was basically empirical, identifying and considering sources of change and impulse as they might be observed in the life of any person or animal. Sheets thinks more existentially, in terms of what it is to live in a world that is correlate, resistance, domicile, and situation all at once, in a dynamically complex but undifferentiated life. Dance is a metaphorical realization of this living-in-the-world, and rhythm, presumably, is the internal life of the symbol. Then one can go a step further (or a step back) and find, as Laban did, that the metaphor of dance can be abstracted as a self-contained complex of movement-as-movement, the dynamics of which, without attention to the specific form of muscular realization or emotive impulse, would be the locus of rhythm (Laban and Ullmann 1971).

9.42 Rhythm and Repetition

In §9.212 I supposed that the rhythm – the functional articulation in time – of a dance or a poem or a musical piece might be either metrical or not. Other analysts prefer to reserve the term 'metre' for the basic articulation of a work, and 'rhythm' for the significant variations on this. The idea is that if we are to recognize a dance, or engage in it, we must pick up the active thread of its continuity in movement, and this can only be a repeated pattern of some sort: to recognize something can only be to experience it as 'the same again.' John Booth Davies, for instance, defines metre as 'the basic, underlying pulse of a piece of music, around which the different rhythms are fitted,' and argues that 'without a grasp of the basic metre, or "time-outline," it is impossible to see the function of the rhythms which occur.'[13] One is inclined to rejoin that, if there is indeed a basic pulse, this will be true, but nothing has been said to show that such a pulse must be present before a rhythm can be identified.[14] But then, what makes identification possible?

Jaques-Dalcroze (1930, 3) defines rhythm as follows: 'A rhythm is a series of connected movements forming a whole and capable of being repeated.' What does (or should) he mean, 'forming a whole and capable of being repeated'? Presumably that the elements in the articulation are grouped, and each such group is followed by another group, of the same sort or of a different sort; but the group must be clearly enough marked off and subdivided that the requirements of being 'the same sort' are unambiguous. Recognizable identities and differences are necessary, then. But recognizable under what conditions? Unless we make some strong stipulation in that regard, we are open to the claim that any movement that is in any way internally differentiated has as many different rhythms as there are ways of discerning and grouping elements and groups of elements, so that any movement that is not an uninterrupted flow has not only a rhythm, but indefinitely many rhythms. Hanna's stipulation that a dance must be 'intentionally rhythmical' suggests that there can be only one rhythm that a given dance was intended to have; but it does not actually say that, and, if it did, we would not have to agree (§9.3). More of this later (§9.6).

9.421 Repetition and Repeatability

Dalcroze makes repeatability a criterion of rhythm. But there is a difference between being repeatable and being actually repeated. At first sight, one might think the latter only a subset of the former – a pattern that is actually repeated is obviously one that can be repeated, though not every pattern of movement that could be repeated actually is so. But that, though true, is doubly misleading.

In the first place, a sequence of identically articulated units has a very distinctive character of its own, generating a family of distinctive dance types. As such, such a sequence is indefinitely extensible. But in any case the repetition imparts a character of insistence, tending to impart a state of excitement or a mood. The use of an ostinato percussion base in today's popular music, often mechanically sustained by repetition of a tape loop, reduces this aspect of repeated rhythms to the grossest terms: a sort of compulsive inner dance, subduing all life to its terms.

In the second place, and by contrast, a rhythm that is repeated need not be 'repeatable' in a strong sense that I will shortly consider. The fact of recognized recurrence suffices to establish the terms of the repetition, which need not be otherwise salient. An articulation that is not repeated, in contrast, must somehow establish itself as the articulation that uniquely determines the relevant movement pattern.

Obviously, any movement is repeatable in the sense that to identify the movement is to specify what is done, and if one can say what is done one can say what it would be to do the same again. Obviously, too, no movement is repeatable, in the sense that each movement occupies a unique spatiotemporal location. If I repeat a sequence seven times, each repetition differs significantly from the others in the number of its antecedents and successors. What must be meant in distinguishing repeatable movements from others is that in those others one did not grasp the principle of the movement and would not know how to repeat it otherwise than by reproducing every discernible detail. And in that reproduction one would not have effected a repetition, because the prototype did not consist in the attempt to produce a given list of items. A repeatable movement must be one for which one can have either something like an algorithm, or a sense of how it goes. The articulated movement must be graspable as a unified totality – and that, we recall, was how Dalcroze defined rhythm itself. There must be a recognizable pattern or point or shape that it would make sense to repeat and that could form the basis of a system of articulation.[15]

One version of the distinction between repeated and repeatable rhythms, then, is that in the former the way time is articulated is made evident, even if it makes no sense, because the repetition of even the most arbitrary set of emphases and divisions establishes its identity as a demarcated set and thereby bestows on it a meaning; whereas in the latter the way time is being articulated is plain, because the emphasis and divisions make some evident sense as a way of dividing and emphasizing. The rather surprising consequence is that whereas in practice we think of rhythmical movement as involving heavily marked repetitions, rhythm as such may seem to be more inherent in movements that are intrinsically repeatable but not necessarily repeated.

9.422 Sameness

If a movement is articulated in time, it must be by some sort (or combination of sorts) of contrasting phases or punctuations. Articulation of a simple movement could be effected internally by starting, continuing, stopping; continuing, resting; tensing, relaxing; accelerating, decelerating; emphasizing, deemphasizing; ascending, descending; moving largely, moving minutely; moving here, moving there. More complex movements can be articulated internally by coming together and moving apart, by changing from one body part to another, and so on. Movements can be articulated externally by correlation with internal changes in other systems – changes in lighting, exposures of different areas of parti-coloured clothing; and above all by the rhythm (itself an equally complex matter) of accompanying music, most commonly and conspicuously in the form of a percussive punctuation. But for any of these to amount to a rhythm we must have some criterion of what it is for one movement to take *the same time* as another.

The paradigm of rhythmical movement is provided by the regular beating of a drum and by movements that keep time with such beating. What it means to keep time, we shall have to see. Meanwhile, what do we mean when we call a drumbeat 'regular'? We mean that the strokes are spaced by identical intervals of time. But what makes intervals identical? That one sounds neither longer nor shorter than another. But what is the standard by which 'neither longer nor shorter' is judged? Plainly we mean that if one stretch of such drumming were sounded simultaneously with a sequent stretch, all the beats would coincide if any of them did. But what is our criterion for asserting that this would be the case?

Nowadays we say: we could make a recording tape and chop it into bits and run the bits simultaneously through a suitable machine. True; but our ideas about identical times go back long before tape recorders were invented, and the idea of a 'suitable' machine seems problematic. Either the criterion of suitability is that things come out simultaneously when we judge that they should (which lands us in a vicious circle), or it is specified in accordance with a theory of mechanics and electronics – and the relevance of any such theory remains to be established.

Mostly, the criterion we use is that the intervals sound identical. If the drummer loses concentration, we may yell without hesitation: 'Wake up! Can't you keep time?' So the drummer does not *establish* the tempo authoritatively. But what does it mean to say that the intervals 'sound' identical? If we are counting to ourselves 'one ... two ... three,' what gives our counting authority? If we have a sort of private internal watch, how do we know it keeps time? If it is to do more than give us an 'authority' that cannot really be authoritative, because it has no basis, we must have a reason for trusting it. What could that reason be? I trust my watch because I believe it has a mechanism that is reliable, in that it will give the same results as other watches. But my 'internal watch' has no mechanism that I know of – and, if it did, it would be the theory of the mechanism that I trusted.

All of a sudden, the idea of 'sounding identical,' so familiar, comes to seem deeply mysterious.

9.4221 Clocks

We could time the drumbeats with a stopwatch. But what have stopwatches to do with it? We design them to 'keep time' – but what exactly is it that we design them to do? We design them to be synchronizable with all other watches. But what does it mean to say that all watches can be synchronized with each other? And why is it important?

The underlying fact seems to be that a large number of repeating movements in nature, including the rotating of the earth, the vibrating of a quartz crystal, and the swinging of a pendulum, bear such a relation to each other that, for instance, the number of times a given pendulum swings in the time it takes the earth to rotate once is constant. And our limbs are pendulums, so their free swings belong to this large set; our menstruations belong to the set, and so do our circadian rhythms. So, to a lesser degree, do our heartbeats,[16] and, on an average and much more approximately, our breaths. The time it takes a hen's egg to become hardboiled after being dropped into boiling water at a given altitude takes (give or take a few) a constant number of units from one of these sets – a fact that should astonish us more than it does. The world might not have been like that, but it is.

It is because so many different sorts of movements, periodic and other, some internal to us, some involved with the work we do, and some simply matters of observation, can be roughly correlated with each other in terms of constant units derived from any one of them that we can form the general idea of keeping time – and, indeed, the general idea of 'time' in the sense defined by Aristotle, as motion in its numerable aspect. In the end, we correlate our movements generally by choosing the most stable set of correlations and building our timepieces (sandglasses, candles, clepsydras, escapement clocks) on the basis of those, by their conformity to which all other local movements are assessed as regular or irregular. But that account makes our procedure sound more arbitrary, more a matter of mere convenience, than it is. There is more to it than that. In very many cases, when some other system of correlations shows irregularity in relation to our preferred set, we can explain why that happens; if some other set were taken as standard, no causal account could be given of the 'irregularities' that would appear in the periodicities of (what is now) our preferred set.

The facts cited show both why we can appeal to our watches to establish equality and inequality of intervals and also why we do not always need to. They also show why it may not be always appropriate to do so: if the movement sequence that interests us is of such a kind that something makes it accelerate and decelerate in an entirely predictable way, as judged by clock time, it might make perfectly good sense to treat it as itself invariant. The fact that we have an all-purpose standard does not mean that it is the best for all purposes.

9.5 More Conceptual Questions

In general, the rhythm of a movement is its dynamic shape as articulated. But is it the resultant shape itself (the dance in its dynamic aspect), or the proportions of the divisions, or the marking of its divisions? Is the term 'rhythm' equivocal, as referring to one of these at one time and another at another? Or does the word always refer to the overall phenomenon, to different aspects of which attention is drawn in different contexts? Or are there actually three kinds of rhythm, three kinds of dynamic movement shape: by flow modulation, by segmental articulation, and by punctuation? Usage suggests something like the following. The rhythm of a piece of music is as defined in the first sentence of this paragraph. To specify what its rhythm is is to specify its articulations in terms of their mutual proportions. But to say in what way it is rhythmical is to assign a qualitative character to its dynamic shaping – such words as 'staccato' and 'rubato' belong to this aspect of the matter. And rhythms may be classified in any of these ways, but ambiguously: what is a necessary aspect of any rhythm (for instance, that it be articulated) may be emphasized (in this case, by clear demarcations), so that to identify a rhythm as having a given character may or may not imply that that is the character that dominates the overall nature of the rhythmicality of a piece.

9.51 Ictus and Modulation

Any beginning, or point of transition, or end is automatically salient, hence a point of emphasis. That is why, in languages, the theoretically clear difference between stress accents and pitch accents is often elusive and unstable. In general terms, however, we can differentiate rhythms by ictus (as, in marching, the sound of bootfall marks the rhythm of legs whose inherent change comes at the beginning and end of their pendulum swing) and by modulation (as in the alternating directions of such pendulum swings, and as breathing in succeeds breathing out).

   The difference between ictus and modulation, as just presented, is one between extrinsic and inherent change: the sound of bootfall is extrinsic to marching legs, since one can march inaudibly on soft soles across grass. One can alter the emphasis by complicating the same distinction into a threefold one. There are rhythms by alteration, in which movement is continuous but changes quality; rhythms by interruption, in which bouts of movement are separated by brief periods of motionlessness; and rhythms by punctuation, in which marks or sounds are made to introduce beginnings and endings in a movement that would otherwise be continuous. Aristotle already argued that in rectilinear motions and in reversals of all sorts an alteration required a cessation of movement: there must be a moment when the system stops moving one way and starts moving another way, and this must be a moment of rest.[17]

   It is at least plausible to say that, either theoretically or phenomenally, all alterations are interruptions. But is it true that all interruptions are alterations? Apparently not: one can simply pause and resume. But it may be rejoined that pause is not a period of non-existence (if it were, it would be unnoticeable, existing only in the mind of God, if at all) but a time of rest or silence, hence itself an element of which the beginnings and endings are themselves interruptions. ... We observe that we are running into a maze of contradictions and regresses. Abstract theories of movement have been unmanageable since Zeno's day, and the antithesis of motion and rest has been relativized out of all recognition. In the practical terms that are the only relevant ones in considering dance and other potentially rhythmical activities, it still makes sense to say that a change is as good as a rest – and, therefore, not the same. There is a working difference between a hiatus and a switch. The only thing we have to bear in mind is that a pause that is an element within the rhythm of an articulated movement is not the same as an intrusive interruption or as any sort of break that is no part of the articulation. When I play a recording of a symphony, a rest is part of the flow of the music in a way in which the break between the movements is not, and the latter is structural in a way in which the interruption when I turn my LP record over is not.[18]

9.52 Beat

The rhythms I have ascribed to 'punctuation' occupy a special place, because the punctuation is functionally independent of the punctuated movement. It provides the 'beat,' a regular series of stresses, by the recurrence of which the internal articulations of a movement are controlled or checked. The concept of a beat involves intricacies comparable to those of rhythm itself. In a piece of music as written there may be four beats to a bar – that is, four equally spaced markers in the smallest systematically noted segment. These are notional, part of the composition and independent of what may happen in performance. In performance, if time is given, some of these beats will be signalled as upbeats or downbeats, weak or strong, and the rest unmarked; but the difference between arsis and thesis and unmarked beats is not notated in the score and is also independent of the phrasing of the music as played. If a beat is given, signalled by hand or foot movements, or by a signal clapper, or however it may be, the players may follow the beat or they may play around it. This is a matter of degree: even if there is a criterion of machine-like precision in making performance coincide with the beat as given, such precision would be a vice rather than a virtue of performance. The performers are supposed to translate the beat into the sort of regularity that vital movements have.

As if this were not enough, it is exceptional rather than normal to have a conductor or a timing device actually giving the beat (whether that be construed as instructing the performers, or as informing them). Players keep time with each other, and a soloist simply keeps time, observing the beat – that is, performing in a way that, in accordance with the standards that musicians learn, complies with or varies on the beat that would be given if any were. Musicians can play together because they know the ways in which they may deviate and return; they follow a beat they do not need to hear. (It may be the case, but it need not be the case, that preserving the beat is the prerogative of one among them.)

Because the beat need not be sounded, it is stylistically possible to play on the beat, or before it, or ahead of it. It is possible for one beat to be sounded and another, unsounded, beat to be inwardly observed. This last possibility is a variation on the situation where the beat is divided – where different members of the group of musicians follow different beats. In such divided beats, the simultaneous rhythms may be hierarchically organized, so that what one leading drummer does is followed by all the others in suitably timing their own beats; or the players may be multiply observant and responsive, any taking a lead from any other (or, of course, giving a lead or imposing a stress).

The range of possibilities thus baldly indicated is explored with great sensitivity and analytic power by J.M. Chernoff (1979), from his experience as a drummer in Africa. It is, however, a musical phenomenon rather than a dance phenomenon: in the first instance, it is a matter of subjectively experienced interactions of independently generated series, rather than of integrated movements. What the dancer does comes together in the rhythmical movement of the body, and the locus of the dance is in the corporeal achievement itself. Not that it is impossible that different dancers should dance together following different beats, or even that one dancer should follow different rhythms (implying different beats) with different parts of the body; this is done; but, when it is done, the description of it will be given in essentially musical terms.[19] These matters must be left to a separate consideration of the relation between dance and music (chapter 12).

9.53 The Unrhythmical

There is a sense in which every movement other than a uniform flow has a rhythm, in that it is divided, and the principle of its division can be repeated in subsequent movements. But there is another sense in which some articulated movements have rhythm – are eurhythmic – and others are unrhythmical. The latter would be those in which the articulation followed no principle, so that the overall rhythm, if any, would consist of the repetition (or even the single occurrence) of what struck one as an arbitrary set of divisions. (This is not quite the same as Aristoxenus's 'arhythmic' movement, in which the mind cannot grasp the divisions in any way at all.) For this distinction to work, as it does, we would have to have, as we do, a fairly strong sense of what divisions are congenial to the mind or the body of the dancing agent, and what are not; the latter must be memorized in all their parts, as one memorizes the value of pi or any other continuing fraction.

There is a third sense in which, among movements that have rhythm in the second sense, some are more rhythmical than others. Rhythm is then a matter of degree, relatively unrhythmical movements may be said to lack rhythm. This distinction, I think, rests on the closeness of the movement principle to the internal principles of vital movement and personal behaviour, in the ways we have already looked at. A movement that is intellectually or artificially generated, even if its generating principle is perfectly plain and intelligible, will be unrhythmical to the extent that one has to keep counting, keep remembering, rather than to encode it by some congenial modification of the muscular memory.

Finally, there is the sense in which the term 'rhythmical' applies only to a relatively small and special class of movements – the sort invoked in singing 'I got rhythm,' or in the technical term 'rhythm and blues.' Movements that are rhythmical in this sense are those in which subjective impulses, within the compass of those that are experienced as expanding rather than restricting the free expression of subjective impulses and the movements of the body, are reinforced rather than manipulated – and reinforcement is, of course, a matter of repetition and emphasis.

In sum, degree of rhythmicality depends on four things. First is salience, the obviousness of the temporal patterning, in itself and in comparison with other aspects of the movement. Second is closeness to the organic, body-centred rhythms we identify in our own lives. Third is the degree to which the rhythm enhances and enforces such a rhythm. And fourth is the extent to which it departs intriguingly or captivatingly from its basic beat, or sets up a counterpoint to it. Conversely, the unrhythmical is what conspicuously does none of these, neglecting them or pointedly avoiding them. Just as it is difficult to generate a truly random number series, I think it must be hard to move in a way that is truly devoid of rhythm; it might be easier to move in a way that makes a parade of its unrhythmicality.

9.6 The Uniqueness of Rhythms in Art

Any movement other than an interrupted flow, I said, must admit of indefinitely many rhythms, because there could be no limit on how rhythms might be identified – unless one made some strong stipulation a priori. Hanna's inclusion of intentionality in her proposed definition of a dance practice was one such stipulation. Even without that, a strong stipulation is in place when we are considering dances as works of art. Most people's idea of a work of art surely requires that it shall have a determinate order in space and time, however complex. If a dance has many mutually independent rhythms, it must be necessary to it as a work that it should have just the rhythms that it has, in just the relation in which they do stand to each other; if its order and rhythm are indeterminate, the precise scope and manner of the indeterminacy will be of the essence of the work.[20] If an order, and hence a rhythm, is determinate, it must be recognizable; and it is surely the work itself that must establish it in a recognizable form. And a rhythm can be established in two ways: by actual repetition, or by being imposed as repeatable either by its inherent salience or by allusion and familiarity.

Setting aside for the moment the question of how one decides what the actual rhythm of a movement uniquely is, we can say in principle that one way of classifying dances would be by the kinds of rhythms they had; and, to establish that, one would have to say what the important differences are among rhythms in general, and among dance rhythms in particular. And what do we mean by dance rhythms? Again we are caught in ambiguities: (1) rhythms used in dances, (2) rhythms conceived in terms that have specific dance significance, (3) rhythms suitable for dances. Like so many of our topics, this one threatens to be interminable and unmanageable. Enough, already.

9.61 A Caveat

The stipulation that a dance as a work of art must have a single rhythm depends on the idea that a work of art is a determinate object of criticism, 'a performance considered with respect to its design,' as I once put it (1982c, chap. 6). But this is an ideal notion: I find it tolerable only as one of a battery of related concepts, corresponding to the realities of art in the physical and historical world, and it was in the context of such a battery that I introduced it. In particular, as Paul Thom argues (1993a), a work *for performance* (such as a choreographed dance) is necessarily indeterminate, and performances have to be seen in that light. Performances of a dance will bring out different aspects of it, not necessarily envisaged by its creator; these will probably include alternative rhythms as optional sub-rhythms. We take a closer look at Thom's position in chapter 14, below. Meanwhile, I would insist once more that a dance cannot in any case be fully understood as a work of art, since our awareness of the dancers' bodies and personalities cannot be properly eliminated from our critical consciousness.

CHAPTER TEN

One and Many

There are essential differences between solo and ensemble dances, whether or not they are performed for audiences. These differences might have been dealt with under the heading of 'dance space,' since the latter includes interpersonal spaces. But the ways people are, and are perceived to be, alone or together are not, on the face of it, a spatial matter.

A soloist, dancing for an audience, dances to be noticed as an individual; but an ensemble member dances as one of a group, so that conspicuousness (even as the only competent member of the group) is an error. What makes a dancer a soloist is that it is proper to attend to her or his individual performance (otherwise than as a talent scout or some such).[1] A soloist and an ensemble can perform exactly the same movements without their status being confused: all that is necessary is that the manner of attention paid to them not be the same.

If the dance is not for show, the contrast is greater, not less. In dances for an audience, all dancers are dancing for the eye; but not now. The soloist is engaging in an individual activity, whatever its purpose may be; the ensemble are taking part in a group activity, and that must be at least a large part of the point of what they are doing.

10.1 One among Many

The distinction between solo and ensemble dances is not a simple dichotomy. When soloists dance with a group, their sense of partaking in a unity and of the unity partaken in is not to be contrasted with that of a member of the group. Being together is something they share.[2]

One might construct a series. At one extreme is the undifferentiated ensemble. Next to it is the ensemble (of which the units may be individuals, or pairs, or subgroups) in which it just happens that one unit is so placed that it sets the time for the rest – just as it is not possible in a rowing eight for the oar nearest the stern not to fulfil the function of 'stroke,' even if the places were taken up at random and no one gives any thought to the matter. Next in our progression we may place the many social group-dances in which each unit (most often a pair) in turn contributes to the overall pattern by making some distinctive movement, such as promenading or forming a bridge through which the others pass.[3] Next to that is the sort of dance in which a soloist from time to time breaks away from the ensemble and returns to it again.[4] Next is that of the chorus and the *choragus*, the leader who is formally separated from the other dancers as their leader, even though the movements danced do not differ from theirs. Next to that we may place antithetical figures within ensembles, typically clown figures (as in the Morris), who dance differently from the rest, not as stars but as foils. Next come starred dancers who dance with the corps de ballet, but are so much the focus of attention that they might almost be dancing in isolation, and the corps mere animated scenery. And at the farthest extreme is the true soloist, dancing alone or with other individuals. There are many variants and intermediate phases; but this will suffice to give the general idea.

The range of formal possibilities here seems isomorphic with that more familiar in music, which has a widely known and well understood vocabulary for divisions of groups and combinations of individuals: concerto, quartet, trio, solo, concerto grosso, and so on. If the correspondence is indeed close, that may be due to the intimate connection between dance and music; but it need not, for these may be the only possible ways of organizing cooperative tasks and of dividing matters for the attention. In any case, it seems that the fuller range of corresponding forms is in the domain of instrumental rather than vocal music. That seems odd, because it is vocalists and vocal groups who bear the closer analogy with dancers; they work with their bodies alone and do not vary among themselves in timbre and mode of production as instrumentalists do with their blowings, scrapings, and bangings. But there may be a sort of explanation. The bodies of different dancers, however similar their movements, remain distinguishable to the eye, but the tones of homogeneous instruments (such as voices) blend into each other, even if they are not doing the same thing.

10.2 Groups

Among groups without soloists, there are a number of distinctions to be made.

One fundamental difference is among the kinds of groupings as such, as differentiated by Sartre (1961). A philosopher who starts with the consideration that each person is aware only of a world of objects, and that one's own consciousness is not among those objects, soon reaches the position that a true communality of persons is impossible. Myself and others cannot be experienced as commensurate. Other people are experienced only as threats to myself and to the integrity of my world. There are then three basic ways in which groups I belong to can enter into my experience. First, since I can be aware of myself as an object for others (because I sense my own vulnerability) I can be aware of myself as passively sharing with others a common character defined by a third party. But then, a functioning group can be mediated by this 'thirdness': I am aware of my fellow group members as all defining all of us as group members. It is not the direct fact of our cooperation that makes us a group, but the fact that we all know that we all know that we are functioning as a group. This is really what defines a team or a corps.

Second, in very special circumstances in which a number of people share a common crisis that they all understand and that absorbs all their attention, they may spontaneously form what Sartre calls a group 'in fusion' – they are too busy, as it were, to notice differences among individuals, including themselves. Such a group is as radically unself-conscious as the mediated group is self-conscious.

The third kind of group is not really a group at all; it is what Sartre called a 'series,' in which all the participants relate in the same way to the same occasion, but not (in any meaningful way) to each other. Sartre's favoured example is a bus queue; but most of what pass for groups are, on his view, no more than series.

Dances in which those dancing together form a series rather than a true group are certainly very common, especially if we count dancing couples as units. A couple may go to a place where there is dance music playing and people dancing to it and may dance along with them, forming part of 'the dance' but not in any real sense dancing *with* them rather than alongside them. The dancers need pay no attention to the arrival and departure of individuals and pairs, unless the result is inconvenient crowding or depressing isolation. Those who attend the dance are united by the band and the floor; the dancers no more form a group than the skaters who come to a municipal rink, united only by the ice.

Intermediate and complex cases between 'group' and 'series' abound. In my one experience as tourist watching the Sardana (at Santa Coloma de Farners, in Catalonia), what looked to be happening was as follows. The music begins; individuals begin to shuffle; small clusters of friends or neighbours form spontaneously and grow as the music continues, but are united only serially, by the occasion and the music and the dance floor (in this instance, the clearing in the grove); then, at the music's climax (the *contrapunt* before the fifth *tirada de llargs*, I am told), the whole company forms into a number of concentric rings, each a true group, but among which it seems to me that the relationship is no longer merely serial, in that a single dance is being briefly danced together. Then the music stops and the whole process starts again.

That Sartre's three types of grouping seldom if ever appear in their pure form should not worry us: he is doing phenomenology, not sociology, analysing the fundamentally different ways in which embodied consciousnesses can realize their compresence rather than giving typical examples of the historical institutions in which these are developed and embedded.

Powerful and illuminating as Sartre's analysis is, its claim to be uniquely grounded in phenomenology is suspect. It owes more to a patriotic devotion to Descartes's metaphysical dualism than to any systematic reduction. No less fundamental to our existence, especially as the embodied entities that dancers inevitably are, is our compresence in a world in which we share thoughts and predicaments. Fellow-feeling is a matter of degree: there are those whose ways of speaking and thinking we share (at the limit, all human beings); those whose concrete situation we share (basically, families and tribes); those whose activities we share for the time being; and, finally, those whose lives we share, ideally as couples in mutual absorption. Within all of these groups except the first, there may or may not be dominating or organizing members, who may be more or less integral to the group. Approaching matters from this end may be more helpful in thinking about dance than beginning with the isolated consciousness that each of us also must be. Soloists, after all, are picked out from the company more often than they are pitchforked into it.

A distinction of significance, such as Sartre's, does not necessarily work itself out in a difference of behaviour. In the latter domain, the most obvious difference is that between dances in which all the dancers perform the same movements (simultaneously; successively; in canon; in mirror-image symmetry – but only the first of these is the pure type) and those in which different dancers perform different parts. Among the latter, the extreme case is that in which the whole dance is an interweaving of individual dances, each different; here, too, we must make a distinction, between dances where each dancer performs a dance that would make sense danced without the others, as if the dance were a counterpoint of solos, and those in which the individual dances, however interesting, are mutually interdependent, artistically or even physically.[5]

Without going to the extreme at which group dancing merges into an interweaving of solos, we may distinguish between group dances in which there are subgroups within which movement is uniform and those where that is not the case. More generally, the distinction is that between dances that rely on blocking effects and those that do not. But, of course, where there are identifiable subgroups, throughout the course of a dance or forming and dissolving, there is no end to the likenesses and differences, and to the mutual references, that can meaningfully arise between them. One subgroup, for instance, may by its movements reveal the nature of what some other subgroup is doing.

Within a whole dancing group, the significance of uniformity may be that of community; but uniformity within a subgroup, where the possibility of an alternative is presented, is more likely to signify regimentation. A dance, or any other concerted movement, in which a number of people make the same movements is one in which the absence or abeyance of personal autonomy is displayed and dramatized. A dance from which such uniformity is absent may in reality be no less regimented and drilled than the other, and the effect of the drilling may be plain to the instructed observer; but the individuality of the person is at least symbolically present. The difference is profound. The extreme case of a dramatized loss of autonomy is the sort of formation in which the limbs and costumes of the dancers are reduced to elements in an overall visual pattern, of which the fascination lies precisely in that loss – in the substitution for patterned human movement of an abstract pattern for which humans provide the ingredients. Such reduction is a common resource of drill displays generally, and its effect is always that of a coup, a witty or otherwise pointed intervention in the ongoing proceedings; typically, it evokes a round of applause in acknowledgment of its special status. These effects are so much a part of general theatre display that some people object to them as taking us out of the domain of dance practice proper; but other people either are indifferent to the existence of any such domain or are happy to slip out of it for a while.

Among dances that do not really on blocking effects, one can distinguish between dances in pattern, in which the performers dance individually but in relation to each other, and dances that form dance patterns in which the changing relations of the dancers to each other are themselves an element in the dance. This is a fundamental contrast in meaning (and one that is as marked for the participants in social dance as it is for the spectators of theatre dance), like Sartre's contrast between group and series; it is the difference between being (in a patterned way) *among* people and being (in a patterned way) *with* people. But, though fundamental, it need not answer to any strict demarcation in practice. As human beings (and even as social animals), we are quick and subtle to detect and respond to multiple aspects of, and rapid and intricate changes in, the grounds on which the fellow-members of our species are acting and interacting. This skill does not desert us when we dance and watch dances.

One obvious way to classify group dances is by their movement forms. Many such classifications would simply follow those used for dances in general, though they might take on a different aspect. For instance, the difference between dancing in place and dancing through space would remain; but among group dances in place the main divisions might be different from those we met before. The most salient contrast might be between intricate and interweaving movements, on the one hand, and cyclic movements on the other; among the latter, those radially organized could be contrasted with countermarching or skin-the-snake movements. Another key distinction is that between asymmetrical and symmetrical movement and among the degrees and dimensions of symmetry. But geometry itself plays no favourites, and such formal classification is perhaps best done either empirically, by enumerating forms commonly used, or ideologically, by social or cosmic significances. Symmetry exemplifies and proclaims one type of order and one kind of meaning; massed, interlaced, and randomized movements traditionally have other meanings, which civilizations have exploited. To build a focal ceremony around a dance in which one specific sort of order is embodied is not a neutral or a trivial act.

One of the most significant formal distinctions among group dances is between those that are extensible and those that are not. It is a distinction that has some affinities with that between group and series. There are many round dances in which anyone can join the dance, if the other dancers will part hands and let one in – in the Sardana, it is specified that any couple may join, provided that they do not break into a pair already dancing. But there are others in which the dance is filled when a certain number are present – an eightsome reel, I take it, can have only a multiple of eight dancers (though I surmise that if Sandy and Maire fail to show up for rehearsal, one can do something analogous to three-handed bridge, *faute de mieux*). This seems to be an independent dimension of variability, for which there might be a variety of grounds (technical, aesthetic, social, religious) but need be no grounds at all, just as there is very little reason why a soccer team should have exactly eleven players so long as both teams have the same number. But eleven is the right number, and that's that.

10.3 Chorus and Solo

I have contrasted group dances with solo dances in various ways but did not discuss the interaction between a group and a soloist who dances with it. Many relations are possible.

As before, an analogy with musical performances may be instructive. There is a difference among the leader ('concertmaster') of an orchestra, and its conductor, and a soloist who plays with them. The leader may well be singled out as an individual, take solo parts, and rehearse the band; as principal player, however, the leader is not contrasted with the other players but plays as one of them.[6] The conductor, in contrast, contributes no sound to the ensemble but operates on the players (or purports to do so), facing the band, back to the audience. The place of conductors is ambiguous, though. On the one hand, they symbolize the unmoved mover generating the music of the musicians, who play in the way they do *because of* the conducting although it does not *cause* them to play (cf. what is said of Siva Natyaraja below, in chapter 22). On the other hand, they perform an interpretative gesture-play for the audience, in which the overall expressive meaning (but not the structure) of the music is symbolized. The conductor makes the dynamics of the sound visible.

It is not always functionally necessary that a well-rehearsed band should have a conductor at its public performances, but at full-scale orchestral concerts it is symbolically necessary. The mediating individual effects a transformation of the occasion, reducing the menacing mass of musicians to a human scale.

The isolated and dramatized conductor differs from the leader, who figures only as activator and timegiver, no more than from the equally dramatized and differentiated solo player. The conductor represents the band to us, and us to the band. The star soloist is visibly not one of the band (even if not their adversary) and appears not to take the conductor's direction – rather, the conductor makes an elaborate show of deferring to the soloist and at the end of the piece makes an equally elaborate show of allowing the soloist to hog the applause. On the other hand, the soloist is hardly on the audience's side, showing rather the absorbed and impersonal concentration of dentists over their drills; at the end, the more obsequious the bow, the more colossal is the superiority conveyed.

The dynamics of the relation between conductor and soloist are echoed in those at a lecture between local chair and visiting speaker. They answer to a common factor in all situations where prominence, prestige, novelty, proprietorship, and power combine and compete in directing attention. What happens if a distinguished stranger joins a dance company that has its own principal dancer and director reflects the power positions of differential prestige, favour, and authority, and this is likely to affect the dancing if not the choreography. Such relationships can form part of the symbolic content of a dance, whatever the real-life relations of the participants. The three types of situation differ, however, in the role of mediator. The chair at a lecture introduces the speaker but stays relatively immobile during the address, merely miming attention and amusement and leading applause when appropriate, and does not attempt or purport to lead the speaker until time has run out. In dance, the position is roughly the converse. Theatre dance has no non-dancing mediator; the trainer of the dancers does not purport to guide them in the course of the dance or show the audience how to react, and may not even appear at the end to share the applause. Of course, if there is a live orchestral accompaniment, the band has its own conductor who conducts the dancers as well; but in such cases the mediating role is not attempted. Well, no more is it in opera, which often presents the odd spectacle of a group of singers, front and centre in a tricky ensemble, their eyes glued desperately to the conductor whom the audience is supposed not to notice. Why this difference? Presumably because dancers and singers are active as humans and their behaviour is as perspicuous to humans as anything could be, so that a mediator could be effective only by misleading; whereas in a lecture or an instrumental work, the performers are active not as humans but as expert manipulators of information or of noisemakers.

There is one phenomenon connected with theatre dance in which a non-dancing mediator figures. In television presentations of dances, it is quite common for the dance itself to be embedded among shots of 'rehearsals,' in which the choreographer or director is seen showing the dancers what to do: by doing the movement itself, by performing a shorthand sketch of it, by guiding an errant limb, by verbal instruction. Of course what we see is not a rehearsal, even if it was at the time: it is part of the show we are being shown. Part of the function may be just to prevent the show being too short, or to take account of the short attention span attributable to a TV audience. Or perhaps the producers surmise that such an audience prefers the human transactions of instruction and correction to the aesthetic experience of dance. But I think part of the function is to show the audience what they are to look for, as the orchestral conductor shows us what to listen for.[7] The question is taken up again when we consider video and television generally, §§20.33ff.

There are, however, social dances in which a non-dancing director does participate. In a square dance, the caller emits a stream of directive symbolism, as stylized as a conductor's beat and as expressive in its dynamic flow. And the caller is necessary to complete the dance, even if all the dancers have the steps down pat. The presupposition of square-dance calling, however, as of 'lining' hymns, is that the performing group know only the general rules of the form, including the practice of calling or leading; whereas no such general knowledge enables the orchestra to follow the conductor without knowing their own parts.

10.31 Sameness and Difference

A soloist with a group may or may not dance as they do. The soloist may do the very same dance as they—except in the sense that a solo demands, as we saw, a different sort of attention. Or the soloist's dance may be a variation on theirs. If it is, it may be more complex or more vigorous or more studied, an enhancement on less ambitious movements. But it may also be simpler, more modest, understated: such a relationship is not rare and achieves a characteristic range of effects and significances because such a dance can be subtle and rich in inverse proportion to the apparent simplification.[8]

If a soloist's movements differ from those of the group otherwise than by augmentation or diminution, they may be recognizable variants on what the group is doing – or, since the possibilities are reciprocal, the group may be performing a recognizable variant of the solo; it may or may not be made clear (as by who watches whom, who is ahead of whom) which of these is the case. Or soloist and group may perform quite different dances. These may be related by a shared time pattern or by an element of common rhythm (remember that the criteria of rhythmic identity are necessarily indeterminate), or they may be formally interrelated in some other way – for instance, through the gestural meaning of the action (semantically corresponding or mutually responsive), or through shared or responsive movement qualities, or both. Or, finally, the two dances may be related in no other way than through the shared context and the knowledge (common to choreographer, dancers, and spectators) that they do constitute elements in the same dance. The movements may not even be contemporaneous (except in the important sense that to be at rest is not to have left the dance), for of course a soloist may move only when the group is at rest, or move only when it moves, or follow an independent distribution of movements and rests.

I have been talking about soloists who dance with an undivided group. But, of course, the group may be subdivided. Complications are then introduced by variations on the different ways the soloist relates to different subgroups; and the soloist may play groups off against each other, and vice versa. As before, the possibilities are endless, and even a partial enumeration would be pointless. But just this set of relationships is a most distinctive, potent, and subtle source of dance meanings, the effects of which are noted by audiences and critics but seem never to be traced to their structural origin. The point is that differentiations among subgroups (whether by block contrasts, or by characterization of their members, or by internal articulation of movements, or whatever) tend to stand out clearly and unmistakably as contrasts between individuals do not, because the latter are systematically confused by the personal idiosyncracies we necessarily impute to them. What belongs to the group is, as it were, ex officio in the public domain. And this holds as true of meanings imputed to dance movement as it does of personal relations in everyday life.[9]

In most of this section, the dances envisaged have been choreographed or traditionally structured, in such a way that one role depends on another. One dancer follows, satirizes, parodies, imitates, and so on, the rest, in all the varieties of mimesis glanced at in §4.2123. In such cases, the target of the imitation is the source of the basic design, but the imitator is active and hence creative in relation to the target, who in this respect is passive. The course of composition need not follow the logic of dependence. One can compose the parody (for instance) first and then compose that which is parodied. But it is of course possible that relationships indistinguishable from those thus constructed should be produced in the activity of dancing itself: someone who dances a parody may be straightforwardly dancing a parody part but may actually be parodying. It is also true that a dancer who is actually parodying may do so with personal parodic intent, or may do so simply because the dance at this point calls on the dancer to perform a parody. Spectators might well not know which was taking place; but, if they did, it would make a big difference to how they saw the dance they were watching. There must, therefore, be a point of view from which such distinctions are aesthetically irrelevant, as well as one from which they are relevant, and neither viewpoint can be dismissed as improper.

10.32 Corps de Ballet

Dances for many people tend to be *choreia*, because what is salient is their joint participation in a figure; dances for one person tend to be *orchesis*, because there is no figure to be participated in, so that what is salient can only be the quality of the movement. But the corps in a professional ballet company is different. Each member of the corps is a dancer whose training is primarily that of a potential soloist; a well-trained corps shows perfection of movement in perfect participation in elaborate figures, and is the hallmark of a ballet company.

10.33 Interrelation

Whichever form the relations between the dances of soloists and groups may take, their mutual relations as dancers may vary. A soloist may dance *to* the group with which the dance is danced, or may dance *with* the group *to* an audience.[10] And it is possible for soloist and group to dance with each other and not to anybody at all. These are different relations and generate different dances. There may even be deviant cases in which a soloist dances to the fellow dancers instead of to the audience, or vice versa, when the institutional or choreographical properties call for the opposite. Meanwhile, psychologically, the dancer may dance *to* the audience but not *for* them. And whether that is good or bad may depend on whether the dancer respects the audience or not.[11]

When soloist and ensemble dance to each other, as it were confronting each other, the dance may be antiphonal, the dancers mutually responsive. But they may not. The dancers may be dancing *at* each other, or even *against* each other: exchanged dances may be supportive, or collaborative, or emulative, or hostile, or imbued with the spirit of any other mode of intercourse. If you substitute any other preposition for 'at' or 'against' here, you will find that many of them at once suggest modes of terpsichorean intercourse – and the same preposition may not be equally suited to the contributions of both parties. Of course, the relationships picked out by such prepositions need not be sustained throughout a dance, or alternate with each other. It is equally likely that the relationship between a pair of dancers may modulate in such a way that at a given time one preposition might seem the most appropriate, if one had to verbalize what one saw or felt – but such verbal pin-pointing would not suggest itself and would be rejected if it did.[12]

Reciprocity among the dancers is not the only possibility. In many old ballets, there were bits in which the soloist seemed to be dancing *to* the rest of the dancers, who formed a passively receptive stage audience, and bits in which the soloist remained passive and accepted the homage of their dance. Of course, both the soloist as spectator and the group as spectators, in such a case, remain engaged in the dance, dancing the parts of audience in a proper exercise of their professional skill;[13] but they are not returning the dance, and the difference between motion-lessly 'dancing' the condition of responsiveness and actually dancing out a definite response remains a striking one.

When soloist and ensemble do not dance to each other, but share an audience, the basic relationship is that of chorus and choragus, the soloist acting as leader and representative for the group. But the converse relation, in which the individual is tag-along for the dominant group, is not unknown, and the relationship has a piquancy of its own – though its purport tends to be dramatic rather than dance-like. And it is conceivable that neither relation should obtain, the soloist simply dancing alongside the group. But this last relationship would be expected to be unstable, since in maintaining the contrast between group and soloist it will be hard to avoid symbolizing some sort of power relationship. In any case, mere otherness without either dominance or exclusion covers a large and indeterminate class of relationships about which further generalization would be neither easy nor rewarding.

The third case was that in which soloist and group join in a dance without an audience, dancing with each other and not to each other.

The leader of the bacchanal simply leads the maenads in the dance. Perhaps the choragus/chorus relationship in the more developed theatre dance should be thought of as a development from this more primitive set-up, following the seductive model of Aristotle's reconstruction of the origins of tragedy (*Poetics*, chap. 4). But perhaps not.

10.4 Couples

The conventional wisdom is that a person can only have one 'best friend,' only look one person in the eye at a time (cf. §3.8 above), only carry on a heart-to-heart conversation with one person. A dancer, too, can only concentrate on one partner at a time. Without prearrangement, I can respond to one other person; if there are three or more of us, we may have to stop and sort ourselves out. So duets occupy a special place among dances, even if some dance traditions leave that place unoccupied.

What are the basic modes of human pairing? We must distinguish coming together, acting together, and being together: bases of attraction, of cooperation, of coexistence. Discarding the latter as not separately relevant for us (we assume there already is a couple dancing), that divides into the nature of the relation put into the dancing and the nature of the relationship on which the dance is based. But, since life is an ongoing activity, the distinction is one to bear in mind rather than to base a discussion on.

Basically, the pair relations that generate different movement forms will be conflict, comradeship, and cooperation in specific contexts. But, if we consider the bases of human pairing as such, we find the parent/child relation and the pair-bonding relation.

The parent/child relation is one of dependence: parent nutures child, child tends Aged Parent. Danceable relations of dependence are many. Stronger supports weaker, more vigorous brandishes more passive, mentor guides follower. These generate a set of special relationships: theme and variation, straight-person and comic. In the last named we ask: which is the leader, which the follower? The comic is the irresponsible child playing around the solemn adult, but the straight person is there only as a foil for the antics of the comic – just as the old exist only to produce and nurture the next generation.

Should we say that there is a family of danceable dyadic relations that exploit the possible variations on the simple relation of dependence, or that this family of danceable dyadic relations explores the range and depth of parent/child dynamics? I want to say both, and not to distinguish between them.

The human pair-bonding relation offers a similar set of possibilities. At one level, it embodies whatever the culture accepts as the appropriate complementarities of role, style, and function: client and patron, supporter and supported (reversible in different functional relationships), mutual alliance, division of economic labour and social energy. At another level, it represents inseparability, and hence conflict in its purest form, that in which the combatants cannot agree to differ and part. At another level again, it embodies the terminal form of sexual energy. In Western dance traditions, sexual metaphors and expressions abound: the typical pair-dance in theatre dance forms enacts the dynamics of courtship and seduction. We are indeed tempted to say that sexuality is virtually coextensive with human dyadic relations, so that every pair dance has a rich sexual meaning worked into whatever other relations may be expressed. This may reflect the profound truth of Freud's theories of psychology; or it may rather reflect the history whereby Western theatre dance, unlike many of the world's dance traditions, has concentrated on athletic display and has consequently chosen its performers among the young and nubile.

The richness of pair-dances owes much to the inexhaustibility and intensity of the relationships generated in families. But we must not overlook the generality of the considerations we began with: that only a dyadic relation allows the partners to respond fully and spontaneously to each other – which means also that an audience can *follow* a dancing couple as they cannot follow the interweavings of any larger group. A stable dyadic relationship not governed by the kinship system is what we call a friendship. What is the danceable basis of friendship?

The primitive philosophical tradition about friendship offers us likeness, complementarily, and congeniality.[14] Of these, we might think that likeness need not concern us much, on the ground that in a dance a like pair is only a group with two members. But that is not true. Two dancers can dance with each other, lift each other, bounce off each other, respond to each other, on a basis of equality or of mutually exchanged leadership and dominance. The non-sexual *pas de deux* has opened up a virtually new world of dance possibilities.

After likeness, congeniality. Congeniality (as the tradition found) defeats theory: or rather, it is what we invoke to explain an otherwise inexplicable pairing. We expect it to break down into a somehow viable complex of complementarities and sharings. But it has a definite meaning of its own. You find me congenial if, without necessarily admiring me, you like to be with me. There is something about me that suits you. And vice versa. We go together as lamb goes with mint sauce (in Britain), or apple pie with ice cream (in America): no explanation suffices, we have only the undeniable recognition of suitability. The analogue in dance would be the duo in which a perceived rightness could not be reduced into anything more elementary, or in which (as in the favourite food pairs mentioned) an obvious explanation fell ludicrously short of the fact to be explained. What *was* it about Fred Astaire and Ginger Rogers? In the aesthetics of dance, however, the congeniality of a pair of friends has no real analogue. The *je ne sais quoi* of aesthetic effectiveness applies to the interaction of couples in just the same way as it does to performances of larger groups or of individuals.

Complementarity is what remains for us to look at. But it turns out that there is nothing to see. In physical type, in dance style, in movement performed, every characteristic (though not, of course, every nameable item) has its complementary opposite as germane to dancing as itself. Supporting and supported, curvilinear and rectilinear, orthodox and heterodox, replete and jejune – anything. Many such complementarities can be subsumed under the dominant antitheses of kinship and sexuality, but not all. We are left with the bleak fact that any syntactic scheme can be analysed out into a set of binary alternatives, so that the fact of complementarity is vacuous in itself. But perhaps that is the most important thing of all: since a dancing couple is itself a pair, its differentiations are a bearer of infinitely rich meanings.

10.41 Mating Couples

The dance traditions of Western civilization – perhaps it would be more precise to say, of Western Christendom and its successor cultures – share a striking characteristic that seems not to be found elsewhere. A high proportion of dances, both theatrical and social, are based on pairs of male and female, among whom the relationships have strong sexual implications. They may not be mating dances, but they are dances in which the fact of sexual communion is essentially present. There are unisex dance groups nowadays: one has only to see them to realize how unusual it has been for it not to matter what sex a dancer is.[15]

The underlying fact about Western civilization that accounts for this singularity must be the peculiar view of marriage, in which a demand for lifelong, monopolistic monogamy used to be combined with a veto on premarital as well as extramarital intercourse and emphasized the unity of the married couple by referring to them as 'one flesh.' This metaphysical unity of the couple goes well beyond the sociological facts (may in fact contradict them, since in practice males and females have at all times enjoyed variously recognized exemptions) and was no doubt reinforced by the sacramental identification of Christ's body with the communion bread.

It is often said that our society is obsessed by sex and that the ideology of romantic love continues to distort all human relationships. It is obvious that sexual activity and matrimonial conjunction must be dominant concerns and powerful institutions everywhere, and it would be unlikely that they would not play a large part in any mimetic dance tradition. What the 'one flesh' mysticism does is to extract the matrimonial couple from the social context on which that universality depends. The significance assigned is that of an unstructured unity that goes beyond and negates both the individualities of the partners and their familial and social identities and involvements.

The peculiarity of the union of the dancing couple of sexual partners is that its meaning in the dance tends to go beyond the fact of actual partnership. It is a mystical bond. If a couple go to a dance together, each may take many partners in the course of the evening, but they are in a strong sense with each other throughout and are expected to leave together. The liminality of dance that dissolves all ties holds the sexual partnership in incomplete suspension.

In old-style ballroom dancing, the placing of hands, and the proximity of bodies and faces ('dancing cheek to cheek') made a complex sexual language part of the dance. It was really part of the dancing and not (or not only) part of the meaning of the dance occasion as mating ceremony (cf. Sparshott 1988, chap. 4); the proprieties of different postures varied with different dances, and the implications of the proximity symbolism were never to be taken literally and applied in extra-dance relations; but it was a subtle and complex matter.[16] In the dances that have succeeded that institution among young people, in which body contact plays little or no part, the couple remain the unit – dancing responsively to each other, dancing in each other's company, dancing introspectively and in isolation in each other's presence, what is danced is still a relation to sexual partnership.

The transition from overt couple-dancing to the sort of solo-pair dancing that replaced it among young people seems to have a certain congruence with the fashion for meditating and drug-taking in groups:

each retired into a private world, but in company; the trips were different, but they were made together. Each bourgeois adolescent desperately needs privacy, but no less desperately needs the support of peers. The modes of dancing extend more widely, and have perhaps lasted better, than the other phenomena mentioned. And, corresponding to the maintenance of the couple relation without physical contact, the disco dance style maintained likeness in difference: there was a repertoire of steps, but one was free to choose from it or to ignore it in any relation or lack of relation to what one's partner did.[17]

In country dancing, square dancing, and popular community dancing generally, the unity of the couple in the dance tends to be maintained. But the form of that unity is perhaps less often a continuous partnering than a continual parting and rejoining. After a more or less baffling sidling, circling, interweaving, or what not, there is the relief of recognition in a renewed encounter. In the classical formula of show business: boy meets girl – boy loses girl – boy gets girl.

10.411 The Gay Scene

The topic of the preceding section is complicated by the peculiarities of human sexuality. Traditionally, in dance as in social life, the behaviour that symbolizes and accompanies coition was associated with the couplings of people who were potential marital partners and parents. It is still most common, and in a sense normal, for couplings on which narratives on stage and in literature centre to unite a young man and a young woman; that is, as it were, the default position, and seems likely to go on being so. However, it now seems certain that a substantial proportion (11 per cent used to be the favoured estimate) of humans are innately attracted to partners of the same sex – though an unknown number of these prefer to live heterosexually, and others whose biological predisposition is heterosexual choose homosexuality.

The sexual and familial relations implied in (for instance) *The Sleeping Beauty* are shadowed by alternative models of sexuality and cohabitation, differing in physical expression and probably in life-style. Each is potentiality a sub-text for the others, the salience of which will depend on the preoccupations of choreographer, performers, and spectators. The same love-dance will look different to people with different sexual orientations.

Bill T. Jones designs for his company love duets that may be danced either by same-sex or by opposite-sex couples. For this to be possible, a profound physical attraction and involvement must be expressed without implying any specific sexual contact. To me at least, the result is deeply moving, especially when one has seen the same dance performed by couples of both kinds.[18]

The situation is complicated by two factors. First, homosexual love appears to be much more prevalent in the dance world and in the arts generally (at least in North America nowadays) than it is in the population at large, or even among dance audiences, and is certainly much more easily accepted, so that there is bound to be a difference of perspective between performers and public – an important difference, which performers and critics alike are curiously slow to acknowledge. Second, same-sex couplings are subject to taboos and disapprovals that vary from place to place and from time to time in society at large, both in their content and in their strength, and all the relevant beliefs and attitudes are so strongly politicized that crude versions of them are likely to form part of the overt meaning of a dance for dance-makers and critics alike.

Same-sex couples are not the only variation on the Romeo-and-Juliet stereotype among mating pairs.[19] The slow and the quick, the old and the young, the old and the old, the ordinary and the ordinary unite in a wealth of danceable meaning of which the depths are perhaps too little explored.[20] And the meanings themselves are multiple in familiar ways. Orgasm is a symbol of ecstasy, ecstasy of orgasm; affection can mean coition, coition can mean affection. And the profundity and variety of all these relations are much more obviously accessible to dance than to any of the other arts.[21]

10.5 Conclusion

Thinking about the prevalence of mating couples in traditional Western dance led us on to think about sexually implicated couples between whom the bond was more remotely associated with procreation; and this could lead us back to the direct relations between pairs of people whose connection is not overtly sexual at all. But such intimate friendships perhaps show only an intense form of what is common to all human relationships and enters into the meaning of all dances with more than one performer.

All relations among human beings have at least three meaningful aspects, even the absence of which is meaningful. First, there is mutual collaboration, offered, refused, promised, implicitly possible or impossible. Second, there is power, exercised or in abeyance, present or ignored. And third, there is sexuality, always at least an undertone in any relationship or encounter, even if only by its repression.

All three of these are ambivalent. Power is facilitating – or crippling; a hierarchy is oppressive – or organizing. Sex is hit-or-miss, say no more, say no more. Cooperation is liberating or cloying. Violence, the enforcement of a form of relationship on those unwilling to enter it, and indifference, the refusal of relationship to those who want it, haunt all three. Such is the dynamism of human relations.

All dance is about dynamic movement, the embodied person's power to move. All dances in which there is more than one dancer are about the dynamics of the relations among moving people, even when the dynamism is not itself choreographed. The relationships mentioned above are of the substance of dance; they are a large part of its meaning, even when the dance has no narrative aspect to order or justify them.

All movements, simply as movements (towards, away from, alongside, crossing, separate from ...), carry different structural dynamics depending on the dynamics of sexuality, power, or mutuality they imply. And the implications for the choreographer may not be the same as they are for this or that performer. Nor need the implications for the dance-makers be the same as those picked up by the audience, each of whom will use (in addition to their ability to see and understand the kind of dance in question) their own life experience and their own ideology. It is within this shifting web of interpretations that dances exist.

CHAPTER ELEVEN

Modes of Dance Organization

The last of our chapters on the kinds of dance looks at the question: what are the significantly different ways in which dances, or dance entertainments, can be structured? The question looks pointless at first, because surely the different part/whole and element/complex relationships we looked at suffice to generate alternative structures. But that is not the whole story.

The question of overall structure arises if a dance-maker, not content to be a miniaturist, wishes to emulate the authors of epics or operas, or if what is articulated as a single dance does not fill the time accepted as proper to a public entertainment. The same question confronted instrumental music in the eighteenth century: when an item stretches beyond what one can immediately grasp, one has to find a way of giving it some intelligible, acceptable, and justifiable order. The question has to arise, as soon as one gets a group together for a performance and assembles an audience to see it. Is one just going to give a recital of bits and pieces, in an order determined by nothing less random than the relative exhaustion of the personnel? Or is the recital to be structured somehow; and, if so, what sort of sequence and totality are appropriate?

The basic question is one of syntax. In language, the internal structure of a sentence is controlled by a strict and complex grammar. In larger forms, no such grammar applies, but there may be rhetorical conventions governing compositional correctness and normality, in addition to social conventions of acceptability. Different modes of articulation may be appropriate at different levels of inclusiveness, and the way these modes nest into each other calls for investigation.[1]

A minimal order is exemplified by the way a variety bill is constructed: what is the most effective combination and sequence (subject to the constraints of performers' vanities and contracts) of grave and gay, quiet and loud, slow and fast, solo and concert: what works as an opener, what as a finale. But then, if unlike the vaudeville manager we are a single troupe presenting a single entertainment, we are already concerned with the internal structure of a *dance performance*. Applying just these considerations within a single art is what led in music to the composition of a 'suite' of dance-based pieces that counts, for both composer and audience, as a unitary work (albeit one of which the components are detachable).

One can, of course, perhaps in the name of 'post-modernism,' confront an audience simply with a sequence of dances, a collage of images, leaving it to audience members to impose or discern significant arrangements, as they see fit. The audience has then to conjecture what actually motivated the sequence, whether consciously or unconsciously, whether the motivation was significant or not, whether structure was absent or concealed, and must decide whether to look for structure, to try to ignore discernible structure, to pay no attention to structural questions, or what. If the dance-maker gives instructions in this regard, the audience must decide whether the instructions are serious, or whether they are being kidded. In general, if the dance-maker can't be bothered, why should the audience? If no structure is intended, are the dance-makers governed by a (perhaps unavowed) feeling of rightness? If the sequence is meant to be random, is the principle of randomness of any interest? The general difficulty is that the dance-makers may have thought of many more possibilities than an audience member could be aware of – but are just as likely not to have thought of all sorts of possibilities that occur to the audience.

11.1 Narrative

The problem of major form arises in all the arts. But a minimal, though satisfactory and in some ways unbeatable, solution is available wherever a narrative sequence of events is possible. Once a *story* of any sort is established (perhaps something implying an initial situation, a plot, and a denouement), the question what happens next is always in place and will always be eagerly asked if the storyteller makes each episode end in a convincing cliffhanger, or if skill has created the confidence that there will be more and as good to come. Our dreams keep us entertained all night with an endless 'and then ... and then ... and then ... ,' without help of flashback or tricky narrator. But the reason that narrative is always available is that our lives make liveable sense to us only in so far as we make stories out of them, flowing into each other, subject to editing and interpretation, ultimately forming a putative story that is coextensive with our lives.[2]

In dance, strictly, the sequential interest of interminable narrative should be maintained simply by making each dance item an event in the story that is the night's dancing. 'What happened then?' becomes 'What will they do next?' But it doesn't quite seem to work that way. A dance as such is not an episode in a possible story; what the dancers do next is not the same as what happens next in a dance they do. The trouble is that narrative order cannot be imposed on movements as such, but only on actions. So it cannot literally apply to any extended dance, without reducing the dance to a sort of extended mime. It is, however, possible to use a narrative as an architectonic framework into which dances are fitted, either as enhancing a situation and expressing an appropriate mood or as advancing the story in a way the more mimelike bits of the ballet set up.[3]

Richard Wollheim (1984) argues that our idea of personhood cannot be divorced from that of living a life, with its structure of care and so on. Dance movement cannot, except at a very basic level, be reduced to bare vital movement, but must be seen as movement of a dancer, and hence of a person. If Wollheim is right, then, dance will inevitably incorporate fragmentary suggestions of an implicit lifeline, even if it does not actually project something like a story. There will then be a constant push toward composing actual narrative dances; it may be necessary to make a conscious effort to avoid doing so.

If an extended dance performance is to be organized by narrative, this may be done in various modes. In one mode, commonly practised in Indian traditions, a narrative poem is actually chanted throughout the dance, and the dance follows the story line. The dance is not necessarily to be construed as illustrating the narrative: from the present point of view, the narrative simply provides the armature for a dance that, as dance, has its own artistic integrity.

In a second mode, the armature is provided not by a text simultaneously presented but by a story that is assumed to be familiar to dancers and public alike: we find our bearings in the unfolding of the dance by anticipating and noticing the points where crises in the story occur. There may or may not actually be a familiar text: there may only be a common story line.

In a third mode, there need be no familar story, the narrative being conveyed mimetically, by whatever mimetic means are available. It is not necessary, for organizational purposes, that the mimetic means employed be sufficient to carry all that a storyteller could recount: all that is needed is that enough be conveyed to articulate the movement/action in terms of what happens next. Nor is it necessary that specific mimetic devices should be used; the relevant relationships could seem to all concerned to be simply *danced out*.

Finally, narrative can be used simply as a source of structural forms without episodic content. That is, some sort of trajectory of tensions and relaxations, convergences and divergences, and so on could be teased out of the repertoire of story forms and used as the formal basis of a dance without regard to any course of events in which those forms have been or might be embodied (cf. §4.2122).

11.2 Music

A second source of extended forms is music. Dance everywhere has been so pervasively mimetic that the use of narrative forms is uncontroversial. Similarly, music and dance everywhere are so closely joined that the question whether dance forms could follow musical forms does not arise. The only questions, in both cases, are whether this should always be so, and what forms it can and should take.

Once solutions have been found to the problem of extended form in music – by the development of sonata form, for instance – those solutions can simply be borrowed for the dance. Again, this can be done in various modes. First, an extended musical piece can accompany the dance and be used as formal basis, in various ways. One way is to base all or some of the articulations of the dance on all or some of the articulations of the music. Another way is to counterpoint the articulations of the dance against those of the music, in such a way that the accepted and familiar form of coherence in the music underwrites a less evident coherence in the dance structure, without actually providing its basis. A third way is for the dancer or dance-maker subjectively to absorb the qualities felt in the progression of the music and make a dance in accordance with that feeling.[4] What that will amount to in practice will vary according to the musical culture of the dance-maker, who may be responding to various aspects of structure more or less correctly identified, or to structurally superficial elements of dynamics or timbre, or to cultural and personal associations of an accidental sort. But that does not matter in this context, since we are concerned with the heuristic problem of arriving at a workable dance form, not with the hermeneutic problem of providing an equivalent for some aspect of the music.[5]

In any case, as Jack Anderson (1987, 246) points out in the course of his penetrating analysis of the problems of the full-length ballet, reliance on a single long musical work to provide the armature of a dance runs into obvious problems. For one thing, such works tend to be solemn and pretentious, imposing a restriction on the dance's scope and running the risk of boredom; for another thing, the musical work itself is likely to be uncongenial to a large part of the audience who might have been receptive to the choreography and performance. And, as Elizabeth Sawyer (1985, 57) observes, if the musical work is powerful enough to perform its structural task, 'either what one is hearing blots out what one is seeing, or each activity becomes superficial and incomplete.'

An extended musical piece can be used as a source of dance form when it is not actually played as accompaniment. Since, when a piece is used as accompaniment, its form can be used as a source of the form that is then the form of the dance, the possible ways of doing this remain open when the piece is not actually being played. The only cases in which this would be an absurd thing to do would be those in which the dance form actually used the musical form as counterpoint, and those in which the dance necessarily embodied a dancer's spontaneous reaction to the music. If it is not for some reason necessary that the dancer *be reacting*, a dance that spontaneously embodied such a reaction could be repeated in the absence of the music that had once inspired it.

Musical forms of a more general sort can be used as sources of dance form. From any piece or group of pieces an architectonic idea can be extracted and used: if it is possible to dance to a piece of music in a way that actually uses its formal properties, there must be a generalizable way of using identifiable musical forms, even when they are not embodied in specific works.

More obviously, abstract musical structures – theme and variation, sonata, fugue, rondo, da capo aria – since they are essential to works that can be and are danced to, must themselves constitute danceable forms in the sense that they must be usable as means of ordering specific dance contents. In fact, it is not unheard of to include such a word as 'rondo' in a dance title; then, just as in music, the audience's mind comes to the work ready primed with an appropriate set of formal anticipations. Again, since music is not dance – both arts have gone their own ways for many years, and the dynamics of dance are not those of musical sound – it is only the architectonic idea of the form that is used, and used no doubt in a metaphorical way. But it can be and is used.

Both musical and narrative form can be used as sources of dance form with any degree of indirection. All we want, remember, is a usable method of organizing extended forms; given such a method in another medium, there is accordingly no limit to the transformations, extensions, and analogies of the given forms that may be of use. At some point, these will lose touch with their origins and become naturalized in the domain of dance organization; but nothing requires us to decide when this shall be deemed to have taken place.

Narrative form and musical form can both be used to provide articulation for extended dance compositions. But these are two of the 'related forms' we will be discussing in part 2. What about the third form, theatre? Well, I already mentioned the examples of vaudeville and music-hall programmes; and the relation of ballet to operatic form is obvious enough – it is discussed in §14.21 below. In general, since dance as we are here conceiving it is largely a theatre art, any organizational device familiar in theatre practice is available to makers and presenters of dances. But there is nothing specific I want to add here.

11.3 Dance Form

It would be absurd to suggest that modes of dance organization must be, like those we have mentioned, extrinsic. Since dances do begin and end, parts of dances can be constructed like small dances and become episodes. Since dance movements differ from each other, passages of dances can be articulated by exploiting distinctive ranges of difference. One could construct a ballet that would be like an opera in being divided into recitative, aria, chorus, overture, and so on, without such a thing as operatic form ever having existed. The corresponding forms are indigenous to dance, and the articulation of them is natural in the sense that to grasp the range of ways of dancing is at once to grasp the way in which they can be used to shape extended forms.

Arnold Schoenberg argued that all musical form could be reduced to theme and variation, and he made this argument basic to his own mature musical practice. Douglas R. Hofstadter goes further and contends that variation on a theme is the essence of creativity in all fields.[6] All concepts, all forms, as the mind grasps them, have inbuilt capacities for variation and combination. This is as true of body-movement forms and dance ideas as it is of anything else.

The eighteenth-century conservative objection to sonata form was that it is arbitrary: since it rested neither on danceability nor on narrative content, it seemed to have no reason for being. Any purely, autonomously musical form was as musical as any other. But, as we know, this objection was refuted simply by the fact that sonata form became familiar and recognized as a standard way of making music: today, it is so obvious that 'absolute' music is the standard way of making music that we can hardly understand, let alone sympathize with, the position to which this was a denial of musical meaning.

There is no reason why modes of dance organization should not become established and win acceptance in just the same way as sonata form did, at least within any dance tradition stable enough for steps and movement sequences to become established. In a classical balletic *pas de deux*, a small-scale pattern of just this sort is established, depending on the pattern of interaction of the two dancers.[7] If patterns of large-scale dance organization based on the sort of distinctions of dance types we have previously made, as well as on dynamic and other contrasts that do not generate kinds, have not become firmly established on a large scale, it is not because anything stands in the way.

Arbitrariness is no objection: fugal form and sonata form are arbitrary, just as is the sonnet form in versification; but they are found to be viable and versatile, and, once established, there is a sense in which they cease to be arbitrary because they are themselves the norm and basis of the law of practice. If this has not happened in dance, it is presumably because no need for it has been felt.[8] And it is worth noting that few if any of the set forms in the other arts are of recent origin. Though still quite often used, they are not the preferred medium of contemporary artistic practice and have not been replaced by other set forms of comparably firm pattern. Today's practitioners and audiences are supposed to be more tolerant of uncertainty than their forebears. There is, however, a tendency for general audiences to become bored and confused by abstract contemporary dance that goes on for more than twenty minutes or so without clearly marked divisions, even when (to me) a clearly marked and well-articulated pattern is being established.[9] So perhaps, if dance-going comes to be as normal a part of cultural experience as musical concert-going is, and if contemporary dance traditions become stabilized, set forms for extended dance performances will become established as they are not now.

11.4 Conclusion

The organization of a large-scale dance structure, we have seen, can be based on materials drawn from narrative, from music, or from the theatre, or developed autonomously within dance practice. An extraneous structure can serve as accompaniment or can be consciously used as model; or the architectonic of the dance may be derived, deliberately or unthinkingly, by an individual or by a whole tradition, from forms that originated in some extraneous source but are now the familiar possession of the culture at large. In any particular case, though, the extraneous model may not have psychological or conceptual priority, since an adept dance-maker will no doubt have interiorized all the material and use it spontaneously, seeing (for instance) dance steps, music, and narrative each through the others. In the televised rehearsal for the reconstruction of *The Rake's Progress* (cf. chap. 4 note 23), all the movements were balletic in form; but almost all the choreographer's instructions to the dancers had to do with the motivation of the action, to get the direction and scale of the interactive movements right. The mimetic aspect of the movement at no point escaped either dance or music. It is as though, if the story were right, the dance would look right, not just as story but as dance, and the movements would lack dance form when they lacked motivation.

Integration of a different sort is exemplified by James Kudelka's *Pastorale* (1991). The ballet is danced to Beethoven's sixth symphony, and the major articulations are those of its four-movement structure. But the observable articulation of the dance is determined by four things. First is the musical articulation of the symphony. Second is the implicit narrative and mimetic content that Beethoven worked into the musical structure. Third is a quasi-dramatic articulation dependent on the social and psychological differentiation of what one has to call the 'characters' in the ballet, though there are no actual characters or incidents. And fourth, there is an articulation in purely dance terms (eked out by a scenic patterning of costumes). Presumably the music, once chosen, was decisive for the main outline, because it is established in the public realm; but the ballet gives no sense of being dominated by any one strand or component. Nothing distracts from anything else.

The problem of large-scale organization of dance performances becomes a problem only if we make it one. When it was not a problem, makers and critics of dance were content to allow such a performance the sort of unity a song recital has – a kind of unity few people find fault with.[10] So a ballet or other dance performance could be likened to beads on a string, or a series of pictures on a wall, or floats in a parade – simply a series of items each satisfactory in itself and bearing no relation to those before and after other than that it was clearly disengaged and demarcated from them. And such a string could be as long as the performers or the audience cared to make it; though too long a sequence of excessively similar episodes becomes tiresome. And has musical culture really gained much by going from Boyce, whose symphonies take ten minutes from tune-up to applause, to Bruckner, whose vegetable movements grow vaster than empires and more slow?

PART TWO

Dance and Related Fields

DANCE AND RELATED FIELDS

In discussing principles of dance organization, I considered how dance can exploit other forms of artistic practice, using their works as an armature or using their structural resources as analogues. I dealt specifically with music and the literary uses of language. I could also have compared dance with the other fine arts: dance and painting, dance and sculpture, dance and architecture, and dance and macramé provide food for thought. But there seems no compelling reason to make separate topics out of these comparisons. The special cases that call for extended treatment, not only for their own interest but because they have played a large part in actual thinking about dance, are music, language, and theatre.

We have seen that people who write about dance, as well as dancers and choreographers themselves, insist on the close connection between dance and music – in many cultures, it is said, these are not two arts but one. And I have continually had to talk about music throughout my discussions. But there is still more to say about the basic likeness and difference between musical procedures and dance procedures, musical structures and dance structures.

Much the same holds for literary language. Hegel and those in his tradition argued that high artistic dance must be mimetic, hence parasitic on literature. We will not accept that; but, as in the case of music, there is an important question we have not taken up. It is still fashionable to take linguistic structures as paradigmatic of all cultural order. The human brain devotes much of its space to language processing; grammatical speech in concept-generating modes is the most distinctive human characteristic. What are the analogies and disanalogies between linguistic order and dance order?

Dance as an art is theatre dance, or, rather, we tend to think only of theatre dance when discussing dance as one of the fine arts of Western civilization. What difference does it make to dance that in its conspicuous public manifestations it is a mode of theatre, existing alongside other such modes and liable to be enriched or contaminated by them?

The next three chapters take up these questions. But the Introduction to this book mentioned another sequence of topics that follows no less directly from the material we have just been through. After considering the kinds of dance, one has to consider other aspects of dance that unite dances as well as separating them. Above all, something must be said about the distinctive values of dance, as one dances for oneself or for others. What spectators see without performing dancers perform without seeing. We have to discuss how one can learn artistic dance, realizing in one's own work the values that will be appreciated by others. And we have to consider the relation between the creation and the performance of dances, between dancer and choreographer. This set of topics might equally well have been dealt with before music and the rest, and our treatment of it will owe little to those other discussions.

CHAPTER TWELVE

Dance and Music

In principle, the meaningful relationships that can be found or alleged between music and dance are of daunting complexity. One would expect this to be the case, if music and dance are from some points of view obviously different – dancers are not musicians, and to learn music does not equip one to dance or to choreograph – but from other points of view have been often declared inseparable, if not identical. Of this unity-in-diversity one may hold that they are originally a single art but have diverged as practitioners became more sophisticated, or that they are distinct arts but have coalesced, perhaps because music habitually makes us want to dance or dancing impels us to provide suitable music. If that is the case, however, music without dance is not in the same position as dance without music. The former also makes a complex practice by uniting with words in song, but dance without music has no such alternative partner.

One thing that makes our topic intractable is that we have no adequate and appropriate characterization of music. This is not because too little thought has been given to the matter. Music has been subjected to more theory than any of the arts. There have, in fact, been too many theories, too variously related to different kinds of musical practice, and there is no usable consensus on how they fit together.

The following are some of the ways in which it has been claimed that dance is meaningfully related to music. It may be conceived, in general, as (a) continuous with music, as though song were a dance of the mouth; or (b) a continuation or overflow of the impulses that lead to music; or (c) related to abstract music in a way closely analogous to the way song is related to abstract music; or (d) analogous in its meanings and divisions to music as a whole; or (e) a natural partner of music (so that either (i) for every dance there is some appropriately accompanying music, and vice versa, or (ii) for every dance there is some fit musical accompaniment, though there is some music that fits no dance); or (f) an expressive outcome of music (which, in Hegel's phrase [1975, II 906], 'gets into our feet'); or (g) an interpretation of music, so that for every dance there is some music that the dance properly means; or (h), like poetry, a source of musical form – and no doubt there are others. All of these relationships are often alleged, and many are argued for; to allege one is not necessarily to exclude others.

Since alleged musical meanings are themselves complex, alleged relations between musical meanings and dance meanings may become very complex: mutual support, unilateral support, conflict, and mutual irrelevance are only the simplest possibilities. Again, since music and dance are both characteristically rhythmic, the relationships of musical and dance rhythms may be complex: the two fields of rhythm may be said to be homogeneous or heterogeneous, structured in like or unlike ways; and the relationships, actual and possible, between the rhythms of specific dances and the rhythms of the music they are danced to (or that follows them) admit of similar variation.

In short, the meaningful relations between music and dance, and between their respective meanings, afford a vast topic, small parts of which have been explored, but which has never been systematically surveyed. The problems are so heterogeneous that I doubt whether such a survey is possible. But one can pick out some salient themes.

12.1 Symbiosis

When Louis XIV established his Royal Academy of Dance in 1662, he found it necessary to ward off the protests of the musicians, accompanying the letters patent with an 'academic discourse to prove that the Dance in its noblest part does not need Musical Instruments, and that it is entirely independent of the Violin.'[1] It has always been assumed, said this document, that dance and the violin have natural affinities but are distinct: music is judged by the pleasure of the ear alone, but 'dance, on the contrary, has nothing that the ear can hear.' Dance, in antiquity, was said to make feelings visible; in France, it confers grace and seemliness in manners. 'The Violin has nothing to do with all of these things, and in connection with dance it adds only pleasure.' Dancers may be led by the violin, but 'they could not follow the Violin's cadences before having learned how to do the steps, to carry their bodies, and to form the necessary figures.' The relation between violins and dance is the same as that between trumpets and war: the trumpets stimulate the troops to fight but do not say how. And, finally, the dance has lasting effect on the dancers' bodies, while music gives only transitory pleasure.

Nothing new here: a string of commonplaces, though a similar string could doubtless have been assembled on the opposing side. What is significant is rather the practised air with which the anonymous author marshals the royal case, and the fact that it was felt necessary to issue the document at all.

'Rhythm without tone may be found in dancing,' said Avicenna (1974, 71), five centuries before Louis; 'dancing, however, is better performed when accompanied by the proper tone – it makes [a stronger] effect on the soul.' In practice, music and dance are inseparable.[2] At least, this is so if one allows the rhythmic beating of a drum to count as music, and I do not see why one should not, in so far as a drum is a musical instrument played musically by a musician.[3] Music has a pulse or beat to which dancers keep time, dancing on, before, after, across, or against the beat but always with essential reference to it (cf. §9.52). Musical pieces also provide introductions and cadences that control entering and leaving the dance ('strike up the band!') and in this way can come to articulate the main structures of a dance. Musical patterns have energy patterns that can interact with dance energy patterns and have affective, dynamic, and textural properties that may be perceived as having dance analogues – though it may not be clear, on reflection, how close the analogies are. Such specifically musical phenomena as gamut, counterpoint, tonality, thematic development, and harmony, however, have no evident dance analogues, and it is not uncommon for a dance to observe the dynamic outline of its accompanying music while ignoring its musical essence.[4]

In much musical and dance practice, the boundaries between dancer and musician may be blurred, with toe-tapping and clapping answered by the swing of a fiddler's body. But in theory, as Avicenna remarked, strict definitions of dance and music exclude each other. Philippe Soupault, for one, makes a great point of insisting that dance and music have nothing to do with each other.[5] Moira Shearer takes the opposite position: in all but the most modern ballets, she claims, 'It is the music which has caused the choreographer ... to want to compose movements and dances. ... When you see a very modern ballet today, with squeals, grunts and groans or no music at all, to me it is a contradiction of what dancing is about. Something, surely, makes one want to dance' (Newman 1982, 105). But this is very strange. One would have thought that choreographers simply wanted to compose dances, and dancers wanted to dance them. She might have said, with equal reason, that something makes musical composers want to compose. It is not surprising, as one reads this, that Shearer abandoned her dancing career – no doubt her heart was never in it.

Dance without music is not only possible but quite common.[6] In such dances, however, at least in our public theatre practice, the absence of music is not merely incidental, but pointed; it tends to strike us as artificial or uncanny (a practice in which dancing was *always* done in dead silence, or to the accompaniment of casual ambient noise, would be downright creepy). Either one feels that the dance really has music (which the dancers are really dancing to, hearing it in their imaginations or humming it beneath their breaths) but it is being suppressed, or, if we are persuaded that there really is no music for the dance, it is as if it were being danced instead to an inherently inaudible music, like the music of the spheres. (Heard melodies are sweet, but those unheard are weird.) Conversely, much music calls for either dance or words to complete or complement it. We have become accustomed to absolute music without either, and may think of that as the best or purest kind in its autonomy and self-sufficiency, but surely there would be something amiss with a musical culture in which people were not often impelled to dance along or to sing along.

'Music can give nothing vital to the body unless it first receives life from the body,' said Adolphe Appia. 'This is evident. And so the body gives up its own life to music, to receive it back again, though now organised and transfigured.'[7] So thoroughly intertwined are the arts of music and dance as we know them that, throughout this work, I keep falling back on musical analogies and structures when aspects of dance itself seem inadequately articulated. The naturalness of this practice is itself more significant than any formal argument about relationships could be.

12.2 The Art of Dance and the Art of Music

Isadora Duncan said many things in the course of her career, and one does not know how carefully she thought them through, or how firmly she stood committed to any of them. But one of the things she said was that, whereas her original inspiration (in America) had come from Walt Whitman, 'afterwards, coming to Europe, I had three great Masters, the three great precursors of the Dance of our century – Beethoven, Nietzsche and Wagner' (Duncan 1928, 48). None of these three precursors was a dancer (any more than Whitman had been): two were musicians, and the third was a philosopher whose claim to precursorship must rest chiefly on his having written *The Birth of Tragedy from the Spirit of Music*.[8]

The specific invocation of Wagner may rest on his predilection for continuous melody and free modulation, as that of Beethoven doubtless rests on the flexibly driving rhythms of which he alone had the secret (and that of Whitman on the apparent spontaneity of his sprawling versification). But Wagner is very much in point here, because his vision of the conglomerate artwork (*Gesamtkunstwerk*) allotted to dance a more important place than the institutions of his day, or his own practice, warranted.[9] His argument went like this. Each of the three 'sister arts,' – poetry, dance, and music – has a different expressive function.[10] The expression of intellectual emotion in words, which Wagner takes to be what poetry is when left to its own devices, is inherently inartistic because organized by the dogmatically abstract principles of metrical prosody;[11] the expression of violent feeling through body movement, which Wagner identifies with the independent nature of dance, is inherently inartistic because organized by the spasmodic movements of passion, the dynamics of muscular contraction, and the heavy impetus of the limbs; absolute music, the expression of deep personal feeling, has the inherent expressiveness proper to art but lacks specific content.[12] But, when the three arts are combined, music acquires a definite content from the legible symbolism of the other two, and its rhythm overrides their ungainly principles of movement, so that verse becomes song and gesticulation and acrobatics become dance. Wagner, being a musician, says that music is the animating principle and the source of the artistic quality of the whole. What he does not say, though his argument makes it plain, is that what is thus ordered and animated has the overall character of a dance. It is as though Wagner were inspired, like many of his contemporaries, by the finale of Beethoven's ninth symphony, which showed, as it were, that it was the destiny of Divine Grace to dance in the streets: in Wagner's vision, music moves out into the world to become a universal and sociopolitical force for world harmony, the basis of an order modelled on and animated by a choric dance.[13]

Wagner's thought enshrines some contentious theses in a deep confusion. The confusion is between the combination of subsidiary art forms in an overarching 'universal art' of music-drama and the conceptual and affective unification of the arts under a single set of principles and values. The tendentious theses are, first, that each of the arts is (as Langer would argue) defined by a separate emotional function, and, second, that the principles of dance order and poetic order arise from the imposition of an order proper to music on orders that are, in the first instance, purely mechanical and purely intellectual, respectively. We are given no reason to think that either thesis is true. They are, however, both popular and persuasive.

Adam Smith, like Wagner but for a different reason, had thought that dancing must depend on music for its artistic articulation. 'In Dancing, the rhythmus, the proper proportion, the time and measure of its motions, cannot be distinctly perceived, unless they are marked by the more distinct time and measure of Music. It is otherwise in poetry. ...' For, he contends, the ear judges 'time and measure' more precisely than the eye (Smith 1795, 236). Why does he think that? I don't know. Perhaps it is only a matter of technology – brief and easily recognizable audible punctuations, like drum beats, were more easily produced than flashes of light. More to the point, perhaps, dancers can always keep ears open for the beat but cannot keep a look-out for visual signals unless the choreography provides for it. However that may be, Smith may be enlisted, more clearly than Wagner, in support of the contention that dance without audible music must be being danced (if it is truly dance) to an inaudible music. The eeriness that I attributed to such dance will be due to the fact that the visible perfection of the dance testifies to a yet higher but invisible perfection that is animating the dancer. Unlike Wagner, Smith is saying that the rhythm of the music cannot be overcoming the defective rhythm inherent in the limbs: however complete the victory of the music, precision of the musical timing must remain inaccessible to limb and eye.

In our chapter 9, we saw that rhythm (as Aristoxenus conceived it, and as we will conceive it if we grasp his argument) is a general phenomenon, extending more widely than music. But music, the art *par excellence* of subjective temporality, is in a way the true home of rhythm – doubly so, as an internally ordered system of mutually commensurate durations and as the real-time dynamics of ordered sound. Wagner's contention that music is the source of artistic rhythm in all performance arts is, however, ambiguous. It could be that rhythms generated in musical practice are exemplary for the other arts, as Anya Peterson

Royce suggests;[14] or it could be that rhythms of all sorts are made conspicuous in music and thus become available for application in such other fields as dance.[15] In any case, musical rhythms are immensely complex, and there is never a unique answer to the question what *the* rhythm of a piece is. A dance may borrow from a piece of music one arguably dominant rhythm or exploit some subsidiary rhythm; in either case, the dynamics of the body are such that no dance can simply replicate a musical rhythm; it is more likely to be counterpointed against it, comment on it, be levered against it in some way. I will have more to say about this soon.

To return to Wagner: Duncan's version of his argument has it that dance alone is not so much ungainly as meaningless: 'The ballet is without true significance, without any accord with art, ... for in the ballet the dance aspires to be everything, to take the place of poetry and drama. The proof that dance cannot exist alone is that it finds recourse to pantomime.'[16] Since Duncan did not use poetry and drama as props, she must have been relying on music to fill the alleged void. But why would music be inherently more meaningful than dance?

In fact, Duncan's claim for the priority of music as personified in Beethoven is ambivalent. On the face of it, she is recognizing that dance is an outward manifestation of a primarily musical impulse that could find (had, in fact, already found) musical expression and is describing the way her own dance practice was animated and organized. But when we reflect that she links Beethoven with Nietzsche and that Wagner may be invoked as theorist and impresario rather than as composer, not to mention that when she was in America she had claimed to be inspired by the American poet Whitman, we may suspect that her claim amounts to little more than a political recognition that her audiences were not predisposed to take dance seriously as an autonomous art, so that she had to appeal to some extraneous source of authority and meaning, whether it really existed or not.

The priority of music over dance can be supported by the old philosophical tradition, glanced at above and chiefly associated with Kant, according to which time is 'subjective' and space 'objective.' I doubt if the distinction can be made precise in acceptable terms, but the idea is, roughly, that what is objective is what physical science deals with, and that what physical science deals with exists in space, time being reduced to a fourth, spatiotemporal dimension. So far as physics goes, the distinction between earlier and later events in a sequence is only one of randomization in energy distribution. Time as we experience it, in contrast, is a real difference between past and future, between memory and expectation. And mental events are inherently temporal, a matter of duration, of enduring. They are not spatial. Neither thoughts nor objects of thought as such are properly locatable in space. To say that time is the form of subjectivity and space is the form of objectivity is a way of referring to these differences.

Since musical performances objectively do take place, and a composer has objectively to make provision for such performances, spatial relations turn out after all to play a part in music; and, since observers observe physical events in ways that involve predicting and remembering, physical reality depends on the supposedly 'subjective' time for its realization. But it is easy to argue that these are secondary phenomena. Music, we can then say, is the dance of the inner life, and its outward manifestation is dance. Dance is the objective counterpart of music. Physical music-making and perceptible music-making are merely cause and effect of the *real* music, which is as such a subjective pattern of temporally structured events.[17] Such a pattern of events becomes dance when its true realization is corporeal. Since we are corporeal beings, through and through, our mode of being can become entirely dance; since we can think of ourselves as systems of pure thought and feeling, we can enter mentally into a world of music in which we simply *are* the music.[18]

I do not think that the analogy between music and dance sketched in the previous paragraph can be worked out. But I have a hunch that the objections to that way of talking about music will be symmetrical with the objections to that way of talking about dance. In any case, those who like this way of talking more than I do can say that, if we are primarily psychophysical entities, music is dance internalized; if we are primarily minds that have the use of bodies, dance is music externalized.

12.3 The Relation of a Dance to Its Music

In actuality – which is not the same as reality, for actuality is what we encounter as we encounter it, whereas reality is what we will eventually have to reckon with when we have mulled over all our encounters – the relations between a dance and the music it is danced to cover a range that is easily seen to be as wide as the prepositional resources of our language. We saw that the same is true of the relations of one dancer to another; no doubt it is true of a wide range of subtly cooperative enterprises.

One can dance *to* the music, a phrase implying that music lays down the structure of the dance. Lays it down, but does not determine it, because there can be different dances to the same music, as in Danny Grossman's *Waltz*, where two contrasting groups of dancers perform contrasted movements in different rhythms, both of which are related equally directly to the music. One can dance *with* the music: the dynamic structures are compatible and parallel, music and dance are in time with each other, and there is at least a suggestion that the dynamic peaks and troughs, if no more, will coincide. One can dance *for* the music, which is what Isadora Duncan sometimes implied she did, subordinating the meaning of the dance to (or even deriving that meaning from) the music, or to the meaning of the music, or to a supposed meaning of the music. One can dance *against* the music, counterpointing some emphasized feature of the dance (rhythm, tempo, affective meaning) against the comparable feature of the music. More remotely, one can dance *around* the music, as descant rather than counterpoint, or *about* the music, as commentary. Metaphorically at least, one can dance into, or out of, or towards, or away from (or up, or down, or alongside ...) the music. When I saw van Dantzig's *Romeo and Juliet* I had the distinct impression that it was choreographed *across* the music, in that major changes in movement and scene seemed not to answer to the articulation of the score. And Nureyev said of Balanchine, 'It's all in his way of dealing with the music: he doesn't follow it, he walks on top of it, just like Fred Astaire.'[19] One can dance *without* the music, and often does, if the tape breaks or the pianist is away – but that is perhaps not a very interesting relationship. One can dance without any music at all, of course, but then there is no specific music one is failing to relate to, so that doesn't count.

Other, subtler relationships are possible. One can, for instance, dance *as if there were* music, that is, in a way that suggests a musical accompaniment of some more or less specifiable sort. (The poet William Stafford [1977, 128] writes that children 'dance before they learn / there is anything that isn't music.') Some of the prepositional phrases we could formulate will have conventionally fixed meanings, and many (especially if we include very long and complicated ones) will be such that it would be arbitrary to assign them any one fixed meaning; but very many, including all the ones I have mentioned, will either have clear potentialities for metaphorical use or be such that one could easily imagine them coming in handy. In fact, I would be surprised if any preposition failed to suggest to a resourceful dancer a way of relating to music. I am not sure I have ever seen anyone dance 'under the music,' but I am by no means sure I haven't.

The indefinitely variable relationships to which we have just issued a charter may obtain between choreographer and composition, or between dancer and performance (or music-as-performed). In general, the expressions introduced first, which are familiarly used for regularly recognized relationships, refer to the practice of fitting a choreography to a musical score; the last ones, the metaphorical repertoire, seem more to be weapons in a critic's armoury for dealing with relationships between a danced performance and its accompanying music. But both relationships can be covered by the same language. One might choreograph a dance *despite* the music as written; it would also be possible, but different, for a dancer to dance *despite* the music as actually being played, whether or not the dance had been choreographed in the teeth of the score in the first place.

I have been writing as though the music came first and the dance then took up a relation to it.[20] That is not always the case. The dance may come first and the music follow on, or both may be worked out together.[21] The relationships are probably symmetrical. If a dance can be danced in any named relationship to a musical piece, it seems likely that a musical piece could be composed or performed in the same named relation to a dance. The metaphors would no doubt be cashed out in different ways in the two sets of cases, but I see no reason why the differences should be of any great interest.

How does it come about, if it does, that virtually any preposition or prepositional phrase can evoke a significant relation between a dance or a way of dancing and its accompanying music, and that the significances are reciprocal? Does it bespeak an inner harmony or analogy between the art of dance and the art of music, such as that one is the inner counterpart of the other? Not necessarily. The possibility of meaningful relationship may be no more than what obtains between any two cooperative activities, at least if they both maintain a comparable degree of freedom and an expressive dimension. An analogy can always be found between anything and anything else;[22] analogies are useful only to the extent that they are fruitful and valuable, and these criteria are hard to apply in any controlled way in the domain of art. If music and dance are felt to be strongly interrelated in the first place, the complexity of meaningful relationships will not weaken the feeling; but, if we were initially disinclined to believe that any such general relationship held, the multiplicity of detailed relationships would not compel us to change our minds.

We must not let all this talk of analogies and prepositions make us forget that, especially for the dancers and musicians concerned, the relation between a dance and its music is an experienced reality, not a matter of theory. Martha Graham (quoted above, chapter 9 note 9) speaks of the music she dances to as if it were a resilient and responsive partner in her dance. One dances into, with, against, or across the music as directly as a swimmer in a fast stream swims with, against, across its turbulence.

The specific relation between a dance and music that Isadora Duncan posited is one in which the form of the dance follows and is suggested by the experience of the music and offers an interpretation of its meaning. In the cases where this seems most obviously to be true, the resulting dance would not necessarily be about the meaning found in the music: it is more likely that what was experienced in and articulated by the music would become, when danced out, a strictly dance meaning. Edwin Denby argues that what Duncan says is impossible, because of the huge differences (on which I have already remarked) between the factors controlling the movement and organization in dances and musical pieces respectively. It follows, though this is not quite what he says, that any dance that followed the formal organization of a musical piece would have a very different artistic meaning: 'The visual rhythm frequently goes against the acoustic one. ... A dance phrase rests on several accents or climaxes of movement which other movements have led up to or from which they will follow, as unaccented syllables in speech surround an accented one. ... The dance accents frequently do not reproduce the accents of a musical phrase, and ... even when they correspond, their time length is rarely identical with musical time units. ... The variations of energy in dancing around which a dance phrase is built up are what make the dance interesting and alive; and they correspond to a muscular sense, not to an auditory one' (Denby 1949, 248–9).

Denby is writing about ballet, not about dancing in all its forms, and one would expect the relations between dance and music in so highly developed an art form to be subtle and complex. One would not expect to find what Denby seems to be excluding, the 'Mickey Mouse' method of fitting movement to sound in which Mickey climbs a ladder to the accompaniment of an ascending scale on the xylophone and falls off it to a beat on the bass drum. Even so, he leaves us wondering why the association of music and dance is so constant and how it is managed. He tries to explain it away: 'The excitement of watching ballet is that two very different things – dancing and music – fit together, not mechanically but in spirit,' he writes (249–50), but this spiritual congruence turns out to be no more than that 'Once the curtain is up the music functions as a spiritual atmosphere for the stage action, as giving the emotional energy of the piece ...' (250). Can that really be all there is to it? Denby might object to that question as implying that spiritual congruence is a small thing, but I would rejoin that it sounds like a big thing only because it seems to reaffirm what has just been denied, an expectation of some positive interrelation of music movement and dance movement. Fitting together 'in spirit' sounds like a more flexible and dynamic but no less concrete relationship than fitting together 'mechanically,' but a mere 'spiritual atmosphere' could be anything or nothing. Denby has saved himself from evident absurdity by a linguistic trick. But he must be right in saying that an interest in dance is an interest in how bodies move and an interest in music is an interest in sequences of pitch relations, and these are different. The fundamental difference is that dance is inertial, one movement transmits energy to the next; but music is not. One note does not cause its successor but implies it logically; tones simultaneously sounded blend into one complex sound, movements remain discrete.

Our disrespect for Denby was, in fact, unfair – as well as rash, considering his intelligence and sensitivity. The harmony between dance and music, at its best, operates at the level of cerebral organization, rather than at the motor level. Marcia Siegel (1985, 221) remarks that Balanchine's choreography *completes the humanity* of Hindemith's music for *Agon*; this sounds very much like a form of Denby's spiritual congruence, and what may lie behind it is best seen from Oliver Sacks's observations of sufferers from Parkinson's disease. What causes their tics and paralyses is a failure in the internal integrating rhythms of their brains; and what most reliably alleviates this arhythmia is music[23] – not any music, but music they can enjoy, music that moves them musically.[24]

How can dance fit music, since the ways they are put together are so different? But of course, if they were not different, nothing would be gained by putting them together. If Duncan somehow dances a Beethoven symphony, what she does would be devoid of interest if the structure of the dance and the structure of the music could coincide. As Peter Kivy has argued (1984, chap. 5), in all artistic representation the recalcitrance of the medium is essential to the effect. The deep answer to how dance and music can fit together, in the end, is that both are profound exercises of the integrating powers of the nervous system. But it is not an interesting answer, since it is only through such exercises that the powers in question are accessible.

The conundrum of relating a dance intelligibly to its music is like the more familiar one about how words and music are related in a song. In a successful song, a verbal order and a musical order, widely disparate, merge in an ordered unity. This is something we all know and appreciate without being able to explain how it is possible. But do we need to explain? We can see, perhaps, what the problem ought to be, but we can't see what the problem is, because there is none.

When I was younger and living alone (or with people whom I didn't mind vexing), I used to prop up a poetry book on the piano and play the poem as I read it. (I can't play the piano properly, but I can do things like that.) What was I playing? Not an equivalent for the rhythmical structure, or for the propositional meaning, or for the feeling-tone and transitions, or for the feelings the poem evoked in me. I just played the poem, the poetic meaning, the way the poem went. I didn't decide how to do it, or figure out what would be suitable, or justify what I was doing or had done, though often I had to stop and think what to do next – I just did it, that's all. I have not the least idea whether or not, if I had been a competent musician, what I played would have been judged congruent with the poem by an impartial observer, nor did I wonder at the time if it would be so judged. I just played the poem. It seems likely to me that Duncan just danced the music – but, because she was a great performer, it came out good.[25] I know of no informed and interested discussions by competent judges of what, if anything, the result seemed to have to do with Beethoven.

To write, compose, and sing a song is to do two things together: it is to poetize to music. We are left wondering why the two things fit together as well as they do. The immediate answer is that singing and song-making come naturally; most of us sing more spontaneously than we make music or verses separately. It is only when developed art has produced unmusical verses and unsettable music that we wonder what the basis of the combination can be. That does not mean that our wonder is out of place. Water occurs freely in our environment; only the advance of chemistry shows that it is a compound of hydrogen and oxygen, neither of which is familiar in an unmixed state. That does not mean that it is illegitimate to wonder how oxygen and hydrogen combine to form water. So, when verse and music have gone their different ways, we may wonder what the basis of the original unity was. Similarly, dancing to music is as natural as anything could be, something people do everywhere; a song-and-dance is an unforced unity. The possibility of developing a musicless dance and an undanced music may lead us to wonder what the basis of the unity was, but it is not as if we were trying to explain how we would set about establishing an artificial connection.

The parallel is not exact. We have a separate word for song; we have no word for dance-with-music that is different from our word for dance as such, and we feel the need for none. And in dance-with-music the dancers and the musicians are usually different people, for obvious reasons – a dancer can hardly combine instrument-playing movements with dance movements and is likely to have no breath to spare for singing. What we have is an initially familiar compound, rather than, as with song, an originally unified individual.

I suppose that in the end there is little in general to be said, more to be gained from examining examples. Any dance has all sorts of formal and structural properties, and all sorts of appreciable qualities, as a whole and in its parts. So does any piece of music. Any such property or quality can be either named and described or at least pointed out and demonstrated. For any such property or quality that is named or described in the one art, an application for the same name or description can be found in the other. For anything recognizably demonstrated in the one, something 'like that' can be demonstrated in the other, though some likenesses will be more striking, more convincing, more piquant, more witty, more literal-minded (and so on, endlessly) than others.

When setting a dance to music, or choreographing to a musical piece, one can take these relationships and exploit them. One exploits them not in any set way but by mirroring, counterpointing, contrasting, pointedly ignoring, and so on; any system of semiotic analysis will chart some of the possibilities. Discussions of the proper relation between a dance and its music are bedevilled by the urge to find that some of these relationships are in every case more proper than others. But there is no reason to suppose that that is the case, any more than there are positive general rules for conducting all human relationships. There are, indeed, general rules governing proprieties and expectations; but one has to know how to relate to those rules, and one cannot even general-ize safely about that.

In the end, it's a simple matter. If you are a real choreographer, someone who makes dances as other artists make things in their own arts, then, if you make a dance that seems to you (as a dance-maker) in your best judgment *right* for the music you are setting it to, it is bound to have a rightness, the rightness you with your trained experience and sharpened sensitivity see and feel in it. And it will be possible for others to see and feel that rightness too (see §17.5). One has only to remember a number of things. First, what you do and see and feel will embody your own style, your own way of dancing and dance-making and your own sense of dance fitness. Second, it will reflect the degree and kind of your own understanding of music in general, of the particular kind of music in question, of the particular piece, and of the actual performance of the piece, at the times when you are doing the relevant listening and making. Third, I have argued elsewhere (Sparshott 1987a) that there are three musics or kinds of musical activity, respectively cognitive, conative, and emotive; that any piece of music can be construed and responded to as belonging to any or all of these, but that any given piece of music will lend itself to such construction and response differentially; and that your own way of listening to music, in general and on a particular occasion, will incorporate a personal strategy of construction and response in these respects. You will also have particular preferences and skills built into your listening habits.

All these complexities go to make up the fitness that you see between your dance and its music. Each spectator of your dance will have a way of seeing, a way of listening, and a sense of fitness, different from yours; and different formations will generate groups of spectators sharing common systems of response that set them off from other such groups. It follows that the fitness you made and found will be congenial to some, perceptible but uncongenial to others, divinable but imperceptible to others again, in endlessly complex ways. That any two individuals should completely coincide in their sense of congruence is little more likely than identity of fingerprints, and the same holds for complete incomprehension, though enthusiasms in acceptance and rejection will mask these failures at the extremes.

The endless complexities in differential awarenesses of fit, perfectly real (because reliably accessible from actual standpoints) but subtly relative to so many variables, do not prevent fitness being the completely simple matter I said it was. This is just how human minds work and have to work, holistically, through cultivated awarenesses of interrelatable perspectives. I can be quite sure that anyone else can see what I have seen, if my own seeing is thoroughly worked into the totality of public practice; if they do not see it now, they could come to see it. No form of reduction or simplification is possible, just because the kind of sympathy and understanding involved is a matter of overall response.

We know little about how the brain works, but we do know at least that it does not work by simply ordered hierarchies of the sort that an engineer might construct.

What I have just said about making dances for music could be said about making music for dances, because the factors involved are the same. What a trained and artistic composer finds right for the dance will be found right by some others, and the rest of us can see how it could be found right. Does that mean that there can be essentially or primarily cognitive, conative, affective dances and responses to dances? No doubt it does.

12.4 Music Structure and Dance Structure

If music needs dance to go with it and ease its inhibitions, if dance needs music to enrich its expression or to point and counterpoint its themes, their symbiosis could rest on shared properties as well as on complementary ones. I will say something about temporal measure in music (and verse) and in dance, and then discuss the concept of a tone as the unit of music and see what that suggests or fails to suggest about dance steps.

12.41 Times

'One ... two ... three ... four ... .' Surely the true voice of dance is the counting voice, just as music is made up of *measures*. The analogy is drawn by Francis Bacon (1605, 401), who speaks of poetry 'Wherein though men in learned tongues do tie themselves to the ancient measures, yet in modern languages it seemeth to me as free to make new measures of verses as of dances; for a dance is a measured pace, as a verse is a measured speech.' I have considered elsewhere the contention that dance is inherently measured, discussing the relation between rhythm in general and metre, conceived as uniform counts of arbitrary units (Sparshott 1988, §8.42, and above, §9.212); what I propose to look at now are some of the complexities of metricality and analogies between measures in different areas. (It is true that Bacon speaks of verse, not of music as such; but the metricality of verse is really a musical property, as we have seen already.)

At least four basic kinds of verse metre are familiar. There is the quantitative metre of classical Latin and Greek, assumed to be the basis of musical rhythm both by Aristoxenus and by Augustine, in which time is articulated by recurring patterns of sub-patterns of longer and shorter units (artificially assumed to be such that two shorts equal one long, so that at set places in the sub-patterns two shorts can replace a long without change of time, with the gap between units counting as zero). This kind of metre has no special relevance to dance, because nothing in body movement forms a plausible basis (as syllabic divisions do) for the quantitative binary code of short/long: one can do it (the foxtrot did) by making one step equal two shuffles, but there is no special point in giving that device prominence.

Second, there is the stress metre of native English verse, in which stressed syllables are separated by notionally equal times, or by equal numbers of unstressed syllables, or by both, in accordance with rules or partial regularities that may take a lot of learning. This again has little applicability to dance, since it depends on the plasticity of an undivided and fundamentally homogeneous string; one could mimic such a movement in dance, but I do not see how one could embody it, and it would be an artificial and rather pointless (and probably unrecognizable) way of structuring one's dance.

Then, third, there are syllabic metres, in which units consist of set numbers of syllables, each syllable being metrically interchangeable for any other – we must not say 'of equal length,' for the concept of metrical length has no application in such systems, and no other is relevant. To use such a metre in dance, one would have to find a clear basis in body movement for something corresponding to syllabic division, and, though one could impose such a division by fiat, I do not know why one would want to, otherwise than by way of experiment. Such metres are at home in Japanese, which is written in the *kana* syllabary, the relation of which to the spoken language is perhaps somewhat artificial. Elsewhere, the very idea of such a metre promotes artificial attempts to produce it in languages where it has no such basis. It can be done, but what is done is never the same as it is where it reflects the way the language is written anyway. The use of a comparable system of division in dance would add a further element of artifice and arbitrariness.

Finally, fourth, in languages that make structural use of pitch variation, there are metres in which what is patterned is the sequence and grouping of pitches. So far as I know, such metres have no direct applicability to dance, because nothing in body movement bears any obvious analogy to pitch variation. But then, nothing in body movement quite answers to speech emphasis or stress either; one can use stamping or punching movements, for instance, but these are special kinds of movement that have an emphatic gestural meaning. These failures of fit are not fatal, because in any case the dance movement will have its own organization in its own terms, as our quotation from Denby showed. Dance movements tend to be those in which extraneous patterns are used as an additional source of formal interest, and it would be the precise way in which such patterns were exploited that would be interesting, not the supposed fact of embodiment or reduplication.

Other forms of metricality, or something close to it, derive not from prosody but from the techniques of drumming. In Indian classical dancing, different 'syllables' correspond to different ways of striking the surface of the drum, producing different kinds of sound (cf. Saxena 1991); in some African drumming, the regularities observed by different drums follow conventions of dynamic interrelation (cf. Chernoff 1979). I do not know enough about these to say anything useful about them. And no doubt there are many other such practices of which I have not even heard, and would not understand if I had.

We must pause for reflection. What did Denby mean, after all, by the inherent organization and rhythm of dance movement? It had to do with the way energies are mustered and impetus developed or checked, setting in motion, changing direction, coming to rest. But how are such movements inherently organized? One famous and ludicrous suggestion is that of Heinrich von Kleist (1810). Only a puppet is truly graceful, because a graceful movement is a natural movement, and the natural movement of a limb is a pendulum swing. This is clearly wrong, equating the natural with the inertial and ignoring the musculature as well as the mind.[26] The inherent movement of the body is in doing things, including dancing. The weights of the limbs, the ways the muscles pull and the joints bend, govern what the movements are and how they are done but not what movements are done and how they are linked. So what is an extraneous order, if not one imposed on the body by external force – or, perhaps, functional failure in the nervous system? I suppose it could only be one that was generated and guided by the very idea of performing such a movement, the idea being abstracted and adapted from the principles underlying and shaping the action of something that was not a human body. It is, of course, quite natural for a human being (and, hence, for a human body) to do that. It is natural to dance.

To resume. When Francis Bacon speaks of 'measures of verses,' I suspect that he has in mind none of the kinds of metre I distinguished, but rather one of the two characteristic metric arrangements of post-Renaissance music. One of these is the metre of ecclesiastical chant, in which the repeated units are strings of syllables equally timed and separated by breath pauses. The other is the standard metric type provided for by staff notation, in which the basic group is a notional number of units of a given length (specified as fractions of a typographically identified unit), the first unit in any such group being notionally stressed: for instance, six eighth-notes to a bar, with stress on the eighth-note written first after a bar line.[27] It is understood, however, that there are no antecedently set limits to how such units may be divided or coalesced, whether they shall be occupied by silence or sound, and to what extent the expected stresses may be displaced, or added to, or ignored. What Bacon has in mind is, I think, that a dance is associated with a particular metre of the kind last named and that a new dance may call for a new metre or a new use of an old one. A waltz, for instance, consists of groups of three quarter-notes, these groups themselves occurring in four groups of four, with the emphasis on the first note heavy and admitting of little variation, played at a set speed, the emphases alternating between a heavier and a lighter. The earlier minuet was much the same only slower, with lighter emphases and more admitted variation, and without the alternation between heavy and light emphases.

In the traditional social dances of our society, musical metres of the type mentioned are isomorphic with the measures of dances – or partly so, for the steps of the waltz are not articulated as the tunes are. But is there any analogy between the kinds of metrical variability I mentioned and a corresponding variability in dances? It is not obvious that there is. Nor do I see any interesting analogy between any dance phenomenon and the tension between formal metre and actual rhythm in verse. The corresponding tensions in dance might be between the articulation of a dance and the articulation of the music it is danced to, or between the inherent rhythms of the body and those imposed on it. But we have just seen that the notion of an inherent rhythm of the body is elusive; and in the other case the tension fails, because there is no expectation of an exact correspondence in the articulations, whereas in verse the formal metre is that of the very verse that has the rhythm with which it conflicts.

The metric properties of music as expressed in our regular staff notation are, in a sense, free-floating. Given a string of notes (for instance, an octave of the scale of G, or any melodic sequence), the relative length of the notes, their interruption by rests or momentary interruptions, and the distribution of emphases can be specified and changed at will, independently of each other. The musical structure and interest, if any, will depend largely on these; but there is no inherent limit to the metrical alterations that can be imposed. Nothing like that is true of dance. That is why musical metrics afford no real model for dance. They are arbitrary schemata. Any interest they have they derive either from their abstract structure, in which case their original musical context is irrelevant, or from the way they articulate the specific music material to which they belong, in which case they have no independent interest that can be transferred to dance. A complex schema abstracted from a musical work can, however, be used as a source of formal ideas; and a metrically or rhythmically interesting piece can be counterpointed against the movement pattern of a dance in any way that proves feasible and promises to be valuable. These can happen in one way if the music is played at the same time as the dance is danced, in another way if it is not. It would also be possible to play the music and dance the dance out of phase, out of tempo, and in other complex relationships; the reason for wanting to do that would, one hopes, be apparent as the proceedings went forward.

One might look for analogy between free verse and unmusical dance. Free verse is verse in which the rhythm has no metrical norm to deviate from; and some hold that, once the habit of metre is lost, free verse suffers not from absence but from loss of measure. That is, in the absence of a norm of metrical expectation, the habit of listening for the rhythm of verse may be lost altogether. Someone can write a poem without thinking about how to read it aloud, concentrating entirely on the sequence of images and word meanings; and in such a case one might say that the poem really had no rhythm of its own, because the actual movement properties in real time (on any occasion of its reading) were left undetermined.[28] So someone might say that in dance that abjures imposed rhythms there is an arhythmy, but if the habit of rhythm were lost the implication of rhythm would be lost as well, and an important dimension of interest would go too.[29] But that would not be quite right. A dance must be danced in real time, and the body must be moved in measure or out of measure, so that what the choreographer specifies always has some rhythmical implication, even if the tasks allotted do not have a specific temporal articulation. (What is arhythmic in the sense that it lacks the expected kind of temporal articulation must have some other kind, and is thus somehow rhythmic, though not necessarily eurhythmic.) The poet, as such, does not move or call for movement but composes semantic entities.[30]

12.42 Tones

Musical systems depend on a gamut, a system of tones strictly inter-defined and identified by uniformity of pitch, a quality found only incidentally in natural sounds. The tuned systems, scales, by which musics are everywhere defined, are themselves the primary products of the musical arts to which they belong. Defining music in terms of such systems excludes much electronic music and any practice that uses natural or raw sounds; but that exclusion can be defended by saying that these other practices are doing something fundamentally different. Once a tonal system (including such offshoots as dodecaphony) is articulated, it establishes a place for itself that is so distinctive, and so inherently significant, that it preempts the very idea of music.

Traditional Western dances, and perhaps most dances of most tradi-tions at all places and times, are based on movement units, 'steps.' Can we say that, as with tones in music, once the idea of a step has been grasped we must see that nothing can be a dance that is not made up of steps – of units defined by their articulation with other such units in a system?

Before we answer that question, we must enter a caveat. What was said of the gamut holds strictly only of learned music, not of popular music. Learned music is based on a theory of musical entities and relations, which do not exist before the theory defines them; but that theory is ultimately derived from analysis of, and extrapolation from, preferred practices. Popular music, based directly on traditional prac-tices, precedes any such theory. A general theory of music must embrace both. Something similar is in principle possible for dance: that analysis of, and extrapolation from, preferred dance procedures might lead to the formulation of a 'dance theory' that defined a new system of entities and relations. It might then be held that anything outside the new system is not really dance at all, or is not worthy of attention by academics and professionals. It is possible, and something close to it has been held for ballet; but the claim has never been generally accepted. Accordingly, no analogy between tones in music and steps in dance can take us very far.

To see whether such an analogy can hold at all, we must look more closely at what a tone is. All tones in music are, as such, alike, differing only quantitatively. Any one tone may be defined by the number of vibrations per second required to produce it; any other tone may then be defined by how the number of vibrations required to produce it is related to that first number, and can be relevantly defined in no other way. Every tone is alike: a pure tone is generated by a sine wave (or, rather, in a way fully represented by a sine wave), and all sine waves are alike except in magnitude. In addition, a tone may be sounded for as long or as short a time as you please, and it is still the same tone (provided there is enough time for the rate of vibration to register on the ear). All tones are alike from this point of view, and it is this point of view that establishes the very concept of a tone. What is called 'absolute pitch' is not an ability to recognize tones by their character; it is an ability to recognize tones by their relationship to an established tonal centre, without any immediate context.

None of the above is true, or can be true, of dance steps.[31] A dance step is a movement of a body or a body part, and body parts have distinctive shapes. Not only do steps differ qualititively, they cannot differ quantitatively without also differing qualitatively, because they stretch and compress the body differently. Also, nothing in dance answers to the fact that an A held for a second is the very same tone as an A held for ten seconds. Poses can be held, but poses are not steps. Nor can we mend matters by saying that the unit in dance should be a pose, not a step (a step answering rather to a musical interval). The most that dance steps and musical tones have in common is that they are identifiably recurrent units. What makes music special is precisely what differentiates tones from steps – that tones are not only recognizably recurrent units but are, simply as tones, differentiated from other tones only by a ratio.

Steps can be the substance of dances, some of which can be thought of as simply sequences of steps, the quality of the whole resulting from their qualities and the patterns in which they are arranged. That is not true of tones, which are alike in themselves. What makes a tone the tone it is is its relation to other tones in a system, a scale; the substance of a tune is the sequence of relationships, of intervals. But intervals, like tones, differ only quantitatively and in being up or down. This indifference has no parallel in anything in dance. A fortiori, the scales that are the basis of musical form, being arrangements of intervals, differ only in the functions assigned to intervals of different sizes and in the relationships thus made possible. A tune may be transposed into a higher or a lower key without any formal change. There will be a real difference, though, because it will lie in a different range of the voice, impose different strains, or be produced by different bowings or blowings of instruments. These samenesses and differences are unique to music and have no analogue in dance or in any other art, and, so far as I can see, they could not have.

The basic features of musical form, then, have no dance analogues. Other aspects of musical form may. This must be because similar or corresponding relationships can hold within systems differently constructed; perhaps some of these will be common to large classes of formal systems, some will answer to necessities shared by all arts of performance, and some may even be shared only by music and dance. I will mention a few, without saying much about them.

Differences in key are watered-down versions of differences in mode. Different modes are different scales, with the intervals differently arranged; and, since scales have no dance analogues, modes shouldn't. And they don't, but differences in modes traditionally go with differences in affect, pieces in the same mode sharing a common emotive coloration. Modes also tend to go with, in effect to incorporate, different musical procedures and styles, as in Indian *ragas*. Is there here an analogue with any differentiation of dances? Not quite. A formal differentiation of structure between two named dances, such as branle and gigue, might indeed go with a difference in characteristic feeling tone and with different repertoires of gestures and gimmicks that go beyond the formal prescription of steps, but the analogy would be forced: the essential, the way the underlying metric was worked into the totality of the work, would not be there.

What about cadence? In music, certain sequences of tones within any given scale have architectonic implications, implying or precluding closure. In dance, too. But in dance the implication tends rather to be the outcome of the mechanics and dynamics. Not all positions are equally easy to start from, or to come to rest at. What goes up must come down. The cadential aspect of dances is built into them because of the way the general dynamics of movement is built into them. That is not true of music, because musical structures (as we have seen) have no inertia. The dynamic aspect of music that supports cadence is partly just 'the sense of an ending,' which is present in narrative and other literary structures as well, and partly a matter of returning to tonal centres and resolving discords, which are very specifically musical matters.

In melody we have a much closer analogy. A melody is just a tune, a recognizably unified sequence of tones. In a complex piece of music there may be a melody that can be picked out, not necessarily because it is emphasized by the way it is played or carried by a distinctive voice or instrument, but by its unity and melodic character. The basis of tune is singability, hence memorability. What about dance? If many people dance together, can there be (should there be) melodic lines? There may be a soloist whose dance has its own sequential unity within the ensemble, but a movement (like a hand-wave, or a droop) may well be passed around the corps from dancer to dancer, as it were a wave rising and falling. In music, however, melody is not just a possibility, it is a focus of musical interest. The corresponding feature in dance is only a formal possibility that may or may not be exploited.[32]

An influential school of musical analysis discovers that, in the musical works generally found most artistically satisfactory, everything in the work can be derived from a series of transformations of a basic idea, the *Ursatz*, fundamentally a cadence with its harmonic and melodic implications. Has this idea any application to dance? Not so far as I can see. If it has not, the way the relevant aspects of music (such as melody) work out must be radically different from the way their supposed analogues work in dance.

What about counterpoint? There seems to be an analogy, in that linear elements in dance can be combined with and played off against each other no less than in music. But in music the requirements of blending and contrast, dissonance and consonance, among melodic lines generate and define contrapuntal form. Musical counterpoint depends on essential homogeneity. The closest and most natural dance analogue is dancers dancing together, each dancer constituting one 'line.' But dancers are individuals, and the relations between them must be the variations of human encounter, which is not the same thing at all. We can certainly say, however, that a dance movement enshrines contrapuntal relationships; no doubt a choreographer of deep musicianship could mine musical practice for a host of specific procedures and effects for which analogues would suggest themselves.

At last, harmony. Harmony started life (in Greek) as a general word for fitting together. Music is harmonious to the extent that the bits that are sounded simultaneously go together right.[33] Rightness is partly a matter of sounding nice and partly a matter of meeting the requirements (internalized by those who share the musical culture) for proper fit and sequences of fit. Some combinations sound discordant, by which we mean, or ought to mean, not so much that they sound nasty as that they are felt to require a certain sort of combination (their 'resolution') to follow them; some sound concordant, not so much nice as stable in the sense that no follow-up is required. There are theories of harmony, having to do with the way things vibrate, which explain which combinations sound concordant and which don't. The theories also give reasons for the difference. The explanations tend to be a bit iffy, ascribing to the nature of human hearing things that turn out to be no more than passing fashions of tolerance and intolerance; but, be that as it may, theories of harmony within our tonal system are elaborate and precise. Dance combinations can be experienced as harmonious or inharmonious: dancers, steps, styles, other aspects of dance can fit well together or may clash, jar, fall apart. Dances have a melodic aspect of linear rightness, a harmonic aspect of synchronic rightness. But there is no such theoretic underpinning as music has: the precise explanations and prescriptions of music theory rest on the numerical relationships underlying the combinations heard. The fittingnesses in dance have no such strict and unified basis but are radically heterogeneous. One cannot predict what will be felt to go with what, or to fight with it, or what reasons will be given to warrant these feelings. That is not to say that harmoniousness in dance is not subject to rational consensus; it is to say that it has no demonstrably single basis.

A resource of music is theme and variation: something is established as audibly recognizable, and the music is structured by recognizably changing that. Interest lies in the possible ways of altering something without making it unrecognizable. We have already seen that this resource is open to dance, and in the same way, since it depends entirely on our general cognitive skills and interests (§11.2).

A resource of music is timbre, instrumental and vocal colour. A tone is identified as a sine wave, but a tone as heard is generated by what answers to a curve complex and variable in outline; it is identified by the fundamental curve. Timbre is important in music just because of the way it varies without destroying the underlying tonality; the actual shape of the curve is of no interest to music theory. What about dance? No analogy, of course, since the concept of a tone has no dance analogue. But, since timbre is contributed by the peculiarities of the instrument and the way it vibrates, there is an analogy, to the extent that a choreographed sequence of steps will come out different as played on the bodies of different dancers. – It is a real problem for ballet that the success of the corps depends on eliminating body timbre, but the success of a soloist depends on restoring and enhancing it. The analogy has little interest, however.

Among dynamic properties in music, those that are properties common to all movement (or to all humanly interesting movement) as such are, of course, shared by music and dance: quicker and slower, smoother and jerkier. But what about loud and soft? Well, dance movements can differ by being more or less emphatic. But, as I said before, such differences tend to change the whole character of the movement, because they change the muscular tension, the impetus, and the human meaning of the movement. In music, too, a tone cannot be *just* louder than another without changing in any other way; but the differences are likely to be less noticeable, and less significant, than in dance.

One last relationship or contrast, not systematically related to the rest. Very broadly speaking, national musics differ from each other, and so do national dances. But people who discuss these differences usually say that the difference in musics reflects differences in the cadence and phrasing of languages, which are related to behavioural traits only indirectly, if at all;[34] whereas the difference in dancing, as we saw in §5.2, is often said to reflect differences in national work habits and conventions of address.

Before I started this survey of possible analogies between musical and dance structures, I was looking at the thesis that, just as the existence of tones and tonal relations and structures preempted the status of music, so the existence of a system whereby dances could be constructed out of steps might preempt the status of dance. But we now see that the system of tonality has a very distinctive character that gives it the status it has and that there is nothing like that in any dance we know, nor could there be. It might at most be true, I suggested, that in a society or cultural tradition in which there are dances made up of interrelated steps, there might be an artificial (gamut-like) repertoire of dance units systematically interconnected, such that nothing that was not so made up could readily be recognized as dance.[35] It might, but why would it be? Bickering between partisans of ballet and modern dance forms used to betray this sort of feeling, but it did not take the same form. The latter taunted the former with being hidebound and rigid; the former ridiculed the latter for being undisciplined and sentimental. But the real disagreement had to do with the underlying motivation of the dance. The trade-off, if any, seemed to be between precision and refinement (and hence beauty) on the one hand, and depth and expressiveness on the other – differences in the way the body is actually trained and moved, not in the presence or absence of a set of purely formal relationships.

Our discussion of tonality and its analogues has assumed that the 'tone' that is basic to music is to be defined as music theory defines it.

But people who hear music, and perhaps some people who make music at a certain level of naïvety, will think of tones simply as recognizable components of music. The late Zygmunt Adamczewski once said, in the course of imagining what a Heideggerian philosophy of music would be: 'You may hear sounds that will be tones *for you*.' He did not say what he took a tone to be. His discourse had been in terms of the supposed phenomenology of music as a mode of care. Clearly, people who know what a tone is, as an old-fashioned musician knows it, could hear a sound that would be a tone 'for them' only if they could relate it to the tonal system, or if they could extrapolate a tonal system from it and hear it in relation to that system. But I suppose people who did not know music in that way could hear sounds that would be tones 'for them' if the sounds smiled along with their souls, or whatever the appropriate form of care would be. Even so, one might insist that really to hear a sound in that way would be to hear it as if it were part of a possible music, to hear the music through or beyond it, whether one realized one was doing so or not.

The same ambiguity, with the same partial resolution, could apply to dance. A movement can be a dance step for me if it does what dance does, and that must mean that it forms part of a possible dance, which I could sense through or beyond it. For it to form part of a possible dance, there must be other possible movements that would form parts (steps) of the same dance in the same way of dancing. What I accept as a dance step *for me* reflects what I know about dancing, the clarity with which I can envisage and accept continuations. If I know nothing about dance and am not any sort of a dancer, what can be a dance step *for me* does not amount to much, because being a step for me is nothing in particular – the catholicity of my acceptance is a function of the vagueness of my notion of what dancing is. And this vagueness in turn reflects my lack of interest in dance, the limited and impoverished extent of my dancing self.

CHAPTER THIRTEEN

Dance and Language

Nobody says you can't have dance without language, in the way that many people say you can't have dance without music. On the other hand, nobody says that dance is a form of music, unless they mean it as a metaphor. But it is common to say that dance is a form of language, and mean it – or think one means it. At the least ambitious level, what is meant is that dance, like all other cultural behaviour, is structured as a symbol system, and that natural languages are the paradigms of symbol systems, so that dance is just as much language as is music or the wearing of clothes. At its most ambitious level, one forces a parallel between dance and natural languages, looking for analogies between grammars and vocabularies on the one hand and dance systems and steps on the other.[1] The argument, or rhetoric, can go both ways.

One can say that language as we know it, dance, and music are specialized developments from an original body-language, including chant. Chant, when bereft of music and limb-movement, is articulated into speech; when bereft of conceptual content and limb-movement, it is modulated into music. The part of the original body-language that corresponds to gesture, when divorced from conceptualization and vocalization, is reduced to dance. But the original integrated means of expression is more of the nature of language than anything else.

Alternatively, one can say that what we call speech has been developed as a specialized dance, a dance of the tongue, from a dance of the whole body; originally, dance was as meaningful as vocalization, but as the dance of the tongue became specialized it took over the task of overtly representing concepts. That left dance to deal with the more global meanings, and with other meanings that for one reason or another could not be put into words.

The relations between dance and language are as multiply pervasive as those between dance and music, but in a quite different way. In the latter case, we find ourselves seeking analogies between musical phenomena and dance phenomena as though there were a special affinity between them. In the former case, it is rather that humans are spectacularly language-using animals, so that any human activity can be discussed from the point of view of the ways language enters into it.

'We now understand,' says Drid Williams, 'that both dancing and deaf-signing are simply different categories of non-vocalized communication systems, and that dances, no less than sign languages, are "... closed systems of mutually agreed, and therefore artificial signs"' (Williams 1991, 72, citing Henson 1974, 10). I do not think we do understand that; it may be wholly true of some dances and partly true of most, but as a generalization what it suggests is quite wrong.[2]

We have already seen that, because of the multiplicity of the reality of human being, a dance as an artistic spectacle must have an indeterminately many-layered nature: visual pattern, physical objects in motion, animal body movement, interplay of social animals, humans in many corporeal and social relationships (cf. §6.2). Different dances will emphasize or suppress one or more of these, in whole or in part, and make them differentially available to different observers.

We can now add that, insofar as dance is language-like, an artistic dance composition will probably be many-layered in the same sort of way that a literary composition is, embodying radically different sorts of meaning in different ways, as in the analyses of Roman Ingarden (1931) and Northrop Frye (1990). Corresponding to the kinds of meaning unravelled by Frye in the Bible (the most heavily interpreted of all literary compilations), we might find several levels: simple statement, individually satisfying units of movement; factual assertion, a formally consistent complex of movement throughout a piece; dialectic, a logical articulation of interrelated episodes; rhetoric, a pattern of rhythmic emphases and repetitions building up an effect; ideology, a systematically closed form with no room for incident or ornament; imagination, a level at which every movement is metaphorical, a 'virtual' reality, and the entire dance is a metaphoric whole, a unified meaning-world of its own; and, finally, an analogic level, at which the dance functions as a vehicle of piercing revelation, as though of some other order of reality.

I do not know whether such a sketch of a Frye-based analysis could be carried through, or whether it would carry conviction if it did; but some such scheme should be as possible for dance as Frye's is for literature.

13.1 Verbal Mediation

Among all the ways in which dance can be meaningful, some meanings are directly mediated by language and some are not. It can be made out that all meanings are indirectly mediated by language, in that our whole way of handling information is moulded by and saturated with language-use, our world is a world for language-users; but never mind that. So pervasive a truth would defy articulation. What concerns us here is, rather, the simple fact that some things have to be explained and some don't, some things can be put into words and others can't. With other things again, you don't have to explain, but it helps; with yet other things, you can put them into words, but it spoils everything if you do.

Some of the words and concepts whereby we mediate dance meanings are expressive; some are mimetic; some are formally descriptive in various ways. People may dance dances of spite, of love, of despair. They may dance lovingly, spitefully, despairingly, in ways full of affect to which neither dancers nor audience put names, and for which perhaps they have no names to put if they would; but they also dance in ways that say 'spite' or 'love' or 'despair' to those who have these concepts, and who put their feelings into them as if they were boxes. Again, someone may dance a dying swan, a dance that can be recognized for the dance it is only by those who recognize that it is 'a swan' and that what it is doing is 'dying.'

I have quoted Balanchine's law, to the effect that there are no sisters-in-law in ballet (§4.2122 and chapter 4 note 19). But there could be. If the dancer knows the named kinship-relations of the characters danced, and the audience knows them too – and there is no reason why audiences should never have this knowledge, even if there are other artistic and historical contexts that systematically preclude it, or discount it – then their shared knowledge of the affective dynamics that such relationships can engender (or are supposed to do, according to the literary and dramatic conventions of the day) makes available to them a whole range of nuances of meaning in movement, a complex of implied deferences and dominations, affections and aversions, prohibitions and permissions, that may shape the cohesiveness of the dance.

More directly, a dance may be articulated in whole or in part as a complex of named parts, specified dimensions and directions. No one supposes that 'arabesque' is a kind of movement whose identity is independent of its having that special name. But it is also true that the factual difference between jumping and sliding acquires a certain sharpness from our having and regularly using the specific words 'jumping' and 'sliding' to identify the classes of movement in question.

It is not only by the naming of feelings, of objects, of relationships, and of movement types that speech may be used to designate movements, and thus affect their choice and their course in ways that would not be possible without language. Where naming fails, metaphor and simile serve to indicate both steps and styles. 'Think of ... ,' 'It is as if you were ... ' (cf. §4.2124). Such language can guide the imagination to envisage what a choreographer has envisaged, or what a dance-teacher requires. Among Balanchine's many talents was an ability to think up a situation or a likeness that would suggest to his dancer the required nuance of pose and style. And a choreographer's discourse on the course of a ballet's intended story or significance may be necessary to show the dancers how the dance is to go, if they are to dance it as it was meant to be, rather than simulate it movement by movement. 'It helps enormously to put the words into your steps,' I have heard Makarova say on just this theme.[3] Many things can be shown but not said, and some things can be said but not shown (as a non-dancer may tell a dancer how to dance, and the dancer may guess what is meant – if it is a possible way of dancing).

Is it really possible to teach a dance without words? Perhaps it is; but only, I would think, if one has used words beforehand to establish the routine, so that the learner knows what in the teacher's demonstration is to be copied, what is to be modified, what is to be avoided, where it is to be understood, and where it is to end. I suppose a good teacher could give a class to students without knowing one word of their language, but it would be a desperate measure, and one would have to resort freely to sign language. Even phrases such as 'like this,' many would argue, are complex verbal mediations: the student must know what to copy and what not to copy, must supplement the 'like this' with the appropriate 'not like that.'

It is in teaching that the place of language in articulating dance movement is most directly evident. Language is a short-cut to the articulation of a skill, with generalization and explanation doing the work of endless sets of demonstrations. But what about other dance relationships? Well, what the teacher says in words the learner must understand in words, obviously. The dancer, when the dance is learned, may have committed the dance to the memory of the body, and verbalize only incidentally as by counting under the breath or reciting inwardly the narrative of a description of the dance, or self-exhortation and self-reproach. Even so, the way the dance was verbally articulated in the first place must govern the way it is held in memory. The body's memory is a wonderful thing, but I don't know whether it can cope with contingencies, and I suppose a dancer's activity is controlled by a set of hierarchies of choice that are conceptually articulated: no matter what, this particular sequence must end up with the dancer upstage left in time for the next solo, and so on. In any complex work, such articulations must take precedence over details of choreography and niceties of quality and style.

In choreography, alongside unverbalized kinaesthetic or visual ideas, there may well be other verbalized, conceptual notions of an architectonic sort. Sequences of choices, too, are framed in verbal terms, so that they are partly shaped by the very availability of the language – 'Three *pas-de-bourrés*, and then two of those things I showed you yesterday, and then do like *this*.' And then, however the dance was conceived, there is the filter of language when the dance is actually to be taught to the dancers. Whatever cannot be clearly or fully shown (for few choreographers are the dancers they once were[4]) must somehow be said – or conveyed by sheer power of personality.

Critics have their own language. That in a dance which the critic can describe has a head start, as it were.[5] Like practitioners of any trade, most critics are incompetent; but not all are, and the words they find may show us what to see. In theory, a good critic's vision (or a bad critic's blindness) might be ingested by dancers and dance-makers and add a new layer of self-understanding to the dance, even if there is nothing in the critique that is useful as advice. In practice, I don't know. Nor do I know how, in general, the practice of theatre dance is affected by this ever-present atmosphere of verbalized public judgment.

Audiences also have their languages. They have names for some of what they see, no names for the rest, and how they see will depend partly on what names they find applicable. If the audience know a language for dance that is different from the one the dancers know, what the audience see may surprise them and, through them, the dancers.

13.2 Gesture

Dance used to be called the art of gesture. The idea probably was that dance was meaningful movement of the body, and any such movement was to be called gesture, as opposed to merely mechanical movements or meaningless gesticulations. Dance as an art was neither meaningless (however stunning or beautiful) nor a means to some practical or mystical end, but existed to convey a meaning. In Indian dance terminology and traditional theory, a distinction is made between *nrtta*, a purely aesthetic dance appreciated for its beauty, and *nrtya*, expressive dance, conveying emotion (typically, the emotive and other meaning of an accompanying text) and centred on those parts of the body whereby we communicate meanings and feeling to each other: face, eyes, hands (§3.77 above; Iyer 1993).

There is a difference between conveying a meaning and being meaningful. All sorts of facial expressions, movements of hands and arms, even shiftings of the body are meaningful; they reveal to us the quality of experience and will of the moving person, without our being able to say in words what it is that is conveyed. But there are also gestures, especially of the hands, that convey meanings that have verbal equivalents.

At one extreme are the finger signs that correspond to letters, phonemes, and common words and that approximate to alternative ways of spelling out linguistic items that are already decided on. The difference between using such signs and talking is like that between talking and writing, they are just alternative media for conveying information in a language. Each medium has its own properties; they are not strict equivalents, and they call for different linguistic skills; but the language is the same, and the information conveyed by one can be conveyed by the other without change or loss. At the other extreme, perhaps, are the gestures of different modes of mime or pantomime, in which there is no vocabulary or syntax as such, but what is conveyed is something that could equally well be put in words, something that functions as it does by being conceptually articulated – 'Go away,' or 'I'm married,' or 'I have to go to the bathroom,' or 'He's crazy.'[6] One can make a dance out of any such material, or incorporate it in a dance, by performing the relevant movements in a way recognized as having a dance quality, or in a context that makes them into dance; though a practice in which they were the whole, or even the focus, of a dance practice might strike us as a bit odd.

Central among practices based on dance-constituting gesture is the classical Indian dance, with its conventionalized dance gestures, *mudras*, mentioned in §4.2124. There are dozens of these; some of them are based on a visual equivalent of onomatopoiea, but all are essentially arbitrary in that their meanings are ascribed by the tradition and have to be learned as one would learn any vocabulary.

Mudras are linguistic items, but they do not function in the same way that words do. Words function as they do because language consists of nothing *but* words and because words are connected syntactically in a way that requires them to hold their meaning constant in a variety of relations: the flexibility of grammar can be exploited only if we admit a certain rigidity in our semantics. A speaker is speaking, a writer is writing, and each of these operations depends on the manipulation of word meanings. But dancers are not speaking or writing, they are dancing, even if they tell a story in doing so; as we saw in §4.2124, the actual use of *mudras* is as much like that of a musical leitmotif as it is like that of a word. As with a Sino-Japanese ideogram component, a *mudra* has a name and a definition, but that is not related in any simple way to what it means in a dance in which it is used: rather, it is a sort of rooted meaning-cluster. Its actual reference may depend on its context in the dance, as the actual meaning of the 'radical' in the ideogram is relative to the actual ideogram it occurs in, though some radicals have more distinctive and robust identities than others. The sense of the *mudra* depends, too, on the position of the hands, their relation to the other parts of the body, and the way the body is moving.

If all this is so, the specific meanings of the *mudras* as they occur in dances is certainly linguistically mediated, but it is not linguistically articulated or linguistically controlled. It is a form of linguistic communication entirely dependent on dance and existing within dance. A *mudra*, at most, comes close to having the meaning of a sentence in which the word corresponding to its definitional identity occurs.[7]

The long and short of it is that dances all over the world embody impersonations and convey narratives. These are likely to be the stated reason for doing the dance at all; they are even more likely to be the reason for the way the dance is done. That being so, the dancers and dance-makers will avail themselves of all conceivable resources to get the impersonation or the story across. Their ways of dancing are likely to incorporate devices that, in one way or another, convey linguistic meanings. A dance or a piece of music can only illustrate a story, it cannot actually tell the story – unless a form of actual linguistic description or narrative is incorporated in the presentation of the work.[8] If the worst comes to the worst, the characters can have their names written across their chests, or dance with placards conveying necessary history. You can say it isn't dancing, and it certainly isn't all that subtle, but who says we have to be subtle all the time? And what is the point of saying that it is not dancing, if the dance-makers and their audiences all agree that it is?

13.3 Dancing and Talking

A dance, I said, like a piece of music, can only illustrate a narrative, it cannot constitute it. But musicians who play piano or guitar, or other instruments that one plays to oneself in solitude, think otherwise. There is a sense in which one talks to oneself through the music, or in which the music talks to one. The music one plays is a narrative in which one lives as one lives in a soliloquy or a conversation, not a narrative *about* anything, but a narrative structure that is its own subject; because one is for the time living in the music, even living *as* the music, the music becomes the narrative of one's own being.

It is often said that verbal narrative is essential to our lives, that our lives have a shaped unity only because we are constantly telling ourselves the story of our past and future (cf. §11.1 above). Our self-knowledge, and hence our human existence, are in this way verbally mediated. If we accept this idea, and add to it what we have just said about living in and through music, it follows that our human existence is, for the time being and in some of its aspects, mediated not by a linguistic structure but by a musical structure that is in some crucial respects language-like.

Can we say the same of dance? Not of all dancing, I suppose, but there could be a mode of meditative dancing of which something of the sort would be true. Such a dance would be language-like, then, not because it could be translated into verbal discourse, and not because it had grammar and vocabulary (or close analogues thereof), but because we could be lost in it as we are lost in talk: because it could constitute, for the time and in one respect, the narrative of our lives.

What are the features that make that possible for music? As we play to ourselves, we can continue, elaborate, simplify, repeat, confirm, deny. We can hurry and slow down, we can wonder and wander and explore, we can contradict and subvert, we can cap our own stories and mock our pretensions, we can hasten and withhold what comes next, we can dawdle and look around. It is like walking through a landscape, or engaging in a dialectic or a rumination.

Is the same true of dance? Not quite the same, or people would have noticed it of dance as clearly as they have of music. But something of the sort should be possible. There is a huge difference, though. As I noodle on the piano, making my way alone through the landscape of my musical mind, you can come into the room and join me, for you will hear me as I hear myself, and you will recognize as I do the shape of my journey. But can that be a common experience in dance? Not if it is more usual for an artistic dancer to dance with a visual effect in mind – an effect that is directly accessible only to others. In that case, if I dance for myself alone, then, when you join me, my dance is not directly accessible to you as it was to me. I return to this conundrum in §§17.3 and 17.5 below.

Where does this leave us? It suggests that the dialectic and rhetoric of talk have a close analogue in music, a far less close analogue in dance. In any case, the matter is relevant to the topic of this chapter only if the linguistic version really is primary, so that solitary dance or pianism is modelled on the soliloquy of a self-making narrative. And is that true? I doubt whether it is really true even in the comparison with music, though it is easy to make a loose sort of argument – as, in fact, I did. In the comparison with dance, the case has yet to be made.

13.4 What Is Language?

13.41 Learning to Speak, Learning to Dance

Plato (Laws II 653D–E) speaks of an infant's lalling, its exuberant use of its vocal apparatus, as analogous to its prancing and gambolling, its exuberant use of its limbs. Once more, dance and speech are parallel: each of them is the developed and articulated version of an originally inchoate form of activity. But the parallel may not be exact. We may feel inclined to say that a child is, in a sense, already dancing when it just prances around, especially when it does so for its adults. A child who has acquired generalized muscle control has already learned all it needs to know in order to dance, though it has learned no dance, has acquired no specific dance skill, and does not really know what dance is, does not know which of its movements should be combined in what ways to be dance.[9] If I have the ordinary sort of control over my muscles, the sort I need to do everyday practical things, I am certainly not thereby rendered able to dance ballet, my body is not trained for that; but there are dances I am able to do, just by knowing which motions I have to go through.

The situation with learning a language is not quite like that. We will not ordinarily say that a child is talking when it is still only lalling or gabbling, not even when its lalling and gabbling begin to contain word-like formations, however often it repeats them. It is not talking at all until it definitely means something by its proto-words and uses them in ways that show a grasp of what it is to address others and be addressed by them. The child at one and the same time learns language and learns a language, and cannot do either without doing the other. In speaking a language, I am not just using a special skill in deploying basic abilities that I already have: linguistic competence is itself the basic ability. There is no such thing as dance competence, at least not in relation to the general notions of dance we generally operate with: there is no such thing as the ability to generate all and only well-formed dance movements.

One thing I do not know is the extent to which linguistic competence, to which so much of the human cerebral cortex seems to be dedicated, is strictly tied to the innervation of the specific bodily apparatus we use to talk with. If it is so tied, people who are dumb from birth will be able to use other means of linguistic communication only by somehow pressing into service the bits of the brain that normally operate the tongue and so forth. But, in any case, linguistic skill is a special set of fundamental encoding and decoding skills, and no such special set of skills seems to be involved in dancing.

In these matters, clearly, I speak as an ignoramus. I simply point to this problem as one in which there is truth to be learned and clarification to be achieved.

13.42 Language as Language

Dance is a sort of language, people say; language is a sort of dance. But the expression 'sort of' covers a multitude of mental sins.

We would expect an anthropologist visiting an unfamiliar tribe to have no more difficulty in recognizing when the tribe (or its members) were dancing than when they were talking (Sparshott 1988, §5.4). One might not know the language, one might not be able to appreciate the dance; but nothing is like language except language, and nothing is like dance except dance.

There are problems with that analogy. For one thing, it does not apply to the avant-garde. The uninitiated cannot always recognize their dances, because part of their point is that they reject the conventional characteristics of dance. They rely on the fact that to count as dance is to be related in some definite way to the established institutions of the art of dance; they derive their dance status, and hence their dance quality, from a conceptual and historical context that may not be available to all observers.[10] Can a stretch of behaviour similarly be unrecognizable (to the uninitiated) as language, because its linguistic meaning and status depend on unobservable features of the context? Hardly. One is using a language or one is not, the syntax and semantics decide. On the other hand, spies and spy-catchers know that a stretch of language-use may be unrecognizable, if it is carefully coded so that its linguistic structure is rendered unapparent – as was supposed to be the case with Sherlock Holmes's 'Dancing Men,' but wasn't, because the disguise was too thin. Could anything of a corresponding sort be true of dance? Could there be a *concealed* dance? One doesn't quite see how: it is the overt features of the dance that constitute the relevant code; signifier and signified are not arbitrarily conjoined (as they are supposed to be in a language).

If I see some people dancing, I can join their dance, or try to, though I am likely to make a fool and a nuisance of myself. It has happened to me, and probably to you: someone grabs your arm and says 'come on!' and you're dancing before you know it. If you are lucky, you pick up enough of the movements quickly enough to join in. Nothing like that is true in language. You simply cannot join in a conversation in an unknown language; you can only grunt and grin like a fool. If you and someone else don't know any of each other's language and want to communicate, you have a problem. Missionaries and anthropologists have their ways, and parachutists from alien skies contrive somehow, but it is a slow and tricky business. Someone who is dragged into an unfamiliar dance is immediately dancing, but dancing very badly; but can people plunged suddenly into the midst of a conversation in a foreign language find themselves immediately talking in an unknown language, however badly?

To deal properly with the questions I have been raising, I would need to say clearly what language is. How could I do that? It would take a library, and I would have to start my career over again. Different scholars offer different criteria, but these have little in common beyond their claims to unique authority and adequacy. Let me just suggest twenty or so features that seem to me to characterize language, and see if dance matches them.

(1) Language is linear: word follows word, sentence follows sentence. It is pretty well impossible, mentally as well as physically, to say two things at once. It is very hard to listen effectively to two people talking at once. Is anything like that true of dance? Not really. A dance may consist of several independent movements performed simultaneously by one or many people, and there is no difficulty in watching a group of dancers dancing together but differently. The only limit is the general one, that one cannot attend to too many diferent things at once. The unilinearity of speech seems to be of a different order.

(2) Language is not only functionally linear, but strictly and structurally so. Two words simultaneously uttered do not constitute a single utterance, let alone a single word. In a dance, two steps performed simultaneously by two dancers do not constitute a single step, but I don't know that there is any principle of dance structure that determines whether they can coalesce into a single movement or not.

(3) Language is essentially segmented, strictly divided into letters and syllables, or into phonemes and morphemes and such. Except for the affective tonalities, it is all basically digital beneath the analog surface of speech. Nothing like that is true of dance, as notaters find. Even in a dance or dance style that depends on articulation into separate steps, the notater usually has to decide exactly where the divisions come. Typical dances are fundamentally analog, the digital aspects representing a sort of theoretical overlay.

(4) The basic segments of speech are limited in number. Every language exploits only a small number of phonemes: if a sound is to count as part of language, it has to be assigned to one of these sets of alternatives. A dance or a dance style can be limited in that sort of way, but no such limitation is characteristic of dance as such.

(5) The segmentations at different levels of the hierarchy of language differ radically. A phoneme has no meaning, the morphemes made up from phonemes are meaningful but have no independent meaning, the words or sememes made up from morphemes have definable meanings and can be freely combined according to rules very different from those governing word-formation. Words have meanings but do not say anything; the sentences in which words combine say things, and may be true or false. In dance, by contrast, though basic movement types may be combined into minimal dance units, which may in turn be combined into admissible sequences, the increment of meaning at each level tends to be merely cumulative.[11]

(6) Sentences have moods – indicative, subjunctive, optative, impera-

tive, and so on. And they may have quite different functions, such as questioning, asserting, praying, and commanding. These can all be clearly differentiated by their formal properties, by sentence shape or word modification. No such distinctions play any formal part in dance structure, anywhere that I know of: one can dance as if one were asking a question, but dance has no question marks, no inversions of order, no interrogative particles or pronouns, among its regular resources. Perhaps most important, dance incorporates no negations.[12] As for anything corresponding to the moods of verbs, I cannot imagine how dance could accommodate anything like that.

(7) Languages have tenses, which are time indicators of various complicated sorts: one can speak unambiguously of what will have been, what had been, what would be. One can say things in the active voice, or the same things can be said in the passive voice. Different languages have different resources in this area, and I have not the least idea what the world-wide picture looks like; but these are, in general, typical features of language. No dance has anything like them.

(8) Many words have synonyms, and a stretch of language can often be paraphrased. True, no words are exact synonyms: there are no pairs of words such that one can be substituted for the other for *all* purposes and in all contexts, and no paraphrase catches all the nuances of its original; but, in practice, paraphrasing and looking for synonyms are things teachers and writers do all the time. So do the rest of us. 'Let me put that another way,' we say. Summarizing is another thing we can do in language, presenting the gist of what we said, and summaries can sometimes be summarized – though we reach a point where it becomes doubtful whether further summary is possible, and a point where it certainly isn't. These phenomena are characteristic of language. Are they peculiar to it? I think they are, if only because they are defined as being so. But do they have analogues in dance close enough for us to say that their absence from dance rests on a mere terminological decision? I doubt it. One step can be substituted for another, freely in some dances, through necessity (from injury, for instance, or lack of skill) in others; but, though the substitute in such cases fills the same niche in the dance structure, it is not clear to me that it ever *means* the same. The question is whether it fits, not whether it is a semantic equivalent. As for summarizing, that probably can be done, though I do not recall instances at the choreographic level. A long and intricate dance sequence could be replaced or followed by a shorter and simpler version that preserved the basic structure and hit the high spots, as it were. What would

almost certainly be missing would be the informative function of the linguistic analogue, the idea that one was trying to get the same meaning and message across by alternative means. At the dancer's level, in contrast, something that might be called summarizing is common, in the form of 'marking': a dancer in rehearsal or in a study session may substitute for a complex and strenuous passage a simpler and less demanding movement or gesture, indicating that the dancer knows what would be done at this point in performance but sees no point in busting a gut here and now. One might argue, however, that the dancer who does this is not offering a précis of the omitted movement but simply alluding to it.

(9) That difference may remind us that speech is necessarily meaningful. You are not really speaking if you are not saying anything. If I doubt that you mean anything at all by what you utter, I am in doubt as to the linguistic status of your utterance.[13] Again, linguistic form supports meaning. In a piece of well-formed nonsense we feel we know what shape its meaning would have if it had any. 'Pirots carulize elatically' was an example logicians used when I was young – the 'words' are made up, but they are clearly a plural noun, an intransitive behaviour-indicating verb in the present tense (agreeing with the noun, so that the noun is its subject), and an adverb of manner, indicating what sort of carulizing pirots do. So far as I know, the only dance forms that support meaning in that sort of way are hand gestures like *mudras;* and even in them the support is weak, for the grammar (the accidence) is missing. And although it may be true that you are not really dancing if you aren't dancing anything, what you would have to be dancing if that were true would be a dance, not a meaningful content.

The general question of 'grammaticality,' as a metaphorical aspect of dance and music, will be touched on again in §18.4.

(10) Languages are or may be opaque to each other, but translation from one to another is usually possible in practice. If one language lacks an expression that the other has, a measure of explanation and periphrasis is usually possible. Translation is no doubt indeterminate beyond a certain point, because the systems of differentiation in two different languages can hardly coincide, but up to a point it works well enough. Adequacy in translation is something on which informed consensus can often be reached, and rational discussion is possible. In dancing, things are different. Two different styles (or methods, or traditions) of dancing are not so much mutually opaque as mutually different, immiscible, and

incompatible. People who speak different languages will often swap equivalences in vocabulary, and even in grammatical devices or proverbs; but, if I see you dance something, I do not know what it would be for me to show you how we do 'the same thing' in our way of dancing.

(11) In language, visual and oral presentations of the same text are equivalent. In a perfectly plain sense, the written version says the same thing as the spoken version.[14] I can write down whatever you say; I can read aloud or recite whatever you write. But dance can only be danced. The notation for a dance is not a dance; what makes the dance a dance is the actual moving of a weighty and muscular frame, trainable and subject to sweat and injury.

(12) Items of language are not, as such, causally interrelated with their predecessors and successors. What I say immediately after saying something is not causally affected by what I just said. My mouth will have to get into position for the next phoneme, and so on, but these changes are even less part of the language than the movements of stage-hands are part of a drama, and no one takes account of them. Some combinations of sounds may be unpronounceable, but languages get around that by setting up modification rules to avoid the clash, or simply by excluding them in the first place. Nothing quite like that is true of dance. The impetus of a movement carries over into the next, or ends in a rest from which the body must start again. Transitions and preparations are part of the dance, even if not an emphasized part.

(13) In language, strict equivalence among tokens of the same type (such as phonemes) is preserved amid wide diversity at the phonetic level. Nothing quite like that necessarily holds of dance, I think. Dancers have their own styles, but the style may affect the substance of the dance in a way that phonetic variation never affects the phonemic constancy on which linguistic identity and mutual intelligibility depend. However, I do not know quite what is the right thing to say about this.

(14) According to what I have remembered and understood of Foucault, language depends on representation. For everything that is said, there is some state of affairs, actual or envisaged, to which it relates and which it arbitrarily traverses: whatever is said is always said about things about which there is always *more to be said*. Our words refer to ideas and entities that in principle go beyond what we call them and what we say about them. Nothing quite like that is true of a dance. Since a dance need not be mimetic at all, no restrictions can be put on the sort of mimetic significance it might have.

(15) Simple sentences tend to have either the form fA or the form ArB

– that is, they either assign a predicate to a subject or state a relation between two entities. In a simple sentence, there is usually at least one referent, and usually one of the referents is the subject of the sentence, what the sentence is about. No doubt there are languages of which that is not true, but I would suppose that those languages also have systems for marshalling facts in basic statements. Whether I am right about that or not, I cannot think of anything of the sort that holds of dance.

(16) Dictionaries can be and are compiled. Not only phonemes, but words as well, are limited in number and determinate in identity. Something comparable could be true of dance, on a limited scale.

(17) The vocabularies of languages are not restricted to nouns and verbs, not even if adjectives and adverbs are added. They contain conjunctions, particles, demonstratives, indexical signs – what used to be called syncategorematic expressions. Without these, languages could not work as they do; I know of nothing in dance that corresponds to them.

(18) Though linguistic utterances are linear and dances are not, the overt syntax of a sentence need not be identical with its deep structure. Nothing like that is true of dance. In dance, what you see is what there is. There is no transformational grammar of dance.

(19) Language in principle *contains* life and knowledge. There is no restriction on what can be known, and no restriction on what can be said. Though there is lots of room for ineffability, language in one way or another encompasses the world. There would be no point in making such a claim for dance, except in relation to specifically cosmogonic or cosmological dances – the dance of a god who dances the world into existence must be comprehensive in its scope. But that would be a divine dance, and the languages of which I am speaking are ordinary, human languages.

(20) Finally, or in summary: each natural language is the chief means of general communication among the members of some human society, and each human society has one natural language as its chief means of general communication. Each member of a society achieves mastery of that language without formal instruction. Any departure from this pattern – bilingualism, aphasia – is pathological, requiring a specific explanation of why the normal pattern has been departed from. No such norm obtains in the domain of dance. There may be societies with one characteristic dance, and there are dances that are specific to a particular society, and there may well be societies in which everyone learns the local dance without having to be taught; but these are exceptional occurrences admitting historical explanations, not the normal state

of affairs. Nor is it the case that dances serve any such overall and pervasive purpose as the communicative function that language fulfils.

The preceding paragraph was written on the understanding that natural languages (and their imitations, such as Esperanto) are the only languages there are. Anything not a natural language is a language only by courtesy. The restriction of language to these all-pervasive, all-purpose media of communication is not just a verbal convention, an arbitrary decision on my part. It is an important, striking, and obvious fact about humans that they use languages of that sort in that way. The ways languages relate to each other, the ways they change historically, are distinctive. Dances, dance forms, and dance traditions are not at all like that. Are they?

13.5 The Semiological Extension

The disanalogies between dance and language are fundamental. But so, it has been argued, are the analogies. It is true that the analysis of dance structures into least discriminable units, least meaningful segments, least danceable units, and least independent sequences, which seems to correspond to the linguistic distinction among letters, syllables, words, and sentences, offers no true analogy, because the linguistic series represents radical differences in function in a way that the dance series does not. But a series such as Kaeppler's sequence of kineme, morpho-kineme, motif, and genre does have a structure analogous to that of a linguistic series, and makes its own sense in terms of how dancers conceptualize and perform their dances.[15]

Alan Megill remarks that the linguistic nature of dance and other systems of communication may be denied on the grounds that nothing in these non-linguistic systems corresponds to the sentence, but may be affirmed on the grounds that they are what they are because they constitute Saussurian systems of signs.[16] If we accept this suggestion, the analogy with language becomes entirely heuristic. Natural languages are the best-articulated and most closely studied sign systems we have and are thus rich in patterns and methods for which, or for analogues of which, dance organization may be scanned. But the real question remains how dance communication does in fact work, and there is no reason to expect the specific structures of language to be replicated in it. The question has to be asked at three levels, that of the scenario and the social context, that of the choreographic design, and that of the actual dancing. And at all three levels the conveyance of meaning may be direct and semantic, relating to something outside the dance at the appropriate level, or it may be variational and syntactic, having to do with the determinate way in which what is done differs from something else that might have been done instead. (It may be taken for granted that a meaning of the former kind must be mediated by a distinction of the latter kind, which has its own meaning, which might have been what was meaningful about it.)

If dance is language-like to the extent that a dance has a determinate meaning, one would expect that it can be notated to record what it is that determines the meaning. Ann Hutchinson Guest's account of the development of Benesh notation quotes Rudolf Benesh to show how hard it is to develop an appropriate language: 'The linguistic laws governing this stage are not fully understood. They are certainly not logical in the ordinary sense. It takes several years of working in the particular dance style before its language is fully understood in terms of notation.'[17] Kaeppler's analysis of Tongan dance shows how a specific dance style thus has its own language. But if all dance styles have their own languages, one should be able to say something in general terms about what dance language is. Is there anything in dance that corresponds to the universal grammatical structures that Chomsky (1983) argued must somehow be innate in all humans to make languge-learning possible? Guest thinks so: '[F]or the past twenty years and more the term "Language of Dance" has come to mean a deep understanding of movement through analysis of its basic content illuminated and reinforced by the use of the Laban system of movement notation. Movement has its own logic. The natural language of dance stems from the movement itself, that is, from the physical "syntax," the intent of the movement and the form that intention takes.'[18]

Reflection suggests, however, that the supposed universal language is not a sort of analogue of Chomsky's necessary linguistic competence, nor of the pre-linguistic coding whereby J.A. Fodor (1979) argued that information must be stored in the cerebral cortex, but a set of movement principles facilitated by certain factors in human physiology and psychology; and the claim to universality rests on the authority one allows to the formulations of Rudolf Laban – an issue in which scientific evaluation is bedevilled by the special pleading of politics and commerce. Dance notations themselves are certainly codifications, more or less systematically applicable to dance movement; what is at issue is whether their applicability is evidence of a pre-existing, codifiable structure somehow inherent in dance movement itself. I return to the issue in §§20.22ff.

How, in general, is dance encoded? What meanings are embodied in dances, and how? The task of enumerating the possibilities is in principle endless, because a dance is something people actually do, not an abstraction.[19] And it is something they do deliberately and self-consciously, involving therefore their full social and personal identities. That being so, a dance must actually reflect (must indeed embody) all the ways in which the society in which it occurs generally encodes things, must pass through the society's general filters of meaningfulness, its standard preoccupations and its standard means of processing data. But also, again because it is something actually done by fully social and human agents, it must reflect (not through embodiment but by analogy and reference) all the ways in which the society *can* encode things, all the dimensions of known and experienced meaningfulness.[20] Whatever a person does establishes a relationship with everything one's society conceives possible, if only by abstention. Not all these relationships are highlighted, but all enter or may enter into hierarchies of relevance – the status and determinacy of these hierarchies being itself a matter for discussion. Third, it must directly reflect all the relevant ways of encoding things of its sort, as revealed in analysis. The sort of thing I have in mind here is exemplified in Susan Foster's book on modern American theatre dance, *Reading Dancing*: one discovers a dimension of actual meaningfulness in a dance, and thereby discovers a dimension of meaningfulness in any dance, because one can always ask how the discovered theme is handled or ignored.[21] In the way that Arthur Danto (1964) has emphasized, making a possibility evident in one dance makes it retrospectively a possibility for all dances, even if, for historical reasons, no such possibility could be envisaged at the time.

I have been entertaining the suggestion that a society's understanding can be analysed into the codes that it uses and their interactions. But that suggestion can be misleading. For such understanding to be possible, humans must have more general abilities: to understand codes, to form them or participate in their formation, and to understand code-formation itself. We understand each other as fountains of code-generating and code-using behaviour. This flexibility is important in dance as a performing art (see chapter 14). A dance in public performance is, in effect, broadcast to an audience that includes connoisseurs, critics, and colleagues from one's own studio and others, as well as members of dance-going and concert-going publics at all levels of indoctrination and with all kinds of special interests. It must be so. This is not an occasional departure from some norm of reception; it is the very condition of public performance, the milieu in which alone dance as a performance art exists. Audience responses cannot be analysed into partial decodings: even if codes are known and agreed on, they will not be the sole determinants of responses rightly deemed relevant by the greater part of the audience. Similarly, in the composition and presentation of dances, promoters, choreographers, and dancers are code-using rather than code-bound; the dance is not less than the totality of what they do (cf. §§19.4ff).

I have been using the words 'code' and 'encoding' with some freedom. But they can be misleading, and I think they have misled many. They falsely suggest two things. First, they suggest that when something is found meaningful it is found so in terms of a set code (in much the same way, Nelson Goodman said that works of art were characters in a symbol system, as though there were an actually developed system in which they were characters). The *Oxford English Dictionary* suggests that 'code' originally meant a systematic collection of statutes, like the Justinian Code, and secondarily any set of rules, like the dress code of a restaurant, and was then applied to a set of military or other signals, like nautical signalling flags. In general, modern techniques for transmitting messages have left us with a fairly clear understanding of what a code is. It is a finite and explicit set of equivalences, like that of the Morse Code or the Chinese Telegraph Code. In the former, each digit and alphabetical sign has its equivalent pattern of short and long sounds or flashes (dots and dashes); in the latter, each of 5,000 ideograms is assigned a four-digit number. One can write the equivalences down in a table and use the table to encode or decode a message. But in modern discussions of meaning, 'code' is often used loosely or metaphorically, equivalences may be determinate or indeterminate, and there is nothing to determine what belongs to the supposed code and what does not. There is no prospect of compiling a table otherwise than as a work of fiction; everything that makes a code usable as a code vanishes, and we are left with a mishmash of ad-hoc observations and heterogeneous analyses.

The second false suggestion is that all meaningful communications are encoded. But, again, modern techniques for transmitting information have given prominence to a distinct idea of what encoding is. A complete and fully formulated message, in its original language or already transcribed from that language in some code or other, is put into an appropriate code according to a set of rules that determine the procedure, so that it can be transmitted by some means appropriate to the code – telegraphy, or semaphore, or wireless beam, or however it may be. The encoding will normally include devices to eliminate noise and to obviate it by redundancy, and probably to frustrate interception. When the message reaches its destination, it is decoded by reversing the procedure of encoding, using the same rules and the same tables. The outcome should be the message as complete and fully formulated, in its original language or in whatever other code it was encoded from.

In a dance, or in an ordinarily occurring use of language, or in most social transactions, nothing like this very special procedure is gone through. The dance as danced, or the speech as spoken, is in its original language; it is not encoded from a previous language or a previous code, for there is none. It is useless to say that something corresponding to dance or speech 'must be' somehow represented in the brain, for no identifiable procedure of encoding or decoding is actually gone through. Who would go through it? It is not just that nothing of the sort is known to happen. The point is that that is not what happens or could happen. For a dance to be a coded version of an original, the original would have to have all the value and meaning that the dance has, the dance as danced adding nothing of value except facility in transmission. The proposal is sheer nonsense.

Semiotics as such is and must be devoid of content, since it aspires to deal perfectly generally with all symbol systems alike. In practice, 'semiotics' is used as a label for the preferences of fashionable theorists, most commonly for the attempt to impose the model of Saussure's general linguistics on everything that can be thought of as conveying a meaning. As such, it is a desperately obscurantist venture. Semiotics is perhaps better thought of as a kind of interest, a topic, the topic of meaningfulness and the fullness of meaning. It stands for the determination to accept no arbitrary limits on the ways meanings can be conveyed. It is not and cannot be a research program. It is rather a call for attentiveness and inquisitiveness and for openness to whatever has been discovered and may be discovered in the field of communication.

One can certainly envisage a semiotics of dance that would take some existing scheme of semiotic analysis and apply it (perhaps in a Procrustean fashion) to some preferred range of dance practice. Such applications are usually instructive and can be illuminating if the theoretical tools are wielded with imaginative intelligence. One can also conceive of a semiotics of dance, more general than Foster's, that looked at a range of dance practice to see what meaning had been found or could be found there, looking to semiotic research for heuristic materials drawn from the widest possible range of communication systems, human and animal (and no doubt vegetable, mineral, mechanical, electronic ...), the semiotic tools serving less to impose a system than to liberate the researcher's mind from bondage to linguistic or other models that might otherwise preoccupy it. I have suggested above that the result would remain heterogeneous; but you never can tell.

CHAPTER FOURTEEN

Dance and Theatre

The kind of dance we buy tickets to see, the kind of dance that writers on aesthetics focus on, is theatre dance. It is a special kind of dance. It exists as a kind of show, transformed from an activity into a spectacle. We do not go to watch people dancing, as we might go to kibitz at a festival; we go to see them put on a show. We join an audience, all of whom have come with us to see that show, with critics who have come to criticize it. There have been rehearsals, and perhaps previews, and now there are the performances. Of course, the dance is not *presented as* being done *for* us, because our demand is that the dance shall be done for its own sake: we do not want to be condescended to. All the same, it is being done for us, because it is done in our presence, and would not be done at all if we were not there. Theatre dance has to be expressive, because it has to be visible to its audience as human activity; but it cannot be expressive in the romantic sense that it is validly derived from artistic integrity. In inviting an audience, the dance-makers are invoking the conventions of a public concert, a show that must go on even if the clown's heart is breaking – and, perhaps more significantly, even if the tragedian is in the best of health and spirits.

14.1 Performing Arts

As a theatre art, dance is *performed* for its audience. That is, the dancers are (as I have insisted) present in their full humanity, but with the implication that what the audience is to attend to is not the totality of what they are being and doing, but those parts and aspects of it that are tacitly understood and agreed to constitute the performance; or, alternatively, the audience is to attend to that totality, but under an interpretation, an interpretation that incorporates a powerful editorial component.

Some of the implications of this performance aspect of dance will be looked at in chapters 16 and 19 below.[1] Meanwhile, the basic conditions of all such performance arts have been worked out by Paul Thom.[2] The dancers or other performers must first agree on a 'reading' of the directives, scripted or implicit, that define what is to be performed; what they present in compliance with these directives is something to which they impart an emotive meaning of its own, something that will be meaningful to the audience that responds to them, and to whose response they themselves respond. Correspondingly, the audience are not passive receivers of a communication but attend to what is done in a way that Thom calls 'beholding': they are vigilantly and selectively – and, above all, playfully – responsive to everything that is going on, not only within the performance and the work but between that and the world outside.

What is essential to the performing arts, Thom argues, is this flexible bond between performers and audiences, so different from the determinate aesthetic object often postulated in theories of the fine arts in general. The bond itself, however, is not necessarily an object of attention. The conditions and conventions of presentation of theatre dance permit any or no overt attention to be paid to the audience. The dance may be broken down into items, each presented to the audience with an introductory courtesy and finished with a bow, or it may be done as if there were no one there but the dancers. It is a difference of conventions, not of inner attitude: nothing says that the dancer who keeps smiling at the audience and acknowledging their applause has to be paying any more attention to them than the dancer who appears lost in a spiritual exaltation of inner solitude. Both conventions are available because both forms of presentation are familiar in the theatrical context: the representational drama at which we are the missing 'fourth wall,' and the 'presentational theatre,' or song-and-dance show, in which the performers do their turns.[3]

It is not that the psychological differences are unreal, but that they need not correlate with the ruling convention. Some dancers are always vividly aware of the presence of an audience; others block it out, as a matter of personal artistic policy; others again may on some occasions be very conscious of the audience, at other times lose all awareness of it. In any case, what they do retains its double aspect, as a proper exercise of their professional skill and as a show. Part of the skill is to be putting on the right kind of show, and part of the show is to show the professionalism and the skill.

14.11 Problems of Presentation

The status of dance as performance art shows most familiarly in the relation between choreographer and dancer, which will be examined below (§18.1). In general, any dance performance calls for at least six questions.

(1) Who controls the presentation? Who is the entrepreneur or the patron, what bureaucracy exercises what oversight, how is the payroll met?

(2) What is the milieu? A concert stage, a club (devoted to dance, or to what?), a public space commandeered or donated for the occasion, a temple?

(3) At what clientele is the performance most directly and overtly aimed? The monarch, the nobility, colleagues, fellow-citizens, fair-goers, captive school-children, subscribers to a TV cable channel, the TV audience generally, critics, subscribers to a season of ballet or some other genre of dance?

(4) How is authority divided among scenarist, choreographer, composer, director, designer, stage manager, star performer, players' union, éminence grise?

(5) What are the rhetorical presuppositions of the performance? Is it to be taken as advocacy, neutral presentation, sincere and straightforward performance, parody, satire, send-up, quotation? These questions may be asked of the slippage, or lack of slippage, between any of the levels mentioned in the preceding paragraph.

(6) What is the relation between personal presence and professional performance, human action and aesthetic presentation?

It is not to be expected that we shall be able to give definite and stable answers to all these questions, and others like them; but our constant willingness to ask them is an essential element in what Thom calls our 'beholding.'

14.12 Theatre

Theatre dance is a kind of theatre, subject to the general conditions of theatre and to the particular forms that theatre admits at particular places and times. Basically, a theatre is a space cleared to be free for action and to be visible. Among us, it is in the first instance a raised platform – a wagon, a trestle, 'the boards,' a stage – on which people can do their thing at a fair or other place where people have come together on holiday. Jugglers, comedians, singers, acrobats, dancers. The theatre is the place where they are possible, and the condition of theatre is that set of expectations. Of course you can have a specialized concert or a drama or whatever you want, but the spectrum of the show maintains its force and is perpetually rediscovered. At its heart is the showperson, the carnival artist, the vaudevillean, who can dance a little, sing a little, juggle or walk a tightrope if need be, dance when a dancer is needed. The specialist, like specialized forms of theatre, emerges against the background of this traditional carnival culture in which (as in a hunting economy) each member is expected to have mastered the basic skills of the culture, except where some taboo forbids it.

The powerful fact of theatre makes all human resources available as material for a unified show. The dancing profession cultivates the most resourceful bodies, and has traditionally the strongest claim to universality of scope. Work movements and gymnastic exercises as well as pantomime are traditionally incorporated in dance along with specific dance movements and may be played with or seriously developed, presented as formal core or subsumed into a unity. Drama itself may be (as it were) melted down, speech and the appearance of speech exfoliating into a theatrical totality that can dance everything.[4] Dance nowadays often aspires to the condition of mixed media, fragments of film figuring in the totality as episode or background, or integrated into it as ingenuity and inspiration suggest. And mixed media shows at their best tend, I think, to be dancelike, if not actually to become dance, if only because the idea of dance involves that of an overall formal unity of human action, and it is dance-makers whose minds are attuned to this comprehensiveness of formal reduction. But it is dance as theatre that does this.

What I was describing or imagining above was temporary or itinerant theatre, theatre on the road. In the time of big cities, theatre becomes fixed, and its procedures become formalized. Theatre buildings approximate a single model, with auditorium and stage and backstage dressing rooms and flies and lighting boards and a management structure – and so on and on. A dance company uses the same equipment, the same methods of advertising and employment, the same methods of selling tickets and subscriptions. Those who attend dance performances come with the same expectations that they bring to other theatrical shows. Of course they come to see a dance and not a play or a concert, and the actual audiences for one form of art or entertainment are not made up of the same individuals who are the audience for another, but it is a familiar cultural form and the patterns are fairly constant. This situation is in strong contrast with what Richard Schechner (1988, 61) says happens in tribal societies, where special spaces are contrived for particular rituals: 'Nowhere do we find a permanent theatre or ceremonial place – a single structure whose shape is "neutral" and "adapted" to all uses. The closest we come to that is an open space for dancing, debating, trading, duelling, trysting. Or the whole village which is a stage for everything that goes on in and around it. Throughout the tribal world events make shapes. In many ceremonies the principal architectural element is people – how many there are, how and where they move, what their interactions are, whether they participate or watch or do both.'

To sum up, theatre dance belongs to theatre in three powerful ways: in its delicate artistic relation to an audience that is to be satisfied but not pandered to, in the way in which dancers belong to the world of show people with its interweaving of skills, and in the way in which dance operates within the powerful and complex institutions of theatrical presentation.

The dances presented in the powerful environment of theatre did not originate there, but in studios and workplaces of an altogether different character. I have heard an Indian dancer testify to the difficulty of moving from the temple where the dance was learned, with its close-set pillars, to the open space of public performance. Even if a dance was created and rehearsed on the performance stage, which seldom happens, the commitment to unfaltering execution before an independent audience of demanding strangers must change the whole nature of the proceedings. There must be a move from intimate intentness on the art to public display – the same move that led Glenn Gould and other musicians to eschew the vulgarizing pressures of the concert hall in favour of the recording studio.

Similarly, when a social dance is taken from the sacral or recreational locations of its spontaneous performance and mounted for a theatre audience, the nature of what the dancers are doing must be changed, try as they may to do only what they have learned. I remarked before how increasing attention to an audience transforms social and ethnic dances into spectacles; but, even without that, the theatre context itself effects a transformation. What may have been cheerful collaboration becomes visible celebration, a sort of manifesto, like that of the audience crowding onto the stage at the end of *Hair*. Writers know a comparable series of transformations, from holograph scrawl to typescript to proofs to bound and printed book, as a personal creation dwindles into one more burden for the remainder table, but this is much less traumatic than the plunge from studio to theatre. How do they manage? But it must be the magnitude of the transition that explains what we so often see on stage: dances and plays so inept that one would have thought the vainest and most besotted artist would have given up long before the dress rehearsal. Either it looked quite different among friends, or they vainly hoped it would look different on the night.

Theatre comprises distinct forms, but the omnipresent theatre culture works against any tendency for such forms to maintain their distinctness. If we look at any book on the nature of theatre or on theatre history, it is worth asking ourselves whether what it tells us is not directly applicable to theatre dance. When Jerzy Grotowski (1968) contrasts an 'impoverished' theatre, in which players interact with audiences without anything other than their own bodies to work with, with a 'rich' theatre, with elaborate buildings and trappings and equipment of all kinds, it seems obvious that the distinction applies to dance in just the same way and that Grotowski's value judgments are as valid in the one case as in the other. When we are confronted with Antonin Artaud's (1958) idea of a 'theatre of cruelty,' we may ask whether the idea of a 'dance of cruelty' has any more or any less validity. Martin Esslin's (1983) 'theatre of the absurd' conjures up the idea of a 'dance of the absurd'; and, if the idea proves empty, we may find ourselves wondering how much substance there was to the idea of a theatre of the absurd in the first place. Francis Fergusson's (1949) idea that a theatre can and should represent the consciousness of a community in a very special way sets us wondering if a dance group or a dance theatre relates to its community in the same sort of way. This whole field of inquiry seems well worth exploring, even if the supposed affinities prove to be no more than the casual likenesses that any two domains of human endeavour are likely to present (cf. above, chapter 12 note 22).

14.2 Dance and Drama

Outside the theatre, dance and drama seem headed in different directions. The divergent tendencies are neatly and deeply caught by Langer's system of the arts, in which dance symbolizes the hidden powers we divine in things, including the power of life itself, while drama symbolizes the various shapes of human destinies.[5] Obviously these would overlap: human destinies are easily seen as manifestations of a blind Schopenhauerian will, which is an occult power if anything is, and vital forces can identify themselves and their power only by being exercised in particular ways.

Inside the theatre, dance and drama are much more closely and obviously related, as different things people can do on stages. And not so different, either; the same people may find themselves doing either or both. In both, the remote authorial *logos* of playwright or choreographer imposes itself on performers who merely represent material for which they disavow responsibility – in contrast with Artaud's 'theatre of cruelty,' in which the players on stage confront their audience without equivocation. Traditional theories of theatre, however, tended to restrict themselves to drama, treating it as a genre of literature rather than a mode of theatre, and assumed that dance exists in effect only as danced onstage. Aristotle, it is true, had called tragedy the imitation of an action and plainly thought of it as performed for an audience; but the action was articulated primarily by the written text, which was all most people (including Aristotle himself) knew, and which sufficed to convey the tragic effect of the pitiful and terrifying series of events that made up the story.[6]

Opposition to this text-centred view of drama was eloquently urged by Gordon Craig (1911), who insisted that a theatrical work 'is incomplete when printed in a book or recited ... incomplete anywhere except on the boards of a theatre' (144). But what about the plays of a Sophocles or a Shakespeare, which readers find to be evidently not incomplete? Well, that just shows that such plays are not theatre pieces. The fact that they are often thought of as the theatre's chief glory, and that the most famous theatrical buildings were constructed expressly to put them on, should not confuse us. A dramatic poet, whose work is a poetic text that may indeed be staged but was not conceived with staging in mind, is not to be confused with a dramatist, whose work is the staged performance of a work conceived for staging (140). But Craig goes further in the opposite direction than Aristotle would allow: a brilliant designer himself, he argues that people want to see plays rather than to hear them, and claims that on a director's first reading of a play 'the entire colour, tone, movement and rhythm that the work must assume come clearly before him' – not, we note, the personal and social situations, the affections and antagonisms, of the characters, or the shape of their action (149). This emphasis enables Craig to conclude that 'the art of the theatre has sprung from action – movement – dance. ... The father of the dramatist was the dancer' (139–40). But that, at least, is surely a mistake. The dancer may be the ancestor of the actor, though I don't quite see why; but the father of the dramatist is just as likely to have been the preacher. Dancers are not the only people who want to be seen and heard by their audiences. However, this may mean no more than that Craig has not distinguished, as the Russian theorists of the day were doing, between drama and generic theatre.

What is the difference, in terms of the practice most familiar to us, between the dramatic actor and the dancer? The actor Simon Callow (1984, 23) tells us that at a certain stage during his training 'I understood what playing a character was. It was giving in to another way of thinking. *Giving in* was the essential experience.' Acting, he says, 'can't be demonstrated and imitated like dancing, because its essence is experience. One learns what a sensation *is*, not what it looks like; and sensation is at the heart of acting' (25). One might reply that acting can indeed be demonstrated and imitated, but not if you want to do it well, and that the same is true of dancing. Like actors, dancers lose themselves in the part. More generally, actors and dancers construct the stage figure that is what the audience sees. This stage figure is neither the same as the performer's own personality, nor the same as the *character* that the members of the audience complete in their imaginations as an extrapolation from what the performer makes for them to see. As a means of constructing this figure, dancers and actors use their imaginations to transform themselves into the danced or acted figure;[7] according to Callow, this is possible for actors only if they passively surrender to the character-type that the audience will reconstruct, but he gives us no reason to think he is right. We are well accustomed to artists describing their own procedures, or the stories they tell themselves about those procedures, and claiming that this is the only valid procedure there is.

What actually is it, in Callow's account, that distinguishes actors from dancers? I see only two possibilities: that actors are passive in a way that dancers are not, and that what actors give in to is a way of thinking. The former is possible, to the extent that actors do what people do when they are not acting: to give in to another way of thinking might then suffice to produce actions and intonations, given that the actor has made second nature of the necessary skills of making oneself clearly audible and visible. But what a dancer does is first and foremost a way of dancing, and from this point of view any dance is more like any other dance than either is like any mode of action that is not dance.[8] What about the thesis that what actors give in to is a way of thinking? Well, the person who dances Giselle may have, and may need to have, an idea of what sort of person Giselle was and what her motivation was, and her performance will be moulded continuously by this idea. What is that, if not giving in to a way of thinking? The only thing is that what is moulded is the dance as choreographed; there is no giving in in the sense that the dancer just makes it her rule to do what Giselle would have done – but then, neither does the actor, who is bound by the playwright's script, the actualities of the stage, and the director's instructions. Perhaps what the dancer gives in to is not the way of thinking that constitutes the Giselle character-type, but something like the idea of how a perfect dancer would dance if she envisaged the role in a certain way.

Actors give themselves in or up to ways of thought by dramatic means; dancers do so by dance means. A ballet, I have suggested, really only illustrates the story it purports to tell; but in an Indian dance-drama, where the recited text is likely to be inaudible or in an unfamiliar language, what is there other than the dancing to carry the story? But then, we say, that is true of the ballet too: the dancing carries the story or the story is not carried. – To which one rejoins that this is indeed the case, and very frustrating and silly the whole business is, when we know or don't know 'what is supposed to be happening' but we certainly can't *see* that it is happening; and one would expect that in the Indian dance-dramas the action would be confined to a limited number of thoroughly familiar stories.

When a dancer dances Giselle, the role remains the same in the dancing bits that simply express feeling as it is in the mimetic bits that advance the story (cf. §4.2). It is still Giselle. But the relation of the dancer to the character being enacted in the role must surely change. This need occasion no difficulty: everyday life makes us thoroughly familiar and at ease with such transitions, even in such mundane operations as calling a meeting to order. And I do not see why we would be disconcerted in a theatrical form in which some of the time what went on was an ordinary stage drama, some of the time a stylized verse-drama, some of the time a miming dance, and some of the time an abstract dance, with the transitions from one to the other not necessarily marked. It probably would not come off, but do we know that it could not? But then, what comes of the claim (§6.12) that dance space and dramatic space are radically different? Nothing, unless we want to make a big deal of the word 'radical' – and perhaps not even then. Most of our lives we are dealing with situations that are equivocal, mixed up, ambiguous, shifting in all sorts of ways. Our minds are such as to make effortlessly all sorts of adjustments that go far beyond our powers of explicit analysis. That does not destroy the value of our analyses; it only shows that analyses is what they are.

14.21 Ballet and Opera

I remarked that dance, though typically practised and rehearsed in mirror-lined studios of distinctive form and construction, tends to share the performance spaces of other theatrical forms – those 'neutral' spaces of which Schechner speaks. A special case of this symbiosis is that of opera and ballet, as represented by their typical metropolitan versions that were developed in European capitals in the nineteenth century and still provide our stereotypical and dominant forms.

Ballet and opera are elaborate forms of stage presentation of which the forms and destinies are closely joined; they have a special import-ance because they belong to the privileged domain of the fine arts as part of the cultural 'establishment.' Both of them are forms of opulent display; it is expected that they will be elaborately mounted and richly dressed, that the principal players will be extravagantly paid and will be celebrities. Both are addressed to the ruling classes: companies and buildings are likely to be Royal, or civic, or national. Each is expected to lose money, to be the creation of extravagant patronage, and to sur-vive on lavish gifts from public funds. Each typically engages many highly trained performers – a big chorus, a stage full of corps-de-ballet or walk-on parts, a full orchestra present in person and not on tape, a big backstage crew. Ballet may be regarded, as Samuel Johnson's dic-tionary defined opera, as an 'irrational entertainment' – they both have a peculiar status in the world of culture. Each is admitted to be a proper field for the exercise of artistic genius; but each is, as a genre, suspect in high-minded quarters. The supposed offstage affectations and onstage oddities of the performers are a traditional target for demotic and journalistic lampoon, even more than other artists are. Both are sur-rounded by the apparatus of glamour, glossy programmes and biogra-phies, the rumour of champagne suppers. Both are conventionally placed as the symbols of old-fashioned 'high life' as opposed to entre-preneurial success: it is the widow of the chief executive of an old-established company whom one imagines as wearing her diamond tiara 'in the front, among the best,' not the spouse of the millionaire founder of a computer company – and this not because the former is supposed to be better educated.

A ballet company and an opera company are likely to share a building, or a financial structure, or a management, or all three. An opera company may have a ballet company as its adjunct. Many operas call for dance episodes; at one time the Paris Opera would not accept a work for presentation unless it included a ballet in the third act, and composers who wanted to have their works performed there had to insert a dance episode, however incongruous. Ballet companies do not, however, ever have opera companies as their adjuncts.[9] Nor do ballets usually incorporate operatic episodes. Why not? Partly, perhaps, because evening-length operas have more consistently been the norm than evening-length ballets, so that there has been less need for padding. But I at least feel that it wouldn't look or sound right. Is this a mere matter of what one is used to, or can the feeling be accounted for? Let us try.

Opera is closer to drama. There is an action, carried by dialogue, in which a dance of one sort or another can become an episode. There is, in any case, a big band playing, and we like to think that, in the kind of all-expressive world an opera necessarily presents, peasants and gypsies and children and other such close-to-nature folks will dance along to any music that may be going. Or the king may wave an imperious arm and sing, 'Bring on the dancing girls.' But although there is a big band at the ballet as well, people are not going to burst into spontaneous song unless the tune is familiar and everyone knows the words; and Prince Charming can hardly wave his imperious hand in a gesture that says, 'Bring on the singing girls.' In short, an opera is enough of a play that it can interrupt itself to incorporate segments of dance or drama or other stage forms as part of its action; but a ballet lacks this powerfully unifying frame, and, if it interrupts itself, it risks falling apart and becoming a generic stage show.

Even if the foregoing explanation of the asymmetry corresponds to the way we feel about the issue, there is nothing necessary about it. It just happens that we construe opera in a way that leans toward the dramatic, and we construe ballet in a way that leans away from it. We can see why it is easy to do this, but it does not follow that we have to. An opera typically starts (after the overture) by establishing the dramatic situation through what the characters 'say'; a ballet may start any old how, but we usually need to look at the scenario to tell what the situation is supposed to be, and how it is supposed to be being established. I, for one, can hardly imagine it otherwise; but a failure of imagination is no argument.

The relationship we are exploring here holds between opera and ballet in the forms they took with the rise of bourgeois society, and in the social milieu thus established as a norm that may still prevail. But opera as it first appeared in Italy was an attempt, half antiquarian and half idealistic, to resurrect the supposed forms and values of classical Greek drama, and this had nothing to do with ballet – though the Greek original interspersed its episodes with 'choruses' that were at least minimally danced as well as sung (Pickard-Cambridge 1968, 251–2). Meanwhile, the court ballets of the same and earlier epochs had little intrinsically to do with theatrical forms but were essentially displays. Their spectators were in no sense connoisseurs of art, but people who came to see a spectacle of the same order as a parade or a public execution. Even in the eighteenth century, the stylistic convergence of ballet and opera was not complete, though the institutional unity-in-separation was forged in the twinned royal foundations of Louis XIV. But it becomes increasingly hard to say what the heart of the difference is, if the difference between singing and dancing is not enough. Perhaps it is that opera remains a form of musical art, in which controversies about musical form are crucial, whereas ballet music could be (and often was) cobbled together by composers of no pretensions.

Aside from the institutional connections, which are decisive, the key to the affinity between opera and ballet in their typical manifestations is that both are forms of non-natural mimesis. In a play, an action is presented onstage in which we see people basically behaving as people behave, and talking as people talk. Most of the abundant artificialities are to be accounted for, first, by the fact that the audience has to see what would not normally be seen and to hear what would normally not be said aloud; second, that everything must be compressed into the time allocated for the performance; and third, that the way everything is said and done is controlled by complex conventions of the genre. Despite these departures from naturalism, the play is a transformation of the presentation of an action of which a 'naturalistic' version lurks in the background. In an opera, the action is presented in a shape that owes as much to the autonomous forms of music as it does to the articulation of the action; in dance, the requirements of the art of dance have the same privilege.

An important affinity between opera and ballet lies in the way each of them typically alternates between two modes, as we saw in §4.2. The ballet alternates between largely mimetic action that advances the story and interludes of pure dance; opera does the corresponding thing, with musical differentiation between recitative and aria. In each case while aria or pure dance is going on, time stops, while the situation in its emotive bearing is celebrated, visibly or audibly. The parallel fails in one respect, that (because arias have words) the emotive content of an aria can be more precise, while a pure dance celebrates life in its more general aspects. Even so, arias tend to celebrate strong rather than subtle emotion; in both arts, the lyrical interludes represent the same switch to a mode of experience that is less tightly bound to the specifics of the situation.

In both opera and ballet, the mimetic function is typically performed in a less realistic mode than drama admits, but the operatic and balletic substitutes for 'acting' are quite different from each other. In a sense, the dancers never stop dancing, even when miming; but the opera performers may stop singing altogether.[10] Opera performers tend to be motionless (or nearly so) in formal passages, while in the narrative episodes they fall into a quasi-acting that might be taken for (may even be) inept hamming; ballet dancers in narrative episodes exploit a movement vocabulary borrowed from ceremonious forms of social dance.

In both opera and ballet, the chorus/corps de ballet operates in the same sort of way, in both narrative and lyrical passages. Common to both opera and ballet, in fact, is a dynamic of solo, group, and ensemble passages, on the interplay of which the form of a work largely depends. There is one interesting difference. Stories in both opera and ballet often depend on a relationship between a male and a female, so that duets play a large part in both. But the duet is not especially at home in music, where harmonic identity depends on a triad rather than a pair of voices. In dance, the duet is right at home, since dancing in male/female partnerships is one of the most distinctive resources and possibilities. So a ballet will often have at least one enormous set-piece for male and female leads, disproportionate to the rest of the work, in a way that has no regular counterpart in opera – even in *opera seria*. On the other hand, volume in music is cumulative: when the chorus joins in, things get bigger and more impressive. In a dance, an increase in the number of dancers increases complexity and flash, but not necessarily impressiveness. A cumulatively crescendo finale is accordingly more typical of opera than of ballet.

14.3 Dance and Scene

A theatre is a special place for shows. Whether stage, trestle, wagon, or amphitheatre, its character as ordinary artifact in a real place in the world is overlaid by its internally determined character as a place apart, a place for theatre. What is shown there may be simply a feat, in which case the theatre place is neutral. But it may be something enacted. If I dance on stage the dance of a horse, the theatre becomes a horse place or places. It may be paddock or stable, but it becomes no less definitely a horse place if the dance leaves it indeterminate what sort of place the horse is in: whatever it is, it is a setting for a horse, to which the horse relates as horses relate to wherever they are. If I perform a passion play, the stage counts as Golgotha. Is Golgotha brought to the spectators, or are the spectators transported to Golgotha? Neither and both: we encounter in a neutral space, which is Golgotha for purposes of the play.

In an 'impoverished' theatre (cf. §14.12), the place is localized by our imaginations or by the words and gestures of the players. 'This castle hath a pleasant seat. ...' Notoriously, perhaps rather tiresomely, the Prologue in *Henry V* asks us to superimpose the fields of France on the 'wooden O' of the theatre. Significantly, the Prologue will ask us to do so even when there is no wooden O but a concrete box – in which case the box stands in for the O, as the O would have stood in for the fields. In a 'rich' theatre, though, the stage will have a backboard or wall, to separate it off, and the backdrop will be some colour or other in some pattern or other. Either it is made a neutral and even shade, or it is painted in a way that suggests or depicts the place of the action. If it comes close enough to depicting a real or possible place, it is called 'scenery.'

In a sense, every dance has a scene, because it is danced as somewhere, however neutrally or vaguely that somewhere is designated. But not every dance has scenery. Does a dance designed with scenery become incomplete, or even a different dance altogether, if it is danced (as, in most cases, it obviously can be) without that scenery? Is a dance that was conceived without scenery transformed into a different dance if scenery is added? Does addition or omission of scenery always improve, or always spoil, a dance?

The word 'scenery' is used by tourists for the visible aspects of the environment they are passing through. But the word itself, etymologically, means theatre scenery. To call the environment scenery is not only to reduce it to its visual aspects, it is to treat the world as a theatrical performance.[11]

Every dance is danced somewhere (see §§6.12ff). It is danced in a space, which it shapes variously as the space of the dance in which or through which it is dance, and it is danced in a place, a dancing place. But spaces are shaped, and places are defined, by objects in them and (especially) around them. So the place a dance is in is defined by the objects that define and limit it. And these provide the setting for a dance. To the dancers as they dance, they constitute and modify the dance space, constraining and inviting their movements. To the spectators, they constitute a scene. Once the idea of a dance as a kind of theatrical performance is sufficently established, any dance that I watch in the appropriate frame of mind is to me as if it were in a theatre; I convert it into a performance if it was not one already. The place where the dancers are dancing becomes the scene of the dance; the more tightly the dance is integrated into its dancing place, the closer that place comes to being reduced to mere scenery.

Dances often exist more as named individuals than as modes of behaviour (§2.3). Some named dances are specific to particular locations. The Helston Furry Dance, for instance, is danced on 8 May every year through the streets and houses of a 'quaint old Cornish town,' houses and stores being thrown open for the occasion. Are the streets and houses of Helston part of the dance? Yes, in a way; but, though I shall dwell on it at length, it is an extreme case. The heritage of the old court ballets has become divided between danced ballets, on the one hand, and pageants and processions, on the other. The Furry is closer to a ceremonial parade than it is to most dances. It may be compared to the Panathenaica, a religious procession in ancient Athens, which ended in a ceremony on the Acropolis. What was necessary was a date, a very specific route for the procession, sacred objects to be carried, authorization and superintendence by the officials in charge of the ritual, a ceremony at the end, and the formation of the procession by those who had a right to take part – and, above all, everyone knowing that *This Is the Panathenaica*. Most of these features are shared with ceremonies and regular celebrations that have no dance or processional component at all. At the Helston Furry, there is so much formal dancing that the whole thing is called a dance. But what identifies it is not the choreography; it is the well-known tune, plus the route through the town, plus Aunt Mary Moses on her Jerusalem pony, plus the date, plus the fact of dancing – and above all the fact that everyone, from the Mayor to the Media, knows that This Is the Furry Dance.

Are the houses and streets of Helston really part of the Furry Dance, then? In a way, yes, since they are an essential part of the ceremony. But in a way no, since the Mayor could take the dance on tour and dance it through the streets of Brisbane and Bombay: 'This is the Celebrated Furry Dance! Brought to you all the way from the picturesque olde-worlde town of' etcetera. And in another way no, since, if Helston were obliterated and rebuilt to a new plan, they could still do the Furry Dance down the new streets. If the original called for specific movements at specific landmarks, the revivers could introduce corresponding movements at new places, or they could make the old movements at places approximately sited *in memoriam*. We old-timers would say, 'This isn't the way it used to be,' or 'This isn't the real Furry Dance, you know,' and people would understand us, but only in the way one does understand old folks for whom things can never be what they were.

There is a third way in which Helston is inessential to the dance. One could teach and demonstrate the dance in other places, and indeed without using houses and streets at all. 'This is the Helston Furry Dance' – and then one shows the steps, humming the tune or having someone play it, and breaking off to say things like: 'This is where we go on to the next house,' or whatever would be necessary or appropriate. Everyone would understand that to do it *properly* one would have to be dancing in and out of the houses, and so forth; but in so far as the dance has a determinate structure and sequence of movements one would unarguably be demonstrating the dance, and demonstrating it by doing it. One would not be doing it *properly*, but one would really be doing it. It would be pointless to start an argument about whether one had or had not actually performed the dance, without explanation or qualification, unless something practical hinged on assent to or dissent from such a form of words – if, for instance, there were a wager, or a government grant at stake. And then the issue would not be a profound ontological one about whether the dance had been fully instantiated.[12] The issue would merely be how to interpret conditions that had not been spelled out with enough precision to determine the outcome of the wager, or eligibility for the grant. The punters should have made it clearer to each other what they were betting on; the agency's guidelines should have been explicit about its requirements.

Helston, it seems, is necessary to the dance in much the same way that any prop is necessary to a dance organized around it. Can one dance a hat dance without a hat, a sword dance without swords? Sure one can, and frequently does, though one may feel the need to add, 'Of course I should really be using a hat,' or 'One needs a couple of claymores to do this properly.' The design by which the dance is identified is preserved.[13] There is, indeed, a difference between preserving a design recognizably, preserving it fully, preserving it substantially, and so forth. With a thoroughly inept dancer, it may be only the swords or the hat that make the dance recognizable, just as in some restaurants you can only tell the tea from the coffee because one comes with a teabag and the other comes out of an urn. But all that belongs to the area of makeshift and approximation that is covered by the notion of 'rehearsal' with its ancillary notions of 'run-through' and 'preview'; to understand how such things are done and assessed is a large part of understanding the performing arts and is not to be dismissed or summed up in a few provisos and definitions.

What is the design of the Helston Furry Dance?[14] It is more of a ceremony than a work of art. In all its vicissitudes, the essentials (partly enumerated above) have included the practice of dancing *through the houses* of the town. If Helston is not necessary, perhaps the idea of Helston is. The Mayor could not take it on tour after all, unless he could persuade municipalities to allow themelves to stand in for his home town. But what would the local audiences need to understand? That there is a foreign way of dancing, that uses houses like this? Or that there is a town in England where they dance like this? Or that this is how they dance in Helston? I suppose, as usual with audiences, some individuals will know more than others, and many will know little and care less. They will all provide that proverbial desideratum in theatre reality – bums on seats.

Some years ago, a show called *Festi Italiani* toured North America. It consisted of versions of the Sienese Palea and other local pageants and festivities, got up regardless, and presented in an arena. These were not presented by citizens of the places in question, but by professional players. They were representations of the festivals, rather than the festivals themselves transplanted. Even so, the promoters' claim that this *was* the Palea and so forth was not wholly untrue, and was not rejected as a falsehood, even though anyone could see that the ceremonies were tarted up, condensed, and packaged. Design conditions of identity retain their force even for such locally rooted phenomena.

The idea of the ceremony is the idea of something performed in a certain place by a certain sort of person. When a version of the ceremo-

ny is staged, the performers do not exactly act the part of, or impersonate, those who would perform it in real life; they stand in for them. The
stage on which they perform stands in for the place where the ceremony would be performed, rather than representing it. The ceremony does
not function as a work of imagination, to which actors and scenery
contribute; it is a device for giving us a vicarious look at something we
would not otherwise get to see, like seeing a rhinoceros in a zoo.

The Italian Festivals, and the Helston Furry, can, in a way, be transported, and carry the idea of their reality with them.[15] Does that work
in the same way for monuments and landmarks? Michelangelo's *David*
is only doubtfully present in its replica at Sarasota, and the Parthenon
is absent from its replica at Nashville. They do not carry their own
Athens with them. Statues (even marble being infected by the example
of bronze) are not very strongly tied to their prime instantiation, but
buildings are. If the Parthenon were pulled down and reerected in Las
Vegas, and a perfect replica put up on in its place on the Acropolis,
which would be the real Parthenon? I suppose most people who might
have an opinion would be too disgusted to want to think about it.
There isn't any real Parthenon any more, they might feel; the links of
history and geography are broken. (If the Florentines like to have an
outdoors David and an indoors David, that's different, it's still
Florence.)

The Palea is put on by different people each year, so it cannot be tied
to a specific human vehicle. Is it tied to a specific social and economic
history? Consider the Oberammergau Passion Play: could that be transported? In a sense it obviously could, in various ways, but who would
want to see it? Its history and its local specificity are all that is interesting about it. It is almost like a Royal Garden Party at Buckingham
Palace, at which neither the company nor the food is worth the effort
– and even the cutlery is not worth stealing, being clearly stamped with
the name of the commercial caterer who does for Her Majesty. The
point is that one was invited to the Palace, and was there.

In a sense, the idea of the place is part of the scenery. You go to
Helston, if you do, to be there when the dance was done. If it goes on
tour, Helston is not there; but if the dance is to be done at all, Helston
cannot be absent in idea. Scenery can suggest its presence, make it more
palpably part of the scene.

We are venturing here on ground Walter Benjamin has made his
own.[16] The camera has changed everything. In the old days, works of
art had to be visited, which took time; they had an aura that belonged

to their setting and status as objects of pilgrimage. Only the rich could make that pilgrimage; art was for an elite. Nowadays, art is for everyone because everyone can own a photograph of anything. Nothing has any aura any more. That is a good thing, because mystery is mystification, and privilege rests on exclusion; but Benjamin seems kind of sad.

Benjamin was no man of the people, and did not foresee the democratization of tourism. Pilgrimage is always a possibility now: we may never make it to Mecca, but we might. And the idea of seeing things in their place was not, after all, weakened by the availability of cheap reproductions, because the reproduction carries with it the idea of its own place. North Americans know this, because almost everyone on that continent knows that almost everyone is *from* some place other than where they now live – the 'old country.'

Every dance is danced somewhere, then, and many dances carry with them the idea of the place where they belonged, their ideal scene. Some dances are so wedded to a particular locale that they cannot be detached from it: when they are danced in other places, as in one way or another they always can be, the place where they are now being danced stands proxy for their original and proper place. The ways in which (and the power with which) this happens are various; but the original place is the real scene of the dance, and may or may not be represented by scenery.

In the case of a theatre dance, notably a ballet, the original production of the dance had a place which was a theatre, and that theatre provided the dance not just with a scene but with scenery. When I saw *La Sylphide* performed by the Royal Danish Ballet in Copenhagen, the quality of my experience was strongly affected by the sense that I was seeing it danced by the company and in the house for which Bournonville choreographed it, and (for all I knew) with the original sets and costumes.[17] The same dance could be danced elsewhere, by a different company in a different house, with the same choreography and the same set, subject only to the limits of reproducibility. It wouldn't be the same, as we say; the aura would be missing. But the mise-en-scène could be preserved. How important is it that it should be? Is the scenery part of the dance?[18]

Once again: the dance is what the dancers dance, the set is what they dance it in. They could do the same dance with a different set, or with none. We are back in the familiar territory of doing things properly versus doing things in a makeshift way, rich and poor ways of doing things, rehearsals and run-throughs and galas. The only question is, for what purposes and in what contexts is the abstraction of dance from set legitimate?

In drama, we remind ourselves, the dramatist's dialogue, and the interpersonal transactions it defines, have a detachable integrity that makes it easy to distinguish them from the productions that embody them. In a ballet, on the other hand, there is nothing with any such independent integrity to be abstracted from what can be seen onstage. The scenario is not enough to stand by itself; it is a mere plan of action (but see §18.1 below). Even the choreography exists only as a set of instructions to the dancers, whereas the text of a play is a readable entity, far more than a playwright's instructions to actors. In a ballet, what you see is what you get; nothing in it forces a distinction between what the dancers do and the set they do it in.

Such a distinction can easily be made. We can tell the choreography from the scenery; we can distinguish what the dancers dance from where they dance it and what they dance it among. But the dancers plainly interact with the floor they dance on, and may do so with the rest of the set. The interaction may be overt, not merely a reality that becomes obvious only on reflection. A stage may have ramps, platforms, and balconies of some complexity, and the dance may be impossible to perform without them – they may define the relationships as well as the physical movements. There may be trapdoors and wires, dancers may be hauled aloft as part of the dance.[19] Dancers may have to interact with engines.[20] Once a situation has arisen in which such devices are accepted as usual, their absence becomes a tacit part of any dance that is done without them.

As well as discontinuous and tilted surfaces, mobile elements, and mechanical transporting devices, a set may – and, now that cheap computers make it easy to program elaborate switching sequences, often does – involve a lighting scheme that goes far beyond accentuation and changing levels. A movement of illumination may be integral to the danced movement; use of darkness as an instant frame makes hidden entrances and exits possible. Like the machinery, such uses of light may be such that the dance cannot be done without them: in the absence of the proper lighting, the choreography might have to be changed and might then lose all interest.

Someone might reply: 'All this is true of ballet, but that only shows that ballet is not dance. Ballet is a show, of which one part is dancing. The scene is part of the show, part of the production, part of the performance, but not part of the dance. What is necessary to make the dance possible is not thereby shown to be part of the dance, any more than the sea is a swimmer.' But the analogy fails: the sea was there already, but the stage devices are produced by the same imaginative agency that devised the choreography, and as part of the design of the whole work, the only work there is.[21] The choreographed component may constitute what could be a satisfactory work on its own; but so may the costumes, or the sculpted scenery, or the music.[22]

Once again, the problems are seen to be factitious. We do not have to choose among oversimplifications. In any complex presentation, it is as proper and easy to consider elements and aspects in isolation as to consider them in interaction, to consider totalities as wholes as to consider them as ensembles, to distinguish artistic failures from mechanical failures as to consider the overall effect. What to emphasize and what to omit, what to combine and what to separate – it is in finding specific solutions to these questions that critics show their skill and audiences show their fitness. Such questions are always difficult, and always worth discussing, not because there are rules for giving right answers but because there are none.

14.31 Stage and Scene

A theatre dance exists only as danced on a real stage in a real theatre before a real audience on a particular occasion. But a dance is also danced as in a place, the scene of the dance, a toymaker's shop or (I have suggested) a shadowy location in the old country that nostalgia evokes. But, as Jack Anderson (1987, 30) points out, the scene of the dance may be envisaged either as a location in a world, or as projected simply by the dance itself; and this makes a big difference. 'Choreographers, then, can treat the stage in at least two ways. For some, it is the only place that exists. For others, though it is the only place we see, it can also imply the existence of other places.' So, when characters exit, one can ask where they are going. 'The answer is likely to be either "nowhere really" or "somewhere else," and that alone will help to define just what sort of a ballet that particular ballet is.'

There is a difference, moreover, between a dancer leaving the stage and a character leaving the scene. Leaving the stage is not necessarily leaving the scene. In an elaborate *pas de deux* in which the partners take turns doing a solo, it may be required that each component take the overall form of a diagonal from upstage left to downstage right, in which case (unless there is a complex convention of invisibility) each dancer must then go off stage and go round the back to be ready for the next entrance. The dancer has then left the stage, but the character has not quit the scene, not even to go nowhere, in the way in which characters in a plotless dance may leave the dance as well as the scene when their turn is over, the choreographer not having envisaged any other place for them to be. Many writers on drama have commented on the complexities of the ways in which playwrights envisage offstage times and places for the characters and actions of their plays. All these complexities remain potentially in place for choreographers, alongside the additional complications introduced by the fact that a dancer in a theatre dance may be a fully fledged character with a (sketched or implied) psychological and social reality, or be playing a 'character' part with little or any such imagined solidity, or may be characterized only in terms of danced interactions, or may be presented simply as a performer of the dance movements and not envisaged as a character at all. Dancers and choreographers have this other range of possibilities, which playwrights and actors lack, because the dancers can be fully present as the doers of the dancing they are doing, but acting is nothing if it is not presenting an enacted person in imagined action.

The ambiguities of offstage reality take effect even before the performance begins, in two quite different forms of anticipation. Sometimes the curtains open on a darkened stage, and then we wait for the light and the scene and the action to come into existence together, a creation *ex nihilo*. But sometimes the lights go on behind the drawn curtains, and then we are impatient to be shown a reality that is already there.

14.32 Body and Clothes

We may think of dance as the human body in endotelic motion. What we mean by 'the human body' is, we have seen, a tricky question; but the simplest and most obvious way to think of it is that the body is what is left when we undress. From that point of view, clothing is its wrapping, added to protect it from injury and the elements, to mask or screen, or to make an attractive package. Dancers are seldom naked; so, if dance is esentially the movement of their bodies, we may wonder what their clothes are for. The most relevant function could only be that of screen, their effect being to confine the dancing body to those parts that are left bare, so that the clothed part of the body becomes a mere armature or connective for those parts in which the dance is wholly present or fully expressive. Thus there could be an eye dance, a toe dance, a finger dance, a belly dance, the movements of the body as a whole being ignored or generalized while specific significance is concentrated in the parts exposed, in conformity with the possibilities canvassed in §7.21.

In the Delsartian analysis of expressive action (§8.2221), the heaviest parts of the body express vital energy, the major articulations express the will, and the extremities express the intellect. That sounds a bit far-fetched, but all it really does is reflect the functions of work and nimbleness and indicate how these can be given orderly expression in a danced or mimed movement. Differential exposure would be an obvious resource for clarifying such expression.

What I have just stated might stand as outlining one range of possibilities open to dance, but as a general account of costume in dance it is just plain wrong. People everywhere dress up to dance, rather than strip off. Starting not with the nakedness of the body but with everyday wear, our dancing dress is more careful and more elaborate. We go to a dance in our Sunday best. Fred Astaire's top hat, white tie, and tails are a familiar and accessible symbol. Naked peoples cover themselves with brilliant and elaborate patterns of paint to dance in. In many dance traditions, in West Africa and elsewhere, the dancers wear an all-over costume that quite hides the shape of the body, culminating in a mask where it is seldom the 'eyes' that the dancer looks through, the whole head typically being displaced upward so that the dancer looks through a disguised slit in the 'neck.'

The masked dancer of West Africa is first and foremost a costume-bearer. What matters is less the steps of the dance than the presence of the dancing mask. Similarly, in the court ballets of seventeenth-century France, the heart of the matter was the entrance and presence of figures in rich and outlandish costumes, attention being divided (differently according to context) between the inventiveness of the costume itself and its symbolic significance.

Such masked dances are epiphanies or pageants. We recall Hegel's strictures on 'symbolic' dance: allegorical movements must be either dull or irrelevant, so that interest and relevance can be combined only in the costumes.[23] Pageantry, still a prominent feature of ballet, with its processions and cortèges and grand entrances, is at the centre of the world tradition of ceremonial dance. Think of the part played by elaborate costumes and masks in the dance theatres of Indian and Chinese civilizations, in which feats of agility are performed not *by* but *around* gods and generals, whose massive and ornate presence renders unnecessary the agility it precludes.

Are we to say that it is the function of costume to conceal what nudity reveals? It has been argued that every aesthetic value is twinned by its counter-value, even if only one of the two is cultivated in a given artistic culture (see §15.2121). If openness of the body is a value in dance, so must concealment be. The very fact that dances reveal and enhance and exploit grace in movement makes it certain that there can be dances in which the natural, expressive surface of the body, where grace resides, is concealed and cancelled. If there are dance customs favouring nudity, there should also be dance customs that favour costume and masque. But, as I was saying, the emphasis here seems wrong. When I put on my glad rags to go dancing, what I hide is not my body but my working self. I do the same if, as some people with white-collar jobs seem to, I dress *down* to go dancing. In either case, it is the working self, the respectable social self, that is put off.

Nakedness or near-nakedness, was established as important to modern dance by Isadora Duncan. One is tempted to associate this connection with the revealed grace of the animal body (cf. §15.22111). But what Isadora actually emphasized was not the quality of movement; it was the unadornedness of the body itself. The ideal is that of a body-based and therefore natural humanity. To this way of thinking, the nobility of savages is one with their nakedness, and the classical Hellenic penchant for nakedness in athletics was taken to be one of the glories that were Greece. The emphasis on nakedness in much modern dance was conceived not primarily as a realization of the true nature of dance as such but as the application within dance of a way of thinking, the back-to-nature and away-from-industry movement, which had little directly to do with dance but provided (for the time being, and in the eyes of some writers and practitioners) the nerve of dance practice.[24]

The vogue of feminism and its association with body-centred thought assigns to dance a new importance, the nerve of dance practice now having culturally central significance. But the association of dance with the freeing of the limbs is misleading. Dance everywhere is social, and social humanity is clothed. Clothes establish social identity. Dance costumes establish dancers in their social roles and identify dancers within the dance. A near-naked dancer is not undressed, but is wearing a very distinctive (and exiguous) costume.

What the audience sees is primarily the costumed dancer. Few dances present a contrast between body and clothes. A dancer in a heavy and stiffened floor-length gown moves as a unit, neither constrained nor concealed, but a person clothed in a certain way, making such dance movements as such a person makes. A female ballet dancer's toe shoe is part of the dancing foot, and the dancer thus shod dances such dances as a person thus footed dances. In the old Lavolta, the stiff busk coming down to a point before the thighs endowed the dancing woman with a carapace, and she was lifted by the point of that carapace – picked up neither by her clothes nor (though the dance must have been given piquancy by that suggestion) by her personal pubis, but by the busk of her dancing self.

Relations between clothes and the clad self are always complex and equivocal, for self and for others. Despite the confidence with which I have sketched some simple relations and identities, matters become still more complex in the case of dance. In social dances, it is partly my clothes that constitute me a dancer. As clowns put on with their paint their identity as clown, I put on my dancerhood when I dress for the dance. In theatre dance, however, things as the spectator sees them are different again. In a social dance I remain, as a dancer, my original social self. I ask someone I know, or someone I do not know, for a dance, and I am accepted as the person I am, not as a character in a play or as a fellow participant in a performance – not even if we are princes and cinderellas at the ball. Next day, the glass slipper will fit the dusty foot. Our invitations and refusals are surrounded and qualified by glamour and the holiday spirit, but we have no separate personas to take on. Whatever we do, we do as ourselves, with social consequences that are qualified but not negated by the specialness of the occasion. Our dancing acts are less disconnected from our weekday lives than *amours de voyage* are from what will follow them on dry land. The specialness and otherness, which it sometimes seems to be the whole mission of dance to provide, transport us into a different mode of being; but in the social dance that different reality is continuously sustained by the mundane reality on which it is superimposed, from which we are never free and to which we may at any moment be recalled. That is what makes masks exciting: they half promise a real concealment, and hence an effective otherness that is more than merely phenomenological.

A dancer onstage, by contrast, is clothed as a person but costumed as a performer. The dance is the entire time in which the dancer is a dancer-for-us-in-that-dance, a performer of that person. Throughout that time the dancer is costumed, and in terms of that performance would have no existence apart from that costume – or, if there are changes, that sequence of costumes – but for one thing. Costume is to performer as clothes are to person. A dancer usually dances the part of a person; and a person, as such, is someone who might change clothes.

What of the swans in *Swan Lake*? The dancers are dressed not as swans but as dancers, abstractly. We as it were imagine swanhood upon them. But only 'as it were' – if we think of them as real swans, black webbed feet paddling away, dabbling in mud and hissing at strangers, able to break a man's arm with one blow of the wing, we start to laugh. For us to imagine swanhood upon them, in whatever way we do that, the costumes must be recognizably dance costumes, but they do have to be white, because swans are white symbolically as well as really, though their skirts *must not* be made of feathers, because ballet skirts are not made of feathers.[25] The enchantment of *Swan Lake* depends on this precise suspension between modes of being, to imagine either of which would destroy the illusion.

The necessary ambiguity of the relation between performer and costume makes possible a characteristic effect in those grandiose spectacles which ballet audiences relish and ballet companies apparently love to put on. Such spectacles abound in processions or throngs of pilgrims, peasants, courtiers, and other gregariously picturesque personages. They may be dressed uniformly, or uniformly with subtle variations, or with piquant contrasts of colour and form. As they swarm, the fabrics recombine into new variations which offer a delight to the audience over and above the actual dance steps. They generate a dance of costumes that is distinct from the dance of dancers, because the significances of the movements are different. The dance of the costumed persons is, accordingly, threefold. They perform a dance as dancers; they act as moving support for the dance of fabrics; and, as a whole, there is the one dance, the procession or whatever it may be. The choreographer may not have envisaged the dance of cloth – the designer may not have been born when the choreography was completed – but it is there for all to see.

Because the dance of performers can be partly separated in this way from the dance of costume, there can be no sharp line between costumes and props, just as there is no sharp line between props and scenery. Portability and detachability are among the chief criteria, but they are not absolute. There seems, though, to be a much firmer division between body and props, so that, if costumes were aesthetically indistinguishable from bodies, props would have been more clearly distinct from costume than they are. Or should we not rather say that in contexts where certain distinctions are sharply made, others inevitably become blurred?

Even in everyday life, hats are not exactly clothes so much as (in the commercial phrase) *furnishings*, to be put on and taken off as one takes up and puts down a walking stick or a purse – and, if a purse, why not an attaché case? Cloaks are not just clothes, either: they can be swirled as well as worn.[26] There are many dances in our theatre repertoire in which cloaks, veils, scarves are swirled, and in many of these the swirling of a veil becomes a leading motif of the dance. Loie Fuller regularly used scarves as props rather than as clothes. Were the undulating draperies always attached to her costume as such? Did anyone notice, or care? Does anything important separate such dances as hers from those in which dancers grab something like a bedsheet by the corners and wave it up and down, without treating it in a garment-like way at all?[27]

The use of fluttering and trailing draperies is linked with the dance of the naked or closely costumed body by a curious and familiar phenomenon, the after-image. Although fluttering cloth can interact with breezes out of doors, or be blown by fans indoors, the movement of draperies worn on a stage indoors most often follows that of the limbs as they move through the still air. But under a bright light the limbs themselves would leave a sort of visible trail: eyes do not see instantly, the sight of a rapidly moving and brightly clad limb is blurred by its motion, and the blurring is enhanced by a brief dazzling that shows where the limb has been. In such conditions, every limb trails a flag of light.[28]

14.321 Dressing and Undressing

If dance is body movement, I was saying, clothing can function not only as part or adjunct of the social self but also as selective screen or focus for the dance movement. A veil, accordingly, may function ambiguously between attached clothing and detachable prop, an ambiguity exploited in the notorious 'dance of the seven veils.' Clothing becomes prop; a part of the social self becomes a movable screen.[29] There is a whole genre of 'tease' dances in which balloons, fans, pigeons, and other objects are manipulated to conceal, and to suggest a failure to conceal, a dancing body. In such dances the spectators are often solicited to conjecture that the dancer is naked, or nearly so; in these cases the expected culmination of the dance is the revelation that the dancer is in fact naked, or is not naked, as the case may be. All sorts of variations are possible, and at one extreme is the straightforward 'striptease' in which nakedness is achieved in the course of a more or less rudimentary dance.

When teaching an elementary course in aesthetics, I was more than once asked (usually by a male sophomore) whether striptease is a fine art. As the term 'fine art' is used, in relation to specific traditions of practice, the simple answer is that it is not; but it is hard to conceive of a definition of the terms 'aesthetic' and 'art' that would exclude strippers on principle. One might prefer the words 'entertainment' and 'entertainer' to the words 'art' and 'artist,' given the likely context of the display and the probable attitudes of those involved, but those are merely probabilities. One might dismiss the stripper as merely seducing or miming a seduction, inviting sexual excitement and release rather than aesthetic appreciation, just as one might distinguish pornography (both in practice and in principle) from erotic art, but such distinctions are notoriously tricky, tendentious at best, self-serving or self-deceiving at worst.

The stripper, after all, is not seducing anyone, but is performing. Bumps and grinds are not seductive actions but symbols of seduction, are in fact dance movements. The context has to remain that of a show; there is a tradition of obscenity that has to be learned. (Matters are complicated because sexual behaviour in any society is itself stylized, and the stylizations may be transferred from bedroom to stage or from stage to bedroom.)

Strippers are not usually categorized as artists. That name connotes either a sort of respectability or a sort of seriousness, or both, which strippers are denied. But they are classed as dancers – 'exotic' or 'specialty' dancers – by themselves and their employers, and what they do may be 'artistically' done in any of a number of ways. They are in show business and are likely to share show-business capabilities at some level. It seems likely that someone who takes up a career as a stripper is someone who once took a job as a stripper and held on to it, and someone who takes such a job does so as part of a more fundamental career choice involving the stage, generically acting or dancing at some level of accomplishment.

A strip is inherently a dance; it is a dance, of sorts, by context; and it is danced by dancers or quasi-dancers.[30] But it is a segregated sort of dance. Its movements are not shared by other dances, otherwise than by quotation and parody, and to move between strip and other forms of dance is probably not a normal career pattern.

Striptease is a very special sort of dance, symbolizing denudation as foreplay. It may differ from other dances in that the symbolization is really valued by its clientele, as pornography also is, in abstraction from any artistic or aesthetic skill brought to its performance. But in this it seems no different from some ethnic or ceremonial dance of which the most important thing is that it shall actually be done, whether it is done well or badly – even though everyone is aware that it could be well done, and could then be appreciated artistically as well.

Though striptease is special in these ways, undressing is an obvious resource for dance in general, with or without a sexual implication. We must remind ourselves here that the social body, the corporeal and encounterable social self, is not the same as the animal body, the physical organism. The social body is *always* clothed in one way or another; when it is naked it is *undressed*. The animal body may or may not be covered with clothes; when it is, the clothing obstructs and obscures it. The social body, by contrast, when deprived of clothing, is either in a special condition or, in a sense, mutilated.[31] Since a dancer's body is necessarily engaged in a dance in both aspects, dressing and undressing have powerfully ambiguous meanings.

The contrast between the revealed nakedness of exposed humanity and the immediate presence of natural animality is close to the phenomenological contrast developed by Sartre between the body as fully animated corporeality and the body as flesh, a mere clog on the spirit (see §5.311 above). Flesh as flesh is shaming; clothing saves the spirit from shame. To the fully animated body, by contrast, which is what dance exemplifies most fully, clothing is either irrelevant, a mere extension of one's embodiment, or a hindrance to life.

The iconography of the arts suggests another complication. H.W. Janson (1969, 488) observes of Carpeaux's group for the façade of the Paris Opera, *The Dance*, that the figures 'look undressed rather than nude. We cannot accept them as legitimate denizens of the realm of mythology, and they slightly embarrass us, as if "real people" were acting out a Rococo scene. ... "Truth" here has destroyed the ideal reality that was still intact for Clodion a century before.' The contrast between the nude, the human body as subsumed in the imagery and techniques of the arts, and the naked, the body exposed by proxy to the voyeur, is as familiar as it is perennially questioned; but Janson's version is something else again. In the Clodion terracotta he cites for contrast, the satyr and nymph are mythological figures, and are not dancing; Carpeaux's figures are dancing, and are not mythological. What has caught Janson's eye, I think, is that Carpeaux's dancers appear not to be performing a dance, but to be frolicking; Clodion's figures appear not to be really performing the action represented, but to be posing. And Carpeaux's jolly rompers have taken their clothes off, it isn't clear exactly why; whereas Clodion's mythological parahumans never had any clothes in the first place. (You can't imagine a satyr in pants.)

There are other complications, too. Think of dance-drama traditions in which the body is elaborately trained as a physical instrument, muscle by muscle, but the dance itself is performed in a mask and heavy robes. Such a dance is an esoteric art, a secret art, as though the visible drama were merely a screen for the invisible exercise of the body's discipline.

All these aspects of and attitudes to the body are always available; we move among them as our predilections or the context dictate, or remain in suspense among them. Isadora Duncan's first dance in Vienna, at an aristocratic soirée, was received in dead silence until a princess asked why she danced with so few clothes on – the dancer's choice of costume was treated as a social act like that of the guests, as though she had first prepared the dance and then decided independently how to dress for the occasion (Fuller 1913, chap. 20). And the newspapers repeatedly commented on her nudity as a scandalous act of exposure, not a social solecism but a public act. Meanwhile, the dance audiences mostly accepted her costuming as part of the dance.

Nakedness stands for poverty, for simplicity, for honesty, for helplessness, for social indeterminacy, and for many other things as well as for sexual availability. It is a powerful symbol; too powerful and too ambiguous, one would have thought, to be used effectively in artistic dance. And it is in the act of undressing that its disconcerting power is unleashed. No wonder dancers use it sparingly. In a successful dance, however, the multivalence of the body and its nakedness can be exploited. In Danny Grossman's *Triptych* (1976), for instance, stripping becomes a symbol of large and undefined significance – a metaphysical act, if you prefer – as well as a sequence of memorable pathos and formal beauty. The dancer is stripped of all defences, ultimately of humanity itself, by the denuding action that seems to take place through him rather than by his decision: the loosening and partial removal of the clothing gives the dismaying feeling that the dancer is dismantling himself. More often, a dance that ends in nakedness is shocking: the body is left without recourse, the dance cannot be continued.[32]

If undressing is a powerful resource of dance, so must dressing be. Donning a costume can affect the meaning of a dance in two ways. It effects a transition from one dance to another, from a dance of nakedness to a dance of sartorial determinacy, from animal body to social self.[33] Second, the act of transition itself can be the subject of a dance: one could dance an investiture. I know of no examples in dance, though there must be many (the device is obvious), but there is a famous example in drama – in Brecht's *Life of Galileo*, where the newly elected pope is seen and heard to put on his official views with his new vestments.[34]

The reverse device is common enough, in a hackneyed form. College dance groups like to put on dances in which the dancers wear some minimal costume symbolizing the liberated body (stripped for action), except for a few who wear street clothes, or something else that can signify social restraint. In the course of the dance, one or more of the latter take off their top layers and join the free spirits. This, one supposes, symbolizes signing up for a dance option to fulfil the PE requirement. But it may be hard to do anything subtle in this line, because it is hard to take clothes off in a way that is neither clumsy nor suggestive, and putting clothes on may be even harder to work into an effective dance. Donning or doffing a crown, or a cloak with a simple hook, is easy enough; beyond that, things may get daunting or awkward. In fact, if one is dexterous enough to do it without awkwardness, the resulting impression may be that of a clever trick, rather than of the meaning that should have been conveyed.

In this section and the last, I have concentrated on some special contexts of Western theatre dance. The restriction is unwarranted. Dance everywhere is dressed up, and every costume is put on at some point and taken off at some later point. The possibility that the donning or the doffing or both should be incorporated (or implied) in the dance must always be present. But this seems to be seldom done; at least, descriptions of dances seldom mention it.[35] Why should this be so?

The obvious answer is that the costume of a dance is most often inherent in the individuality of the dance itself. The dance cannot properly begin until the costume is on. A costume cannot then be assumed as part of a dance, because the act of dressing up is esentially a nondance act, belonging to the background world in which the special context of the dance is established.[36]

A less obvious answer is that the significance of changing costume, and hence changing social role, is peculiar to societies in which it is accepted that social roles can be assumed and changed: mobile, pluralist, function-oriented societies. But I doubt if that is true. Even in hierarchical, caste-ridden, ossified societies, there must always be transitions from one time of life to another, with recognized rites of passage. One assumes widow's weeds or the *toga virilis*; one passes from pubescent to nubile to matriarch, from lad to warrior to councillor. What the possibilities are here, how they are realized in different circumstances, which of them are effected or symbolized in dance, and what part is played by costume in all this – that is for the empirical investigator to find out for us. And it may be that what the investigator finds out will be that the terms in which I have posed my questions here are not applicable at all to societies that are differently conceptualized.

PART THREE

Aspects of Dance

ASPECTS OF DANCE

The fundamentals of the philosophy of dance are not the issues most people want to discuss. The fundamentals have to do with how the practice and arts of dance fit into the meaningful world of humans as symbol-using and culture-making animals. These are what I have been writing about. But, just because they are fundamental, they are not what first comes to mind when people wonder about dance.

Most students, especially young ones, encounter the philosophy of dance in the form of dance aesthetics; they expect to learn the rational basis, if there is one, of the difference between good and bad dancing, so that they can be secure in their own tastes and in their criticisms of others. Their expectation seems reasonable – what else could aesthetics be for? But older people find it hard to take much interest in it. They are content to trust their own experience as practitioners and critics, and as consumers they see no reason to consider anything other than their own appreciations. The rest is commerce, or public relations. All the same, the question is obviously legitimate, and it is first of the remaining aspects of dance to be considered here.

For professional philosophers, the most intriguing question is the basis of the identity of dances, since they mostly exist only as what the minds and bodies of individual practitioners retain and transmit, in forms that are as distinctive as they are fugitive. Accordingly, our last substantive chapter deals with the identity of dances – or would do so, except that the ways in which dance is recorded, ways that have been rapidly and decisively changing in recent decades, promise or threaten to change our understanding of what constitutes sameness and differences of dances, and this has to be taken up as a separate topic.

Before we can deal with the conditions of identity of dances, we have to confront something we have been rather casual about up to this point: the inner articulation of the process of dance-making, from planning to execution.

Meanwhile, the chapter on dance values reminds us of a split between dance as something to do and dance as something to see, which calls for a short chapter on this diversity of viewpoints, which we have previously encountered more than once in its public context as the relationship between performers and audiences. And that in turn raises the question of how one learns to be a dancer, an artist in whose experience the work performed must take a form radically different from that which is encountered by the public for whom, one supposes, the art exists. And, since the fusion of viewpoints rests on the imagination of a choreographer and the will-power (and fund-raising capacity) of an impresario, this brings us round to the organizational question that grounds our discussion of dance identity. And promenade home.

CHAPTER FIFTEEN

Dance Values

By what standards and values are dancing and dances to be judged? What makes them good or bad? It must seem odd that I have been able to talk about dance for so long without confronting this question. But in fact I have been dealing with it all along. Dance is a practice, something people do on purpose, knowing that they are doing it. And, in practices, facts and values can never be separated. One cannot learn to dance without learning what it is to dance well, to improve, to get things right and get them wrong in dancing. To engage in any practice is nothing other than to act in conformity with a specific set of rules, standards, and ideals, even if these are never put into words; and one cannot describe the practice intelligibly without explaining what at least some of those rules, standards, and ideals are. One could not even recognize a practice without knowing what values governed it; there is no other way of sorting out what belongs to the practice from what does not.

To explain the values that govern a practice, then, all one has to do, and all one can do, is give a good description of the practice itself. But people who are engaged in the practice of dancing are never merely dancers, and nothing else. They engage in other practices as well, and their dancing may be their way of doing so. Also, the dancing they do may fall essentially within the scope of some such practice, in their own eyes or from some other point of view. Dance enters into the whole economy of human life in all sorts of ways, so that all the values of human life may be relevant to dance in all sorts of ways.

In general, the values of any practice, the things about it that make it good or bad, involve any interest actively taken in it by anyone. Practices exist only as what people actually do, and what actually happens, and this reflects the totality of the forces that impinge on it. Practices, however, are things people do on purpose, and for a purpose. Among all those impinging interests and interventions, accordingly, we can distinguish a subset that we allow to be legitimate, in that the interveners can justify their interventions, and the hopes and demands they represent, in relation to those purposes. This is an entirely indeterminate restriction, of course; but, in principle, it makes sense to allow some privilege to the concerns of those who recognize what the practice is, and can say how it concerns them. Within the legitimate interests we might distinguish a further subset: relevant interests, those related to the nerve of the practice as something distinctively undertaken, with its own cultural integrity and point.

The values of a practice, in short, especially of a practice so complex and pervasive as dance, must inevitably be multiplex, involving motivations, constraints, and payoffs of all sorts. A general study of value must pass under review the whole economy of human life, and any part of that study may be relevant to dance. Obviously, I cannot go into all that here. All I can do is make some general remarks (of the kind I am making now) about what basic sorts of values can be distinguished and how these distinctions relate to our understanding of dance.

My basic concern here is the following. Given the special nature of dance as art and practice, is there anything special about the valuational aspect of dance? Are there any special value terms and considerations that enter into discussions of dance in interesting ways? There are, I think, three main possibilities.

(1) First, there might be some value terms or considerations that are uniquely appropriate to dance, applicable to other modes of activity and other phenomena only by metaphor or by palpable extension. This first possibility itself admits of two alternatives: that such special terms and considerations should play a key part in the evaluation of dance, or that they should be marginal.

(2) The second possibility is that there should be no terms or considerations that are unique to dance, but that among those of wider applicability there are some that are especially appropriate for dance – as it were, the evaluative core for dance.

(3) A third possibility is that, though neither of the other two really obtains, it has become a literary convention or cliché to say that some terms are especially appropriate to dance and to keep using them for

that reason. Since such terms are really no more applicable to dance than to anything else, serious evaluations of dance would not use a special vocabulary; nor would there be an implicit vocabulary into which what is actually said should be translated.

The above three possibilities are not the only ones. It might well be, for instance, that there is a special vocabulary for discussing dance but that this vocabulary answers to no distinctive set of values – they are just words the use of which reminds us that it is dance we are talking about. In that case, the status of a certain activity as dance might depend on the decision of critics to use a certain language in discussing it.[1]

One thing we can be sure of: the situation will be complex. If there are universal values, they must apply to dance as well as anything else. If there are values appropriate to any of the wider domains within which dance falls (such as art), they must apply to dance as falling within those domains. And if there are values that are strictly appropriate only to dance – and that there are such values becomes obvious as soon as we consider that only a dance can literally be *well danced* – these will be metaphorically applicable to other domains. A Mozart divertimento is well danced by its composer and, if we are lucky, by its performers. By parity of reasoning, values literally specific to other domains will be applicable by extension or by metaphor to dance. A dancer's solo may be finely etched or melodious, chiselled or moulded, fine-spun or well-woven.

15.1 Singularities

In a practice such as dance, the most apposite and accurate description of what is done is at the same time the most satisfactory account of its value. But supposing that the whole universe has to be looked at in that way, as an intelligent and purposeful creation? In that case, the best description of any reality will also be the best account of its value.

The scholastic philosophy of the Judaeo-Christian tradition did hold that the universe was a divine creation and accordingly worked out a very general theory of reality and value of the kind described.[2] Beauty and goodness, it held, are proportionate to reality. A thing is good and fine in so far as its reality (its being the thing that it is) is fully achieved; and, though everything is to be prized for being what it is, this esteem belongs especially to things that in some clear way are what they are, celebrating or emphasizing their own reality. Artefacts, especially works of art, are what they are in a singularly emphatic sense, as many philosophers of art have argued, because their being is defined by the intentions they exist to fulfil; in a perfected work of art, the coincidence between intention and achievement is complete.[3]

From this point of view, fact and value in dance cannot be separated, because the value of each particular dance lies in its being exactly what it is. Its value cannot be transferred to or shared with other dances, let alone with performances or entities of other sorts. This argument, however, has nothing to do with dance in particular; it applies equally to anything to which the concept of perfection can be applied. It applies to, among other things, the whole body of dance practice. A specific dance, realizing the unique value inherent in its being just the dance it is, might therefore still fail to embody the value defined as appropriate by the 'nerve' of dance practice itself. It is in such cases that we say of a performance that it was fine in its own way, but not much good *as a dance*.

More significant, perhaps, the thesis that the primary value of any dance lies in its being just the unique entity it is holds equally of all dances and all works of art. It is quite consistent with the contention that all dances are unique in the same set of ways: that their unique values have a common structure, or share common dimensions whereby they are values. Theories that stress the uniqueness of works of art and their values tend to overlook this point.

On Judith Hanna's account, the values that regulate any dance are determined by the judgments (anticipated and actual) of the dancers' reference group. They are thus internal to the culture of the dancers, and one could not usefully generalize about them. The thesis postulates that there is a single homogeneous reference group, that the dancers share the same standards among themselves and with all those whose judgments are relevant. That would be true only in a very limited and stable society – the sort that used to figure in anthropological studies of exotic cultures, and nowhere else. In most actual societies, reference groups are multiple.[4] These groups may be interrelated in a hierarchy that is more or less determinate at a given time and more or less persistent through time. Without such clarity and stability, it will hardly be possible for anyone to dance without effectively deciding who the appropriate reference group is to be – God, or the priestly class, or the critics of the New York papers, or the choreographer's smile, or the dancers' artistic conscience, or who. In any case, the question of what the values are will come down to who sets the standards. We will thus be left with a prima facie confrontation, as envisaged by McFee, between an endotelic work, establishing the standards it meets and creating the taste by which it is to be enjoyed, and the reference group or constellation of groups without whose recognition and endorsement the pretensions of the work are idle.

It sounds as if it would be an open question whether any generalizations can be made about what sort of values will meet this double challenge. But it is not quite open, as we saw at the beginning of this chapter. If it is possible to talk about dance at all, dance must be a specific practice; both the claim that what one is doing is dance, and the claim that one is criticizing what is done *as dance*, must impose some limitations. The conceptual link must be established in some way that is evidently not frivolous. Even the cultural commissars who purport to judge a ballet solely by its propensity to advance the cause of revolution are presumably able to tell the difference between a poster and a dance and must have some idea of what it is to express political attitudes in a balletic way rather than in a street-corner harangue.

In the first instance, no doubt, the judgments passed on dance are internal to a practice and a cultural group. But a distinction that can be made anywhere can be made everywhere. Any practice that is successful in its own terms thus throws out an implicit challenge for the world to meet. You can do what you do, it says, but can you do what we do? And wouldn't it be better if you did? Besides, if the values of any culture are clearly articulated and hierarchically arranged, what is thus articulated must be a set of real distinctions. Even if no other culture uses the same articulation, the possibility is always there.

The judgment that a connoisseur of ballet passes on a ballet-dancer's style is basically that it is balletic or non-balletic. The same judgment can be passed on a dance not in the ballet tradition, or even on a dance from outside the culture within which ballet is a dominant dance form. Such judgments are not necessarily stupid, but their relevance is clearly in question. It would have to be established by showing either that one was doing more than taking the criteria peculiar to a specific style and applying them to a different style with its own different criteria, or that such use of those criteria is justifiable – as it could be; it could, after all, be a source of new profundity or enlightenment.

My discussion so far has supposed that values can be articulated, as if the dance-makers as well as their reference groups could say what was good and what was bad in what was done, how they succeeded and where they failed. And it makes sense to say that, if there is to be evaluation, there must be justification. I think that is true, but must there always be evaluation? Obviously there need be none, unless there are choices to be made in a forum that is either public or established by one's own internal economy. Someone who simply does a dance may relish and prize it not *for* what it is, as though it had an extractable essence, but simply *as* what it is.

There is a double trap to be avoided here. On one side is the danger of supposing that, because one can say a great deal about what it is one likes about a thing or a person, one's liking must be a sum or resultant of factors one's explanation has isolated. On the other side is the danger of supposing that, because one loves something or someone in their full uniqueness, there can be nothing one could say about what one treasures. A compromise that may get the worst of both worlds is to say that what one treasures is what one thus enumerates plus an extra, ineffable something – *je ne sais quoi*. But what will get us the best of both worlds? That is a long story, which American philosophers, from the pragmatists of the 1930s (Prall 1929 and 1936) through Arnold Isenberg (1949) to Mary Mothersill (1984), have laboured to tell.

15.2 Generalities

This chapter is called 'dance values' but might equally well have been called 'dance and values.' Values extrinsic to dance may well be intrinsic to the life of which dance is a part. Dance is an enclave, we say; but there are no enclaves in life.

Each dance is prized just as what it is. Nothing else will be an exact equivalent of this dance as I experience it now, at just this time in my life and in my professional career, with my sensibilities attuned and sharpened just as they are now, my present action and experience interacting with the unique set of memories and expectations that can never recur again. But I can, after all, do the same thing tomorrow night; and whatever is 'the same,' and hence repeatable, in what I do will have the same repeatable values. If what I am dancing now is a waltz, its specialness will include its having the character and hence the value that 'the waltz' always has. Since it is a dance, it will have its proper subset of dance values. If it is a work of art, an exemplification or application of the art of dance, then the special nexus of values that belong to art will belong (or significantly fail to belong) to it. And since whoever is dancing, assisting in, or attending at the dance will be a social being, with all the responsibilities that come from membership in a human society, all social values will impinge on it in one way or another.

It may be absurd, I said, though it is not impossible, to take the values specific to one dance practice and apply them to what one acknowledged to be a different practice. But it is not evidently absurd to take the general dance values, or the general art values, or the general social values, of one's own culture and apply them to the dances of another culture. One's general ideas about dance, about art, and about social comportment are comprehensive views on how life can and should be conducted. Such views make no sense for one's own culture unless they can be applied cross-culturally. If I admit that they cannot be so applied, I am saying that they are not really standards for dance and art generally, but simply lay down what is accepted within an admittedly arbitrary practice. And if that was all I meant, I could have said so. On the other hand, to say that standards and values at a certain level of generality can be applied cross-culturally is not to say that any one such application is more legitimate than any other.

I have been dividing the general values applicable to any dance into social values, art values, and dance values. About social values this is not the place to write. Instead, I will say a little about the general structure of value systems and value terminology and then say something about art values and general dance values, in turn. I do not know how useful this can be, but my project requires me to point out the topics with which the philosophy of dance must cope, and this is certainly one of those.

15.21 Values in General

My early training in 'ordinary language' philosophy left me not knowing what the word 'values' meant. Nowadays I use it all the time, and I can hardly remember what it was like to be troubled by not knowing its meaning. Actually, though, it is very hard to say what it does mean. It is perhaps important that we find ourselves using in our philosophy a word that is neither well entrenched in the vernacular nor securely established in technical jargon, as though we were using a puff of ink to hide our confusions. The word seems partly to be a symptom of a determination to parcel the world into aspects – fact and value – on grounds that seem clearer at some times than they do at others, and partly to be an orator's word, part of that rhetoric of uplift and suasion for which no sort of clarity is required. But what precisely was the difficulty of understanding that I felt as a young man? A juvenile philosopher's balking at a word, in those days, was a sort of self-conscious declaration of mental purity. What I did not realize was that it is never enough to say one does not understand. There must be some definite obstacle to be cleared away; otherwise one is only suffering from the sort of queasiness of mind that any topic can generate at any time, like the sudden conviction that one does not really know how to spell one's own name.

The difficulty I sense now is that the word 'value' is a sort of catchall, lumping together various things the status of which was much clearer than that of 'value' as a presumed unity. 'Value' was once defined as 'any object of any interest' (Perry 1923, 115). That may be all right so long as you know what interests are, which I'm not sure I do; and so long as all interests are mutually commensurate, which has yet to be shown.

The word 'value' seems to cover at least the following. First, the standards by which performances are judged to be well or ill done. Second, the criteria by which things of a given kind are judged to be good or bad specimens of that kind. Third, the objects of desire and the objectives of action, that which we seek to attain or obtain. Fourth, the second-order standards by which such objects and objectives are judged to be worthy of the desires and aspirations we admittedly devote to them. Fifth, ideals: notions about what is admirable, beautiful, noble, glorious. Sixth, things that we would hesitate to call desirable, because they are not exactly to be obtained or attained, but which make life worth living: notably, love. Seventh, perhaps, the constraints we impose on ourselves, imperatives and prohibitions, considerations of right and wrong. Are these all somehow commensurate with each other? In a sense, it must be so. Whatever each of us is to have and do must be encompassed by our limited powers within a limited lifetime. Even if no common measure is possible, we must act as if we have one. At any given moment, there is one choice I have to make (or act as if I had made): what to do *right now*. Perhaps the use of the single word 'value' simply stands for this necessity, and the elusiveness of its meaning reflects the mixture of muddle and pain, boredom and delight, that makes up the confusion of our lives.

15.211 Basic Values

A traditional way of dealing with the multiplicity of values is to compile short lists of terms whose meanings may be contrasted, and to sketch their relationships. One such triad, made popular by Victor Cousin in the nineteenth century, distinguishes the true, the good, and the beautiful (together with their negative counterparts, the false, the bad, and the ugly).[5] Of the seven kinds of value listed in the previous section, objects, objectives, and second-order standards come under the second member of the triad. Ideals belong to the third, the beautiful. It is not really clear where constraints come, if they come anywhere, but it would really have to be the second. And such things as love would come somewhere under the second and third, but do not fit well.

An older version of the triad, which goes back to Plato, puts the 'right' where Cousin put the 'true.' The 'right' here stands for the morally obligatory and lawful, an entrenched set of what I am here calling 'standards,' and in this capacity corresponds exactly to what I called constraints; but it also stands for what is correct and right in connection with other sets of standards. The general idea is that of compliance and conformity. The good, in this version, is construed as incorporating the useful – what is good for some purpose – which takes care of criteria; but it also extends to all objects and objectives, including general welfare. It would thus include love, and whatever fits with that. And beauty functions in relation to ideals, as before: the beautiful, the fine, the noble, is what we admire and yearn for. Yet another related triad, which we find in Aristotle, says that people always act from one of three motives: the good, the beautiful, and the pleasant. The idea seems to be that rightness and morality, as such, do not motivate anyone; one has to have a sense of duty that presents morality as an ideal (transforming it into 'beauty'), or as the line of conduct that is called for by the state of things as they really are, and must therefore be to one's own long-term advantage (hence 'goodness'). In addition to the good and the beautiful there is the residual value of 'pleasantness' – the status of being an actual object of desire or satisfaction, without that desire or satisfaction being itself in any way evaluated. In this way, all value reduces to 'pleasure,' the fact that there are things we want and like; but, just for that reason, pleasure in itself cannot function as a value – it can never afford a basis for preference among alternative courses of action or experiences.[6]

The sets of value terms we use differentiate the various ways in which we think well or badly of things, the ways we articulate our choices and avoidances. The lists of preferred terms just mentioned show how one tradition of reflective thought has argued that such articulation could be ordered and simplified. The tradition is limited and obsolete, and doubtless enshrines cultural bias of many sorts. But no one has tried to do anything like this for a long time, and these lists will serve our turn. My point is not to argue for their specifics, but to suggest that any evaluation of dances and dancing rests on the basis of an overall system of values. The status of the evaluation is equivocal unless we have some idea of what that system is, if there is one; whether it is clearly articulated; whether it is stable or shifting; whether it is consciously present or merely implicit; whether it is finite or open-ended; and so on. Meanwhile, whatever its status, the upshot of our discussion is half a dozen terms or categories, with their contradictories and their contraries: the pleasant, the useful, the noble or beautiful, the good, and the mandatory – including (something I did not mention) the appropriate.[7]

Each of these terms represents a type of value applicable to dance in three ways. First, they may be values assigned to the practice of dance, as a whole or as defined by its nerve. Dance may be a pleasant pastime; a useful distraction or recreation; a locus of beauty, or a part of the finest way of life; something good in itself, appropriate to the human condition or to certain times of life – and it may be immoral in itself, to be forbidden as conducive to sin.

Second, as values operative in society at large, the terms may reach over into discriminations among dances; not all legitimate evaluations need be made in terms internal to dance practice. Some dances may be honourable and some dishonourable, social dancing may be conducive to good citizenship while theatre dancing threatens it, and so on. So it is useful to have a working notion of how many basically different kinds or dimensions one is prepared to admit into one's categorical schemes.

Third, the basic kinds of value picked out by our preferred terms operate internally within the practice of dance, as they must within any practice. There is a difference between the right and the good. Someone who has learned to dance, who has acquired the art of a certain kind of dance, has learned to do it *right*, to dance (it) correctly. Someone who has truly mastered the art has learned to do it *well*, to display the appropriate excellences of that kind of dance. And such a person need not necessarily do it right, because masters of the art have earned the privilege of doing things in their own way: rules are for people who have not sufficiently grasped the basis on which the rules were formulated, and on which accordingly the rules may be broken. But the privilege is not to be abused. Nothing is more notoriously problematic than the self-indulgence of virtuosi who believe their prowess exempts them from regularity and propriety. We put up with them, but we wish they wouldn't.[8]

Both rightness and goodness as thus conceived are distinct from beauty. The beautiful, as understood here, is what compels wonder, admiration, and delight. As such, it has nothing to do with the mastery of any art or with any excellence in it, because the assessment of mastery and excellence calls for comparative judgments and estimations and these differ from aesthetic acknowledgment in the same way that drawing a conclusion differs from assenting to a premise. Someone could, and many did, gaze spellbound at what Isadora Duncan was doing without admitting that she was dancing well or going the right way about dancing.

Rightness, goodness, and beauty are none of them quite the same as appropriateness or fittingness, which is a matter of meeting specific expectations based not on the inherent requirements of a branch of skilled accomplishment but on what is to be expected from someone (whether adept or inept) in the operative social context of their action. The interrelation of different values and standards is a matter of some subtlety. Friedrich Zorn, a dancing master at Odessa, remarks that in the quadrille no one dances the steps properly. He is resigned to that. What he cannot stomach is that nowadays people won't even move in time to the music; they simply walk through the figures of the dance (Zorn 1887, 168–9 and 182–3). What Zorn does not see, or will not admit, is that if everyone is indeed doing that, that is the right thing to do in an Odessa ballroom, whether or not it is the right thing to do as specified by the manuals that embodied Zorn's professional and artistic standards. To be either more or less expert, either less or more graceful and elegant, than one's actual role in the specific dance requires is to announce oneself as the wrong kind of dancer for the occasion.[9] That is what the young people of Odessa knew, and they weren't going to commit a social solecism by dancing *properly* just to please Dr Zorn.

We have, then, within the domain of dance, distinguishable values of rightness, including perhaps correctness and appropriateness, goodness, and beauty. As we saw in §3.74, there is a tendency for rightness to be digital and goodness to be analog – or to use an older language, for rightness to be quantitative and goodness to be qualitative. If I do something right you can check off the things I have got right. If I do a dance right I have made no mistakes. For this to be possible, it is necessary that the dance can be analysed into discriminable features; it is perhaps even necessary, and it certainly helps, if the dance can be broken down into 'steps,' action units that I can be said to perform or fail to perform (or not to perform 'properly,' that is, in such a way that I can be clearly seen to do them). But checking off points will seldom enable you to say confidently whether I have done it well or not, though you should be able to point to the aspects or features of my performance in virtue of which you give me your seal of approval.[10]

After goodness, rightness, and beauty, what else? What about morality, in dance terms? There is a morality of art, dancers keep faith with and do their duty by their publics, their choreographers, their fellow dancers, themselves. But I am not sure to what extent this would be a morality internal to dance, rather than an application of general morality to specifically dance behaviour. John Ruskin insisted that there was a probity of art, hence of the art of dance in particular, but his critics complain that he is moralizing about art in a way that is extraneous to art itself. Other artists, who are convinced that there is a morality of the art they practise that is distinct from general morality, may be accused of merely thinking moralistically about restrictions that they impose on their own practice on what are really subjective grounds, personal hang-ups that have nothing to do with art. But one could retort that artistic communities often are guided by moralities of both sorts and regard them as essential to the serious practice of the art.

What about pleasantness and unpleasantness, enjoyment and unenjoyment? The young people who take my ticket at the door of the theatre have taken to telling me to 'enjoy the show,' and I suppose they should know. But all the general arguments about the concept of pleasure are in place here (cf. Sparshott 1982c, 132–6). A dance (unless it is a magical utility, or a liturgical obligation, or something of that sort) must be a rewarding experience in one of the ways dance is rewarding, or why would anyone do it? But to be pleasant, or agreeable, or fun, or enjoyable, or a gas, is to offer only one special set of rewards.

15.212 Art Values

Some kinds of value pertain to art just because it is art; like the general values we have considered, these will also be dance values, to the extent that dance is art. Their application should be unproblematic and should require no such special discussion as the one we have just gone through; the general problems about considering dance as a fine art have already been dealt with, as have those distinctions among dances that become prominent in the context of art (§§3.7ff).[11] But there is much that could be said, and I will say some of it.

Now that art has become so self-conscious, and often so arcane, philosophers often say that art should be seen as art, with the idea of art in mind. One looks on a work of art as susceptible of interpretation, as having some meaning in relation to the practice of art. The ways in which works of art handle this relationship generate a double interest: they make the work interesting in itself, and the way the artist does this is interesting in itself. A further source of value lies in the way this specifically artistic interest relates to whatever other values the work is experienced as having – its beauty, its ideological soundness, its skilful execution, or whatever it may be.[12]

The distinction between the interpretation-based values of art as such and the various other values that works of art may have calls to mind the distinction between the primary standards of an art, those that relate directly to whatever the art is primarily practised for, and its secondary standards, which govern the ways the primary aims of the art are usually achieved (§3.3, above; Sparshott 1982c, 30). Given that the value of art lies in its being expressive, or authentic, or semantically rich, or whatever it may be, a beginner who is learning to produce works that will have that character and value will also have to learn various specific skills that are matters of mere technique. Virtuosity in these technical skills may come to be prized for its own sake, whether or not it is also held to be of artistic value.

Secondary standards in dance could be generated even if the only recognized primary standards were those internal to a specific dance, in the way considered in §15.1. Suppose that in dancing the saraband all one could say was that one had to learn the saraband. Still there might be certain skills, neutral in themselves, that were contributory to doing that, and proficiency in them might be assigned a certain value of its own. Then suppose it turned out, as it well might, that the same skills were contributory to the equally irreducible abilities to dance the courante and the fandango. If that were recognized to be the case, then these secondary standards would have to be recognized as general standards of excellence or propriety applicable to many (if not to all) dances. And since this 'many' was arrived at inductively, we would have to say that the criterion or standard, whatever it was, was prima facie applicable to dance in general. We would then be recognizing an ability to dance that would be logically distinct from the abilities that sufficed for excellence in any specific dance. It sounds quite absurd; but I am not sure it is.

Once secondary standards in an art are fully recognized, emphasis may be variously divided between these and the standards that remain primary. Nor is it merely a matter of the relative weight they are accorded; interest may be taken in the way they are related, the way they modify each other, the degree of their mutual independence, the way they are played off against each other, and so on. Their situation, as described above, may even be reversed: secondary standards may coalesce into a comprehensive academic style, and the supposedly primary standards be reduced to a manner of achieving this new primary goal.

M.H. Winter (1974, viii) quotes a review of a Charles Bernardi ballet from the Brussels *Gazette des Pays Bas* of 21 June 1763: 'The entire plot was generally well understood, the different groups well-arranged, the positions elegant and picturesque, the action well-ordered, the passions elegantly expressed, everything could be divined. ... ' Winter remarks on how uninformative such criticism was; to find out what the dance was actually like, she says, one would have to find a contemporary drawing. It is quite right to say that the critic tells us nothing about this particular dance. We are, however, told a great deal about dance in general. We learn what demands were made on theatre dance, the dimensions of dance value, and the foci of critical concern: plot, grouping, position, action, passions; understanding, arrangement, elegance, picturesqueness, order, energy in expression, clarity. It is as if we had a list of things to look for, a troubleshooting chart, and checked off each item on the list as we came to it. Assuming that we have the critique in its entirety, this performance of the Bernardi ballet is being given a clean bill of health.

Critics might use such check-lists in several ways. First, the critic might compile in advance a list of things to look for and check each of them out. The critic could do this on the basis of long experience of the ways things go right and wrong in dance, or simply sit down and work out a priori what the possible merits and demerits of a theatre dance performance could be. Alternatively, the critic might attend a performance with open mind and simply wait for favourable and unfavourable impressions to be made, relying on long experience and acuity to guarantee that nothing would be missed, so that a check-list could be compiled from a thorough critique (or, more probably, from a series of such critiques) without the critic ever having given the matter explicit thought. Or, as quite often does happen, a critic might have an explicit set of things to look for, things that every critique should say something about if there is room, and be alertly open to other things that might need mentioning but do not always. For instance, a critic needs to note the quality of the music, its appropriateness, and how well it was played (though the Brussels critic concentrated on what was actually danced and how it was danced and left the music out of account, unless Winter omitted that bit) but does not always need to say whether the air in the auditorium smelled of frying onions or of patchouli. And this residual set of possible topics might itself be determinate (one knows that one does sometimes have to mention the smell), or might be quite open-ended – who knows what might come up? In reality, I suppose, critics approach performances with a loose hierarchy of considerations ranked by importance and probable relevance, tailing off into a misty area where things are marginal or surprising. A historian could go through a set of critiques and come up with a ranked list of considerations deemed important or relevant to the criticism of dance. The value of such a list would be questionable, though; what people find it necessary to talk about depends on what happened.

The kind of value structure I have been describing does not depend on applying a range of diverse value considerations to an entity initially conceived as homogeneous but allows for the complexity of the entity, simply registering that in certain named respects the performance was OK or not OK. A more elaborate critique would, of course, unpack the OK and not-OK into explanations. If a work of art is a performance considered with respect to its design, the relevant complexity of any work of art will have a fairly constant structure, answering to the complexities of peformances and of designs.[13] Performances involve what is performed, the performing of it, and the action of the performer; design involves the hierarchies and cooperations of the design act, the human action that generates the design. In the case of dance, as of other performing arts, this involves the interaction of scenarist, choreographer, and dancers (see §18.1 below); it also involves everything necessary actually to produce a theatre dance onstage. In the dancing there must be movement/stillness, action/rest, passion/resistance, expression/-impassivity; in the interaction of the dancers there must be interaction or compresence (and a lot of things we mentioned before); for the dance to be visible onstage there must be place and space, light and dark; and there must, it seems, be sound (music or noise) or silence, if only because feet thump. The basis of evaluation in theatre dance lies in the necessities of dance action and production, and at the heart of these are the common necessities of performance art and of art generally.

The necessities of which we speak are partly discovered, partly produced. An art must develop, as Richard Wollheim (1987, chap. 1) explains, in a dialectic. We appreciate something; we find a way of producing something that can be appreciated in that way; what is produced is appreciated in a new way; we find a way of producing what can be appreciated in that new way; and so on. In a sense, the possibility was always there, but its uncovering is a historical process.[14] So we say, the quality of the music is always an issue in theatre dance. But it need not have been. It could be that, at first, a stamping and clapping served only to encourage and to keep time. Then people found they could clap expressively. ... And so we go on. Now we are in a sense stuck with music, because, although some dancers may pay no attention to that, their paying no attention to it becomes an integral part of their way of dancing.

15.2121 Dimensions of Art

In §4.11, I introduced the three dimensions of significance that aestheticians of very different theoretical and cultural affiliations have ascribed to works of art as such. The first dimension is that of sheer presence, answering to the status of the work as aesthetic object, as contemplable or contempland. The second dimension is that of structure and form. The third dimension is that of the way humanity is manifested in it, its expressive aspect – not its quality of being expressive, for it might not be, but the way it relates or fails to relate to the world of human praxis and affect of which art is a characteristic manifestation. The three dimensions of art correspond roughly to the three kinds of dance I distinguished – the mimetic, the expressive, and the formal – which in turn answer to the three stock theories of art described in textbooks of elementary aesthetics. The simplest version of the triad is perceived quality, expressed and conveyed feeling, and understood meaning; a subtler version invites us to look at the work itself, to look inward to its human origin, and to look outward to its meaningful relations. Alternatively, we are to attend to the sheer presence of the work, to its structure as spatial reality, and to its quality as belonging to the temporality of vital experience. Whether these are really different or not is hard to say; it seems to be a matter of interpretative strategies, which involve much ambiguity.

Where versions of the three dimensions clearly differ is in where they put mimesis or representation. They reflect different emphases in discussing art, concentrating respectively on aspects perceived in it or relations ascribed to it. On the latter view, mimesis is, properly speaking, a mode of articulating a work: the formal structure of a painting depends heavily on the units constituted by the objects and persons depicted and their relationships; the structure of a dance is articulated largely by the episodes and relationships in the story being danced, if there is one. Dufrenne (1953) and others accordingly put mimesis in the second dimension. On the other view, representation as such is an aspect of meaning that takes us away from the work and refers us to the supposed objects depicted in the work; expression also takes us away from the work itself, to the supposed artist that the work projects, so that expression and representation belong to the same dimension. Both positions have their difficulties; neither set of difficulties is insurmountable; neither way of surmounting the difficulties is free from problems. To decide between them is unnecessary; to reflect on both is worth while.[15]

If we apply the threefold schema to dance, in the simplest way we can, we come up with an element of pure presence, the immediacy of the human body to which we are united in a sort of I/Thou relation (Buber 1984); an element of skilfully patterned and controlled and presented choreography, the form of the dance; and an element of what old theorists called 'gesture,' humanity deploying itself in characteristic motion, dance as a mode of living. And each of the three will have its associated values. There will be the dance variant of stage presence, epiphany; the values of agility, deftness, forcefulness, economy of movement; and the values of grace, majesty, vigour, and other aspects of humanity in meaningful motion. And now we may appreciate better that ambiguity in the placing of mimesis, because the mimetic aspects of dance plainly afford both a rich structural resource and a repertoire of affect.

The values associated with the three dimensions of dance, presence, structure, and expression, would be values of the unity, of the articulation, and of the totality, respectively, since it is in its totality that the work bespeaks the humanity from which it seems to issue. Can we say more about the typical forms of those values?

The special value of dance presence might be something like authority. The human person as source and centre of movement, rather than as a node of social interaction as in drama, would establish a simple dominance over the imagination. Any sort of radiant beauty would belong equally to the dimension of presence but would be less specific to the dance.

What of the second dimension? The general qualities of aesthetic excellence in animal movement, the triumphs of evident ease and economy, are in place here, and the word 'graceful' (though often confined to human gesture) is sometimes thought to capture these in a special way. But there are also general qualities of appreciable form, such as symmetry and asymmetry, balance and imbalance, rhythmicality and arhythmicality, which become thematized in dance works. I say something about these three pairs in particular.

I have already introduced the thesis that what aestheticians misleadingly think of as aesthetic qualities, such as symmetry, are aspects that creators have chosen to thematize, to make centres of interest and objects of appreciation in their work.[16] But it could not be an object of artistic concern just to make something symmetrical – that would be too easy to be interesting. Interest must lie in the way symmetry was achieved. That being so, it could equally be a matter of artistic concern to achieve asymmetry in an interesting way. If symmetry can be a term of critical encomium, so can asymmetry be: in both cases, it is the symmetry/asymmetry axis that can be a focus of artistic concern and, consequently, of appreciative and critical interest.

What is the special status for dance of the three pairs of terms we chose? Symmetry is relevant because human bodies are bilaterally symmetrical but imperfectly so (§§6.13–6.131 above). Right hand can match left hand in a pose, but humans are right-handed or left-handed. We can turn left or turn right, but it matters which way we turn. Left and right are socially significant. So the values of symmetry and asymmetry should be important in an art of specifically human movement.

As for balance and imbalance, it has been argued that the basic experience in balletic and much other artistic dance is the loss and regaining of equilibrium, so that dance would be above all the art in which values of balance and imbalance would be crucial.[17] Why? Because, in any discrete phrase of dancing, the dancer must start in a stable position (or the pose could not be held), from which any departure must be loss of stability, and must end again in a pose that can be held. For a dance to be perspicuous in its character as a dance, the beginning and the end, the departure and the return, must be thematized. So first position is first position.

The most obviously central value in the analytic dimension of dance is rhythmicality. 'Rhythm,' we saw, is basically just a word for the clear articulation of movement in time, and not a value term at all. The word 'rhythmic' is typically reserved for patterns that are attractive because they are specially marked and insistently recurrent; 'unrhythmicality' could be used for the converse quality, not lack of evident pattern but significant avoidance of obviousness of pattern. As in many such pairs, it may be, in some practice or even in all practice, that one is the value normally pursued and the other serves as a change, as a reaction, as a protest, or as a foil, because the opportunities it offers for exploitation are less obvious. Attractiveness, however, as we saw in §15.211, is not the only source of value.

Among the rhythms to which we ascribe the special value of rhythmicality, some are insistent, and are valued because they endorse the heyday in the blood; others are subtly seductive, teasing or massaging. Rhythms of both kinds are musical, singable, invite us to live along with them. Other patterns of movement repel such surrender, offering interesting or intriguing patterns for us to observe and tease out. Such rhythms may be called unrhythmical – not arhythmical, because there is a recognizable order, but not rhythmical either, because they do not invite us to move with them. Such rhythms might also be called unmusical and undancelike, on just the same grounds. Some music invites us to sing along, some does not; some dances invite us to join in, some do not. Perhaps we should recognize that there are unmusical musical pieces and undancelike dances, the work of a sensibility denying and transcending itself.

The fundamental value of the expressive dimension, one might think, is grace. Gracefulness is the best obvious word for that condition of the body in which it appears as totally ensouled, a perfect and full manifestation of generous life, and is what dancing masters existed to impart. Children and parvenus went or were sent to them to learn deportment. Deportment is, precisely, grace, and that in turn is simply the absence of awkwardness, awkwardness being that condition in which the body as a whole or in part seems not to be the integral person but becomes an awkward mass of stuff to be controlled. An awkward person 'doesn't know what to do with his hands'; graceful people don't know that either, because their hands are a part of them, not something one has to dispose of like an empty coffee cup.

Unfortunately for this suggestion, I already said that grace was preeminently the value of the second dimension, as the natural excellence and economy of animal movement. Human beings can be gracious as well as graceful (see chapter 22). Animals show unthinkingly the integrity of their life processes. Humans show the quality of humanity in responsibility and care as well as in joy.

The ambiguity in the notion of grace (on which I will have a great deal more to say presently) is a special case of a more general difficulty. A dancer is a human being; a dancer is the dancer's own instrument. We have seen that some thinkers object to that way of talking, reasonably, as a confusing metaphor. I cannot be my own instrument, something I use; who would be using it? The notion of an instrument requires separation of used and user. At most I can think of myself as other than the body I am in, and as using that body; but such dualism requires a strong theoretical commitment that many philosophers think cannot be consistently made, and I doubt if many dancers would find it congenial anyway. One could argue, however, that the arts always do require such reflective doubleness, in which one cultivates and exploits one's own personality without pretending to abandon it. Or 'everything happens as if' one were doing that; an artist adopts this stance of reflective self-exploitation, whatever may be the best way of describing it. But other artists, no doubt, do not, or are not aware of doing so, or do not play the game of pretending they do.

Whatever the best way to talk may be, many dance qualities are bound to belong ambiguously to the structural and expressive dimensions, because one performs as a created dance what one also does as a person. A typical movement quality, such as deftness, will certainly belong to structure; it is a quality of the movement of the body, not a global quality of a dance or a moment in a dance. But deftness is also a human way of being in the world, expressive of a fundamental project, and so forth. A racoon may open a garbage can deftly, with the neatness and efficiency that constitute deftness; but it does not do it deftly in the way a person rolls a cigarette single-handed, as an aspect of their being the person they are. Susanne K. Langer (1967, Introduction) pointed out that the vocabulary of art criticism is the best vocabulary we have for all vital movement, because the ways animals move are a special sort of movement, movements of organisms, and differentiated accordingly by differentiae of lives. Art exploits and develops and symbolizes movements of this order. Dancers are animals in fine fettle; that is not all they are, but it is an independently important part of what they are.

15.21211 Rasa Reviewed

Given that the work of art has the three dimensions of presence, structure plus representation, and human expression, we may argue as follows. The beauty, the impact, of a work depends on its making in its beauty a unified effect, a unity to which every formal and representational element of the work contributes. Because expressiveness is a dimension of the same work, this unified effect must be a humanly expressive one. The expression itself must be correspondingly unified. Consequently, each work must have one dominant affect, connected with a powerfully affective aspect of life. This affective unity is what the classical aesthetic theory of India called *rasa*; I discussed it before under the heading of expression (§5.1), but we now see that it more properly represents an integrated approach to all the values of art, specifically of the dance dramas to which it was originally applied. Every aspect of a work – music, formal structure, vocabulary, episodes – must be of a sort beautiful in itself and beautiful in a way clearly associated with that dominant tone, its relish or *rasa*. An artist's task is not to find new depths of experience to plumb or new outrages to jolt complacency, but to achieve this unity in an excellent way, in relation to one of the established modes of human feeling; the mission of art theory is to work out what the requirements and possibilities of the task are.[18]

This approach to art has had no effect on Western art practice and theory, and the dance-drama which is its supreme manifestation is admired but not followed. But the central idea is a powerful one: that the aesthetic appeal of art must be affectively tinctured, and essentially so.

15.22 Values in Dance

If it is true and meaningful to say that dance is a practice, and that there is an art or arts of dance, dance must have some determinate character, and this character must necessarily mark out certain ranges of value. Among all the things we favour or disfavour in any given dance, some will pertain to those aspects of the object of our concern that unite it with other dances.

It may be that there is nothing more to be said. I have already done three things. I have suggested that we can compile a general inventory of value terms and see how these cash out in relation to dance. I have proposed a general analysis of works of art and asked how this would apply to the evaluation of dance. I have argued that the real values of a specific dance (type or token) are determined by what precisely the dance is, so that the value lies in that and nothing else being achieved well, properly, and in accordance with all the more specific laudatory adverbs we can think of. We can now add that any enumeration of kinds of dance, such as the ones I essayed, is at the same time an enumeration of ways in which such specific values can be achieved. A dance that is characterized as a dance of one person (soloist) with many, and as being danced *against* those many, can in those respects be danced well, or correctly; it can also be danced with bravado, or sneakily, or cautiously, and to earn those adverbs unequivocally would in itself be a sort of merit.

More specifically, whatever is identified as the 'nerve' of dance practice will establish a set of central values for dance. If there is a limit on what that nerve can be, or on how nerves can be identified in specific cultural or historical contexts, that will establish a determinate structure for central dance values. Then again, any sketch of 'dimensions of dance meaning' (see §2.4 above, and Sparshott 1988, chap. 4) must support a corresponding structure of dance values; where we find meaning, there we assign value, and where we find value, there we postulate meaning.

In all this chaotic multiplicity of dance values, some are salient, and the upshot of our discussion should be to bring out the ways in which such salience emerges. This should leave us with a set of considerations that function from time to time, in specific cultural contexts, as importantly relevant to how a dance should be evaluated *as dance*. None of these considerations, once identified, can ever be ruled out a priori when one is considering the merits of a dance as dance, even if we decree, or conclude, that on some occasion, or in some age, they are not relevant. What has once been seen is proved not to be invisible, and may be seen again.[19]

We have seen how the three dimensions ascribed to art have their specific manifestations and values in art. But the peculiar relation of artist to art in dance offers us an alternative triad, which we encountered when we found that the same value terms appeared as aspects of form and of expression. The dancer's medium is the body, which is at least three things at once (§6.2). It is a physical thing that is set in motion, a human body that is set to perform personal feats, and the person himself or herself in action. Dancers are people, and dancing is a way of being a person if not a demonstration of personhood, and people cannot be indifferent to people. Actors in a play are also persons but hide their personhood behind the assumed personages whose parts they play. A dancer has nowhere to hide; if a character is being danced, the emphasis remains on the process of mimetic dancing, as in opera it remains on the singing (cf. §14.21). Nijinsky's leap is at once a visible arc and the feat of someone so controlling a leap as to give an impression of soaring and suspension; it is also the actual leap of a man exerting male strength.

It may be a mistake, though, to set up an alternative dimensional triad in this way. Rather, our sharing a common humanity with the dancers as dancers makes the spectacle of dancing a deeply ambiguous phenomenon, on which we have many perspectives. For instance, the fact that our senses are finely attuned to human physiognomy and posture, as they are to no other range of phenomena, and that this attunement has a preemptive force (which is why a neighbour's whisper distracts one's attention at a musical concert), means that our reading of a dance as an organization of movement risks perpetually running counter to our reception of cues to a human significance of a different order. Similarly, our awareness of dancers in their full humanity interacts in all sorts of ways with our sense of their corporeality – and human corporeality itself, as we have seen, is a many-sided thing.

In general, all the ways in which physicality, corporeality, social identity, and humanity may be meaningfully vested in dance must always be present, and may always be discerned and afford the ground of evaluation. But specific dance styles may characteristically single out one of these ways for emphasis and celebration and perhaps make one or more others unconsciously evident. And an audience can always read the dance according to the emphases its choreographers and dancers have given it, or in the way the dance's tradition prescribes for it, or in other ways dictated by their own predilections.

Meanwhile, it is probably better to reserve talk of 'dimensions' for the three introduced in §15.2121, which represent the convergence of a theoretical consensus.

Throughout this chapter, I have been discussing values of dance as considered from a spectator's viewpoint. The dancer's viewpoint has been taken into account only to the extent that it internalizes the judgment patterns of the culturally accepted judges that they identify as their reference group or groups. But dances must also have direct value for their dancers. Dancers must find multiform satisfaction and delight, and their opposites, in the very activity and achievement of dancing. To the extent that that is true, though, the values achieved can have little to do with theatre dance as performance art. Learning to practice an art involves discounting subjective experiences, perspectives, and gratifications, and learning to perceive and assess what one is doing as would an ideal member of the public. Dancers who think of particular works as 'fun to do,' 'challenging,' 'murder on the feet,' and so forth usually tell us this in an anecdotal or confessional tone, rather than as a privileged contribution (or counterpoise) to critical judgment. We are being let in to a private world where we are not expected to belong, the values of which are not expected to pass current in the public domain (see further, chapter 17 note 15). A great deal needs to be said here; but I am in no position to say it.

15.221 Special Values

What would be the most central values of dance as dance, that are neither general life values nor versions of the general values of art? On the account I have given so far, they might include the values of self-transformation and self-recreation, revelations of vital capacity. But we do not habitually use this as a category of dance value, even if reflection suggests that we should; if we did, one could argue that this is after all only a special version of the 'strangeness' that reflection shows to be at the heart of all art as such (§3.7).

Aside from that, the central values of dance as dance should be the excellences of the trained body in dance movement, in abstraction alike from the semiotics of art and from the reality and symbolization of personal motivation and social engagement. Of all arts, dance is the one that takes as its medium the admirable and expressive movement of human bodies. Its typical values, then, will be values of comportment, as realized in exquisiteness and vigour of development and control. Edwin Denby is the theorist who has most emphasized the way dance directly involves bodily posture and movement – the beauty, strength, and person of the performer.

Denby's collection of essays (1949) starts with an irresistible panegyric on this aspect of theatre dance as we mostly know it. The youthful charm of the dancers, he says, includes good build, open face, spring in standing, good carriage, strength in stopping, knowing what to do and where to go, and the enjoyment of their parts in a performance. On this base is superimposed an unusual control over movements, visible clarity of movement, differences of emphasis and urgency within motion, the continuity of impulse and culmination of phrase within simple movements and sequences. This, he says, is *showing* a dance, and includes showing how steps are related and how they make coherent sense, in relation to the music and to the story and 'as dance phrases purely and simply.' After mentioning how dance phrases may cohere in time and space, and in dynamics, he says that to dance intelligently is to make all these and their relationships plain to see (3). But, he goes on, we must add to these the look of individuality and spontaneity, originality in bringing the choreographer's dance to life; in addition to which, some dancers can give 'the sense of amplitude in meaning which is the token of emotion in art.' This last, he says, is 'the pleasure of the grand style' (5–6).

Denby insists that everything he has said applies equally to any dance technique, though he must be implicitly confining himself to Western theatre dance. The immediate relevance of this deeply considered review of values by an exceptionally experienced and thoughtful dance critic is that, though Denby insists that serious dancers never break out of the illusion, the whole pyramid of values rests on the pre-artistic qualities of actual youthful charm and returns to them again. This breaks with the venerable and austere tradition in aesthetics that contrasts charm with beauty, holding that the seductions of charm distract us from the beauties proper to art. That tradition of thought would hold that a high art of dance would not merely reduce youthful charm to one form of excellence among others; it would repudiate both charm and its opposites, on principle, as beneath the dignity of art. In fact, if ballet has been despised by artists more often than not, it is precisely because it is felt to trade on natural charm and facile glitter. If such charm is not to be dismissed as a false value of dance, dance itself must be dismissed as false art. But that, of course, does not concern us here, where we are prescinding from the special status of dance as 'fine art.'

15.2211 Grace and Vigour

Long before Denby, Adam Smith (1795) had identified two alternative systems of aesthetic value in specifically human movement, two ways of manifesting prowess. He identified these as grace and agility, two aspects of versatility that may be emphasized and assessed independently, corresponding respectively to the enhancement of bodily powers and their control. Some dances astound us by their vigour and nimbleness, some charm us by their harmony.

Rather obviously, this duality in dance values answers to a duality in natural processes, the yin and the yang. These are commonly thought of as a projection of male and female stances, as normalized in many societies. There are values of assertion, and values of discretion. (There is also an opposition of aggression and submission, which may be the brutal reality underlying the ideal.) There is a glorying in individuality and self-expansion; there is a sweetness in cooperation and self-giving.

It is a really perplexing question whether the connection between these two values and the two sexual orientations is intrinsic or adventitious. In Indian classical dance tradition, no bones are made about it: there is the dance of Siva and the dance of Parvati, the dance of male strength and power and the female dance of acceptance and tenderness. But there is also an obvious point to the contrast in value that has nothing to do with sexual orientation or role. In developing an art of human body movement, strictly as movement, one can go in the direction of greater and greater feats of strenuousness, together with their visible and eloquent synthesis in an artistic unity; or one can go in the direction of greater and greater refinement of harmony. There can be new and amazing feats of agility, there can be no new and amazing feats of grace. Grace may become more profound, more deeply affecting as qualities of heart and mind become more accessible. Agility as such has no profundity of affect. These are not abstractions and projections of alternative social roles or human types; they are developments and celebrations of complementary aspects of all human lives. And yet I, for one, feel that without the association with sexual stereotypes the contrast would never have been put in that way, or would never have been given the paramount emphasis it has.[20]

The grace and vigour that are the male and female versions of the stereotypical attractions of youth may be thought of as special cases, erotically tinged, of the more general perfections of the control and release of the body's energies to which the names 'grace' and 'athleticism' are also applied. These, in turn, are related to the yet more general contrast between the sublime and the beautiful, which has played an important part in the history of aesthetics (cf. Sparshott 1963, 70–88). In Kant (1790), the sublime is what delights the mind by overwhelming it in magnitude or strength, whereas the beautiful delights it by satisfying its propensity for order. In Edmund Burke's (1757) sentimental version, the sublime and the beautiful are equally universal in scope but derive their influence over us from symbolizing, respectively, rough male domination and soft female submission. More recently, Raymond Bayer (1956, 223–7) made the sublime and the graceful the major categories of aesthetic value. All works of art, he argued, are traces of artistic activity, signs of success in overcoming resistance. But there are two ways of succeeding. The sublime is the mark of a dominant idea fighting its way through opposition and obstruction; the graceful demonstrates power in the easy maintenance of control, whether in relaxation or in tension. The sublime emphasizes subject matter, the graceful is manifested in form and technique.

These oppositions between the rough and the tender, conquest and concord, vigour and grace, remind us of the ancient Greek distinction between *orchesis* and *choreia*, dances of individual vigour and of civic order, as well us of Plato's recommendation of two styles of dance – both for men! – for war and peace, respectively (chapter 2 note 6); not to mention Plato's demand for two kinds of dance in education, one to instil freedom and self-control, the other for physical fitness (*Laws* VII 795). Are all these dualities different aspects of one major opposition between aspects of reality, or alternative interpretations of such an opposition? Or are they a set of quite different antitheses, only loosely associated? Or is the whole area of discourse so vague that no such question can be definitively answered? I suspect that what people say about that will depend on large ideological or existential commitments. But it does seem that such a contrast as Adam Smith points to – between the beautiful and the graceful on the one hand and the sublime and the exuberant on the other – is centrally relevant to dance values.

15.22111 Grace

It was not Smith's dyad of grace and agility that became conventionally established as the dominant value of dance, but grace alone. How could that be? One possibility is that dance came to be thought of as essentially feminine; but surely there is more to it than that. An appropriately general account of the nature of grace was worked out by Raymond Bayer, not in the general work cited above but in an earlier work that massively explores the ramifications of a general aesthetics of grace.[21] In general, grace is always a manifestation of life, of the way animate beings integrate their movements, not simply with economical efficiency (as Herbert Spencer argued) but in such a way that all components of a movement are modified by each other and by the whole.[22] At the animal level, this shows itself in an integration of movement that is not merely hierarchical but unified in a single rhythm; at the level of human rationality it is shown not in the successful imposition of an intellectually conceived plan but in the integration of activity that is suffused with intelligence throughout.[23] 'Grace is a politics of dissimulation,' Bayer says (1933, II 275), and his final definition (323) makes the essence of grace 'the suppleness of the structural bond, a *play* in structures.' The structures of grace become concrete where system disappears.[24] In short, the artistic success shown in the achievement of grace lies in the victory over all enemies of freedom in the organization of body movement.

Bayer's aesthetic of grace pervades all the arts, to the extent that they manifest the kind of dynamic he is exploring. Why, then, is grace typically thought of as the special value of dance? Obviously, because of the special nature of dance itself, which in its most typical form represents precisely what Bayer has in mind: the permeation of human movement by intelligence and spirituality, cultivated for its own sake. And the elusiveness of the concept reflects the peculiar status of dance as a special art, in which humanity makes its corporeality visible: humanity is so complex and diverse, so many things are there to be seen.

Setting the results of Bayer and his compeers aside for the time being, we note that the word 'grace' covers at least four things: the perfection of animality made manifest; a special kind of sinuosity (identified in Hogarth's 'line of grace') that seems especially characteristic of that perfection;[25] the Greek *charis*, the charm that supervenes on carefree youth, the evident ease of life itself; and the graciousness of condescending majesty (including divine grace in all its forms). If we talk about 'grace' in dance, and do not somehow account for all of these, we may feel uneasily that we have left something out. Walter Sorell (1971, 105) tells us that 'John Martin once advocated the erasure of the word *grace* from the dance critic's dictionary' but gives it as his own opinion that such trite words are indispensable. Perhaps, though, the attraction of this word for careless critics is not its triteness but its multiple suggestiveness, which seems to contain in itself a world of thought – which the critic is, accordingly, spared the trouble of actually thinking.

In addition to the multiplicity just noted, the word 'grace' is used in ambitious ways that serve to explain the importance of dance itself. We saw in §5.311 how Sartre suggests that a dancer's body is permeated with conscious vitality, so that dance has a special phenomenological significance. 'Grace' would be a good word for this permeation, and grace would accordingly be a fundamental value of dance.

Gregory Bateson (1972) pursues a similar theme without specific reference to the body. He equates grace with 'psychic integration' in general: 'I shall argue that the problem of grace is fundamentally a problem of integration, and that what is to be integrated is the diverse parts of the mind – especially those multiple levels of which one extreme is called "consciousness" and the other the "unconscious." For the attainment of grace, the reasons of the heart must be integrated with the reasons of the reason' (129). Art, he says, is 'a part of man's quest for grace,' aiding and celebrating in various ways both the successes and the failures of such integration, and he remarks that different cultures seek psychic integration in different ways, sometimes opting for 'avoidance of complexity by crass preferences either for total consciousness or total unconsciousness.' It is because all art addresses this universal task and problem that we can appreciate arts of cultures with which we are unfamiliar – just as, he says, 'The physical grace of cats is profoundly different from the physical grace of horses, and yet a man who has the physical grace of neither can evaluate that of both' (129).

There is some confusion here. If grace is psychic integration, I see no reason to think that tortoises, millipedes, sloths, and hippopotami are less well integrated than cats and horses, even if we find the results of the integration less seductive.[26] The word 'evaluate,' which Bateson uses to insinuate an analogy between interspecies admiration and cross-cultural comprehension, gives the game away. What we *appreciate* in the cat is the perceived quality of movement – the delicacy, precision, lightness, and economy; what we purport to *evaluate* would be the psychic integration, and we have no grounds for thinking we can infer that from the sinuosity and the quality of muscular control that we relish. 'The central question,' says Bateson (129), 'is: In what form is information about psychic integration contained or coded in a work of art?' But we have no grounds for thinking that such information is contained or coded in a work of art, or that, if it is, that information is the ground of our cross-cultural esteems.[27]

Bateson admits that grace has many species: physical grace, as in animals and dancers, would be one; the general coding of psychic integration in art, not all of which is graceful (or interestingly graceless), would be another. If we could accept his general account of art, dance would be the art in which the inner value of all art was most evident.[28] But it seems more reasonable to associate the graceful aspects of dance (in those styles where grace is sought and achieved) with the fact that dance directly involves bodily posture and movement, the beauty, strength, and person of the performer. As Denby (1949, 34) puts it: 'Susceptibility to ballet is a way of being susceptible to animal grace of movement. Many people are highly susceptible to the pleasure of seeing grace of movement who have never thought of going to ballet to look for it. ... Art takes what in life is an accidental pleasure and tries to repeat and prolong it.' Denby, who uses language with precision, here relates physical grace not to the developed appreciation of ballet but to 'susceptibility' to it. Spontaneous, youthful grace, on this showing, would not be the supreme value of dance, but rather a basic value, belonging to the *Vorlust* rather than to the *Endlust*. The disciplined grace of conscious control, manifested in art as conceived by Bayer, would be superimposed on this or (especially in mature performers) substituted for it. After all, if grace is the specific value of the art of dance, it cannot be any sort of animal or spontaneous endowment, but must be some high-level integration. It is because of the many-levelled nature of dance that we keep slipping away from that truth.

High-level integrations cannot be expected to be obvious or easy. On Aschenbrenner's principle (cf. §15.2121, with note 16), to the extent that gracefulness is a value in artistic dance its converse should also be. We cannot deny to an artist the challenge of making artistic use of difficult materials. If grace expresses vital ease, there must be a less charming but no less valid mode of dance that expresses struggle and frustration in graceless, awkward, choked, jerky, and abortive-looking movements.[29] Such dance would be recognized as artistic by Bateson, as being seriously concerned with problems of psychic integration; but then, we may reflect, what isn't? Certainly, 'grace' is hardly the word that would come to mind here. But we might reflect, combining this thought with what we cited from Denby, that a body appears graceful because it *is* graceful, and that a dancer's first task is to make the body a fully expressive instrument, hence a vehicle of grace. Perhaps the movements people praise as graceful are those that not only possess but exemplify grace, whereas the dance movements we praise but call awkward or graceless are those that really possess grace but *express* its absence.

The position we have just reached seems not merely wrong but silly. It would be better to concede that grace is at most a specific sort of excellence in one sort of dance, seeming to have a privileged position only because it is directly connected with the bodily accomplishments that make for facility in dance, and the natural possession of which gives people an aptitude and often a taste for dancing. Making such a value central to the art of dance risks wedding that art to the raw charms of youth and beauty. And to stretch the meaning of the word 'grace' to cover artistically controlled movements of all sorts is mere obfuscation. But we should remind ourselves that kinds of art may be privileged when they come close to what gives the art itself a reason for existing (§3.76); graceful dancing as Bayer conceives it, a celebration of the triumph of integration, or as Bateson conceives it, a manifestation of the integration on which psychological and cultural flourishing depend, would certainly earn such privilege.

In an address on 'Both More and Less Than a Matter of Taste,' Calvin Seerveld (1987) proposed a reappraisal of the concept of taste that may help us here. In the days when people talked about judgments of taste, he argued, the good taste that such judgments manifested was an important human quality, the quality on which civilization rested. Civilization still rests on human qualities and sympathies, but not on the ones the eighteenth century valued: a country's war memorials show what it thinks of war and death and sacrifice and may thus be justly assessed as in good or bad taste, as expressing a good or a bad human attitude, even though a good war memorial should strike us as anything but 'tasteful.' In a rather similar mood, we may suggest that the movements in dance that one thinks of as graceful are those that, though describable as qualities of integrated movement on the one hand or evidence of psychic integration on the other, are those that are a metaphor for harmony and decency in social life. People who carry themselves well in social life, in the ways some of which Denby celebrates, attract us as expressing a fitness for a good society in ways that are already metaphorical. Grace in dance is the transformation of the gracefulness that dancing masters once sought to effect in their lay pupils, to make them look as if they ought to belong in polite society (see §3.3). When Rousseau, who took them literally, called such movements *singeries*, monkey business (cf. Sparshott 1988, 65 note), he was forgetting that the apes are above all social animals and no doubt rejecting outright the use of anything so artificial as metaphor in the serious business of human relations.

The dancing master has been a durable figure in our courts and polished societies. He was not just a trainer of professionals and a rehearser of amateurs, composer and timegiver, he was in the fullest sense a master of ceremonies. And ceremonies were important. When there were no more courts and no more ceremonies, the dancing master survived (from medieval times well into the nineteenth century) as the maker of social metaphors for the bourgeoisie. And the values he imparted were, precisely, the values of grace.

Today's society is not only corrupt and commercial, as all nice people complain; at its incorruptible core it is rough, various, improvised, changeable, not so much egalitarian as provisional. The frontier is in our souls.

The specific values of integration for which the qualities of grace were an appropriate metaphor do not have the commanding status they once had. But the status that grace had, that of the danceable metaphor of sociality, retains its importance. Let us give it one last try. Adam Smith's influential contemporary, the critic Henry Home (Lord Kames), distinguished human grace from the mere beauty of animal movement, which he thought could never amount to grace. In a horse trained for war, 'every single step is the fittest that can be, for obtaining the purpos'd end. But the grace of motion is visible chiefly in man ... because every gesture is significant.'[30] It is not the mere fact of integration that counts, not even the pervasiveness of intelligence throughout the motion, but the meaningfulness: to use modern language, a dance movement is a sign in a system of signs.

Kames's appeal to significance is not innocent. He couples grace not with the antithetical value of vigour as Smith did, but with the human value to which it contributes, the overall value of civilized human life. And this, oddly enough, is dignity: 'dignity alone with elegant motion may produce a graceful appearance; but still more graceful, with the aid of other qualities, those especially that are the most exalted.' And one needs 'an expressive countenance, displaying to every spectator of taste, with life and energy, every thing that passes in the mind.' Grace is accordingly defined as 'that agreeable appearance which arises from elegance of motion, and from a countenance expressive of dignity.'[31] But what is dignity? It is the species of propriety that reflects man's 'sense of the worth and excellence of his nature,' what attracts respect; it properly corresponds to virtue rather than to mere grandeur, but courage and generosity are more dignified than wisdom and justice because they make a more positive and direct impression on the beholder.[32] It is no wonder that his account of grace goes on to say that 'dancing affords great opportunity for displaying grace, but haranguing still more.' One is inclined to say of all this that the noble judge is speaking of graciousness, rather than gracefulness, and is doing violence to the concept of grace. But he might reply that not all dance deserves a gentleman's esteem and that a work on the elements of criticism should concern itself with what is truly valuable, not what people happen to like. Grace is significant, and its significance is the value of human comportment in the face that it turns to others.

In sum, the reason for making 'grace' the supreme and distinctive value of dance is the confluence of two lines of thought. First, the integration of the body trained for dancing, as epitomized by ballet training, has just the quality that our theorists extol as graceful; and second, gracefulness in behaviour and posture relates the practice of dance to a central value of humanity, civility in self-presentation, whereas agility and virtuosity are associated with the 'sheer unmeaning dancing' of show business. But the reason is not good enough; as we have seen, other values can be expressed in dance, including those of vigour and endurance, and these may be no less central to individual and social life.

In the last resort, the reason for the preeminence of grace may be something as simple as an emblem. The names of the Muses claim dances for themselves; but we have no image of the Muses themselves as dancers, rather than as patrons of dance. It is rather the three Graces who stand, not for creative art and skill, but for the intimate and universal generosity of the personality giving itself in community; and the three Graces are known, not by the names of their provinces, as the Muses are, but by the painted and sculpted image of their dancing selves. We meet them again at the very end of this book.

What is at stake in all these disquisitions about grace? Is the word 'grace' a mere label of prestige, which every theorist wants to sew into his or her own coat? Is it an elusive but easily recognizable property that proves hard to describe, like the smell of sweet-gale? Or is 'grace' just a vague word that means no more than 'excellence in dance of the non-flamboyant sort,' so that different analyses and descriptions of grace express preferences for different dance styles? That may be part of it; but it cannot be all, because the word 'grace' is applied to other things besides dance.

The word 'grace' and its cognates seem to be at home in metacritical contexts where we discuss whole realms of value. In such contexts, very vague and general words like 'grace' recur almost obsessively. But is the word any use in the actual criticism of dances? John Martin, we saw, thought not; but Walter Sorell demurred. It may be that, even when a movement is exquisitely graceful, that is never the most appropriate word to use of it; there are so many ways of being graceful, and the crucial question is which one we have here. One might use the word to refer to a movement in a context where grace is not looked for – in emptying a garbage can, for instance. But to use it of a dancer in the course of a dance is merely irritating. Its appropriateness is too general and too obvious: it merely refers the movement back to the common level of dancing.[33] For more precision, one would attempt a description or essay a simile; for a general encomium, one would rather resort to a current colloquialism like 'far out' or a loud whistle.

A word like 'graceful' is useful mostly in range-finding contrasts, as one might say that someone was the most graceful of dancers but someone else was more ethereal or more precise.

The main reason, however, why the bare word 'grace' seems as futile in criticism as it is unavoidable in theoretical discussions is not that it is the wrong word to use but that single words by themselves contribute little that is distinctive to their contexts. As Ted Cohen (1973) showed once and for all in his critique of Frank Sibley's (1959) article on aesthetic concepts (so influential at the time), to fasten on the word as unit is almost always a mistake. It distracts attention from the actual procedures and experiences of appreciation and enjoyment and falsifies the whole nature of critical discourse.[34]

To sum it all up, then: no one disagrees that the quality of grace is a good one (we would not normally use the word 'graceful' in disparagement), or about what sort of quality it is, or that it is relevant to dance. Theorists disagree about what other good qualities it is related to and needs to be differentiated from; about what bad qualities it is to be contrasted with; about where it fits on the spectrum of vitality between the physical and the spiritual; and about what place it holds among dance values. At stake in these disagreements are the true values of human life, as the life of a civilly corporeal being; the place among such values that belongs to a generous self-control, and how that relates to hardier and more obstinate virtues; the place dance holds in such a life; and the place dance should properly be assigned in that life, whether it now holds that place or not. These are not questions about the definitions of terms but about the orientations of our lives. And they relate to the chimerical ideal of complete virtue, the dream of a life that somehow combines the disparate excellences of divergent roles and contrasting life-styles: saints and heroes, nurturers and controllers.

The nature of grace and its place in dance is a properly contested issue. But, before we seek to resolve it, we must remind ourselves that what immediately confronts us is not a mysterious reality of which 'grace' is the name, but the endless multiplicity of occasions when people use the word 'grace' to apply to things of their own choosing, in situations and for reasons that reflect the histories and strategies of their own lives as they are living them at that moment. Let theorists debate as they will, nothing is going to change that.

15.22112 Athleticism

Gracefulness, when properly understood, has been held to be the one supreme value of dance, though in other senses the word picks out a more general excellence or a more specific virtue of some dances. That is why I have rehashed the issue at such length. But we recall that Adam Smith made grace one of two mutually complementary ranges of dance value, the other being the combination of vigour and precision that I called athleticism. However, while grace in dance is a basic excellence because it stands for a value that is fundamental in human life generally, athleticism has no such obvious basis among art values. Its human foundation seemed to lie in individual assertiveness as opposed to social compliance. That would explain why only one of the two complementary sets of values was ever built into the institutional warrant of dance practice. But could we find among the ideologies of art a place prepared for athleticism? It would be odd if we could not, in an age when the survival of the fittest was so variously appealed to. And we can, because Herbert Spencer and many others argued that all art is a form of play, and play is the manifestation of excess energy, so that art becomes the expression of individual exuberance (intellectual, spiritual, moral, physical, or other) in leisure. The dance of athleticism is an artistic metaphor for dancing for joy, dancing in triumph – the joyful triumph that was built into the Parthenon.[35] The men of the Bolshoi jump high and often, to loud applause, and why not?

None the less, despite Smith, there is no developed ideology of athleticism as the value of art dance. This may be because straightforward feats of muscular prowess and control, such as acrobatics and juggling, have their own status. In the Peking Opera, one of the most successful set pieces is a battle between crustaceans and something else, monkeys if I remember – a most spectacular display of bodies in intricate, precise, and exuberant movement. We wouldn't call it dance, exactly; it doesn't need to be dance. Perhaps it isn't even art. The performers are showing us how strong and clever they are, glorying in their prowess as humans in the fullness of their bodily powers.

It appears, then, that the emblem of the three Graces stands alone. But there is a vacant space alongside them, and in the Afterword we will see how it is to be filled.

15.222 Other Values

What other specific values of dance deserve mention? Any value can have its special manifestation in dance; the specific quiddity of any dance generates the idea of a value that could be sought and perhaps found anywhere; any dance could be danced in such a way as to earn any adverb of praise or dispraise. None deserves mention here, unless it is either central to dance practice or endemic in critical discourse. I will mention a couple.

Dance was once thought of as primarily the art of gesture. We would not say that now, because dance and dance values have shifted, but the point remains. The artistry of gesture is not a distinctive part of the actor's skill, and it is not a part of mime, being a mode of address rather than impersonation; but it is at least a recognized part of the art of dance. Its virtue must be gestural eloquence and remains a permanent possibility of dance, even if different traditions or even whole civilizations neglect it. It cannot be reduced to anything else, but is distinctive of dance and a distinct element within it.

R.F. Thompson (1974) singles out a value of West African dance traditions that he calls 'coolness,' a sort of aware dignity of self-possession; it is a quality recognized wherever African dance has spread its influence, which is almost everywhere. It comes close to what Bateson thinks of as grace but is not the same, having less to do with psychic integration than with social presence. As we did with grace, we ask of coolness whether it is a quality of comportment esteemed in the society at large, and recognized in dance only because dance participates in the values of the wider culture (and, of course, especially its values of comportment), or a specific dance value that has spread its influence everywhere. The difference becomes negligible if a culture is saturated with dance values, dances itself as it were, as people (for example, Gorer 1949) used romantically to imagine was the case in Africa; or if the pervasiveness of the value is itself enough to give dance, in which it is so fully and prominently exemplified, a special place in the culture.[36]

Finally, we must not forget the specific values that define a style no less definitely than the steps associated with it. Terms such as *ballon* and *aplomb*, as the French language suggests, are inseparable from ballet; the qualities are excellences and accomplishments in areas pertinent to many kinds of dance, but it verges on absurdity to apply them to anyone other than a ballet dancer. This is partly because they are qualities highlighted in typical ballets, but principally because the terms really designate the qualities in question *as they are manifested in ballet*. I do not know of any such terms appropriated to any other dance tradition. This is probably because I just don't know them or cannot now call them to mind; but it could be because no other dance tradition is so stable, so formalized, and so self-consciously cultivated as to generate such a specialized vocabulary.

15.3 Dance Criticism

Throughout this chapter, I have been referring to critical discourse as though this were the proper domain of dance values. But, apart from the comments on check-lists in §15.212, I said nothing about critical discourse as such. Should there not be a chapter on dance criticism? Perhaps; but I have nothing specific to say about dance criticism in particular, and I have written at such length elsewhere on criticism in general that I confine myself here to a few cursory remarks.[37]

Graham McFee, we recall, says that understanding dance is entirely a matter of understanding explanations of dance, and such explanations are the work of critics. If that is true, criticism is vital to dance; in fact, dance as such could not meaningfully be said to exist without a practice of dance criticism to sustain it. But what is dance criticism? Criticism of dance, presumably; so that it purports to depend on the practice of dance, rather than the other way round.

What, in general, is criticism? One answer is that it is 'discourse apt to ground evaluation.' The idea is that the critic starts from a description of what is done, then provides an explanation and interpretation that shows how that description supports an evaluation with which the critic concludes.

Evaluation, though, is something we are seldom called on to do, unless we are judges in competitions. And how is the initial description arrived at? Is a description ever anything other than the justification offered for an interpretation? Does the formula I offered do more than suggest a theoretical articulation of an attentive appreciation to which any verbal exposition is secondary? If that is all it is, critical discourse may be what many say it is – a web of words concocted from the residue of other such webs, connected loosely if at all to what the critic really saw and felt. In any case, the alleged three-stage process should be replaced by a dialectic. One might equally start with an evaluation, then produce an interpretation that would support the evaluation, then formulate a description that would warrant the interpretation. Or the interpretation, the divination of meaning, might come first. Most likely, all three would be developed in relation to each other, and which was the most important would depend on circumstances.

Let us try another tack. From concepts, let us turn to facts. Dance critics are people who publicly say and write things about dance and dances, dancing and dancers. As such, they will say, inividually, what they want to say about whatever interests them. Why ever should they not? They will, collectively, write about whatever they think will inter-est their readers; if they did not, a market would go unsatisfied, and that would not last. They will write, or publish, what their editors and employers demand, approve, or tolerate. All that, and only that. How could it be otherwise? There are, no doubt, societies in which discourse is otherwise controlled, but I am not aware that there are any dance critics in such societies.

Given this mass of heterogeneous writing on everything anyone finds relevant to dance, two questions arise. The first is, are any of these interests salient enough to be worth mentioning in a general account of criticism? The answer to that is that the salient interests would answer to salient aspects of dance. Books like this one would be where to look for an answer. The second question is whether the word 'criticism' marks out any distinctive area in this immense field. And the immedi-ate answer to that, though it will have to be modified, is that there really is none. Criticism is not a discipline. There is no tradition or skill of criticism in which one could be trained, no accrediting body for dance critics; in fact, one cannot conceive how such an accrediting body could gain authority.

The first modification we have to make is that dance criticism can indeed be contrasted with other sorts of writing. Criticism is not sociol-ogy, is not history, is not theory; reviewing is or is not really criticism, depending on context. But none of these contrasts can be detached from particular contexts: almost all critics will on occasion do biography, or history, or sociology, or aesthetics, or ethics, as part of their criticism. Dance works as we encounter them are as many-sided as the interests taken in them and the influences exerted on them; the dancers, creators, and producers of dances are real people in real situations, and all of this reality affects what is done; people who are interested in dancing may be interested in all or any of it. Someone may dismiss some of this interest as aberrant or irrelevant; but this dismissal, though it may be supported by argument, has no authority. Whence could such authority be derived?

The second modification to the thesis that dance criticism is not a discrete part of discourse about dance, but the totality of that discourse when it is carried on in the public domain, requires us to turn from the factualities of criticism to the institutions of theatre art dance in a large, multicultural society. For all the multiplicity of human interests that goes to make their work, the art of dance is carried on by professionals working in the terms of traditions to which they are related in complicated ways, with skills they have laboured to perfect in ways whose full appreciation requires a skill in connoisseurship comparable to their own. The public for the art of dance as such is interested in the outcome of these traditions and skills; that, and the imagination released by their means, are what the public wants to appreciate. No member of the public, however, just because it is a public, has time and opportunity to develop connoisseurship in all such skills and traditions; in relation to any given style of dance, each member may have any degree of understanding and love.

In such societies, critics fulfil the needed function of intermediary. They tell us about the tradition a work belongs to, about the ideologies that go with the tradition, how it relates to other traditions. They tell us what to look for, so that we can see the design in the work and discern the relation between work and performance. They tell us how a work relates to its own tradition, exemplifying, advancing, or denying. They may discern for us what in the work is part of the design, what is unconsciously betrayed as subtext, what is accident; they may tell us things about the background which explain how it came to be the way it is. All of these things do help. They help us to appreciate the work as we experience it.

That is how critics operate within the institution of theatre dance in a large and diverse society. It is the people who do this who are called critics, because they practise criticism in an institutional way in the context of the overall institutionalized practices of dance and art. People of high culture used to deplore the necessity of such criticism, attributing it to the unfortunate admission of plebeians into what once was an aristocratic audience well attuned to the nuances of the best artistic practice. But they were quite wrong; they were able to maintain this stance only by remaining ignorant of most of what was happening in the arts.

Within institutionalized criticism, there is a variety of functions. Some critics keep up with all the latest happenings in the newest studios. Some confine themselves to one tradition and demonstrate the appreciation of its finest points. Some – the reviewers – act as truffle hounds, discerning which of all the stuff on offer will most or least repay the public's scanty supply of available attention and purchasing power.

The rich diversity of dance, which makes institutionalized criticism a necessity, also makes for a rich diversity of critics. Do we need a supercritic who will do for the unmanageable diversity of criticism what critics do for the diversity of dance? No. Who would judge the supercritic? Anyway, the available practitioners of criticism are few enough that we soon get to know them pretty well.

Having commented on the concept of criticism, the realities of criticism, and the institution of criticism, we are left to observe that what critics do is write or (less often) speak. A critique is a performance, no less than the performance it comments on. The best critics are good writers – they have to be, for their task demands large resources of observation and language. They create imaginative experiences in powerful and evocative words. Sometimes their creative power detracts from their usefulness as intermediaries, but not often, because it is the sharpness of their vision and the depth of their love, without which they would not have become critics, that lend their language power.

Like those of literary critics, the writings of dance critics are freely read by people unacquainted with the works criticized. With literary criticism, one can perhaps propose or pretend that some day one may read the books; but the dance performances are gone for ever. Why do so many people find it worth while to read the collected critiques of a Denby, a Jowitt, a Siegel? Is it merely the pleasure of fine writing, the cadences of a supple prose and the quality of mind it conveys? Or is it rather the pleasure of gossip, the aimless fascination with which we learn on the evening newscast of the fires, fêtes, and crashes that have ruined, enriched, or terminated the lives of strangers? Is it the illusion that the critiques enable us somehow to conjure up spectral dances in our imaginations? Is it the hope that, should we find ourselves at a party amongst people who are discussing dances they have seen, we could understand the conversation and might even join in? Or is the delight we feel akin to that we imagine in *Piers Plowman*, the vision of the dance world as a field full of folk, going exuberantly and gallantly about their multifarious business?

15.4 Conclusion

The admitted values of dance are distinctive and elusive. Gracefulness, gestural eloquence, the manifestations of vigour and vitality, the power of personal presentness, the revelation of new possibilities for life – these all call for elucidation and interrelation. Philosophers need to discuss which of them, with their cognates and surrogates, have their true home in dance and and are present elsewhere merely by metaphor; which of them are ubiquitous in art and perhaps in natural beauty as well, but in dance take on specific forms that need to be identified and elaborated; and which of them are associated with dance only through rhetorical traditions. Perhaps these terms, or a selection of them, are generic aesthetic values, specific to dance only in the manner of their interrelation. Perhaps, too, there are other values of equal or greater importance that my treatment here has missed.

In any case, what is open for enquiry is not what words we should use in criticizing dance, for we should be prepared to use all the words we have. Nor will our enquiry teach us how we should dance, or how we should look at dance, which we can learn only in the long practice of apprenticeship and spectatorhood. The best we can hope for is that we might better identify and neutralize temptations to misdirect our attention, to confuse what unites all dances with what categorizes some of them, and to speak of dancers as though something other than a dance were being performed. Meanwhile, it is an old habit with us to use key terms like 'grace' to mark the turns in our discussions, and it will be a long time before we are convinced that the habit is always a bad one.

CHAPTER SIXTEEN

Dancer and Spectator

One of the ways I classified dances was by their relation or lack of relation to persons, other than the dancers, for or to whom the dance was performed. Social dance does not require spectators, though part of the meaning of our social dances is that any pair of dancers may stop dancing and become part of the context, an informal audience, for the others, and those others dance as in the presence of these and other bystanders. French court ballets attracted masses of spectators, but they came to see the king and his court rather than as an audience for a dance – to be there and to be seen to be there, to look at the king being looked at, as worshippers rather than as connoisseurs. Many ritual dances are danced *for* initiates, but as a present force rather than as a spectacle: the initiates are to be impressed rather than pleased, are danced *at* rather than *to*. In a dance of healing, the dancer is likely to dance *to* the invalid, or the spirit that has invaded the invalid, but to dance *for* the relatives of the invalid – who, however, are not so much spectators as witnesses and coadjutors of the healing act.

In many ritual dances and ceremonies that have or approach the status of dance, the dance is performed neither *at* nor *to* those present, and certainly not *for* them; but it is danced *before* them, and could not properly be done otherwise than in their attentive presence. Some have speculated that all art is descended from practices having this status, to which the appropriate response hovers between awe and appreciation. Some have thought that art, in losing this status, has lost most of its value. Lukács, however, thought it was the essential mission of art to secularize and defuse such dangerously mystifying practices, so that their victims attain the dignity of true spectators.[1]

Theatre dances exist, or have come to exist, for spectators, in so far as a theatre exists for a public. It is not only that they are performed for audiences, and conceived with such performance in mind, as Paul Thom explains (1993a); the very kind of dance that they are could exist only within the institutions of theatrical presentation. They are aesthetic dances in a visual mode. There may be other dances, too, that depend on spectators for their meaning: there is a gradation, as we saw in §3.3, from dances that people find worth watching, through dances that the dancers know that people find worth watching and dance with special care for that reason, to dances that exist to be watched. Once such dances exist, however, they can be danced in isolation; it is possible to develop in solitude a dance that no one will ever see, even though the kind to which it essentially belongs exists only to be seen. As soon as the spectator's viewpoint is established, choreography becomes possible; and it is obvious that one can choreograph dances that never come to performance, and that dancers can be their own choreographers.

Practitioners of dance as a performance art must surely, like practitioners of any other performance art, develop a mode of awareness of the dance they are dancing in which its visual qualities are primary, even though they are not visible to the dancer in the act of dancing. The awareness of the dance as such is an awareness of how it would be looking.

What comes of such a mode of awareness when there is no spectator? One dances as if there were one, in anticipation of a public. But how can one justify maintaining the visual mode of awareness, as against the kinaesthetic mode through which the body is actually perceived, if no spectator is expected?[2] The obvious thing to do is what other artists do when no public is in prospect: to postulate a real but ideal spectator, to dance for God, whose power of seeing all things becomes, for once, a blessing rather than a threat.[3]

It would be too simple to say that a theatre exists for its audiences. It exists for the artistic satisfaction of playwrights and players, for the prestige and civic health of its community, and for many other things besides. But it can hardly do those other things without appreciative and discriminating audiences. So it is not too much to say that theatre dance as danced in a theatre is done at least partly for an audience; and, I would add, for the whole audience. Such audiences are heterogeneous. Among us, they are likely to include most of the following.[4] First, show-goers, people who will go to see anything that is presented with sufficient éclat in a large enough and posh enough hall. Second, show-goers who go to shows mainly to be seen going to shows by other show-goers, whose demands on performance may be only that they shall be mildly entertained in no specific way. Third, body-lovers, who like to see young and healthy people jump around in ways that gracefully or athletically show off their youthful attributes. Fourth, art-lovers, who take interest in the art of dance, or in the specific genre to which this evening's dance belongs, or in art generally.[5] Fifth, dance-lovers, delighted denizens of the world of dance, learning and exploring all its ways. Sixth, connoisseurs of technique, who are interested primarily in perfect fulfilment of the secondary standards governing this evening's kind of dance. And seventh, balletomanes, ballet freaks who like to lose themselves in the glamorous world in which ballet seems to operate, and their counterparts in the counter-culture in which contemporary dance operates.

A public performance is necessarily directed to all of these, as well as to such fringe members of the audience as students and critics. They are there, they have paid. A dancer may be guided by the precepts of the ballet mistress and dance in the first instance for teachers and colleagues, who constitute the real reference group by whose judgments the operative standards of dance are immediately defined; but the pressure of the known presence of those others cannot but make itself felt. That coarse phrase 'bums on seats' expresses the crassness and ineluctability of the pressure they exert. The dancer must therefore be sustained by a very complex body-image. The elaborate bows and curtain calls for which ballets are notorious embody a deep irony, but a deeper sincerity: they are a danced acknowledgment of an impossibly complex but wholly legitimate set of demands.[6]

What I am saying here is not the same as what Thom says about performance art generally. Performers, he says, respond to the overall response of their audience as a whole (which, we recall, takes the form of a 'beholding' that includes attentive awareness of the surroundings as well as of the performance as such) and tune their performance accordingly. Such response may enhance their performance, or damage it. My present concern is with the performance that the dancers prepared, the realization of their rehearsals; and with the spectators who, whatever their state of preparation, came to see just that. My point is that, even on this restricted understanding, what was rehearsed for is an ideal entity radically different from what will take place before an audience. The shock of actual presence is something that cannot be anticipated.

A spectator is someone who is not a dancer – at least for the time being.[7] Different ways of not being a dancer (see §3.6) generate different ways of being a spectator. A dance into which I am unable to enter because I am unathletic and untrained cannot mean the same to me as a dance into which I cannot even imagine myself entering. If, for instance, I think of a dance as a 'work of art,' its aesthetic nature may depend on my assigning it to a realm of imaginary or virtual objects, or on its status of essential objecthood; in either case, I could hardly imagine myself as participating. And neither of these kinds of dance can mean the same to me as one into which I *must not* enter, because it is sacred or the privilege of a special caste. On the other side, my experience in watching a dance into which I might enter – it is a free country, I could train for a dancer – is not that of watching a dance into which I habitually enter, in which tomorrow it will be my turn to perform and theirs to watch. And neither of these is the same as my experience of a dance into which I have to enter because I am compelled or commanded, as Tiresias tells Cadmus in Euripides' *Bacchae*: 'The God made no distinctions, whether it was the young people who must dance or their elders: it is his will to receive a common honour from all.'[8] All these ways of not being the dancer of the dance I watch will determine how I see it, what I look for, what I see, in what frame of mind – what I am as spectator, what the dance is for me.[9]

Dance as an occasional exercise is an elaboration and extension of such aesthetic movements as everyone from time to time makes anyway, so that everyone is incipiently a dancer; but art dance, made up of steps that have to be learned, can be performed only by a specially disciplined body. The latter sort of dance is especially tantalizing for the spectator. When I watch such a dance, the body I see in motion is a human body, like mine and yet not like mine. The unlikeness rebukes me, because the fact of its excellence is more evident than the special training that bars me from competition.

The rift between participation and display is in fact wider in dance than in most other arts. Such verse-writing, play-acting, music-making, drawing, and so forth as we learn in school are continuous with the highest achievements in the corresponding fine arts. That is not true of dance. Neither the dances children learn at school, nor the dances adults learn socially, have any real continuity with the high art of ballet, or with its counterparts in other civilizations. We have all danced in rudimentary ways, but theatre dance is remote from our experience. We all dream of dancing, of flying, of performing movements beyond the capacity of our bodies; it is the proximity to our dreams and the remoteness from our waking bodies that is poignant. The classical dance arts of India and Europe, in which the body is made over from childhood on, and kept in condition for the art only by rigorous constraint continuously renewed, are arts from which we are alienated, exposed to a manifestation of humanity from which our experience of our own humanity is excluded.[10]

There are, then, different ways of being a spectator. Some of these different ways of being other than the dancer one is watching are generated by the situation of spectatorship itself – whether one's exclusion from the dance is merely a temporary condition, or a matter of life divergence, or a downright prohibition. It follows that there is a clear sense (the sense defined by such plain facts) in which the spectator one is is different from the person one primarily is. That remains true even if one regards the 'person one primarily is' as a construct, or as a product of impure reflection, or as a set of roles assumed in interpersonal relationships, or in some other non-naturalistic way. Whatever view one takes, it still makes rough sense to think of a human being, in society and in solitude, as either a totality or a privileged set of traits that define the target of that individual's biography or autobiography, the psychic and social facts most constantly associated with the body's lifetime. It is this totality or privileged set that can be contrasted with the role and the role-player associated with the highly specialized context of dancing and dance-watching. It is true that if we probe too indiscriminately the contrast may fall apart, for the very concept of a 'person' clings to its etymological origin as *persona*, a player of roles, and in discussions like the present these origins return to haunt it; but, as soon as we relax and revert to our everyday acceptance of the glaringly obvious, the contrast reinstates itself.

The relation between spectator and person corresponds to that between dancer and dancing person. In the artificial concept of 'performance' I introduced elsewhere, the agent correlated with a performance, such as a dance, is the postulated performer of precisely that dance as it is taken to be danced, in abstraction from any biographical facts or contingent acts that we know to be in reality inseparable from that performer (Sparshott 1967 and 1982c, 38–43). We make an abstraction, knowing it to be one. Just so, watching a particular dance performance has itself the nature of a performance. The spectator (as such) of the dance (as such) is abstracted from the individual who has a whole life before and after the dance-going, and who, even while spectating, is liable to distraction by extraneous worries, physical discomforts and diversions, and associations with the dance or the dancer that are admittedly irrelevant but intrude to disrupt spectatorship.[11]

The performer of the act of spectatorship is like the perceiver of the aesthetic percept, the experiencer of the 'aesthetic experience' as Virgil Aldrich (1963) described it. In such experiences, a person deliberately abstracts from the general context and everyday modes of some episode of looking (or listening, or sniffing, or tasting, or palpating, and so on) and fastens on a special way of doing so, in which only certain beautiful or striking features are isolated and developed in and for attention. We would be doing this in our spectatorship if we used our eyes and our skills of looking in a way that enabled us to perceive the maximum of beauty or interest in the danced movements.

The mind-set in which we select for maximum beauty and interest may be called the 'aesthetic attitude.'[12] But what I am thinking of as spectatorship goes beyond this: I am concerned with the spectator's prior potentiality for an involvement that is not actually taking place, and how that affects the way dance is received.

The symmetry between spectator and performer has seldom been explored in depth. An exception is Sartre's discussion in *L'Idiot de la famille* (1971, 785–90), in which he combines his early phenomenologizing from *L'Imaginaire* (1940) with the qualified Marxism of the *Critique of Dialectical Reason* (1961 – cf. Sparshott 1988, 291–2).

Sartre's earlier idea was that to regard a statue as a statue (and hence as a work of art), or a landscape as beautiful, or for that matter an impersonator as the character impersonated is to discount the material reality of what confronts you and use it as the armature for an imaginative reconstruction which is the object of one's attention and which is *de-realized*, that is, postulated otherwise than as being part of the real world. We concentrate on the appearance of the landscape and whatever aspects of it fit together into a determinate *landscape* as opposed to a chunk of terrain; we allow ourselves to see and hear Maurice Chevalier in the tilt of the impersonator's head and the huskiness of her assumed voice, discounting her female plumpness; we see the Venus in the marble, disregarding the stoniness of the stone.[13]

In Sartre's later treatment, the perspective shifts to emphasize that the terrain, the impersonator, the marble are necessary in these cases to the act of imagination. They are what Sartre had come to call the 'practico-inert' of the imaginary. An actor, a stone statue, a famous landscape, a professional impersonator have the status of permanent incitements to an act of the imagination that will de-realize them in a way that, in its context, is socially realized. When we see an actor in the theatre we are ready for him to act; he is a *centre réel et permanent d'irréalisation*. Like the marble of the statue, the actor is a support of the de-realization – but, says Sartre, 'the de-realization gives it its necessity because the object is necessary in order that the de-realization may take place,' it is an 'in-itself' that has taken on a 'being for others.' That is, we recognize the actor as an actor who will function as inciting us to see him act, to lend him precisely the imaginative reconstruction that playgoing demands; we recognize the marble as matter that has been worked on to be seen imaginatively as art, that demands of us an artistic interpretation.

What Sartre is saying here is a dressed-up version of what everyone who talks about art has to come to terms with in some language or other.[14] He now adds that, in coming to a performance to see the actors act, to see the real dancing persons de-realize themselves as dancers in whatever dance they may put on, we come to de-realize ourselves as spectators. We come, not of course to become unreal, but to enter by complicity into the role of imaginer, related to the persons we habitually are as the dancers are to the persons who dance. We come to the dance to make ourselves spectators. Our spectatorhood is superimposed on our personality and cancels it – but without eliminating it, because the *act* of self-de-realization of course depends on there being a self that is being de-realized, just as the dancers' acts of de-realizing themselves for the public depend on there being real people there who are actively de-realizing themselves in the dance.[15]

A statue of Venus carved out of white marble, with its 'immutable consistency' and 'radiant inertia,' retains some of the hardness and brilliance of the marble in a transfigured form: the statue as statue is not the marble, but it is such a statue as could be carved from that marble. In an analogous way, when I transform myself into a spectator, de-realizing myself in the way that the dance elicits from me, the spectator I am is such a spectator as the person I am could be: it depends on the character I have as well as on the experience I bring to the performance.

As I see it, the point of Sartre's approach is that the symmetry of de-realizations between dancer and spectator is complete but not perfect. Since my spectatorship on any occasion is a manifestation of the spectator I have it in me to be, which is a transformation of the continuing personality that supports it, there is no way in which that act, however disinterested, discerning, pure, or whatever, can be the precise counterpart of the performance I see, which for its part is a manifestation of the performer the dancer can be. The performer I as spectator project from the performance on the basis (the 'armature') of the body I perceive is constructed from the network of possible intentions that I can conceive on the basis of my imagination, not that of the dancer.

CHAPTER SEVENTEEN

Learning to Dance

What is it that one learns when one learns to dance? Thinking about this question may be the best way to understand what, in practice, dance is. Like most of the questions raised in this book, this one is two-sided. It is partly a question of fact. What do dancers actually do when they learn to dance in this or that way? What is their regimen, how are they recruited and trained? What part is played by peer pressure, what by formal drill and instruction, what by autonomous self-formation? How do the answers to these and similar questions differ for different modes of dance, and for dances in different cultures? But the question is also partly conceptual or epistemic. What is dancing competence? What is it one learns when one learns to dance? As usual, intuition without concepts is dumb, concepts without intuition are blind; we need the factual and the conceptual as well. But at the present unformed and pre-scientific stage of enquiry, I will not try to keep them separate.

17.1 Learning Dances

In the beginning, I suppose, one does not learn dancing, one learns dances. Similarly, in music one learns first to play a simple tune – a scale is a simple tune and, as one first learns it, differs from other tunes mainly in that one knows it is not even meant to be interesting. But in learning a tune one learns to produce the tones that make the tune – a simple matter on the piano, less simple on a flute, harder on a violin. Just so, in learning a dance, one learns the steps that make the dance, and the positions one starts from and stops at; and one learns how to stand and how to move in the dance.

When one learns a second dance, one will find that some of the steps, positions, stances, and ways of moving recur. But in fact one will know that already from the tone of instruction, from the way the teacher says 'to the side' or 'hands on hips' as something that has been said innumerable times before and will be said innumerably more times. One of the first things one learns is what it is that the teacher takes for granted. Also, even in quite simple dances one will encounter recurrent sequences, the dos-à-dos of a square dance or the hay of a country dance. As one learns more dances one already learns styles, concatenations and associations of steps, regularities and probabilities; one learns a way of dancing, and so one begins to learn what a way of dancing is. Here too the teacher's tone and words will guide: we are warned to prepare for something quite new or merely introduced to something a little different, we hear what is 'always' and what is 'this time.'

17.11 Step by Step

As one learns dances, one learns to dance. A plausible sketch of the principles of such learning is often extracted from Aristotle's *Ethics*, where it serves as a clearer and simpler case of the principles by which we learn morality. It goes like this. At first, one simply makes the moves one is told to make in the way one is told to make them. Even to do that, one must be able to identify what the recurring moves are (to copy the waving and not the twitching, and so on) and what the 'ways' are. 'Purse your lips as if you were going to kiss,' 'fingers like little hammers' – one has to *understand* even down-to-earth instructions like those. Because understanding is involved, the habits one thus acquires are not mere reflexes; they are ways of using one's intelligence in action. And so one goes on, through a series of more comprehensive and more complex instructions and practices. One has to grasp the point of each of these, simply in order to follow it.

At each later stage in such a learning process, one grasps the point of the earlier and simpler practices in a new way. One comes to see, in the light of what one has now learned, the reasons why the points one had to grasp earlier had to be grasped. In acquiring step by step the techniques of whatever one learns, one inevitably acquires the values by which the practice is judged, not as a superadded ideology, but as what gives the practice its cohesion and its learnability and makes it a practice (see the beginning of chapter 15). It's no good talking and arguing: you have to learn to do, and when you have learned you know.

In the later stages of such a learning process, one comes to grasp the underlying principles of organization, so that Liszt was able to play Mendelssohn's new violin concerto from the manuscript in short score, at sight, and in doing so to give a performance that (Mendelssohn felt at the time) could not be improved upon. So an experienced dancer learning a new dance may see at once 'how it goes' and, on the basis of a sentence or two of instruction from the choreographer, will be able to rephrase the whole structure of a sequence.

At a deeper level, one comes to understand how dances are built. Choreographers are almost all experienced dancers. At a yet further stage, by extracting (or divining) yet deeper principles of organization, one may come to see how entire styles of dance can be built; one may even, by extrapolation, learn to generate new art forms. In these further reaches, one need not put one's understanding into words, though analysis may help; what is necessary is that, through more and more practice, more and more varied experience, and more and more reflection on what one is learning, one should become practically aware of more and more remote and general, more and more subtle and profound, ways in which dances are put together and their various successes achieved. I know of no other way in which this can happen. Different learners will learn different things more quickly, will be differentially aware of and responsive to different rules and tendencies that may legitimately be found to underlie the practice they are mastering. Such complex practices as one finds in the arts are not governed by rules, but are such that partial rationalizations in terms of different selections and hierarchies of apparent rules afford alternative plausible interpretations (Sparshott 1988, 113–30). As one learns dances, one acquires a learning style – a way of scanning and packaging experience.

In short, learning is acquiring autonomy at ever deeper levels and in ever more thorough ways, as one masters and interiorizes more and more of a rationale (one's own rationale, and whatever rationale may be in the public domain) of what one had at first to learn by rote. And this is possible because even what we call rote learning is largely a matter of grasping and using principles, whether or not those principles are consciously formulated.[1]

17.12 Holistic Learning

It is not necessary that everyone who learns to dance should begin by learning dances. One might begin by learning what were in fact dance disciplines and dance movements without knowing what they were, in a gymnasium rather than a studio, much in the way that children used to learn Latin by memorizing grammar and vocabulary. Even if one does start by learning dances, one may do so not step by step but holistically, as I understand Balinese children and Japanese students of artistic dance may. One is shown the dance and then made to do it or take part in it, gradually learning how to do it by repeated performances of the whole. This makes no difference, that I can see, to the analysis I proposed. It is still true that, to learn the dance properly, one will have not simply to copy the movement-sequence that one observes but to extract from it the system of analysis it is based on, and how it is based on it, the style of posture and movement, and everything there is to learn about it, in the same way that children learn to speak their mother tongue correctly, idiomatically, and eloquently, without necessarily having any formal instruction. The only difference between such holistic learning and step-by-step methods is that the latter tend to emphasize accuracy over style in the early stages, whereas the former gives easier access to whatever resists analysis. In both cases, the student has to learn and internalize whatever is necessary for satisfactory participation, and this internalization is something one has to do from one's own resources.[2]

17.2 Learning Dancing

Is there such a thing as learning to dance, learning dancing in general? What I have described is a structure of skills widening and deepening from a simple base, but such a structure assumes a strong internal connection among the skills acquired. Does such a connection obtain among all dance skills, or among some dance skills that are common to all dances? It might rather be that in learning one way of dancing one unfits oneself for learning another way of dancing. It is hard to imagine a bel canto singer being able to sing like a rock singer or like a winner at a Hebridean Mod, which develop quite different modes of voice production, intonation, and projection.

   If one's skill is strictly associated with the technique of one strongly marked style, it will at best help only coincidentally with the technique of a different style, and may well hinder. But it might help indirectly with the acquisition and use of the new technique. The dancer has learned what a dance is, what it is to learn a dance, what mastery is – has learned how to learn. Such a dancer has less to learn than a beginner, and more chance of learning it successfully, even if the body formation and ingrained movement skills that have already been acquired make it impossible actually to learn the alien style without forgoing something too valuable to give up. To learn dance$_1$, one has to learn dance$_1$ and also to learn dance-learning; then, to learn dance$_2$, one may have to unlearn dance$_1$ but one will not have to relearn dance-learning.

Dance differs from other arts in the democracy of the barre. The muscles of all dancers, whatever their experience and eminence, need the same toning by daily classes.[3] And even the best dancers may need the same regimen of correction to ensure that their bodies conform to the standards they know so well – one can get 'out of synch.' This is not, I think, true of other arts, where solitary practice enables artists to judge themselves. But this democracy, of course, may extend not only to a common competence but to a common style, the requirements imposed on the body by a specific habit and technique.

A question that still has to be faced is whether a dancer's understanding of what it would be to achieve mastery of a dance in an alien style is any greater than, say, a musician's understanding of what it must be to achieve mastery in painting. For there is a deep sense in which all artists understand each other, as well as a sense in which they do not.[4] And we see at once that there can be no hard and fast answer to that question, because we have seen that the practice of dance is indeterminate both in its extent and in its assigned nerve.

What I have just said about the transferability of dance-learning skills may be misleading. The action programmes of skilled performers (as of all organisms, I suppose) are organized in multiple hierarchies, neural and muscular. The information could be stored in the pattern and duration of activation habitual in muscles and muscle collectives; in body-feedback responses; in environmental feedback responses; in organizational programs, sorting methods, and so on. And it seems to me likely that different performers may organize their skills differently for the same outcome – nothing is more characteristic of the spontaneous activities of natural systems than the availability of many different procedures for the same end. If so, different hierarchies of control might well correspond to different degrees of transferability of training and skills. What one performer has mastered as an autonomous system, another performer might have mastered as a special case of something more generally applicable, without there being any clear sense in which one way of organizing the skills in question was either better in itself or more true to the inherent articulation of the art.

17.21 *Primary and Secondary Standards Again*

Because learnability and reconditeness are no less characteristic of an art than its practical relation to an end to be achieved, the distinction between primary and secondary standards can always arise, and what is secondary from one point of view can be primary from another. 'Artistic' value may function simply as an occasion for the development and manifestation of prowess; the latter, no less than the former, can be an ornament and embellishment of life, and a stretching of the confines of human capacity (see §15.212).

At the highest reaches of accomplishment, one is no longer taught a hierarchically organized repertoire of skills, nor even the organizational know-how of one's guru; it may rather be the subtle practice of exploiting the untaught and cultivating the unteachable – to develop one's own way of doing things. Technique as such, we are told, belongs only to the moment of teaching. Where there is technique, it is taught only as something to be reassimilated into the learner's undifferentiated capacity; but what is taught may itself be the sharpening of the learner's own gifts.

In the fine arts, and hence in dance-making to the extent that dance is assimilated to our ideas of art, the conventional wisdom has it that the aim is to produce something original, imaginative, expressive, beautiful – in any case, something worth considering for its own sake, as if it were unique.[5] But can there be arts of such things? Will there not inevitably be a complete split between the primary standards of the art, as so conceived, and any secondary standards that may be cultivated?

In a way, the split will be inevitable. But in practice it is not. The basic idea of such an art as dance, and the experience of it, must give rise in artist and public alike to a functioning notion of the area in which the art operates, and of the kinds of successes and failures that have proved possible in that area. This notion does not, in the present understanding, operate as a set of standards or rules; it simply provides the background against which our attentive expectation seeks objects for it to appreciate, in surprise no less than in fulfilment. And, to the extent that dancers and their public do work with an autonomously functioning set of secondary standards, the personalization of techniques and the development of one's own way of exploiting the common resources converge on a personal practice of the art that is as original and unique as a personality.

The long and short of it is that teaching and learning operate flexibly and variably within these possibilities, with emphases that vary according to the prevailing tradition as well as to the ideological choices and personal temperaments and capacities of the people involved. All the options are open, but any may be closed off. It is not for the philosopher to make judgments here, though many do.[6]

One cannot understand any art, or the arts in general, without grasping the actual dynamics of instruction, ability, expectation, and practice that prevail, as well as the exceptions that are tolerated or rejected.

17.3 Learning to Dance for the Public

Dancers may dance for themselves alone, or for spectators who are not interested in the visible quality of what they see, but only in (say) the fact that a dance is being danced before them.[7] Other dancers, the ones with whom we are chiefly concerned, perform for a public, a set of people who watch them dance and appreciate what they see. What, in principle, does such a dancer-for-the-public have to learn?

By way of preliminary, we must remember an ambiguity in the idea of dancing 'for a public.' It may mean dancing in such a way as to please a public, taking acclaim as sufficient testimony to success; or it may mean dancing in such a way that the values of one's dance are accessible to and appreciable by a public, and are such that a public ought to appreciate them, whether it does or not. It is easy to incur misunderstandings here. It is easy to suppose that making a performance accessible to a public must mean pandering to whatever tastes and preferences that public might happen to have (even if it is an audience shouting 'Take it off!' at Martha Graham). It is also easy to confuse trying to please a public and seeking acclaim as a dancer with seeking to entertain and win applause of any sort. Liberace played piano in such a way as to please, by his piano playing, a certain public who were not exactly connoisseurs of musicianship; but that is quite different from what he also did, to surround himself with glitter in order to please as a showman, someone who might equally well have been doing something quite other than playing piano.

The situation is complex, not to say delicate, because the values are more easily separated in principle than in practice. In at least some genres of rock music, for instance, the showmanship seems inseparable from the music. One might like some punk rock as music, but one's liking it would be somewhat perverse: punk rock was not properly separable from the *idea* of punk, from a certain sort of stage behaviour and costume and the convention that these were to be taken as symbolizing social protest. Such ambiguity pervaded nineteenth-century ballet, in which the artistic ideas of such poets and scenarists as Théophile Gautier and such inventive choreographers as Perrot cohabited with the demands of the Jockey Club for lots of visible flesh.[8]

There is, then, an unstable relation among three things: dancing before a public, in such a way that it is essential that the relevant values of one's dance be visually accessible; dancing for a public, in the sense of doing the sort of dance that will please a given segment of the existing public for dance as dance; and dancing in a way that will give pleasure to a public, though that pleasure has nothing to do with dance as dance. It is not always easy to keep these apart. The development of dancing *sur les pointes*, for instance, seems to give an authentic dance pleasure, since it makes available a whole new range of movements and effects. But it has been argued that the reason men like it is not because it generates a certain sort of floating movement, but because it cripples, disfigures, and hurts the dancer, and men like to see women crippled, disfigured, and hurt. Men, after all, do not wear these shoes.[9]

In principle, learning to dance as for an audience must be primarily a matter of making oneself visible. That is, one must learn to bring it about that the movements that are significant to oneself in one's dancing bear the same significance to an appropriately prepared audience who see the dance. Or, what may come to the same thing, one must learn to find and feel in one's own dance movements the significances that will be found and felt by such an audience. And the audience's training must surely be to see directly the aesthetic quality of the dance, not to divine the satisfaction the dancer finds in it.

But what is that aesthetic quality to which the audience responds? There seems to be a vicious circle. An adequately trained audience would surely respond not to the mere look of the moving limbs, but to the movement as the dancer made it, and that would mean empathizing with the movement as intended, so that they would after all be transforming their visual data into clues to kinaesthetic events; while, at the same time, trained dancers would convert their kinaesthetic experience to a symbolism of (visible) movement. In fact, Dr Sheets-Johnstone reports that dancers who describe what they take to be their kinaesthetic experience (that is, their sense of the body's movement and location in terms of its own inward organization as released to proprioception) are in fact always reporting that experience in terms of their *body image* – not that they are thinking of how they look, but that the body as they feel it is a body perceptible in space.[10]

If there is a circle involved in the collusion between the empathies – the spectator's adoption of the dancer's way of feeling and the dancer's adoption of the spectator's perspective – the circle is not after all a vicious one. It is more like the familiar circle whereby the teller of a tale envisages the understanding of an ideal reader, and the reader (or hearer) envisages the intent of an ideal storyteller. No practice exists otherwise than in the shared understanding of the practitioners as to what the practice is. Storyteller and listener, dancer and spectator, can play their parts only in so far as they know what it is to tell and be told to, to dance and be danced to. And this is something, as Piaget documented, that we all learn in childhood. We have to, because all conversation and all society depend absolutely on it.

The best account I know of the process of learning an art like dance is Vernon Howard's (1982). His sole topic is the art of singing in a *bel canto* style; but I take that to be closely analogous to the art of dancing in a style like ballet, in that it involves developing the perceptibly effective use of a particular set of body movements. For Howard, the development of a voice is the whole art of song. Once one has learned to sing in the sense of producing one's voice, there is no further critical question. For instance, there is no question of artistic or inartistic interpretation. If the voice as voice is perfectly used, it follows that the song is perfectly rendered.[11] Similarly, one might argue that ballet technique, as acquired in the development of positions, movements, and transitions, has built into it everything that is required for artistic perfection. That would be to say two things. First, that one has not achieved technical perfection if one dances in a way that the ordinary critic might call 'technically perfect, but ... ' – but cold, but without feeling, but without conviction, but without magic, or whatever. For then there would always be a point of ballet that one had not mastered, a way of making transitions or a way of controlling the face muscles that would produce the effect the critic calls 'inner conviction,' or 'tenderness,' or whatever it might be. But, second, it would also be to say that there must always be some things in a dance performance that are critically irrelevant, even if audiences respond to them. And, of course, we know that that is the case. 'Star quality' is partly a matter of personal brilliance in the art, the extra spellbindingness that sets a Nureyev off from a Martins, and partly a matter of successful publicity and fame.[12]

Howard deals with, among other topics, the different sorts of things that teachers say to students at different phases of their career, partly technical (in terms of physiology) and partly metaphorical. Some of this discourse fulfils a special function, as follows. One never really hears one's own voice as others hear it. What one hears of oneself is transmitted through the head bones, which is not the same as the sound publicly produced. But people who sing in public have to control their voices by what the public can hear. Howard argues that the vocabulary teachers use and transmit to their students is part and parcel of the process of acquiring the actual skill of voice production, so that, in learning to speak in the required artificial language, we are at the same time learning to experience our new voices in a way that corresponds to what an audience will be able to hear.[13] The new language is associated only with the new voice, not with the old voice and how we heard it.

If what Howard says is true of singing, something comparable must surely be true of dancing for a public. In the most advanced stages of learning to dance, one must also be taught the language of dance at ever more precise and esoteric levels. In this way, one is in effect learning to develop one's body image and make it available as a conscious critical resource, so that one comes to feel one's body as visible.[14]

In visual experience, one inevitably sees things and people as things and people, not as constructs from the coloured patches that, according to old-fashioned theories, are the strictly visual data from which we build the visible world, and which we 'interpret' in so doing. Again, one quickly learns to see things and people 'in' pictures although it is obvious that what one is looking at is patches of pigment. Yet again, experts who read scratches on bullets and traces on aerial photographs learn first to see faint marks which the lay person does not see at all, then to interpret these marks as signs of this or that activity past or present, and finally to see the signs as signs immediately, without really noticing the forms of the traces from which they are constituted. Just so, one may suppose, a trained dancer learns to feel in the kinaesthetic body-feelings, and in any other internal 'sensations' there may be, only those that are relevant to the dance as visibly danced, and to feel in them precisely the direct testimony to that visible dance.[15] To a philosopher who is deeply indoctrinated in the eighteenth-century dogmas that still pass as conventional epistemology, it may seem strange that people should be able to learn such skills; but it is just the sort of thing that people do do, it is the way the mind of any animal has to be able to work if it is to find its way around in the world.

Some dancers and theorists, as we have seen, speak of making the body over as an instrument.[16] This seems to involve two things. First, one has to develop the ability to make certain movements, to construct chains of movements apt to be conjoined in the dance style aimed at. This is a matter of training the body to move in a certain way, and it makes sense to think of this as transforming the body into an appropriate tool for making dances. But, second, one also has to develop the habit of analysing one's movement, of thinking and imagining it, in a certain way. The supposed new instrument cannot be separated from a new way of using an old instrument, and that is why so many people object to calling the body an instrument at all. ('Is my body he, she, or it?' a dancer asked.) Once again, new ways of doing call for new ways of thinking and symbolizing, from which they cannot be cleanly separated.

To sum up, it looks as if learning to dance as for an audience requires both a remaking of the moving body in the interests of visibility (if nothing else) and the developing of a correspondingly new way of thinking and feeling one's own movements.

It remains to make a mundane point that may deflate much of the foregoing. Howard's treatment of song depends on the impossibility of hearing one's own voice. If one sang into a microphone with a loudspeaker monitor (as peformers often do), what one thus heard would still fuse and compete with what one misheard through one's head bones. But dancers can and do use mirrors. Of course, one cannot watch oneself dancing as one dances. But one can practise movements before a mirror, and there is no other visual access to one's own movement to compete with the reflected image. And suppose one were to learn one's dancing in a room walled with mirrors, so that one had continual access to one's visible self? Surely it would then become second nature to associate how movements felt with how they looked, since this was what one wanted to do anyway? Granted, one's access to the look of one's dance would not be continuous, but the gestalt mechanisms of our mental and observational processes enable us to use discontinuous data for the construction of wholes – again, we could not live in the world if we could not do this. And there would be no competing signals that would need to be circumvented, as is the case with singing. One dancer has told me that this is indeed the heart of the matter, that the mirror (and, hence, the way one looks in dancing) is one's constant companion as one learns, so that the problem of access never arises. Other dancers seem to say that a mirror can help only to a limited extent. I am not entitled to an opinion on the practical issue.

17.4 From the Particular to the General

17.41 Learning Dances, Learning Dancing

To learn one dance thoroughly would be to learn its organizing principles. It would therefore be to envisage how it might be performed in various manners, if not in various styles.[17] It would also require envisaging how the dance might be varied, as the choices it involved suggested the alternatives of which they were the rejections. But to learn only one dance, however thoroughly, could give one no practical sense of specific sets of significant choices made, and to learn only one style of dance would give one a practical sense only of those modes of variation that it embodied. What one would have actually acquired, by way of a knowledge of dancing as such, could only be a sense of the meaningfulness of the practical alternatives one's experience encompassed, together with a vague nimbus or aura of alternatives that would make sense as extrapolations and exfoliations from what one knew.

'What do they know of England, who only England know?' There is a sense in which one does not fully know any dance unless one knows all dances, because one does not know all the possibilities it rejects. There is another sense in which one does not fully know a dance unless one knows all *and only* the dances its habitual dancers know, because one cannot otherwise know the specific range of practical choices it involves. But there is yet another sense in which a person can know one dance perfectly without knowing any other dances at all, just as one might know the Twenty-third Psalm by heart without knowing any other poetry. If one did know only one dance (or only one style of dance, if 'style' were suitably identified), one might be a very good dancer (of it) without progressing beyond, or digressing from, one's practical understanding of precisely what one had learned to do. Similarly, I know musical performers of high skill whose only ambition is to perform as well as possible the music of the masters, and whose general idea of music seems not to extend consciously beyond the specific music they play. Their understanding, even if we insist that it must really extend to the nature of the music itself (for otherwise they could not perform musically), is entirely implicit in their performing skill as exercised on specific pieces.

There could not be a unitary process of learning to dance, because dance comprises many specific practices. But there could be a complex grasped as unitary, in the way some people seem to comprehend music as a whole that comprises technique, memory, institutional attitudes, values, and appreciation, all at once. How? One cannot say, except that a 'compleat' musician must possess and integrate all these, and the intricate convolutions of the human brain are no doubt adapted to integrate disparate components of complex practical abilities. Learning to dance as a general skill probably requires the cultivation and integration of gracefulness, muscle memory, muscular coordination, adroitness, a sense of dance form, rhythmicality, and an ability to master non-rhythmical rhythms. Perhaps one could enumerate and analyse the requirements, although this has never been properly done, even for music.

All the factors in such general dance ability would be differentially learnable, so that dances in which the factors weighed differently would themselves be differentially learnable. But the latter differentiation would not follow directly from the former, because the ways the factors combined in the central processing system would not be determined at any lower level. In practice, people to whom we ascribe a natural aptitude for dancing, and who find dancing easy to learn, differ widely among themselves in what precisely it is that they find easy to learn and do.

17.42 Learning Dancing, Learning Choreography

A dancer can hardly fail to be aware that there are always new dances that can be learned, and new ways of dancing, as well as further refinements of skill in performing dances already mastered. But if one's understanding of the dances that one has learned extends to a grasp of alternatives, and hence to an understanding of dancing as a general practice that might be variously manifested, every dancer should be able to learn choreography. Knowing alternatives, and knowing how alternatives multiply and generate ever new possibilities, could surely be put to practical use. And yet it is notorious that dancers abound but choreographers are scarce. 'Many are the wandbearers, but few are Bacchus.'

Any skilled dancer could invent a dance, if it were necessary to do so and if the requirements to be fulfilled were light, just as anyone who knew what a piano was could invent a tune on the piano, provided that it did not have to be interesting or beautiful. But few performers actually compose music or show any interest in doing so. Why not? Perhaps the next chapter will suggest some answers. Meanwhile, our question should be this: what has even a thoughtful and reflective dancer not learned that must be learned if one is to be a successful choreographer? Dancers have learned how the dancing body works, at least in their own case, and how what is specific to oneself differs from what is common to all who share one's professional skill. That is something one could hardly fail to learn in the process of learning to dance with others, since the accommodations that have to be made when one dancer substitutes for another must be a familiar part of the fabric of one's life. But dancers do not need to learn how to devise new and effective sequences that will make new kinds of sense, how to select specific movements that will surprise and delight in the context of a specific sequence, how to devise new lifts and relationships that will be both unexpected and right. Dancers have learned what options there are and how one chooses between them. Choreographers create the options among which choices have to be made. What has to be learned is the habit of creation itself.

Much has been written on the art of making dances, but there is no technique of teaching choreography as there is a technique of teaching ballet dancing.[18] At the heart of ballet is the daily class, the routines of sequential exercise; these are as far as possible from teaching choreographic principles. One would think that a ballet school would include in its curriculum classes in choreography, if only as the most direct way to get the students to think deeply about dancing; but this seems to be seldom done.[19] Perhaps one can see why. The destiny of the students is to perform dances choreographed by others, in the company of others similarly trained; their task will not be to think, but to obey.

What do choreographers have to learn, that might be taught? The habit of creation, I said. Perhaps that could be taught, not only as problem-solving is taught, by setting tasks calling for various mental gifts, but also a mental discipline is taught, by habituating the student to meet demands regularly and confidently. The poignancy and pathos of an inspired genius cannot be taught directly, because they are just what goes beyond anything anyone yet knows; but may it not be possible, up to a point, to teach people to inspire themselves?

For the most part, though, what can be taught in choreography would be three or four sorts of thing. First, to exploit systematically the resources available: the uses of space, the different ways of using music, and so on. Second, the basic aesthetics of dance-making: ways of shaping a dance acceptably, beginning and ending, dynamic variation. Third, collaboration in the profession: what lighting designers, set designers, stage managers, costume makers, theatre managers can do and will put up with. And fourth, as phenomenologists argue, how to access one's own spontaneity and authenticity and maintain their life in one's dances.

17.43 Learning Choreography, Learning Dance-making

Learning to choreograph is not the same as learning to create a ballet, and these have not always been done by the same people. Ballets at one time were devised by grandees, or poets, or impresarios, who may have had no skill in dancing or in the invention of dances, and who would not know how to instruct a dancer.

The same division of labour can take place in architecture. There is a charming building at Magdalen College, Oxford, that was designed by a fellow of the college, a man of taste who had no experience in building. He drew the elevations and, no doubt, the floor plans and handed them over to the master builder, who figured out how to make it stand up and what materials to use and instructed the stonemasons and carpenters accordingly. There can be whole chains of such skills; the people at each level know what they have to do to satisfy the people at the next level up, but need not themselves have all the necessary techniques.

To learn choreography, one must add to a dancer's knowledge of the possibilities of dancing the ability to invent sequences of steps and combinations of the movements of one or more dancing bodies. But the devising of a ballet requires only that one have seen enough ballets to grasp what the acceptable range of ballet form has been, and how it might be continued and varied in the future, together with a certain sort of stage imagination: the ability to envisage as a whole what the shape of a danceable ballet might be. This involves more than just writing a scenario or synopsis, such as you may read in your programme at the theatre. One must compose such a scenario and envisage it as the basis of a danced significance, as a danced action that might be fleshed out in specific musical and dancerly incarnations. One need not oneself have any distinct idea of what those incarnations might be, so long as one could convey to the actual choreographer and composer enough of what one had in mind to instruct and inspire them in their own creations.

This original devising of (the idea for) a ballet might be the work of the composer of the music, or of an impresario who commissions music of a certain character, or of the choreographer who will actually compose the dances (which of course is the most usual practice in recent years), or of some third party who has and conveys to the others an idea they can use – or of no one in particular, for music and scenario and choreography may all develop together.

Movies are the prime example of an art calling for complex collaboration among people of highly technical skills, so that it is notoriously often impossible to say who, if anyone, bears responsibility for the general character of the finished film as a whole – who is the *auteur*, as French critics used to say. But it is at least possible for the same question to arise in the case of a ballet. Who, for instance, is the inventor – author – originator – deviser of *Sacre du printemps*? Whoever summoned forth the music to fit its central meanings, or selected the meanings to fit that music. One or many, it was none of the many choreographers who have produced danceable versions; it was whoever produced the powerful *Gestalt* by which *Sacre du printemps* holds a distinctive place in the dance world. Who devised the *Gestalt* depends on what identifies the dance as a distinct creation (see §19.4).

If the invention of ballets in this sense is a skill that can be learned, it differs radically from the skill of the choreographer and even more radically from that of the dancer, even if one person combines all these skills in a single creative act. But perhaps there is nothing to learn. There is certainly no dense texture of work involved in any such learning, such as is involved in learning the techniques of engravers, or violinists, or ballet dancers.

I return to the interrelation of these skills in the next chapter.

17.5 The Solitary Dancer

How could one learn to dance, as an artist of dance? A difficulty here stems from the idea of art current in the early years of this century and still effectively dominant in old-fashioned circles.[20] The idea in question is that a work of art is essentially the direct expression of something important to the artist, to which critics and public have only indirect access. The work of art can be this because it grows under the artist's hand, or before his or her eyes and ears, and thus is directly and immediately accessible to the artist in the act of working. Artists are sustained by their appropriate sense of the rightness and wrongness of what they are doing; their artistic sense as critics and appreciators is directly engaged in the work and guides it. It is this immediate conjunction of creative impulse and critical sense that is the hallmark of the true artist.

The difficulty is that this immediate conjunction cannot obtain in dancing. A dance as a work of art must be achieved visually, but dancers have direct and immediate access to the dance only kinaesthetically. It makes no sense to dance for oneself alone, or for God. So there cannot be an art of dance in this privileged sense. Mirrors and special techniques of instruction, we have seen, enable dancers to learn to dance in ways that will look well to others, but the connection remains indirect.

One way of responding to this challenge is to say that it rests on a false model of art. Photographers, for instance, do not see their photographs as they take them. But one could rejoin that the photographer is in suspense between the closing of the shutter and the drying of the print – or, of course, that photography is not an art anyway, just because of this lack of immediacy. But, in any case, the photograph on completion is accessible to the photographer in exactly the same mode as it will be available to the public, as the dance will never be available to the dancer.

Again, an actor's working up of a performance is never available to him or her as it is to the public. Actors never see themselves from beyond the footlights, a fact that grieves many. But then, it might be rejoined that an actor in isolation is not an artist. A performance is a proper part of a play. The public imagination has no acceptable figure of the solitary actor; the closest we get is the ham mugging and mouthing to the mirror. The figure of the solitary dancer, by contrast, is popular in myth and legend.

One may, however, go further. Sartre (1948) argues that novelists can never read their own novels – to read a novel, one must genuinely not know, and have no responsibility for, what will happen on the next page. Novels do not really exist until their readers have confirmed in them what their authors could only hope was there. And something of the same sort would hold of all arts. Artists never know that what they think they see in their works, and think they see because they know they put it there, is really there for anyone to see. To all of this we may retort that all it shows is that artists may be mistaken, suffer from bias. But it is not necessary that they should. They read the same words, see the same pigment on the same canvas, as the rest of us. Even novelists, though they cannot be first-time readers of their works, can be re-readers. And it is from this sort of possibility that the dancer is cut off. The solitary dancer is an absurd figure, unless the dance is a sort of therapeutic work-out.[21]

I suggested in §5.311 that dance as art must primarily be a dance of what Sartre identifies as the second bodily dimension, the body-for-others, the aspect of one's corporeality that is the manifestation to others of one's status as a living thing. According to Sartre, it is in principle impossible that one's awareness of oneself in this mode should not be mediated by one's knowledge of other people. The present hypothesis, however, is that a dance that has the status of art must be, at its core, the autonomous work of a dancer as individual creative artist. Are these requirements not incompatible? Perhaps they are. But Sartre's phenomenology is ontological. He is not saying that one's self-knowledge is psychologically indirect. The point is rather that the viewpoint of the Other (*Autrui*) is structurally built into this aspect of one's self-knowledge. Even if one accepts Sartre's argument, then, it is not easy to see what its implications are; Sartre himself is blatantly unreliable on just this issue, as many critics have pointed out.

The figure of the dancer as true artist, dancing for herself alone, is best exemplified by Isadora Duncan – paradoxically, because she was very much a show-business phenomenon from the start. But she did appear to be an artist in the act of her dancing, not an executant giving one performance of a dance that could be given again and again, even if something like that was factually the case.[22] And it is this ideal autonomy, rare and even illusory though it be, that presents a crucially interesting case for the philosophy of art.

The ideal of artistic autonomy, the idea that artists should be guided by nothing other than the rightness in the work itself as they see it, leads to an appearance of paradox, since we also recognize that artists typically practise their art as a profession before a public, and one does not see why that public should be concerned with what was designed to suit someone other than themselves. But the resolution of the paradox is easy and familiar. In satisfying themselves, artists are satisfying people who would not have taken up their art professionally if they were not already exceptionally avid, or sensitive, or assiduous members of the public for it. Artists can therefore practise their art in the confidence that their own judgment has been developed from that of the public at large only by improvement, refinement, specialization, and extrapolation. Despite the misgivings expressed in §12.3, it is rational for such artists to demand that the public catch up with them and (see §15.22) to hope that some of them will.

Artists, then, in the actual course of their work, need not think about the public. They cannot but be exemplary members of that public, and in satisfying themselves they satisfy the most exacting of connoisseurs. That is true even of revolutionaries like Schoenberg, who insisted that his least appreciated procedures were logical applications of principles that already lay beneath traditional practices. The simplest process of learning to dance, we saw, essentially involves just this successive penetration of principles ever more deeply buried. If revolutionaries can genuinely see and feel the rightness in what they are doing, they can be confident that others could come to see the same rightness by following the same path of learning, a path of the sort inevitably involved in all learning in the arts.

Meanwhile, as we have seen, the artist's representative critical faculty is directly engaged in the act of making, because what one is working on is available to eye and ear as one shapes it, in the form in which it will be publicly available. It is only this direct engagement that makes the responsible practice of an art possible in simultaneous relation to one's work, one's freedom, one's skill, and one's public. And it is just this engagement that is impossible to the autonomous dancer, to whom the dance is directly accessible only as a feeling of body rightness, whereas it is directly accessible to the public only as visible movement. We have seen how the two rightnesses can be correlated. In fact, they must be correlated. But how can they be the same, in the way that our paradigm of responsibly autonomous art seems to require?

We must not forget how narrow the scope of our problem is. For most artistic dance no such problem arises; perhaps there is no actual case where it is urgent. There is no problem, for instance, with the correspondence between a virtuoso's rejoicing in the same prowess that a spectator takes admiring delight in. There is no problem with a choreographed dance in which the executant's sense of rightness in movement extends only to the movement's being performed according to the choreographer's intent and without constraint. There may be no problem in ballet or any form of dance that has a set vocabulary of movement, in which the sense of body-rightness could be just the awareness of performing well and easily the specific task to which one's body has been trained and adapted. There is certainly no problem with any sort of dance conceived as mobile sculpture, in which the dancer's body is reduced to a passive medium for the visual imagination. And there is obviously no problem with any form of dance that is heteronomous from the start, in which the sustaining values are those of entertainment or showmanship. The problem is confined to that ideal case of an autonomous dance, in which it appears that the artist must find satisfaction in movement-as-felt and the audience must respond to a movement-as-seen which must somehow be the same.

I suggested, on the basis of Vernon Howard's account of singing, that the dancer learns a special proprioceptive language in which kin-aesthetic sensation is immediately and unreflectingly experienced as a revelation of one's visible body, so that one's imagination of oneself as visible is veridical and evidential. But perhaps I should not have taken that last step. What an audience responds to is not the sheer sight of human forms in motion, it is people moving – not indeed the humanly meaningful praxis as a social or instrumentalizing transaction, but a setting oneself in motion. An ugly arm line, on this showing, is ugly not because it bruises the optic nerve (so to speak) but because it bespeaks awkwardness. In one of those elaborate lifts that intrigue us in the work of choreographers like Cranko, what delights or disquiets us is the way the people's bodies are twined around each other as human bodies, arms and legs functioning in all their armishness and legginess. So what a dancer's developed awareness perceives is body movement from the inside. It is the very same movement in the very same aspect that the audience sees, though 'seen from a different angle' – sensed with a different modality. One does not after all need to have an image of one's moving body, one senses it in the moving of it. The shared hu-manity is the link, though cognitively the bridge between inside and outside views has to be constructed.[23]

If shared humanity is the link, and society depends on human agents understanding immediately the human actions of other human agents, perhaps we should think again about the actor. An actor learns to act primarily by learning projection, learning to make tones and gestures fully readable. Once the subtle skills of audibility and visibility are mastered, actors play their parts by learning to be someone doing something. Instead of concentrating on each movement and gesture and inflection, actors need only bear in mind just who they are (who the characters they are playing are) and exactly what they are doing and why. Stanislavsky at least argued that if actors succeed in making every detail of their situation real to themselves, their visible and audible actions will automatically emerge as especially visible and audible versions of what they are acting. Actors act parts by doing what their characters would do, but doing it through the medium of an eloquent voice and body. What feels right will look right.

Can we now reinstate the analogy between the dancer's art and the actor's, and say that once dancers have made their bodies over into a dancer's visible body, whatever feels right as a dance will look right, and in just the same way? I refused to use the analogy before, on the ground that the actor's performance was not an autonomous creation but existed in the public space among the actors; but the same objection does not hold against the bond of shared humanity.

The analogy still will not sustain us. What the actors' audience is interested in is not the movements of the bodies as such, but the actions, the meaningful relations among them and between them and the furniture. The audience reads the actions at once, as things humanly done.[24] It does not matter that they have access to them in different ways. But in the case of dance it does matter; it is not the action that makes the dance, but the movement. Granted that the movement is essentially that of a human body, even of a human being in the act of making those movements, the actual movement remains essential. Whatever human or social significance it has is secondary, enabling us only to see the movement for what it is. It remains true that to the visible form of that movement, which essentially constitutes the dance as a work of art, the dancer has no direct access. No doubt it is true that the shared humanity, together with the painfully acquired trick of visibility, guarantees that what feels right as a dance will also look right. But the two rightnesses cannot be the same.

No doubt I am making too much of this. The only problematic case, we recall, is that of the solitary dancer creating a dance which is to have the status of a true work of art, but which no one will ever see. One might think such cases significant because of the heroic days of modern dance, in which the pioneers devoted themselves to an art for which there was no audience, labouring to perfect dances without regard to the possibility of anyone seeing them. But that is hardly right: mostly they worked in groups, they had each other and they had each other's eyes.

What would one say of the true solitary? Such people, one might say, are beguiled by the idea of 'art for art's sake,' their inner motivation derived from their ideas of themselves as devoted artists rather than from the substance of their performance. But it need not be so. To envisage clearly the possibility of a work of art is in a sense already to have created it; to dance unseen is to achieve something that has chor-eographic meaning, and it is to have rehearsed a possible dance, even if on reflection we would have to deny that the dance has been fully achieved in any appropriate medium.

Suppose the solitary dance is improvised, rather than worked out as a composition? Such a dance might only have the status of a preparation, or rehearsal, or testimony, or reassurance; and it might be that to take a strictly aesthetic satisfaction in dancing for oneself would involve some self-deception, and incur the risk of more. But the fact is that in all the arts there is a hiatus between the moment when the artist thinks all the answers are complete and the moment when the result is presented to a public and no more excuses and self-deceptions are in place.[25] Perhaps the solitary dancer is only an extreme case of this hiatus. True, the case differs in kind from all others, in a dramatic way that catches the imagination. But all the others differ in kind from each other.

No doubt it is because of the dramatic difference between a performer's access and a spectator's access to a dance that the solitary dancer figures in popular myth as a symbol of relations between the human and the divine. On the one hand we have the *jongleur de Dieu*, the mute acrobat dancing at night before the altar in the deserted church; on the other hand we have the God who creates the universe by dancing it into existence. In the latter case it is precisely the discrepancy between the inner access to the meaning and the outer evidence of the movement that symbolizes the ontological gap between two levels of reality, between the essential world gods know and the existential world they create.

17.6 Conclusion

The relation between a dancer's perception and the audience's perception has at least three aspects. First, in a ritual or social dance, or any dance that exists for its participants, the meaning must be for the dancers, not for any audience. The meaning, therefore, need not be primarily mediated by visual appearance; the sense of human relations may be primary. The meaning of a dance that exists for an audience, by contrast, must be mediated visually and need not be accessible directly to the dancers. Among the human relations involved, that between audience and performers is primary; the relations among the dancers are not themselves part of the meaning of the dance.

Second, the meaning of a dance for its dancers might be released in the act of dancing itself, or it could be accessible through their dance knowledge. The audience, in contrast, need not be aware of the dancers as exerting and testing themselves. To the audience, a dance is primarily a spectacle, a show, not an action of which they are witnesses.[26] The audience, as such, see dancing as they know dancing, as seen from the outside.

Third, as in all art, the dance performance is, for the practitioners, the culmination of their endeavours; for the audience, it is the beginning of their experience. Only the dancers and their colleagues have the sense of the dance as something achieved at the end of their fundraising, their training, their rehearsal.

When we ask how dancers know their dance is right, we are asking a question whose answer is not only complex and difficult, but tragic.

CHAPTER EIGHTEEN

Dance and Choreography

This chapter is dedicated to the memory of George W. Beiswanger, who encouraged me in these enquiries. He died 10 September 1993.

18.1 The Basic Hierarchy

In theatre dance, or any kind of dance that is put on show, the following considerations hold good.

An impresario, or anyone who plans and puts on a show consisting all or mostly of dance, operates within certain constraints. Some are physical: the time frame, the available space. Others are social: budget, available performers and publics, stylistic imperatives.[1] Within these constraints, the teleological articulation of practice requires at least three interrelated phases or factors, which I distinguished in §§17.42–17.43. At one extreme, there must be a scenario, an operative general notion of what is to be done. At the other extreme are the actual dances as danced by the dancers. Between these two lies the domain of choreography, the specification of what movements or actions shall flesh out the scenario and be danced by the dancers. It is not necessary that these three functions shall be performed by three separate groups of people. Nor are the three functions sharply distinguished from each other, either in theory or in practice, except that only the dancers at the moment of performance can actually perform the dance, and what they actually do is neither scenario nor choreography but dance. Within their dancing, one must distinguish between the actual movements of their bodies, as perceived by themselves and by the audience, and their performance of the dance as choreographed; but we need not go into that again.

Over and above the scenarist is the impresario, or whatever agency arranges for dances to be put on; and above the impresario are whatever social and political powers provide the world in which impresarios can operate. But I will not concern myself with them now, though the philosophy of art needs to bear them constantly in mind.

Among the three factors, scenario, choreography, and dancing, there is no a priori general requirement as to what comes first, either in the order of composition or in degree of firmness of the hierarchy. In any given dance show, identified and named for the public or for the dance world, the scenario may be more variable than the actual dances, or a piece of choreographic design may be the *sine qua non*, or a showpiece by a star dancer may be what the show is all about. We can, however, conceive the sequence as a chain, and we usually do. It is really a logical sequence, but we habitually envisage a model in which what is logically prior also comes first in time.

First, then, the scenarist blocks out a story line or formal sequence, indicating perhaps no more than *where* the dances come, with general classifications and episodic significances, in whatever terms correspond to the articulation of the general shape of the show as conceived. On this basis the creative choreographer devises the dances, specifying (or completing the specification of) what is to be danced.[2] The essential specification, as given to the dancers, may be a demand for movements of a certain scale and character; may specify steps or expression (or both); may call for movements of a certain formal sort; or may call for danced *actions* (on the part of the dancer, or on the part of the character whom the dancer is dancing – the dancer Natasha is to kiss the dancer Boris, or the character Snow White is to kiss the character Dopey). In whatever form and at whatever level of specificity the instructions are given, the dancers will have to supply any missing parts or specifications – expressive character, stylistic shape, formal realization, mimetic significance – in the light of the scenario, or in the light of the known stylistic parameters shared by those engaged in the enterprise as participants or as public. In whatever system of choices prevails, each dancer has at every moment to do something definite, if only by default, because choice and failure to choose will alike be construed as choice within the actual dance context.

What is said here of the dancing holds also for other elements in the performance. At the scenario level, there are vague notions of the type of setting and the quality of light; at the choreography level, the scenery and costumes are designed and a lighting plan worked out; at the executant level, someone has to paint and mount the flats, make and fit the costumes, wire up the lights and work the switches. In every such case, there are inevitably places where the executants have not been told exactly what to do and must rely on their native wits and their professional know-how.

Any intermediary figure between originating choreographer and dancer (on any given occasion) – teacher or trainer or ballet master/ mistress or reviver of a dance – will have to choose what (in the original choreography and system of presentation as it has been transmitted) is to be preserved as sacred in the tradition, what is artistically essential, and what is negotiable (and on what terms). Meanwhile, other systems of constraints and opportunities will impinge, including those I named at the start: limitations and availabilities of special talents and resources, legal and moral inhibitions and encouragements, which affect the original judgments about what can and what cannot be negotiated. Whatever the priorities are, all relevant decisions must be made, well or badly, consciously or unconsciously, by design or by default, because the dancers will be doing *something or other* in all relevantly identifiable respects. The sequence of decisions is a matter of anecdote; the relative emphasis is a matter of taste or of convention; the completeness of the decision system is unavoidable.

All the foregoing interactions and adjustments take place within a tissue of understandings. All the people involved, from scenarist to dancer, must share an understanding of what a dance is – or rather, of what counts as a dance – though the precise extent of this understanding is indeterminate. Choreographer, ballet mistress/master, and dancers must share knowledge of a way of dancing, which corresponds to a way of devising dances, a way of teaching those dances, and a way of learning dances, the shared parts of which constitute that way of dancing. The participants, of course, will differ widely in the depth and extent of their knowledge, and may well have patches of ignorance; and how they understand what they know will correspond to differences in their training, their life experience, their spiritual and intellectual bent, and their individual personalities. All agreements issue from disagreements, and the disagreements remain. But what makes the disagreements possible is a more basic agreement in what it is that one is disagreeing about.

The shared understanding will most likely be less complete at the beginning of the joint operation than at its fruition. One of the things that must be involved in choreographing and performing a specific dance is a shaping and reshaping of the common notion of what dance is, through a clarified understanding of what *this* dance has been, has succeeded in becoming, has failed to be. (It is possible that the opposite should happen: that a promising collaboration should break down because the participants become less and less agreed on what they are trying to do, or even on what kind of enterprise it is they are engaged in. In such cases, one looks for an explanation of why they got together in the first place.)

As we saw in the preceding chapter, shared knowledge does not extend to everything in a dance. A dancer must know how to dance a dance, which neither scenarist nor choreographer need know. The choreographer must know how to design a dance, which neither of the others need know. There is nothing specific, however, that the scenarist needs to know, because the evening might consist of a series of turns and divertissements – the imperative of unity of concept may impose stringent demands, but there is nothing to say what the appropriate range of this unity is. Just as Edgar Allan Poe said that no long poem could be more than a series of short poems with a neutral filler, so one might say that a perfect dance evening could consist of a set of items, each internally unified but mutually unconnected (cf. §11.4). In such cases, all the scenarist requires is an impresario's sense of what will work in a theatre and what will not.

A choreographer can specify what a dancer is to do by saying what movements are to be performed (which bit of the dancer goes where, when, how) or by saying what is to be done (in terms derived from the social world). But a choreographer can also specify what a dancer is to do in terms of a known language of dance, like that of ballet. In this last case, it is perhaps not clear whether we should say that the specification is in terms of action or in terms of movement, or whether the distinction becomes inappropriate: probably we have to think about the situation and then decide what to say about it, rather than rely on reach-me-down distinctions from general theories of action. In any case, it is remarkable to the outsider how little a choreographer actually has to say to a dancer when they are working within such a known system. Even when the steps to be performed are not stereotyped, the dancer quickly picks up what the choreographer means and wants, in style as well as in movements, because the overall artistic intention is immediately perspicuous from the way in which the vocabulary is being used.[3]

As a matter of practice, all possible relations among dancer, scenarist, and choreographer are realized. Philosophically, all sequences are open: the hierarchies and determinations can be systematically worked out in terms of any general action theory, in ways I have sketched here. Artistically, there are ideological and conceptual constraints on what can be done, or on what must be claimed to have been done, if the status of art is to be bestowed on the upshot. On the personal level, different artists impose constraints on themselves and on their colleagues that they treat as mandatory. First, there is what they insist on because they are psychologically or socially incapable of operating otherwise. Second, there is what they insist on because without it they cannot take their own work seriously as art. And third, there is what is demanded by their conception of art itself. These last demands may be subjective, part of their creative activity as such; or they may be forensic, part of their public stance, without which their presence to the world will be damaged. On this personal level, it is not necessary that all participants should share the same view as to what hierarchy is operative, or how the hierarchies operate.

As a matter of practice, I said, all possible relations within the hierarchy are realized. There are no standard ways in which all dance companies operate on all occasions. It was rather misleading to say that, however, since it implied that some hierarchical relations must obtain. But that is not necessary. Of course, if scenarist, choreographer, and dancer(s) are all different people, then the scenarist will be making decisions for the others and the choreographer will be making decisions for the dancers, because making decisions is all they do. But the separation need not obtain absolutely, or at all. Ideally, some would say, they do not. Among the group making a given dance, one could trace a flow chart of actual decisions; but any idea might have been originated at any point, any decision might have been initiated at any point. Ideally, all suggestions and decisions are subject to feedback, to the point where the consensus of the group effectively decides everything. Nothing else will work properly, because a failure of consensus means a failure of understanding that must lead to a faltering in practice. And it makes no difference where an idea or decision originates, because in the normal case it will be so modified in the forming of the consensus that the upshot no more has a single point of origin than a river system has a single source. 'One is the river of life, but into it flow streams whose sources are manifold.'

Now we can take a further step. Ideally, it is the group that decides, as it is the group that dances. In the act of true joint creation, individuals are not aware of themselves as separate agents or centres of decision; the dance of the dancing group takes over. Similarly, architectonic decisions are not separate from decisions of detail or from specific movements: everything is governed by the conscious praxis of the collective in its entirety, governed spontaneously by a single operative awareness of the dance. Any departure from this unity is a temporary retreat, to be cancelled in the restored unity of the common life of the dancing community.

To the position advanced in the last paragraph, one is inclined to object that things do not work like that, that the indissoluble unity of decision and action it postulates is an ideal limit, further from any possible realization than the rigid hierarchy in which the functions of scenarist, choreographer, and dancer(s) are exercised by individuals who have no more contact with each other than is necessary to communicate instructions intelligibly. What happens happens. But, however things are done, the functions remain separate, it is as if they were separately performed; and the functions unite in a single praxis, it is as if there were no division between planning, decision, and execution.

One also hears it said, of course, that a hierarchical separation of functions reflects the evil patriarchal insistence on power and violence, the male way of doing things that has brought the world to the brink of destruction; the communitarian absence of separation stands for the womanly (not matriarchal!) manifestation of loving sisterhood that might yet lead the world to salvation, if 'leading' were not a (male) way of exercising power. But the world is not forced to choose between bullying and dithering.

18.2 Composition and Execution

Music theory has been much more thoroughly worked over than dance theory has, and in music theory a lot has been written about the relation between composers, who invent pieces of music, and the executant musicians who play the pieces from instructions that a composer provides. The relation between composer and performer must have a lot in common with that between choreographer and dancer. It may be more useful to say what some of the more obvious differences are.

First, the composer typically provides instructions in the form of a score that the musicians read. Or, in the case of an orchestral score, there are multiple sets of partial instructions, one for each player, and a conductor who leads the players through the actual playing of it. In a sense, the conductor teaches the band how to play the piece. But an experienced band can perfectly well read the score for themselves, and keep in time with each other; what the conductor teaches is one specific way of playing it together, to make a unified performance out of it. Choreographers, by contrast, usually teach the dance directly to the dancers. There is seldom a score, and if there is it may not be used. Not all dancers can read dance notation, and of course one cannot read a dance at sight and dance it as one reads, in the way that any trained executant can read and play a piece of music at sight. There may be no determination of what exactly is to be danced before the choreographer starts working with the dancers; whereas in music, even if the composer is present with the orchestra, most of the information will be transmitted from the score, the composer merely adding such nuances as escape notation and clearing up any ambiguities that initial attempts at performance may reveal. The choreographer, for reasons that will appear, is usually the initial *répétiteur*, though that function may be taken over by someone else once the dance has been invented – or rather, invented and taught, because the teaching is normally the first effective locus of the invention. Composers, in contrast, quite seldom act as their own first *répétiteurs*, even if the conductor of a first performance likes to have the composer around to resolve problems. In fact, many composers are very bad conductors, and there is no essential reason why a composer should be able to conduct at all (except that anyone who is not paralysed can wave an arm in time to the music, if that counts as conducting). But I do not know that it is even possible for a choreographer to be unable to teach a dance to its originating group. In theory, one could compose a dance in notation, or on a computer, and give it to the dancers in that form; but, outside the classroom, does it often happen?

In short, what a composer typically works on is the score, which, together with its copies, will be the score for all performances. What a choreographer typically works on is the prime instance of the dance itself.

This difference in focus reflects a deeper difference. George Beiswanger (1970, 88) says: 'Dances are made not *out of*, but *upon* movement, movement being the poetic bearer, the persistent metaphor, by which muscular material is made available for the enhanced, meaningful, and designed *goings-on* that are dance.' We are in error, he says, when 'we think of choreography, not as putting dancers in motion, but as taking

dance movement and putting it in order.' Composers may have particular singers and players in mind, and compose music for them to sing in
their characteristic fashion. But that is very different from setting a
specific human dancing person in motion in a particular way, even if
the motion in which the dancer is set constitutes a dance that others
could also dance. Composers *could* set singers in voice, but that is not
the way they usually work; choreographers *can* devise motions that any
dancer can perform, but, according to Beiswanger, they typically do not
work that way.

The second difference follows from the first. Composers nowadays
are typically freelances. If a composer works with one group, it will
most likely be because it has commissioned a work, not because the
composer and the group habitually work together. But a choreographer
is more likely than not to be attached to a specific company and to
work mostly with and for that company.[4] In a large organization,
though, today's choreographer is not usually the same person as the
artistic director or general manager.

The hands-off relation between musician and composer may owe
much to the development and use of a musical notation that any working musician can read at sight. If so, the circumstances that prevent
dancers 'reading at sight' from even the most lucid dance notation may
prevent dance from ever becoming a notational art in the way that
music has, as Nelson Goodman speculates that it might. But Beiswanger's remarks suggest rather that the use of dance notations has been
restricted because choreographers and dancers have good reason for
wanting to work directly with each other.[5]

I suppose the sharpest difference between musical composition and
choreography is that most pieces of music, once composed, can be
realized on many different combinations of instruments. So long as the
melodic, contrapuntal, and harmonic relations are preserved, it is the
same music, at most a different 'arrangement.' Maybe the practice is
frowned on in the highest circles of today's musical art (cf. Adorno
1984), but it is a standing possibility none the less. Nothing of the sort
seems to be true of choreography. A given dance can be danced by
different groups of dancers, and the dancers need not all be of the same
size, but it cannot properly be danced by anything other than groups of
dancers. It can be 'danced' by marionettes or by humanoid figures in an
animated film, but only in so far as they simulate human dancers. The
human body is the only instrumentation. This would be true even if
Beiswanger is wrong about the dancer's musculature being itself the

focus of the choreographer's attention. Of course, choreographers can arrange 'dances' for mechanical mice, or squadrons of army tanks, or anything that can be manipulated in motion; but then, they can also juggle billiard balls, if they have a mind to, and neither this activity nor the others would usually be regarded as an exercise of choreographic skill.[6] A group dance can be developed out of a solo, and other such transformations are possible; but I suspect that the new dance would not be considered identical with the old.

People dance with their bodies. Even if they make their bodies over into dancers' bodies, instruments for the dance, the transformation does not make them cease to be the individually shaped and talented bodies of different individuals. Whereas it is not uncommon for a composer to write for a particular voice or player, as Britten wrote for Pears and Pears's voice become more and more unusual the more Britten he sang, that is not the most usual way of doing things in western music. It is much more usual for a choreographer to make dances for and with specific dancers. 'For years he didn't create on me at all,' I heard Nora Kaye say of Antony Tudor, and the precise choice of words (standard in this context) is worth meditating on. The choreographer creates, invents a new dance, but it is not clear that Tudor can do this without a specific body, to the peculiar exigencies of which the dance can be moulded, even though other dancers can then dance it with their own bodies. (One could even say that in some cases it is not the dancer who realizes the choreography, but the choreography that is abstracted from the dance.) Even when choreographers do not proceed in this way, and not all do, they may well have a particular sort of body formation in mind.

Because dances regularly begin as tailored to a specific set of dancers, it is quite usual, when a dance is revived, for the choreography to be adapted to the new bodies and spaces. No one thinks anything of it, unless the revival is done with antiquarian rather than artistic intent. Choreography is seldom sacrosanct in the way that (at least in some people's minds) the letter of a musical score may be. Though music history abounds with adaptations of scores, cuts, and re-orchestrations, these are felt to be aberrant in a way that much more radical changes in choreography are not. In both cases, of course, actual audiences seldom know, and are even more seldom told; but among those who are conversant with what is being done, I think the prevailing attitudes do show this difference.

The procedures differ, as well as the attitudes. Musical changes seldom go beyond cuts and modifications of orchestration and omission of repeats, leaving melody and harmony inviolate,[7] and they are typically felt to be expedients that leave the original form of the music intact, to be returned to when times get better. But in choreography things are often changed without too much regard for the original detail, even if anyone can quite recall what it was, because that detail is felt to be appropriate to the original company rather than to a timeless entity, the repeatable dance. It follows that the conditions of identity of a particular named dance are not strict in the way that obtains in music, a matter to which we return in the next chapter.

The extent to which an original choreography is specific to a particular group of dancers varies, as I said. Not only may different choreographers have quite different ways of working, but the same choreographer may quite well work differently on different occasions, depending on circumstances – for instance, on the amount of time actually available for working with the group. A dance may be conceived abstractly, and then taught to (and adapted for or by) the dancers. A dance may be inspired by particular dancers or body styles or movement styles, but conceived as being for anyone, in a way remotely analogous to that in which a painter may use a person as a model without producing a portrait of that person. Or a dance may be worked out for dancers from whose individuality it is inseparable; in that case, it may be (usually, no doubt, will be) worked out *with* that dancer, or simply designed *for* that dancer – and, if it is worked out with the dancer, the dancer may be to any extent and in any manner a collaborator in the design of the dance, or may be simply the person (in Kaye's phrase) on whom the dance is created.[8] But even here it must be remembered that, on the one hand, dancers are not choreographers, so that their input will be directed rather to the detail of the dance than to the totality; and, on the other hand, dancers are humans with the full human equipment of intelligence and will, so that, however determined they may be to assume a passive and subservient role, their very manner of submission and passivity cannot but contribute a shaping effect to the mind of even the most arrogant choreographer.[9]

The threefold division between scenario, choreography, and dance oversimplifies the structure of movement control. From the devising of a scenario, with characters, scenes, and dance numbers, one may proceed to movement blocking, the rough shapes; and from there to the gross movements, who goes where how fast. Then come the fine movement decisions; and finally the movement style, the first thing lost in transmission between generations because it cannot be reduced to instructions. All of these are included in what choreographer and *répétiteur* must instil into their dancers, and it is obvious that the professional and personal negotiations will differ at different levels. Because of the intricacy of these relationships, choreography does not travel well. In many modern dance groups, the choreography is typically that of the leader of the company, or at least of someone associated with it permanently, and is relatively seldom danced by any other company. The style of dance goes with the style of dancer.

This situation does not so notably obtain in ballet, where technique is more standardized; but even there the repertoire is much less mobile than in music. The idea of ballet is so firmly wedded, in the ideology of proponents and opponents alike, to the idea of a uniform technique practised in classes wherever the arts of Western civilization hold sway, that we sometimes forget how diverse ballet companies are. Companies that excel in Bournonville may do rather miserably in Balanchine; dancers at home in Balanchine and Ashton may find themselves at odds with each others' ideals of humanity. The civic ballet of Left Overshoe may find much of the Bolshoi's repertoire beyond its competence; the Bolshoi may find what they do in Left Overshoe beneath its dignity. But I suppose it is true of any ballet in the repertoire that any ballet company can give it a whirl, whereas a free interchangeability of repertoires becomes dubious if not unthinkable where that technical basis does not prevail.

Throughout this section, I have written as though sharp contrasts can be drawn between practice in music and practice in dance, or between conditions in ballet and conditions in modern dance. But all these contrasts, when taken absolutely, seem wrong. The situation is rather that practices and traditions differ in all sorts of ways, because of factors that vary greatly in the resistance they offer to exceptions. There are these familiar and explicable tendencies, but tendencies are all they are. People are able and willing in different degrees to resist them or to embrace them, or simply to carry on as if they did not exist, like the Road Runner continuing to run in mid-air because he has not noticed that he has gone over the edge of a cliff.

18.3 Choreography and the Dimensions of Dance

Not every aspect of a dance can be choreographed, and undanced choreography has no independent artistic standing. Choreography, accordingly, is not a complete art. If one of the three aesthetic dimensions of dance is sheer presence (§15.2121), that cannot be provided for by devising steps. A choreographer can provide for it in the dance movements and stillnesses devised, but its realization is up to the dancers (and, indirectly, to those who originally trained them to dance with power). Choreography deals in the first instance with the second dimension, form and representation, prescribing movements that can be describably differentiated. It also deals with the expressive dimension; in teaching their dances, choreographers do not simply prescribe movements of bodies and actions of characters but describe imaginable situations and metaphors by which a dancer can unify a particular movement with expressive grace and force and, by so doing, manifest a quality of human personality that the dance will embody.

A composer of music cannot compose everything. One cannot intelligently say 'Play this *magically*,' though some directions come optimistically close. But one can, in composing for a specific artist, rely on that artist's magic and (since magic cannot exist in a vacuum) write what lends itself to that. The same must be true of the choreographer. However, though a composer cannot compose everything, many theorists argue that a piece of music, as composed, is already complete as a work of art, so that performances of it are either secondary works or partial realizations of the composer's work. Few would argue with equal confidence for the artistic self-sufficiency of a choreography.

Since a dancer dances with the whole person, whether or not the body is at the same time transformed into a specialized instrument, one would expect the part played by a personal and idiosyncratic magic to be much greater than it is in music, and equally out of the choreographer's reach. A distaste for ballet has often reflected a feeling that ballet choreography was too complete, offering scope only for feats of dexterity and technical accomplishment, and leaving no room for the dancers' artistry or humanity. Ballet was felt to be inherently oppressive. But surely nothing in the inherent dynamic of choreography requires it to be oppressive. Choreographers, however precise their specifications, may be thought of as providing opportunities rather than as imposing demands (see §18.4). And in ballet, as in other dance styles, choreographies may be tight, specifying every least movement, or loose, allowing much leeway in details, or quite open, leaving extensive areas open to the decision of the dancer, or even in places randomizing; and this may be just a matter of how the choreographer happens to go about things, or it may answer to deeply thought ideas about the choreographic process itself. A choreography may permit, or may require, ornamentation; may permit, or require, variation; may permit, or require, improvisation.[10]

I keep coming back to Isadora Duncan, not so much for what she did as for what she seemed to the artistic world to be: a dancer who was a great artist in her dancing, whether or not she was a great dancer. One way of putting the matter is that the overpowering effect of her art lay in what, it seemed obvious, could not be choreographed. Robert Henri, for instance, used her as the prime illustration of his general thesis that human beings can 'deal in an unconscious way with another dimension than the well-known three,' because differences in significance in art do not seem to correlate with measurable differences: 'Isadora Duncan, who is perhaps one of the greatest masters of gesture the world has ever seen, carries us through the universe in a single movement of her body. Her hand alone held aloft becomes a shape of infinite significance. Yet her gesture in fact can only be the stretch of arm or the stride of a normal human body.'[11]

People often complained that Duncan's attempts to impart her technique were futile: she could only say 'Not like this, but like this' – and there was no visible difference between the *this* and the *this*, except that the right ones were of the kind Henri describes, and the wrong ones were just ordinary. But the things people said about Duncan often confused two issues, her independence of technique and her lack of skill as a teacher. Certainly she had a technique; it could be taught, and it still can. But she left the running of her school mostly to her sister and other more or less willing victims, and perhaps others could teach her methods better than she could. The point remains, however, that the Duncan style of dancing, however charming and historically important, did not and does not go much beyond a rather facile prettiness. What Duncan's admirers prized in her were the moments of power.

18.4 What Choreographers Need to Know

Rachel Isadora Maiorano is quoted as saying: 'In ballet, the dancer isn't really a creator. You're there to dance, not to think or suggest, but just to focus. The difference between the dancer and other artists is that in dance, you don't use your experience. You can get by being a superb technician and being entirely unthoughtful' (Gordon 1983, 107). It is a puzzling statement, on the face of it. Are creating and suggesting the only kinds of thinking there are? If you can 'get by' by being a superb technician, what about people who want to do more than just 'get by'? Is their experience no use to them? Frankly, she sounds like a hack who thinks like a hack, expects to be used like a hack, and is used like a hack. No doubt there are companies and choreographers and dancers of whom all this is exactly true. But is it the normal condition of dance? Is it even the normal condition of ballet? In the course of a discussion in 1988 (see chapter 17 note 2), a panel of former dancers from the Ballet Russe de Monte Carlo in the 1940s were comparing experiences, horrible stories of oppression and chicanery. But when at the end the person chairing the panel asked them to sum up their impressions, they rejected the strongly implied invitation to condemn their tyrants; the feeling most strongly and consistently expressed was one of gratitude for the opportunity to dance the classical repertoire and get to know it really well with representatives of the great Russian tradition. And this fits what one has always understood to be the attitude of executant musicians, that there is no conflict between compliance with the score and the development of an artistic understanding.[12]

The Australian choreographer Graeme Murphy once said that a dancer's artistry comes when the physique starts to fail; a dancer cannot dance expressively without a knowledge of, and an interest in, life. Dancers should be contributing artists, he said, not mere instruments of the choreographer; their minds should be appealed to more than they are.[13]

Dancers, it seems, must at least be good technicians, so that, in so far as they are instruments of the choreographer, they will be good instruments. To be expressive instruments, they must have experience and knowledge. Their dancing is an intelligent contribution, then, and that intelligence can and should be put to a fuller use. And I have suggested already that, in learning to dance, one acquires an ever-deepening understanding of the principles of all the kinds of dancing one learns. But none of this is choreography. Someone might have all these without having the least inclination or ability to set up as a choreographer, just as that supremely intelligent musician Gerald Moore devoted his career to accompanying singers without ever stepping into the limelight as a soloist, much less setting up as a composer.

What is it that a choreographer must have that a dancer need not have? A dancer's understanding, I said, grows in depth until it becomes mastery of the whole art. But there is more in knowledge of the whole art than a dancer can use, except in the sense that any knowledge about dance (or anything else) may affect practice somehow or other. It may not, however, affect it for the better, for the most erudite practitioners are not necessarily the best. And even within the domain of practice, as distinct from history and theory, a dancer need not know all a choreographer must know. The meaning of any dance depends largely on its internal relations, its architectonics, the relation of each present moment to earlier and later moments. Some of this the dancer needs to know, where the relations are internal to the meaning of the dance as danced. But if the relations hold between discrete items, dancers need not be aware of them – unless one holds that dancers must know whether they need to dance with them in mind or not. Such relations may demand preservation of mutual indifference, hence the integrity of the several parts. But the choreographer must always have them in mind. The architectonics of the proposed piece, the relation between whole and parts, occupy a space in the choreographer's mind quite different from any they hold in a dancer's.

The definers of choreography in *The Dance Encyclopedia* put it very well: 'The art of composing dances; the science of putting together steps to form a dance and separate dances to form a dance composition or ballet.' And they borrow from Lincoln Kirstein the formula: 'the design by a dance composer of dance patterns which comprise ballets'.[14] This is very different from Beiswanger's idea that a choreographer as it were moulds muscles. For the encyclopedists, it is neither making dances nor moulding dancers, it is literally constructing, putting together. And that is certainly something a dancer does not do, implying an essentially external approach to the art. This is emphasized by calling choreography a 'science'; but perhaps this only means an 'art' in the old Platonic sense, a systematic use of the practical intelligence that proceeds on the basis of rational principles.

A choreographer has to be able to generate shapes. There is no reason why a dancer, however sensitive to the expressiveness of a dance or of a whole performance, should have any skill in putting steps together into sequences. 'It is easy to understand,' says Balanchine (1967, 203), 'the importance of connecting movements one to the other with subtle care, yet at the same time emphasizing by contrast their continuity.' It is equally easy to see that not everyone could comply with that requirement, or with other stipulations that he makes in the same context.

Choreography may well depend on a level of movement analysis that dancers cannot readily extract from their dance training. The difference might correspond to Aristotle's distinction between 'experience' and 'art' (*Metaphysics* I 1). Experience leads, in the way sketched in our account of learning, to deeper and deeper insight into underlying principles. But after a certain point, something else becomes necessary: a codification and conceptual reconstruction that will uncover connections of a new sort, making the field intelligible as a whole. This may well be what those choreographers have in mind who argue that their own compositions depend on an analysis of the basis of human movement: 'Choreographic movements are the basic movements which underlie all gesture and action and the choreographer must train himself to discover them. ... It is natural that these basic movements will at first seem affected and artificial to the body which is accustomed only to the practical movements of everyday life. ... The choreographer ... turns, not away from life, but to its source' (Balanchine 1967, 202).

I do not know how Balanchine determined that these movements, presumably discovered through some process of analysis, are basic, or who he thinks performed the analysis in question. Perhaps he means that each choreographer must work out afresh what is basic; more likely he thinks what is basic is the standard elements of ballet movement as worked out by the joint efforts of generations of choreographers. Even less is it clear how Balanchine thinks such a claim would be substantiated; less still is it clear how it could be substantiated to the satisfaction of someone not disposed to be credulous. But none of that discredits the main contention, that choreography requires an analysis of movement more fundamental than any that a dancer needs or can use. Perhaps all choreographers have to be anthroposophists or something of the sort – though it would still remain to be determined whether, if that were so, the necessity would be psychological, or culturally generated, or functionally integral to the choreographic process, or what (cf. Sparshott 1963, 32–3 and 48–51).

It is notorious that choreographic analyses of the fundamentals of human movement are not all compatible with each other. If they are basic, what they are basic to is probably never more than a particular highly generalized style or method of dance-making. But that would not defeat their claim to be basic; it is possible that all could be related, differently but equally directly, to identifiable principles of musculature or kinesiology, or of visibility in movement, or something of similarly irreproachable fundamentality.

In discussing what choreographers need to know that dancers do not, we may once again seek analogies from music and elsewhere. In music, a composer needs the ability to write correct harmony, to manage voice-leading, to write parts that will lie within the range of voices and instruments. The first two of these are technical skills that do not lie within the professional competence of a performer as such. (A church organist must be able to improvise in acceptable harmony and arrive at a convincing cadence at a moment's notice; but to improvise is not to perform.) Is there any parallel to such technical skills of composition in dance? I do not know of any, but there could be: there could be dance traditions incorporating a syntax of forms that a choreographer would have to learn, on pain of having dances dismissed as ungrammatical and hence unperformable.

In considering the place of such technical requirements in composition, in music and dance alike, the metaphor of 'grammar' may lead one astray. Violating the rules of grammar in writing makes one literally unintelligible.[15] The corresponding rules in music are much closer to being rules of acceptability: there is no semantics that relies on the syntax in the strict way that is typical of language. And I suppose it would be the same in dance. An 'ungrammatical' dance would be incoherent and unintelligible in the sense that the dance was pointless, one could not tell what the dancers were up to; but there would be no *message* that was failing to be delivered. The dance would be a solecism rather than a nonsense.

An analogy for the combination of high skill in dance with effective inability to choreograph might be found in the familiar combination of ability to read a language easily with almost complete inability to speak or write it.[16] This curious combination appears to the layman to have three components. First is the ability to recognize grammatical relations without being able to generate them. Second is the ability to recognize vocabulary without the ability to recall it – whenever I see *bac* I know it means 'ferry,' but I can never remember the word for 'ferry' when I need it. Third is the sheer difficulty of producing speech *ex nihilo*. A dancer may know how to do whatever is called for, without knowing when it is called for or why; may recognize a dance as satisfying to do, and have a good feeling for why it is satisfying, without knowing how one would produce something that was satisfying in that way;[17] and, above all, does not have actually to *invent* something to dance. This last element, this sheer power to initiate, is the most elusive element in creation and is indispensable.

Being able to read a language and not write it differs in an important way from being able to play music but not compose it.[18] A musical performer can play a piece of music without recognizing the rules of harmony in any way at all, or even suspecting that there are such rules;

one need only play what one sees so that it sounds right, and the music will come of itself. But if one just reads the marks on the page without knowing the grammar of the language, no linguistic meaning will come at all. Does dance have a meaning-producing grammar, like music, or a meaning-constituting grammar, like language? Or are the conditions of dance meaning significantly different from both? I suspect that the last is true, that there is really nothing for the expression 'dance grammar' to refer to; but, for all that has been said about the ways in which dance meanings are special, I am not confident that I have laid the issue to rest.

Another thing that may separate dancer from choreographer is close to the difficulty of actually initiating speech in a language of which one has reading knowledge. A choreographer undergoes the risk of creation, of standing out in the light as creator, taking responsibility for the whole of the dance. A dancer, like any other artist, takes the artist's risk in performance, of chancing success and failure in a number of ways as executant; but the dance is always there, as at least a partial standard of correctness. One may fall by a standard, but one may also stand by it; and the standard itself is more a support than a threat, because it is something for which one is not responsible. Not everyone may wish or be able to take the extra step beyond the support.

Similarly, but more subtly, a choreographer takes responsibility for imposing a dance on the world. Does one have a right to do that? Some artists feel that they have no right to impose a work by their own will. The work must demand to be made. One is not to say nothing. Perhaps what Diaghilev supplied to his neophyte choreographers was the conviction (self-justifying, possibly) that they had something to say.

A dancer may fail to be a choreographer neither from lack of know-how nor for the existential reasons just mentioned, but for practical reasons. A choreographer does not have merely to make something that *could* be danced. The upshot has to be rewarding to dancers and interesting to audiences. Many highly accomplished persons prove unable to think of anything to do with their skill. Even a work that 'demands to be made' may turn out to be a bore when the making is done.

18.5 The Necessity of Choreography

The relationship between choreographer and dancer is an essential topic in the discussion of dance. But my examples have mostly been from ballet and other theatre dance. In fact, though the distinction between invention and execution is conceptually sharp, the idea of choreography as a practice seems internal to Western theatre dance. It seems absurd even to think of the word in some other practices. What I am told of the way an Indian guru teaches a dancer seems to leave no space for the idea at all.[19]

The notion to which the idea of choreography is really internal is that of a dance theatre in which new dances are shown as new, and old dances are shown, not as ritual, but as taken from a repertoire. Dances are not merely presented, but worked up for presentation. These ideas and practices are not confined to Western traditions, and wherever they are found the concept of choreography is in place. Why, then, do we not apply it in traditional Asian or African contexts, though we apply the word 'dancer' there without hesitation? Is it just that we happen not, in most cases, to recognize or even to know the name of whoever composed a dance? Perhaps; but the institution (and hence the distinct practice) of choreography requires, not only that the question 'Who composed this?' have a determinate and discoverable answer, but that the question be one that is customarily asked and answered. Han Suyin says somewhere that Chinese dances were *traditionally* traditional, so that only a dancer recognized as great could modify the choreography of a dance. If that was really so, then it appears that great dancers were named but great choreographers were not, so that it would be appropriate to say who changed a dance but not who composed it in the first place.[20]

Realistically, the idea of a choreographer is internal to the very specific practices of Western ballet and its successors (for modern dance did not so much displace ballet as aspire to replace it, occupying the niche it had prepared in the arts establishment) when the original functions of dancing master were split up among impresarios, regisseurs, and dance inventors.[21] And part of what is built into the idea of choreography is that of private property – the very idea that a dance is originated and owned by someone, an idea that takes palpable shape in the laws of copyright.[22] But everything said in this section is subject to the proviso that the spread of international cultural organizations is changing the way things are done and conceived everywhere. Travel is envisaged, self-consciousness is encouraged, labour is divided. Everything is changed utterly; a terrible vulgarity is born.

18.6 Margins of Choreography

18.61 Routines

My treatment of choreography has been excessively high-minded. Basically, a choreographer is merely someone who devises routines for dancers to perform. And not only dancers. Gymnasts and figure-skaters perform routines that are well put together, elegant, and conformable both to the tastes and capacities of those who are to perform them and to the requirements of whatever competition and display is in question. In such cases, rather than the choreographer finding dancers to flesh out an artistic conception, it will more likely be the competer or performer who hires a choreographer to put things together as one might hire a costume designer – and yet, behind every successful Kurt Browning, there stands an Anne Bezic.

The essential thing in such cases is the context, which is that of the show or the competition, the thing to be done and shown. The choreographer is frankly an artisan, because it is the performer alone who is to succeed or fail. The career of Fred Astaire is exemplary in this regard, as in much else. When he and his sister were little, their dancing master devised little routines for them, to show off their specific charm and incipient skills in specific exhibitions. To the end of his career, Astaire was devising routines for himself and his partners to perform in specific slots in specific shows. Balanchine repeatedly called attention to this aspect of his own work. I think people felt this was false modesty on his part, and certainly there was a rather ostentatious lack of ostentation involved, but it seems to me entirely likely that he was struck by the practical seriousness and responsibility of coming up with something of the right sort and the right length that the dancers will actually be able to do on the night.[23] He was, after all, right to be proud of having made a dance for circus elephants.

18.62 Improvisation

Improvisation is the complement of composition. What the choreographer does not specify the dancer must supply. The relation, as I remarked, may be anything. In many sorts of case, the dancer makes the decisions that the choreographer does not make, so that the dance as finally performed is fully choreographed, but in collaboration between the choreographer who does no dancing and the dancer who has done some of the choreography. In other cases, the dancer leaves the complements to ad-hoc decisions, made for the occasion, so that audiences on successive nights will see rather different dances, though each will in a sense be fully choreographed. But a dancer may simply leave it to the spur of the moment to do whatever comes to mind and body. Should we say, deciding on the spot? Maybe, but not necessarily. 'Deciding' suggests some consideration of alternatives, however fleeting; and the dancer may simply trust to the inspiration or impetus of the moment, without considering alternatives at all. It is largely a matter of degree: how clear does the consideration of alternatives have to be, before one speaks of *deciding* what to do? At one ideal extreme, everything is worked out and planned beforehand; at the other extreme is a total spontaneity in which there is no conscious consideration at all, but a stream of action that sustains and develops itself. From the present point of view, however, there is not even a single continuum, because one may have more or less clearly in mind, in a more or less fixed form, plans and possibilities at all sorts of levels, together with a more or less shadowy set of strategies for changing one's mind about any of them.

There is no sharp distinction between knowing and not knowing what one is going to do, between having made up one's mind and not having made it up, until the relevant moment of action or public commitment. None the less, an important difference is to be noted. Composition for oneself or others, in which one makes a complete set of decisions that determine what a work is to be, what is to count as an example or performance of the work because it complies with that set, and what is to be excluded as not complying, differs fundamentally from improvisation, in which there is no such set of decisions and, consequently, no determinate work that could be correctly or incorrectly performed. Like many such distinctions, however basic, this one does not divide actual phenomena into two discrete sets; in principle, though, it demands different criteria of assessment, and implies different values in action.

In discussing the solitary dancer as true artist, I started from the supposed basic value of art, the fashioning of something deeply satisfactory to the maker, the quality of which is corroborated by its being an object of satisfaction for others. The devotees of improvisation find an analogous but perhaps even deeper value in spontaneous creation. Instead of labouring to capture and refine an artistic idea, the nature of which is revealed only in the process of creation or revelation itself, improvisers launch on an unguided process of self-discovery, finding and developing within themselves a new kind of rationality of which they had not known themselves to be capable. Someone who is good at improvising can do this most of the time, as perhaps Beethoven could, the very process of improvising transposing him into a new, uncharted world of discovery and creation in which he was both supremely rational and entirely free. Less gifted people find this happens less regularly; their spontaneities usually amount to no more than discursive ramblings, but now and then they are taken over by a force of unwilled formal and dynamic creation that is no part of their everyday selves. And this can be done with other people; with a congenial group it is even better. Their joint improvisations make them regularly free of each other's minds, so to speak, in a joyful community of free interaction, combining the purest satisfactions of art with the promise of a better world of human harmony. Such joint improvisation is possible in any performance art, notably in theatre and music; but it is most at home in dance, where the interaction is most free from preconceptions.

One may wonder whether the value just described is really a dance value. Suppose the improvisation were remembered and recorded; the improvised dance could then be repeated, but it would no longer be a spontaneous creation. Would that make it any worse as a dance? Is it inconceivable that the dancers, when they saw the film of themselves doing it, might make improvements that would make it a better dance? Should we not distinguish delight in the act of successful creation from satisfaction in the quality of what one had succeeded in? After all, this is a cliché in the philosophy of science, that the heuristic processes of scientific discovery are but loosely related to the validity of scientific demonstrations. Are the advocates of improvisation not making an elementary mistake?

Not necessarily. In science, the methods of discovery and their joys have one sort of value; the discoveries themselves have a quite different sort of value. But all the values in dance improvisation, aside from the social delights of camaraderie, are those of dancing itself; there is no independent realm of values to be entered. There are problematic relations between the value of a dance to the dancer and the value of that dance to an audience, and between the excitement of doing something that is coming off and the satisfaction of doing something that is being got right; but these relations presumably hold in a reciprocal or dialectical way within a single unitary context of action.

Cynthia Novack (1984) has reported her observations of a congress devoted to dance improvisation, the participants in which were devotees of the sort of rational spontaneity I am discussing here. What unites those who profess these practices, it seems, is less a common belief than a commitment to the use of certain set words and phrases, together with shared attitudes to other parts of the dance world. Novack points out that, despite their professed belief in freedom, the practitioners as individuals were all in the job market, competing with each other and with dance professionals from other camps. Not that that matters, perhaps, since nobody in the educational world can reconcile professional practice with ideals. What is more significant is that the context within which the improvisers operated was not that of art and the art school, but that of physical education and its departments, departments which in recent years have acquired, as it were inadvertently, a responsibility for the individual as physical and social organism – a sort of sanitary Sunday school.

Novack reports that one audience member said that a special delight in watching dancers improvise was to see them taking a risk in public. It is not clear whether this is like watching dangerous stunts in a circus, where there is excitement in the real danger that the performer may fall and be killed, or whether it is more like sporting events in which a team may win or fail, and at any moment something exciting may happen. In any case, the specifically artistic risk improvisers take is in one way like that taken by choreographers, who (like any artist) put career and personality on the line in every work, in a way in which dancers of a choreographed work hardly do; in another way, it is special and more immediate, because the improviser has to come up with something *now*. But that is true only if one improvises in public. The self-discovery of the improviser in the physical-education context involves no risk beyond that of disappointment, the risk that nothing may happen this time.

In §18.61 I mentioned professional stage dancers like Astaire, for whom the context of creation was that of the spot to be filled, the show to be put on. The same kind of performer, in the same kind of context, is relevant to our present concerns. A vaudeville or music-hall performer, other than a singer, traditionally was not an improviser, but by the same tradition was not the executant of a choreographed routine. What the great comedians did was what Astaire did for his films, gradually work up and polish a routine which was then presented unchanged. One went to the music hall to see the performer go through the famous act, which the performer had developed and for which the performer took responsibility. Such performers did their own material. It was in this tradition that Isadora Duncan and her contemporaries worked. It was a tradition of complete freedom, in one way; but it was also a tradition of total responsibility.

In line with my usual practice of looking to the world of music for parallels, I should now say something about musical improvisation, especially in jazz. What any kind of music afforded the improviser, until recently, was a universally accepted set of organizational devices: a harmonic structure, a system of countable measures and notes, a repertoire of cadences. With this methodical apparatus it is easy to devise frames, and to operate within them singly or jointly, establishing degrees of freedom and fixity, places to join and places to separate. All who combine effectively in joint improvisation must understand what the framework is and how it will be used, and must be able to tell from what is being done what options are being opened and what are being closed. What Western dance generally lacks, so far as I am aware, is frameworks for improvisation, understood everywhere, comparable to what music provides in generating known ways of improvising. Some African and Asian traditions of dance, it seems, provide something of the sort. What one learns in them is how to dance along with others who have learned in the same way without there having to be a specific dance one has learned. But the accounts I have read of these traditions have not answered quite the questions I would ask: the precise ways in which dances are improvised rather than choreographed, or the extent to which our own distinctions in this realm fail to apply.

CHAPTER NINETEEN

The Identity of a Dance

When are we justified in saying that two performances are performances of 'the same' dance? What are the conditions of identity of dances,
and why are they what they are? It is the sort of question philosophers
like to ask.[1] But it is only now, when we have discussed the choreographic hierarchy, that we are in a position to consider it.

19.1 Dance and Dancer

We can tell the dancer from the dance. The same dancer may dance
both Odette and Odile in *Swan Lake*, but she must dance them differently; her audience will be specifically interested in how the one dancer
expresses the duality in these linked roles. Another part of the interest
lies in seeing how her rendering of the duality differs from other
dancers' ways of rendering it.

Things are different when we are watching an improvised dance, or
when we see unfamiliar dancers in an unfamiliar repertoire. We can still
compare these dancers with other dancers, these dances with other
dances; but we can do so only on the basis of a distinction between
dancer and dance that we have to make within a single phenomenon,
a single observed performance. It is then that we ask Yeats's famous
question, how can we tell the dancer from the dance?

To recognize a dance as a dance at all, we must recognize it as an
alternative to other possible dances. If we had no sense of what other
dances there might be, we could not be recognizing it as a dance rather
than something else – 'moving around,' perhaps. And to identify a dance

as a particular dance is to recognize it as inherently repeatable. It is a distinct thing that has been done; so it is something that can be done, and therefore could be done again. It is obviously possible, though it might be ruled out by vanity or etiquette, that a dancer who made a mistake or a slip, or simply did not do a dance very well, might say, 'I'll try that again' and do the same dance better (or, of course, not so well; or just about as well, but a bit differently). If we did not know what was meant by 'the same again,' we would not have understood the dance at all;[2] and, since the first attempt was (ex hypothesi) defective, the second attempt is likely to sharpen our ideas about what 'the same again' was.[3]

To see a dance, I must see it as repeatable by the same person. But people keep changing. If the dance were repeated by the same person, it would be on a different occasion, or later on the same occasion. Between the two occurrences the dancer would have tired, or matured, or both, or would have got warmed up or invigorated. In any case, the dancer would have had the experience of doing the dance one more time, and knowing it that much better – or becoming that much more bored with it. The changes might be too small to notice, but they would be real; a sharp enough perception could surely find the hair's-breadth of difference. And we can certainly imagine the same dancer doing the same dance years later; and then, perhaps, he will always put his hand out to save his balance at the same point in the dance, and we old-timers will say, 'I remember when he used to do that bit without using his hand.' The dancer is the same, and the dance is the same, but the same dancer will not always do the same dance in the same way.

Dancers are beset by perils and promises of age, fatigue, injury, illness, enthusiasm, inspiration, dejection, and luck; occasions are beset by good and bad audiences, resilient or slippery floors, efficient or inadequate or ill-timed lighting, goodness knows what accidents of costuming; and the choreography of a dance is hedged around with a haze of expedients, emergencies, fallbacks, and options, as well as stylistic alternatives that the necessary variability of human affairs dictates. A choreographer can seldom be sure that the dance will always be danced by the same dancer (injuries cannot always lead to cancellations) and can never be sure just what the conditions of the dancers or the circumstances of the performance will be; whether consciously or not, every choreography must have variability built in. To know what 'the same again' will be in a dance, we must have the same sort of sense that the choreographer had of the ideals of repeatability and the limits of variability.[4]

In short, we know the dancer from the dance because we cannot know either dancer or dance without knowing the different but intimately related ways in which each may vary.

If we can know the dancer from the dance, because we cannot know either without knowing how each might stay the same and hence might *not* stay the same, we must have some notion of how the same person would do the same dance when changed in some specific way (when older, for instance), or when dancing it differently. To know that, we must have some notion of how a different but (in some specified ways) similar individual would dance it, and of how a very different dancer would dance the same dance in essentially the same way, or again in a different way. So we must have some grasp of how, by continuation, we could come to a scarcely recognizable version of the same dance. (We could not imagine the version, perhaps; but we can imagine what it would be to be confronted by it.) And if we can envisage the same dance by a quite different dancer, we can envisage the same dancer dancing a quite different dance – an everyday experience, of course. But that raises a question. Could there not be a series of transformations, each recognizable (in terms of our dance-going skill) as a new version of the same dance as the one before, the end of which might be indistinguishable from what (in terms of that same skill) would have been unequivocally judged to be a quite different dance, if the intermediate stages had been left out? But, to answer that question we must consider more generally the conditions of identity for dances (§19.4, below). There are other things to attend to first.

19.2 Performance Type and Performance Token

I have introduced the term 'performance' in a special sense, to mean what is done by the agent of an action in the doing of that very thing (cf. chapter 15 note 37). Such a performance is the proper object of criticism. When critics of art or literature criticize something, they implicitly single out from all other phenomena a set that answers to a single possible intention, which, for purposes of their criticism, they take to be that which the criticized performers achieved or failed to achieve. All other actions and happenings, including irrelevant actions of the persons performing, are deemed extraneous, to be taken into account, if at all, only as disturbing or concealing or accidentally enhancing factors.

In many kinds of situation, what is performed is a task, the specifications of which can be laid down in advance. A person simply does or fails to do, more or less completely and efficiently, what was to be done. In the fine arts, by contrast, there is no such task to be performed. The critical act, which determines how well the artist. did what was done, also and principally purports to determine precisely what it was that was performed. The critic describes the artwork in a way that, in effect, interprets it as the fulfilment of an imputed intention. Whether or not the artist or anyone else ever entertained that intention is of no independent critical importance, though knowing what the artist had in mind may help to explain why an ambiguous or doubtfully successful work is to be taken in one way rather than another.

19.21 The Choreographer's Performance

A choreographer's making of a dance is the performing of a performance in our sense. The dance as composed is a performance with a character that can be isolated for attention and criticized. But what the dancer dances is not necessarily identical with what the choreographer composed. In a sense, it can never be. A work for performance, as Paul Thom explains (see §14.1 above), is meant to be realized for and beheld by audiences; works differ in the flexibility they admit, choreographers differ in the rigidity of their stipulations; but in any case, as I said in §19.1, what the choreographer composes can only be a series of dance movements which, because in principle danceable by many differently equipped dancers (and by dancers each of whom will be in different conditions on different occasions), must leave open options of manner and nuance. As in music, there are three levels of indeterminacy. Some composers are more pernickety than others in what they specify (by way of bowing, dynamics, accent, expression, and so on), but even the most obsessive must leave something to the performer, including the precise interpretation of the attempts to introduce precision. Here are two levels, then: the latitude necessary for the executant to make sense of the composition, and the extra leeway that composers allow or demand by leaving open options that they might not have left open. Things are made more complex, but not fundamentally different, by 'aleatoric' practices, where some things are left to the performers' choice or chance; here, too, composers differ in how meticulous their instructions are as to when and how choice and chance are to enter, and here, too, the executants have to decide how to follow these instructions to produce a performance that will make sense – one they can actually *perform*.

There is, however, a third level of indeterminacy. Choreographers and composers are not, as such, producers or impresarios. Their task is to create, to prescribe a work, not to issue commands to performers. It is up to performers and directors to follow their directions or not, and it is a familiar fact that they do not always do so.[5] They depart from script or score from necessity, or for convenience or economy, or for artistic reasons. What is permissible in this regard, or what is even noticeable, varies in very complex ways. It depends on the context of production,[6] and on the wider cultural context that generates specific sorts of expectations about how scores will be used. Nicholas Wolterstorff (1980) has taught us to think of works of art (especially in performance arts) as normative kinds: the artist, in accordance with prevailing conventions, lays down what is to count and what is not to count as a performance of the work, leaving the rest indifferent. But many works are so complex that a production can fly in the face of many such prescriptions and still pass muster as a production of the work, and there may or may not be a consensus as to what is beyond the bounds of whatever it may be.[7]

It is so obviously and inevitably true that what the dancers do need not coincide with what the choreographer proposed that in a new dance, where choreographer and regisseur are the same, we expect that parts of the choreography will really count only as options, and that if the dance stays in repertoire it is unlikely to stay the same. The attempt to reconstruct the original performance of a work is a very special sort of undertaking, more archaeology than art. (Notoriously, when choreographers are enlisted to help in such reconstructions, they often keep trying to change things.)[8]

One notorious example of the instability of a choreographer's initial proposals is the place of Benno, the Prince's friend, in *Swan Lake*. Gerdt, the immensely popular dancer scheduled for the original performance, was no longer strong enough to support his partner reliably, so Benno was written in to lend a hand. But what then? On the one hand, nobody thinks that Benno would have been there if the Prince had been a younger dancer, so people often say he is not really part of the dance, and a revival should omit him. On the other hand, Benno was really part of the original choreography, and some people say that once he had been written in it would be false to the artist's intention to leave him out. Even if the dance had been fully worked out in a version without him, that version was not adopted for the actual performance, and might be thought to have no higher status than such abortive sketches and rejected alternatives as fall by the wayside in many works. Someone might complain that Benno is ridiculous, an embarrassment, an expedient that spoils the effect of the ballet with the pretence that a third party would be present at an encounter so intimately romantic. But someone else might retort that the Prince is after all a Prince, shown in the ballet as oppressed by court conventions, and it is natural that he should be accompanied by an aide-de-camp, whose presence is no more intrusive than that of a sofa. So what, after all, is the choreography that the choreographer created? If 'he' (allowing this pronoun to stand for the team, or collective, or succession, of dance-makers jointly responsible for generating the ballet *Swan Lake*) made an alternative Benno-free version, he did a very complex thing. He created *Swan Lake* in its original version(s), a ballet with a distinctive shape and story and theme(s) and music, such that a number of alternative versions could equally be said to realize it. Also, when you see one of those versions, what you see is unequivocally and authentically the *Swan Lake* 'he' composed. And 'he' also created the totality, the whole bundle of alternatives together with the historic occasions and contextual justifications of their introduction. Of each of these three alternative constructs it is true that it is the authentic work, as choreographed by its original choreographer. There are no good theoretical or practical grounds for pushing the matter further than that. What decisions you then make about how to mount or appreciate or criticize a production of the ballet will properly rest on something other than the authority of the original artist.

Gregory Currie (1989, 68) argues that a work of art is to be regarded neither as the outcome of a segment of the artist's biography, nor as a self-contained phenomenon, but as the terminus of a heuristic path, the rational process of production whereby the artist evolved a work from the problems faced and the antecedents confronted. A critic's task is to reconstruct that path and thus make the work fully intelligible. That's all very well; but, as we have just seen, in the performing arts the path has no determinate end. There are a multiplicity of contingencies and expedients, heuristic highways and bypaths leading to alternative classes of performance options, any or all of which may remain accessible for future opportunities or emergencies. A choreographed dance is a bundle of such actual possibilities, more or less determinate in scope, more or less loosely tied.

19.22 The Dancer's Performance

A dancer who takes on a role in a ballet works within limits imposed by artistic conscience and by the instructions of choreographer or regisseur. Within those limits, a dancer has to work up a way of dancing the part. The part, the role, then assumes the function of *task*, and the dancer's dancing is the performance of this task. But the performance itself is what has to be worked up, and when this is achieved it assumes the function of a secondary task. The dancer dances, again and again, not just Giselle, but *her* Giselle.[9] We can tell her Giselle from another dancer's because of the different stylistic choices she consciously or unconsciously makes. And we can tell her performance on Thursday from her performance on Sunday, possibly by stylistic shifts as her understanding of the role changes, but more probably by whether she is on form, and by more specific variations in the way she looks and moves.

Like other signs, it can be held, a dance as dance is constituted entirely by its relevantly meaningful aspects.[10] It is a complex of meaningful movements.[11] But, like all other signs, it can in principle be identically repeated, and exists only as token or tokens, as actual exemplar of its inherently repeatable features.[12] But the actual movements of the dancers' bodies neither constitute nor are constituted by signs or their meaningful aspects; they are what the men and women are actually doing. What the 'sign' in question is is a matter for interpretation; that being so, it could be many things at once. We have seen that, on each occasion, a dancer in the role of Giselle is dancing Giselle. From her point of view, though, that is not immediately relevant. What is relevant is that she is dancing *her* Giselle, giving a rendering of the interpretation of the role that she has got up for the current production.[13] But that is not the whole story. On any given occasion, she is crafting that evening's peformance, autarchically if not autonomously. The construction that is her Giselle functions, as does the role of Giselle itself, only regulatively: the actual object of her attention and endeavours is the performance she is giving right now – itself, of course, a sign constituted by its meaningful features. There is no mechanical process by which the dance is being produced, however much of it she has made automatic so that she can 'dance it in her sleep.' She is a thinking person, and the dance is necessarily the product of her thought at the time – necessarily, because at any moment her partners may falter, or some variation in her surroundings may call for instant adjustment. Just as the choreographer's Giselle allows for individual variations, so the dancer's Giselle admits of variations from evening to evening. Such variations do not make each performance what anyone would call a fresh creative act, but they do make it an achievement of craft and artistry, to be appreciated for its own sake and not merely as the trivially successful realization of a design on which the real interest is concentrated.

What I have just presented is a hierarchy of types.[14] At the top is the hypertype of Giselle, the schematic design exemplified in all true performances of the role. Below that there is an array of megatypes, distinctive ways of interpreting and dancing the role. At the bottom are the specific interpretations fully and uniquely exemplified by a particular evening's performance of a specific dancer's definite interpretation of the role. It is a hierarchy in this way: what the dancer is doing right now is an example of one way of performing the role, that way itself being a specification of a more generalized way of doing it, and so on up to Giselle itself, which is what the others are successively differentiated versions of versions of versions ... of. Where such lines cannot be definitively traced, there is no determinate hierarchy and the term should not be used. And we must not forget that, at the bottom, the individual performance is both type and token, unique in fact (and necessarily so in practice) but in principle repeatable.

To an audience, the relation between the choreographer's Giselle, the dancer's version of Giselle for the current production, and the Giselle being danced on the present occasion fluctuates. It differs for differently informed and differently interested members of the audience and need not be stable or simple for any of them. Few of the audience will assign the dancer's Giselle any independent status; they will be interested to see Giselle being danced, and danced well, and will probably divide their attention between the ballet as an artistic unity and the dancer's dancing of the role on the present occasion. If their interest in the dancer goes beyond the immediate occasion, it will probably go not to 'her Giselle' but to 'her in Giselle' – we know Karen Kain by experience and repute and are interested to see how well she does in this ballet. Her performance as a repeatable invention is not likely to be an object of interest for most spectators. But for a good many of them it will be.

Interest in a dancer's rendering of a role can be separate from considerations of how well the role is being performed. Suppose one were to go to see (as I have done) the late Donald Wolfit in *King Lear*: how disappointed one would be if Wolfit were not to do *his* Lear, but were instead to play the part *well* in some normal or contemporary understanding of the actor's art! Such a performance as Wolfit's takes on the status of a shtick. Pavlova's dancing of *The Dying Swan* must have been like that. It was, no doubt, a supreme manifestation of the dancer's art;

but, even if it had not been, its status as an institution would have made it as worth seeing as Disneyland.

19.3 Performance and Performing

In my artificial use of the terms, performer and performance are correlative. The performer is no more and no less than the agency of the performance as such, and the performance is just what the performer does in the doing of it. There is a third term: the performing of the performance by the performer. This sort of trinity-in-unity was invented by Aristotle, to account for the unity of thought, in which the mind as thinker, the thought that the thinker thinks, and the act in which the thinker thinks that thought could not be conceived as having any existence separate from each other, though to think is not the same as to be thought about, and neither the thinker nor the object of the thinker's thought is the same as the act of thinking. There is only the act of thinking, in which 'thinker' and 'thought' are necessarily abstractable as poles. This is the pattern of thought that Augustine borrowed and slightly adapted for his theory of a divine Trinity; Husserl used the same triad of nous/noesis/noema in later versions of his phenomenology; Sartre used what was essentially the same pattern for his analysis of free action, in which action and aim and motivation spring simultaneously into inseparable existence (Sartre 1943, part IV chap. 1 §2). So we see that thinkers of very different temperaments and methods have found the pattern useful in the analysis of action as such.

I have distinguished the dancer from the dance. Do I need to add anything about the third term in the relation, the dancer's dancing of the dance? Not necessarily. I began with the dancing, from which dancer and dance are projected as polarities and then identified, respectively, with the personal and product aspects of the existing institution of dance. To distinguish the dancing from the dance would be to differentiate the pattern of energies from its discernible outcome as a pattern of movement. To distinguish the dancer from the dancing would be to differentiate the intender and designer from the fact of execution. These theoretical distinctions become real separations only when the artefact or performance has an embodiment that does not coincide with its production. To the extent that a dancer's dancing of her Giselle simply realizes the very same that she realizes whenever she dances it, the separation has some reality. But I have nothing more to say of it here. I would only remind the reader that the self-contained unity of a performer performing a performance is compromised not only by the audience's more comprehensive awareness, in the manner indicated by Paul Thom, but by the background reality of the not-yet–de-realized personhood of dancer and spectator, as recognized by Sartre. The human density of dance experience and the abstract concentration of performance do not compromise each other but mutually resonate.

19.4 The Identity of a Dance

When do we think of a copied, or modified, or disguised, version or similitude of a work of art as actually being that work, and when do we not? I began by using Peirce's vocabulary of 'type' and 'token' to discuss this issue, saying that a performance is a token of a work of art, and hence is that work, in so far as it can be traced by the appropriate means to the design act originating the work, and in so far as the design is discernible in the performance (Sparshott 1982c, 168–87); we have just seen how this must be modified in discussing the performing arts. Do we need to say anything different when we are talking specifically about dance?

One difference is that not all dance is art. Dance in general, we saw in §2.3, tends to exist in the form of named dances that are recognized as scattered particulars within cultures, identified institutionally by various contextual and formal criteria. In such cases the concept of a 'design act,' activity coalescing in the generation of an aesthetic object, has no bite. We may say that someone must have invented the polka, or that it emerged from a definite consensus in a specific dance-making milieu, but who cares? What makes the polka the polka is the way it is taught and disseminated, the intercommunicative mass of dance practice within which it circulates (Keil and Keil 1992). It is a historical entity like an epidemic. And since within our culture there is a rough and ready sense in which dancing is dancing, there may be something to be said for treating *Swan Lake*, another named dance, in the same way. What makes *Swan Lake Swan Lake* is the way its unity is recognized within a dancing, dance-making, and dance-going community that understands itself, for practical purposes, fairly well, and which has an extensive but not infinite tolerance for distortion and perversion.

What at first looks like a quite different consideration within the art of ballet tends in the same direction. I have spoken of 'the choreographer's *Giselle*' as if the design act of choreographing *Giselle* gave it a form that was determinate within the practical limits imposed by human variability. But what Vernoy de Saint-Georges and his colleagues did was in some ways closer to inaugurating a tradition that then became self-sustaining.

The distinction between designing and inaugurating is brought out sharply by the entry 'Dauberval, Jean' in *The Dance Encyclopedia*, where we read: 'Dauberval's best known ballet, *La Fille Mal Gardée*, first produced in 1789, is one of the oldest ballets still being performed, although probably in an entirely different form, his original choreography having long disappeared' (Chujoy and Manchester 1967, 272). What does that mean? Does calling it 'entirely different' mean that the ballet now called by that name has nothing in common with Dauberval's except the name and the mere fact that each successive version somehow or other allies itself with some earlier version, and thereby with the forgotten original? Surely there is a little more to it than that.[15] At least, the theme (a young woman in a position of dependence who escapes the vigilance of those responsible for her and marries or makes off with the 'wrong' man) must remain, together with some basic pattern in the sequence of events in which the theme is realized. I suppose all the *Encyclopedia* means is that today's choreography is entirely by Ashton, or by someone else who was not Dauberval. In calling what we see *La Fille mal gardée*, we are tracing it not to Dauberval's design act but to his inauguration of the practice of composing ballets with the same name and something (we cannot say exactly what) of the same outline.

The complexities of the identity conditions of dances are notoriously exemplified by *Swan Lake* (Selma Jeanne Cohen 1982). What confronts us is a sort of family resemblance among dances that are linked by a complex set of intentions and references. Petipa and his colleagues (notably, in the second and canonical version, Ivanov) set about composing a ballet to music by Tchaikovsky, who (and whose colleagues and successors) more or less simultaneously set about constructing a score. After a while, a pattern in dance and music became more or less established but was still subject to unlimited alteration and variation (including, as we have seen, the introduction of a sort of flying buttress for the male lead). We end up with a set of strongly diagnostic features: a basic story line, certain key moments and dances for which the ballet is famous, a musical score of which some passages have become cynosures, and a problematic ending. But though these are severally and jointly very strongly diagnostic they are not, strictly, necessary and sufficient conditions of *Swan Lake*'s being performed. Just as important is the informed intention by those putting on the dance to do *that familiar ballet* and to orientate themselves by it and not by anything alternative to it. If they do it in a new and different way, still they must be intelligently intending – that is, intending with a dance intelligence, in the light of an artistically informed understanding of what a ballet is – to do that ballet and no other. It is the familiar and live tradition (or, in the case of monuments from the past, the reconstructable tradition) that guides them and serves as a point or frame of reference to which they allow a certain authority. What ultimately guides them is not Petipa's and Ivanov's choreography, but rather a diffused sense of just the sort of variability of which Cohen gives such a striking account.[16] I say 'variability,' but a more apt word is 'elasticity.' A known ballet has a sort of topological tendency; it admits of endless changes, so long as the sense of limits established by the historical pattern of change that has come to prevail at the moment of performance is not flouted.[17]

The identity of an artistic dance cannot be determined, as is standard practice in other arts, with reference to its origin. The choreography of the original production can usually not be recovered and, in the absence of a notated score, cannot be known to be recovered. The necessity of practical modification means that the original choreography, even if it be allowed authority, exists only as remembered, and individual memories are fallible. Ann Hutchinson Guest (1984) observes how hard it is for dancers, once one way of performing a piece has been memorized by the body, to consider any alternative way, whatever its authority. And when one has been collaborating with others it soon becomes impossible to remember, even if one wished to do so, who contributed what at what stage. The memories of a group may reinforce and correct each other in such a way that a tradition is preserved intact, but ballet companies seldom have the cohesiveness that would make this effective; if they do, what is remembered is the joint tradition and not the original invention. Guest (130) remarks how incredulous both choreographer and dancers may be when confronted with the notated score from which they have insensibly drifted away in the course of time.

Another factor that encourages the dance world to identify a ballet with its history rather than its ideal form is that this world is rather a small one. There are not very many ballet companies large and powerful enough to mount a major ballet with conviction. In the same way that in a small oral community, where everyone knows everyone else, individuals are instantly identified by the sum of their relationships and the course of their lives, so that it is as if every member of the group knows everything everyone is doing and will do, the overall history of a ballet like *Swan Lake* is intimately familiar to everyone seriously involved in ballet. It is known as an individual with its own fortunes and vicissitudes, rather than as a formula or a type of artifact.

Even among classical ballets, what counts as identity in one need not be what counts as identity in another. In many cases, it seems to be a matter of indifference whether one speaks of a new production of an old ballet or of a new ballet on the same theme or to the same music. I consider three cases.

Some years ago I saw *Napoli*, 'choreographed by Peter Schaufuss after Bournonville.' Although some of the music had been changed and the second of the three acts substantially rethought, this was presented unequivocally as a new production of *the same* ballet. Why? Clearly, because the second act had never worked (it still doesn't) and so could not be canonical; because the music never had any strong unity or independent value; and because the mark of the ballet was that of a basic story, a contrastive triptych design with a local-colour setting in the first act and a tour-de-force ensemble in the last, and Bournonvillish choreography. People go to see *Napoli* with that in mind; if you keep that you have kept *Napoli*, and there is nothing else essential to be lost. But, perhaps more directly, Schaufuss knows the ballet as he knows an old familiar friend; I imagine him saying to himself and his associates, 'Let's do *Napoli*,' after which the only problem is how to do it effectively. The possibility that the outcome might somehow fail to be *Napoli* would be too ludicrous to cross anyone's mind.

Le Sacre du printemps is identified essentially by Stravinsky's unmistakable score and a strong and simple two-scene idea (probably Nicholas Roerich's) about fertility and sacrifice among primitive people.[18] The original choreography by Nijinsky never caught on, and Massine's version was therefore thought of as the same ballet because it had no successful rival.[19] Since then, there have been alternative choreographies by MacMillan and Vasilyov/Kasatkina, a highly idiosyncratic version by Béjart, an offbeat one by Tetley, and others. Read the article *Rite of Spring* in *The Dance Encyclopedia*, and ask yourself: is one ballet being spoken of, or many? Even allowing for dislocations introduced by revisions in the second edition of the *Encyclopedia*, it is impossible to say. The question is not raised; there is no reason why it should be. But I am left with the impression that the imperiously individual music and the straightforward outline of the story define the ballet in such a way that the post-Massine versions, if they keep those, are to be classed as different versions of the same ballet – even if in other respects they are so strongly characterized and rethought that we recognize them as individual and integral works. In seeing Béjart's *Sacre*, one has and has not seen *Sacre*. Having seen that version and no other, prudent people, if asked whether they had ever seen *Sacre*, would (unless pressed for time) answer neither yes nor no. They might say, 'Well, I've seen Béjart's *Sacre*,' and go on to say what they had *not* seen.

In *Romeo and Juliet*, our third example, the basic story of the star-crossed lovers existed before the ballet did and is better known; so it cannot serve as an identifying mark, as the narrative form of *Sacre* does. Nor is Prokofiev's score as strikingly individual, as strongly ordered, or as historically notable as Stravinsky's. But it is a memorable and popular composition and does serve to discriminate one class of ballets from others that use a Romeo-and-Juliet story, and the title, but use different music.[20] No one supposes that Tudor's ballet to Delius's *Village Romeo and Juliet* is in any sense the same ballet as any of those using Prokofiev, even though it uses the same Shakespeare story.[21] But what of the others? *The Dance Encyclopedia* handles the matter as follows. First we have a general article on 'Romeo and Juliet' ballets other than those using Prokofiev's or Delius's music. Then there is an article on the original Lavrosky/Prokofiev production, ending with the note 'for more recent productions see entries below.' Next comes an article on the Tudor/Delius ballet. Then there is a separate article on a version by Ashton to Prokofiev's score; it makes no reference to Lavrosky or to the article on that version, though Ashton's is surely one of the 'more recent productions' there referred to. The Ashton/Prokofiev article ends with a list of 'other versions to this score,' concluding with MacMillan's (1965). Then a separate article deals with MacMillan's ballet, again as though it were an independent work, but ends by comparing it with 'the two other great productions of the ballet,' namely, Lavrosky's and Ashton's.

It is obvious that the encyclopedia's way of handling the matter does not represent anyone's considered opinion but is simply an outcome of editorial exigency, compounded by the failure effectively to integrate with the existing text the new material added for the second edition. But the result of this somewhat negligent procedure is to leave naked and exposed what more cautious editing would have hidden. There is, in principle, a difference between a new ballet, a new version of an old ballet, and a new production of an existing version of a ballet. It is not even very difficult to say what the difference is. But in practice, setting aside the question of paying royalties, it is not important. It is at most a matter of which factors one wishes to emphasize, and what connections one wishes to make, in a given context; and it is often simply an editorial matter of dividing material into manageable pieces.[22] In scientific taxonomy, notoriously, some scientists are splitters, dividing genera into many species, and others are clumpers, recognizing only a few variable species; and it is the same with encyclopedists and librarians.

That little matter of royalties does make a difference. With recent works, in which a proprietary interest could be claimed, questions of identity become crucial. Or do they? It is not clear a priori that the legal question is relevant to the conceptual one, or to the artistic one. The conceptual question has to do with the circumstances in which, and the reasons for which, one dance is properly described as 'the same as' another (same dance, same version, same production, and so on); the artistic question has to do with whatever is artistically or aesthetically relevant to the integrity of authorship and authenticity, however that relevance may be determined. The legal question has to do with the legitimate use or the expropriation of another's labour and depends essentially on a practical way of identifying creative work. Recent revisions of copyright legislation in the United States were supported by numerous briefs solicited from experts in the productive arts, which had previously been inadequately if at all protected by legislation.[23] How far could such briefs be expected to be relevant? All the way, actually, since their concern will have been with what deserved and needed protection, and to an author this must be the integrity of the work. The effect of giving sharp and formal expression to these concerns must be to clarify and modify the conditions of conceptual identity. It was not always so. Before the 1978 legislation, the choreography of a dance could not be copyrighted in the United States, even if a complete notation existed: to copyright an abstract dance, one had to invent a theme and a narrative for it, in terms of human involvements (Guest 1984, 321–3).

Setting aside the issue of property rights, questions of identity may be changing. First, in these days of film and video, a choreography can be fixed and recorded from the beginning, or at any stage. A film or a tape is not a perfect record, and it does not contain anything to show what exactly it is a record of; but, so far as it goes, it is determinate. Similarly, the development of detailed notations, and of sophisticated ways of using them, means that a firm decision about what a choreography is to be can be recorded unambiguously. I return to these issues in the next chapter.

There may be a difference between the ways dances tend to be identified in ballet and in more recently developed dance styles. In ballet, with its elaborate formal vocabulary and fixed training procedures, a choreography may approximate to a selection among a set of pre-existing possibilities. In contemporary styles, a creation is more likely to be inseparable from its dancing by a particular group, whose leader and trainer is the choreographer; in such cases, neither the system of training nor the range of available alternatives has any definite existence in advance of the generation of the particular dance. Identity becomes more a matter of proximity to the prime instance of the dance as done by the originating company. Reviving or reconstructing such a dance successfully must be rather like painting a portrait: the criterion of success is not the number of warts portrayed, but the acceptability of the outcome as a good likeness by those who are in the best position (by acquaintance, or by authority) to say. This contrast, however, is fading as ballet companies loosen up and contemporary companies stabilize their techniques and procedures.

Criteria of the identity of works are not really fixed in any of the arts. Typically, alternative possibilities are open to us in any context; what the context fixes is a range of proprieties among which we remain free to choose, depending on what we want to emphasize. The situation is pretty well understood in practice, as are the reasons that lead people to take one well-known line rather than another, and the reasons why they insist more or less violently that theirs is the only rational or decent line to take. In dance, matters are at least as indeterminate as in any other art, and proprieties change as practices change. That does not mean that it is arbitrary whether we speak of two occasions of dancing as being the same dance or two different dances. It means that the proprieties are intricate and are learned in the course of informing ourselves about the practice of dance and the arts of dance.

19.41 Idealism and Materialism

Jack Anderson, in a widely discussed article (1975), contrasts two ways of thinking of dance movement, and two corresponding ways of establishing the identity of a dance. If one thinks of dance movement idealistically, as the 'incarnation of ideas and effects,' the steps may be changed provided the same idea is expressed and the same effect achieved. If one thinks of it materialistically, as an assemblage of steps, different ideas and effects may be derived from it. The 32 fouettés in

Swan Lake are a case in point. They were included as a brilliance, a tour de force on the part of the ballerina Legnani. They no longer perform this function, since ballerinas nowadays can do them routinely; for an idealist, a dancer may substitute some other dazzling display, which will have the same effect. Materialists, with whom Anderson concurs, hold the fact that the 32 fouettés were derived from the speciality of a particular dancer to be irrelevant: though inspired by Legnani, they were choreographed for Odile, and they are now part of the ballet.[24]

A difficulty with 'idealism,' Anderson points out, is that one can never be sure what the 'effects' are, or what precisely (in abstraction from the actual movements) the embodied 'ideas' are; but the steps are verifiably what they are. In fact, idealism reflects a primitive stage of the art, in which communications were imperfect or ambitions were inflated. Materialism reflects higher standards of precision in choreography, in transmission, and above all in artistic integrity. Idealism answers to the old feeling that 'dance is not really an important art.'[25] But it represents a constant threat: 'the classics are constantly eroding.'

As often in questions of definition in the arts, the line between the conceptual question of what a dance is and the normative question of how dances ought to be conceived is hard to draw. Anderson acknowledges that idealism is a view still widely held – at least, it has to be held, if certain current practices and judgments are to be supported. It is not clear what the underlying values are from which the superiority of materialism is derived. Is it that most actual changes are for the worse, and result from compromises and economies? Surely not, because such changes might result from materialistically being content with 'going through the motions' no less than from an idealistic use of cheap substitutes. Either view may be used as an excuse for one or another form of slackness; either may be invoked to condemn weaknesses attributed to exclusive adherence to the other.

The only value that unequivocally supports materialism is historical accuracy, in the spirit of Leopold von Ranke's slogan 'the way it really happened.' If we go to see *Swan Lake*, we want to see that ballet and not another ballet, and the only way to be sure of satisfying that demand is to provide a step-by-step replica of the original. But the limitations of Ranke's ideal have long been as notorious as its worth. Facts have their own instability. Two dancers performing the same choreography do not perform the same movements, but movements that are similar in certain relevant respects. We cannot even assume that relevant similarity can be equated with equivalence in a specific notation, for notation presupposes interpretation.[26] And dancers are not the same shape as they were a century ago. Today's dancers cannot do what they did and would look silly if they tried.

Once a work no longer belongs to a living tradition, the split between idealist and realist considerations creates an insoluble problem for anyone who would revive a dance. If one reconstructs the steps precisely, one can be sure that their effect will be quite unlike what the original dance-maker intended and achieved; if one aims at what one supposes was the original effect, one can achieve it only by sacrificing the recognizable identity of the original. It is like translating from a foreign language, where one must often choose between the literal meaning of a text and the effect for which alone the text was written as it was. Mark Franko (1989) suggests that the attempt at reconstruction should be abandoned altogether, at least for a general audience, and be replaced by reinvention – that is, using a new dance to achieve in today's terms something analogous to what the original did for its own time: '[R]einvention can practice cultural critique as a form of active theorizing on dance history. ... It consists in inscribing the plurality of visions restoring, conceptualizing, and/or inventing the act' (74).

Be that as it may, Anderson's polarity takes it for granted that a dance is a system of visible movements in space. And so it is. But that does not require us to ignore the history of performance traditions, or Beiswanger's thesis that choreography sets human bodies in motion. The equation of human movements with their spatial manifestations, as opposed to their significance as action, which Anderson presents as a maturation of the art of dance, might equally be regarded as a denaturing or impoverishment.

What looked like an embodiment of Anderson's polarity appeared in a discussion about Antony Tudor between the executive director of the Dance Notation Bureau and a distinguished dancer.[27] The director, Muriel Topaz, argued that no one other than the choreographer has any right to change the steps of a dance; certainly the dancer in a reconstruction has no such right. The dancer, Nora Kaye, who had worked closely with Tudor, argued against her that it was all right to adjust the steps 'as long as the intention stays the same' – though she agreed that the *dancer* had no such right. She pointed out that it was the intention that Tudor himself clung to; while composing a ballet, he might well forget from day to day precisely what steps he had prescribed. A more direct (and deeply felt) confrontation between idealism and materialism could hardly be imagined. Since this was an unscripted discussion, the speakers are not to be held to their precise wording (even if I have got it right). But I recall wondering, in relation to Topaz, what standard was being appealed to when the producer of a reconstruction was denied the right to change the steps. Presumably not just the legal right, for in artistic matters the law cannot be presumed not to be an ass. What right, then? An obligation to the audience, which relies on the name of the dance as an assurance of what will be done? (But who is to say exactly what expectations are legitimate?) A moral right of fidelity to a sacred object, to the work as fetish?[28] (But who is to say where its mana lies, what is subject to taboo?) Or what? It is hard to say. However, Kaye's apparent support of idealism may be more equivocal than appears. The 'intention' she appealed to did not have to be an idealist's general 'effect' or 'idea,' but could have been a quality of action or movement that was quite specific, though not to be identified with a specific sequence of steps.

Kaye remarked that Tudor did want things to be done exactly the way he wanted them, *at the time*, though the content of these precise demands might change. What that suggests to me is that Tudor was guided throughout, as artists in other arts are, by a regulative idea of the work to be achieved. Such an idea often, if not always, develops as the work progresses, each new stage in its completion evoking a new idea of the whole. Ideally, when the work is completed, the actuality of what has been accomplished coincides with the idea of the work as it should be. From this point of view, idealism and materialism as Anderson conceived them both appear as pernicious abstractions; in fact, both are unintelligible, for the materialist has no answer to 'why?' and the idealist has no answer to 'how?'

19.42 The Basics

The first thing to say about problems of identity is this. It makes sense to say that x is the same as y only if x and y are distinguishable to begin with. And they always are, if only because they are designated by the terms 'x' and 'y,' respectively, and the writing or utterance of 'x' is inevitably separated spatially or temporally from that of 'y.' The question 'Is *this* the same as *that*?' could never be answered with an unqualified yes, if the context did not make the point of the question plain.

In practical contexts, questions about identity and difference are questions about expectations and disappointments. Sometimes we want continuation or (after an interruption) 'the same again.' Sometimes, when we would have liked continuation but cannot have it (because something broke or wore out), we want repetition, 'something just like that.' Sometimes we want a change, 'something different.' The criteria for sameness and difference depend on the circumstances, and above all on our reasons for *wanting* a change, or a continuation, or a repetition. With beer, 'the same again' means not the same pint we just drank, but another just like it; with human beings (cygnoid or other) it means the very same person – Odette again, and not Odile, however good a replica the latter may be. With drill bits, a different one may be just the same only neither blunt nor broken; with occupations, only a radical difference in kind may fail to evoke the cry 'same difference!' Because circumstances of action and requirements of value and use vary so widely, we cannot lay down general criteria for what counts as the same or as different; we can only say what, on a certain kind of occasion, is likely to satisfy an actual demand for continuity or change, repetition or alteration. We dispose of a large vocabulary ('substitution,' 'replacement,' 'surrogate,' 'stand-in,' and so on) for different ways in which such demands may be met or frustrated. And, as we know from our experiences when shopping in a consumer society, vendors and customers may honestly differ as to whether what we get this time is or is not 'just the same' as what we got last time.[29] 'The original' may be spurned as 'not the same as it used to be'; the 'new and improved' may be scorned as 'just the same old stuff.'

In general, questions of identity turn on three kinds of criteria: formal, material, and historical. The old wooden ship is just the same ship it always was, even when every plank and every inch of cordage has at some time or other been replaced. The form is the same. But if the ship were dismantled, the pile of boards and rope and stuff would still be the ship, if anything is; the form is gone, but the material is all there. Whether that really counts depends on how people think about ships. When it comes to people and institutions, though, formal and material considerations alike are subsidiary to historical ones. With human individuals, as people have argued since Locke, the chains of memory and foresight that run from birth to death may have priority;[30] with institutions, like the Roman empire, what primarily counts is the intricate history that begins with the rise of Octavianus Augustus.

To the extent that dances are named individuals of one sort or another, which I have suggested is often the best way to think of them, what counts as the same dance will be primarily a historical question. An extreme case is that of the Helston Furry Dance, described above in

§14.3, where the identity of the dance is fixed only by the place and time and by a vaguely conceived ceremony, conjured into existence by a mixture of antiquarianism, sentimentality, and civic pride. But even in the case of so palpable a choreographic reality as *Swan Lake*, what the dance is can be properly explained only by recounting the principle features of its generation and its survival in the repertoire – what counts as 'its' generation and survival being determined by what the relevant people meant to do, did, thought they were doing, and (above all) were accepted as doing by those people whose acceptance counted. History is double: the working of a force through channels in which it becomes ever broader and fainter, and the development from unidentifiable origins of a finally ineluctable reality.

History is not everything, though. And not everyone knows it, or understands what they do know in the same way. If everything of *Swan Lake* were lost in a cultural cataclysm, with the exception of what one company knew how to perform under that name, what they danced would surely still be as much *Swan Lake* as anything ever was. (Its history would, as it were, start afresh.) And audiences are not assemblages of historians. What counts to the public, and to all whose interest in the dance is practical, is what the dance is valued for. And this, we have seen, varies from dance to dance. But it also varies from individual to individual, and from group to group. It is to explain the warrantability of these variations that we have to invoke the history of the dance, even though historical justifiability as such is not a dance value.

It is with ballets that have survived many vicissitudes of modification and reconstruction, of oblivion and recovery, in various forms in various traditions, that the historical nature of their identity most forcefully presents itself.[31] But what we said about *Swan Lake* could also be said about 'The Waltz,' as discussed in §2.3. The waltz had an origin and a vogue and a social significance, and has existed in many varieties. If it is still danced today, I do not know if it is danced the same way everywhere. But, as with the polka, few people care.[32] No doubt, somewhere, at some time, in some ballroom, disappointed strangers have confidently taken the floor, only to find that everyone else was doing it wrong. 'That's not a proper waltz,' they might grumble, or, if broadminded, 'That's not what we call a waltz where *we* come from.' But the story is too intricate and trivial to be recorded or bothered with: everyone knows more or less what a waltz is, and we can adjust to the local variations as we go along. It's the difference between history and folkways: it isn't really history unless a historian can make a story out of it, and a story that explains something. Historians can chart innovations and major changes, and explain their meanings; but they cannot chart every twist and turn, and it is these minute particulars that make up the life of a social dance.

I said above that, in general, questions of identity that do not depend on historical factors may be determined by formal or material considerations, or both, depending on the interests involved. The contrast between form and matter here sounds rather like Anderson's contrast between idealism and materialism. But it is not the same at all. Crudely, matter is just stuff: bricks and mortar, planks and nails. Form is the shape or order in which the matter appears. Less crudely, in the terms established for philosophy by Aristotle, form and matter are correlative terms. In a ship, it is the timber and cordage that are the matter; it is the way they are shaped and combined that is the form of the ship. But in each of the planks that make up the timber, the matter is oak, and the form is the way the oak is shaped; and in oak it is the molecules of carbon and hydrogen and so on that are the matter, the form of oak being the characteristic way those molecules are combined. So, in a dance, it is the steps (or other movement units or quantities) that are the matter; what gives the dance its form is the way the steps are put together. And it is that form, the way the steps are put together, that Anderson's 'materialists' identify with the dance. But that formed dance, in turn, could equally be regarded as the matter of which the dance, as artistically performed, was the form.

When asked of things of almost any sort, the question 'Is it *really* the same?' admits of no definitive answer. Different considerations yield different solutions. That is especially obvious with culturally emergent entities, such as dances, in which the entity itself is the resultant of many interests and demands: something to join in, something to appreciate, something to make money from. Whose demands shall take priority in such cases is a question of cultural politics, and any resolution will be a political decision rather than a scientific discovery.

Specifically, in the case of an artistic dance, two radically different interests are involved. On the one side, there is the proprietary interest of those who invent, mount, and perform the dance, the moral and legal interest of copyright. Like other property rights, these are a necessary condition of the production of goods and services: those who undertake the labour and expense of producing works of art must have their expenses defrayed somehow or other. On the other side, there are the interests people take in various aspects of the experience of the dance once created. These two sets of interests are obviously both legitimate, but they do not coincide, and no one way of harmonizing them imposes itself.

Among the interests taken in the dance as an object of experience, different well-marked groups of people want different things repeated or continued. Whether they judge a modification or a performance as being the specific dance, whether it makes them say 'the same' or 'not the same' and attach importance to that judgment, depends on the satisfaction of expectations that are central to the whole way their experience of art and their approach to life is organized.

Any instance of artistic dance, like the institution of the art of dance itself, is the product of many artistic endeavours, in harmony or in tension. Even if we dismiss some of these as mere personal distortions of the work of art as such, and concentrate on the work itself as sign or as 'performance' (in my artificial sense), what confronts us is ambiguous, in at least the three ways we have considered. First, it may be a true, a typical, or a malformed token of a number of types: scenario, choreographic design, danced psychodrama, danced realization of music, dancers' realization of choreographic intent. Second, it is the issue of a complex design act of creations working on each other, a single dynamic realization of all the potentialities involved. And third, it is an episode in the historic evolution of the dance it is, produced in the particular circumstances that have governed its performance and its reception. None of these three can be legitimately denied. Anyone may choose to ignore any of them, but such refusals are not binding on anyone. How could they be?

Despite all that, questions of sameness and difference can often be given quite definitive answers, provided that we spell out the interests involved. Questions of identity continue to be raised, because demands for (and promises of) continuation and change can be explained and justified. Such justifications may well conflict, and are an important area of agreement and disagreement in the fields of human cooperation and interaction. To say that something really is or is not 'the same' is to downgrade or delegitimize one set of demands in favour of another, by denying its socially effective existence.

To look for a definitive answer to problems of identity, then, is futile. But to refuse to debate those problems is to deny oneself a familiar and precious tool for exploring the most vital problems in the philosophy of art.

CHAPTER TWENTY

Recording Dance

The lack of any reliable and generally accessible way of recording dance has given it a fugitive nature. It has rendered dances unstable, depending on generations of dancers whose uncertain memories are associated with their own styles and body habits. It has also made dance hard to study, because knowledge of specific dances cannot be widely diffused; very few people can grasp from their own experience the range of the art or arts of dance, even in their own time.

This fugitive nature of dance is widely deplored. But at one conference I attended, a number of speakers independently insisted that the ephemerality of dance is part of its value.[1] I heard no explanation of this insistence, and perhaps it was only a reaction to the insistent propagandizing of dance notators which is a feature of such conferences; but it can be defended. First, the vital indeterminacy and fragility of dance, in its context of intense effort and labour, may give it an intense human value like that of love, a value that is lost in arts where there is some guarantee of repeatability and permanence. Of all the arts, dance is least likely to succumb to the deadly illusion of immortality (cf. Sparshott 1983). A second justification lies in the ambiguous relation of dance to the human person. What can be preserved and repeated is the sequence of movements through which all those who dance a given dance must go. But each of those who go through those movements is a different person. Imposing a definite formula that prescribed exactly what the dancer must do would make it easy to think of the dancer's body as an instrument to be manipulated like a puppet. In a formal dance, of course, the dancers sacrifice their individuality to the plan and the ensemble; but everything that reminds us that each time the dance is danced it is a new endeavour and a new occasion does something to counter that killing tendency. Further along the same line, we have seen that some dancers and theorists think of a dance as ideally a manifestation (partly symbolic, partly direct) of the dancer's way of being in the world (§5.3); to this way of thought, anything that emphasizes how dances are repeatable and recordable goes against the whole spirit of dance.

In the heyday of abstract expressionism in painting, some critics thought up the idea of 'action painting': the value of painting, they argued, lay in the act of painting itself, and the value of the painted canvas was only that of a record that such an act had taken place. They had a good point, but it was not good enough to prevail against the way paintings continued to be treated [cf. Sparshott 1982c, 441–7 and 563). Similarly, insistence on the transience of dance, however profound its motivation, is not going to prevail against the widespread practice of preserving and repeating theatre dances as named individuals, and that practice depends on methods of preservation. So long as continuity is maintained, memory serves, though not reliably, and may be eked out by notes and sketches. But when continuity is lost, we have to rely on what has been recorded. And such records have in the past been seldom available and never adequate.

The art of dance lives in tension between transience and permanence, as all arts do. From this point of view, nothing could be better than the 'imperfect' preservation whereby tradition, recollection, and *aide-mémoire* endow dance creations with a variable longevity and mortality. It is good that much that is precious should be quickly lost and forgotten and that something should endure. Never to let anything go, never to hold on to anything: these are profound passions of beings who are capable of love but incapable of immortality, and the fragile forms of dances that depend on our minds and our bodies for survival are well suited to them.

In principle, there should be two ways of making a record of a dance. One is to make a moving likeness of it, the inspection of which is like inspecting the original dance itself. The other is to make a symbolic description of it, so that anyone who consults and understands the description has enough information to reconstruct the dance. Both these methods have become fully available for the first time within the last century, in the form of film or video and of effective notational systems, respectively.[2]

One obvious element in the complex contrast between video and notation is the difference between mechanical and manual methods. On the face of it, to make a video one simply points a machine and presses a button – many of our most treasured film records of old dances were made just like that. To make a notation, one has to translate every aspect of the dance one wishes to preserve into the terms of a notational system one has learned. A second obvious element is the contrast between pictorial and propositional form, between showing and telling. A notational record gives information but does not show what the dance is like. A film seems to show what a dance is like but does not in itself say what it is that it shows: it does not distinguish between choreographer's intention and dancer's execution, or between correct and incorrect practice. A notated score may be authoritative, but I doubt if it is possible for a film to be so.

If a film cannot be authoritative, that is because, like a recording of an opera, it is prima facie a 'historical record of what was then done, and nothing more. The score constitutes the real work and every artist will wish to go back to it' (Benesh and Benesh 1977, 121). What you see on the film is a performance, and even a perfect performance cannot be authoritative. But the score enshrines the work that is antecedent to any performance of it. However, neither musical score nor dance notation is inherently authoritative, unless it is similarly antecedent; otherwise it, too, merely records the performances on which it was based, and 'the notator's major problem lies in deciding which aspects of the dance are structural components, and hence integral to the choreography, and which are matters of interpretation' (Adshead 1988, 189–90; cf. Benesh and Benesh 1977, 131). I suppose a dance-maker could compose a dance in notation, or make a film of a dance, and in either case could assign authoritative status (for authorial, rather than critical, purposes) to the product. In a sense, it would be possible to say definitely that a notated score had or had not been complied with, whereas with a pictorial record it would always be a matter for judgment whether a performance was 'sufficiently' like the paradigm in all 'relevant' respects; but, realistically, it would equally be a matter for judgment whether a performance had complied with the score in an artistically responsible manner.

Film and notation both rely, to an indeterminable extent, on the user's understanding both the practice recorded and the recording system itself. Film is perspicuous only because it is so familiar; we can follow a film without thinking, because the kinds of selections film-makers make and the conventions they follow have become 'second nature' to us. Notation is not perspicuous at all, except to those who have laboriously set about learning its language. And film-maker and notator alike choose what to record on the basis of their understanding of what in a dance is significant, what goes without saying, and what makes no difference. It remains true and centrally important, however, that a film record works by being like what it records, in a way that most members of the culture find immediately recognizable and do not need to learn, whereas any likeness between dance as danced and as notated is discernible only to those who have made a study of the relevant system.

What did people do before film and notation were evolved – or if they did not own a camera, and had not learned a notation? They tried to remember, of course; but dancers often eked memories out with memoranda, designed for their own use, but such that an ingenious person can often reconstruct much of the dance. They could write down the sequences of such steps as had names, using abbreviations for the commonest ones; where special vocabulary failed, they could write out a description of the movements to be made by each part of the body. These descriptions could be supplemented by sketches showing what poses looked like, by diagrams showing the dispositions and directions of limbs, and by diagrams of stage positions and lines of movement.

A dancer's informal *aide-mémoire* tends not to rely on any one system: each aspect is recorded in the form that best combines informativeness with ease of inscription and access. This should prepare us to learn that no single method of recording dance is best, that ideally a number of methods should be combined. Professional notators consider a score incomplete unless it is accompanied by full information on all aspects of the production, including not only dress designs but actual swatches of the materials employed (Guest 1984). But what one actually does will depend on time and resources available, as well as on the specific purpose for which a record is required. In this respect, the use of notation in dance differs from that of staff notation in music, which is taken for granted as the one all-purpose way of writing the music traditional in Western civilization.

In considering the variety of ways of recording dances (or any moving systems), we may construct two series, a pictorial and a propositional.

The pictorial series starts with the film or video, mechanically preserving what seems to be a visual trace of the movement. It is not really such, for a film is actually a series of images following each other so closely that they seem continuous, and a video tape is the trace of a scan; but what matters is that there is no time for relevant information to be lost in the interstices. Next in the series is a sequence of still photographs. Such a sequence does not give the impression of continuity, unless the pictures are very numerous and used as a flip pack, and relevant information is lost in proportion to the length of the intervals between shots. The loss in practice is minimized by photographing the significant movements, the unpredictable ones, and the points of articulation.

In real life, 'stills' are usually posed, almost never actually taken in actual performances, and the posing may be consciously or unconsciously deceptive in many different ways. A film, too, is not always a true record of what it purports to show; the dancers may distort things by dancing to the camera, the film may be edited in the direction of some idea or ideal.

The fact that a still photograph is posed does not necessarily destroy its value as a record: it may record the actual less faithfully because it represents the ideal more fully. The trouble is that nothing in the picture tells us which it is doing.

Next to photographs in our series come drawings and (especially) the engravings which for centuries were the most usual means of recording the look of a dance or a dancer. In a way, such an engraving can be even more informative than a still photo as to what the ideal of dancing was, untrammeled by the weaknesses of the actual dancers. But here the fact that a picture does not tell what it is a picture of becomes more important than ever. What we see in an engraving may be not the way dancers held their arms, but the convention artists were using for representing dancers' arms. Engravings may show the clothes people wore, or the kind of clothing artists and their publics thought appropriate in dance pictures. Even a known intention of fidelity does not protect us against a change in the understanding of what one should be faithful to. Photographers betray their intentions by showing what they did not intend to show, because it was automatically recorded by the camera's impersonal lens; artists' intentions are betrayed when their drawings show what they did not intend to show, the conventions of representation they employed.

Looking at a collection of old dance engravings puts one in mind of the *Nuremberg Chronicle*, in which one and the same woodcut is used as a picture of whichever city the chronicler is writing about (see Gombrich 1960, 68–9). Such a woodcut shows nothing of the individuality of the city it purports to depict; instead, it shows something of cities in general at the time, something of the way the artist thought cities looked, and something of the way artist and publisher thought cities ought to be depicted in books.

Dance engravings are not merely informative devices. They also serve as souvenirs, evocations of recalled or imagined objects of vision. As bearers of information, however, they belong in the same series as the instructive illustrations of dance manuals, which are essentially diagrammatic, even if the diagrammed positions are embodied in little naturalistic drawings of human figures. Users of such manuals encounter the same ambiguity that we met before: is one supposed to hold one's arm so that it looks just like the arm of the little person in the picture, or is the picture indicating only the approximate pose – or the bare fact that the arm is to be raised? To avoid such puzzles, the diagrammatic figures may be converted into regular diagrams, using some disambiguating notation in which the naturalistic element remains, if at all, only to make things look less forbidding to the reader.

The other series, the propositional one, starts with prose descriptions and narratives that use only the means a natural language affords for general purposes. The next step, because the task is so specialized, is to introduce a supplementary vocabulary of technical terms and a system of abbreviations; we may also get rid of grammatical complexities, because everyone knows the text is a dance description and prescription. We are now using a specialized sub-language generated within a natural language. The next step, which is the last, is to devise a notation ad hoc, a mini-language in which one can do only one thing, describe/prescribe, and can describe/prescribe only one thing, body movement, and can describe/prescribe only those aspects of body movement that the deviser of the notation has provided a way of recording.[3]

Each of our series has a notation at the end, but the notations bear within them different conceptual histories. Benesh and Laban notations may be thought of as endpoints of the two series; they are not alternative scripts or spellings, nor are they alternative languages in the way German and French are. The fact that both are widely used, and are often spoken of as if they are rivals, is one more testimony to the deep ambiguities within the arts and practice of dance.

20.1 Score and Transcription

Music employs an unchallenged system of notation, which composers and performers of music are expected to know. But writing and reading scores do not replace playing and hearing music, and the difference between propositional and pictorial records of dance has its analogue within musical practice.

Many music lovers nowadays have a fairly comprehensive acquaintance with the whole of the popularly current repertoire, little of which they have heard in concert. This has been true for a century and a half at least, since the domestication of the pianoforte. Works for any combination of instruments were transcribed for two or four hands at the piano, and sold cheap; the ability to play from such scores was widely diffused, and a lot of people could get a fair idea of what a piece would sound like from reading the score itself. Radio and phonograph differ from piano in many ways, both musically and socially; but this does not prevent them from both being means of diffusion. Anyone can listen to a recording and get an excellent idea of what a piece sounds like. But the recording may conceal some feature of the structure that a piano transcription would have made plain to all who could read it. The transcription emphasizes structure, making selected aspects of it unambiguously clear and available for study, but may be misleading about what a piece would sound like. It gives information about what the sound would be like only indirectly, through structure, to those capable of imaginatively or mechanically realizing the structure in sound; whereas the recording, which reproduces sound, relies on the hearer's knowledge to divine the structure in what it reproduces.

These differences between transcription and recording reflect those between score and performance. A single hearing of a complex piece at a concert can seldom release its whole structure, not only because most of us are rather ignorant of principles of musical composition and analysis, but also and primarily because one cannot attentively hear all that is going on.

In dance, none of the notations now in use was devised before the present century, at a time well after the development of movies. The historical and cultural relation between written notations and pictorial records of dance is very unlike what obtains in music. But the differences in the way they can be used have much in common. Notation releases structure, pictures release appearance. But no film of a complex dance can show everything; an image that gives the overall appearance cannot comprehensively cover every detail.[4] And the written notations necessarily lack any device comparable to the piano transcription, which makes structure palpably available to a wide public of unambitious performers and readers. Arts of dance lack systems of simplification, transposition, and transcription. A dance score is, and seems likely to remain, cumbrous and expensive. And a person can hardly dance to a score while reading it (though a portable desk for hanging round a performer's neck has been invented); the blessed musical accomplishment of playing or singing at sight, which is at the heart of musical enjoyment, has no likely analogue in dance.

20.2 Notation

Saying that dance has suffered from lack of an adequate notation is misleading. Adequate for what? There are many ways of recording different sorts of dance that have served various purposes perfectly well. This is a matter in which I lack expert knowledge and confine myself to marginal comments.[5]

To the extent that a dance is made up of standardized components it can be, and often is, specified by naming the components and their sequence. A simple version of this is the calling of a square dance. At a more complex level, we have the kind of *aide-mémoire* notebook already described, giving the sequence of steps by their familiar names and describing or sketching any nameless components, providing them with ad hoc names if they recur. In other cases, annotated sketches and diagrams suffice. In the heyday of ballroom dancing, newspapers regularly carried descriptions of dances and steps illustrated by little diagrams indicating the successive placings of the feet. So far as I know, these were quite adequate for anyone who knew the basic positions and moves of ballroom dancing. As all notations do, such a device informed one as to how specific choices were to be made, it being assumed that one already knew what there was that had to be chosen between.[6] The square-dance caller does no less, and no notation, however pretentious and elaborate, can do more: it cannot include the rules for its own interpretation, for those rules would themselves need rules to interpret them, and so on ad infinitum. What modern notations do is vastly to increase the number of choices that are allowed for, and the precision with which the choice itself is guided.

The idea of a comprehensive diagrammatic notation for dances is not new. More than one such method was published in the late seventeenth century, when professional dancing began to take on a distinctive form of its own. They were devised by professional dancing masters who made great claims for them, but none of them acquired anything like the general acceptance, the cumulative modification and development, and the institutional acceptance that staff notation did in music. Why not?

The first thing to say is that even staff notation is not universal and immortal.[7] A few decades ago, it was rare for a highbrow modern work to be published in a form that the ordinary musician had been trained to read. Why was that? The obvious answer is that staff notation lasted a long time because the progress of musical procedures was steady and was such that staff notation could accommodate it; but that state of affairs did not last for ever. (Much of the supposed revolution was sheer affectation and ostentation, and the mainstream of the musical world continues and will continue massively to use the old notation, and to sing and play what can be written in it; but the old monopoly has been broken.)

The fate of staff notation is relevant here, because one system of dance notation, that devised by Feuillet, was hailed in terms such as are nowadays used for Labanotation and lasted in quite general use for a century. What happened to it? Like staff notation, it corresponded to the prevalence of a steady practice. What stopped it was the social changes clustered around the French Revolution, which destroyed the courtly consensus of method within which Feuillet had worked. Specifically, Feuillet gave a floor plan, with indications of the movements a dancer was to make at each point of the journey. The method would have become intolerably cluttered if applied to movements of any complexity. It rather relies on the presumption that, as John Weaver remarks in his presentation of the method (1706b, 55), 'The Carriage and *Movement* of the *Arms* depend more on the Fancy of the Performer, than on any certain Rules.' I suppose Carlo Blasis and his contemporaries changed all that.[8]

Obviously, effective notations would have been devised and perfected soon enough if anyone had needed them as badly as, for example, missionaries needed a script to write Cree in. So I suppose nobody did.

What does one need a notation for? At least five different things. First, as a shorthand or *aide-mémoire* to remind one of a dance that one might otherwise forget. For this purpose, the record need not be complete, and the notational or other system need not be comprehensive; it depends on what one is likely to forget. One can guess wrong about that; the likelihood of error depends on the length of time that elapses between making and reading the record and on the quirks of the individual's memory.

The second use is as a (public) record of the dance. In this case, the notation must be comprehensive and convey the sum of the information required by the putative user. But though notators cannot rely on the user's memory of the specific dance, they inevitably rely on the user's general understanding of dance practice and (of course) of the notation itself. One can guess wrong about that, too: what misses notation, because everyone knows it and nobody notices it, may be just what will nonplus a distant generation.

Related to its use as record or reminder is the third use, as teaching device. Instruction in how to perform a given dance or sort of dance typically takes place within a dancing community that shares a common culture; what has to be imparted is only the differences within a familiar practice, as with a knitting pattern or a wiring diagram.

Fourth, a notational system may provide an alternative medium for dance. A choreographer might compose a dance at a desk, with pencil on paper, as many musical composers do, without any feeling that there is a veil between the act of composition and the musical reality. And certainly a notation might afford access to the structure of a dance as direct as that which a physical performance provides.[9] Some experts do claim that they can envisage a dance from its score. But one wonders, in such cases, how they envisage the dance being performed;[10] and one wonders how far a dance can be equated with its structure, which is what the notation records.

The fifth use of notation is more problematic. When use of a notation becomes second nature, it could provide not an alternative means of access to dances but the unique means of access to possible ways of dancing that could not be performed but exist only as notated. The Eshkol/Wachmann system seems to have been developed as a way of notating Noa Eshkol's own 'undanceable' choreography (Guest 1984, 108), and there is nothing impossible in the idea of a movement-form that existed only in notational form and could be appreciated as such. But we may doubt how practically important that possibility is. In music, it is easy to write down what cannot be physically performed, but this has never really caught on as standard practice. There is a lot more music that cannot really be appreciated otherwise than by studying the score, but that can be performed; and then there may be a special satisfaction in listening for the subtleties one knows are there.

Would such undanceable choreography, capable of existing only as projected by its notation, fall outside the scope of dance, because it is outside the scope of human corporeality? Not necessarily. Just as multidimensional geometries go beyond our experience of three-dimensional space but remain within our grasp of spatiality, it may be said that what is notatable but unperformable extends the imaginative bounds of human mobility. But this may be an empty possibility. We must trust the sincere, informed, and sensitive testimony of those who report such enlightenment, while rejecting empty posturing and deceptive or delusional boasting. Now all we have to do is tell which is which.

The supposed delights of notatable but unperformable 'dance' present us with an ambiguity. A film record of a dance serves the purposes of dance enthusiasts, but a dance film pleases lovers of film. A film may do either or both, separately or in conjunction or in such a way that each function enhances the other. Analogously, the notated score of a dance might please a public of notation buffs. But the analogy of film fails at its most vital point: there is an independent art of film with its own public; there is even an independent art of calligraphy that might be realized in inscribing a musical score; but we do not yet know what an art of notation would be that was independent of what was to be notated, and I doubt if we ever will.[11]

20.21 Four Uses of Notation

The fact that dance notations can perform five or more different functions does not suffice to explain why people should actually go to the trouble of devising and using them. From the practical viewpoint, four functions suggest themselves: as a medium of choreographical composition, for dissemination, for identical preservation, and to establish legal identity.

20.211 Composition

Choreographers have not been used to composing on paper; the demand for the ability to do so could arise only in new social circumstances, in which choreographers were physically separated from dance companies. In fact, no such demand has arisen. The very idea of notational composition has aroused hostility. One eighteenth-century dance-master (Gallini 1762, 123) says that the use of a notation 'only serves to obstruct and infrigidate the fire of composition'; a musician working in an oral or improvisatory tradition (e.g., Mezzrow and Wolfe 1972) can say the same. Similarly, André Levinson, not himself a dance-maker but speaking for what he conceived to be the classical tradition, wrote that attempts to revive Petipa ballets from written scores were useless: 'In this way one can collect and fix each little bone and each muscle of the artistic organism as if it were an artificial cadaver for an anatomy lesson. But it is possible to breathe life into this 'Homunculus' only when the performers themselves preserve a living memory of the original production. Thus the only way to preserve the precious choreographic works of the past is to continue their performance traditions without interruption. ... The forms of dance must be guarded vigilantly just like the fire at the vestal sanctuary. Once extinguished, it will not flare up again' (Levinson 1982, 49).

This mistrust of notation could change – one has only to transpose Levinson's remarks into terms of musical practice to realize that people used to working from a score are also accustomed to breathing life into scores. What gives the position solidity is the strength of George Beiswanger's thesis that choreography is not a matter of inventing dance forms directly but of setting human dancers in motion, not to produce a visual effect but to make bodies move visibly. It follows that there is a very strong tendency for choreography to be in the first instance production-oriented rather than work-oriented.

20.212 Dissemination

A dance production is, however, the production of a work; and some works, once produced, are found to be worth keeping. They become famous. A second need for notation now comes to the fore, the need for a means of dissemination. The actual use of Feuillet's notation was to circulate knowledge of new dances throughout the civilized (that is to say, French-speaking) world. What can be thus diffused can last as long as print lasts, so that the dance-maker can be a monument of civilization, as ancient sculptors and Renaissance painters were. The position is spelled out by Soame Jenyns in his poem on *The Art of Dancing*:

> Long was the dancing art unfixed and free;
> Hence lost in error and uncertainty:
> No precepts did it mind, or rules obey,
> But ev'ry master taught a different way:
> Hence, e're each new-born dance was fully tried,
> The lovely product, ev'n in blooming, died:
> Tho' various hands in wild confusion tossed,
> Its steps were altered, and its beauties lost:
> Till Feuillet at length, great name! arose,

And did the dance in characters compose:
Each lovely grace by certain marks he taught,
And ev'ry step in lasting volumes wrote.
Hence o'er the world this pleasing art shall spread,
And ev'ry dance in ev'ry clime be read;

...

Hence with her sister-arts shall dancing claim
An equal right to universal fame,
And Isaac's rigadoon shall last as long
As Raphael's painting, or as Virgil's song.[12]

What can be taught, recalled, and transmitted must depend on what can be codified. A ballet dancer's classical training itself affords such a codification, but complex and innovative choreography resists it. In any case, however, a written notation is necessary if the dissemination of dances is to be made independent of the travels of choreographers and dancers. Feuillet's method corresponded to an enlightened age in which arts and ideas were the common property of an international civilization. Our contemporary notations enable dance to take its place in the 'museum without walls' that is so important a factor in this century's experience of art.[13]

The rise of notation in the present century cannot be attributed to the desire for precise records or the difficulty of personal communication, because it coincides with the age of rapid and regular travel around the globe. The time when the scholarly world became obsessed with historical precision, in the late eighteenth century, was just the time when Feuillet's method lost ground and was not replaced. Nor should we think of today's more complex notations as separating the dissemination of dances from the travel of persons; one would not normally mount a ballet from the score alone, without the guidance of someone from the notation bureau. 'No known system records the synchronization of steps to music with anything like the precision that it takes to dance Balanchine,' says Arlene Croce (1987, 123).[14] We must think again about why notations were called for when they were, and not before.

20.213 Precision

Three conditions have to be fulfilled if it is to be worth developing an elaborate notation. First, there must be something of such complexity that an elaborate codification is required. Second, there must be a demand for information thus codified. And third, and most important, that demand must be for the precise replication of what was originally notated. That means that there must either be agreement about what counts as precision or a realistic belief that such agreement could be reached.

In the case of dance, there must be a demand, distant from the point of origin in place or in time, for the precise replication of a specific dance. For there to be such a demand, the idea of a determinate dance, identified with a precisely specified choreography, and a habit of esteem for such determinate dances, must be established. And I find it hard to believe that this could come about without photography, providing a living idea of *this dance and no other* as opposed to a dance answering to some general description. If I am right in this, photography, so far from rivalling notations as a means of record, may be among the chief conditions that make them seem desirable.

At the same time that photography highlights the possibility of visual replicability, the general context of mass-media saturation both establishes reputations and demands at long range and raises the standards for acceptable reproduction. Loie Fuller's (1913) account of her early career illustrates the relationships involved. She invented a kind of stage performance with lights and draperies, first exemplified in her 'Serpentine Dance.' The producer of the show in which she presented it stole the idea, and had it performed by a dancer in his own entourage. Later, similar plagiarism was perpetrated in Paris, without direct knowledge of Fuller's original version. A little later, however, the reputation, first of the Serpentine Dance, then of Fuller herself, generated a demand that only she could satisfy; people could see the difference between her and her imitators. But if precise information had not been able to catch up with reputation, her imitators could have satisfied the demand. Nowadays, our normal level of expectation calls for effective assurance that what we see is the original or a true copy, not someone else's version or imitation. The whole context in which touring companies operate has undergone a radical shift in the age of television.

Another factor that gives rise to a need for notation is a shift in emphasis in the identity of a dance work. In considering the conditions of dance identity, we noted that the criterion might lie in the scenario and the music rather than in the choreography. In the days when ballet technique was highly conventional, a ballet could be sufficiently identified by its scenario and general tenor and choreographic scheme, with only a limited number of set pieces, high points at which the precise sequence of steps really counted. And these set pieces, it may be thought, could easily be memorized. It is unlikely that anyone cared precisely how *Giselle* or even (pace Levinson) *Swan Lake* was originally danced. The general effect, and such details as anyone might remember, would suffice.[15] There would be no incentive for anyone to take a choreography, in all its detail, away from the company and house it belonged to. If a choreographer were to take a ballet to a new house, she or he might as well remake it on the spot; even if a company were to travel and take a production with them, they would make no special point of *making no changes*, which is what notations are for. Why should they care?

What makes notation essential is an attitude to choreography in which each step is considered and composed for its unique contribution. It is not that choreographers should actually consider each step to be essential, for no one denies that accommodations must continually be made for the specificities of bodies and temperaments; the point is rather that, as Anderson said (cf. §19.41 above), dance cannot claim parity of esteem with the (other) fine arts unless the right to unalterability is acknowledged. Strict identity is essential because, as hinted in chapter 19, the prestige claimed for the arts in their heyday rested on reverence for individual genius. Genius was supposed to show itself in the complete integration of a perfected work, in which nothing could be changed without spoiling it. The obvious truth that virtually all known works could be changed in all sorts of ways without anyone greatly caring, or even noticing, and that many had been arrived at by makeshifts and compromises, or simply developed to a terminal point determined by fatigue rather than triumphantly achieved, was beside the point. The point was that it ought to be *possible* to think thus of any authentic work of art, if one set aside trivial anecdotes.

20.214 Copyright

Chapter 19 mentioned another factor that calls for a complete and precise system of notation, adequate to specify a dance and distinguish it from any other. This is the introduction and spreading recognition of international copyright. In a thoroughly organized international economy, property rights have to be systematically established, and that includes rights in artistic property. However highminded we like to be about it, so long as art takes work to produce and present and so long as there is property, art is going to be property.[16] So property rights must be established, and that means that criteria of identity for all forms of art must be set up. To the extent that the criteria of identity for dance are choreographic, that means that a precise and comprehensive dance notation will be useful. Such a choreographic record is not, in itself, either necessary or sufficient to sustain a legal claim. The determining factor is not even the consensus of the dance community as to what one can claim proprietary right to. What counts is the practice of the courts, asinine as they may be, starting with their willingness to recognize artistic ownership at all. Once more, Loie Fuller's tribulations are a case in point.

20.22 Notation and Notations

20.221 Varieties of Notations

In §8.22 I said that a system of movement analysis and a method of notation are likely to be developed together, interdependent parts of a single enquiry. In any case, any well-articulated system can form the basis of a notation; and any movement analysis, however poorly articulated, can affect the way a notation is developed.

What kinds of notations are there? The biggest difference is between those that result from some general analysis and those that are worked out ad hoc for a specific body of material. Among analyses, some are etic, based on the notator's preferred observational categories, and some are emic, based on the way a practice is articulated by its practitioners.

Analyses may vary in the extent to which they are scientific rather than empirical – that is, in the reconditeness of the organizational principles uncovered by the notator's observation or research. The depth of analysis need not reflect any correspondence to a basis that is both practically relevant and interculturally recognizable; reconditeness is an independent variable.

Just as a notation may be intellectually abstruse and counter-intuitive for some or all users, it may be rebarbative as a transmitter of information. The completeness of the information it conveys is independent of the ease of memorizing its code and becoming fluent in its use.

Finally, notations vary in their relation to praxis – that is, in the amount of information they give their users. A notation that instructs one in the performance of unfamiliar sorts of movement is different from one that merely indicates key choices in a familiar practice, and even a simplified version of the former sort may be ill-adapted to the latter purpose.

The basic problem with dance notation is this. In a written language, the notation is based on a spoken language that is already articulated in linguistic terms; a written language tends to be a system rendering a system, though (as notably in Japanese and Gaelic) conceptual and historical considerations of one sort or another may foul things up. Similarly, a musical notation is applied to material that is already firmly formed, tuned strings and keyboards, pipes of graded lengths or with regularly drilled holes. A lot of ordering went on before notation began. But a general dance notation has to cope with material that has not been submitted to any such comprehensive and preemptive order. The kinesiological scope and limits of the human body are not the operative framework of human action, and the conventions of a specific dance or dance practice are only temporary and superficial restrictions: in both respects, humans remain and must remain ready for anything. To the philosopher, the hermeneut of understandings, these relationships of order and freedom are of great interest; the possibilities and limits of dance notation are accordingly of great potential interest.

20.222 The Bias of Notation

Actual notations are not neutral. We found Jenyns remarking, in his encomium on Feuillet, that the introduction of an agreed notation has the effect of fixing and regularizing style, detaching it from the manner of an individual teacher or choreographer. A notation affords a finite repertoire of signs, allowing one to use this sign or that in this or that form to record what one wishes to record. However flexible, what it affords is a system of choices. The options one is to choose between are determined by the system, not by the subject matter. Unless the deviser of the system and the performer of the movement are using the same set of elements and the same syntax, the notator has to decide how the movement is to be described. Experts on notation recognize that notators are like translators, rendering what performers do in the idiom of performance into the language of the notation, and are faced with the same indeterminacy of options.[17] A wise notator will, if possible, watch a whole dance through several times, to see how it is articulated and how its structure can be best represented with the means available, before starting to notate it.

Among systems in contemporary use, Labanotation, the one most generally used and most comprehensively elaborated, was in its beginnings strongly connected with the origins of modern dance. Mary Wigman describes how Laban originally worked out his system as an essential part of an attempt to develop a rational analysis of the movements of a human body, an analysis that could form the basis of a refined way of thinking about dance (cf. §4.2 above). This analysis itself had to be developed slowly, through trial and error.[18] His own account of the basics of his theory of movement, and of how his notation records it, makes it plain how this was so. As we have seen (§8.2222), the basis is a general geometry of movement, substantially ignoring the details of human anatomy and without regard to any existing dance conventions. Specifically, there is no reference to the nature of ballet or any other form of theatre dance. The basis of the notational system is an abstract way of thinking about movement, which is highly general in its coverage and very specific in its approach, though it can be used, with or without extensions and modifications, to record any sort of body movement.

Laban's way of thinking of movement in terms of circumferential movements of a hinged system of limbs, with the centre of the body as its point of origin, is dynamic rather than visual in its approach, and his later 'effort-shape' analysis supplements this with a task-oriented dynamic organized around the interface between the working body and an instrumental world (Heidegger's *zuhand*). Both dynamics are diametrically opposed to those of Delsarte (as presented by Shawn), who conceives and analyses human movement centrifugally, in terms of the animating force of an organism as it expresses itself meaningfully through the articulation of the limbs in a system of gestures. The Delsartian body is neither moving nor working, but making signs in a rhetorically ordered world.

Labanotation, with its modern dance affiliations, is not especially suited to the notation of ballet, which is still the culturally dominant form of theatre art dance in our civilization. It is not surprising, then, that a system of notation should have been built up around the choices confronting ballet dancers.[19] The Benesh notation, like Labanotation (and worked out in ignorance of it, apparently; the widespread diffusion of the latter is a quite recent phenomenon), is said to be applicable to movements of all sorts, but its approach is very different. It is basically visual, diagramming a dancer's movements in a way derived from stick-figure sketches; the user is enjoined not to memorize them as signs, but to use them visually, reading the language of the notated dance rather than the notation itself, just as one reads English or French rather than the Roman alphabet in which both are written (Benesh and Benesh 1977, 3). Though the notation is visually conceived, and dance is a visual art, the figure is seen from the back – not the spectator's view, but that of someone standing behind the dancer in class, or as if one could imagine oneself directly into it, limb for limb (17). What Benesh shows, in contrast to Laban, is movement as observed rather than as undertaken, the pattern of action rather than of energies. Which one prefers may depend less on what is to be notated than on one's own cognitive style – whether one is a visualizer or an analyst.[20]

Most abstract of all well-known notation systems is Eshkol/Wachmann, which specifies the values of certain movement parameters without reference to any concrete embodiment. As noted above, the practice to which this notation relates is the idiosyncratic choreography of Eshkol herself, which is conceived (I am told) without relation to any conventions or traditions of danceability.[21] Unlike any of the other notations, it really is equally applicable to any movement of articulated bodies and, perhaps just for that reason, is more discussed than used. Or is that the reason? 'Movement Notation enables us to free ourselves of the interpretation of movement in terms of the attainment of goals,' Eshkol writes (1975, 5); 'and by removing all interpretations, to discover the visible phenomena of movement.' But human movement is not independent of the attainment of goals, nor of the shapes of human limbs and the workings of muscles and joints. Eshkol's system is based on a geometrical analysis of the articulation of a system of straight lines pivoting in circles, arcs, and cones, on points located on other pivoting lines; the physical systems of living creatures are not at all like that. Rather than neutral in respect of vital and volitional models, the basis of the notation is an abstract model substituted for any possible embodiment. (The notation itself consists mostly of a set of numbers corresponding to positions located in terms of this model.)

At the furthest extreme from the schematics of Eshkol/Wachmann are the utilitarian systems worked out by makers and teachers of dance without theoretical pretensions. One development of this sort is Sutton Movement Writing, a 'pictorial movement handwriting' that uses stick-figures and other simple forms.[22] Since the main criterion is that the writing shall be easy for the uninitiated to learn and use, such systems should teach us a lot about how movement is conceived in the communities within which it is developed.

Another ballet-centred system, that of Conté, is different again, neither energy-centred like Laban nor visual like Benesh, but essentially a mnemonic system. It uses the conceptual scheme of ballet and represents the dancer's crucial choices by the standard symbols of musical staff notation, suitably reinterpreted. Unlike either of those others, it is essentially a shorthand system, dependent on the verbalizable descriptions of what it records; it cannot, therefore, be extended to unfamiliar movement idioms, though it is said to be easy to learn and use within the restricted conventions of French classical ballet. Essentially, I think, it is a drive towards systematization of the ad hoc mnemonics that dancers develop for themselves, exploiting and adapting the resources of extant sign-systems likely to be within a dancer's purview, whereas Sutton achieves general accessibility by developing means of symbolization already informally current within the culture at large.

Because dance notations are at least partly ideological in origin and tendency, they give a new twist to a well-known thesis of Nelson Goodman (1968), to which I have alluded before (§8.2). He argued that when an art became notational (that is, habitually recorded in an authoritative notation) the very concept of the art must be altered, because the conditions of identity of every work would be changed. A work would now be defined by what the notation could capture – the work is the score together with its compliance class. Everything not defined by the score would become, from the point of view of identifying the work, secondary. And this would necessarily change the way the art was thought of, because the logic of notational systems is unique.

Does this mean that the use of notation will really cause the art of dance to change, and change differently according to which system of notation comes to prevail? Not necessarily. Goodman's thesis, as he keeps saying, is not meant to reflect the actual conditions under which any art operates. No art is notational, as Goodman defines that term, nor should it be. Notationality is defined not by the way scores and notations are actually prepared and used but in terms of the logical relations and conditions of identity that Goodman specifies. And the sole function of strict notationality, as he conceives it, is to ensure that a performance can be derived from a score, and a score derived from that performance, and so on in perpetuity, without any loss of identity. But that is an entirely useless function. Even in music, which comes closest of the arts to being what Goodman would call a notational art, what is acceptable as a performance of a work is notoriously more variable than he stipulates. It is not necessary that a score be complied with precisely; nor is it sufficient, for a performance may be literally 'correct,' in the sense that it complies precisely with the score, and yet be musically 'impossible.' The entrenchment of staff notation in musical practice has done nothing to eliminate these acceptabilities.

Although Goodman is explaining logical relationships and not describing practices, however, I suspect that he is as right about practice as he needs to be. Regular use of a notation must lead to some measure of reliance on that notation, and this must encourage some changes in practice. A notation directs the attention in certain directions, emphasizes certain relationships, fosters a certain way of thinking. How could it be otherwise? In dance, however, notation remains effectively the domain of experts, and this must limit its influence on the mass of dance practice.[23]

20.3 Film and Video

Forty-five years ago, an anthropologist reviewing the resources for dance study regretfully dismissed the use of film: 'A consideration of motion picture techniques in the study of the dance has been omitted for various reasons. First of all, it is necessary to have the services of an expert cameraman to get good motion pictures of dancing. Secondly, no dances performed under field conditions have been recorded on film in such a manner that they can be reproduced by watching the film. Successful motion pictures of dance are those in which the routines are arranged specially for camera technique. Obviously, if these difficulties were overcome, the motion picture might solve most of the problems facing the comparative student of the dance' (Pollenz 1949, 435). Have things changed? Not altogether, though film and video equipment and its lighting needs are less obtrusive than they were. It is still true that a dance cannot be fully reconstructed from a single film, and the compilation of a comprehensive filmed record is seldom practicable.

We have to distinguish at least five uses of film. One is to compile information about a dance, in such a way that a dance can be reconstructed from the various segments and aspects recorded. Another is to record the general look of a dance, something a notated score might fail to preserve. A third, significantly different, is to film a dance in such a way that an audience can then see the dance on film. An important variant on this presents the audience with a dance *in* film, not just *on* it, the totality of the film making up an environment within which the dance is embedded. A fourth use is to make what I shall call a dance-film (as opposed to a film of a dance), a film that might give an audience the impression of seeing a dance but in which there may be no separate dance to see, the technical aim and aesthetic value being primarily cinematic rather than choreographic. Marcia Siegel had this in mind when she observed: 'I have often thought dance on TV is treated as if it were information, and it's televised for its information qualities and not for its art qualities. It's clear to me that the same art qualities cannot come across on television that come across on the stage, but television does have its own aesthetic possibilities, as Merce Cunningham and Twyla Tharp have shown in their television work. I think it can be another experience entirely which we haven't even begun to explore the possibilities of.'[24] Since then, exploration has begun, and I will say a little about it later. Meanwhile, note that Siegel does not make quite the distinctions I did. I contrasted giving information with conveying the impression of watching a dance. Siegel says that the latter is impossible, so that to preserve any aesthetic interest new values have to be added from the resources of the technology. What she has in mind is a situation in which the dance as choreographed exists, and remains as the target of the filming. This is not the same as the creation of a dancefilm in which the target is the film as experienced. But such a dancefilm is not quite the same as films where the camera viewpoint shifts in such a way that the viewer, for whom the camera stands proxy, seems to be somehow a participant in the dance. They represent my fifth use of film.

Let us suppose we are looking at a film someone has made of a dance. There are several different things we can say we are doing: some of these will mean the same as each other, and some will not, and it will not always be clear which.

We may say simply that we see the performance (on film). Or we may say that we see a film of the performance, concentrating (as it were) on the medium rather than on the message. In this latter case, it is not clear whether we would claim to have seen the performance itself or not: in fact, it is something we often say precisely when we want to leave that open. We might even say that we had seen an *image* of the performance, though I have never actually heard anyone say that. It would, after all, be correct in a way: we weren't there, we didn't see it, in a more straightforward sense than that in which doctrinaire philosophers used to say that people never see anything but sense data (or, of course, bits of their own brains).

As well as the above, we could say that what we saw was an interpretation of the performance. The film-maker had to choose where to put the cameras and what to do with them, and this implied an interpretation of the performance as a spectacle, if not as a dance. Even if the film-maker was not making conscious decisions about these things, the making of the film constituted an interpretation, as though it had a mind of its own. Or we could say that we had a *view* of the performance – the word 'view' here having a splendid ambiguity between visual vantage point and personal interpretation.

Alternatively, we could put the word 'dance' wherever we had 'performance' before, saying that what we saw was the dance, or a view or interpretation of it. Like the film-maker, we could have been concentrating either on the dance as choreographed or on the performance of it, or dividing attention between the two; the film-maker's point of focus need not be the same as the viewer's, nor need all viewers share the same with each other.

All of the foregoing are things we can truly say we are doing when we look at a film made from a dance. None of them amounts to saying that we have seen a dancefilm.

Narrative films can, but need not, base their structures on extant versions of their story in another medium and may not even be such that another medium could capture their essential structure. Similarly, the film of a dance may derive its structure from an actual dance, or even from an actual performance of a dance, but need not do so. The people involved in making the film may be vividly aware of the impossibility of enabling an audience actually to experience anything like being present at a dance performance, and may accordingly think of their film itself as the performance (or the work of art) and concentrate on its filmic qualities. These will include filmic equivalents or versions of dance qualities, just as an ordinary feature film has filmic equivalents of narrative qualities. As before, any of the people involved, choreographer or producer or dancer or film-maker or viewer or anyone, may differ from any others on the issue of whether what they are involved in is a (filmed) dance, or a dancefilm, or ambiguously either, or something between the two.

In any case, a film can never offer viewers a replica of any view of a dance performance that they might get at first hand.[25] Even if the camera is placed (literally or virtually) in a particular seat in the theatre, it cannot put the viewer in that seat. The camera may look just where we would look, but it does not do so in answer to our will. Nor can it offer any true substitute for the variable focus of the eye. Whatever lenses or filters a film was made with, the viewer's scanning of the flat surface of the screen cannot be at all like scanning a dance as it is performed in the depth of the real space of the stage. What the viewer of the film singles out for attention is always an in-focus or out-of-focus, clear or fuzzy, image on a flat screen. The screen is always at the same distance from us and therefore does not call on us, or even permit us, to refocus our eyes at all (except in so far as the different parts of the screen, though each keeps its unchanged distance, are at different constant distances from us). The effect must be very different from that of shifting attention from one part of a dance to another. It cannot throw what is peripheral into the background in at all the same way. The bit of the screen surrounding what we are looking at is still in focus. When we watch a dance on stage, the changing focus of the eyes answers to our attending will.

Filmers of dance and makers of dancefilms usually alternate between close-up and normal shots, or split the screen, or superimpose one or more close-ups on a shot of the whole stage. In a dancefilm, such moves have to be construed filmically by the viewer, as artistic or functional parts of the whole. But, to the extent that what is being made is a film of a performance, the function of such devices may be presumed to be to offer a substitute for the viewer's normal transfer of attention from soloist to ensemble and back, supplemented perhaps by the use of opera glasses. (In real life, film-makers' uses of these devices will inevitably serve their own creative or interfering urges as well as their will to please; but that can't be helped.) But the film-maker's devices cannot succeed in this. As before, the change of attention, even when it coincides with our wishes, does not follow our will: we are not now looking at something else that we have chosen to look at, we are being shown something we were not being shown before, and still have the same option of concentrating on part or all of what is on the screen (or, of course, off it). Split-screen and ghosting (image-over) effects as well as close-ups are simply given and perceived as such, as modifications of what is screened, and tend to distract attention away from the performance rather than to direct attention within it.

The difference between watching a dance on film and watching it in reality depends less on the failure of the manipulated images to conform to the viewer's will than on the fact that they are not perceived as things coexisting with each other and with the spectator within a surrounding space. In watching a live performance, an important factor is the sense of an actual space surrounding both ourselves and the dancers. A dancer, I said in §6.12, may be sensed as creating a sort of moving force field that fills the dancing space, and even those who think such language fanciful may respond to the sense of the dancers as being *there where they are* in real space. I doubt whether film can ever provide that sense, although such devices as 3-D or an extra-wide screen may (briefly) provide the illusion.[26] But, if film can do it at all, I would suppose it can do it only by being unobtrusive;[27] the devices used to make the dance more visible succeed only in drawing attention to themselves and thus risk making the dance vanish altogether.

A dance on TV or film necessarily lacks presence.[28] The medium itself precludes it: we cannot be in the same space together. Film and video are means of indirect presentation such that a freeze-frame or rerun, a flashback or a slow-motion, causes no shock of surprise; we switch our attention from what is presented to the manner of presentation without even being aware of doing so. In addition, a sense of presence depends on minute expressive cues and intimacies, like facial expressions and breaths, that are either lost by the camera or are preserved by it out of scale with the overall presentation. Above all, the personal dimension is abolished. Everything on film or video, things and people alike, is reduced to the common medium of reflected and transmitted light. Even while we are ignoring this mediation, it remains the background reality of our experience.[29] We always know, really, that we can walk out or switch off.

20.31 Dance in Film

Between films of dance, in which the information is about dance and the aesthetic and artistic values are principally dance values, and dance-films, which give no information about anything other than themselves and of which the values are basically film values, there is a large intervening space. This is occupied by narrative films in which dancers dance as part of the narrative.

In such films, dances do occur and are presented as such to our attention, but they have two aspects. They are dances in their own right. But they are also part of the narrative. At one extreme, they are formally danced episodes, shows that we see characters in the film attending as an audience – though the dancers may also, in another capacity, be characters in the story. At the other extreme, characters in the film burst into dance 'spontaneously,' in the way that characters in a musical burst into song. In between, the characters who do the dancing figure in the narrative as dancers by profession or commitment, and the dancing is part of what they do in the course of being themselves. In all types of case, the dancing, or what takes place inseparably from the dancing, may or may not further the action of the film.[30] One thinks of

The Red Shoes (1948, by Powell and Pressburger), in which many of these possibilities are explored; or of the 1930s films (which seem innumerable in retrospect) in which the young, locked in each other's arms on the ballroom floor, are suddenly seen to be dancing through moonlit clouds or along a palm-lined shore, as metaphor for their ecstasy.

In the general run of such films, including those of Astaire, the dances, though emphasized in their individuality, are assimilated to their context in the film by being kept short and keyed into the narrative; but this need not always happen.[31]

Dances designed for such films are designed as dances, to be seen and appreciated as such, but specifically as dances-to-be-filmed, and, in many cases as dances-in-films. From its beginnings, film has moved easily between realism, facilitated by the expectation that a camera will have recorded what took place in front of it, and fantasy, encouraged by the film-maker's freedom in putting together the images that the projector will throw on the screen. Even the most straightforward narratives use non-literal devices of all sorts, and audiences take them in their stride. When what the film presents is presented as dance, the opportunities for such freedoms are multiplied, because every audience knows that dance belongs in the domain of creative expression from the start. And of course, in most cases, the characters would not in real life be dancing at all in the given circumstances, so there is no reason why the dance they are doing should be plausible or physically possible.

When choreographers design dances, they seldom if ever confine themselves to devising sequences of steps. The dances they design are integral to a stage setting, the general nature of which they work into the dance, because human movements are necessarily performed in relation to physical reality anyway, and it would be hopelessly irresponsible to take the specific setting for granted. Even more so, designing a dance for film is not merely designing a sequence of movements that can be performed on any flat surface. Even when dance-makers ignore the storyline of the film, they must take account of the intense artificiality of sets and cameras. If the dancers dance on the floor, it is because of a decision made to that effect; the film could equally place them on a shelf, a wall, a ceiling, on the lens of a kangaroo's eye. The dance-maker designs the whole visual reality of the episode to which the dance belongs.[32] But in this great and popular genre, unlike dancefilms, what the film audience sees and relishes is not the movement of images on the screen, but the dance that is being performed before them.

In these films, as in so many adventure films, the audience may often not know whether it is seeing the work of a skilled acrobat, or a clever director, or both. Its admiration and delight, if it discriminates at all, may be redirected again and again.[33] It takes a tactful director and an experienced viewer to avoid the feeling that one is being cheated and deceived. Fortunately, such tact and experience abound. One is sometimes inclined to say that these films are not really records of dances at all. But what better record do we have, or what better could we desire, of Astaire's dancing?

20.32 Dancefilm

One of the earliest films of dance verges on being a dancefilm. Made by Thomas Edison and shown (and abandoned) in a small Ontario town in about 1897, it shows a 'Butterfly Dance' a few seconds long. The draperies (it is unclear whether they are worn as dress, or held and manipulated on sticks) form two pairs of wings, as of the lepidoptera, which are swirled in and out. The film is coloured by hand, very simply and crudely but effectively, mostly tinting the drapery in primary colours which change according to a rhythm of their own. The uniformity of the tint and the rhythm and nature of its change bear little relation to the form of the dancer, or to any movements she may be making; consequently, what we see is not a film of a dancer dancing, but a pattern of movement that is neither on the screen (because it is the draperies that bear the colour) nor on the dancer (because of the way it changes) but in a filmic space of its own.[34]

The problematic nature of dancefilm may be illustrated by a PBS presentation I once saw of a dance, choreographed or at least revised for television, directed by the choreographer himself.[35] Although the setting was that of a dance, with dancers dancing together on a surface, a large part of what we viewers saw consisted of 'atmospheric' shots of small parts of the dancers' bodies – elbows, tops of heads – presented in such a way that it was neither the dancers nor the bits of them that were perceivable as moving to the music, but the shots themselves. There was no way in which viewers could relate what was shown to any choreography, unless they happened to know and remember the dance from previous exposure to it. In fact, a viewer could not know that there was or ever had been any choreography, or that anything was being danced: there was really nothing to extrapolate from.[36] In a case like this, where there is no choreographer separate from the film-maker, the implication that there is a dance being danced could be as false as the impression that a film set has a ceiling out of camera range. That is not necessarily a moral or artistic defect, or even a Terpsichorean one; but in this instance I found it a displeasing experience, because what I seemed to be being shown was a sort of meditation on a dance that the film-maker knew and had in mind, but that I did not know. Perhaps it was really a film of the experience of dancing, or the experience of feeling a dance one was dancing. But my experience was rather like that of someone in a very bad seat at a theatre, confined to frustrating glimpses of what should have been the show.

In the case just described, the viewer was vexed by the supposition that there was a complete dance that might have been seen but was being withheld. But the supposition could have been mistaken. Less disconcerting was a telecast of a studio performance of *Nutcracker* by Baryshnikov and the American Ballet Theatre (29 November 1984), directed by Tony Charnoli. In this case, a specific performance of a well-known ballet was named as the target of the film. It seemed to be assumed either that the audience had no interest in dance (but then, why were they watching?) or that the dance itself was of no interest (but then, why do it?), for *Nutcracker* was presented as filmed *action*, relying on fragmentary gestures and facial expressions to convey the nature of the praxis. Such things do not carry the weight of the dance, and the viewer seldom had any sense of what the dancing was like. There were frequent and quite long periods when the camera showed us the reactions of the audience to what they were seeing – to what we ourselves might have seen and reacted to, if the camera had allowed us. One might reply that this was, after all, a studio performance, and that in the studio there really is no dance overall; the stage dimension, with its curtains and ceremony, is what decisively converts the most episodic of ballets into a single work. But a better reply might be that *Nutcracker* nowadays is presented less as a dance than as a Christmas party and that the film we saw was really a kind of festive celebration rather than any sort of film of a dance performance.[37]

How can one film a dance so as to make a dancefilm, allowing for the artificiality imposed by the camera's intrusion and compensating for the lack of the staged occasion, while making up for the camera's inability to show us everything our eyes could seek out if they were free? One popular solution is to build a programme round the rehearsals of a short dance, shown piecemeal so that we see the separate movements as information but see the film as narrative art, and allowing the pro-gramme to culminate ceremoniously in the straightforward filming of a performance of the entire dance in its theatre setting.

At the other extreme, annoyance is avoided by blocking the illusion that there is or could be a performance to be seen, destroying any cues from which a real space and time could be inferred in which the dancers might be moving together. Here, dancefilm and animated film often converge; if there is no spatiotemporal constraint to impose a human reality of dance practice, dance movements can blend into three-dimensional and two-dimensional renderings and simulations of vital movements of all sorts. If relatively little of this is done, it may be because of the immense amounts of rehearsal time and laboratory work required to service a very restricted market.

Advances in the design of portable equipment mean that in filming a dance performance the camera can wander among the dancers, seeing angles that no theatre audience could ever see. The resulting dancefilm is not any sort of record of anything a choreographer envisaged as to be seen; what it records is the trace of the travelling eye. The visible result is a fusion of two sets of decisions and movements, those of the dance-makers and those of the film-makers' (real or constructed) eye. As a result, one sometimes hears people talking about the camera as participating in the dance, dancing along with the dancers. But the camera-holder, however athletic, is not dancing. The camera's physical movements do not have the qualities of the movements it captures, and the camera's suppositious eye is that of a mobile spectator, not that of a participant in the strenuous and elegant rigours of the dancing bodies. If the camera viewpoint represents a participant in the dance, the dance itself is reduced to a pattern of images; and then what we have is not a dancefilm at all, but a composed film in which dancers' movements are among the sources of the imagery inscribed on the film for projection on a screen.

20.33 Video

20.331 Video as Record

I have been assuming that whatever can be said about film goes for video as well, despite all the technical differences. But that is not true. The flexibility and immediacy of video encourage a different sort of use in recording dances, halfway between film and a mirror.[38] The light video camera instantly produces a tape that can be immediately reviewed, and then may be erased or preserved without penalty – in sharp contrast with expensive filmstock, which must be slowly developed and printed and cannot be reused. A video camera can be used like a visual scratchpad. This could revolutionize dance-making.

As video becomes a normal part of dance-recording and hence of dance-making, it naturally enters into the creative process as well as the manufacturing process. I am thinking of some things Twyla Tharp has done. She has taken a video record of a part of a rehearsal and made a dance by reproducing the taped movements, giving the remarkable effect of a truly repeatable spontaneity, such as one would have by making an audio tape of a pianist's improvisation.[39] More subtly, she has had a dance danced dispersedly by dancers moving throughout an office building or other busy place, dances or bits of dances taking place where they might – but having all the dancing captured on the closed-circuit TV of the building's security system (suitably modified, of course), with monitors throughout the building, so that by reference to the banked monitors one could get an overview of what was being done where.

20.332 Video as Medium

The uses made of video as an adjunct to choreography merge into uses of video as a medium of its own. I want to refer only to what would correspond to the making of dancefilms (as opposed to filming dances). In such a work, the specific resources of the medium are so exploited that the result no longer functions as a filmed or taped dance but has to be thought of as a mixed-medium work, or simply as a creative piece of film or video.[40] In this regard, video is radically unlike film. The electronic manipulability of the video image is not governed by rules susceptible to visual intuition, as film is; its transformations have topologies of their own. Video dance, or dance video, is a new medium, as dancefilm really is not, because 'TV no-space,' as Twyla Tharp has called it, really is a no-space; it is not a muddled or compromised or sublimated version of experiential space.

The video screen, no matter what Marshall McLuhan said, is just a phosphor-lit (approximate) rectangle, as spatial as you please; it sustains what Susanne Langer would presumably have called the virtual space of the video dance. But if 'special effects' are used, they easily destroy the sense of a space in which the dance is being performed. In dancefilm, too, as we have seen, this sense may be undermined and become vestigial; but this is more likely to affect limited aspects and episodes of the film. The electronic maskings and transformations of video, in contrast, work like a kaleidoscope to cannibalize and destroy forms, subjecting them to a comprehensive metabolism, even if some undigested gobbets retain recognizable shapes. Patterns are created in which life is cancelled.[41]

Tharp points out, however, that for a dance-maker video can be disconcerting. At first, the possibilities are dazzling; but soon they become almost an annoyance. They do not offer enough limitations. The endless possibilities they offer are unrelated to the specific choices a dance-maker is used to making and can meaningfully make. But all that means is that the maker of dance video must be a video artist, with creativity geared to specific sets of choices in video terms, as well as a dance artist. This is where so many mixed-media artists fail: they do not have a genuinely synthesized artistic sensibility attuned to the specific potentialities of the various media used and to their interaction, so that one is painfully aware of what was supposed to be happening, rather than enjoying what is actually going on. The few most successful operators in the field are individuals equally gifted in music, dance, and showmanship, like Michael Jackson and Madonna.

20.3321 Dance on Television

Dave Allen remarks that: 'Viewers tend to create their own *programmes* (or viewing experiences) which may well consist of chunks of *The Red Shoes* or *Swan Lake* interspersed with advertisements, contest announcements, telecast information, cups of tea, trips to the toilet, flashes of [network television] and conversations with family and friends. This experience and the continuity and *flow* of television is significantly different from the more ritualistic experience of the communal darkened auditorium of the cinema with collective and relatively unbroken attention on the *silver screen*.'[42] He argues that people preparing dance programmes for television need to bear these differences in mind. This seems reasonable. But there seems to be a suggestion that, because viewers do not always give a continuous presentation their undivided attention, programmers should not provide continuous presentations to which they may attend if they wish. The effect of thus second-guessing the choices viewers might make would be to preempt their power of choice altogether. My attention may wander in a cinema or a concert hall, too; but that does not mean that I do not wish to be confronted with a performance from which my attention may wander and to which it may return. And the fact that viewers often switch channels or even practise 'channel surfing,' as well as reading or conversing, when what is on the TV is something they regard as nothing special, does not mean that they will not watch attentively when there is something on that they really want to see. Nor are such variations in viewer practice at all the same as the predictable interruptions of programmes on commercial channels by the advertisements and other foreign matter to which Allen alludes, which may indeed call for dance-makers and others to divide their works by optional breaks at the appropriate intervals. But between the time I write this and the time you read it the practices of television transmission and reception will have continued their incessant changes, as cable and satellite dissemination alter the balance between broadcasting and narrowcasting. Allen's words, published in 1993, already had a musty smell when I read them before that year ended; what remains fresh and sound in them is the urgency of attending to the real world in which televised dances go forth to meet their fate.

20.4 Conclusion

A notation, if widely adopted, must shift the whole nature of dance within the dance community that takes it up. But film works quite differently. Because it is immediately legible, it changes the possibilities of artistic dance by fusing with it. Film presents us with dances in impossible spaces, dances transformed by the distortion and transformation of images, dances where the camera seems to become a participant, dances reduced to strange formal patterns by electronic masking. The relations among dancers, choreographers, scenarists, video wizards, and technicians change into something unknown to theatre dance. And we see many theatre dances in which a film is screened all or part of the time. This film may simply embellish or counterpoint the dance, as an added ingredient. But it may also show the same dancers in a different space, participating in an impossible union across the divide; or it may show a transformation of the very dance that is being performed before our eyes.

The fact that film enhancements, embellishments, and transformations are possible does not directly change the practice of most dance artists, who may well prefer to continue as they always have, without benefit of camera. But indirectly it affects them a great deal, because they are now dancing in a world where the new possibilities are familiar, both to themselves and to their public. The meaning of every movement is changed, because it represents a choice that nobody ever had to make before.

In the same way, in a dance community where notation is rife, one might think that the many practitioners who remain notationally illiterate will be unaffected by the shift that a notational base must effect in the basic understanding of what dance is. To some extent that may be true, in the same way that the medieval invention of a learned and literate music left untouched the rude mechanicals revelling in their tongs and bones. But they were not entirely untouched; popular music now is a music that uneasily or defiantly operates in the interstices of the score-driven universe of the conservatories. When notations were rare and ineffectual, to dance without regard to them was the normal way to dance, if not the only way. One would give no thought to the matter, any more than people in 1900 were consciously dispensing with the use of automobiles. When notations become ubiquitous, ignoring their use becomes a political act.

CHAPTER TWENTY-ONE

Conclusion

Dance is peculiar among the fine arts for the way in which it involves the humanity of the artists themselves. Dancers dance with their bodies as instruments, but they dance as people. In the theatre, they are seen as people as well as the characters and graceful animals they also are; in a social setting, they dance as participants in formal ceremonies, but also as their very selves. In the first volume of my investigations, where the emphasis lay on what it is to dance and to be a dancer, the theme became that of liminality: dancers do everything they can to make themselves special, in place, occasion, dress, sound, and movement.[1] They lose their selves, not by impersonating others but by placing themselves in a disengaged and disengaging reality. From this point of view, the inner reality of dance, whether consciously embraced or not, is self-transformation.

In the present volume, centred on dance undertaken professionally as a performance art for a public, the self-transformation of the individual dancer fades from sight. Many dances still have self-transformation as their theme, for obvious reasons: the non-ordinariness of the movements being undertaken by the human bodies of the dancers makes the dramatization of a complete change in agency an easier theme for dance than it is for drama.

For the public of dance as an art form, however, what has come up again and again in this book is that insistent ambiguity of the dancer, as visual image, as physical object, as animal body, as human body, as character, as person. Above all, it is the presence of the dancer as person that is so striking. This is quite unlike what happens in drama, where theorists once fastened on a *Pendelbewegung*, an alternation of the attention between impersonator and impersonated.[2] The dancer, even in character, is still *dancing* the character, never quite becoming it or taking it on. It is the movement quality, not the human action, to which the choreographer moulds the dancer, even if the movement is specified by the human action to which it pertains.[3]

The salient themes of this enquiry do not suffice to ground any general conclusion. My endeavours, though as much philosophical as they are anything, and intended to exemplify a way of philosophizing, have after all been merely propaedeutic to a philosophy of dance. I have assembled and discussed problems and considerations which, in my view, philosophers of dance should be cognizant of, if they are not to risk going astray by sheer inadvertence. All this, I have been saying, is what philosophers of dance should give themselves good reasons for leaving out of account, if out of account is where they choose to leave it. But we are still left asking whether a philosophical consideration of the dance is likely, in the foreseeable future, to blossom on the boughs of any considerable thicket in the groves of academe.[4] The answer depends on three prior questions. In what conditions is the philosophy of an art possible? In what conditions can the philosophy of a fine art be meaningfully practised? And what conditions make it worth doing?

First, what makes the philosophy of an art possible at all? That the relevant practice can be identified. That identification must be carried out either by recognizing some inner coherence in the practice (however complex), or a coherent succession of such coherences; or, if no such coherence can be found, on the basis of some conceptual unity (however complex) that can be seen to warrant the initial supposition that such a practice exists. Wherever these requirements are met, a systematic and critical discussion is possible, and such discussion is what we mean by philosophy. To impose any more stringent condition on what discussions may be deemed 'philosophy' is to violate the conditions of philosophy itself, by excluding from consideration certain possibilities about what the world may be like. And, once the practice is recognized, whether it is an art or not is always open for discussion, on lines with which philosophers are familiar.

Next, in what conditions can the philosophy of a fine art flourish? The basic concept of the fine arts is that the arts of painting, poetry, sculpture, music, architecture, perhaps dance, and certain other arts, of which we do not need to stipulate a list, form a set of arts that are worth discussing as a group. This would most likely be if they were assigned a niche, or a coherently interrelated set of niches, in the ensemble of the cultural activities of our civilization; for I take it that the concept of a civilization carries with it the requirement that its cultural activities form an ensemble, the nature of that ensemble determining what kind of civilization it is. We cannot say 'mankind' instead of 'our civilization,' though some people do say that, and more people used to; but we may be confident that there will be a niche or niches assigned to something like the fine arts in any civilization in which we can take more than an anthropological interest.

The fine arts can fill such a niche if they are arts of cognitive appreciation and enjoyment, or imagination. The idea would be that they afford access to some distinctive level or mode of understanding ourselves and our world, or that they afford insight into some distinctive set of realities or possibilities, or that they afford a kind of exquisiteness in enjoyment that constitutes a positive accomplishment of humanity. A work of art will be an entity that is institutionally or technically linked to such activity in a way that is recognized as appropriate; a work of art *worthy of the name* will be one that itself contributes to the filling of the appropriate niche. The philosophy of the fine arts is possible to the extent that it is possible to develop and criticize the idea of such a set of arts, with its appropriate works and activities.

Next, in what conditions can there be a philosophy of *one* of the fine arts? When is a specific fine art worth dealing with in the philosophy of art? There could well be an art, a technique and a medium, in which excellent and important works are achieved, but not in any distinctive way, so that there would be no point in discussing it. For instance, general works on the philosophy of art seldom discuss drawing, even though drawing is not at all like painting as a set of skills, presumably on the ground that any kind of aesthetic and artistic significance that drawings have will be of the same sort that paintings have – they will fill the same niche. And such works used often to omit dance for the same reason, supposing dance to be no more than what a poet would be reduced to if afflicted with laryngitis.

A specific fine art will clearly be worth mentioning in the philosophy of the fine arts if its medium offers special opportunities and challenges, special resources for meaning and affect, in such a way that it may be presumed to open up a distinctive range of insights. It may not be enough that it affords a distinctive range of delights, or of cognizables, because the exploring of those ranges will be sufficiently done by the critics of the arts in question, leaving nothing for philosophers to do.

It is clear that dance has its own technique and medium, its own delights and cognizables. But it is also clear that it offers to open up a distinctive range of insights, exploring the human body as corporeal involvement in the world, the intersection of the necessities and glories of the human body with the will and the imagination of the human as personal agent, the celebration of the embodied human. It ought to be an important art, as it seems to be a universal one. Its persistent place in the education of children is a fitful recognition of that importance. But somehow its hold on a central place in our civilization is insecure. We persist in finding it less important than we feel it should be. Why is this? Well, perhaps it is not so. Perhaps the rather discreditable reasons why the philosophical profession has neglected the dance suffice to explain this wider indifference (Sparshott 1988, chap. 1).

But could it not simply be that dance is after all, in an obvious way, limited? Human bodies come in a limited range of shapes and sizes, and dispose of limited energies. We have only so many limbs, and only so many ways of moving them. And in the world of human exercise, someone who is deprived of speech is cut off from the deepest and most flexible means of communication. Perhaps what is most important in dance is what is least amenable to aesthetics. Dance is basic, indeed, but as a fine art its scope is limited. It is very down to earth.

I have spoken with choreographers who felt that way – that they were working a shallow and easily exhausted soil. But that sort of talk is common in all the arts and is no more than a sign of fatigue. All the arts evidently retain their power to astonish. Dance, in the last few decades, as much as any other of the arts, has shown its power to unfold new possibilities of meaning. How this can be so, and why it should be so, it has been the purpose of this whole enterprise to explain; that it really is so we are reminded again and again, when new dances give us that sense that only new art and new science can provide: that nothing like this was seen or suspected from the beginning of the world until now; and that, among so much poverty, and cruelty, and meanness, and pain, and despair, it is a privilege to be alive in an age when such things are made real and made known.

But let us get back down to earth again, one last time. Suppose there is a special occasion – an occasion which, for whatever reason, you want to *make* special, a festival. What are you to do? Either you do ordinary things in some special way, or you do special things. How many sorts of special things are possible? Perhaps not a great many.

1. You can make a display, do something beautiful or interesting or striking, with or without some material or equipment in addition to the resources of your own person.
2. You can engage in some special sport, contest, or competition, a matching of prowess.
3. You can engage in feats of special skill or strength, agility, dexterity, endurance.
4. You can engage in special speech: rhyming, riddling, orating.
5. You can engage in special sound, musical or unmusical: singing, ululating, chanting, scraping, blowing, banging.
6. You can engage in play-acting, mime or drama.

These categories, and a few others like them, will probably cover most of the special things you can do at a festival, to make an occasion special.

All of these things can be done together, separately, continuously, interruptedly, communally, individually. Their being done as a festival may mean that they are done as in the presence of the gods, or as emanations of a timeless order; or it may not. The things you do may seem specially appropriate to the festival; or they may not. They may somehow refer to the festival of which they form part; or they may not.

A festival may be open or closed in form. There may be accepted limits on what can be done, and on what it can be taken to mean. But to name a limit is to invite its transgression; all forms of special action that can be conceived will always be present as options, and all possible meanings may be entertained, if only to be rejected.

Anywhere in the above field of possibilities that we find bodily movement performed for its own sake, or watched for its own sake, we can call it dance. And people are always moving, and often watching, and whatever they do they can do for its own sake.

The exploration of the whole field of possibilities which the idea of festival opens up is the philosophy of dance. Even if we decide in the end that dance is something very limited and special, the first demand on the philosophy of dance is that it respect the extent and density of the domain of thought and action in which dancing is done. And that respect requires us not to formulate theories about dance which we can then adopt as creeds but to keep up a level of vigilant, intense, and exploratory thinking. First and foremost, the mind must maintain access to its own powers; the cunning whereby we survive in the physical world must not be allowed to fail us in the world of thought. Theories, definitions, metaphors, and demonstrations are instruments of thought, not thought itself.

Helen Keller, blind and deaf, her hands on the body of Merce Cunningham as he danced, said: 'How like thought. How like the mind it is' (Graham 1991, 149).

CHAPTER TWENTY-TWO

Afterword: The Three Graces

Wagner introduced his notion of a comprehensive artwork through the traditional emblem of the Three Graces, with their lightly touching hands. He used these figures to image the three sister arts of poetry, music, and dance – the three 'time arts' as some have called them, the arts that depend on relationships deployed through temporal modification and succession (cf. Sparshott 1988, 70). But no one else read the image that way, and it seems wrong: the sister arts combine in their difference to make a single art, but the Three Graces are all alike.

The configuration of the Three Graces has remained a constant presence in our art, in a way that has no parallel among figures from pagan antiquity. In my first version of what became this book (Sparshott 1982b, 18–19), the following observations came in the exact centre of my discourse, just as the Graces themselves in their self-absorption were the still centre, the eye in the storm of the dance.

Now that my discourse has lost its centre, the image of the Three Graces is displaced too. And whatever place it has it must share with a no less powerful and familiar image, that of Siva as the Lord of the Dance, Natyaraja.[1]

Siva is surrounded by a ring of fire, to which he appears indifferent. He is poised on one leg in *demi-plié*, the foot planted on a small, prostrate figure – said to be a demon, or the dwarf of ignorance, but looking in some versions more like a dead or frightened child. The other leg is raised, free of the world of illusion and death. His arms are divided. Of his four hands, two hold emblems – the drum of creative sound, the flame of annihilation – and two make signs – the *abhaya mudra* of reassurance, and 'a hand that points to the lifted foot to indicate the refuge of the individual soul' (Kar 1952, 45, quoting Coomaraswamy) – but we do not need to read the signs, since they are plainly of no concern to him. If there is a world, he faces it down; but it is not evident that there is a world. His pose would be triumphant if there were anything to triumph over, but in all renderings the expression on his face is beyond triumph, beyond indifference. It is evident that he is a god, and he is dancing. His pose in this dance is full of energy, but we cannot imagine any movements that would lead to this charged equilibrium or follow from it. In this, he is as far as possible from the jackal in the Dogon legend, whose steps create the world by tracing out in the dust the future inscribed in his skirt.[2]

The Graces are very different. They are neither gods nor women, but dancers.[3] They are quite ordinary. They are unaware of any possible onlookers, not because they gaze out into a void, but because their attention is held within the confines of their dance. They are absorbed, not in themselves or each other, not in the pose they are holding or the movements they are making, but in the dance itself that seems to be their sole reality.

Siva is in a dance pose. The Graces in their dance are not posing, and their position suggests no movement before or after.[4] There is a world, and they are at home in that world as Siva is not; but they neither embrace it nor exclude it. They are as feminine as Siva is masculine, but no more than Siva do they need any relation with others to define this aspect of their reality. They are not dancing the compliance of Parvati, they are not mothers or consorts, neither sisters nor companions. They are the Graces. Hesiod names them Thaleia (festivity), Aglaia (splendour), and Euphrosyne (good cheer), but others give them other names.

Evidently there is something in the triune image of the Graces that appeals strongly to the imagination. But the strength of that appeal is more evident than its ground. It may be that the variety of decorous nudity contributes something to its popularity; but surely that cannot be all. There must be something in the symbolic suggestion of their pose. But what?

Sir John Davies (1596, lxxiv [p. 189]) takes them to symbolize all dance –

those gracious Virgins three;
Whose ciuell moderation does maintain

All decent order and conueniencie,
And faire respect, and seemlie modestie –

but does not feel it necessary to elaborate or explain. The grace that his
lines invoke seems ambiguous, combining an inwardly motivated generosity, graciousness, with the gracefulness of a movement that is natural
to a body animated by a harmonious and peaceful spirit; but these are
taken to be aspects of the same quality.[5]

The posture of the Graces accords with the view of sculpture and
painting we associate with Lessing, according to which such immobile
representations show movement most fitly in moments of repose
between agitations.[6] It is clear that the Graces are dancing and that they
represent the quintessence of dance; it is less clear what they are dancing.
They may not be moving at all. They are evidently not moving much.[7] If
dance orbits elliptically around the twin foci of grace and vigour, as
Adam Smith thought it did, then grace is the focus where the sun is.

The Graces, I was saying, represent the quintessence of Dance. But
how can they do that? Dance being a kind of practice, it is hard to see
what would be meant by ascribing an essence to it, and harder to see
how one could determine what its essence is. I used the fancy word
'quintessence' to warn the reader that an element of metaphor was
seeping in. What is meant is that a statue or picture of the Graces
should interpret them as dancing in a way that perfectly expresses that
motivation which most typically moves humans to dance, rather than
to do something that would be equally well or better designated by
some other word. It follows that, if no such motivation can be established, the iconography of the Graces represents an unsubstantiated
claim. One would be purporting to deify or attribute authoritative
permanence to the 'nerve' of dance as interpreted in one's own here-
and-now. Or, to put a better face on things, one can say that the Graces
represent the quintessence of dance – but only as dance would be
understood in a culture for which the Graces could be effective symbols.

One thing that seems clear about the Graces is that they touch hands.[8]
According to an old classical dictionary, which I take to represent a
received opinion of the eighteenth century, 'The moderns explain the
allegory of their holding their hands joined, by observing, that there
ought to be a perpetual and never ceasing intercourse of kindness and
benevolence between friends' (Lemprière 1801, s.v. 'Charites & Gratiae').
Their triplicity symbolizes the three phases of generosity: giving, receiving, and returning.[9]

If the Graces represent the intercourse of benevolence, we may take them as figuring a Neoplatonic interpretation of the cosmic dance.[10] In a Neoplatonic scheme it is giving, receiving, and returning that are the fundamental dynamic of the world, not that whirl of the heavens which round-dances have so often been held to symbolize. Grace is an outgoing generosity of spirit, and it is the generosity of Being that in a Neoplatonic scheme causes each level of reality to generate the one below it. On this view, if 'Divine Grace is dancing,' the dance is a movement going out into bodies from an unmoved centre. So a human dance, it might be said (and nearly has been said; it is only a slight modification of Langer), presents the image of powers moving out into the world and becoming visible and thus beautiful. This is that dynamic version of 'the Idea made perceptible' that Hegel, by omitting dance from his scheme of the fine arts, failed to exploit.[11]

Siva as Lord of the Dance cannot, for all his manifest power, symbolize a Neoplatonic cosmic emanation. For one thing, his isolation is absolute; we would not be surprised to learn that in a world that conceived such an image we and our world were an illusion. What the god makes, he destroys; it is nothing to him. But also, what moves each level of reality in a Neoplatonic scheme to generate the level below it is love for the level above, to which it aspires to return; and grace is, above all, the quality in things and people that evokes a pure love.

Dance thus conceived as powers moving out into the world can function (as calligraphy, tracing the hand's 'dance,' can also function) as the central art of a culture, because activity expressive of life assumes therein a form that is at once natural and eloquent; its technical transformations (like that whereby calligraphy yields to typography) change it into what symbolizes natural movement by violating it.

The above reverie (it is no more than that) yields a reading of the *pas de deux* that remains the emotional centre of romantic ballet and its heirs. The static dancer spins his mobile partner like a top. The force of his presence is to be seen as creating the dance.[12] Fonteyn is doing most of the dancing: but a large part of the point of the dance is that, even so, she divides our attention equally with Nureyev. This reading, however, conceals another: that it is the woman who does all the work, while the man just stands there and takes the credit.

Meanwhile, the Graces and their grace are there for us to see, and we see that they are not two, but three, dancing equally and dancing together, but by themselves, and in need of no presence to stand in the midst of them and divide them from each other.

Notes

CHAPTER 1 Introduction

1 Most writing on the philosophy of dance, especially that part that falls within conventional aesthetics, has concentrated on ballet, the dance genre most conducive to objectification and 'disinterested contemplation' and hence allowing the least significance to self-transformation. This emphasis, though understandable, is misguided and has led aestheticians to misconstrue the values of dance, which in turn has contributed to the tendency of the philosophy of art to neglect dance (cf. Sparshott 1988).

One must not, however, forget the proviso in the text, that a dancer may dance a dance as routine or job. In that case, the dance is subjectively a task to be got through, involving no sort of self-transformation other than that involved in any absorbing occupation. According to Drid Williams (1991, 46–7), an African masked dancer explains that for him the dance is primarily 'hard work,' not a self-transforming experience. But that tells us nothing about the significance of the drudgery that is being undertaken.

CHAPTER 2 The Problem of Classification

1 Class G covers 'geography, maps, anthropology, recreation' and ends with anthropology (GN), folklore (GR), and manners and customs (GT), before getting round to recreation and leisure (GV), which is where we find dance. Dance follows outdoor recreations, physical education and training, sports, and 'games and amusements,' which range from hobbies

and parties to parlour magic and tricks. Dancing comes after games and
amusements, to be followed by circuses, spectacles, and the like. Class G
as a whole is separated from music (M) and the fine arts (N) and literature (in P) by social science (H), political science (J), law (K), and education (L). I will not describe the internal arrangement of the section on
dancing, beyond observing that although 'ballet' is a separate heading
under theatrical dancing, as are tap dancing and clog dancing, 'modern
and expressionistic dancing' (coupled with 'revival of classical dancing'
and with 'religious dancing' as a subdivision) is not, but is treated as a
more general and descriptive grouping – it comes before the biographies
of dancers, not after. That gives one food for thought. One might guess
that the scheme was originally set up after Diaghilev and Duncan but
before Graham; in any case, it suggests that ballet was a dance form but
modern dance was not.

2 That is why I do not discuss the specific methods used by the Dance
Collection of the New York Public Library. I note from the introduction to
the catalogue that 'the dance collection has developed a comprehensive
list of 8,000 subject headings and cross-references which take into account
all facets of the field' (NYPL 1974, vii). I see the forest and the trees, but no
interesting pattern in the plantings – someone else might see more. But
the main thing is that the organizers are not seriously faced with the
problem I discuss in this section – the place or places assigned to dance
on a general map of knowledge.

3 I say 'in the first instance,' because the waltz can also be performed as a
theatre dance and can be thought of as an ethnic dance, the characteristic
behaviour of a specific 'tribe.' What was a folk dance yesterday may be a
court dance today and a theatre dance tomorrow, as Louis Horst (1940)
observed. However, if what is done on stage is done as a waltz and
meant to be seen as such, it is surely being done 'in quotes,' in allusion to
its social and recreational origin elsewhere, and the sense in which the
waltz is 'ethnic' is one in which no behaviour is other than ethnic (the
alleged 'tribe' being constituted ad hoc by whoever engages in the behaviour).

4 My use of this example does not mean that I endorse the old notion that
all dance is somehow descended from a supposed 'primitive' dance in
which our ancestors impersonated animals for magical purposes. The
significance of animal impersonation for the dance is examined in
Lonsdale 1981.

5 *Choreia* and *orchesis* are extensively discussed in Sparshott 1988, especially
§2.1.

6 Plato's *Laws* VII 814d–816d proposes (or recommends) two kinds of civic dances: the 'Pyrrhic' war dances, which involve 'the motions of eluding blows and shots of every kind by various devices of swerving, yielding ground, leaping from the ground or crouching,' and corresponding motions of attack; and the dances of peace (*emmelia*), which embody 'the graceful style of dancing in a way becoming to the law-abiding man' – these being divided into joyful dances of deliverance and sedate dances of contentment (trans. A.E. Taylor, in Plato 1961, 1385–6). This proposal has something in common with the distinction I am making in the text, as well as with the one introduced in §15.2211. However, Plato's distinction holds only within the 'serious' dances held fit for citizens of a conservative utopia; there is a corresponding class of 'comic' dances unfit for such citizens. The latter are loosely characterized as parodic, vulgar, and obscene, and all mimetic dances are relegated to this category. Plato clearly has not thought the matter through. The issue is explored at length by Lonsdale (1993, chap. 3), who draws on recent anthropological theory to refurbish Nietzsche's distinction between Apollonian and Dionysian strains in Greek ritual. Some dances, the ones approved in the *Laws*, reinforce the hierarchical order of the city; but the disorderly dances which the *Laws* disdains as irrelevant to the city are in fact no less vital to it, because they celebrate *communitas*, the shared membership without which there is nothing for hierarchy to order.

CHAPTER 3 Classification by Context

1 What Geertz says of art generally may be said more specifically of dance. I return to this question under the heading of 'expression' in chapter 5.
2 The point of specifying a reference group is that ill-informed, or flaky, or stupid individuals will differ widely as to what they admit to be dance. One can really speak of what 'we' call dance only in so far as some authoritative group is conceded to speak on our behalf.
3 Such self-consciousness may of course vary among members of a dancing group. Suppose, for instance, some of them have taken part in an international dance festival and then returned to a wider group that had no thought of such things.
4 I doubt whether what I mean is quite what Wittgenstein had in mind – he associates *Lebensformen* with 'language games,' another cloudy notion. For discussion of Wittgenstein's meaning, see Hunter 1968.
5 'Students of Ballroom Dancing set themselves a very light task compared with that of the students of any other Art. In Operatic Dancing, three

years' hard work will enable the student to realise in some degree what remains to be learned. ... In Ballroom Dancing, the whole subject is comparatively small, and six months should see intelligent students well on the way to becoming Artists. ... In case the reader should form a wrong impression, it should be clearly understood that students should not expect to reach their zenith as actual executants of the Ballroom Art in less than two years. ... It is, however, true to say that in no other Art is proficiency gained at such a low price in time and work as in the Ballroom Art' (Rumsey 1928, 91–2).

6 This is not to say that a person may not derive great personal satisfaction from studying or privately practising an art of which the successful practice requires qualities one lacks and will never attain.

7 'The village Morris-men ... are few in number, especially chosen and trained, and form a close society or guild of professional performers. Admission into their ranks is formal and conditioned. It is not enough that the probationer should be a good dancer, lissome and agile; he must, in addition, undergo a course of six weeks' daily instruction at the hands of the elder dancers' (Sharp 1909, 9). Sharp goes on to say that the Morris is a ritual dance, not a pleasure dance; he does not mention its use as a money-making display.

8 Great offence is often given to expert practitioners of ethnic dance or music by audiences, officials, and others who dismiss their work as unserious and amateurish simply because it does not belong to an official branch of 'high art.'

9 The relation between primary and secondary standards is discussed in Sparshott 1982c, 30; see also §15.212 and §17.21 below.

10 Quoted (without reference) in Van Vechten 1980, 154–5. (Not in Gautier 1986.) Another viewpoint on the Spanish approach to dancing is that of a ballet mistress engaged to transform a folk-dancing group into a ballet company: 'Within my experience, Spanish dancers differ from those in the theatres of other countries by the fact that in most cases they have had no theatrical training whatsoever, and in many cases they had never set foot on a stage in their lives. It is not surprising therefore that they found it hard to understand why they had to rehearse once they had learnt the dance sequence, and the daily routine of class and rehearsal was far beyond their comprehension! They indignantly maintained that they knew how to dance and had no need to "learn" and what was more, with their independent spirit, they were not prepared to follow anyone, or keep in line with their colleagues, either! To ask them to do so, they considered a gross interference with their personal liberty!' (Ivanova 1970, 13).

11 The relevant sense of 'style' is that articulated by Richard Wollheim (1979).

12 In *Die Meistersinger*, both Beckmesser and Walther lack style: the former because he and his colleagues identify art not with mastery of a range of choices but with skilled compliance with a set of requirements; the latter because, as Hans Sachs points out, he has not grasped the idea of mastery at all.

13 This was not sheer ignorance: like Ruth St. Denis, Duncan had studied ballet in New York, with Marie Bonfanti (Ruyter 1979, 8).

14 This way of putting things may be contested. One way of thinking about the difference between amateurs and professionals is that the former think of self-expression, the latter think of art: the loss of personal control is the acceptance of public responsibility. H.R. MacCallum (1953), however, follows R.G. Collingwood in arguing that this apparent loss of control may be a self-recovery: from the subjective release of 'commotion' the artistic dancer passes to the realization and expression of 'emotion,' accessible to the audience as well as to the dancer. What the amateur thinks of as putting on a show may really be the discovery of what the dance was about all along.

15 See Sparshott 1988, 62–3, for Bournonville's report on Petipa's comment on this phenomenon.

16 This section is basically about dances for audiences. But, whether there is an audience or not, a group of dancers may well number among themselves persons with all the predilections that give rise to such tensions.

17 See Hanna 1988, chapter 4, for varieties of male/female differentiation throughout the world.

18 And presumably by some knowledgeable chamberlain or appointed successor, or who will teach the new king?

19 My knowledge of Shklovsky is all derived from Jameson 1972, 50–5.

20 Outside America, the aspiration has sometimes been greeted with some skepticism. It used to be said in the 1950s that the CIA had been given the task of discovering and surreptitiously promoting some art form in which the United States could claim cultural leadership, suitable to the political leadership with which World War II had saddled it. They came up with abstract expressionist painting and modern dance, art forms whose repute fusty Europeans professed to find otherwise inexplicable. The vogue for attributing supernatural powers to the CIA seems to have subsided, however.

21 There is also a political side to the concept of a high art, related to the function of arts in the hierarchy of an imperial civilization. See §3.761.

22 See Sparshott 1982c, 293–5. The conditions of learning are, however, more complex than such simple contrasts allow. For example, Beryl de Zoete writes that Balinese Sanghyang dancers have never had dance training and dance only in trance, but then 'dance as if it were their constant occupation'; she infers that 'dance-movements enter since infancy into the consciousness of every Balinese and become stamped on their muscular memory' (de Zoete and Spies 1938, 71). But it appears from what she says that this cannot happen to the trance dancers in the same way that it happens to other Balinese.

23 I say 'presumably' because the children may assume that the adults are misguidedly trying to help them have fun, whereas it is more likely that the adults are trying to tie the children up in group activity and thus *prevent* them having fun.

24 Recent British writing emphasizes the opportunities and constraints imposed on dance education by the introduction of a nation-wide curriculum with common examinations and, consequently, examinable standards (Adshead 1988; McFee 1994).

25 For the development and vicissitudes of this idea, see Ruyter 1979.

26 The distinction made here may be questioned. In ballet, for instance, one has not performed an arabesque correctly unless one performed it gracefully. In general, in performances for a public, one has not fulfilled one's implied contract unless one performs *well* at the appropriate level and in appropriate respects. An insight similar to this plays a fundamental role in Wittgenstein's aesthetics, according to which *getting things right* is (always?) the appropriate standard. All this is true, but nothing in the text is overturned by it.

27 The classical statement of the institutional theory is that of George Dickie (1974). A later version (1984), more nuanced and refined, lacks the challenging force of the original statement. McFee (1992, chap. 3) remedies what he sees as the wilder implications of Dickie's original theory by stipulating that a work of art must actually be endorsed by the 'Republic' of art, but this apparent hypostatization of a notional entity makes one wonder if he is not inclined to give too much credit to the examining bodies of the educational establishment.

28 The concept of authenticity in art has been examined in detail by Bruce Baugh (1986).

29 Do cutting edges really widen horizons? Perhaps they widen peepholes. I do not know why the advocates of outré art find the idea of a cutting edge attractive. At my age, one prefers a cushion.

30 This lies behind a celebrated article in which Monroe Beardsley (1984)

argues that what is distinctive of dance is 'an overflow or superfluity of expressiveness' (46). He was taken to task by Carroll and Banes (1989), who pointed out that this is untrue of much artistic dance.

31 Some of the implications of such a position are worked out by Susan Foster (1986).

32 Or, of course, she; but few of those who heard Thomas Rainborowe at the Army debates at Putney in 1647 will have noted the omission.

33 For instance, 'The manipulative attitudes of superordinate peoples can force adaptation by subordinate peoples that is not the same as internally developed evolution' (Kealiinohomoku 1980, 42, quoted by Williams 1991, 59). Kealiinohomoku is referring to the specific practice of transferring the dance practice of one group to the performing context of the other group, thus destroying as much as it preserves; but the principle is the same, treating the administrative and educational structure of an imperial civilization as if it were necessarily identical with the ethnic traditions of a dominant group. Students of the Roman Empire have known better than that, ever since Juvenal observed the effect of Greek culture on it. (But the same students have also known that imperial powers often destroy the cultures of their subjects, if not their lives, ever since Tacitus said of the Romans that 'they make a desert, and call it peace.')

34 The functioning of imperial cultural systems in relation to a public life accessible to everyone has been explored in a very practical but philosophically rather innocent way by E.D. Hirsch, Jr (1987); for the application of Hirsch's ideas to dance, see Sparshott 1991. I say a bit more about the phenomenon of empire in Sparshott 1994a.

35 Alessandra Iyer (1993, 13 note 4) maintains that the Sanskrit terms *margi* and *desi*, usually construed as referring to India's 'classical' and 'folk' dances, respectively, have no hierarchical connotations, but simply differentiate the pan-Indian tradition of the *sastras* from local traditions: 'Complex and refined artistic forms are not only an urban cultural feature; they can equally be found at a rural level.' If she is right, this is a more straightforward recognition of the status of imperial culture than any that is current in Western thought; but the ideology of Indian art history is too intensely politicized for outsiders to assess. But see the next section.

36 Bose (1991, 260) notes that contemporary traditions in classical Indian dance are based on later treatises, not on the *Natyashastra* itself; but the latter lays down the basic lines within which all the traditions have developed.

37 Drid Williams argues (1991, chap. 2) that one should ask not why people dance but what they are doing when they dance. I do not see why the

latter question should invalidate the former: what people are doing is one thing, what they purport to be doing is something else.

38 See for instance Hanna 1983, in which the notion that both dancers and audiences should be able to say what a given dance 'expresses' is not accompanied by any recognition of the ambiguities involved. Not much is said on this theme in chapter 5, below.

39 The dances here envisaged are not to be confused with such dances as the Balinese Sanghyang (cf. note 22 above), which are danced throughout in a trance state. Whether or not the meaning of these dances is a communion with some beings other than the community and its available gods, they are a social affair and involve the dancers as a group, even though the group is in a special state: they are not a means of inducing and exploiting a special solitude.

CHAPTER 4 Mimesis

1 Janet Adshead (1988, 1) urges that in dance analysis the dancers' movements are simply observed; the system of movement can be discerned; interpretations of the dance can be rendered plausible by observational analysis and contextual research but cannot be demonstrated; evaluation follows on interpretation. Some critics are inclined to question the first two points. See §8.2 and §8.223 below.

2 Until recently, the word 'imitative' was used for this notion; then 'representational' was tried. But the everyday associations of these words were found confusing, so recently people have used this Greek adjective (with its associated noun 'mimesis'), which is the word Plato and Aristotle used when they introduced the notion into philosophical discussions. The ways they used the word were vague, equivocal, and downright misleading; people nowadays use it as a quasi-technical term – that is to say, stripped of misleading connotations, but not furnished with definable meaning.

3 For Peirce's system of categories, see Buchler 1955, chapter 6, and Savan 1987, 7–14.

4 Royce (1977, 204) similarly prefers a more profound, threefold classification (adapted from Curt Sachs), according to which a dance may be mimetic, or abstract, or metaphorical, the point being roughly that one's dance may have the meaning of referring to or embodying something that it in no way resembles. I am here lumping the first and third together, distinguishing dance that in *some* way refers from dance that in *no* way refers.

5 Martha Graham writes: 'It used to be that when dance was staged, a

flurry of the hand meant nothing more than the representation of falling rain. The arm, moved in a certain way, suggested a wild flower or the growth of corn. Why, though, should an arm try to be corn, or a hand, rain? The hand is too wonderful a thing to be an imitation of something else' (Graham 1991, 108). That sounds wise, but it is stupid: everything hangs on the 'nothing more than,' which is then forgotten. Otherwise one asks *why* the hand is a wonderful thing, to which the answer is that it is the tool of tools, a noble part, the embodiment of intelligence in manipulation, expression, gesture. What Graham castigates is using the hand stupidly, like a semaphore. And when was that ever thought to be good choreography?

6 The distinction in Indian dance practice between *nritta* (pure dance) and *nritya* (interpretive dance) is similarly one between organized wholes: the former may well contain mimetic elements, what distinguishes the latter is that it interprets a text that is being sung (cf. §3.77 and Saxena 1991, 11).

7 The introduction to a collection of André Levinson's writings begins by posing the contrast between dance as having 'autonomous value' and dance as deriving from its expressing or communicating something 'in the way that literature or painting might' (Acocella and Garafola 1991, 1). But the phrase quoted begs the question: why should not the mimetic potentialities *specific to dance* be important, without detracting from the autonomy of dance? For a moving tribute to the 'white ballet' as the ultimate refinement of pure dance, see below, chapter 6 note 25.

8 Frederick Ashton, 'Notes on Choreography,' in Walter Sorell, ed., *The Dance Has Many Faces;* quoted from Sorell 1986, 8.

9 Arlene Croce (1987, 164) writes: 'For a generation or more, our most progressive dancers have lived by the rule of purity which lies at the heart of modern expression in the arts. The historic shift of non-representationalism ... has been the principal factor in the emergence of dance as an art. In the other arts, reaction sets in when liberating developments have run their course. But a reaction against pure meaning in dance threatens the life of the art.' It doesn't do to look into this sort of rhetoric too closely, but it is relevant here to ask how Croce gets from 'non-representationalism' to 'pure meaning.' What is pure meaning? It can't be meaning that means nothing; it can only be meaningfulness that means nothing other than itself, that is exhausted in being the significant entity that it is experienced as being. Such a dance means *itself.*

10 Some people find this language alienating, as though the body was reduced to a tool to be manipulated. Wigman clearly does not: she thinks

of it rather as a musical instrument which she must tune and learn to play, so that she can perform on it the music she wants to make. Beryl de Zoete, a former student of Dalcroze's, writes in the same vein (1953, 12–13): 'In all forms of dance I believe it is possible and indeed essential to achieve that transformation of the body into an instrument for the expression of something beyond itself and beyond the scope of its ordinary expressive capacity without which no dancing is really interesting.' There is a certain ambiguity in this language: it could mean either (a) that the achievement of a new level of expressiveness *ipso facto* transforms the body into a more expressive instrument, or (b) that one changes the body into a new kind of instrument with new expressive capacities. Wigman means (b), but de Zoete may only mean (a).

11 It is on the implicit denial of this possibility that Martha Graham's denunciation of mimetic gesture (note 5 above) depends.

12 In this connection, it is worth noting that the revolution that Fokine wished to effect in ballet style had two aspects. The mimetic aspect was an idealizing of gesture, movement of perspicuous meaning, and the formal aspect was an expansion of the range of dance movements themselves. These were not two changes, but two ways of describing a single change in the way of dancing.

13 Compare the distinction between artistry and virtuosity in §3.3 above.

14 There is a film showing Baryshnikov's performance of Petrushka: every mimed movement is immediately recognizable as a dancer's movement, the movement of a dancer's body moving as a dancer.

15 The distinctions drawn in this paragraph owe much to Kivy 1984, chapter 3, on 'A Typology of Musical Illustration.'

16 The 'one' who so immediately sees may or may not be relying on an agreed familiar code; that is an important difference, but not relevant here.

17 James Miller (1979, 489) quotes Honorius Augustodunensis (*Gemma Animae*, PL 172, 587–8) on 'the ancients': 'In their choral dances, they wished to represent the revolution of the firmament; in the joining of their hands, the connecting of the elements; in the sound of the singers, the harmony of the resounding planets; in the gestures of the body, the motion of the constellations; in the clapping of their hands, or the beating of their feet, the crashing of thunder.' In the light of the distinctions made in the text, we may ask ourselves to whom these meanings were available, and how.

18 Twyla Tharp (1992, 52) says she could never dance in character, being unable to imagine herself as anyone other than the person she really was,

namely, an Indiana farm girl. But her readers have already learned that she never was an Indiana farm girl.

The practice of masked dancing at balls enabled the dancer, behind the disguise of the mask, to dance as the person he or she really was – like one of Shakespeare's boy actors playing the part of a girl disguised as a boy, a double transvestite.

19 For Balanchine's law, see Taper 1984, 251; I will enter a caveat in §13.1. Twyla Tharp (1992, 90) tells how in *Re-Moves* 'I solemnly pulled three eggs from a black bag and allowed them to roll from hyperextended fingers to smash on the floor – a reference to my recent abortion.' What can she mean? Was this action supposed to inform the audience that she had recently had an abortion? Was it supposed to tell the audience something about an abortion which they already knew she had had – for instance, that she had been expecting triplets? How did she expect the audience to know?

20 There is an extensive (though not exhaustive) treatment of the topic in Sparshott 1982c, 65–84. The artistic significance of mimesis in general is elaborately discussed by Kendall Walton (1990). The thesis he develops is that works of mimetic art are props in a game of make-believe and to be understood on the analogy of such imaginative games, as children play them. If we suppress our doubts that adults understand children's games better than they understand the mimetic arts with which they are currently familiar, and our feeling that the arts are being patronized by big grown-up Uncle Ken, we may recognize here a subtle and fruitful idea. Children's toys are assigned character and enter into games that are thoroughly structured, but do so in ways that are not predetermined; similarly, a work of art is elaborately structured and is appreciated and interpreted in exercises of the imagination that are centred on its definite features but retain their own freedom in relation to it. I recommend this important work to the reader's attention, though I have not found it useful in developing my own arguments here.

21 These generalizations have exceptions. An elderly dancer reminiscing for a conference audience related that after a rehearsal, some time in the 1940s, the choreographer told him: 'I forgot to tell you – in this part you are B17 bomber dropping bombs.'

22 The correspondence between my 'personalizing' and the Indian *rasa* is limited, because it is the perfection of *rasa* that uniquely moves the connoisseur to aesthetic ecstasy (Saxena 1991, 137–40); one would not claim any such unique status for perfection in personalization.

23 All this is evident in a televised video of de Valois reconstructing *The*

Rake's Progress with members of the Royal Ballet (an IFPA production directed by Jolyon Wimhurst, 1982, shown on TVOntario).

24 See the illustration in Humphrey 1962, 120–1.

25 Such demonstrations may go through a transition from the attempt by a historian to reconstruct a lost dance style or form, through a student presentation to a scholarly audience, to the development of a version of the new discovery (as a delectable antique) for the enjoyment of a general audience. After a while it is no longer relished as an antique but becomes something to be enjoyed 'in its own right.'

CHAPTER 5 Expression

1 Compare Edward Schieffelin's description of Kaluli dancers: 'Dancers are coached to "be like a wild pig" – that is, anonymous, like a person from a distant area whom nobody knows. As their individuality is submerged, so their image is elevated to an abstraction. The effect is magnified by the dancer's isolation. Moving in the firelight, the dancer seems to be the only living thing in the vast, motionless interior. ... Coming through the avenue of lowered torches, he seems remote, archetypal, a figure emerging from an infinite distance, another time and place' (Schieffelin 1976, 177). I do not know whether the Kaluli would agree that 'archetypal' is the *mot juste*, however.

2 In practice, the expressive side of a performance may be experienced as complex. If I am watching a performance of *Giselle*, I may well be aware of the artistic personality of the scenarist and the choreographer; of the general creative tone of the genre and the epoch of the ballet's invention, and also that of its presentation; of the dancer's artistic personality as expressed in her characterization and performance; of the personality of the character Giselle in the ballet, as variously written into the scenario, the choreography, and the interpretation of the character in the present production; of what the character Giselle is feeling and expressing at this moment of the action; and of the actual attitudes and feelings of the person who is dancing, and who has general attitudes towards the business of dancing, and the role she is dancing, as well as thoughts and feelings about them that she is having at the moment. And no doubt there are other aspects I have not called to mind. Some of this we may dismiss as artistically or aesthetically irrelevant, or irrelevant to some present concern, but such dismissals are precarious (see Thom 1993a, discussed in §14.1). What about those dances in which the dancers are called on to say how tired the dance is making them? Their complaint is part of the per-

formance, because it is in the script, but we have misunderstood unless we refer it to the actual fatigue the dancers as humans are undergoing. Tiresome as this sophomoric ploy may be (the 1960s were the triumph of the sophomoric), the point is a good one and reminds us once more that dance is the art in which it is least possible to separate the artist from the work – and, consequently, the art in which the concept of expression is most intractable.

3   Steven David Ross (1982, 128) writes: 'It is worth emphasizing here the familiarity of bodily movements in dance. Unlike arts whose craft cannot be appreciated by a novice – instrumental music or sculpture – the medium of dance is apparent. We live with our bodies and have a strong sense of our capacities and limitations. Perfection of craft is apparent in all dance performances, more available for general appreciation than the craft of many other arts. The presence of the body and its possibilities in dance offers an extraordinary range of surface-depth contrasts that are inherent in the dance medium. Dance discloses to us possibilities for bodily movement that we could not imagine for ourselves, but which we can appreciate in manifold ways when we encounter them.' Nearly every sentence here could be replaced by its contradiction with almost equal plausibility; the relations between our own bodies as we live them and dancers' bodies as we see them are profoundly ambivalent.

4   This is the method followed in Hanna 1983, with mixed results.

5   The idea that dance not only can and does express feeling in some way, but that this is a striking and important achievement of dance, is not new. Aristotle's *Poetics*, whatever his detractors say, simply mentions in an aside that dance movement is among the mimetic media and includes the representation of feeling in its repertoire. But Quintilian, following Xenophon, finds it remarkable that states of mind, which are in principle accessible only subjectively, should be readable in face and body. 'Dance is often understood and moves us without speech,' he writes, 'and states of mind are perspicuous from face and gait. Even in animals that lack discourse rage, joy, and love are discernible from the eyes and from other bodily signs. Nor is it surprising if these, which after all are involved in a certain movement, should have such psychological force, when a picture, a work that is silent and never changes expression, so penetrates into the inmost feelings that it often seems to surpass the very power of speech' (Quintilian, *Oratorical Education* XI 3 66). Such expression, it seems, is a more striking achievement in the graphic arts but more central in the domain of dance.

6   Compare D'Israeli's strictures on calligraphy, §4.2 above. The position is

hard to make precise. Why should the design and exquisite execution of precise movement be thought of as less humanly expressive than emotive gesturing? Is controlled skill a defect in humanity? A rationale may be found in the Chinese ideology for Sung landscape painting, itself spiritually akin to calligraphy: a prolonged discipline of eye and hand brings about a condition in which a spontaneous movement can embody a profound vision (Chiang 1935; Sirén 1936). But such ideologies, like Martin's theories, have about them an air of wilful fiction. Further reflection requires us to enquire into the aesthetic value of grace (§15.22111).

7 For a sensitive modern exposition of the theory, see Saxena 1991, chapter 5 and Appendix 1 – in which, however, the relation between historical reconstruction and the actualities of current connoisseurship is not easy for the uninstructed reader to make out. For a fuller exposition, see Masson and Patwardhan 1970.

8 According to Hanna (1988, 82), Javanese dancing recognizes five basic types of human disposition: the refined (female); the truthful, refined, modest, and self-confident; the honest, unexcitable, self-confident, and determined; the harsh, excitable, arrogant, and dynamic; and the coarse, conceited, uncontrolled, and rough. Each of these is embodied in a different movement motif and dance style (*ragam*). 'Because the Javanese recognize the movement code,' Hanna writes, 'even non-narrative dancing implies personality.' Hanna does not say whether the movement code has to be learned as such, together with the underlying conceptual scheme, or whether it is something every Javanese learns as part of the general culture. In any case, the likenesses and differences between this phenomenon and the Indian *rasa* theory (not to mention the *ragas* of Indian music) offer food for thought.

9 Graham McFee (1994, chap. 4), concerned to vindicate the place of dance education in the mandatory curriculum of a state school system, says that every artistic dance must relate to 'life issues' – otherwise, why should we care? An issue, surely, is something that is debated; and David Best (1985, 159), from whom McFee borrows the term, had argued only that an art form must be *capable* of dealing with such issues. McFee, arguing that *every* art work must so relate, has to emasculate the term so that everything of human concern counts as a 'life issue.' It is apparently taken for granted that beauty itself is of no human concern, but any connection between dance and everyday affairs should suffice to satisfy Her Majesty's Inspectors. The difficulty of making out precisely what McFee means is commensurate with the difficulty of the problem with which he is wrestling.

10 Since the word 'expression' is used loosely to cover all aspects of the meaningful disclosure of subjectivity, the topic is enormous and intractable. I have written on aspects of it elsewhere. In Sparshott 1982c, 85–91 and chapters 11–12, I distinguish between two radically different ways in which the concept of expression enters into the theory of art; in Sparshott 1994b, I discourse on the impossibility of reducing the topic of expressiveness in music to a single problematic or confining it to the domain of a single theory.

11 Despite their historical importance and occasional brilliance, the sort of dance typified by the Judson Dance Theater (Banes 1983) must seem to the philosopher to suffer from inherent instability, depending on factitiously holistic contrasts between their own procedures and a past conceived as monolithic, and sustained by a network of argumentative rhetoric that no conscientious lover of truth can easily bear. Look at Deborah Jowitt's sensitive account of Trisha Brown's brilliant and influential work (Jowitt 1985, 67–72), and see what you think.

12 Ruyter 1979, 92–3, paraphrasing Staley and Lowery's version of Luther S. Gulick's advocacy of folk dance. She quotes Staley and Lowery (1920, 31) as saying, 'Modern psychology advances the theory that children live their fullest lives when they recapitulate the experience of the race. If this is so, there is nothing we can do that would be of as much value as the simple folk dance.' The 'modern psychology' in question is that of G. Stanley Hall, who maintained: 'Although it may become a highly technical art, dancing is best conceived as an originally spontaneous muscular expression of internal states, primarily not with the purpose of imparting, but for the pleasure of expressing them' (Hall 1911, 42–3, quoted by Ruyter 1979, 97). Ruyter comments that Hall mistakes the use of dance in a homogeneous, traditional culture for the possibilities of dance in a multicultural society.

13 Personally, I never felt that my zest in dancing 'Gathering Peascods' was inhibited by the fact that my agricultural experience was limited to digging potatoes and pulling flax. But Lomax is not thinking of the pastimes of an alienated bourgeoisie.

14 Drid Williams (1991, 119) reminds us that understanding the function of dance in society is not the same as understanding dance. To equate them is to deny the meaningful reality of dance.

15 The contemporary dance groups that visit my town often insert in their programmes statements about the deep human or cosmic meaning of their work. The statements are invariably jejune and banal, but the dances are often brilliant and original. One wants to say, 'Shut up and dance!'

16 I am influenced here by Sartre's explanation of the attractiveness of various forms of sport (see §6.1213 below).

17 Cf. §4.2125 above. In athletic dance, *orchesis*, the body tends to the extreme of animal nakedness; in social dance, *choreia*, the body tends to the other extreme of the invisible centre of its clothing and decorum. See §14.321 below.

18 One form (but only one form) of this celebration is to glory in the triumphs of bodily health and strength (§15.22112). 'Dance is always a perfection in bodily movement, and nearly always at the very limits of bodily capabilities. Moreover, a good dance is seldom good enough: we expect more than perfection, even bedazzlement, yet with a sense of ease. Dance is like sports in which the extreme possibilities of the body are continually being tested, and the celebration of consummate achievement is a central and supreme value' (Ross 1982, 129). Ross here, like many theorists and enthusiasts, identifies dance with one of its popular kinds.

19 Some of these are extensively discussed in Sparshott 1988, 352–70 – but as alternative interpretations of the meaning of dance, rather than as alternative possibilities for artistic expression.

20 See Hanna 1988 for a rich study of these themes.

21 Sartre 1943, part 3 chap. 2. Much of what follows excerpts my paper 'The Dancing Body' in Sheets-Johnstone 1984.

22 Sartre 1943, 506. Why 'she'? Is it because Sartre was an inveterate sexist of an old-fashioned French bourgeois sort? Partly; but partly because it is part of our folk sociology that ogling people carnally is something done principally by males to females. The suggestion must be that nude female dancers at stag parties, if they are really dancing, succeed in resisting a determined effort to neutralize their humanity.

23 The word 'Other' gets a capital here because it renders Sartre's *autrui* (not *l'autre*): individuals encountered in the world are representatives of The Other, an inescapable aspect of the world as harbouring our possibility of being seen, and hence our status as objects and potential victims.

24 This is not to be confused, Sartre insists, with the cadaver, the assemblage of tissues to which I will be reduced after death. The cadaver is not an aspect of bodily living at all; it is something I know about and apply to myself through physiological theory.

CHAPTER 6 Formal Principles of Movement

1 Jack Anderson (1987, 5) says: 'Theoretically, one could say that, from all the possibilities for motion that exist, choreographers select the move-

ments they consider most appropriate for a given work' but are usually subject to traditional and practical limitations. But even the theoretical possibility does not exist: there is no initial set of determinate and discrete movement-units that confronts the dance-maker and invites selection.

2 Hanna 1979, 19. My reasons for not defining dance are explained in Sparshott 1988, §5.1 Hanna's definition is based on extensive knowledge of world-wide dance practice, rather than on virtuosity in the formal requirements of definition-making. Another anthropologist ends a survey of theories of dance by saying: 'It follows that *dance* may be defined in whatever way seems most appropriate to the study of any specific situation or society. Dance is not an entity in itself, but belongs rightfully to the wider analysis of ritual action, and it is in this context that one can approach it analytically and grant it the attention it demands' (Spencer 1985, 38). He pays no attention to the problem of how something that is not an entity in itself can be identified with enough certainty for him to edit a book about it. (This is what gives rise to the misgivings expressed by Drid Williams, as cited above in chapter 5 note 14.)

3 This is not strictly true, if the envisaged viewpoint is located over the centre of the dance space: movements will then be toward, or away from, or around the centre, and not all parts of a level surface will be equidistant from the 'eye.' A truly two-dimensional pattern requires no viewpoint, or an infinitely mobile viewpoint at constant rectangular distance from the patterned surface.

4 See §20.221, where we will see that in the Benesh analysis the 'moving system' that is the dancer is conceived visually, but as from behind, so that dancers can, as it were, imagine themselves forward into their own body image as if it were dancing in front of them in class.

5 Williams says (1991, 63) that a theory about energy expenditure and muscle-work is not a theory of dance as such, any more than a theory about a sculptor's muscles is a theory about sculpture. The analogy is inexact, since the completed sculpture will exist independently of the movements that went to its making. Otherwise, she is right, if one is thinking of the physics of kinesiology, but not if one is thinking of the dancer's expenditure of effort, which is what the text is about.

6 Boundary and centre are definable variously, in geometrical terms or in terms of the dynamic organization of a system.

7 This is why I inserted in §6.1 my proviso about spheres that grow, shrink, or change conformation. These possibilities arise when something that is a unit in respect of one kind of movement is a complex in respect of

another. This is true of a group of dancers (or a school of fish) which move all together as a single entity, but also move as individuals within that entity. The individuals move farther apart, and the group expands; they change relative position, and the group takes on a different configuration.

8 Laura Dean, for instance, 'has become known for dances involving constantly changing, but always clearly defined, patterns and extended passages of spinning' (Anderson 1987, 194). The person who spun on a ball-bearing was recalled by Selma Jeanne Cohen, in an oral communication to some conference or other.

9 Seldom employed in ballet, but I seem to remember some dung beetles in Andrée Howard's *Spider's Banquet* (1944). ...

10 Frye 1990; see especially the diagram on page 179. Versions of the same material are to be found in Frye's earlier writings.

11 Place and space obviously correspond to Frye's second and third levels, though his paradisiac interpretation of place is more restricted than mine (which is close to Aristotle's); the first level corresponds to the dancer's presence as the unique focus of attention. About the demonic level I am more doubtful, but there is a great gulf fixed between the laird and the sylphide, or between the jockey club and the tutu.

12 In Western theatre dance, the relation between dancer and audience belongs to the public region; in African dance forms, it may belong to the social region.

13 That is why Wordsworth's lines 'I've measured it from side to side: / 'Tis three feet long, and two feet wide' ('The Thorn' 3, early version) jar on many readers.

14 The idea of a 'virtual' reality, in the sense used here, was introduced into aesthetics by Langer (1953) and has been hotly contested ever since. The virtual properties of a work of art are those that it is perceived as having as a work of art of the relevant kind, relevance being determined by history in the ways that have been explored and explained by Arthur Danto (1964 and 1981).

15 A change must be a change from some condition to some other condition; there must be a time before the change, a time while the change is taking place, a time after the change. Aristotle pointed out the significance of this for both science and art, both of which have to isolate happenings from their backgrounds for attention.

16 It also milks the audience for applause, if they have not started yelling their fool heads off already, so that they can be heard over the radio by the folks back home in Dismal Seepage.

17 Astronauts in zero gravity find that they tend to identify wherever their feet are as *down*, in the sense of the direction *in which they might fall* – or so I read in an article picked up in an Air Canada in-flight magazine, April 1983.

18 A widdershins movement is 'right-hand' in the sense that a circle of dancers all holding hands and facing inward move widdershins if they move toward their own right hands. Deasil is 'clockwise,' I suspect because clocks mimic the course of the sun, which (if you face it, north of the Equator) is deasil.

19 Agrippina Vaganova, for instance, says that in describing ballet steps she specifies starting with the right foot rather than the left only for brevity's sake: 'The left foot may and should be used as often as the right one' (Vaganova 1969, 3).

20 In ballroom dancing, the male held the female's body with the right hand and her hand with the left – the female used (usually) the same holds, but with the hands reversed. Why not the other way round? Because the male is given the more masterful grip, and the female's dominant hand is prevented from interfering by being kept out of the way? Or did it have something to do with the way gentlemen wore their swords in the days when this style was developed? I have been told that it did – but did dancers not remove their swords?

21 Cf. note 1 to this chapter.

22 Comparable sets might be generated by asking, instead of 'What is a dancer?' 'What is a dance spectator?' or 'What is a dance critic?'

23 To a dancer at a bad moment, one's partner may be primarily a heavy mass of which one is about to receive the impact, as we will see in chapter 17 note 15.

24 If, as in the palmy days of the Judson Dance Theater, the 'dancer' was some chance-seen pedestrian identified as 'my dance' by a sophisticate peering from a window in Greenwich Village, he or she could not have been seen *as* a dancer otherwise than in terms of some notion of what it was to be a dancer and hence to be seen *as* one. For this to make any solid sense, the sophisticate would have to have a lifelong, practical knowledge and commitment to dance. Otherwise, the sophisticate would be just faking, a pretentious booby like so many others in that precious decade who uncomprehendingly mimicked the gestures of their betters (compare the comments on Yoko Ono in Goldman 1989, 260–4 and passim).

25 After the first big-time performance of Ballet Creole, a Toronto group with a substantially Caribbean base, we were pontificating in the inter-

mission about how they were going to have to make some tough technical decisions if they were going to sustain a public presence. One of us
said something about sloppy arabesques. Something in me wanted to say
that this was wrong, that in that style of dancing nothing could be an
arabesque, sloppy or not; it could only look like one. But I bit my tongue,
because after all it could not have been anything other than an arabesque,
and the choreographer and dancer could not have designed and danced it
as anything else. None of us is innocent. Only an overpoweringly strong
choreographer could wrench such a posture away from its own tradition.

An instructive claim for the traditional ties of the arabesque was made
by Vadim Moiseyewich Gaevsky in his *Divertissement*, 10–11 (quoted from
Wiley 1990, 85–6): 'White ballet was bequeathed to us by the nineteenth
century. It is, perhaps, the principal discovery of the ballet theatre in the
last 200 years. Like many other discoveries in ballet, it is impossible to
date precisely. ... We are dealing with a discovery which was extended
and developed, which realized itself. ... In all times it was understood as
a professional absolute. From the ballet-master, from the performers an
ideal mastery is demanded, a professional perfection. Both the technique
and the school of the artist must be infallible, the line of the arabesque
must be infallible. The arabesque is the principal participant in this
play. The romantic arabesque is a graphic formula of the absolute. The
subject-matter of white ballet is the movement of the action towards the
arabesque.'

26 A favourite ploy is to fix a mask to the back of a dancer's head, so that
forward and backward become confused. But I do not remember any use
of this ploy that becomes much more than a trick or a joke.

27 More will be said about such prepositional relations, in chapter 10 and
elsewhere.

CHAPTER 7 Anatomy

1 Frank Richards (1936), an acute though unsophisticated observer, relates
that when he was a private soldier in India it was possible to engage
'nautch dancers' who would perform naked for an extra fee. The soldiers
enjoyed the resulting spectacle but could not appreciate the dance as
dance, because it consisted of movements of the hands of which they did
not know the significance. It is clear from the context that he means not
only that they could not read the language of the *mudras* but that they
did not know how to appreciate a dance of hand movements as such.
Comparable combinations of titillation and sophistication are reported

elsewhere without the element of cultural confrontation: the attraction may often lie in the very tension between Will and Idea.

2　A classical account of this distinction is given by Condillac (1746, II 1 i, §11). After describing the generalized expressive behaviour from which language and dance developed, he goes on to say: 'As men perfected their taste, they gave this dance more variety, more grace, and more expression. They not only subjected to rules the movements of the arms and the attitudes of the body, but traced out the steps that the feet should form. In this way, dance divided naturally into two subordinate arts: one ... was the *dance of gestures*, and was reserved for contributing to the communication of human thoughts; the other was mainly the *dance of steps*, and was used to express certain situations of the soul, especially joy: it was employed on occasions of rejoicing, and its main object was pleasure.' He adds that the 'dance of steps' retains the general nature of the dance from which it originated, but that in France, by contrast with Italy, concern for gravity and simplicity had so impoverished it that it comprised too few signs to constitute a language for a 'figured dance' involving several dancers.

3　Though not subjected to detailed criticism, bodily posture may be important to the style of a dance genre or to that of a particular dancer. The rigidity of the Irish jig style, noted above, is not the only possibility: some tap styles demand an unobtrusive and negligent grace, others call for a vigilant tension. It is not always clear what the requirements are, or how they are imposed, though they tend to be noticed and recognized. It is easy to be sure that a singer's platform manner is not part of the singing, though it is part of the performance; but in the case of dance such a separation is not easily made.

4　The flexibilities of the torso can constitute part or all of a dance, and legs can be planted on earth while the body sways. In dances danced for women by women in Saudi Arabia, for instance, 'With demure, downcast eyes and flat-footed steps, the dancer's movements begin and radiate from the pelvis in 360-degree rotations that spiral up the trunk' (Hanna 1988, 52). Such dances belong to the large and widespread class of 'belly dances,' of which it has been conjectured that they are fundamentally and originally celebrations of female fecundity (Buonaventura 1983). My text is not intended to downgrade these but only to make the commonsense point that human locomotion and manipulation depend on legs and arms hinging on the mass of the trunk which, relatively to them, is necessarily inert, and that this cannot but affect the way dancing is done.

5　It is possible that the human ear and scalp cannot do much in the way of

waggling, because of the poverty of the relevant musculature or something. But, for all I know, it may simply be that no one has tried.

6 The standard version of this encounter may be found in McDonagh 1973,
82–3. Agnes de Mille (1991, 163–4), an eyewitness, tells a different story,
less piquant and less relevant.

CHAPTER 8 Units and Systems

1 Collingwood 1938 (cf. also Frye 1990, 27: 'Literary works communicate in
mythical wholes'). This thesis upsets many people, unnecessarily.
Mallarmé, they point out, said that poems are made out of words, not out
of ideas. And it is perfectly true that poems are made out of words and
(however unified the original creative act may have seemed to be) are
revised by coldly substituting one word for another. Yes, but the substitution changes the meaning of the poem as a whole, and of every word in
it; and it is to this overall change that the revising poet attends.

   Merleau-Ponty (1962, 150) suggests that all part/whole analyses of
actions are misleading, because what we project is always an engagement
of the whole, which must be grasped before any such analysis makes
sense. On a practical level, Twyla Tharp said in the TV program on *The
Catherine Wheel* that if a choreographer gives dancers too many instructions they will spoil the dance by concentrating on movements, instead of
doing the action in the way that is best for their bodies.

2 Or, of course, a pointedly continuous abstention from movement.

3 Use of the corresponding technical vocabulary (phoneme, morpheme,
sememe, lexeme, etc.) would not change anything; all the distinctions I
refer to would still need to be made, because they are functional in literary practice.

4 The terms 'emic' and 'etic' are borrowed from the distinction, in linguistics, between phonemics and phonetics. Phonetics studies the actual
sounds made by people in speaking, using oscillographs and such; phonemics studies the differentiations in sound that are used and recognized
in distinguishing one spoken word from another. The slang abbreviations
are used to remind us of how important the difference between these
studies is, in all its ramifications.

5 This position is vigorously argued by McFee 1992, part IV, drawing on a
powerful philosophical consensus. A satisfactory understanding of the
issue would require us to balance McFee's claim against Adshead's separation of observation from interpretation.

6 I have mentioned (chapter 6 note 25) how an arabesque may suddenly

turn up in a dance of which the vocabulary and ethos are primarily Caribbean. More strikingly, the Shobana Jeyasingh Dance Company, all of whose members are fully trained in Bharatha Natyam, perform dances in which the movement units and postures mostly belong to that school, but the music and prevalent choreography are uncompromisingly Western. (Or so it looked to me; but Iyer 1993, 15 note 22, ignores or denies the association.) Usually, when this sort of thing is attempted, the synthesis embarrassingly fails, but Shobana Jeyasingh makes it work. What happens in all such cases is presumably that a unit from a dance tradition has a sufficiently distinctive character that it can be recognized in isolation and can then be incorporated in a different tradition without losing its distinctiveness, but substituting a new set of connectives for those that linked it to its place in its original home. How this is done in any particular case is something that requires and repays study.

7 Similarly, there is a sense in which M. Jourdain had been talking prose all his life, and a sense in which he really had not.

8 Contrast what is related of Isadora Duncan's more fluid practice and technique: that she could show her students how to perform a movement well, and how to do it badly, but although the students could see which was the one that looked good neither she nor they could explain or demonstrate the difference in a learnable way.

9 You might challenge this, remembering that Chinese children learn to write in a system where each word has a different ideograph; but remember that the ideographs are based on fewer than 120 'radical' components, and are built up from a very few standardized ticks and strokes.

10 Weaver's writings are all reproduced in facsimile, with introduction and commentary, in Ralph 1985; they are referred to here by their original pagination. I have no doubt that Weaver merely exemplifies an extensive tradition, of which I am ignorant: then as now, writers claim originality for what everyone has been saying for decades.

11 '... we shall be able to prove, That the Rules and Institutions of our Profession are built upon the Fundamentals of *Anatomy*; agreeable to the Laws of *Mechanism*; consonant to the Rules of *harmonical Proportion*, and adorn'd with the Beauty of a natural and cultivated Gracefulness' (Weaver 1721, 2).

12 'From the Symmetry, and Harmony of all the Parts of a Body, of a regular Proportion, *Beauty* arises. From a just Position, Disposition, and Contrast of such proportionate Parts, Grace arises. ... How much then ought the Art of Dancing to be valu'd, which, by a just Disposition, and by an harmonious Motion of all the Parts, adds Gracefulness to this just Accord,

or Symmetry of the Members; and, at the same Time, by the Exercise arising from it, contributes so much to the preserving of Health?' (Weaver 1721, 89).

'... The rules laid down, for these and the following Actions, or Motions, are according to the Dictates of Nature; agreeable to the Laws of Mechanism; and consonant to the Rules of Proportion: And ... whatever Positions, or Motions, derogate from these Laws and rules; such Attitude, or Action, will be absurd, awkward, disagreeable, and ungentile' (Weaver 1721, 133).

13 This quotation is from Weaver's earlier work on dance notation, which is similarly concerned with common dancing rather than with stage dancing (Weaver 1706b, 55).

14 'What *Rhetorick* is to the *Orator* in Speaking, [Gesture] is to the *Dancer* in Action; and an Elegance of Action consists, in adapting the Gesture to the Passions and Affections; and the *Dancer*, as well as the *Orator*, allures the Eye, and invades the Mind of the Spectator; ... ' (Weaver 1721, 144).

15 I deal with this in my 'Foreword' to Souriau 1889.

16 The intricate history is unravelled by Nancy Ruyter 1979, chap. 2.

17 Quoted from Samborn 1890, 6, by Ruyter 1979, 18.

18 Stebbins 1902. A modern reader's reaction is likely to take the form of one of two 'decomposing exercises,' from Lesson I: either exercise 12 ('Let jaw fall so you feel its weight') or exercise 11 ('Let lids fall as if going to sleep'), 86.

19 Shawn 1968, 22. Such dicta, for which Laban's writings provide parallels equally pretentious, provoke one to ask what the function of such 'mystical' and anthroposophical components of movement analyses may be. Are they merely to bolster the authors' conviction that the system they are using is important and irreplaceable? Do they serve some obscure practical purpose? Can they be dispensed with? Or are they merely stating humble truths that supercilious critics refuse to acknowledge?

20 Notations, including Labanotation, are discussed in chapter 20, where we see that every system of dance notation implies a system of analysis and, by the orthographic decisions it imposes, enforces a way of identifying, dividing, and linking the elements of movements.

21 This line of thought, so influential in its day, may be the origin of the 'inner man' whose identity puzzled us in the speculations of John Martin (§5.1).

22 Jaques-Dalcroze 1917, 28. Compare Weaver's recommendation of the use of poses from paintings and prints, §8.221 above. Weaver's reason for invoking this material was not reverence for the past but the availability

of a readable vocabulary of pose and gesture. It is the idea of such a vocabulary that Dalcroze is rejecting.

23 Michael T.H. Sadler in Jaques-Dalcroze 1917, 63–4 note.

24 In the passages cited, Laban writes of 'training,' not of 'education,' whereas McFee is careful to explain that his topic is education, not training. However, Laban does not consider that his recommended training is complementary to dance education, and McFee suggests that, whereas all children need to be educated, not all need to be trained dancers.

CHAPTER 9 Rhythm

1 The history of art in this century shows that anything can be a dance that is presented and accepted in a dance context. But the significance of acceptance varies, as do the authority and efficacy of accepting groups. Avant-garde works that can be effectively 'seen as dance' only in the light of an experience of dance built up through other dances, viewed as normal, are parasitic: either they cannot themselves form part of the body of practice through which dance is carried on and understood, or they do so only by serving as constant counterfoils. Not everything that is presented and accepted as dance within a coterie can sustain itself as a part of dance practice. This theme is tellingly developed by Richard Wollheim (1993, 30–4).

2 In chapter 15 we will make this into a general principle, associated with Karl Aschenbrenner: unless it is bad by definition, the converse of any excellence can itself be an excellence.

3 Eryximachus, the crackpot medico in Plato's *Symposium* (187B), says that 'we produce rhythm by resolving the difference between fast and slow.'

4 Aristoxenus 1959. Pighi's edition is not easy to follow, and I am not aware of any adequate commentary in any language.

5 The insistence on real least parts is highly unaristotelian and no doubt comes from Aristoxenus's Pythagorean heritage. The standard form of early Pythagoreanism thought of the universe as essentially countable, consisting of separate units in configurations, so that the key to understanding the world was what they understood as mathematics, a sort of combination of arithmetic and geometry.

6 Dancers in difficult works rely heavily on counting. To judge by what they say, the measures that enter into this 'dancers' count' cannot be identified with any attribute of the music or the choreography: it is an inherent articulation, sometimes subjective, identifiable only as the count that will get you through the passage in question. I have had this

explained to me, but did not understand the explanations. The topic is well discussed by Elizabeth Sawyer (1985, 100–1) and in an anecdotal way by Joseph Mazo (1978, chap. 2).

7 Devotees of Ludwig Wittgenstein's polemic against the possibility of a private language may doubt whether the idea of an individual rhythm is coherent. How can one be sure of identifying the units, if there is nothing to measure them against? But the objection holds only against ascribing a determinate individual rhythm to a dance of one's own. One could not, however, claim that an individual rhythm *followed a rule* that was in principle inapplicable to any other movement.

8 Marching itself is not a form of dancing, so the orders cited are not specifications of even minimal dance structures. But why is marching not dancing? Because the dominant value is uniformity, which is not a dance value; and, of course, the context is not that of dance (cf. Sparshott 1988, §7.522). What is immediately to the point is that the demand is for uniformity in keeping to the beat, taking no other rhythmic consideration into account.

9 These and other practical complexities of musical rhythm in relation to dance are admirably dealt with by Sawyer (1985, chap. 6). Compare also what Martha Graham has to say (1991, 75), though it is not about rhythm as such: 'Your body does not feel the same when you dance to strings as when you dance to woodwinds. It simply cannot. It doesn't even feel the same when you dance to a flute or a bassoon. There is a different thing which hits against your body. The wall of sound holds you in a certain way. You rest on that tone.'

10 Saxena points out (1991, 75) that dance movements, being rhythmical, cannot be simply sensual; a rhythm as such, being a form of order, is ideal.

11 Humphrey 1962, 104–9. John Booth Davies remarks, however, that the connection between rhythmicality in general and the periodicity of body processes has not been established. A correlation has been suggested, he says, between cultural differences in the uses of musical rhythms and different practices of child-carrying by parents (1978, 192–3).

12 The concept of an organism, in this sense, goes back to Aristotle. But Langer's thought here seems to have specific affinities with some metaphysical formulations in Schelling (1805). Music, he says, as the art of time, is associated with our self-awareness. Rhythm, as 'a periodic division of the homogeneous, whereby the uniformity of the latter is combined with multifariousness, that is, unity with diversity,' transforms 'the chance element of succession into necessity' and is the basis of our

sense of our own unity as conscious beings, not to mention the universe itself.

13 John Booth Davies 1978, 178–9 (his chapter 12 is all about rhythm). He concedes, however, that rhythm thus understood as 'a pattern or group superimposed on top of a basic beat or metre is hard to make out in rhythmically advanced music' (183).

14 I have remarked that dancers do a lot of counting – apparently not only in rehearsal, because I have heard Karen Kain say that she was 'too busy counting' to notice some aesthetic aspect of a performance she was in. But Kain may well have been brushing aside a question she thought silly or impertinent – not all artists' answers have a purpose beyond shutting the questioner up. Gelsey Kirkland says she tells her dancers that they must not count; the implication is that they should be able to rely on dramatic feeling to carry them through (Kirkland and Lawrence 1990, passim).

15 Note how close this comes to what was said about style (§3.31).

16 The late Stillman Drake told me that Galileo was able to time his experiments in mechanics with great accuracy by using his own pulse. I had previously supposed that his accounts of his experiments involved a good deal of fiction, since no extant chronometer could have justified his results.

17 I previously mentioned how Aristoxenus, rather incomprehensibly, generalized this quite intelligible notion into the thesis that *any* articulation of movement requires a momentary rest at the joints, to keep the articulated members distinct. Aristotle argued that matter and processes (and hence, time) were infinitely divisible; Aristoxenus, as a Pythagorean, may not have accepted that view (cf. note 5 to this chapter).

18 The break between the movements in a musical work is of indeterminate length in the score; of definite but imprescriptive length in a concert performance; and of invariant but musically irrelevant length on a recording.

19 An exception could be made for such practices as those of Merce Cunningham, in which movements of unrelated tempo were simply compresent in the dance space, subject to the choreographer's general directives. But it is not irrelevant that Cunningham's use of such methods developed in the ambience of the musician John Cage; and, in any case, no precise account of the relation between two contemporaneous movement sequences was envisaged or attempted.

20 Or, if not this, the precise scope and manner of the indeterminacy of the indeterminacy. Cage got annoyed when performers of his works forgot this.

CHAPTER 10 One and Many

1 Isadora Duncan wrote, 'To unite the arts around the Chorus, to give back to the dance its place as the chorus, that is my ideal. When I have danced I have tried always to be the chorus. ... I have never once danced a solo' (1928, 96). This is odd, because the impression she made on others was often that of incommunicably individual genius. What can she have meant? Perhaps nothing much, a mere cloud of disingenuous self-effacement. But what she said makes sense. She often danced alone in her dance space, and she was then not a soloist, not singling herself out from rivals. When she danced with others, she danced in the same way, not transforming herself into a performer the meaning of whose dance includes setting herself apart from others; she was simply joined by other dancers. Her dance was like the chorus in a Greek tragedy, an impersonal comment on the world.

2 When Nureyev was dancing with a second-rate dance company he tended to forget this, contriving not merely to ignore his fellow-dancers but to dance out his disdain. I found the result painful to watch, but reactions like mine were not expressed by criticisms I have read.

3 The words 'active' and 'passive' are generally used for the pairs in such dances. The relationship has much in common with that in children's games of tag.

4 In general, it is a prime resource of choreography to organize movement into fluid separations and rejoinings of individuals and groups of different sizes. The constant changing of personal relations that this involves is a source of deep delight but need not be presented or experienced as a formal structure. The analysis in the text is not faithful to the phenomenology of this aspect of dance, which reflects the continuity of adjustments in human compresence in the world.

5 Of dances that would make sense on their own, the extreme case is that in which the dances are indeed independently conceived and the total dance consists simply of their compresence; of *this* the extreme is that in which the component dances were even chosen at random, without thought for congruence and compatibility.

6 In ballet companies, in which it is more common than in orchestras for individual dancers to dance more or less briefly in separation from the group, and in which frequent injuries call for dancers to be pressed into service at short notice, it is common for there to be a more elaborate nomenclature for dancers in accordance with the importance of the individual roles that they may expect to be assigned: corps member, soloist,

principal dancer, and so on. (Mazo [1978] explains how the system operates, or operated, at the New York City Ballet; Peter Martins [1982, 159]
compares the NYCB's nomenclature with that of the Royal Ballet;
Khudekov [1896, 266–7] gives the nomenclature *and the corresponding pay
scales* for the St Petersburg ballet in 1873 – commenting that the most
junior grades were so badly paid that they were forced into prostitution,
which, given that the ballet management was drawn from the same social
set as the 'balletomanes,' may not have been unforeseen.)

7 In the televised reconstruction of *The Rake's Progress* (cf. above, chapter 4
note 23), the last function was certainly performed; it was in fact instructive to see how few of the movements we had seen being laboriously
inculcated were separately identifiable, let alone interpretable, in the finished performance (or what one could see of it on the small screen). In
this case, however, part of the purpose was to show homage being paid
to the venerable choreographer.

8 Along these lines, there was recently a vogue on British television for
comedians to 'dance' as soloists with a professional back-up group: we
were first to deride their incompetence (and sneer at the professional
dancers for doing so well something so trivial), then to admire the expert
way they handled their incompetence. Precision in clumsiness is the
clown's stock in trade and requires that the spectators recognize just what
the movements are that the clown fails to get right.

9 Graham McFee (1992, passim) seems to think it follows from his preferred
interpretation of Wittgenstein's demonstration of the impossibility of a
truly private language that the motivations and thoughts of others are as
transparent to us as our own. But, if that is indeed the conclusion, it is
plainly false, so the premises (whatever they are) would be wrong. Even
when people are not putting on an act, their thoughts and feelings are
partly veiled from each other; conversely, people can deceive themselves
about their own motivations in a way they cannot deceive other people.
No doubt some of the formulations we habitually use to describe these
phenomena could be misleading (to a visiting Martian, perhaps), but
nothing could be more familiar than the phenomena themselves.

10 Cf. §6.2. I refer to their relations *as dancers*; as before, I am talking about
the dynamic shape of the dancing, not the personal attitudes of those concerned. Not too much weight should be placed on the prepositions used
here: any preposition, to be serviceable, has to stand for a multitude of
significantly different relations. I may be said, equally aptly, to be dancing
'with' someone if what we are doing is like having a conversation with
each other, or if it is more like singing with each other a cappella.

11 Cf. Tanaquil LeClercq: 'You have to dance for somebody. You don't do it for yourself; that's like contemplating your own navel. You do it for people. That's why I can't understand those modern dancers, dancing away in lofts for just a few people' (in Newman 1982, 166).

12 In §12.3 I will point to similar 'prepositional' relationships between a dance and its music. Dance and music alike function as vital and expressive agencies, which it makes sense to personalize in this way.

13 It was the apparent loss of this perspective that made Nureyev's performance in roles he had inflated for himself distasteful for some observers (cf. note 2 to this chapter).

14 See Plato's *Lysis* and the somewhat quizzical comments on the issue at the start of Book VIII of Aristotle's *Nicomachean Ethics*.

15 Or what sex the danced character is: in many dance traditions, only one sex dances, some dancers specializing in representing the opposite sex.

16 For the immense complexities here, see the material compiled by Hanna 1988. And compare what was said in §6.12131, above, on the belly dance, in which a dance of person-to-person intimacy relies on the suggestion of real-life invitation being held in tension with the performer/audience relation – not to mention the sub-text of a 'women's dance' of childbirth and fecundity.

17 In this paragraph and some preceding ones, the lapse of a few years between draft and final version has made me change many present tenses to pasts. No doubt many more such changes will have been called for between final version and proofs, or between proofs and publication. The conventions of sexual and social pair bonding, like the dance conventions and styles that go with them, change at a pace with which university presses cannot compete.

18 The intertwinings of Pilobolus, based on a sort of intimate gymnastics, are equally free from specific sexual suggestion, but in a quite different way. In the Jones dance, a passionate personal attraction is shown as working itself out in sensual contact; in Pilobolus, a sort of pansensual ecstasy of touch seems to be expressed in a way unconnected with love or even affection. The implied relationship is like what one sees among lionesses, who lie piled on each other as indiscrimately as coats on a bed at a party.

19 An artistic stereotype, not a social one; there seems never to have been a time when European couples tended to get married before their mid-twenties, even among the aristocracy.

20 Glen Tetley's *La Ronde* (1987) shows one of the problems here: the supposedly contrasted couples, though dressed differently and given different moods and steps, all look alike, because their dancing all shows their

youthful prowess and vigour, which it expresses so strongly that the subleties of characterization are obliterated. (This may have been what the choreographer intended, the homogeneity of virtuoso dancing standing for the obsessive nature of sexual passion that obliterates all social reality.) Here again, it seems to me that Bill T. Jones is exemplary, admitting into his company a variety of shapes and sizes that he exploits eloquently and imaginatively in ways that no other company (among those I have seen) seems even to envisage. But no doubt I am wrong about this – the best critics seem not to find this aspect of his work worthy of remark.

21 Here too Hanna's (1988) amassing of possibilities is invaluable, though her own politics highlight certain options and interpretations that not all readers will share.

CHAPTER 11   Modes of Dance Organization

1 Yvonne Rainer's dances of the 1960s, made up of task-like assignments, used energy-phrasing as the mode of movement organization (Copeland and Cohen 1983, 327; Rainer 1974). Theoretically, this method could be applied to a whole evening's dancing, if tasks and sub-tasks were combined in a complex endeavour. The method remained experimental, however, successful as generating endless talk (such as this) but little used by other choreographers.

2 The idea of a 'Last Judgment' perhaps shows less the wish for unarguable certainty in moral judgments than the wistful hope that our life might turn out to have had a single, determinate narrative shape.

3 Less literal uses of narrative are possible. Robert Desrosiers's surrealistic extravaganzas, for instance, strike me as pseudo-narratives of quasi-actions with metaphorical digressions, the whole being superimposed on a subtle and frenetic (and, I am told, very difficult) choreography, which gives the impression of varying little in tempo and substance but acts as a sort of carrier wave, so that one cannot forget for a moment that the whole shebang is being vigorously but (in a way) unobtrusively *danced*.

4 Similar language is used of Balanchine by Joseph H. Mazo: 'Whatever it was that Balanchine felt as he listened to *Symphony in Three Movements*, he translated into physical action for his dancers. It is not a conscious process, but a subconscious mutation of felt emotion into visualized emotion' (Mazo 1976, 87). The idea here seems to be that since musical structure is not dance structure, there must be some common currency in which equivalents of both can be found, and this must be 'feeling.' This 'feeling' is (as the context suggests, and as the venerable theory of aesthetic

'empathy' would have it) conceived kinaesthetically. The salient qualities of the music as heard give rise to certain felt movements in the body; the dance consists of visible movements that have the same kinaesthetic equivalent. But actually the 'feeling' serves no purpose, unless we insist on some unconscious process. Balanchine, as a gifted musician, might well respond to features rendered salient by intelligent observation, rather than by going with the flow, and might well devise choreography that he judged to be in some specific way congruent with (or a comment on) the features observed.

5 For the confusion, exemplied in the preceding note, see Sawyer 1985, 18–22. For the problematic idea of identifying and dancing out the feeling of a piece of music, see the remarks on Dalcroze in §8.2224.

6 Hofstadter 1985, passim, especially chapter 12. His reasons are largely ideological, part of a campaign to eliminate the idea of originality as creation *ex nihilo* and the associated 'mysticism,' but this quirk can be discounted.

7 The names of the parts (adagio, variations, coda) are borrowed from music, but it is not clear why.

8 Blasis (1828, part IV) has a long section on 'The Composition of Ballets' but is devoted entirely to traditional theories of dramatic form, concluding that 'the Ballet consists of as many varieties as other theatrical performances' (208), without any hint that being *danced* might make any difference.

9 This is what my experience suggests; but a friend from New York objects. Audiences vary, she says – and, of course, they do, even general audiences, because audiences are self-selected on various grounds, not all related to receptiveness to the entertainment predictably on offer. My friend's objection, however, refers to the reception of programs of abstract contemporary dance *in general*, not to the specific problem referred to in the text.

10 When the Beatles issued *Sergeant Pepper's Lonely Hearts Club Band* and proved the possibility of an internally structured pop song sequence, setting an example widely followed ever since, it remained possible and even quite usual to issue LPs (cassettes, CDs ...) that were merely collections of songs. No one thinks twice about it.

CHAPTER 12 Dance and Music

1 Translated as Appendix III of Franko 1993, 182–5.

2 See Sparshott 1988, §8.461. The dancing-master Guglielmo Ebreo of Pesaro (1993, 107) argued (in 1463) that dance should follow the musical con-

cordance of four voices, paralleled by the four elements and integral with the four virtues: 'without this harmony or consonance, the art of dancing would be nothing, nor would it be possible to do. Imagine trying to dance without instrumental music or any accompanying voices. What pleasure would there be, or what delight would it offer either the dancer or the listener? None whatever! Rather it would prove to be something unpleasant, foolish, and unnatural.' One has to bear in mind, of course, that there are high-minded artistic circles in which 'unpleasant, foolish, and unnatural' would be high praise.

3 Is drumming really music? If I hit a drum made as a drum, with a drum-stick made for the purpose, or with a hand technique that demands train-ing, surely it is. But what if I only hit an empty can with a stick? If I use a musically interesting rhythm, of course it is – if it is 'musically' interest-ing, *whatever* that means, what I am doing is music. (Less interestingly, it is so if I do it in a regular musical performance; a *Kitchen Symphony* by Richard Strauss might well have had a part for a chime of empty cans.) But what if I merely hit the can in a simple repetitive tempo? Again, if I do so in an ensemble or a performance already recognized as music, it is. But if I do so as part of a practical task (beating my cans into plough-shares), or if I am simply battering away at a bit of vulnerable metal, presumably it is not. If I do so for a dancer to keep time to, or to dance to, I am providing 'the music' for the dance; does it follow that what I do is music? The information I have given is not sufficient to determine an answer. Whether what I am doing is properly to be called music depends on exactly what I am doing on the given occasion, and also on the precise context in which the question 'Is that music?' (or 'Would you call that music?') has arisen.

4 The notorious poverty of the run-of-the-mill ballet music in nineteenth-century Russia is partly accounted for by the composers' (such as Minkus, Drigo, and Pugni) deliberately scanting those aspects of their music which the choreographers could not directly use (cf. Sawyer 1985, 196–7 and passim).

5 Soupault 1928, 24. One is reminded of Descartes's insistence that body and soul must be separate substances. Descartes, however, recognized and emphasized that soul and body function as an inseparable unity. Soupault does not interrupt his brilliant silliness long enough to ask whether the same might not hold for dance and music.

6 Twyla Tharp (1992, 99) says that a reason for dancing without music is that 'music communicates emotion and structure more easily to most people than movement, and it was movement we wanted to explore.'

Other choreographers might respond that what they wanted to explore was movement-with-music.

7 Adolphe Appia, *L'Oeuvre d'art vivant* (Edition Atar), quoted in Jaques-Dalcroze 1930, 120.

8 See Stodelle 1978 for this view of Nietzsche. It is possible that Duncan was thinking of *Thus Spake Zarathustra*, however.

9 This was big of him, because he had been compelled to insert an unwanted ballet into the second act of *Tannhäuser* to get it performed in Paris. The *Gesamtkunstwerk* is discussed in Sparshott 1988, §1.341.

10 To make dance one of the sisters was already a tendentious move; attempts to join dance to the established pair, poetry and painting, were regularly made and as regularly resisted and ignored (cf. Sparshott 1988, 24–6 and elsewhere). But Wagner's threesome was not based on that pair: these three sisters are all arts with a temporally extended, sequential structure. Painting in this context would be relegated to the status of scenery. The reason for this is that Wagner's universal artwork should bring a community together in a great secular ritual, such as the theatre at Bayreuth might embody. Architecture, sculpture, and painting can contribute to the setting of such a ceremony but cannot form part of the *dromenon*, what is actually going on.

   Menestrier (1682, 1), by the way, says that dance is not one of the three sister arts, but their elder brother – the Branwell Brontë of the arts?

11 Wagner fails to observe that metre is a late and sophisticated device, superimposing on the rhythm of the voice a specifically musical order. But, if he had observed it, it is unlikely that it would have changed his mind. He would regard the relationships he unveiled as unaffected by accidents of historical sequence and could derive strict tempi in music from the necessity of accompanying verse. We may recall that Aristoxenus's treatise on rhythm, though based on abstract and universal principles, equates practical rhythm with metrical prosody (cf. §9.21 above).

12 This contention, most familiar from Hanslick, had been common ground for up-to-date musicians since the middle of the eighteenth century. Adam Smith too had pointed to the symbolic poverty of music: 'In the power of expressing a meaning with clearness and distinctness, Dancing is superior to Music, and Poetry to Dancing' (Smith 1795, 236).

13 The choral finale of Beethoven's Ninth Symphony was widely held to announce the artistic bankruptcy of absolute instrumental music in general and sonata form in particular. As Wagner saw it, the earlier symphonists had tried to rescue the beauty of absolute music from its

inherent insignificance by shaping it into the forms of ethnic dance but had only partly succeeded. This finale of the Ninth impatiently rejects these half-measures – *Nicht diese Töne* – in favour of a hymn that turns into a military march. And everyone knew that Schiller's 'Joy,' extolled in the hymn, really meant Freedom: it is the latter word, *Freiheit*, that fits Beethoven's spondaic accentuation.

14 'Since dance is bound to music, its movements have to proceed at a certain pace and maintain a certain flow. One may slow them down, perform a piece in slow motion, as it were; but that would have the same effect as slowing down the rate of normal speech. It would break the rules of the medium' (Royce 1984, 68–9). The medium, we note, is that of music, not that of dance per se. It is not clear what the rules are, or what their authority is; the analogy suggests that they may be conventions of social acceptability rather than intelligibility, and in any case the place of 'rules' in art is notoriously equivocal.

15 Compare L.B. Alberti: 'We follow the practice of a musician who teaches a young person to dance: he begins by following with his sound the movement of the student, and so, by playing less irregularly from step to step, he teaches the beginner to be less irregular' [Cosi adunque a noi; e in questo così esserticarci faremo come fa el musico che insegna ballare alla giuventù: prima sussequita col suono el moto di che impara, e così di salto in salto meno errando insegno a quello imperito meno errare] – L.B. Alberti, 'Profugiorum ab Aerumna,' in Alberti 1966, 130 (quoted from Jarzombek 1989, 232; my translation).

16 Duncan 1928, 95. Rather similarly, Henry Prunières argued that ballet, shorn of the literary underpinnings with which the composers of court ballets had often provided it, could only become opera or degenerate into mere spectacle (Prunières 1914, 246–7).

17 'In music I experience an animate motion which is neither my own nor someone else's and which I perceive directly, rather than through the intermediary of a body whose motion it would be – pure self-motion, bound to no body, no 'self.' The act of perceiving this motion must itself be a motion. ... Hearing tones, I move with them; I experience their motion as my own motion' (Zuckerkandl 1973, 157, quoted in Sawyer 1985, 17).

18 Compare what I wrote in the Introduction about self-transformation in music and dance, summarizing one of the themes of Sparshott 1988.

19 Rudolf Nureyev, interviewed in *Le Monde*; *Manchester Guardian Weekly*, 30 June 1985, 12. Doris Humphrey (1962, 132) says of 'mood music' generally that '[n]one of this is intended to be danced "to" but only "on." '

20 Doris Humphrey (1962, 132) says that dance 'is not an independent art; it is truly female, needing a sympathetic mate, but not a master, in music.' Perhaps the enriched understanding of matrimonial politics that we owe to feminist thought may deepen our understanding of the relationships between dances and their musics. Meanwhile, Projesh Banerjee (1983, 157) holds that 'Music is the mother, dance its child and offspring. Dance sucks the milk oozing out from music's bosom.'

21 Someone like Ludwig Minkus, employed at a miserable wage as staff composer for the St Petersburg ballet between 1871 and 1886, was hardly an autonomous source of artistic authority.

22 Richard Feynman (1986, 53) argues accordingly that showing how the theory of one practice can be applied to another practice is always a waste of time. But what makes it always possible to find such analogies, if it is? Are all such analogies and disanalogies equally plausible, equally fruitful, equally interesting? Can anyone always find such analogies, or does one need to be a very clever fellow? Feynman's argument should be received with caution: he was so extremely smart that he was often quite stupid about the ways the minds of duller people worked.

23 'This power of music to integrate and cure, to liberate the Parkinsonian and give him freedom while it lasts ... is quite fundamental, and seen in every patient' (Sacks 1987, 294). I am obliged to Andy Silber for drawing my attention to this material.

24 'Rhythmic impetus has to be present, but has to be 'embedded' in melody. ... Would any music, then, provided it was firm and shapely, serve to get Frances D. going in the right way? By no means. The only music which affected her in the right way was music she could *enjoy*; only music which moved her 'soul' had this power to move her body. *She was only moved by music which moved her.* The 'movement' was simultaneously emotional and motoric, and essentially autonomous ... ' (Sacks 1987, 295–6). Some allowance must be made for the possibility that Sacks's choice of words reflects his own ideas about music as well as his clinical findings.

25 Deborah Jowitt writes: 'I don't think it would have occurred to Duncan to consider a symphony in terms of tonal variety or harmonic richness and thus hesitate to tackle it: she thought she heard Beethoven speaking and wished to respond' (Jowitt 1988, 74). I am sure that's right, provided one does not take 'speaking' as having anything to do with words.

The statement in the text that it 'came out good' reflects the impression made by Duncan on the artistic world of her time. Elizabeth Sawyer, in the course of an incisive attack on what she calls 'this subjective orgy of personal response,' claims that 'judging from most accounts' Duncan's practice was a warning against her methods (Sawyer 1985, 21); but the accounts in question are probably written from the exclusive standpoint of nineteenth-century ballet technique at its most hidebound – or, even worse, from that of the St Petersburg balletomanes whose exploitative and pornographic 'connoisseurship' is displayed in the documents collected by Peter John Wiley (1990). Fredrika Blair (1986, 184–90) considers at length the objections to Duncan's use of great music. Her justification was that dance must express great emotions, and that meant using great music or none. Blair considers three objections: that the composers did not intend their music to be used in that way, that the dancing distracts the listeners from the music, and that dancing to the music implies that the music is not complete in itself. The first objection she dismisses, rightly, as irrelevant; to the second, she opposes Duncan's claim that the dance should make you listen more closely to the music (to which one may add that audience members are free to attend performances of the music without dance accompaniment); and to the third, she retorts that, on the contrary, the music and the dance should 'make the same statement in their separate ways.' And that, of course, is the nub of the matter: it is assumed that a musical piece is a *statement about* emotions, not a piece of music at all.

26 The same notion – that all animal movement is unnatural – is implicit in Galileo; see Sparshott 1987b. Perhaps it is meant as a joke; or perhaps it is a hangover from a creationist mythology in which life (especially human life) comes from a miraculous intervention in an inherently lifeless world.

27 But see Sawyer 1985, chapter 6, which explains how far notational indications are from determining a metre, let alone a rhythm.

28 In saying that, one would be ignoring Aristoxenus's recognition that linguistic rhythms constitute one of the three main classes of rhythm, though not in real time. But one might prefer to ignore that.

29 In the Toronto Dance Theatre's *Legends* (1971), if memory serves, part of the musical accompaniment takes the form of recorded birdsong. My feeling was that, though music always is or is not in time with a dance it accompanies, the birdsong was neither in time nor out of time *nor independent* of the dance (as it might be in a piece by Merce Cunningham), but in a different auditory space altogether. That is what it would be for the implication of rhythm to be lost.

30 The 'composition by field' advocated by Charles Olson was essentially a repudiation of the of the very idea of metricality, which was to be

replaced by an audible ordering based on the interrelations of all aspects of the words in a poem, within units determined by the breath.

31 It is also untrue of tonal sounds as actually produced and heard, which cannot be divorced from their means of production, from their proximity to the top or bottom of the range of the voice or instrument that produces them, or from their proximity to the upper or lower limits of human hearing.

32 Gregory Scott presented a paper on this concept, under the name of 'chorody,' to the Canadian Society for Aesthetics a few years ago.

33 The word got into the musical vocabulary by way of the 'fitting together' of a lyre with its strings, hence the tuning of the strings.

34 See, however, Sawyer 1985, 155–6, on the propriety of using national music to accompany national dances.

35 We must remind ourselves that such exclusions and privileges as we are considering here cannot be preemptive, because the social institution of dancing at dances is decisive. We turn back the rug, turn lights down or up, and put on a tape, and *whatever* we do then is dancing, provided that it is in *some* way distinctive. The proviso is necessary because it has to be possible for someone at a party or a hop not to be dancing – it must be *clear* that such a person is not dancing. And, if that is clear, I think it must also be clear that someone could be seen to be trying to dance, or to be dancing but not dancing properly.

CHAPTER 13 Dance and Language

1 The Villaris, for example, invite us to think of 'isolations' (that is, particular movements of specific parts of the body) as letters of the alphabet, and continue: 'Trying thinking of the steps as nouns, and the turns and breaks as verbs. Once you have mastered them, so that you understand the use and expression of each, you can form dance sentences by combining steps, turns and breaks to make your own statement. Finally ... you can move on to whole paragraphs, or the disco dances themselves' (Villari and Villari 1978, 41–2). The authors' faith that people wanting to learn disco will have a firm grasp of grammatical notions is rather touching.

2 What it suggests, not necessarily what it says. Who knows what constitutes a closed system, or agreement, or communication, or categories, in the minds of these authors? The word 'simply' is hardly appropriate here.

3 Interviewed in 'Live from Lincoln Center,' in an intermission during MacMillan's *Romeo and Juliet*, PBS, 7 May 1988.

4 Compare Cham's caricature of Théophile Gautier demonstrating to Amalia Ferraris the steps for his new ballet *Sacountala*: the frock-coated poet soars like a blimp, while Ferraris looks worried (Gautier 1986, plate 72).

5 Graham McFee (1992) argues as follows. To understand anything is to grasp its meaning. The meaning of anything is nothing other than the content of an explanation of its meaning. Explanations are verbal constructs. In the arts, the provision of such constructs is the work of critics. Therefore, understanding dance is entirely a matter of understanding what critics say.

6 American Sign Language, as I understand it, lies between the two extremes, but closer to the former. The syntax is not that of the written or spoken language, but it is often called on to provide strict translations for specific verbal utterances in a specific language. But I confess to ignorance here.

7 I am relying here on a lecture-demonstration by Rajika Puri at the 'Dance in India' conference at the University of Toronto, April 1985. See La Meri 1964.

8 Compare what is said of programme music in Kivy 1984, especially chapters 9 and 10.

9 See what was said of 'educational dance' in §8.223. A psychoanalyst of my acquaintance, learning of my project in this book, simply took it for granted that a newborn child's undirected movement of its limbs was the very paradigm of dance. No one but a psychoanalyst would think that. But I suppose the argument would be that these movements represent the primary process of dance, on which what adults know as dancing is superimposed as part of 'civilization and its discontents.' What is sublimated retains a certain priority over its sublimation.

10 Avant-garde goings-on cannot always be used as counter-examples to generalizations about dance: if Clayton Clevarass puts on a 'dance' the whole point of which is that it runs counter to everything people accept as and expect from dance, it is foolish for an aesthetician to use it as an example of what it is meant to contrast with. But it is an important truth that, in general, such performances are possible and are accepted as legitimate and that some of them do severally or collectively change the expectations and acceptances that they challenged. See §3.76.

11 Cf. Sparshott 1988, 284–5, commenting on Kaeppler 1972. In Kaeppler's usage, kinemes are the minimal movement units as defined by the variables recognized in a dance tradition; a morphokineme is 'the smallest unit that has meaning in the structure of the movement system' (185) –

that is, it is recognized as a unit by the dancers and may be named by them; a motif is a structurally significant movement, such as 'conventionalized ways of beginning, ending, and dividing sections' (202); and genres are kinds of dance (classified in Tonga by occasions for performance, p. 214).

12 The 'newspeak' imagined by George Orwell for his *1984* would never have worked. A language with a free negative allows for speakers to deny whatever they can affirm, and vice versa, and Orwell's linguistic engineers, who were working on the basis of a language like English, did nothing about that. I suppose Orwell didn't think of that, and people who compare dance to language don't often think of that sort of thing, but it is just the sort of thing you have to think of.

13 The Brussels avant-garde dance company Ultima Vez, presenting *Her Body Doesn't Fit Her Soul* in a Canadian city in 1993, frequently addressed the audience. Occasional passages in French and English were embedded in a lot of what was probably Flemish – but also a great deal (from the dancer Saïd Gharby) of what may or may not have been Arabic, and a lot of what may well have been gibberish. It was suitable to the company's style that they moved easily from one to the other, from certainty to conjecture.

14 They are not identical in *every* way, of course. Each has its own advantages: the written text is unambiguously spelled out and available for reference, the spoken version conveys emphases. In a sense, the spoken version is prior, because speech came before writing in history and precedes it in individual development; but, as Derrida has taught us, writing can develop only because language was *writable* from the beginning. See also chapter 18 note 15.

15 Although Kaeppler's are constantly referred to, her system seems neither to have been developed by others nor to have been widely used.

16 Megill 1985, 205–7, comparing the views of Philip Pettit with those of François Wahl (1968, 10).

17 Benesh 1978, 264–5, quoted in Guest 1984, 103. When Benesh says the laws are not 'logical in the ordinary sense,' it should be borne in mind that he is not himself a logician, so that one cannot be certain what he is excluding.

18 Guest 1984, 103–4. A footnote explains that the alleged change in the meaning of the phrase 'Language of Dance' came about because it was registered in the United States as a service mark, rather than through any recognition of the 'deep understanding' embodied in Labanotation.

19 Some possibilities are enumerated in Sparshott 1988, and I have no wish to add to their number here.

20 The same considerations are powerfully articulated throughout Merleau-Ponty's *Phenomenology of Perception* (1962), from a psychological and phenomenological point of view.
21 Foster (1986, 59) distinguishes five categories of convention in contemporary theatre dance: frame, mode of representation, style, vocabulary, syntax. 'In the interplay among these conventions, a complex system of resonances establishes the symbolic field of the dance.' Foster's analysis is weakened by failure to dwell on the concept of a convention itself and bedevilled by a tendency to take for granted that pre-existing linguistic categories are adequate for her purposes, but it is a major contribution to its subject.

CHAPTER 14   Dance and Theatre

1 The concept of performance, in a more general sense, is developed in Sparshott 1982c, especially 38–43. Richard Schechner (1988, 72) distinguishes among 'drama,' a written text; 'script,' which is 'all that can be transmitted from time to time and place to place, the basic code of the event,' which must be carried by people who know it and can teach it; 'theatre,' the enacted event, what the performers do; and 'performance,' everything that goes on from the arrival of the first spectator to the departure of the last spectator. I find the terminology awkward, but the analysis is useful, though I will not in fact be using it.
2 Thom 1993a. For my immediate response to this important and exciting book, see my short review in the *Journal of Art and Art Criticism* (Sparshott 1994c).
3 The distinction between representational and presentational theatre is well treated, with continual reference to dance, by Faubion Bowers (1960).
4 I remarked above (chapter 13 note 13) on the flexible way the Belgian company Ultima Vez uses speech and the appearance of speech. Equally remarkable is the thoroughgoing fusion of dance and drama achieved by Karen Pearlman and Richard Allen (THAT WAS FAST Productions), in their *Blue Cities* (1993). With astonishing control of breath and voice, they contrive to combine dramatic interchange of speech with vigorously expressive dance. The overall effect is unique in my experience; but the drama is danced, rather than the dance dramatized.
5 Langer 1953. For some general remarks on dance and drama in general, cf. Sparshott 1988, 327–30.
6 Aristotle, *Poetics*. That Aristotle's text is incompatible with the idea that tragedy is in itself a written rather than an enacted form is vigorously (and, I think, irrefutably) argued by Gregory Scott (1992).

7 The necessity of insisting that performers imagine their characters, rather than somehow transforming themselves into them, is pointed out by Paul Thom (1993b) in a critique of Diderot.

8 In the practice of the avant-garde, this may be true only institutionally, contextually, ontologically, and semantically; in traditional practice, the resemblance extends to observable characteristics as well.

9 The fame of the Ballets Russes makes people forget that Diaghilev's missionary zeal was originally directed more to opera than to ballet. Bournonvile found it hard to clear a space for ballet amid his management's insistent demand for opera. And an article from *Der Tanzlehrer* in 1892 plainly treats ballet as competing with opera for funds and space and complains that '[t]he ballet is welcome as an extra, but its right to independent existence nobody will recognize' (Crompton 1984, 163).

10 This is partly a matter of stage convention. In a presentation delimited by participation, a dancer can fall out of the dance simply by assuming a casual posture and demeanour noticeably unlike the sort of presence maintained by non-dancing participants; a singer can cease to be part of the performance by a similarly nonchalant withdrawal of presence, quite different from the silent maintenance of a position in the action. But the sounds of unpitched speech differ from any sort of singing in a more radical way than any sort of body movement differs from dance; and singers can achieve inaudibility more readily than dancers can achieve invisibility.

11 Similarly, the word 'landscape' was used of a kind of painting before it was used of the kind of subject matter that figured in such paintings. It seems that we don't have a word or a convenient phrase for the environment as visible object, apart from these words derived from artistic practice. Perhaps this is because an environment, as such, cannot be an object.

12 For the point that questions of identity are not primarily ontological, see §19.42.

13 The relevant sense of the word 'design' as used here is explained in Sparshott 1982c, 154–6.

14 It is of no consequence to my argument just what the specifics of the design are. What concerns us here is only that there really is or could be a ceremonial dance, of the general sort that people describe, that is tied to the actual buildings and places of a named location. But here goes. An impressionistic eyewitness account from 1897 mentions a fair, streets hung with 'green boughs and garlands and strings of flags,' a circus tent by the river, and a pageant of the kings and queens of England; then, starting at 1 p.m., a procession led by a volunteer band playing 'that

quaint old hornpipe tune,' parties of dancers starting down the steps of the corn market, who 'dutifully twirl each other round' to a 'clumsy dancing step,' the procession consisting mostly of a few embarrassed-looking 'ladies and gentlemen gaily arrayed'; and the whole procession marches in through the back doors of stores and houses and leaves by the front, changing partners (apparently) after each one (Norway 1897, 284–7). The only skilful and unselfconscious dancers are a party of naval ratings from HMS *Ganges*, who 'follow on behind dancing together, two and two, wholly in their element.' This answers fairly well to A.J.H. Jenkin's description of the refurbished version introduced in 1930: 'In through the front doors of the houses the dancers pass, pealing every bell and rapping every knocker as they go, and so out through the back. Sometimes they dance around a garden or through a room. Shop doors are left open for their progress, and in some places the party files in at one entrance, dances through a department, and out by another; descending in one place even into a cellar' (Jenkin 1945, 450–6). Jenkin details the figures of the dance, citing J.D. Hosken, *Helston Furry Day*; but the eleventh edition of the *Encyclopedia Britannica* says that the dance itself was modern (c. 1910). Since the dance procession had always been called 'the Hal-an-tow' it was presumably done with a heel-and-toe tripping step – which may help to explain why the sailors were so at home in it.

The festival had a chequered history. The *West Briton* newspaper for 12 May 1865 complained that 'a most disreputable practice, which has died out for some years, known by the name of the "Hal-an-tow," was revived on Monday, but the inhabitants were so disgusted with the doings, that it is not likely again to be allowed,' because 'the most hideous noises were made' by 'half a dozen men and boys' from three to six in the morning and resumed at nine, carriages being stopped as they entered the town and held up until money was given (Barton 1972, 129). Thirty years earlier still, Davies Gilbert writes of it as a festival of misrule, in which young people went out into the country and entered certain houses where they 'appeared to seize what they wanted' and returned to the town in triumph, 'dancing and decorated with flowers' (Gilbert 1838, 165). He derives 'Furry' from 'foray,' meaning a raid; Jenkin derives it from the Middle English 'ferier,' a fair; but everyone agrees that the equation with 'floral' is a fanciful invention of sentimental eighteenth-century classicists. Jenkin thinks the festival was intended to bring in 'the summer and the may, O'; but Douglas Kennedy (1949, 85) holds the depressing view that it was a spring-cleaning festival, since the dancers at one time 'carried sprigs of may blossom or green broom, and used these to brush different objects in the rooms through which they passed.' It seems to have been a very variable feast, its most constant features being the dancing into and out of houses, and Aunt Mary Moses on her donkey.

15 I don't know how well this works. *Festi Italiani* never reached New York, but I never heard whether that was because audiences were too small or because costs were too high.

16 Benjamin 1969. This article seems to me to say something other that what everyone says it says; it is at least deeply ambivalent. But the approximation in the text will suffice.

17 I was wrong: the building I was in was not the building Bournonville worked in. He lived to see the new opera house, and hated it. I do not know how much of the original choreography, settings, and costuming the Danes have preserved, but it looked 'authentic' to me. I am happy to be the sort of person for whom tourist-traps are made.

18 There is a terminological problem here. The word 'scenery' is traditionally appropriated to the physical embodiment – what the actor chews. 'Scene' is too general and too vague. I shall use 'mise-en-scène' or 'set' for the type of which the physical scenery is the token.

19 Not a good idea, says Théophile Gautier (1986, 55), even if the machinery does not jam: 'We find nothing graceful in the sight of five or six unfortunate girls dying of fright, hooked up high in the air on iron wires that can so easily snap. Those poor creatures thrash their arms and legs about with the desperation of frogs out of water, involuntarily reminding one of those stuffed crocodiles hanging from ceilings.'

20 In Constantin Patsalas's *Nataraja*, as done by the National Ballet of Canada, most of the stage is filled with an enormous statue in two pieces that rotate independently, while the costumes by Sunny Choi consist mostly of elaborate swirls of body paint. A member of the audience was heard to wish that the scenery was as well painted as the dancers, and that the dancers moved as well as the scenery.

21 The unifying imagination need not be that of the choreographing individuals; see Sparshott 1982c on the 'design act.'

22 Consider, for instance, the costume designs of Léon Bakst (see Schouvaloff 1991).

23 Compare Flo Ziegfeld's 'showgirls,' still to be seen at Las Vegas, whose talent was to look spectacular in extravagant concoctions of feathers and jewellery. A showgirl was not exactly a dancer, but she was not exactly not. What made her not a dancer was the presence, in the same context of exhibition, of dancers who danced. For Hegel, see Sparshott 1988, 37–8 and 83–4.

24 For the concept of the nerve of a practice, see Sparshott 1988, 128–30.

25 Parodists get an easy laugh by letting a few feathers fall. (The feathers become a snowstorm in Kudelka's *Making Ballet*, 1993.) One might ask oneself why the effect is not pathetic.

26 Guglielmo Ebreo (1993, 233), writing in the fifteenth century, distinguishes three types of dances: short dancing, long dancing, and cape dancing. In long dancing, 'all his gestures and movements should be grave and as refined as his attitude requires,' because the long robe *non savia agire movendo troppo in qua & in la.* In short clothing, one can make leaps, turns, and flourishes *con misura & con tempo*; grave movements are unsuitable, and show that the dancer does not know what he is doing. With a short cape, 'the cape catches the wind, so that as you do a jump or a turn, the cape swings about. And with certain gestures and movements, and with certain rhythms, you need to hold your cape by an edge, and with other rhythms you have to hold both edges, which is a lordly thing to see when done in time.'

27 Loie Fuller's dance was not so much a borderline case as a deeply ambiguous one. According to the article on Fuller in Chujoy and Manchester's (1967) *Dance Encyclopedia*, she was not really a trained dancer, and developed her scarf-dances from experiments with manipulating the cloth and the lights, not from developing and enhancing dance movements. Although she used the word 'dance' for what she did, her creations might equally well have been thought of as moving sculpture. Chujoy and Manchester call her a 'performer' and not a dancer, and that seems fair enough (cf. Sparshott 1988, 358). The poet Robert Finch, who saw her at the end of her career, tells me that what he saw seemed to have nothing to do with dancing. But we have to remember that swirling draperies were a feature of the theatre dance of her day, and that such contemporaries as Isadora Duncan thought of her as a dancer without any apparent misgivings. And in the films I have seen, what one sees is a dance.

28 Paul Souriau points out the importance of such optical effects (1889, last chapter), though he does not think them relevant to the higher reaches of art and beauty.

Telecasts of dance have made us vividly aware of the after-image effect, because the brightly lit dancers burn their image into the TV camera. I am not aware that choreographers or video artists have made much use of this resource, though they may have. If they have not, it may be because the effect is too hard to control, or because it is bad for the equipment. It could, of course, be because the resource is trivial and basically uninteresting; but that sort of thing doesn't usually stop people.

29 In the choreography devised by Graeme Murphy for the Australian Opera's 1993 production of Strauss's *Salome*, the seven veils were danced by seven grey cloudy figures, entwining a passive Salome with seductive revelations and concealments. I thought this a splendid idea, bringing out wonderfully the inner meaning of the dance; others thought otherwise.

30 This is probably more true of female strippers than of male strippers, for whose dance there is no established performance tradition and for whom there is no set pattern of normal career choice. The only male stripper I have seen was just taking off his clothes and showing himself to the patrons of a bar, and clearly had no idea of how to go about it. The only one I have talked to was on a bus, on the way to his first job, and simply following up the recommendation of a friend. He was quite unaware of any methods or skills that might be involved.

31 Roland Barthes (1972, 84) says that 'Striptease – at least Parisian style – is based on a contradiction: woman is desexualized at the very moment when she is stripped naked.' I suppose his point is that the show ends at that moment. What strikes the reader is rather that the performer is described as impersonal (woman, not a woman) and passive, stripped rather than stripping. I think the desexualization he speaks of is what I am referring to as the social mutilation that results from the lack of any distinctive clothing.

32 Some of these thoughts are pursued further in Sparshott 1995.

33 Similarly, a change from one costume to another involves a change of role; both roles can be expressed in dance, so can the contrast between them, so too can the transition from one to the other.

34 'As powerful as the effect of the clothes on your body is the effect of your appearance on your imagination. The moment you see yourself, your brain starts to work differently. In this way costume acts exactly like a mask. The costume, as it were, travels inwards. You start to form the bodily shapes of the man who looks like *that*' (Callow 1984, 155).

35 The Monkey King, in the Peking Opera presentations of his saga, is the sort of character who might try on the mask or paraphernalia of a defeated or absent opponent. But the Peking Opera is not pure dance; it is a 'mixed' genre of danced and sung drama and acrobatics. I do not know that the Monkey King does this, but it is within the scope of his established character to do so, unless there is a compelling reason for him not to. There might be such a reason. It could violate some deep religious or cosmological sense for such a divine/demonic being to be disguised, or it could equally violate some deep dramatic feeling for a disguise to be symbolized by a disguise.

36 In Kathakali it takes many hours for the actors to put on their costumes

and make-up. The fact that it should take so long seems to be a large part of the reason for it – Kathakali seems to do things the hard way, on principle. Dressing up could not be part of the dance, because it is fixed as a major part of the pre-dance. See de Zoete 1953.

CHAPTER 15 Dance Values

1 Graham McFee (1992; cf., above, chap. 13 note 5) advances an argument that could be pushed in this direction. A work of art is not such until it is accepted as such by the 'Republic' of art; the meaning of a dance is what it is explained to mean, and such arguments are preeminently the work of critics. One may infer that a critic's use of a specialized dance terminology establishes that the work's meaning is a dance meaning and thus issues a passport to the dance province of the Republic of art.

2 This way of thinking is not confined to monotheists, though it works best for them; it was originally developed by the pagan philosophers Plato and Aristotle, who thought of the world as a single, stable, intelligible reality without a creator.

3 Other philosophers argue the opposite, that works of art are not what they are, being intensional objects that exist equivocally as variously perceived and understood. One can say, for instance, that a work of art is an artefact subject to an interpretation, the interpretation being negotiated between artist and critics in a historical situation.

4 In a class on the dance of Rotuma, an island of Polynesian culture but politically part of Fiji, the lecturer, Vilsoni Hereniko, himself a Rotuman, told us that dance was a way people communicated their identity to each other: 'This is what we are like as an ethnic group.' But the tape he showed us was of a group participating in a dance competition in Suva, the Fijian capital.

5 Cousin 1853. This triad answers to Kant's three critiques, of pure reason, of practical reason, and of judgment, specifying the dominant value of each. But it goes back beyond that to the scholastic systems referred to in §15.2: whatever is perfect is *truly* what it should be, fulfils its functions in a useful and *good* way, and evokes admiration by its *beauty*.

6 I give more details in Sparshot 1994d – see the index under 'values.'

7 The actual terms that play key roles in our evaluations need not fit easily into our categories. Words like 'dumpy,' 'glorious,' and 'grotesque' have variable and complex implications. The value implied by the word 'interesting,' which I will soon be making much use of, probably belongs in the category of the beautiful; but this is by no means clear.

  Similarly, in the sad case of Dr Zorn (referred to on 311, above), nothing depends on terminology. Such words as 'well,' 'properly,' 'appropriately,' and 'right' are to a large extent interchangeable in a given context. They do not suffice to establish a particular distinction; rather, it is the distinction being made that establishes what the words are being used to mean. It makes perfectly good sense to say that it is wrong not to do something wrong, that it is appropriate to act unsuitably, and so on. A word like 'inappropriate' (or even 'wrong') carries an implicit reference to a context and conveys more subtly an attitude toward the legitimacy and cogency of that context, in ways that resist codification but admit of extended discussion (which they are not going to get here).

8 Compare the discussion of primary and secondary standards in §15.212.

9 There is a splendid illustration of this theme in W.P. Kinsella's story 'Feet of Clay' (1993).

10 The difficulties here are evident to anyone who considers the judging at international figure-skating championships. Technical and artistic features are assigned separate marks. In the former, points are supposed to be deducted for specific flaws and failures; but it seems obvious that this is not always what the judges do.

11 R.G. Collingwood (1938) notoriously contrasted art (the unified expression of a state of mind) with craft (the expert realization of a plan, even if the plan was devoted to the production of something beautiful or powerfully moving). He conceded that in fact all works of art involved craft; what he did not allow was that the relation between art and craft in these senses was itself a major object of artistic interest. Similarly, Graham McFee argues that a dance conceived as a work of art cannot also be conceived as some other kind of performance, such as a magical rite. He says nothing about any interest that may attach to the way these two functions may be interrelated.

12 In the present context, a good way of seeing the difficulty about treating dance as a fine art is to consider how ill-suited the traditional aesthetic concepts of 'disinterestedness' and 'disinterested contemplation' are to the embodiedness and person-involvement of dance.

13 The formula used here is introduced and elaborately explained in Sparshott 1982c, chap. 6.

14 The breakdown of this dialectic, in which artists and public encourage each other in the development of new possibilities of creation and appreciation, may lead to the sort of separation between primary and secondary standards I mentioned above.

15 Another problem with the three-dimensional analysis has to do with qualities and textures: are these aspects of a work's presence, or of its

structure, or both? Or does the impossibility of answering this question show that no three-dimensional analysis is workable?

16 §14.32 above. I shall refer to this as 'Aschenbrenner's principle,' because it was Karl Aschenbrenner (1974) who gave it a central place in critical theory; but Arthur Danto (1964 and 1981) had already emphasized that the introduction of any new quality that some artwork relevantly possesses has the logical effect that all artworks, old as well as new, are hereafter to be characterized either as possessing or as not possessing that quality (cf. §2 and §13.5 above).

17 The centrality of balance is a theme of Doris Humphrey. But Edwin Denby's magnificent assay 'Forms in Motion and Thought' begins as follows: 'In dancing one keeps taking a step and recovering one's balance. The risk is part of the rhythm. One steps out of and into balance; one keeps on doing it, and step by step the body moves about' (Denby 1986, 556).

18 Saxena (1991) makes it clear that this view of art depends on the existence of a kind of trained connoisseur, the *rasika*, whose taste enjoys unquestioned authority. The authority of the connoisseur is one of the things that Western civilization has jettisoned.

19 We may illustrate the point from Aristotelian ethics. One may hold that a person's moral worth depends partly on whether that person is generous with money. If so, the question whether someone is generous can never be ruled out a priori as irrelevant to a moral appraisal; but it does not follow that the question of generosity is always relevant, for the person may be without possessions or may live in a culture where the concept of private property has no application, or where the economic set-up depends on people never doing anything that could be described as generous. Cicero pointed out centuries later that Aristotle said nothing about a central Roman virtue, *frugi* – thriftiness, more or less. No one asked at the time whether any of the Greeks had this quality. The question would have made sense, though, had it been asked.

20 An interesting sidelight is thrown on the contrast between grace and athleticism by Agrippina Vaganova's comments on the style of Russian ballet, as she developed it. She effected a synthesis, she says, between the French style taught by Gerdt and by N. Legat, full of 'soft and graceful, but unnecessarily artificial and decorative, movement,' and the Italian style as taught by Cechetti, which cultivated aplomb and vigour but tended to be angular and harsh. The contrast here is not connected with sexual stereotypes but simply with two traditions, which happen to be nationally identified but are not explicitly linked with national, racial, or

generally cultural characteristics. And the actual contrast is not quite that drawn by Smith, but between a rigorous-appearing and discipline-emphasizing style and an appealing and affective one. The synthesis of, or compromise between, the two is, however, itself identified as a distinctively Russian style – again, one developed by Russian individuals (Pavlova, Karsavina) without its being claimed that anything ethnically and culturally distinctive of Russia is involved. The synthesis thus suggested to and aimed at by Vaganova has, however, a character that is not straightforwardly intermediate between the others; it possessed a 'poetic spirituality, a purely Russian "cantilena" of dance movements, a wealth of expressive plastic nuances' (Vaganova 1969, vi–viii). And one can see how such expressiveness might be achieved by giving a determinate content to the flowing style of the French, and a humane meaning to the rigours of the Italians, though it could not be thought of as a compromise between them.

21 Bayer 1933. Chapters 8 and 9 of volume 2 are devoted to dance; they are concerned almost exclusively with ballet, and include a charming disquisition on the various ways in which dancer's attitudes to their self-image as dancers may affect the grace of their movements.

22 Cf. Spencer 1891, 381. Paul Souriau (1889, part 3) similarly differentiates between actual efficiency and the expressive appearance of efficiency, the latter of which is the more significant aesthetically.

23 Compare Félibien's observation (1685, I 31) that beauty depends on the symmetry and proportion of physical parts, whereas grace is born from the uniformity of interior movements caused by the affections and sentiments of the soul.

24 Bayer 1933, II 361: 'Les structures de grâce, equilibres d'abstraction saisissante, se concretisent alors parmi la disparition des systèmes.' I seldom know how to translate Bayer, and I do not always know what he means. Nor have I succeeded in tracing his argument throughout his two volumes.

25 Hogarth 1753. The 'line of grace' is defined on 39: 'That sort of proportion'd, winding line, which will hereafter be call'd the precise, serpentine line, or *line of grace*, is represented by a fine wire, properly twisted round the elegant and varied figure of a cone.'

26 Hegel (1975, 124) put his finger on the spot. We do not find animal movements in general beautiful, just because we have no insight into the psychic mechanisms that motivate them. So, I would add, when we do find animal movements attractive it must be for some other reason. One might suggest that Bateson's examples are of animals so deeply domesticated

that their motivations mesh with the human world and are thus accessible to us; but I doubt if that is true in all and only relevant cases, and it does not help Bateson, because it suggests that what attracts is not the fact and quality of psychic integration but its accessibility.

27 Richard Schechner (1988, 180) maintains that animal movements remind us of dance because they are graceful – that is, unambiguous and simple; the integration is not psychic, as Bateson would have it, but semiotic. He cites Ray Birdwhistell as saying that 'the things we call graceful are always multi-message acts in which the secondary messages are minimized, and then the role of the whole is maximized' (Schaffner 1959, 101–2). In the same vein, Konrad Lorenz says that 'with the elimination of noise in the movement, when the movement becomes graceful, it becomes more unambiguous as a signal. ... [T]he more pregnant and simple the movement is, the easier it is for it to be taken up unambiguously by the receptor. Therefore, there is a strong selection pressure working in the direction of making all signal movements, then releasing movements, more and more graceful, and that is also what reminds us of a dance' (Schaffner 1959, 202–3).

28 If we follow the scholastic way of thinking, referred to above, in which everything is both good and beautiful to the extent that it is real, expressive grace may be thought of as the special form that beauty takes in dance. (Not all dances are graceful; but then, not all are beautiful.) It appears, according to the account we have been giving, as the supreme quality of human aliveness. Beauty, according to scholastic theory, requires three conditions: brightness (*claritas*), integratedness (*unitas*), and wholeness (*integritas*). What would be the corresponding three requirements to the expression of vitality in dance? The 'brightness' would be the sheer visibility of the vital movement: a dancer labours to make the body visible, to impart to it just that 'radiance of form' that Maritain glossed brightness as. (Thomas Aquinas, an earthier person, may have had no more in mind than that things look better when they are freshly painted.) The wholeness lies in that the body is alive in every part, nowhere inert; grace pervades the entire body. And the integratedness lies in that the vitality made visible is that of a single life, not a multiplicity of agitations.

29 Compare Jacques Rivière's (1913) remarks on Nijinsky's choreography for *Sacre du printemps*, in which much of the pathos derives from the body's recalcitrance. For some discussion, see Sparshott 1988, 344–8.

30 Kames 1788, 256. Compare Bayer's invocation of the concept of 'success' to explain artistic value: the concept of success requires that actions be interpreted as meaningfully contributing to an assigned end.

31 Kames 1788, 364. The term 'elegance' seems nowhere to be defined; he does not include it in his index.

32 Kames 1788, 353–5. Kames here comes close to his fellow Scot, Thomas Reid, who says that 'grace, as far as it is visible, consists of those motions, either of the whole body, or of a part or feature, which express the most perfect propriety of conduct and sentiment in an amiable character' (Reid 1785, 763).

33 This is not always the case. A recent comment on Michael Jackson's 'Smooth Criminal' says that 'we are treated to a virtuoso performance of fluid sensuous grace which is always under precise rhythmic control and which merges almost imperceptibly back and forth between everyday gestural interaction and dance structure,' and refers a little later to Jackson's 'feline controlled flow' (Fiske and Hartley 1993, 66). Note how close this comes to the very terms of Bayer's exposition, and observe the resumptive use of the word 'feline': 'grace' is, for once, the *mot juste*.

34 Actually, Cohen is being unfair. The point of Sibley's article was not really to effect a classification of terminology but to point to a level of discourse that required taste for its correct use. Some of the things we say about works of art seem merely to describe them but at the same time seem to give direct support for a favourable or unfavourable judgment. How can this be? Answer: they are descriptions, but such that their aptness can be seen only in the light of a developed aesthetic appreciation. The position is well explained and discussed by Betty Redfern (1983, chap. 6).

35 It seems at first odd that Bayer, saying that art is the trace of artistic success, should allow no place to sheer exuberance alongside the finesse of grace and the doggedness of the sublime. I suppose it is because exuberance carries no suggestion of difficulty overcome, hence no true success, no effort to leave its trace in the aesthetic object.

36 In Rotuma, we were told (cf. note 4 to this chapter, above), the quality most prized in dance is *maru*, which our instructor described as unself-conscious grace. It is easy to imagine that dance traditions everywhere must recognize and prize such a quality, as Bateson suggests. One would need deep knowledge of the culture to tell how closely the prized quality was tied to the specifics of the dance tradition in question. Is *maru* all that different from 'coolness'?

37 I expatiate on the formula about 'discourse apt to ground evaluation' in Sparshott 1967, where I anatomize the general concept of criticism in terms of Aristotle's 'four causes' and relate the concept of criticism to that of performance, a relation further explored with specific reference to art

criticism in Sparshott 1982c, chapter 6. In Sparshott 1981b, I explore the difficulty of distinguishing criticism from other talk about literature and art. In 1982a, I make some general remarks about the place assigned to criticism in the academic chatter of the day.

CHAPTER 16 Dancer and Spectator

1 Lukács 1963. I discuss the issue in Sparshott 1982c, chap. 13.
2 The priority of the kinaesthetic mode of awareness is actually doubtful. It is on the basis of kinaesthetic sensations that I know, in a sense, where my limbs are, but they do not make the posture of my body directly available to me; one is not kinaesthetically aware of one's dance as a dance, or of the movements and positions that make it the dance it is, in any immediate way. Nor does my proprioception inform me of the position and movement of my body in any public space. McFee (1992, 265–70) launches a vigorous polemic against the very notion of a kinaesthetic sense, on the ground that it would be a sense without either sense organ or distinct perception. I suppose the idea of such a sense rests on the presumption that, because dancers obviously cannot *see* what they are doing, they must somehow be able to *feel* what they are doing; these feelings must be specific enough to encode the visual data that constitute the dance for spectators. That may not be true. But the whole problem of the mechanics of perception and its integration into knowledge is full of perplexities. Merleau-Ponty (1962, especially chaps. 2 and 3) discourses elaborately on the inappropriateness of the language of perception to our experience of our bodies and to our ability to relate to the world we live in.
3 Strictly speaking, an omniscient God would be aware of the dancer's kinaesthetic sensations and would have no reason to isolate for attention that dancer's quasi-visual awareness of dance movement – unless that were being specially offered to God as a sacrifice or something, as, in the legends, it usually is. But thinking strictly about God seldom pays off; one attributes to one's deities just those tendencies and capacities one needs for the moment.
4 A similar situation confronts dance impresarios in India: ' ... there are gradations in the minds of people, Paamara, Pandita, and Gnani, (the layman, the educated, the enlightened). Hence the dancer must be careful in drawing up programmes for different kinds of audience. ... Generally an experienced dancer can gauge the audience by the organisation, occasion and environment. In my career, as a dancer I have always tried to present programmes to suit the predominant audience' (Dhananjayan 1984, 53).

5 Where I come from, the audience for ballet and the audience for contemporary dance of comparable artistic and professional pretensions have few members and few visible characteristics in common. Again, art lovers are never seen at the ballet and seldom at any sort of dance. But that says nothing special about dance. In the same city, the publics for specific arts and specific art forms are highly differentiated; chamber music, symphonic music, opera draw audiences that overlap very little with each other and with the publics for drama and the visual arts. (Ethnic differentiation is equally evident: a Belgian troupe brings the Belgians out in droves, a Japanese quartet attracts the Japanese, each stays home for the others.) Perhaps it is because no one has the time and few people have the money to go to everything in a big town. In a smaller centre, there may be a relatively large nucleus of people who go to almost all 'cultural events,' just because there are few enough for it to be possible. (It is a familiar and well-supported contention that where such separations occur they correspond to recognizable and explicable socio-economic classes; what has been less studied is the precise manner and extent to which the correspondence holds and fails.)

6 The late pianist Glenn Gould stopped giving concert performances because he was aware of these pressures as inescapable but as conflicting with the demands of the music. An intelligent and sensitive man, he did not deceive himself into thinking that even a dedicated musician could avoid responding to the presence of that mixed audience, not all of whom would be exclusively interested in the art of music. In the recording studio, one's real and postulated audience cares only for the quality of the music as music; what is absent is the direct social pressure of impure interests in the moment of performance itself. (Ironically, it seems as if Gould came to play for studio technicians and imagined his ideal audience as knob-twiddling owners of studio-type equipment.) I am not aware of any dancer who ever gave up dancing before an audience for artistic reasons.

Dr Eileen Or (in a seminar on dance aesthetics) illustrates this aspect of performer/audience relations by the following analogy. A Chinese person cooking for Canadians in a Canadian home will prepare chop suey as 'Chinese cooking,' because that is what they expect. Similarly, one adopts a version of one's 'ethnic' dance slanted towards what one takes the host country's stereotype of one's ethnicity to be: the cultural artefact is not only hermeneutically mediated, it is changed to conform to this stereotype of stereotypes.

7 Can dancers be spectators of each other? Of course, each must be aware

of what the others are doing and may be critical or appreciative of the quality of their performance; it is a nice point whether this can ever amount to spectatorship.

8 When I quoted this before (§3.6), I remarked that this was not true: it was a women's dance, and Pentheus is killed for joining it. There is no contradiction: a Greek god is quite capable of imposing lethal commands and compulsions. Whom the gods wish to destroy, they first drive mad.

9 For a different angle on the same phenomena, see Sparshott 1988, §4.531.

10 Post-modern dance sets out to reinstate the democracy of movement, uniting dancer and spectator in their common humanity. But it may be just for that reason that no significant body of spectators has accepted that practice as an art. M.J. Friedman grapples with this question in his underestimated monograph *Dancer and Spectator* (1976).

11 This seems to go against my acceptance of Thom's concept of 'beholding,' the proper spectatorial stance in which one playfully entertains extraneous associations. But it does not. Some associations add resonance, others intrude distractingly. Learning to manage one's responses is part of growing up.

12 The pitfalls of this approach and the attendant vocabulary have been pointed out by George Dickie and others and are discussed in an appendix on 'Aesthetic This and Aesthetic That' in Sparshott 1982c; but these need not concern us now.

13 These 'de-realizing' modes of awareness are treated as particular cases of imaginative experience in general, in all of which the straightforward assignment of the experience to the status of report on the real world is cancelled in some way or other. The ways are quite various: it is the variety itself, and the pervasiveness of forms of de-realizing cognition, that is the point of Sartre's treatment.

14 Another way of dressing it up is the distinction between 'earth' and 'world' in Heidegger (1960).

15 Compare what Marcia Siegel has to say about American dancers (1985, 236–7): 'The ordinary look of American dancers, the characteristic way they dance as themselves, not as made-up personages, is something we're used to. ... We notice a distinct contrast when a dancer from another tradition joins an American company. ... There is a suggestion of bygone aristocracy in the way Europeans dance, a pretext that the dancer's social status is more imposing than that of the audience who's watching him or her.' Of course, it could be only that the Americans dance as though their performance were a continuation of their college PE option.

CHAPTER 17   Learning to Dance

1 Aristotle says that learning to be good is acquiring a way of making choices, but that this is not true of techniques because we do not (for example) have to *deliberate* about how to spell a word. Is he right? Not in the case of such complex and open-ended arts as those of dance and the other fine arts. The kind of learning discussed in the text fails to be the development of a way of making choices only because neither making conscious and verbalizable decisions nor finding yes-or-no answers plays a predominant role in it. But, as one progresses, one deliberates more and more, as the questions one faces have less to do with skill and more to do with how one is to conduct one's life in the art. The concept of a practice, in fact, breaks down the traditional distinction between 'art' and 'prudence.' The procedures of the reflective practitioner are explored and illuminated by D.A. Schön (1983).

2 The difference between step-by-step and holistic learning appears in what some professional dancers say. In the course of a discussion among former members of the Ballet Russe de Monte Carlo, at a meeting of the Society of Dance History Scholars, at the North Carolina School of the Arts in 1988, James Starbuck was talking about the difficulty of finding a congenial place to train after moving to a strange town and spoke of attaching himself to different studios for different aspects of technique. Igor Youskevitch commented on this that there are two stages in learning to dance professionally. In the first stage, one should find a single teacher, any competent teacher, and stick with him or her until one's formation is basically complete. Later, when it is merely a matter of maturing oneself in one's practice, one may pick up fine points here and there; but one should not remake oneself as a dancer.

3 Contrast the attitude ascribed to Spanish dancers by Anna Ivanova (quoted in chapter 3 note 10, above). I have heard the great Indian dancer Ram Gopal speak of the value of such regular classes when one is away from one's home base; I have also heard him challenged on this point, as compromising the purity of one's style. The point at issue was that, on the one hand, dancers who regard their technique as a secure possession risk becoming flabby; on the other hand, dancers who maintain their muscle tone by working out in an alien technique risk perverting their technique. It is not irrelevant that Gopal is a controversial figure in Indian cultural politics.

4 My lifetime practice of poetry at the professional level helps me to a certain understanding of the arts in general, including dance. I 'know what it

is to' – certain important things. But at any moment this may lead me astray; I have to be constantly on the watch lest a common experience suddenly become a false analogy.

5 Actual uniqueness, and originality in the sense of being unlike anything hitherto seen, are of no consequence: what is at issue is the relation to the prevailing expectation of the artistic community and its public, its making a distinctive impression, and its distancing itself fruitfully from its tradition, respectively.

6 You might say that it is not for me to say what it is not for philosophers to say – but who are you, to say what it is not for me to say?

7 See the opening paragraphs of chapter 16. Priests or potentates may have dances danced ceremonially in their presence, in which the important thing is whom the dance is danced for and on what occasion, the priest's or potentate's interest extending only to the fact that it is danced with some respectful degree of correctness: there would be no connoisseurship of dance, only a stickling for ceremony.

8 The same ambiguity was noted and explored by Kenneth Clark in *The Nude* (1972): the highest artistic achievement and the most direct erotic concern do not get in each other's way, but it is hard to generalize about what the relationships are.

9 To maintain this position, one would have to hold either that no women ever like to wear toe-shoes or to see them worn, or else that women who like to wear them are masochists and women who like to see other women dance in them are rejoicing in the humiliation of their fellow women. See further, note 15 below.

10 Dr Sheets-Johnstone explained her position in a seminar at the University of Toronto in the 1980s. As I remarked in the last chapter, it is hard to say what kinaesthetic awareness, all by itself, would be. The kinaesthetic body as perceived has no perceptual aspects – it cannot be inspected from close up or from a different angle, as visibilia can. The kinaesthetic body is not an object of which we are aware. Proprioception gives us a sense of our inner integrity in relation to the world we perceive but is not a supplement to percepts in the way that sights and sounds complement each other. I know I don't have wings or a tail, because surely I would feel them; but what it would be to have wings or tail is something I would have to find out in other ways. I know I have a left leg, because I feel it, but the feeling gives me no information about what it is like, over and above what I get from observing my legs and other people's by looking and touching.

11 Howard does not actually say this, and perhaps he would never say it –

he may actually think it a thoroughly silly view, as I do. But it certainly follows from what he does say. A possible explanation for this discrepancy between what he says and what I hope he means is that he trained himself to sing (was trained to sing) professionally to the highest standards but never devoted himself to singing as a career. It is conceivable, then, that he never reached the point at which the lay person's concern with 'artistic' as opposed to technically perfect rendering could once more become paramount. But this is sheer speculation, and impolite speculation at that.

12 On not being a superstar, see Martins 1982, passim, and especially the introduction by Robert Cornfield, p. xi.

13 We can do this because in learning to sing we must also thoroughly learn to hear singing, if only because we come to listen to it in a more urgently focused way.

14 Paul Ziff once told a meeting of the American Society for Aesthetics, in reference to advanced sports training, that the instructions given by a coach to a really advanced player would be unintelligible to a player at only a slightly lower level of training. Similarly, it appears that in music there are at any given time only a handful of really advanced teachers in any given area, so that one's whole career may depend on being taken on by a particular teacher, not only because that teacher has the ear of the producers, but because there are things that only that teacher can teach (compare the delay in Edward Johnson's career, when he was already established as a professional singer, because he could not get taken on by the one man whose instruction he needed to bring him to international stardom – Mercer 1976, 20–39). Yet that teacher may not be a first-class practitioner. The teacher is rather the only effective wielder of the language in which the instruction of ultimate refinement has to be given. In the 'democracy of the barre,' to which I referred earlier, I suppose the same language is needed and used but takes on a different meaning because the tuning of the body takes place at a higher level of precision. (This democracy goes with that aspect of social dance whereby anyone can join in, because the ensemble effect is unimportant – unlike an orchestral rehearsal, which depends on all players sharing a similar notion of what it is to play in tune.)

15 In §15.22 above, I remark that dancers distinguish what they feel as people from what they experience as dancers. Julie Van Camp, in the course of a symposium on dance criticism, commented on a recently choreographed ballet in which the dancers were required repeatedly to land on their toes. It was obvious to any dancer, she said, that this must

be extremely painful; in fact, it seemed to be evidence of sadism in the choreographer. But, she said, the critic had to disregard this obvious fact as irrelevant to the dance as performance. Other contributors to the symposium took issue with this view, and I myself thought at the time it was perverse purism. Surely, I thought, the critic was entitled to comment on all aspects of the dance, the personal-interest as well as the artistic and technical aspects, the unintended as well as the intended features of the presentation, the events backstage as well as the show itself. That the dance was painful was no more irrelevant than that it was difficult. I take it, however, that what Dr Van Camp had in mind was that the dancer would not be aware of her sore feet *as a dancer*; as a dancer, she would be aware of nothing but the dance as a dance, and the critic would be failing to respect her professional and artistic integrity unless a similarly austere concentration and relevance were maintained in observation and comment. In the act of working at any art, one is aware of many things, marginally, but as artist one is aware not of the artist in oneself but of the privileged status of those aspects of one's experience that the artist in one unites as relevant. In fact, I would say that the excitement of maintaining this edge of attention is one of the fullest and most immediate rewards of the masterly practice of an art.

Like anyone else engaged in a taxing performance, a dancer while dancing has many thoughts and many awarenesses and in looking back on that night's dance may recollect them rather than the actual dance; but that does not detract from the integrity of the dance. Maria Tallchief related at a conference, many years after the event, how at one moment in an exceptionally early morning rehearsal after a celebration she caught the look in the eye of the partner who was about to catch her as she leapt towards him: he was visibly wondering what he was doing there at that hour, and how in God's name he was expected to hold on to this vast weight hurtling towards him. But that, in a sense, was dance business, not dance; it was a good and funny story just because of its combination of human aptness and artistic irrelevance.

Even as I revise this chapter, Isabelle Brasseur has placed second in a figure-skating competition in which she had a broken rib. The television announcers made sure that the audience knew how much it was hurting and how uncertain it was that she could complete the performance. But there was nothing in the performance itself, including her facial expression, to show that anything was wrong. How was one to judge the performance? Technical and aesthetic judgment, sympathy, anxiety, and admiration seemed to exist side by side in my mind. The case differed from the one that troubled Van Camp, because the source of the pain was not the design of the movement as such; but part of the task in athletic championships is the overcoming of incidental pains and weaknesses, even though no points are awarded. The likenesses and differences between these two cases deserve prolonged meditation.

16 See §4.2 (with note 10) above, on Wigman and de Zoete. A certain mystique attaches to the rigours of training. Writers keep saying that ballet dancers must start training before they are eight, even though they know that many of the most famous dancers began in adolescence and even, if they are males, in college. A similar mystique seems to surround Indian classical dance. Projesh Banerjee (1983, 35) writes that in Kathakali 'the students used to live with their master (*Asan*, as they were called), during the period of their study. Intensive and strict training for a period of twelve years enabled the student to bring under control every part of the body, solely for the sake of aesthetic expression. His eyes are ever vibrant, his facial muscles eloquent, his fingertips creative and his whole person visible rhythm.' But a professional dance teacher writes, 'One can go on for ever learning and practising. Though the recommended age to start is 7 years, they really start learning the art and its nuances only after 12. Till then they exercise and the physical training gives them the stamina for any kind of hard and arduous work. So really speaking, four years of serious study from the age of 12 will make one a good dancer, who has all the necessary qualities. I mean, a professional standard' (Dhananjayan 1984, 70).

17 Could it be the same dance, if it was performed in a different style? See chapter 19.

18 Something can be taught, and something useful and valuable; one thinks of Humphrey's *Art of Making Dances* (1962), and of Patricia Beatty's useful handbook (1985), as well as *The Choreographic Art* by Van Praagh and Brinson (1963). A systematic method for taking a student from a personal idea to its technical realization is presented by Blom and Chaplin (1982); but the necessity of starting from an individual means that the objective must be 'aesthetic shaping of the inner experience' (xi), which militates against the development of a technique.

19 McFee (1994, 61–3) argues that dance composition is a necessary component in learning to understand dance; but he insists that what was thus learned would not be art.

20 The idea is eptimized in the writings of C.J. Ducasse (1929). The treatment in this section is based on Sparshott 1981a, written when I thought this was more of a problem than I now think it is.

21 Frances Rust (1969, 118–19) comments on the oddity of the dances popular among British teenagers in the 1960s. They precluded body contact with the partner, combined maximum rhythmicality with minimum grace, and were ruleless but uniform: the dancers were exhibitionist in manner but seemed oblivious to the outside world. The music was too loud for conversation – and valued on that account, according to her informants. The hip movements characteristic of the Twist were developed not from any dance tradition but from the pop singers familiar from television. These are clearly solipsistic dances, though Rust does not use that word: just as the geniuses of the rock video, Madonna and Michael Jackson, make a display of self-absorption, the adolescent dancer moves in a solipsist fantasy, dreaming the irresistibility of his or her conversation and bodily eloquence without engaging in any personal intercourse that might put the image at risk. They are a crowd of solitary dancers, each dancing for an imagined audience that responds to the dance of their daydreams rather than to the movements they are actually making.

22 Duncan's dance was not an unprecedented invention of spontaneous genius, and if it had been it would have been less effective than it was. What is really unprecedented does not look original, it looks like nonsense. Her dance relied on sentimental ideas (ubiquitous in the nineteenth century) of Greek art as a freshening and purifying proximity to nature; on the equally ubiquitous ideals of a return to the spontaneity of the body from oppressive industrialism; and, in her early days at least, on the ideal of the saving freedom of the New World, as we find it in Whitman.

23 There used to be a fashion among Wittgensteinian philosophers of saying that one is not aware of one's own movements, in the sense that one's sense of moving does not rest on evidence; one simply moves, consciously only because not unconsciously. It is not only the sense modality that differs: there is a whole world of difference between (consciously) doing something and being aware of something, whatever form that awareness might take (cf. Melden 1961). Existentialists and phenomenologists make the same point in different ways (cf. Merleau-Ponty 1962, 94). In what I do, my consciousness is simultaneous with, inseparable from, my action; in what anyone else does, I must wait and see. The difference is indeed fundamental, but I am not sure it affects the present argument much. Artists' critical awareness of what they are doing in the actual doing of it belongs to an attentive attitude that is far from the spontaneous and unreflective action which the philosophers have in mind.

24 None of this quite applies when actors are seen to be hamming, or putting performances together tone by tone and gesture by gesture rather

than in the Stanislavsky way, and are seen to be doing so. In such cases the audience has a very special and rather different pleasure, not in the apparent action but in the appearance of an action – in the tatters to which the passion is torn.

25 Some theorists argue that no improvisation can ever be a work of art, because it represents no commitments and involves no choices. No norm is laid down, compliance with which is necessary for a performance of the work. That seems not to be entirely true of improvisation in public, where indeed choices are made, including the choice to improvise, and the performer is committed to continue what has been begun in a way that responds to the decencies of the art and of the performing situation; all that is excluded is the mulling over of alternatives and the principled rejection of all lines but one. But the main point is correct, that an essential moment in the composition of a work is the decision to let something stand and to stand by it. I expatiate on the theme of improvisation in §18.62.

26 That is the point of those dances in which the choreographer has the dancers tell the audience how hard they are working, and so forth (chapter 5 note 2). The device fails to undermine the contrast, because either the utterances are part of the dance, hence not true communications from the dancers, or they are true communications, in which case they are no part of the dance as a choreographic work.

CHAPTER 18 Dance and Choreography

1 No doubt there are others. See in general Foster 1986, 59–64, on 'frames.'
2 The distinction between scenarist and choreographer is clearly stated by Martha Graham (1991, 225): 'When I work with a composer I usually give him a detailed script. ... There is a kind of order, a sequence I try to bring to the script in terms of placement and the means of the dancers. Here, for instance, I will note that there is to be a solo, and here a duet; this is to be the company, and this is to be a return to the solo, and so on, throughout the script. ... When I get the music, I start to choreograph.' A little later (236) she says of Antony Tudor: 'He was what was known as a choreographer. Such an impressive word. I had never heard the word "choreographer" used to describe a maker of dances until I left Denishawn. There you didn't choreograph, you made up dances. Today I never say, "I'm choreographing." I simply say, "I am working." ' Graham was not one of those little minds of which consistency is the hobgoblin; but we can take her as meaning that she uses the word 'choreography'

only when she wishes to distinguish it from 'script-writing' within the dance-making process.

Peter Martins (1982) makes no such conceptual distinctions within the process of dance composition. He says he begins by listening repeatedly to the music, after which the whole thing gradually jells. But he presents himself as a journeyman, charged with providing something for his company to dance, rather than as someone with a dance idea that he wants to make concrete. Such experiential sequences, whatever they may be, do not directly affect the conceptual analysis.

The typical libretto of a mid-nineteenth-century Russian ballet, like *The Little Humpbacked Horse* (1864), is a literary composition; it contains almost no suggestion even of the blocking of the stage action, let alone of its articulation in dance, and contains a lot of description that could not even be approximated or suggested in a stage production. It simply told a story that might move someone to compose a danceable equivalent. (In this case a group of enthusiasts concocted it, on the basis of Yershov's fairy tale, to persuade Saint-Léon to do a Russian subject for once; see Wiley 1990, 130–1 and 238–49, for the story and the text.) Such productions are not scenarios in the sense considered here.

3 A well-known dancer reported at a CORD conference on 'Dance and Culture' (Toronto, July 1988) that a choreographer with whom he had worked for some years, and with whose style he was thoroughly familiar, would never tell him what to do in mime passages when he was not in the forefront of the action, beyond telling him to 'do something.' Ordinarily the choreographer would simply accept what the dancer did; if not, his correction was usually confined to 'Do less' or 'Do more.' In learning to dance in that style, the dancer had learned to choreograph in the same style, in a modest way.

4 This pattern was once common in music. An eighteenth-century *Kappelmeister* was hired to compose music, train musicians, and supply musical performances on a regular basis, to a specific institution, court or church.

5 As the etymology suggests, the word 'choreography' once meant a dance notation. A choreographer, we may suppose, was contrasted with a dancer as someone who invented dances without dancing them; the devising of a notation, and the introduction of dances through its means, testified to the sharpness of the difference.

6 Yes, Balanchine *did* make a dance for elephants. Everyone mentions this; nobody lists the result among his masterpieces.

7 There are notorious exceptions: the massive reworkings to which

Mussorgsky was subjected by Rimsky-Korsakov, for instance. But in such cases we tend to use such phrases are 'revised version,' 'original version,' or even 'arr. Rimsky-Korsakov.' Though I must admit that when you buy a ticket to an opera you don't know what you are going to hear, and most often the programme won't tell you either; if you buy a record, you are unlikely to know what's on it until you get it home, because the sleeve won't tell you. The necessary accommodations of practice combine with the lapses from candour in merchandising to defeat any generalization.

8 *Icefire* (1982), choreographed by Fred Benjamin for the Alvin Ailey Repertory Ensemble, looked when I saw it as if in some passages the steps of the various dancers were conceived as the same but had been modified by or for the individual dancers, both as to their styling and as to their timing. They were certainly not synchronized, but equally certainly not independent sequences that happened to be proceeding simultaneously. The dancing was neither in unison nor not in unison. To some extent, this is a feature of much modern dancing, in so far as it eschews the regimentation of ballet without embracing the dialectic of freedom as the post-moderns do. But what one more often sees is a loose approximation to uniformity and synchronicity, a compromise between design and spontaneity; what Benjamin presented us with looked like a blend of choreographic theme with dancerly variation. This sort of thing makes dances very hard to follow for strangers, who have no initial reason to trust or to mistrust any aspect of the choreographer's intelligence and competence or those of the dancers.

9 Toni Bentley (1984, 89) writes of an industrial dispute as follows: 'Those who love themselves more than Balanchine have made their stand and demonstrated their lack of faith in him. They cry they have belief in him as an artist but not as their dictator. But how can one separate the two when his art can be produced only out of a state that he himself must rule? It's a pity he needs a hundred individuals as his tools rather than paintbrushes. What would have happened if Van Gogh's brushes one day had refused to be manipulated because they wanted better living conditions?' The obvious answer is that, if paintbrushes were animate, painting would be something other than what it now is; and that, if paintbrushes were rational beings, painters would control them by talking to them, not by pushing them around. Nor does one see why Balanchine's absolute choreographic authority would entitle him to dictate working conditions.

10 An eminent dance teacher has explained to me that Fokine's choreography has proved unstable because it was originally amorphous; Balanchine's choreography, like Petipa's, can be preserved because it was originally precise.

11 Henri 1923, 54–5. As in so much writing on the arts, Henri's use of language is sloppy rather than metaphorical. Why appeal to an unknown spatial dimension, when all he means is that the significance and effect of the gesture cannot be described or explained by giving its measurements? Why is the way we deal with it any more unconscious than any of the ways in which we process sensory information? What suggests 'carries us through the universe' as a helpful way of saying what Isadora does, as if she were a space ship? What basis have we for comparing her greatness with the greatness of other masters of gesture the world has formerly seen? And so on.

12 In music, John Cage's notorious pretence that composers infringe on the liberties of performers is grotesquely silly, unless it is a joke; one is to suppose that someone who sits down at the piano with a volume of Beethoven's piano sonatas dreads the bondage that is about to be imposed, rather than looking forward to the liberating treat of playing that glorious music.

13 In a talk on New Zealand radio, Concert Programme, 4 August 1987.

14 Chujoy and Manchester 1967, 201, quoting Lincoln Kirstein, *Ballet Alphabet*. They further quote Kirstein as saying: 'Its science is difficult to acquire and its practice, rare. There may be a hundred good dancers to a generation, and but half a dozen choreographers.' The use of the word 'science' suggests that the few good choreographers are good because they have mastered a difficult discipline, like nuclear physics. If that were correct, one would expect the few good choreographers to have studied with the best teachers and done well on their exams. One has only to think of the career patterns of the most distinguished choreographers to see that what happens is nothing like this at all. Diaghilev seems to have made his choreographers out of whole cloth, largely on the basis of their sexual attractiveness (unless it was the talent that turned him on), and it worked at least as well as anything else ever has.

15 I specify writing, because there is a sense in which no mis-speaker of a language violates grammar. Rather, one acquires or fails to acquire linguistic competence. The word 'grammar' originally meant correctness in writing, because in writing we produce language in an abnormal way in which our competence may desert us. We have to stop and think 'what one says'; and we may be unable to do so, because the rhythm of our saying, which ordinarily would carry us unfailingly along, is lost. That is why there are grammatical rules. The written language is different, too: there is less redundancy, because readers can stop to check, whereas listeners cannot, and writers can subject their language to a process of

selection and revision, whereas speakers must rely on what they find on the tip of their tongue. When Derrida said, truly and profoundly, that language was 'writable' from the start, he did not mean that what people write transcribes what they would say. Spoken language and written language are alternatives, and grammar relates essentially to the latter. Neither music nor dance has anything that corresponds to this complementarity of skills, so far as I can see.

16 These are two separate inabilities. Speech requires readiness, but admits imprecision; writing allows one to take one's time, but inhibits imprecision, because one must definitely decide which word to put down in what form, without feedback to indicate where one is going wrong.

17 This is because (as we noted when discussing values) something that accounts for the excellence of one thing (is what is good about it) may be quite different from what accounts for the goodness of some other good thing. One cannot abstract the good-making feature and use it to guarantee success on another occasion. Film reviewers have commented on this in comparing *Crocodile Dundee* with *Crocodile Dundee II*.

18 One difference is that one can compose music one could not perform, just as one can choreograph dances one could not perform – can't play that fast, can't jump that high – but there is no interesting sense in which one can write a text one could not read; but that is not what I have in mind here.

19 'The word is entirely unknown to Indian dance,' says Banerjee (1983, 169). When S.K. Saxena (1991) composes a *kathak* dance, what he does is provide a string of danceable syllables (*bols*). Is this choreography? Not exactly, I think; the relationships involved cannot really obtain outside the specific dance culture.

20 In Irish traditional song, it is normal to speak of A's version of B's version of C's version of D's song; it is clear that the origin of such a train of adaptation might be lost or mythologized.

21 Just so, in music, the word 'composer' really refers to the division of labour in the Western culture industry, although musicians throughout the world make and invent music.

22 The idea of artistic proprietorship is not strictly linked to property rights. There are cultures in which a song is known as that of its inventor, though it never occurs to anyone that it should not be freely sung by any who will. I do not know whether there are any cultures in which dances are assigned to their authors in this non-exclusive way, but it seems likely, especially in Australia and Melanesia (cf. Sparshott 1988, 182).

23 There is a notable contrast between these often-quoted obiter dicta and

the rather exalted claims he made for choreography as such in the *Dance Encyclopedia* (Balanchine 1967).

CHAPTER 19 The Identity of a Dance

1 Notable discussions are by Armelagos and Sirridge (1978), Margolis (1984), and McFee (1992, chap. 4). Gregory Currie's ontology (1989) lays the foundations for a many-sided discussion of the identity conditions for art generally.

2 This often happens in aleatoric music; we read the obfuscatory programme notes, and we hear the performance, and we do not know at all what would count as performing the same piece again.

3 The other evening, I saw a dancer support himself momentarily by an outthrust hand. The gesture was in keeping with the choreography, but I supposed he had landed a bit off centre and was restoring his balance. A few minutes later the same movement was repeated without the outthrust hand, and I was reasonably sure. But, of course, I was not *quite* sure; I would have been quite sure if I had come back another night and seen him to do it without the outthrust hand, or if I had been a more expert dance-viewer and had known for certain that a choreographer of that competence would never invent a move like that. (I could still have been wrong, of course; expert dance-viewers run the risk of being absolutely certain about things they are quite wrong about.)

4 'Limits of variability' may be a misleading phrase. It implies that variation is all right up to a point and then stops being all right. That is not the way things are. Different kinds and measures of variation are 'acceptable' in different ways, in different circumstances, for different reasons. In dance as elsewhere in the performing arts, experience is largely a matter of learning the intricacies of appropriate attitudes to variation: what is quite all right, what must be excused, what condoned, what ignored as far as possible, what allowed for, what taken as an added piquancy, and so-on without definable limit. It is seldom that a simple choice between acceptance and rejection is in question (acceptance for what? rejection from what?); even when it is, that need not be the end of the matter.

5 Composers and choreographers do not, as such, issue commands or directions: they merely provide something playable and danceable, respectively. Whether anyone actually plays or dances their work is not up to them. They can, however, in our society, so long as they retain the copyright, prohibit anyone from using their work in ways of which they disapprove.

I would say they do this as proprietors, not as creative artists. Meanwhile, more and more judicatures are developing legal means of protecting works of art from abuse, independent of copyright protection.

6 For example, certain sorts of compliance are not expected of amateur and student groups. But certain sorts of licence may not be allowed to them, either. If a group is so weak that we acquiesce in its cutting corners, it may arouse resentment if it claims the right to be uppity in its interpretations. See the next note.

7 In the most recent production of *Lohengrin* by the Canadian Opera Company, a bedraggled body was carried onstage in the closing measures. The programme notes explained that this was the corpse of the young man the heroine was accused of killing. This proved that she was really guilty, and her knight was all in her imagination. You would never have guessed that from watching the proceedings onstage and listening to the music, because Wagner had written music for the opera he wrote, not for the one the director thought would be cleverer. But no one supposed that it was anything other than *Lohengrin* that was being performed. It would still have been *Lohengrin* if it had been done on roller skates, which I thought would have made about as much sense. (The director, however, who knew the opera much better than I do, thought otherwise, and persuaded a professional opera company to go along with him; as I say, there may or may not be a consensus.)

8 Elizabeth Sawyer (1985, 240) observes that 'Chopin ... seldom played a composition twice in the same way, but altered it according to the mood or situation at the time. Later, for publication, he would settle on one version, which was then frozen within the printed score, thus misleading music-lovers of later times into the belief that this was the original "composition." ' However, Chopin did choose one version to be frozen, and published it, so I do not see how later musicians were misled. Balanchine's ballets have been copyrighted, and people who want to perform them nowadays must do so in accordance with a notated score and under the supervision of the curators of the choreographer's legacy. But the choice of a version to be the definitive one does not necessarily answer to a fixity in Balanchine's mind; it is simply part of the age-old necessities surrounding the editing and publication of texts. Peter Martins (1982) remarks that Balanchine would always revise a dance when he revived it, not only to fit the new dancers, but to prevent it from becoming stale.

9 Wolterstorff (1980) argues that a dramatist (or the choreographer of a mimetic work) does not create an individual: he or she specifies a type of

person – the type of whom everything in the work, and everything that follows from that, is (subject to certain restrictions) true. What the actor or dancer, in working up a performance, ideally does is to pick out a more specific type within the type defined by the work and pretend (as it were) to be a person of that type. The dancer developing her Giselle is determining (explicitly, or implicitly by her actions) what sort of person, of the type defined by the choreography, will be the sort she will, every time she performs the part until she changes her mind, pretend (as it were) to be. (I say pretend 'as it were,' because acting is not exactly pretending, but it is close enough.)

10 We must keep reminding ourselves that the equation of a dance, even a theatre dance, with a sign or a system of signs is deeply questionable. Beiswanger's (1970) emphasis on the primacy of the dancer's body in choreography makes this point. One can hold that it is essential to dance that it is actual people dancing, being what they do, not merely constructing something or furnishing the vehicle for a system of meanings. In so far as that is the right way to look at it, it is misleading to apply to dance even the most safely grounded generalizations from semiotics or the general theory of the fine arts.

11 To say that a dance is a complex of movements is not to imply that a dance must be made up of preconceived units ('steps'), even if it is. The movements of which it is a complex could be arrived at by abstraction from the dance as a continuous whole and would be elements only in terms of the articulation of that whole as such.

12 Nelson Goodman (1968) identifies a class of 'autographic' arts, in which there is only one true exemplar of a work, the one worked on by the artist, as opposed to allographic arts (like poetry) in which innumerable inscriptions of a work may exemplify it equally well. A work of art in dance is autographic if it is strictly identified as what a dancer actually dances, just as a painting is identified as what a painter actually paints: any process of copying or mechanical reproduction, however meticulous and sophisticated, must in principle fail of its aim because it is in principle impossible to specify conditions for its success. The point is indeed well taken. If you tell someone to do again *exactly* what they just did, without further specification or restriction, neither of you could be sure that they were complying, because there could always be something that neither of you noticed that a different observer might have observed and counted as a difference. All I need, however, is that it should be in principle possible that a performance could be repeated so exactly that no observer within the relevant dance community could tell the difference,

even though we may be convinced that in practice this would never happen. The difference between allographic and autographic is one of logical ontology, a matter of what *counts as* an exemplar; its relationship to the facts of creation and connoisseurship is oblique.

13 Her Giselle is not necessarily hers for a lifetime, but is hers for this production. If she dances the part again in a later production, she will get the part up again, and is most unlikely to do it in quite the same way, even if we discount changes in age and experience. She may rethink the role afresh, or simply revamp her old version. Even if she thinks of herself as reviving it unchanged, the new series of rehearsals can hardly fail to lead to a slightly different outcome.

14 I explain this language at length in Sparshott 1982c. The distinction between type and token is derived from C.S. Peirce; the elaborations about megatypes are introduced, after C.L. Stevenson, by J. Margolis (1965). Currie (1989, 76) says that 'the work is a type, and its instances are tokens. But the type of which the instances are tokens is not the work itself. It is the work's pattern and structure' – the sign as sign, not the concrete outcome of a heuristic path.

15 The discontinuity should not be exaggerated. Didelot, who produced it in St Petersburg as late as 1851, was a student of Dauberval; and in 1851 Petipa, who put it on as late as 1885, was already well established in St Petersburg. Koegler (1982, 154–5) gives a succinct account of the ballet's history of variations and recombinations, with bibliography.

16 For *Swan Lake* as culminating in present performance practice, see Beaumont (1952), who writes a history from the viewpoint of the problems faced by the Royal Ballet in its then-current production.

17 Notoriously, in the canonical presentation of *Swan Lake*, Odile performed 32 fouettés, not because the choreographer demanded them but because that was the dancer's *pièce de résistance* (Selma Jeanne Cohen 1982, 9–10). And this piece of display has become traditional in a curious way. In the last *Swan Lake* I saw, as Veronica Tennant stopped spinning, the lady on my left muttered 'twenty-eight,' and afterwards the lady on my right observed that Tennant had done 28 fouettés. *Swan Lake* is the ballet in which, at a certain moment, either one stops watching and starts counting, or the ballerina does something else instead. It is no essential part of the ballet that 32 fouettés be done (though the same stalwarts who say that *of course* a Prince makes love with an aide-de-camp in attendance say that 32 fouettés are *exactly* what a phony like Odile would do at that point), but it has become essential to it that there is a point when either they are done or they are not. The pure lover of art, presumably, would

not make this abstraction from the artistic totality of the dance; but the ballet-goer does, and not to notice how the point was met or got around would in fact count against one as a fit member of the audience for this particular ballet. To say 'I wasn't counting' would be priggish, snobbish, a pose; if one were in fact so carried away that one was not counting, one would never admit to the fact. (Of course I was counting; I made it 29, but arithmetic was never my strong suit.) At the very very best ballet houses, of course, they don't need to count, they just know there are 32. They count them only so that they can congratulate themselves that *of course* there are 32.

18 André Levinson, discussing the original version, attributes the ballet to 'Stravinsky and Roerich,' not to Nijinsky. In fact, he seldom ascribes Diaghilev's ballets to their choreographers, more often to their designers (Levinson 1983). I don't know how he decides: perhaps this is how Diaghilev advertised them. But there may be an element of parti pris, since he complains that Diaghilev's practice took the art of ballet away from the dance-master and gave it to the designer. The prevailing view assigns the scenario to Roerich, who was interested and expert in that sort of thing. Stravinsky contrived to give the impression that it was all his own idea; but then, he was rather possessive about *Sacre*. When a riot at the opening performance became an exemplary event, and fixed the original version in the public consciousness, Stravinsky jealously insisted that the riot was occasioned by his music, not by Nijinsky's choreography. In this, he seems to have been right, in that the booing began before the dancing started. Since later performances were not disrupted, by the way, the motivation of the brouhaha must have been political rather than immediately aesthetic; but popular historians persist in attributing it to artistic outrage.

19 Now that Nijinsky's version has been painstakingly reconstructed and presented to great acclaim by the Joffrey Ballet, this may change. Since the choreography is no longer scandalous, it may establish a definitive priority. But perhaps the very fact that it no longer shocks may, when we have all got over our initial impressions, tell against its eventual authority. Time will tell, as much as time tells anything.

20 In a telecast on the Arts and Entertainment Network on 21 October 1993, a ballet performed by the Northern Ballet Theatre was described throughout as 'Prokofiev's *Romeo and Juliet*'; the choreographer was not once named by the announcer, and one had to await the credits to discover that it was Massimo Moricone. Mind you, almost none of Moricone's work appeared on the screen, which was filled by the expressive and

handsome faces of the characters. (Adshead and Layson [1983, 125–46] have a useful exposition of the relationships among the ballets based on the Prokofiev score, centred on that by MacMillan; another account, more sharply pointed, is in Croce 1987, 256–9.)

21 In the winter of 1993–4, the headmistress of a London school refused to accept free tickets for her students to attend a ballet performance of *Romeo and Juliet*. The refusal was widely reported and ridiculed; but the ballet was uniformly attributed to Shakespeare. I suppose it never occurred to the media that it mattered whether it was a play or a ballet, let alone whose ballet it was. To do them justice, the headmistress prob- ably did not care either, since her reported objection was that the story placed too much emphasis on heterosexual love. (In terms of the ballet, this is an odd complaint; Cranko's choreography, at least, makes the erotic significance of the teasing and jostling of the youths, which lead to the deaths of Mercutio and Tybalt, unmistakable, whereas it can easily be missed in reading Shakespeare's text.)

22 The New York Public Library's Dance Collection says that '[e]ach version of a ballet is treated as a distinctive work and appears as a separate head- ing. Entries regarding productions of a particular version appear under that specific heading rather than under a general heading' (NYPL 1974, viii). To the cataloguers, the differences among versions determine what the headings shall be; to the reader, the headings indicate what the library deems to be a different version.

23 Extensive material is collected and discussed by Van Camp (1982).

24 Compare the rather different case of Benno, discussed in §19.21 above. It is objected to my text here that the fouettés were choreographed for Odile *as danced by Legnani* – that is, as a brilliance. It would follow that any dancer to whom they were routine would not be conforming to the chor- eography by performing them. One sees the point; but to say that is to deny determinacy to any choreography, since it substitutes the choreogra- pher's supposed intentions for what was actually prescribed.

25 Ann Hutchinson Guest notes (1984, 126–7), using Frederick Ashton as an example, that 'some choreographers put forward movement ideas and allow the dancers considerable latitude in shaping up these ideas into a setting most comfortable to them,' which the choreographer then accepts. Would that mean that, in Anderson's eyes, Ashton was not a serious choreographer? Not necessarily, since the choreographer decides where the dancers are to be allowed such freedom, and has to find the result acceptable.

26 Ignoring the problem of interpretation, McFee (1992, 106) says that, ideal-

ly, questions of identity should be decided by reference to an appropriate notation; but he recognizes that different notations are best suited to different purposes and different types of dance. He thinks that questions of identity are, therefore, historical; but he does not explain how this is supposed to work. Perhaps the idea is that problems of identity can be settled only within classes of cases for which a specific notation is, for the time being, agreed, and membership of which is also agreed.

27 At the annual Conference of the Society of Dance History Scholars on 16 February 1985.

28 I have argued elsewhere against the practice of defending such a taboo by treating a work of art as a quasi-person with rights (Sparshott 1983).

29 Philosophers used to say that in questions of sameness and difference one must specify 'the same what?' The Evening Star is the same planet as the Morning Star, but perhaps a different phenomenon. This clears up some confusions in some kinds of case but does not get to the heart of requirements and disagreements in complex practical situations.

30 This is because questions of personal identity involve responsibility: what can I be held guilty of, how can I commit myself? Locke (1694, Book II chap. 27) invokes the idea of a Last Judgment, when all my lost memories will be fully restored. But, because responsibility is a social matter, the subjective links of memory cannot altogether override the visible continuity of a familiar personality. The Athenian citizen Socrates, son of Sophroniscus, of Alopece, is responsible for educating Critias, even if he cannot remember ever meeting the man.

31 This is perhaps the real basis of Anderson's advocacy of materialism. To treat a dance as a historical entity is, as he says, not to take it seriously as a work of art in the romantic understanding, as formulated by Ducasse (1929). But the idea that Ducasse formalizes is basically idealist, rather than materialist: the reason why the work is to be preserved meticulously is that it is the perfect expression of the artist's emotion (see Collingwood 1938).

32 Frances Rust (1969, 189–90) notes that the waltz was stabilized in the United Kingdom by a conference of dance teachers in 1920–1. The purpose of normalizing the steps of this and other social dances was to enable more customers to share the same dance floor without hurting each other.

Charles Keil and Angeliki Keil (1992, 3), tracing six polka styles current in America for over a century, remark that 'there was no polka scholarship when we started' and that 'from the 1870s to the early 1970s, universities did not encourage a single person to write about any of these ethnic working-class musics for a scholarly journal' (15).

CHAPTER 20   Recording Dance

1 Conference on 'Dance and Culture' (CORD, Toronto, 13–17 July 1988). One might add that the familiarity of an 'official' canon of approved artists and works seriously distorts the impression of these arts given in the literature of aesthetics generally (cf. Sparshott 1994a).

2 In much of what follows, I use the words 'film' and 'video' indiscriminately where what matters is only the fact that the record is a moving picture.

3 This restriction may reflect a decision to omit some aspects from the notation, or an inability to find a way of recording them, or an unawareness of their existence. I use the expression 'describe/prescribe' to suggest that what is thus notated my be regarded indifferently as record or as recipe.

4 This restriction holds only for the use of film to give an overall impression of the dance, a surrogate for the dance experience, which is how it is most often used. Someone gets a camera and takes a film to show what it looked like. But one could use film to record every detail of a dance, with one camera (one film sequence) showing the entire stage or dancing area, and as many other cameras (entire or partial film sequences keyed in to the first) as were necessary to record every detail that needed separate noting in each dancer's movements. Similarly, one could make a taped record of a musical performance with any desired degree of completeness, by using a pair of microphones for the overall tonal effect and balance, and as many directional microphones as necessary to fix each detail of the sound produced by each player. One does not usually think of such comprehensive techniques of visual and sound recording, because they are never used outside the technician's studio. We do not want as much information as such documentation would provide, or not at such expense and in so unwieldy a form. There are lots of things we could do with our technology but don't, either because there would be no point or because they would be too expensive or bothersome for the trivial purpose they would serve.

5 For a full account, see Guest's (1984) historical and systematic treatise on dance notations, which, as my frequent citations will have suggested, is full of shrewdness and wisdom as well as information.

6 A similar notation is used for contredances in Magri 1779, part II chapter 7, in which the dancers are represented by semicircles linked by arrows. All you need to know is which body goes where, just as in the ballroom notation all you need to know is which foot goes where.

7 The discussion in the text ignores guitar tabulations, tonic sol-fa, shape-note systems, and other devices for students and amateurs.

8 Magri (1779, chap. 59, 'Of the Use of the Arms') says that '[t]he use of the

arms is so necessary, that upon it depends good or bad dancing, so much so that without it the *Ballante*'s body would be reduced to a walking statue without expression and without grace' – but arm movements are nowhere specified in the descriptions of particular dances.

9 Computer programmes exist that enable a choreographer to envisage the three-dimensional effect of a movement, just as architects use them to judge the coherence of designs. I do not think we are sufficiently familiar with this technology yet to see where it might go, or where we might go with it.

10 The experimental psychology of envisaging, and the artistic pragmatics of imagined performances, are a field of study that requires sympathetic scepticism. When we hear such claims, how are we to understand them? What questions should we ask, to evaluate them properly?

11 The Feuillet notation of a dance, if finely engraved, may be a beautiful thing, though some have called it 'hen-scratchings'; but its beauty is calligraphic and is independent of its function.

12 Jenyns 1729 [Canto II], 31. Isaac's Rigadoon, in Feuillet's notation, is in Weaver 1706a (Ralph 1985, 296–308). The claim in Jenyns's concluding lines is echoed by what the Beneshes (1977, xiv) say of their own nota-tion: 'We can now envisage the dawning of a renaissance in the world of dance, when dance will enjoy the status and respect which is given to music, art and drama.'

13 For the 'museum without walls,' see Malraux 1953 – though Malraux was speaking specifically about photography.

14 The person from the notation bureau is not likely to be able to remedy this deficiency. Does that mean that Levinson was right, that a living tradition must be maintained? Not necessarily, since even dancers trained by Balanchine will be unlikely to share the precision of his musical ear. Erosion will set in. Musical insight is needed, not memory.

15 Similarly, in music, at a time when procedures were standardized, many passages could provide the continuo player merely with a figured bass, it being understood that any professionally competent way of filling it out would count as a performance of the work.

16 The word 'property' used to be a red rag to the bull-headed: 'property is theft.' But any society, whether capitalistic, socialistic, traditional, or com-munistic, has to make some arrangements about who gets to use what, when, and how. And in the international context, or the context of any but a closed traditional society, the arrangements have to be formalized, so that they can be explained. The content of those explanations is all we mean by property rights.

17 Discussions of literal translation usually say at this point that all transla-

tions must be to some extent misleading. Experts on notation do not always make that explicit. This is at least in part because the analogy is imperfect. In a verbal text, there is a syntactic pattern, which is to some extent detachable from the structure of meanings to be conveyed, but interacts with it in a way that no other verbal text can reproduce. The translator must decide where fidelity is most important. In a dance, this duality does not obtain; dances are not linguistic structures but movement structures. For the foreseeable future, notated versions of dances are means to the recovery or dissemination of a dance as performed, whereas a translation of a linguistic text functions as a text in its own right and is seldom used as a means of reconstructing the original.

18 To say that Laban worked out or developed a system can be misleading. He was, by general report, an idea man, working up one general idea after another and leaving the detailed elaboration to others. Labanotation is not a system devised and perfected by Laban, but one conceived by him and elaborated by others. The extent of collaboration in its perfection and adaptation may partly account for its general utility; the bias of its origin, suggested in the text, has not been much noted in practice.

19 There have been more than one; but Stepanov's system, taught at St Petersburg at the beginning of the century, fell before a change of regime in the institution and the stylistic transformations effected by Fokine. See Guest 1984, 73ff.

20 Remarked by Ronda Rhyman at the Toronto CORD conference, 14 July 1988.

21 'In contemporary dance,' says Eshkol (1975, 5), 'composition is still largely the result of *ad hoc* decisions, continuity being ensured by a heavy reliance upon musical accompaniment and literary theme. In order to reach the mature stature of an art such as music, the composition of dance will have to enter a phase in which the material itself is explored. The focus of this exploration should be upon the search for structure. ... The person who makes no order in anything does nothing for others and nothing for himself. ... Order makes possible agreement and understanding, by exposing relations and connections.' The model proposed here can only be that of twelve-tone music, in which the accidental relations generated by equal-tempered keyboards are subjected to manipulations which have no other purpose than to frustrate attempts to produce and discern the meaning structures of extant musical practice. But the twelve-tone system did at least anchor itself on real keyboard instruments and the ways their potentialities had actually been exploited. Eshkol is not talking about anything at all.

22 The system is described and its origins narrated by its inventor in Sutton 1982. As might be expected, adherents of more sophisticated systems adopt a rather haughty tone when they talk about it, which they rather seldom do.

23 It seems odd that Labanotation, a visual system encoding visual data, should be so remote from our visual intuitions and habits that the uninitiated cannot even guess what it is recording. See Tufte 1990, 114–19, for some pithy remarks. But Tufte does not consider the possibility that this notation, though counterintuitive, may in fact be the best for the specific purposes it is designed for. He also mistakes the Eshkol/Wachmann drawings of the model underlying their notation for the notation itself, and says pithy things about them, too. ...

24 Fancher and Myers 1981, 32. Adshead and Layson (1983, 77) warn the history student to 'be aware of the distinction between the kind of film or video produced as a direct record of a production, likely to have been viewed from the front with minimal or no changes of camera angle, and the "presentation" film or video where the director arguably is acting in the role of "second choreographer." Here selection for the camera, in the form of close-ups, focusing on certain dancers and alternative camera angles, means that the dance as presented to the audience has changed.' Cynical observers of media techniques will reflect that there is a difference between what is actually the record of a performance and what only looks like a record because the style of presentation is what one would get by shooting head-on with a single camera.

25 Dave Allen (1993, 19) warns that 'any act of dancing which is reproduced on screen is at once mediated by all the conventions of that act of recording and transmission.' True, but one must not be carried away. The dance is certainly mediated by all the methods and mechanisms used; but not everyone is aware of all conventions, or subscribes to them. And a study of the senses as perceptual systems reminds one that they are targeted on the world we live in, of which we need to inform ourselves; they embody robust tendencies to discount distortions of indirection, malformation, incompleteness, and obscurity. These normalizing tendencies immediately get to work on the novel mediations of the new technologies.

26 Such illusions seem to work by contrast with a more familiar mode of presentation. Long-lived audio buffs will recall how perfectly 'lifelike' each advance in recording technology seemed, until after a few months one became used to it and realized that this too was 'only a recording.'

27 This is the argument for the usually frowned-on practice of filming a dance or play with a single, unmoving camera placed in the stalls.

28 Deborah Jowitt (1985, 29) lists among the things Merce Cunningham found out about dance on TV: 'That side-to-side movement doesn't always register, because it crosses the small screen so quickly. That, because the camera's eye has no muscle, the intensity of a movement tends to dissipate before it reaches the viewer so that what's gentle becomes bland.'

29 Clive Hirschhorn (1974, 118) relates that after viewing *Me and My Girl* (1942) Gene Kelly realized that dance routines that succeeded onstage were flat on the screen. 'What lasts on the screen for a minute could last on stage for three to five minutes, the reason being that the stage is three-dimensional. ... There is a lack of kinaesthesia on the screen. ... On stage, if he threw a kick or a punch to the audience, there would be a reaction. ... But on the screen the very same gesture would receive no reaction at all.' (Kelly notes that, oddly, a stronger effect is given by rushing the camera right up to a stationary object.) In an elaborate set piece from a film I saw on TV the other night (probably *Take Me Out to the Ball Game*, 1949), Kelly dances all round the set, with a variety of things and people, on an assortment of surfaces. Onstage, it must have been wonderful. On film, the obsequious camera drained it of immediacy and excitement. On TV, one had to keep telling oneself what a triumph it was.

30 Ethan Mordden (1981, 110) says of Eleanor Powell (unlike Astaire): 'In the end, her musicals were Powell films rather than dance films: she didn't spread dance all over the screen. *She* danced; the other characters sang, joked, and ran the plot. Powell, too, sang, joked, and plotted, but by focusing on *her* dances as the special things in her films, she eliminated the need for dance as expression of person or story.'

31 'The genius of Astaire movies, for instance, lies not only in the quality of the dancing, but in the organization of the dance in small, bite size pieces set in an everyday context to which a wide audience can readily relate,' says Robert Penman (1993, 115), urging producers of dance for television to do the same. Astaire's vaudeville background would perhaps predispose him to the meticulous preparation and presentation of short pieces.

32 Hirschhorn (1974, 255) remarks that according to Jack Cole Gene Kelly 'is far more interested in the staging of a number than in the actual dancing of it'; this may reflect the fact that on film the actual performances always play a much smaller part in the overall effect than on a stage.

33 A film such as *Top Hat* (1935), in which Astaire's methods matured, required not only a suitable partner (Ginger Rogers), but a sympathetic director (Mark Sandrich), a devoted producer (Pandro S. Berman), and a like-minded dance director (Hermes Pan). Sandrich's analysis of a film from this period (*Follow the Fleet*) is reproduced in Arlene Croce's classic

study (1972, 186–7). For a massive and fully illustrated account of Astaire's work in films, with an illuminating introduction, see Mueller 1985.

34 The film is said to be now in the National Archives of Canada. The dancer may be Loie Fuller.

35 My notes say it was Balanchine, but in the absence of data it is better to keep to the generality of the case as recollected and described.

36 The director may have forgotten the history-erasing nature of film editing. A film sequence is not caused by the sequence that went before it, shots being assembled on the cutting table, and film-goers know that a scene in a film is not necessarily in the causal ancestry of the next scene. Early film-makers learned that an appearance of narration could be generated by intercutting suitable images from a variety of sources; audiences soon learned that, too, and this knowledge may undermine any tendency to interpret a series of shots of dancing as the chronicle of a continuous dance performance. In the 1983 TV presentation of Tharp's *The Catherine Wheel*, viewers see and hear the dancers talking about how long and demanding their parts are – but, though we are told the presentation was based on a theatre production, what we saw was only brief snippets; if, in fact, the dance was danced straight through, that was done for reasons irrelevant to what was shown on TV.

37 This *Nutcracker* case differs from that of the *Romeo and Juliet* described above, in which there was never any doubt that it was a ballet that was being shown. The fact that we saw more narrative than choreography may have resulted from simple acquiescence in the fact that cinema and television are overwhelmingly narrative media, in which it is easier to follow stories than to delineate forms (Allen 1993, 33; Rubidge 1993, 188). Ethan Mordden observes (1981, 200) that in TV versions of musicals the songs and dances are the first things to go when footage is snipped.

38 In much the same way, a Polaroid 'instant' camera is halfway between a standard camera and a mirror.

39 Some caution is in order here. The dancers in rehearsal were dancers, and were moving as dancers if not dancing, so that in reproducing the taped movements they were not simulating or imitating an action, but simply doing 'the same again.' Besides, it is unsafe to take literally Tharp's statements about what she is doing; what one sees is seldom what one is told one is seeing. (Unallocated allusions to Tharp's dicta refer to her comments on televised presentations of her work, notably *The Catherine Wheel* [1983].)

40 A 1991 programme in the *Dance in America* series, called 'Everybody

Dance Now,' dealt with the treatment of dance on music videos and included a variety of thoughtful statements by choreographers. One remarked that, whereas in a musical the dancing is worked into a love story, in a music video the movement is simply abstracted and exploited 'for profit.' Another complained: 'It is impossible for a non-dancer to edit a dancer's work; I'm a dancer, I want the dancing, not the cinematography.' Someone else argued that these videos are the first universally accessible showcase of American dance.

41 Busby Berkeley achieved similar effects with standard film techniques, in his more imaginative numbers (see, for instance, the 'By a Waterfall' number from *Footlight Parade*, 1933, illustrated in Thomas and Terry 1973, 66); but he had no artistic heirs.

42 Allen 1993, 13, modified to remove an inscrutable allusion to specific British TV channels.

CHAPTER 21   Conclusion

1 The same emphasis predominates in Lonsdale 1993.

2 The *Pendelbewegung* comes from Konrad Lange, who also calls it a *Hinundherschwanken* (1897, 257; cf. Sparshott 1963, 215–17).

3 This statement is easily defeated by a counterexample; any choreographer who read it could refute me by telling a dancer simply to do something. That is a fact about the institution of dance; and that is why the institutional theory of art needs to be supplemented by other kinds of discourse.

4 How long is the foreseeable future? That depends on who's looking. The phrase refers to what may be plausibly extrapolated from currently conspicuous tendencies, and what can be confidently predicted is that the future won't be like that.

CHAPTER 22   Afterword: The Three Graces

1 A magnificent rendering of Siva Natyaraja (South India, 12th–13th century CE) is illustrated in Zimmer 1955, plates 411–14. The stability of the iconography and variability of the expressive rendering can be seen by comparing (for instance) the versions in Kar 1952, plates 31–2 (11th century) and 55 (16th century).

2 For the dance of the jackal see Sparshott 1988, 105, where the comparison with the Natyaraja gives more weight to the cosmogonic significance of the latter than I do here.

3 Historically, they are gods – daughters of Eurynome, the third wife of

Zeus, according to Hesiod's *Theogony*, though others give them other parentage. They may be seen in a wall-painting from Pompeii, after a Hellenistic sculpture, in Boardman 1964, figure 248, together with Raphael's famous rendering of the same group (figure 249). Other renderings may be found in Deichgräber (1971) and in Clark (1972).

4 Lonsdale (1993, 274) reproduces a Hellenistic relief that shows them in a quite different pose, of which this is not true – or seems not to be. They are fully clothed, striding across the carved panel, tiptoe to tiptoe, each holding in her right hand the hand of the one in front. The free hands hold their flowing robes. The leading Grace gazes downward; the middle one looks back to meet the eye of the third. As we look more closely, we see that the middle one's torso is fully turned toward us: she cannot be striding as her companions are (for her legs, entirely concealed by a small altar in the foreground, must be close together), nor are her clothes taken, like theirs, by the wind of her movement. So, as in the more familiar stance, their position suggests no possible movement before or after, or even present; it is an undanceable dance. We would not know this relief represented the Graces, had the sculptor not provided a dedicatory inscription.

5 Deichgräber (1971) observes that the ambiguity is inherent in the Graces themselves, who begin their career as goddesses of benediction (etymologically connected with *chairein*, to rejoice or prosper) and become associated successively with a divine beauty of person, the spirit of fifth-century (BCE) Athenian culture, and the 'beauties' of a poet's style. 'Grace' may stand for whatever the Graces at any time may be thought to bestow, and in addition to the two specific meanings mentioned in the text it may be used in aesthetics to stand for the uncovenanted '*je ne sais quoi*,' that aspect of beauty which is attested to by experience but cannot be accounted for by any system (cf. §15.22111).

6 Lessing 1766, interpreting another famous Hellenistic sculptural group, *Laocoön*.

7 For an interpretation of their stillness, see Sparshott 1988, 247–8.

8 'Hence is it that these *Graces* painted are / With hand in hand dauncing an endless round; / And with regarding eyes, that still beware / That there be no disgrace amongst them found; ... ' (John Davies 1596, lxxv, p. 190). I say 'seems' in the text, because in most versions of this group (including the Pompeii fresco and Raphael's rendering of it) the hands do not touch. Each Grace has one hand on a shoulder of one of the others; in the free hand she holds a nosegay or a flowering twig – for which Raphael substitutes a ball. In some versions the pose is asymmetrical, in

that each of the Graces facing us has a hand on the shoulder of the one with her back to us, so that the one on the right has no hand on her own shoulder; others are symmetrical, in that the one on the left has her hand on the shoulder of the one on the right. I do not know if this has any iconographic significance – it may be that the asymmetrical one simply brought the hand forward to make it visible. In Botticelli's free version in his 'Primavera,' the fingers of the Graces are entwined, and it may be this version that Davies and Wagner are thinking of.

9 Boardman (1964, 265) says that ' "The Three Graces" type is said to have served as a brothel sign in Renaissance Italy,' but he does not say who says it. If true, it would explain the popularity of the image in some quarters, but not its literary interpretations.

10 According to Deichgräber (1971, 58), a cosmic interpretation in Neoplatonic terms is first found in Proclus. The moral interpretation exemplified by Lemprière is Stoic; Seneca, citing Chrysippus, gives three versions of it.

11 Hegel's exclusion of dance from the scheme of the arts is discussed in Sparshott 1988, 33–45.

For this cosmogonic reading of dance, compare Gregory Nazianzen (*Adv. Jul. Or.* 4 chap. 43): 'And if you must dance, being addicted to feasts and festivals, then dance; only, not the dance of the shameless Herodias, whose end was the death of the Baptist, but the dance of David at the resting of the Ark, which I believe to be symbolic of the mobile and agile outgoing of the Divine (*tēs eukinētou kai polustrophou kata theon poreias*).' On the human scale, it is this sense of movement as an outgoing of the inward person that is captured in Martha Graham's much-quoted formulation of what it is to *dance significantly*: 'Through the medium of discipline and by means of a sensitive, strong instrument, to bring into focus unhackneyed movement: a human being' (in Rogers 1941, cited from Selma Jeanne Cohen 1974, 136).

12 Fokine's duplication and inversion of this theme in *La Spectre de la rose* is as profound an invention as his metamorphosis of *La Sylphide* into *Les Sylphides.*

References

Acocella, Joan, and Lynn Garafola, eds. 1991. *André Levinson on Dance.* Hanover, NH: Wesleyan University Press

Adorno, Theodor W. 1984. *Aesthetic Theory.* London: Routledge and Kegan Paul

Adshead, Janet, ed. 1988. *Dance Analysis: Theory and Practice.* London: Dance Books

Adshead, Janet, and June Layson. 1983. *Dance History: A Methodology for Study.* London: Dance Books

Alberti, Leon Baptista. 1966. *Opere Volgari.* Ed. Cecil Grayson. Vol. 2. Bari: G. Laterza

Aldrich, Virgil. 1963. *Philosophy of Art.* Englewood Cliffs, NJ: Prentice-Hall

Allen, Dave. 1993. 'Screening Dance.' In Jordan and Allen 1993, 1–35

Anderson, Jack. 1975. 'Idealists, Materialists, and the Thirty-Two Fouettés,' in Copeland and Cohen 1983, 410–19. First published in *Ballet Review* 6

Anderson, Jack. 1987. *Choreography Observed.* Iowa City: University of Iowa Press

Aristoxenus 1959: Aristoxenus of Tarentum. *Elementa Rhythmica.* Ed. and trans. G.-B. Pighi. Bologna: R. Patron

Armelagos, Adina, and Mary Sirridge. 1978. 'The Identity Crisis in Dance,' *Journal of Aesthetics and Art Criticism* 37, 129–39

Artaud, Antonin. 1958. *The Theatre and Its Double.* Trans. Mary C. Richards. New York: Grove Press

Aschenbrenner, Karl. 1974. *Concepts of Criticism.* Dordrecht: Reidel

Avicenna 1974: *Avicenna's Commentary on the Poetics of Aristotle.* Trans. Ismail M. Dahiyat. Leiden: Brill

Bacon, Francis 1605. *Of the Proficience and Advancement of Learning, Divine and Humane.* London: Henrie Tomes. Cited from his *Works*, vol. 3, ed. James Spedding, Robert Leslie Ellis, and Douglas Denon Heath. London: Longmans and Co., 1857

Balanchine, George. 1967. 'Notes on Choreography.' In Chujoy and Manchester 1967, 201–4

Banerjee, Projesh. 1983. *Indian Ballet Dancing.* Atlantic Highlands, NJ: Humanities Press

Barnes, Sally. 1983. *Democracy's Body.* Ann Arbor, Mich.: UMI Research Press

Barthes, Roland. 1972. 'Striptease.' In his *Mythologies*, 84–7. New York: Noonday Press

Barton, Rita M. 1972. *Life in Cornwall in the Late Nineteenth Century: Being Extracts from the West Briton Newspaper in the Two Decades from 1855 to 1875.* Truro: D. Bradford Barton Ltd

Bateson, Gregory. 1972. *Steps to an Ecology of Mind.* San Francisco: Chandler Publishing Co.

Baudrillard, Jean. 1972. *Pur une critique de l'économie politique du signe.* Paris: Gallimard

Baugh, Laurie Bruce. 1986. 'Art and Authenticity.' PHD dissertation, University of Toronto

Bayer, Raymond. 1933. *L'Esthétique de la grâce : Introduction à l'étude des équilibres de structures.* 2 vols. Paris: Felix Alcan

Bayer, Raymond. 1956. *Traité d'esthétique.* Paris: Armand Colin

Beardsley, Monroe C. 1984. 'What Is Going On in a Dance?' In Sheets-Johnstone 1984, 35–47

Beatty, Patricia. 1985. *Form Without Formula: A Concise Guide to the Choreographic Process.* Toronto: Underwhich Editions

Beaumont, Cyril W. 1952. *The Ballet Called Swan Lake.* London: C.W. Beaumont. Reprinted New York: Dance Horizons, 1982

Beiswanger, George. 1970. 'Chance and Design in Choreography.' In M.H. Nadel and C.G. Nadel, eds., *The Dance Experience*, 383–90. New York: Praeger

Benesh, Rudolf. 1978. 'Birth of a Language,' *Theoria to Theory* 11, 261–73

Benesh, Rudolf, and Joan Benesh 1977. *Reading Dance: The Birth of Choreology.* London: Souvenir Press

Benjamin, Walter. 1969. 'The Work of Art in the Age of Its Mechanical Reproducibility.' In his *Illuminations*, trans. Harry Zohn, 217–52. New York: Schocken

Bentley, Toni. 1984. *Winter Season: A Dancer's Journal.* New York: Vintage Books

Best, David. 1985. *Feeling and Reason in the Arts*. London: George Allen and Unwin

Blair, Fredrika. 1986. *Isadora: Portrait of the Artist as a Woman*. New York: McGraw-Hill

Blasis, Carlo. 1828. *The Code of Terpsichore: A Practical and Historical Treatise, On the Ballet, Dancing, and Pantomime; with a Complete Theory of the Art of Dancing: Intended as Well for the Instruction of Amateurs as the Use of Professional Persons*. London: James Bulcock. Reprinted Brooklyn: Dance Horizons, n.d.

Blom, Lynne Anne, and L. Tarin Chaplin. 1982. *The Intimate Act of Choreography*. Pittsburgh, Penn.: University of Pittsburgh Press

Boardman, John. 1964. *Greek Art*. London: Thames and Hudson

Bose, Mandrakanta. 1991. *Movement and Mimesis: The Idea of Dance in the Sanskrit Tradition*. Dordrecht: Kluwer Academic Publishers

Bournonville, August. 1865. *Mit Theaterliv*, vol. 2. Trans. Patricia N. McAndrews as part 2 of *My Theatre Life*. Middletown, Conn.: Wesleyan University Press, 1979

Bowers, Faubion. 1960. *Theatre in the East: A Survey of Asian Dance and Drama*. London: Evergreen Books

Buber, Martin. 1984. *I and Thou*. Revised edition, trans. Ronald Gregor. New York: Scribners

Buchler, Justus, ed. 1955. *Philosophical Writings of Peirce*. New York: Dover Books

Buonaventura, Wendy. 1983. *Belly Dancing: The Serpent and the Sphinx*. London: Virago

Burke, Edmund. 1757. *A Philosophical Enquiry into the Origin of Our Ideas of the Sublime and Beautiful*. London: R. and J. Dodsley

Callow, Simon. 1984. *Being an Actor*. London: Methuen

Carroll, Noël 1981. 'Post-Modern Dance and Expression.' In Fancher and Myers 1981, 95–103

Carroll, Noël, and Sally Banes. 1989. 'Working and Dancing: A Response to Monroe Beardsley's "What Is Going On in a Dance?".' In George Dickie, Richard J. Sclafani, and Ronald Roblin, eds., *Aesthetics: A Critical Anthology*, second edition, 645–50. New York: St Martin's Press

Chernoff, John M. 1979. *African Rhythm and African Sensibility*. Berkeley: University of California Press

Chiang Yee. 1935. *The Chinese Eye*. London: Methuen

Chomsky, Noam. 1983. *Cartesian Linguistics: A Chapter in the History of Rationalist Thought*. Lanham, Md: University Press of America

Chujoy, Anatole, and P.W. Manchester, eds. 1967. *The Dance Encyclopedia*. Revised and enlarged edition. New York: Simon and Schuster

Clark, Kenneth M. 1972. *The Nude: A Study in Ideal Form.* Princeton, NJ: Princeton University Press

Cohen, Marshall. 1983. 'Primitivism, Modernism, and Dance Theory.' In Copeland and Cohen 1983, 161–78

Cohen, Selma Jeanne, ed. 1974. *Dance as a Theatre Art.* New York: Dodd, Mead & Co.

Cohen, Selma Jeanne. 1982. *Next Week, Swan Lake: Reflections on Dance and Dances.* Middletown, Conn.: Wesleyan University Press

Cohen, Ted. 1973. 'Aesthetic/Non-Aesthetic and the Concept of Taste.' *Theoria* 39, 113–52

Collingwood, R.G. 1938. *Principles of Art.* Oxford: Clarendon Press

Condillac, Etienne Bonnot de. 1746. *Essai sur l'origine des connoissances humaines.* Reprint Paris: Galilée, 1973

Copeland, Roger, and Marshall Cohen, eds. 1983. *What Is Dance?* New York: Oxford University Press

Cousin, Victor. 1853. *Du Vrai, du beau et du bien.* Paris: Didier

Craig, Edward Gordon. 1911. *On the Art of the Theatre.* London: Heinemann

Croce, Arlene. 1972. *The Fred Astaire and Ginger Rogers Book.* New York: Vintage Books

Croce, Arlene. 1987. *Sight Lines.* New York: Alfred A. Knopf

Crompton, Robert Morris, ed. 1984. *Dancing: A Journal Devoted to the Terpsichorean Art, Physical Culture and Fashionable Entertainment.* Toronto: Press of Terpsichore

Currie, Gregory. 1989. *An Ontology of Art.* London: Macmillan

Danto, Arthur C. 1964. 'The Artworld,' *Journal of Philosophy* 61, 571–84

Danto, Arthur C. 1981. *The Transfiguration of the Commonplace.* Cambridge, Mass.: Harvard University Press

Davies, John. 1596. *Orchestra or a Poeme on Dauncing.* In his *Complete Poems,* ed. Alexander B. Grosart, vol. 1, 155–213. London: Chatto and Windus, 1876

Davies, John Booth. 1978. *The Psychology of Music.* London: Hutchinson University Library

Deakin, Irving. 1956. *At the Ballet.* London: Nelson

Deichgräber, Karl. 1971. *Charis und Charites: Grazie und Grazien.* Munich: Ernst Heimeran

de Mille, Agnes. 1991. *Martha: The Life and Work of Martha Graham.* New York: Random House

Denby, Edwin. 1949. *Looking at the Dance.* New York: Pellegrini and Cudahy

Denby, Edwin. 1986. *Dance Writings.* New York: Alfred A. Knopf

DES. 1972. *Movement: Physical Education in the Primary Years.* London: Department of Education and Science

Dewey, John. 1934. *Art as Experience.* New York: Minton Balch

de Zoete, Beryl. 1953. *The Other Mind: A Study of Dance in South India.* London: Victor Gollancz

de Zoete, Beryl, and Walter Spies. 1938. *Dance and Drama in Bali.* New York: Thomas Yoseloff

Dhananjayan, V.P. 1984. *A Dancer on Dance.* Adyar, Madras: Bharata Kalanjali

Dickie, George. 1974. *Art and the Aesthetic: An Institutional Analysis.* Ithaca, NY: Cornell University Press

Dickie, George. 1984. *The Art Circle: A Theory of Art.* New York: Haven Publications

D'Israeli, Isaac. 1859. 'The History of Writing-Masters.' In his *Curiosities of Literature,* vol. 3, 167–77. London: Routledge

Ducasse, C.J. 1929. *Philosophy of Art.* New York: Dial

Dufrenne, Mikel. 1953. *Phénomenologie de l'expérience esthétique.* Paris: Presses universitaires de France. Translated as *Phenomenology of Aesthetic Experience* by Edward S. Casey and Albert A. Anderson, Evanston, Ill.: Northwestern University Press, 1973

Duncan, Isadora. 1928. *The Art of the Dance.* New York: Theatre Arts

Ellis, Havelock. 1923. *The Dance of Life.* New York: Houghton, Mifflin

Elyot, Sir Thomas. 1531. *The Boke Named the Gouernour.* London: Thomas Berthelet

Eshkol, Noa. 1975. *Right Angled Curves.* Holon, Israel: Movement Notation Society

Esslin, Martin. 1983. *The Theatre of the Absurd.* Third edition. New York: Penguin Books

Fancher, Gordon, and Gerald Myers, eds. 1981. *Philosophical Essays on Dance.* Brooklyn: Dance Horizons

Félibien, André. 1685. *Entretiens sur les vies et sur les ouvrages des plus excellens peintres.* Second edition. Paris: S. Mabre-Cramoisy. Reprinted Geneva: Minkoff, 1972

Fergusson, Francis. 1949. *The Idea of a Theater.* Princeton, NJ: Princeton University Press

Feynman, Richard P. 1986. *Surely You're Joking, Mr. Feynman.* New York: Bantam Books

Fiske, John, and John Hartley. 1993. 'Dance as Light Entertainment.' In Jordan and Allen 1993, 37–49

Fodor, Jerry A. 1979. *The Language of Thought.* Cambridge, Mass.: Harvard University Press

Foster, Susan Leigh. 1986. *Reading Dancing: Bodies and Subjects in Contemporary American Dance.* Berkeley: University of California Press

Fraleigh, Sondra Horton. 1987. *Dance and the Lived Body: A Descriptive Aesthetics*. Pittsburgh: University of Pittsburgh Press

Franko, Mark. 1989. 'Repeatability, Reconstruction and Beyond,' *Theatre Journal* 41, 56–74

Franko, Mark. 1993. *Dance As Text: Ideologies of the Baroque Body*. Cambridge: Cambridge University Press

Friedman, James Michael. 1976. *Dancer and Spectator: An Aesthetic Distance*. San Francisco: Balletmonographs

Frye, Northrop. 1990. *Words with Power: Being a Second Study of 'The Bible and Literature'*. New York: Harcourt Brace Jovanovitch

Fuller, Loie. 1913. *Fifteen Years of a Dancer's Life*. Boston: Small, Maynard and Co. Reprinted New York: Dance Horizons, n.d.

Gallini, Giovanni-Andrea. 1762. *A Treatise on the Art of Dancing*. London: Printed for the author

Gautier, Théophile. 1986. *Gautier on Dance*. Ed. and trans. Ivor Guest. London: Dance Books

Geertz, Clifford. 1976. 'Art as a Cultural System,' *Modern Language Notes* 91, 1473–99

Ghosh, Manoman, ed. and trans. 1967. *The Natyashastra Attributed to Bharata-Muni*. Vol. 1. Calcutta: Manisha Granthalya Private Ltd

Gilbert, Davies. 1838. *The Parochial History of Cornwall*. Vol. 2. London: J.B. Nichols and Son

Goldman, Albert. 1989. *The Lives of John Lennon*. New York: Bantam Books

Gombrich, E.H. 1960. *Art and Illusion: A Study in the Psychology of Pictorial Representation*. New York: Pantheon Books

Goodman, Nelson. 1968. *Languages of Art*. Indianapolis: Bobbs-Merrill

Gordon, Suzanne. 1983. *Off Balance: The Real World of Ballet*. New York: McGraw-Hill

Gorer, Geoffrey. 1949. *Africa Dances: A Book about West African Negroes*. Second edition. London: John Lehmann

Graham, Martha. 1991. *Blood Memory*. New York: Doubleday

Grotowski, Jerzy. 1968. *Towards a Poor Theatre*. New York: Simon and Schuster

Guest, Ann Hutchinson. 1984. *Dance Notation: The Process of Recording Movement on Paper*. London: Dance Books

Guglielmo Ebreo. 1993. *De Pratica seu Arte Tripudii – On the Practice and Art of Dancing*. Ed. and trans. Barbara Sparti. Oxford: Clarendon Press. (Manuscript c. 1463)

Hall, Edward T. 1966. *The Hidden Dimension*. New York: Doubleday

Hall, G. Stanley. 1911. *Educational Problems*. New York: Appleton

Hanna, Judith Lynne. 1979. *To Dance Is Human: A Theory of Non-Verbal Communication.* Austin: University of Texas Press

Hanna, Judith Lynne. 1983. *The Performer-Audience Connection: Emotion to Metaphor in Dance and Society.* Austin: University of Texas Press

Hanna, Judith Lynne. 1988. *Dance, Sex and Gender: Signs of Identity, Dominance, Defiance, and Desire.* Chicago: University of Chicago Press

Hegel, G.W.F. 1975. *Aesthetics.* Trans. T.M. Knox. Oxford: Clarendon Press

Heidegger, Martin. 1960. 'The Origin of the Work of Art.' In his *Poetry, Language and Thought,* trans. Albert Hofstadter, 15–87. New York: Harper and Row, 1971

Henri, Robert. 1923. *The Art Spirit.* Philadelphia: J.B. Lippincott

Henson, H. 1974. *British Social Anthropologists and Language: A History of Separate Development.* London: Oxford University Press

Hirsch, E.D., Jr. 1987. *Cultural Literacy.* New York: Houghton Mifflin

Hirschhorn, Clive. 1974. *Gene Kelly: A Biography.* London: W.H. Allen

Hirst, P.H. 1989. 'The Concepts of Physical and Dance Education. A Reply.' In G. Curl, ed., *Collected Conference Papers in Dance,* vol. 4, 38–43. London: National Association of Teachers in Further and Higher Education

Hofstadter, Douglas R. 1985. *Metamagical Themas: Questing for the Essence of Mind and Pattern.* New York: Basic Books

Hogarth, William. 1753. *The Analysis of Beauty.* London: J. Reeves

Horst, Louis 1940. *Pre-Classic Dance Forms.* New York: Dance Observer

Howard, V.A. 1982. *Artistry: The Work of Artists.* Indianapolis, Ind.: Hackett

Humphrey, Doris. 1962. *The Art of Making Dances.* New York: Grove Press

Hunter, J.F.M. 1968. ' "Forms of Life" in Wittgenstein's *Philosophical Investigations,'* *American Philosophical Quarterly* 5, 233–43

Ingarden, Roman. 1931. *The Literary Work of Art.* Trans. George G. Grabowicz. Evanston, Ill.: Northwestern University Press, 1973

Isenberg, Arnold. 1949. 'Critical Communication.' In his *Aesthetics and the Theory of Criticism,* 156–71. Chicago: University of Chicago Press, 1973

Ivanova, Anna. 1970. *The Dancing Spaniards.* London: John Baker

Iyer, Alessandra. 1993. 'A Fresh Look at Nrtta,' *Dance Research* 11, 3–15

Jameson, Frederic. 1972. *The Prison-House of Language.* Princeton, NJ: Princeton University Press

Janson, Horst W. 1969. *History of Art.* Revised edition. Englewood Cliffs, NJ: Prentice-Hall

Jaques-Dalcroze, E. [ed.] 1917. *The Eurhythmics of Jaques-Dalcroze.* London: Constable. First edition 1913

Jacques-Dalcroze, E. 1930. *Eurhythmics, Art and Education.* New York: A.S. Barnes

Jarzombek, Mark. 1989. *On Leon Baptista Alberti*. Cambridge, Mass.: MIT Press

Jenkin, A.K. Hamilton. 1945. *Cornwall and Its People*. Newton Abbott: David and Charles

Jenyns 1729: Soame Jenyns. *The Art of Dancing: A Poem in Three Cantos*. Reprint London: Dance Books, 1978

Jordan, Stephanie, and Dave Allen. 1993. *Parallel Lines: Media Representations of Dance*. London: John Libbey

Jowitt, Deborah. 1985. *The Dance in Mind: Profiles and Reviews, 1976–83*. Boston: David R. Godine

Jowitt, Deborah. 1988. *Time and the Dancing Image*. New York: William Morrow

Kaeppler, Adrienne L. 1972. 'Method and Theory in Analyzing Dance Structure with an Analysis of Tongan Dance,' *Ethnomusicology* 16, 173–215

Kames, Henry Home, Lord. 1788. *Elements of Criticism*. Edinburgh: John Bell and William Creech

Kant, Immanuel. 1790. *Kritik der Urtheilskraft*. Translated as *The Critique of Judgement* by J.C. Meredith. Oxford: Clarendon Press, 1952

Kar, Chintamoni. 1952. *Indian Metal Sculpture*. London: Tiranti

Kealiinohomoku, Joann. 1980. 'The Non-Art of the Dance,' *Journal for the Anthropological Study of Human Movement* 1, 83–97

Keil, Charles, and Angeliki V. Keil 1992. *Polka Happiness*. Philadelphia: Temple University Press

Kennedy, Douglas. 1949. *England's Dances: Folk-Dancing Today and Yesterday*. London: G. Bell and Sons

Khudekov, Sergei Nikolaevich. 1896. The Petersburg Ballet during the Production of *The Little Humpbacked Horse* (Recollections),' *Petersburgskaya Gazeta*, 14–21 January 1896. Cited from the translation in Wiley 1990, 250–75

Kinsella, W.P. 1993. *The Dixon Cornbelt and Other Baseball Stories*. Toronto: HarperCollins

Kirkland, Gelsey, and Greg Lawrence. 1990. *The Shape of Love*. New York: Doubleday

Kivy, Peter. 1984. *Sound and Semblance: Reflections on Musical Representation*. Princeton, NJ: Princeton University Press

Kleist, Heinrich von. 1810. 'Über das Marionettentheater.' In his *Sämtliche Werke*. Leipzig: Insel Verlag, n.d., 1134–42. Translated as 'Puppet Theatre' in Copeland and Cohen 1983, 178–84

Koegler, Horst. 1982. *The Concise Oxford Dictionary of Ballet*. Second edition. London: Oxford University Press

Laban, Rudolf. 1963. *Modern Educational Dance*. Second edition, revised by Lisa Ullmann. London: Macdonald and Evans. First edition 1948

Laban, Rudolf. 1974. *The Language of Movement.* Boston: PLAYS Inc.

Laban, Rudolf, and F.C. Lawrence. 1974. *Effort.* Second edition. Plymouth: Macdonald and Evans. First edition 1947

Laban, Rudolf, and Lisa Ullmann. 1971. *The Mastery of Movement.* Third edition enlarged by Lisa Ullmann. New York: PLAYS Inc.

La Meri (Russell H. Carreras). 1964. *The Gesture Language of the Hindu Dance.* New York: Benjamin Blom

Lange, Konrad. 1897. 'Gedanken zu einer Ästhetik auf entwickelungsgeschichtlicher Grundlage,' *Zeitschrift für Psychologie und Physiologie der Sinnesorgane* 14, 242–73

Langer, Susanne K. 1953. *Feeling and Form.* New York: Scribners

Langer, Susanne K. 1967. *Mind: An Essay on Human Feeling.* Vol. 1. Baltimore, Md.: Johns Hopkins Press

Lemprière, J. 1801. *Bibliotheca Classica; or, a Classical Dictionary.* Fourth edition. London: T. Cadell Jun. and W. Davies.

Lessing, G.E. 1766. *Laokoon.* Berlin: Voss

Levinson, André. 1982. *Ballet Old and New.* Trans. Susan Cook Summer. New York: Dance Horizons. Russian edition, St. Petersburg, 1918

Locke, John. 1694. *An Essay Concerning Human Understanding.* Second edition. Ed. Alexander Campbell Fraser. London: Oxford University Press, 1894

Lomax, Alan. 1968. *Folk Song Style and Culture.* AAAS Publication No. 88. Washington, DC: AAAS

Lonsdale, Steven. 1981. *Animals and the Origins of Dance.* London: Thames and Hudson

Lonsdale, Steven H. 1993. *Dance and Ritual Play in Greek Religion.* Baltimore, Md.: Johns Hopkins University Press

Lukács, Georg. 1963. *Ästhetik, I: Die Eigenart des Ästhetischen.* Darmstadt: Luchterhand

MacCallum, H.R. 1953. *Imitation and Design.* Toronto: University of Toronto Press

McDonagh, Don. 1973. *Martha Graham: A Biography.* New York: Praeger

McFee, Graham. 1992. *Understanding Dance.* London: Routledge

McFee, Graham. 1994. *The Concept of Dance Education.* London: Routledge

Magri, Gennaro. 1779. *Theoretical and Practical Treatise on Dancing.* Trans. Mary Skeaping. London: Dance Books, 1988. Italian edition, Naples: Vincenzo Orsino

Malraux, André. 1953. *The Voices of Silence.* Garden City, NY: Doubleday

Margolis, Joseph. 1965. *The Language of Art and Art Criticism.* Detroit: Wayne State University Press

Margolis, Joseph. 1984. 'The Autographic Nature of the Dance.' In Sheets-Johnstone 1984, 70–84

Martin, John. 1939. *Introduction to the Dance*. New York: W.W. Norton. Reprinted Brooklyn: Dance Horizons, n.d.

Martins, Peter. 1982. *Far from Denmark*. Boston: Little, Brown and Co.

Masson, J.L., and M.V. Patwardhan. 1970. *Aesthetic Rapture: The Rasādhyāya of the Nātyasāstra*. 2 vols. Poona: Deccan College Postgraduate and Research Institute

Mazo, Joseph H. 1976. *Dance Is a Contact Sport*. New York: Da Capo Press. First edition, New York: Saturday Review Press, 1974

Megill, Alan. 1985. *Prophets of Extremity*. Berkeley: University of California Press

Melden, A.I. *Free Action*. London: Routledge and Kegan Paul

Menestrier, Claude-François. 1682. *Des Ballets anciens et modernes selon les règles du théâtre*. Paris: René Guignard

Mercer, Ruby. 1976. *The Tenor of His Time: Edward Johnson of the Met*. Toronto: Clarke, Irwin

Merleau-Ponty, Maurice. 1962. *Phenomenology of Perception*. Trans. Colin Smith. London: Routledge and Kegan Paul

Mezzrow, Mezz, and Bernard Wolfe. 1972. *Really the Blues*. Garden City, NY: Doubleday (Anchor Books)

Miller, James Lester. 1979. 'Choreia: Visions of the Cosmic Dance in Western Literature from Plato to Jean de Meun.' PhD dissertation, University of Toronto

Miller, James. 1986. *Measures of Wisdom: The Cosmic Dance in Classical and Christian Antiquity*. Toronto: University of Toronto Press

Mordden, Ethan. 1981. *The Hollywood Musical*. New York: St Martin's Press

Mothersill, Mary. 1984. *Beauty Restored*. Oxford: Clarendon Press

Mueller, John. 1985. *Astaire Dancing: The Musical Films*. New York: Knopf

Newman, Barbara. 1982. *Striking a Balance: Dancers Talk about Dancing*. Boston: Houghton, Mifflin

Norway, Arthur H. 1897. *Highways and Byways in Devon and Cornwall*. London: Macmillan

Novack 1984: Cynthia Novack. 'Ethnography and History: A Case Study of Dance Improvisers,' Society of Dance History Scholars, Seventh Annual Conference, *Proceedings*, 1–9

NYPL 1974: New York Public Library. *Dictionary Catalog of the Dance Collection*

Penman, Robert. 1993. 'Ballet and Contemporary Dance on British Television.' In Jordan and Allen 1993, 101–25

Perry, Ralph Barton. 1923. *A General Theory of Value*. New York: Longmans

Pickard-Cambridge, Arthur. 1968. *The Dramatic Festivals of Athens*. Second edition. Oxford: Clarendon Press

Plato. 1961. *Collected Dialogues*. Ed. Edith Hamilton and Huntington Cairns. Princeton, NJ: Pantheon Books

Pollenz, Phillippa. 1949. 'Methods for the Comparative Study of the Dance,' *American Anthropologist* 51, 428–35

Prall, D.W. 1929. *Aesthetic Judgment*. New York: Crowell

Prall, D.W. 1936. *Aesthetic Analysis*. New York: Crowell

Prunières, Henry. 1914. *Le Ballet de cour en France avant Benserade et Lully*. Paris: Henry Laurens

Rainer, Yvonne. 1974. *Work 1961–73*. New York: New York University Press

Ralph, Richard. 1985. *The Life and Works of John Weaver*. London: Dance Books

Redfern, Betty. 1982. *Concepts in Modern Educational Dance*. London: Dance Books

Redfern, Betty. 1983. *Dance, Art and Aesthetics*. London: Dance Books

Reid, Thomas. 1785. *Essays on the Intellectual Powers of Man*. Edinburgh: J. Bell

Richards, Frank. 1936. *Old Soldier Sahib*. London: Faber and Faber

Rivière, Jacques. 1913. 'Le Sacre du printemps.' In his *The Ideal Reader*, 125–47. New York: Meridian Books, 1960

Rogers, Frederick Rand, ed. 1941. *Dance: A Basic Educational Technique*. New York: Macmillan

Ross, Stephen David. 1982. *A Theory of Art*. Albany: State University of New York Press

Royce, Anya Peterson. 1977. *The Anthropology of Dance*. Bloomington: Indiana University Press

Royce, Anya Peterson. 1984. *Movement and Meaning: Creativity and Interpretation in Ballet and Mime*. Bloomington: Indiana University Press

Rubidge, Sarah. 1993. 'Recent Dances Made for Television.' In Jordan and Allen 1993, 185–215

Rumsey, H. St. John. 1928. *Ballroom Dancing Explained*. London: Methuen

Rust, Frances. 1969. *Dance in Society: An Analysis of the Relationship between the Social Dance and Society in England from the Middle Ages to the Present Day*. London: Routledge and Kegan Paul

Ruyter, Nancy Lee Chalfa. 1979. *Reformers and Visionaries*. New York: Dance Horizons

Sacks, Oliver. 1987. *Awakenings*. New York: Summit Books

Samborn, Frederick, ed. 1890. *A Delsartean Scrapbook*. New York: Lovell, Gestefeld

Sartre, Jean-Paul. 1940. *L'Imaginaire*. Trans. Bernard Frechtman as *The Psychol-*

ogy of Imagination. New York: Washington Square Press, 1965. French edition, Paris: Gallimard

Sartre, Jean-Paul. 1943. *Being and Nothingness.* Trans. Hazel Barnes. New York: Washington Square Press, 1966. French edition, Paris: Gallimard

Sartre, Jean-Paul. 1948. *What Is Literature?* Trans. Bernard Frechtman. New York: Philosophical Library. French edition in his *Situations* II, Paris: Gallimard

Sartre, Jean-Paul. 1961. *Critique of Dialectical Reason.* Trans. Alan Sheridan-Smith. New York: Schocken, 1983. French edition, Paris: Gallimard

Sartre, Jean-Paul. 1971. *L'Idiot de la famille.* Vol. 1. Paris: Gallimard

Savan, David. 1987. *An Introduction to C.S. Peirce's Full System of Semeiotic.* Toronto Semiotic Circle Monograph Series No. 1. Toronto

Sawyer, Elizabeth. 1985. *Dance with the Music: The World of the Ballet Musician.* Cambridge: Cambridge University Press

Saxena, Sushil Kumar. 1991. *Swinging Syllables: Aesthetics of Kathak Dance.* New Delhi: Sangeet Natak Akademi

Schaffner, B., ed. 1959. *Transactions of the Conference on Group Processes of 1957.* New York: Josiah Macy Jr. Foundation

Schechner, Richard. 1988. *Performance Theory.* Revised edition. New York: Routledge

Schelling, Friedrich Wilhelm von. 1805. *Schriften zur Philosophie der Kunst und zur Freiheitslehre.* In his *Sämtliche Werke,* first edition 1805. Leipzig: Fritz Eckhardt Verlag 1907, vol. 3. Excerpted and translated in Ruth Katz and Carl Dahlhaus, eds., *Contemplating Music: Source Readings in the Aesthetics of Music. Vol. I: Substance,* 315–32. Stuyvesant, NY: Pendragon Press, 1987

Schieffelin, Edward L. 1976. *The Sorrow of the Lonely and the Burning of the Dancers.* New York: St Martin's Press

Schön, Donald A. 1983. *The Reflective Practitioner: How Professionals Think in Action.* New York: Basic Books

Schouvaloff, Alexander. 1991. *Léon Bakst: The Theatre Art.* London: Sotheby's

Scott, Gregory Lawrence. 1992. 'Unearthing Aristotle's Dramatics: Why There Is No Theory of Literature in the Poetics.' PhD dissertation, University of Toronto

Seerveld, Calvin. 1987. 'Both More and Less than a Matter of Taste.' Paper presented to the Canadian Society for Aesthetics, Hamilton, Ont.

Sharp, Cecil J. 1909. *The Country Dance Book, Part I.* London: Novello

Shawn, Ted. 1968. *Every Little Movement: A Book about Delsarte.* New York: Dance Horizons. First edition 1953

Sheets, Maxine. 1966. *The Phenomenology of Dance.* Madison and Milwaukee: University of Wisconsin Press

Sheets-Johnstone, Maxine, ed. 1984. *Illuminating Dance*. Lewisberg, NY: Bucknell University Press

Sibley, Frank. 1959. 'Aesthetic Concepts,' *Philosophical Review* 68, 421–50

Siegel, Marcia. 1985. *The Shapes of Change: Images of American Dance*. Berkeley: University of California Press

Sirén, Osvald. 1936. *The Chinese on the Art of Painting*. Peiping: Vetch

Smith, Adam. 1795. 'Of the Nature of that Imitation Which Takes Place in What Are Called the Imitative Arts.' In his *Essays on Philosophical Subjects*. Edinburgh: Wogan. Cited from Karl Aschenbrenner and Arnold Isenberg, eds., *Aesthetic Theories*, 227–52. Englewood Cliffs, NJ: Prentice-Hall, 1965

Sobel, Bernard. 1951. 'Vaudeville – The Last Days of a Glorious Profession.' In Doris Hering, ed., *25 Years of American Dance*, 49–51, 202. New York: Dance Magazine

Sorell, Walter. 1971. *The Dancer's Image*. New York: Columbia University Press

Sorell, Walter. 1986. *Looking Back in Wonder*. New York: Columbia University Press

Soupault, Philippe. 1928. *Terpsichore*. Paris: Emile Hazan et cie

Souriau, Paul. 1889. *The Aesthetics of Movement*. Trans. Manon Souriau. Amherst: University of Massachusetts Press, 1983. French edition, Paris: Alcan

Sparshott, F.E. 1963. *The Structure of Aesthetics*. Toronto: University of Toronto Press

Sparshott, F.E. 1967. *The Concept of Criticism*. Oxford: Clarendon Press

Sparshott, Francis. 1981a. 'The Solitary Dancer: A Problem in Aesthetics,' *Philosophic Exchange* 3, 69–80

Sparshott, Francis. 1981b. 'The Problem of the Problem of Criticism.' In Paul Hernadi, ed., *What Is Criticism?*, 3–14. Bloomington: Indiana University Press

Sparshott, Francis. 1982a. 'The Last Word in Criticism,' *Transactions of the Royal Society of Canada, Series 4*, 20, 117–28

Sparshott, Francis. 1982b. 'On the Question: "Why Do Philosophers Neglect the Aesthetics of the Dance?," ' *Dance Research Journal* 15, 5–30

Sparshott, Francis. 1982c. *The Theory of the Arts*. Princeton, NJ: Princeton University Press

Sparshott, Francis. 1983. 'Why Artworks Have No Right to Have Rights,' *Journal of Aesthetics and Art Criticism* 42, 5–15

Sparshott, Francis. 1984. 'Medium and Convention in Film and Video,' *Millennium Film Journal* 14–15, 72–88

Sparshott, Francis. 1987a. 'Aesthetics of Music – Limits and Grounds.' In

Philip Alperson, ed., *What Is Music?*, 33–98. New York: Haven Publications. Reprinted College Park: Pennsylvania State University Press, 1994

Sparshott, Francis. 1987b. 'Aristotle's World and Mine.' In Mohan Matthen, ed., *Aristotle Today*, 25–50. Edmonton: Academic Printing and Publishing

Sparshott, Francis. 1988. *Off the Ground: First Steps to a Philosophical Consideration of the Dance*. Princeton, NJ: Princeton University Press

Sparshott, Francis. 1989. 'Philosophical Theories of Human Nature,' *Philosophic Exchange* 19–20, 89–104

Sparshott, Francis. 1991. 'Contexts of Dance.' In Ralph A. Smith, ed., *Cultural Literacy and Arts Education*, 73–87. Urbana: University of Illinois Press

Sparshott, Francis. 1993. 'How Can I Know What Dancing Is?' In Jolanta Brach-Czaina, ed., *Primum Philosophari*, 148–61. Warsaw: Oficyna Naukowa

Sparshott, Francis. 1994a. 'Aesthetics and the End of Civilization,' *Philosophic Exchange*, forthcoming

Sparshott, Francis. 1994b. 'Music and Feeling,' *Journal of Aesthetics and Art Criticism* 52, 23–35

Sparshott, Francis. 1994c. Review of Thom 1993a, *Journal of Art and Art Criticism*, 52, 357–8

Sparshott, Francis. 1994d. *Taking Life Seriously: A Study of the Argument of the Nicomachean Ethics*. Toronto: University of Toronto Press

Sparshott, Francis. 1995. 'Some Aspects of Nudity in Theatre Dance,' *Dance Chronicle* 15, forthcoming

Spencer, Herbert. 1891. 'Gracefulness.' In his *Essays: Scientific, Political and Speculative*, vol. 2, 381–6. London: Williams and Norgate. Essay first published in the *Leader*, 25 December 1852

Spencer, Paul, ed. 1985. *Society and the Dance*. Cambridge. Cambridge University Press

Stafford, William. 1977. 'Keepsakes.' In his *Stories That Could Be True*, 128. New York: Harper and Row

Staley, S.C., and D.M. Lowery. 1920. *Manual of Gymnastic Dancing*. New York: Association Press

Stebbins, Genevieve. 1902. *Delsarte System of Expression*. Sixth edition. New York: Edgar S. Werner. Reprinted New York: Dance Horizons, 1977

Stodelle, Ernestine. 1978. *The Dance Technique of Doris Humphrey and Its Creative Potential*. Princeton, NJ: Princeton Book Co.

Sutton, Valerie. 1982. 'Sutton Movement Writing and Shorthand,' *Dance Research Journal* 14, 78–85

Taper, Bernard. 1984. *Balanchine: A Biography*. Third edition. New York: Times Books

Tharp, Twyla. 1992. *Push Comes to Shove: An Autobiography*. New York: Bantam Books

Thom, Paul. 1993a. *For an Audience: A Philosophy of the Performing Arts.* Philadelphia: Temple University Press

Thom, Paul. 1993b. 'Truth and Materials in the *Paradoxe sur le comédien*,' *Diderot Studies* 25, 119–33

Thomas, Tony, and Jim Terry. 1973. *The Busby Berkeley Book.* Greenwich, Conn.: New York Graphic Society

Thompson, Robert Faris. 1974. *African Art in Motion: Icon and Act.* Los Angeles: University of California Press

Tormey, Alan. 1971. *The Concept of Expression.* Princeton, NJ: Princeton University Press

Tufte, Edward R. 1990. *Envisaging Information.* Cheshire, Conn.: Graphics Press

Vaganova, Agrippina. 1969. *Basic Principles of Classical Ballet: Russian Ballet Technique.* Trans. Anatole Chujoy. New York: Dover Publications

Van Camp, Julie. 1982. 'Philosophical Problems of Dance Criticism.' PhD dissertation, Temple University. Ann Arbor, Mich.: University Microfilms International

Van Praagh, Peggy, and Peter Brinson. 1963. *The Choreographic Art.* New York: Knopf

Van Vechten, Carl. 1980. *Dance Writings.* New York: Dance Horizons

Vatsyayan, Kapilar. 1976. *Traditions of Indian Folk Dance.* New Delhi: Indian Book Co.

Villari, Jack, and Kathleen Sims Villari. 1978. *The Official Guide to Disco Dance Steps.* Northbrook, Ill.: Quality Books

Wahl, François. 1968. 'La Philosophie entre l'avant et l'après du structuralisme.' In Oswald Ducrot et al., *Qu'est-ce que le structuralisme?*, 299–441. Paris: Seuil

Walton, Kendall L. 1990. *Mimesis as Make-Believe: On the Foundations of the Representational Arts.* Cambridge, Mass: Harvard University Press

Weaver, John. 1706a. *A Collection of Ball-Dances Perform'd at Court.* London: J. Vaillant. In Ralph 1985, 287–336

Weaver, John. 1706b. *Orchesography. Or, The Art of Dancing, by Characters and Demonstrative Figures.* London: H. Meere. In Ralph 1985, 171–285

Weaver, John. 1712. *An Essay towards a History of Dancing, in Which the Whole Art and Its Various Excellences Are in Some Measure Explained.* London: Tonson. In Ralph 1985, 387–672

Weaver, John. 1717. *The Loves of Mars and Venus; A Dramatick Entertainment of Dancing, Attempted in Imitation of the Pantomimes of the Ancient Greeks and Romans; As Perform'd at the Theatre in Drury-Lane.* London: W. Mears and J. Browne. In Ralph 1985, 733–62

Weaver, John. 1721. *Anatomical and Mechanical Lectures upon Dancing.* London: Brotherton and Meadows, Graves, Chetwood. In Ralph 1985, 853–1031

Weiss, Paul. 1961. *Nine Basic Arts*. Carbondale: Southern Illinois University Press

Wigman, Mary. 1975. *The Mary Wigman Book*. Ed. and trans. Walter Sorell. Middletown, Conn.: Wesleyan University Press

Wiley, Peter John. 1990. *A Century of Russian Ballet: Documents and Accounts, 1810–1910*. Oxford: Clarendon Press

Williams, Drid. 1991. *Ten Lectures on Theories of the Dance*. Metuchen, NJ, and London: Scarecrow Press

Winter, M.H. 1974. *The Pre-Romantic Ballet*. New York: Pitman

Wollheim, Richard. 1979. 'Pictorial Style: Two Views.' In Berel Lang, ed., *The Concept of Style*, 129–45. Philadelphia: University of Pennsylvania Press

Wollheim, Richard. 1984. *The Thread of Life*. Cambridge, Mass.: Harvard University Press

Wollheim, Richard. 1987. *Painting As an Art*. Princeton, NJ: Princeton University Press

Wollheim, Richard. 1993. 'Danto's Gallery of Indiscernibles.' In Mark Rollins, ed., *Danto and His Critics*, 28–38. Oxford: Blackwell

Wolterstorff, Nicholas. 1980. *Works and Worlds of Art*. Oxford: Clarendon Press

Zimmer, Heinrich. 1955. *The Art of Indian Asia*. 2 vols. New York: Pantheon

Zorn, Friedrich A. 1887. *Grammar of the Art of Dancing*. Trans. Alfonso Josephs Sheafe. Boston: International Publishers, 1905. Reprinted New York: Dance Horizons, n.d. German edition, Leipzig: J.J. Weber

Zuckerkandl, Victor. 1973. *Man the Musician*. Princeton, NJ: Princeton University Press

Index